Windows Vista™ Timesaving Techniques™ For Dummies

C000280813

Coaxing the Most Out o

In Technique 19, I take you through high-payback steps that make Google work q…
Google search tricks that I keep taped to my monitor:

- **Put the most important words first.** Searching for `phuket diving` brings different results than `diving phuket`. Capitalization doesn't matter.

- **Google returns pages with all the search terms.** They're "AND"ed together. Refine a search by adding more terms: `phuket diving` can be narrowed down with `phuket diving beginners`.

- **Use OR (capitalized) to search for multiple items.** `phuket OR samui OR similans diving` returns pages about diving in Phuket, Samui, or the Similans.

- **Put specific search phrases in quotes.** `diving phuket "day trip"` is more restrictive than `diving phuket day trip`.

- **Use a hyphen to indicate words you want to exclude.** `diving phuket -overnight` returns pages that don't include the word *overnight*.

Use these keywords to get answers quickly:

- **To convert units, use `in`:** `10 feet in centimeters` or `20 dollars in euros` or `350 f in c`.

- **To calculate, type the equation:** `1248.3/7.1` or `pi * (7.5 squared)`

- **To get a definition, use `define`:** `define booty` or `define supercalifragilisticexpialidocious`

- **For local time, try `time`:** `time redmond` or `time irkutsk`.

- **For movie reviews, use `movie` followed by the movie name:** `movie birds` or `movie borat`.

- **Quick facts:** `height mt st helens` or `length amazon river` or `nepal currency` or `weather auckland`.

- **Just type:** USPS, UPS, or FedEx tracking numbers; flight numbers; UPC codes; telephone area codes; stock ticker symbols.

Browser Shortcuts for IE7 and Firefox

To Do This	Press This Shortcut
Start a new tab.	Ctrl+T
Open the linked page in a new tab.	Ctrl+Click on a link
Bring back the last closed tab (Firefox only).	Ctrl+Shift+T
Open a find box to find text on a page.	Ctrl+F
Expand a URL. For example, type **dummies** and press Ctrl+Enter, and your browser looks for `http://www.dummies.com`.	Ctrl+Enter
Return the search results in a new tab.	Alt+Enter in the search bar
Force your browser to "refresh" — go out to the current Web page and retrieve the latest results.	Alt+F5
Close a tab.	Center click (scroll wheel click on most mice) on a tab title

For Dummies: Bestselling Book Series for Beginners

Windows Vista™ Timesaving Techniques™ For Dummies®

What You Need to Do Now to Protect Yourself

- **Get Firefox.** Internet Explorer is bundled with Vista, but is an unremitting pain in the security posterior. Dump it. Firefox is free (www.getfirefox.com), and it works independently of IE. See Technique 18.

- **Buy, install, update, and religiously use a major antivirus package.** I recommend the free-for-personal-use package called AVG Free from Grisoft. Avoid Windows Live OneCare. See Technique 45.

- **Clobber scummy programs before they clobber you.** Vista ships with Windows Defender, a competent scum-buster backed by a company with a spotty scum-fighting record. Better to add a second layer of protection with a top-notch anti-scum program such as Webroot SpySweeper. See Technique 47.

- **Force Windows to show you filename extensions.** Microsoft's decision to have Windows hide filename extensions — the letters at the end of a filename, such as .doc or .vbs — is a dangerous design mistake that every Windows user can and should fix. See Technique 15.

- **After you can see filename extensions, watch out for suspicious extensions in e-mail attachments and downloads.** See Table 45-2 in Technique 45.

- **Never open or run a file attached to an e-mail message until you**
  - Contact the person who sent you the message and verify that he or she specifically sent you the file.
  - Save the file on your hard drive, update your antivirus software's signature file, and run your antivirus software on the file.

- **Get Windows Firewall working right.** See Technique 48.

Getting the Most from Your Music

- **File formats count.** Microsoft and Apple intend to make a whole lotta money from their file formats, and you're the one who will ultimately pay to play. Micrapple restricts your use of the songs you've bought, and the rules get more complicated (and more onerous!) all the time. If you want your music to be free, it has to be MP3 (Technique 25).

- **Windows Media Player** *can* **"rip" audio CDs to MP3 files**, which can't be locked or restricted (Technique 27).

- **Your iPod isn't chained to iTunes.** If you have an iPod, you've probably discovered that (1) you can't copy songs from the iPod onto your computer, and (2) your iPod is "married" to one computer: you can move all the songs you want from one computer to the iPod, but you can't transfer songs from a second computer without resetting the iPod. You don't have to live with those restrictions (Technique 31).

- **Each music store has different rules.** See Technique 27.

- **Not all music trading is illegal.** *Most* of it is. Not all of it. Some bands encourage no-cost trading: the Grateful Dead blesses the free exchange of fans' concert recordings, for example, and has since the sixties. The best place to find files? On the newsgroups (Technique 20). What a long, strange trip it's been.

Copyright © 2007 Wiley Publishing, Inc. All rights reserved. Item 5368-3.

For more information about Wiley Publishing, call 1-800-762-2974.

For Dummies: Bestselling Book Series for Beginners

Windows Vista™ Timesaving Techniques™ FOR DUMMIES®

by Woody Leonhard

Author of Windows Vista All-in-One Desk Reference For Dummies

Wiley Publishing, Inc.

Windows Vista™ Timesaving Techniques™ For Dummies®

Published by
Wiley Publishing, Inc.
111 River Street
Hoboken, NJ 07030-5774

www.wiley.com

Copyright © 2007 by Wiley Publishing, Inc., Indianapolis, Indiana

Published by Wiley Publishing, Inc., Indianapolis, Indiana

Published simultaneously in Canada

For general information on our other products and services, please contact our Customer Care Department within the U.S. at 800-762-2974, outside the U.S. at 317-572-3993, or fax 317-572-4002.

For technical support, please visit www.wiley.com/techsupport.

Wiley also publishes its books in a variety of electronic formats. Some content that appears in print may not be available in electronic books.

Library of Congress Control Number: 2006939463

ISBN: 978-0-470-05368-3

Manufactured in the United States of America

10 9 8 7 6 5 4 3 2 1

WILEY

About the Author

Curmudgeon, critic, and perennial "Windows Victim," **Woody Leonhard** runs a fiercely independent Web site devoted to delivering the truth about Windows and Office, whether Microsoft likes it or not. With up-to-the-nanosecond news, observations, tips, and help, `AskWoody.com` has become the premiere source of unbiased information for people who actually use the products.

In the past decade, Woody has written more than three dozen books, drawing an unprecedented six Computer Press Association awards and two American Business Press awards. Woody was one of the first Microsoft Consulting Partners and is a charter member of the Microsoft Solutions Provider organization. He's widely quoted — and reviled — on the Redmond campus.

Woody lives in Phuket, Thailand, with his wife, Add; his father; and his ornery all-American beagle, Chronos. Add and he own and run Khun Woody's Bakery and Patong's very first and finest Sandwich Shoppe. If you're ever in Phuket, feel free to drop by for the best bagels in Asia.

Dedication

To Duangkhae Tongthueng (occasionally known as "Mrs. Leonhard"), my trusted advisor, mentor, and companion for many years.

To George Leonhard, my dad, who took the plunge and came to live with Add and me in Phuket. I love you, Dad. Thanks for all you've done.

Author's Acknowledgments

I would like to thank my wondrous agents, Claudette Moore — who's been with me since the beginning — and Ann Jaroncyk, who keeps it all running; Becky Huehls, who got all the hard work, including the nail-biting task of ensuring this book made it out on time; Steve Hayes, who approached me with a fascinating idea that ultimately turned into the first edition of this book; Andy Hollandbeck and John Edwards for yeoman's work on the copy edit; and Erin Smith and all the hard-working folks in production who help ensure the graphics and layout look wonderful.

Thanks, folks.

Publisher's Acknowledgments

We're proud of this book; please send us your comments through our online registration form located at www.dummies.com/register/.

Some of the people who helped bring this book to market include the following:

Acquisitions, Editorial, and Media Development

Project Editor: Rebecca Huehls

Sr. Acquisitions Editor: Steve Hayes

Copy Editors: John Edwards, Andy Hollandbeck

Technical Editor: Lee Musick

Editorial Manager: Leah P. Cameron

Media Development Manager: Laura VanWinkle

Editorial Assistant: Amanda Foxworth

Sr. Editorial Assistant: Cherie Case

Cartoons: Rich Tennant (www.the5thwave.com)

Composition Services

Project Coordinator: Erin Smith

Layout and Graphics: Denny Hager, Melanee Prendergast, Heather Ryan

Proofreaders: Laura Albert, Laura L. Bowman

Indexer: Slivoskey Indexing Services

Anniversary Logo Design: Richard Pacifico

Special Help

Susan Christopherson

Publishing and Editorial for Technology Dummies

Richard Swadley, Vice President and Executive Group Publisher

Andy Cummings, Vice President and Publisher

Mary Bednarek, Executive Acquisitions Director

Mary C. Corder, Editorial Director

Publishing for Consumer Dummies

Diane Graves Steele, Vice President and Publisher

Joyce Pepple, Acquisitions Director

Composition Services

Gerry Fahey, Vice President of Production Services

Debbie Stailey, Director of Composition Services

Contents at a Glance

Introduction 1

Part I: Making Windows Work Faster 7

Technique 1: Experiencing the Windows Experience Index 9

Technique 2: Tracking Performance and Reliability 19

Technique 3: Keeping Programs from Starting Automatically 30

Technique 4: Getting Your Drives Up to Speed 40

Technique 5: Making the Screen Run Faster 49

Technique 6: Scheduling a Nightly Reboot 55

Part II: Convincing Windows to Work Your Way 61

Technique 7: Streamlining the Start Menu 63

Technique 8: Building a Power Desktop 76

Technique 9: Tricking Out the Taskbar 90

Technique 10: Using Built-In KeyboardShortcuts 98

Technique 11: Making Your Own Keyboard Shortcuts 103

Part III: Packing Programs and Files 115

Technique 12: Launching Your Most-Used Programs Quickly 117

Technique 13: Making Programs Run Your Way 123

Technique 14: Removing and Reinstalling Programs 129

Technique 15: Exploring Effectively 136

Technique 16: Finding the Files You Want Fast 149

Technique 17: Listing Files Quickly 169

Part IV: Making the Most of the Internet 177

Technique 18: Customizing Internet Explorer and Firefox 179

Technique 19: Saving Time with Google 203

Technique 20: Downloading from the Newsgroups 211

Technique 21: Instant Messaging with Microsoft and Trillian 221

Technique 22: Using Windows Live Mail Desktop — Or Not 237

Technique 23: Zapping Junk Mail 247

Technique 24: Surfing Anonymously 256

Part V: Cranking Up Your Audio 265

Technique 25: Fighting for Your Musical Rights 267

Technique 26: Using Windows Media Player 272

Technique 27: No-Nonsense Music Gathering 282

Technique 28: Creating Your Own Music CDs and DVDs 289

Technique 29: Picking Up Podcasts 294

Technique 30: Transferring Music to iPods and MP3 Players 299

Technique 31: Getting Music Off Your iPod 304

Part VI: Having Fun and Saving Time with Visual Media 311

Technique 32: Organizing the Photo Gallery 313

Technique 33: Touching Up Photos Quickly 318

Technique 34: Managing Pictures from a Digital Camera 324

Technique 35: Editing Your Home Movies 331

Technique 36: Doing More with Your Pics and Videos 339

Technique 37: Posting Pics on Flickr and MySpace 351

Part VII: Networking at the Speed of Light 357

Technique 38: Installing a Small Network 359

Technique 39: Securing Your Wireless Network 370

Technique 40: Adding and Configuring a New User 376

Technique 41: Sharing Drives and Folders 384

Technique 42: Meeting with Meeting Space 389

Technique 43: Controlling Your PC from Afar with LogMeIn 394

Part VIII: Fast Security Techniques 399

Technique 44: Updating Vista Cautiously 401

Technique 45: Protecting Your PC from Viruses 408

Technique 46: Plugging and Unplugging Windows Firewall 419

Technique 47: Zapping Scumware 429

Technique 48: Checking Your Security Perimeter 435

Part IX: Keeping Your PC Alive 439

Technique 49: Running Disk Chores While You Sleep 441

Technique 50: Running Periodic Maintenance 449

Technique 51: Requesting Remote Assistance 456

Technique 52: Getting Help Fast 462

Part X: Fast (Nearly Painless) Disaster Recovery 469

Technique 53: Making Backups — Fast 471

Technique 54: Restoring Your System after Calamitous Change 478

Technique 55: Recovering a Lost Password 486

Part XI: The Scary (Or Fun!) Stuff 491

Technique 56: Changing the Registry without Getting Burned 493

Technique 57: Making Screen Shots with the Snipping Tool 502

Technique 58: Fast, Easy, and Safe Online Shopping 509

Technique 59: Create Your Own Desktop Theme 517

Technique 60: Saving Time (And Your Eyes) On-Screen 522

Technique 61: Top Ten Tiny Timesaving Tweaks 529

Technique 62: Top Ten Tiny Timesaving Tips 535

Index 541

Table Of Contents

Introduction   1

About This Book   1
Foolish Assumptions   2
What's in This Book   2
  Part I: Making Windows Work Faster   3
  Part II: Convincing Windows to Work Your Way   3
  Part III: Packing Programs and Files   3
  Part IV: Making the Most of the Internet   3
  Part V: Cranking Up Your Audio   3
  Part VI: Having Fun and Saving Time
    with Visual Media   3
  Part VII: Networking at the Speed of Light   3
  Part VIII: Fast Security Techniques   3
  Part IX: Keeping Your PC Alive   4
  Part X: Fast (Nearly Painless) Disaster Recovery   4
  Part XI: The Scary (Or Fun!) Stuff   4
Conventions Used in This Book   4
Icons Used in This Book   4
Where to Go from Here   5

Part I: Making Windows Work Faster   7

Technique 1: Experiencing the Windows Experience Index   9

Problems with Performance Benchmarks   10
Analyzing Benchmarks   10
Calculating the WEI   11
  Maxing out the WEI   12
  Breaking down components   12
  Assembling a base score   14
Analyzing the WEI   14
Digging Deeper   16
The Most Important Benchmark Score   18

Technique 2: Tracking Performance and Reliability   19

Watching for Redliners   19
  Trolling the Task Manager   20
  Bringing up the CPU Meter   21
  Starting with the Task Manager   21
  Interpreting the CPU monitors   22
Monitoring Resources   23

Monitoring Performance Your Way   25
Reading the Reliability Report   26
Generating a System Health Report   27
Slogging through the Event Log   28

Technique 3: Keeping Programs from Starting Automatically   30

Recognizing That You Have a Problem   30
Finding and Eliminating Auto-Starting Programs   31
  Understanding where auto-starting programs
    hook into your computer   32
  Detecting and deleting auto-starters   33
Getting the Junk out of Internet Explorer
  and Firefox   36
  Escaping the endless add-on cycle   36
  Removing rogue toolbars in Internet Explorer   38
  Removing rogue toolbars in Firefox   38
Preventing New Auto-Starters   39

Technique 4: Getting Your Drives Up to Speed   40

Cleaning and Defragging Your Hard Drive   40
  Understanding fragmentation   40
  Cleaning unnecessary files   41
  Running a manual defrag   43
  Defragmenting — the advanced course   43
Expanding Paging Volumes   45
Changing Partitions on the Fly   46
What about Drive Accelerators?   47

Technique 5: Making the Screen Run Faster   49

Understanding Aero Glass   49
  Running Aero   49
  Superimposing Glass   52
Tweaking the Display for Speed   53
Reclaiming Automatically Zapped Visual Elements   54

Technique 6: Scheduling a Nightly Reboot   55

Hibernating with a Hot Key   55
Using Other Shutdown Switches   57
Restarting Overnight   57

Part II: Convincing Windows to Work Your Way   61

Technique 7: Streamlining the Start Menu   63

Navigating the Start Menu   64
Pinning and Unpinning   64
  Unpinning your Web browser and e-mail program from the Start menu   64
  Pinning what you like to the Start menu   65
Reining In the All Programs Submenu   67
  Where All Programs comes from   67
  Rearranging the All Programs submenu   69
Cascading to Save Time   72
  Introducing the options   72
  Choosing the options you want   73

Technique 8: Building a Power Desktop   76

Desktop Brevity: The Soul of Wit   77
  Adding key icons   77
  Cleaning up old icons   78
  Aligning icons   80
  Moving icons so you have more room on the desktop   81
  Getting the most from the Sidebar   82
Generating One-Click E-Mail   82
  Setting up the e-mail   82
  Improving one-click e-mail   83
Opening Multiple Documents at Once   85
Arranging Multiple Windows Side by Side   88
Shooting a Picture of Your Desktop   88

Technique 9: Tricking Out the Taskbar   90

Customizing the Taskbar   90
  Making the taskbar taller   90
  Changing taskbar settings in one fell swoop   91
  Grouping Windows   93
Blitzing the Address Bar   95
Navigating from the Taskbar   97

Technique 10: Using Built-In Keyboard Shortcuts   98

Shortcuts Everybody Needs   99
Important Windows Key Combinations   100

A Grab Bag of Application Shortcuts   101
Odds 'n' (Sometimes Useful) Ends   102

Technique 11: Making Your Own Keyboard Shortcuts   103

Putting Custom Hot Keys to Work for You   103
Knowing What You Can't Do with Hot Keys   104
Creating and Organizing Hot Keys   104
  Starting a program with a hot key   105
  Opening a folder with a hot key   106
  Surfing to a Web site with a hot key   107
  Sending e-mail with a hot key   108
  Opening a file with a hot key   111
  Running presentations with a hot key   112
  Undoing hot keys   113
Using ActiveWords for Expanded Hot Keys   114

Part III: Packing Programs and Files   115

Technique 12: Launching Your Most-Used Programs Quickly   117

Using the Quick Launch Toolbar   117
Making the Quick Launch Toolbar Appear   118
Adding Programs to the Quick Launch Toolbar   118
Making Room for More Programs on the Quick Launch Toolbar   118
Changing Quick Launch Screen Tips   119
Opening Documents Quickly   121
Opening Web Pages Quickly   121
Adding a Blank E-Mail Message to the Quick Launch Toolbar   121

Technique 13: Making Programs Run Your Way   123

Running a Program When Windows Starts   123
Allowing Other Users to Run Your Programs   125
Bringing Back Word's Last Document   126

Technique 14: Removing and Reinstalling Programs   129

Removing Programs Thoroughly   129
Cleaning Up before a Reinstall   131
Adding Windows Components   132

Removing Windows Patches 133
Using Non-Microsoft Replacements 134

Technique 15: Exploring Effectively 136

Making Windows Show Filename Extensions 136
Customizing Explorer for Speed 138
Seeing all your files and folders 138
Seeing pathnames in Explorer 139
Choosing the Right View 140
Working with Details view 141
Sorting files by group 143
Setting Folders' Behaviors 143
Copying Files Quickly 145
Changing Filename Associations 146
Renaming Files En Masse 147

Technique 16: Finding the Files You Want Fast 149

The Cardinal Rule of Searching 150
Building an Index 150
Setting index file type options 151
Adding locations to the index 152
Rebuilding or moving the index 154
Engaging Your Brain Before the Search 156
Searching from the Start 156
Searching Simply 158
Modifying a simple search 159
Searching with OR and AND 160
Changing Simple Search parameters 161
Searching Advanced 163
Saving and Reusing Searches 165
Finding Files That Got Lost 166
First, don't panic 167
Second, get determined 167

Technique 17: Listing Files Quickly 169

Showing Directory Listings 170
Writing a program to show directory listings 170
Adding the program to the right-click menu 172
Embellishing the File Listings 173
Listing files by filename extension 173
Printing a file list automatically 175

Part IV: Making the Most of the Internet 177

Technique 18: Customizing Internet Explorer and Firefox 179

Using IE and Firefox Together 179
Hardening Internet Explorer 180
Tweaking Firefox 184
Getting used to tabs 184
Put the Close button on the active tab 185
Squeeze more tabs on the screen 186
Speeding Up Your Browser 186
Choosing a fast home page 187
Showing placeholder pictures 188
Bumping up the cache 189
Speeding Up Yourself 191
Feeding on RSS 192
Using important shortcuts 195
Unhijacking the Back button 196
Creating custom shortcuts from the Address bar 197
Keeping Your Browser Under Control 197
Removing "saved" passwords and usernames 197
Checking for add-ons and parasites 199
Choosing Antiphishing Technology 199
The Internet Explorer approach 200
The Firefox approach(es) 201
Comparing the two 202

Technique 19: Saving Time with Google 203

Using Google Effectively 203
Saving time with search terms 204
Using Advanced Search 206
Posting on the Newsgroups 206
Finding Images, News, and More 208
Refining Browser Choices 208

Technique 20: Downloading from the Newsgroups 211

Understanding Newsgroups 211
Working with newsgroup limitations 212
Spreading messages around 212
Legally speaking 213

Using Newsgroups   213
   Breaking up and posting files   214
   Assembling files   215
   Connecting to a news server   215
   Setting up a good news reader   216

**Technique 21: Instant Messaging
with Microsoft and Trillian**   **221**
Saving or Shooting the Messenger?   221
Choosing a Messenger   222
Using Windows Live Messenger   223
   Messaging in a Microsoft World   223
   Installing WLM   224
   Getting the skinny on user IDs   225
   Setting up your Messenger account   226
   Adding contacts   229
   Making contact   231
   Using the fancier features   232
Using Trillian   232
   Weighing Trillian against the competition   233
   Installing Trillian   233
   Using Trillian   233

**Technique 22: Using Windows Live
Mail Desktop — Or Not**   **237**
Counting Microsoft's E-Mail Programs   237
Choosing an E-Mail Program   238
Starting Windows Live Mail Desktop   239
Mauling Windows Mail   242
   Arranging Your Windows Mail desktop   242
   Making Windows Mail wait to send and receive   243
   Dealing with read receipts   244
   Using signatures the smart way   244
   Dealing with e-mail attachment security   245

Technique 23: Zapping Junk Mail   **247**
Understanding Spam   247
Phishing Phor Phun and Prophit   250
Avoiding Spammeisters and Phishers   251
Lurking in Web Beacons   251
Crawling and Trawling   253
Unsubscribing — Not!   253

Fighting Back   253
   Taking spam action   254
   Biting the phishers   254
   Don't add to the problem   255

Technique 24: Surfing Anonymously   **256**
Understanding Anonymous Surfing   257
Using Anonymous Sites and Toolbars   258
Hooking into Anonymous Proxy Servers   259
Routing the Onion Way   261

Part V: Cranking Up Your Audio   *265*

**Technique 25: Fighting for
Your Musical Rights**   **267**
What's Going On Here?   267
What You Need to Know about CRAP   268
Comparing Music Formats   268
Making Your Own MP3s   269
Sorting through the Stores   270

**Technique 26: Using Windows
Media Player**   **272**
Getting the Right Media Player   272
Running WMP for the First Time   273
Making Media Player Improvements   276
Running WMP   278
Controlling WMP from the Keyboard   279
Working with Codecs   279

**Technique 27: No-Nonsense
Music Gathering**   **282**
Adding Music to the Media Library   282
Ripping CDs You Own   284
   Ripping ethics   284
   Choosing a file format and sampling rate   285
Ripping from A to Z   286
Looking for Music in All the Right Places   288

**Technique 28: Creating Your Own
Music CDs and DVDs**   **289**
Choosing the Type of CD/DVD to Burn   290
Picking Songs and Burning the CD   291

Technique 29: Picking Up Podcasts   **294**

Understanding Podcasts   294

Finding Worthwhile Podcasts   295

Rolling Your Own Podcast Quickly   297

Technique 30: Transferring Music to iPods and MP3 Players   **299**

Choosing an MP3 Player   299

Copying Files to an MP3 Player   301

Technique 31: Getting Music Off Your iPod   **304**

Disabling the iPod's Automatic Sync Feature   304

Copying iPod Music to Your PC   306

Restoring Missing Information   307

Part VI: Having Fun and Saving Time with Visual Media   **311**

Technique 32: Organizing the Photo Gallery   **313**

Coping with Photo Gallery Limitations   313

Futzing with the Photo Gallery   314

Scanning into the Gallery   316

Technique 33: Touching Up Photos Quickly   **318**

Changing Pics   318

Bringing Back the Old Version   321

Technique 34: Managing Pictures from a Digital Camera   **324**

Transferring Pictures to Your PC Automatically   325

Using a Camera's Memory Card as a Storage Device on Your PC   329

Technique 35: Editing Your Home Movies   **331**

Understanding the Limitations of WMM   331

Importing and Combining Clips   332

Trimming Clips   334

Using Transitions and Effects   334

Adding Titles and Credits   336

Saving the Movie   337

Technique 36: Doing More with Your Pics and Videos   **339**

Putting Your Pic on the Desktop   340

Using Your Pictures and Videos for a Screen Saver Slide Show   341

Burning Pictures on a CD   342

Burning a Slide Show on a CD   343

Recovering Deleted Pictures from Your Camera   345

Decreasing Picture Download Times   347

Understanding digital pic file sizes   *347*

Changing the resolution of pictures   *348*

Technique 37: Posting Pics on Flickr and MySpace   **351**

Sharing with Flickr   351

Gabbing in MySpace   355

Going for the Yahoo! Groups   356

Part VII: Networking at the Speed of Light   **357**

Technique 38: Installing a Small Network   **359**

Putting the Pieces Together   360

Choosing the right hardware   *360*

Pulling cable through your office or house   *361*

Locating the hardware   *361*

Preparing for Vista Networking   362

Cranking Up Vista Networking   362

Checking the Pieces   365

Understanding Addresses   366

IP addresses on the Internet   *366*

IP addresses on your local network   *367*

Assigning local IP addresses   *367*

Technique 39: Securing Your Wireless Network   **370**

Running the Wireless Router Setup Wizard   371

Propagating Changes   374

Technique 40: Adding and Configuring a New User   **376**

Grasping User Accounts   376
   Recognizing account types   *377*
   Working with account types   *378*
   Increasing security with passwords   *379*
   Using simple, common-sense protection   *379*
Creating a New Account   380
Modifying an Account   381
Hobbling the Guest Account   382

Technique 41: Sharing Drives and Folders   **384**

Sharing the Vista Way   384
Opening Up the Network   385
Sharing Folders   386

Technique 42: Meeting with Meeting Space   **389**

Setting Up Meeting Space   390
Holding a Meeting   391
Collaborating   392

Technique 43: Controlling Your PC from Afar with LogMeIn   **394**

Installing LogMeIn   395
Starting, Stopping, and Disabling LogMeIn   396
Using LogMeIn   396

Part VIII: Fast Security Techniques   *399*

Technique 44: Updating Vista Cautiously   **401**

Reining In Windows Update   402
Downloading the Big Updates   405
Checking for Small Updates   406
Retrieving and Installing a Declined Update   406

Technique 45: Protecting Your PC from Viruses   **408**

Understanding Viruses — and Hoaxes   409
Dissecting a Virus   410
Discerning Whether Your PC Is Infected   413
Dealing with Your Infected PC   414
Protecting Yourself — Quickly   416
Installing AVG Anti-Virus Free   417

Technique 46: Plugging and Unplugging Windows Firewall   **419**

Understanding Firewalls   420
Coping with Windows Firewall   421
   Checking out the inbound firewall   *422*
   Watching a program poke through the firewall   *423*
   Making your own firewall exceptions   *425*
Closing the Inbound Firewall Fast   426
Getting at the Outbound Firewall   427

Technique 47: Zapping Scumware   **429**

What Is Scum?   430
Knowing When You've Been Slimed   430
Using Windows Defender   430
   Understanding the problems with Defender   *431*
   Removing scum with Defender   *431*
   Running the other parts of Defender   *433*

Technique 48: Checking Your Security Perimeter   **435**

Approaching Your Security Perimeter   435
Running Steve Gibson's ShieldsUp!   436
Running Microsoft's Baseline Security Analyzer   437

Part IX: Keeping Your PC Alive   *439*

Technique 49: Running Disk Chores While You Sleep   **441**

Fragging Fragmentation   442
Running a Disk Cleanup   442
Scheduling Disk Cleanup   445
Checking Up on Scheduler   447
Adjusting the Timing of Defrags   447

Technique 50: Running Periodic Maintenance   **449**

Making Your Maintenance Shopping List   449
Weekly Cleaning   450
   Vacuuming strategies   *450*
   Dusting tips   *450*
   Cleaning screens   *451*
   Ungunking the mouse   *451*
   Checking the floppy drive   *452*
Monthly Cleaning   452

Fixing Components As Needed 453
   Cleaning CDs and DVDs 453
   Recovering from spilled coffee or soda 453
   Pulling out a stuck disk 454
   Pulling out a stuck CD 455

Technique 51: Requesting Remote Assistance **456**
Using Remote Assistance Wisely — Quickly 457
Coping with Remote Assistance Limitations 457
Requesting Remote Assistance 458
Sending a Remote Assistance SOS Using IM 458
Fine-Tuning Remote Assistance 460

Technique 52: Getting Help Fast **462**
Exploring the Help and Support Center 463
Using Help Effectively 465
Saving and Retrieving Help Articles — Quickly 466
Using Other Help Sources 467

Part X: Fast (Nearly Painless) Disaster Recovery **469**

Technique 53: Making Backups — Fast **471**
Using Different Types of Backup 472
Understanding Vista File Backup 473
Running a Quick File Backup 473
Restoring Backed Up Files and Folders 475
Using ZipBackup 477

Technique 54: Restoring Your System after Calamitous Change **478**
Understanding System Restore's Limitations 479
Turning on System Restore Everywhere 479
Creating a Restore Point 481
Deleting Restore Points 482
Restoring to a Restore Point — Quickly 483
   If Windows isn't running and won't start 483
   If Windows runs 483

Technique 55: Recovering a Lost Password **486**
Creating a Password Reset Disk 487
Using Your Password Reset Disk 488
Getting Around Your Own Password 489

Part XI: The Scary (Or Fun!) Stuff **491**

Technique 56: Changing the Registry without Getting Burned **493**
Don't Mess with This? 493
Understanding the Registry 494
Backing Up Data the Registry Way 496
Making Changes Safely 497
Running My Favorite Quick Registry Tweaks 497

Technique 57: Making Screen Shots with the Snipping Tool **502**
Using Fast Keyboard Shortcuts 503
Cranking Up the Snipping Tool 504
Making Paint Behave Itself 506
Going Beyond the Basics 507

Technique 58: Fast, Easy, and Safe Online Shopping **509**
Searching for Reliable E-Tailers 509
Paying It Safe 511
   Choosing a payment method 511
   Getting what you pay for 511
   Using reputable Web sites 512
   Handling credit card fraud 513
   Keeping private information private 515
Complaining Effectively 515
Mastering eBay 515

Technique 59: Create Your Own Desktop Theme **517**
What's in a Theme? 517
Creating a Theme 518
Distributing Your Theme 520

Technique 60: Saving Time (And Your Eyes) On-Screen   **522**

Applying Basic, Vision-Saving Tactics   522

Understanding How Characters
   Appear On-Screen   523

Adjusting Resolution Settings   524

High-Resolution Tricks   526

Fine-Tuning ClearType   527

Technique 61: Top Ten Tiny Timesaving Tweaks   **529**

Tweak 10: Bring Back Menus   529

Tweak 9: Show Filename Extensions/Hidden Files   530

Tweak 8: Adjust Power Settings   531

Tweak 7: Use Trillian   532

Tweak 6: Bring on the Eye Candy   532

Tweak 5: Get Al Roboform   533

Tweak 4: Run Webroot Spy Sweeper   533

Tweak 3: Dump Your AV Program   533

Tweak 2: Get More Gadgets   534

Tweak 1: Use Firefox   534

Technique 62: Top Ten Tiny Timesaving Tips   **535**

Tip 10: Watch Autostarting Programs   535

Tip 9: Get a USB Drive for Backup   536

Tip 8: Learn How to Run   536

Tip 7: Change Icon Sizes Quickly   536

Tip 6: Use Quick Launch Quickly   537

Tip 5: Check Your Experience Index   537

Tip 4: Plug into the Grid   537

Tip 3: Turn Off Automatic Updates   538

Tip 2: Don't Buy CRAP Music   538

Tip 1: Get a Faster Internet Connection   538

Index   **541**

Introduction

Tell me if you've heard this one before: You're supposed to be at your son's school play in two hours. You're typing away on the computer, putting the finishing touches on a rush report, and all of a sudden Vista freezes tighter than a drum, taking your work along with it.

Blecch.

Whatever happened to the old-fashioned notion that PCs are supposed to save time, not waste it by the bushelful? What can average people do to make Windows work for them, not against them?

That's where this book comes in. This book isn't limited to dry "click this, press that" tips: *Windows Vista Timesaving Techniques For Dummies* goes outside the traditional computer box to solve real-world problems that Vista users encounter every day.

About This Book

Microsoft says that Vista contains 60,000,000 lines of programming code. Half a *billion* PCs run Windows, and a big chunk of them run Vista. Heaven only knows how many people have used Windows. Nobody — absolutely nobody — understands more than a tiny part of Windows. Yet everybody — everybody outside an ashram, anyway — has to come to grips with it.

Not an easy task, eh?

Windows Vista Timesaving Techniques For Dummies concentrates on high-payoff techniques that save you time. These techniques make Windows work faster, more reliably, and more like the way you work, day in and day out. Use these Techniques to spend less time spluttering and futzing with your machine.

Foolish Assumptions

I assume that you know how to use a computer and that you can navigate Vista without fretting or asking a lot of questions. In fact, that's the first way this book saves you time: I don't cover old ground.

I assume that you're not scared to get under the hood, monkey around, and make changes to Vista — especially if those changes are going to make your computing life easier, more productive, and more hassle free in the long run.

I assume you're using Vista. If you're still using Windows XP Service Pack 2, put down this book and pick up a copy of *Windows XP Timesaving Techniques For Dummies,* 2nd Edition — that's the one for WinXP Service Pack 2. I generally assume that you have Vista Home Premium Edition, although most of the Techniques also apply, at least in part, to Vista Home Basic. There are a few exceptions — some Techniques apply only to Vista Business, Enterprise, and/or Ultimate.

When a given Technique applies only to a specific version of Vista, I'll be sure to give you some advanced warning. If you're stuck with Vista Home Basic, I think you'll see rather quickly that you will want to upgrade to Home Premium — or maybe even Ultimate.

When there's a difference in Vista between the way it acts in a peer-to-peer network setting (a *workgroup* in Microsoft parlance) and the way it acts on a Big Corporate Network (a *domain*), I usually stick with the peer-to-peer approach, simply because that's usually the only configuration you have control over. If you have to wrestle with your network administrator, don't use this book as a blunt instrument, though. You can say, instead, "Hey, it says here that I can do that in piddling little Vista Home; why can't I do it with Vista Business Edition here at Flummox Corporation?"

You should assume that I'm not going to waste your time. I don't dillydally around, explaining why you may want to do something. Everything here has a common theme: Use these Techniques to save time.

What's in This Book

To save you time, I organized this book into Techniques — groups of related tasks that make you or your computer (or possibly both!) more efficient and effective. Some Techniques are short 'n' sweet, tackle one specific topic, and get you in and out of the machine in record time. Other Techniques are more involved and explore the pros and cons of various options.

Wherever an important ancillary topic, shorter tip, or loosely related timesaver may be of use, I include it. Watch for the icons. They can save you gobs of time. And don't be surprised if you bump into a tip or two that urges you to change the way you work, as opposed to simply making changes to your computer.

This book is laid out in a unique, easy-to-read, two-column format full of figures and other visual cues that make it easier for you to scan and jump into a Technique at the point most appropriate for your circumstances. Linear thinking is good. Nonlinear scanning is better.

 Lay the book flat so you can see exactly what you're doing without flipping a bunch of pages (and tearing your hair out in the process).

You can read the book from front to back, or you can dive right into the Technique of your choice. Either way works just fine. Anytime a concept is mentioned that isn't covered in depth in that Technique, you'll find a cross-reference to another Technique to find out more. If you're looking for something specific, check out either the table of contents or the index.

The Cheat Sheet at the beginning of the book lists my choices of the most important Timesaving Techniques. Tear it out, tape it to your monitor, pass it around to other folks at the office, and be sure to tell 'em Woody shares their pain.

The two final chapters — Top Ten Tiny Timesaving Tweaks and Top Ten Tiny Timesaving Tips — explore the best of the best. Quickly.

All Gaul may have been divided into three parts, but this book needs eleven (a particularly, uh, galling admission). Here's what you'll find.

Part I: Making Windows Work Faster

If you want to save time, dive right into the heart of the matter: What you really need to know about the Windows Experience Index — it doesn't mean what you think. Looking at performance and shutting off performance-robbing programs. Getting the cobwebs out by rebooting every night.

Part II: Convincing Windows to Work Your Way

Fine-tune Windows so that it helps you work faster. Get your Start menu squared away. Change the desktop so it works for you, not against you. Plumb the depths of the Vista taskbar, and use keyboard shortcuts in ways you probably never thought possible.

Part III: Packing Programs and Files

You discover how to launch your most frequently used programs quickly. You see how Microsoft built the search engine, then rebuilt it, and rebuilt it again, with the end result a bit hard to follow but quite powerful. I also show you how to print a list of all the files in a folder, quick as a click.

Part IV: Making the Most of the Internet

Take back control of the World Wide Timesink. You can find out about configuring and customizing both Firefox (my browser of choice) and Internet Explorer and setting up both to save you gobs of time. I also show you how to make the most of Google. I take you through the newsgroups, the last Wild Wild West bastion on the Internet frontier. You may want to check out the steps for using Instant Messaging, both with Windows Live Messenger and with the far more versatile Trillian. I also show you how to surf the Internet anonymously. It's quick and easy.

Part V: Cranking Up Your Audio

A surprising number of pitfalls await the unfortunate. Here's how to avoid them. Avoid buying copy-protected CRAP music. Get no-nonsense, person-to-person music-gathering techniques; recommendations for buying music; and inside tips on ripping and burning. Customize Windows Media Player and manipulate playlists, create your own music CDs, transfer music to players and other PCs, and tune in to podcasts. No, you don't need an iPod — although it doesn't hurt to have one.

Part VI: Having Fun and Saving Time with Visual Media

Video and pictures take time to handle, but they're such fun. So here's how to spend less time while having more fun. Vista has a new Photo Gallery that handles pics remarkably well. Edit your home movies, manage digital pictures, and decrease picture download times. Ever wonder how to retrieve pictures that you accidentally deleted from your camera? The answer's here. You can also find techniques for posting pics on Flickr and MySpace.

Part VII: Networking at the Speed of Light

These days, everyone's networked, or so it seems. But how efficient is your network? Here you can find out how to get the most out of your peer-to-peer network, get home and small office network installation tips, find out the best way to share one Internet connection among several machines, and add (and configure) new network users. If you're looking for help installing a wireless network, look no further. I take you through the fastest way to set up your network — and, far more importantly, secure it.

Part VIII: Fast Security Techniques

This part contains full behind-the-scenes coverage of the Windows Security Center, showing you not only how to protect yourself from the bad guys who are trying to break into your computer, but also protect yourself from Microsoft's faulty patches. Protect your PC from real viruses with a thorough, free antivirus program and get the best spyware protection. If you need to set up and monitor your security perimeter, look no further.

Part IX: Keeping Your PC Alive

An ounce of prevention is worth a ton of painful cures. Here you can discover how to run periodic maintenance automatically while you're off lounging somewhere (or meeting some insane deadline). I show you how to decide how much maintenance is enough and how to determine when to run maintenance checks so that your workflow isn't affected. I also step through getting Remote Assistance and other forms of help.

Part X: Fast (Nearly Painless) Disaster Recovery

Has Windows gone to Hades in a handbasket? Again? Here are the tricks you need to try in down-to-earth language. Find out how to back up your computer reliably, easily. Find out how to get your PC to boot when it doesn't want to, restore your system to its pre-calamitous condition, and recover lost passwords. It ain't pretty, but sometimes you have to take the Windows bull by the horns.

Part XI: The Scary (Or Fun!) Stuff

Most of the Techniques in the first ten parts are pretty straightforward. In Part XI, I take you deep into the belly of Vista. Find out how to make changes to the Registry without getting burned, and go through several of my favorite Registry tweaks that aren't covered by Microsoft's programs. I also show you how to put together your own desktop theme and work with ClearType. It's much better this time around.

Finally, I have two little Techniques that emphasize the neatest, coolest, bestest tweaks and tricks I've found. Bet the last trick — Trick #1 in the whole book — will really surprise you.

Conventions Used in This Book

I try to keep the typographical conventions to a minimum:

- The first time a buzzword or concept appears in text, I *italicize* it and define it immediately so that you can easily find it again if you need to reread the definition.

- When you see an arrow (⇨) in text, it means you should click, click, click to success. For example, "Choose Start⇨Control Panel" means you should click Start, then click Control Panel. Rocket science.

- When I want you to type something, I put the letters in monospace font. For example: Type `myfirstfilename1.doc` to name your new file.

- I also set off Web addresses and e-mail IDs in monospace. For example, my e-mail address is `woody@AskWoody.com` (true fact), and my Web page is at `www.AskWoody.com` (another true fact).

- All filenames, paths, and just about anything you see on-screen are shown in monospace font, as well. For example, this bad boy, found in the Windows Registry, is set off like this: `HKEY_LOCAL_MACHINE\SOFTWARE\Microsoft\Windows NT\Current Version\WinLogons`

- I always, absolutely, adamantly include the filename extension — those letters (like `.doc` or `.vbs` or `.exe`) at the end of a filename — when talking about a specific file. Yeah, I know that Vista hides filename extensions unless you go into the program and change it (which I recommend in Technique 15).

Icons Used in This Book

While perusing this book, you'll notice some icons in the margins screaming for your attention. Each one has a purpose.

Here's how I call out the inside story — pointed facts that Microsoft might find embarrassing, school-of-hard-knocks advice, the kind of straight (sometimes politically incorrect) talk that shows you what's really happening. Hit my Web site, `AskWoody.com`, for the latest.

 When time is of the essence, this icon emphasizes the point. More than a tip, but not quite a full Technique, this icon points out a quick trick that can save you time — either now or later.

 You don't need to memorize the stuff marked with this icon, but you should try to remember that this icon indicates something special that you need to know in future Vista endeavors.

 When I'm jumping up and down on one foot with an idea so absolutely cool that I can't stand it any more — that's when I stick in a Tip icon. You can browse through any chapter and hit the very highest points by jumping from Tip to Tip.

 Achtung! ¡Cuidado! Anyplace you see a Warning icon, you can be sure that I've been burnt — badly — in the past. Mind your fingers. These are really, really mean suckers.

Where to Go from Here

If you want your voice to be heard, you can contact the publisher of the *For Dummies* books by clicking the Contact Us link on the publisher's Web site at `www.dummies.com` or by sending snail mail to Wiley Publishing, Inc., 10475 Crosspoint Boulevard, Indianapolis, IN 46256.

You can contact me at `woody@AskWoody.com`. I can't answer all the questions I get — man, there ain't enough hours in the day! — but I take some of the best and post them on `AskWoody.com` frequently.

Speaking of `AskWoody.com`, drop by! I bet you'll be pleasantly surprised by the straight story and coverage of important news items that you can't find anywhere else. And I have hundreds of volunteers who have written about half a million answers to computer questions, all accessible by clicking the Ask A Question tab on my Web page.

Confused about where to go next? Well, you can flip the page. Or you can flip a coin. Or you could hire a hundred monkeys and have them sit down at a hundred PCs and see how long it takes them to come up with the first Technique.

Choices, choices . . .

Part I

Making Windows Work Faster

The 5th Wave   By Rich Tennant

"I really think the Home Basic version will work fine for you. Besides, there is no Yurt Basic version of Vista."

Technique

1

Experiencing the Windows Experience Index

A performance index by any other name would smell as sweet. Microsoft refrains from calling the *Windows Experience Index* (WEI) a "performance index," but that's precisely the function it performs. You get one number, backed up by a small handful of ancillary numbers, that together are supposed to tell you how well Vista performs on a specific piece of hardware. Since the dawn of computer-dumb, people have been trying to measure how fast a particular computer works and report on the speed as a single, easy-to-understand number or index. To date, nobody has succeeded. Vista's no exception.

A small handful of developers inside Microsoft know precisely how Vista calculates the Windows Experience Index.

None of them are talking.

A legion of hardware and software manufacturers are trying at this very moment to hack, crack, reverse engineer, out-psych, and out-bamboozle the Windows Experience Index.

Why?

Money.

For the first time in Windows' long history, Microsoft has put its imprimatur on a performance benchmark. Everybody and his brother wants to beat the Windows Experience Index. Stakes are high. A chip manufacturer that can eke out, say, a 5.7 rating instead of a paltry 5.4 can "prove" that its hardware works faster, thus potentially selling zillions of additional chips. Powerful incentive to jigger the results any way they can.

You can save yourself a heap of time and money if you understand the inner workings of the Windows Experience Index — both its strengths and its limitations. This Technique shows you the mechanics and the dirty underbelly of the beast. At the end of this Technique, I reveal the most important benchmark of all — one that Vista doesn't even touch.

Problems with Performance Benchmarks

You can't boil down a computer's performance to a single, simple number. You know that. Microsoft knows that. The world knows that. But it sure doesn't keep people from trying.

Performance ratings have been around since the very first computers flipped their bits. For decades, computer magazines thrived on benchmarks. Whetstones and Winstones, Dhrystones and Fhourstones, SYSMarks, PCMarks, 3DMarks, MarkMarks, and dozens more all achieved levels of notoriety but ultimately failed to produce a simple answer to a simple question: Which computer runs faster?

 There's a reason why the answer proved, and proves, so elusive. A computer's speed depends quite dramatically on what you're doing and how you're doing it. Benchmarks can try to replicate a typical (or even atypical) workload, but in the end, performance differences that you can feel in your gut rarely get translated accurately into numbers you can see on a graph.

Historically, after a specific benchmark test reached critical mass (for example, as soon as *PC Magazine* or *PC/Computing* based recommendations on a particular benchmark test), hardware manufacturers built and tweaked their hardware exclusively to improve those specific benchmark test scores, regardless of the effect on real-world performance.

 Now that Microsoft has codified a specific benchmark test, you should expect more of the same — and take that natural propensity into consideration when looking at WEI results.

Analyzing Benchmarks

A good performance benchmark can help in four very different ways:

✔ **If one of the components of your computer isn't pulling its own weight, the benchmark should pinpoint the laggard.**

In my, uh, experience, the Windows Experience Index benchmark accurately identifies parts of a system that aren't up to snuff — but fixing the problem may be considerably more difficult than throwing money at it.

✔ **Conversely, if all your computer's pieces are reasonably well-balanced, the benchmark should tell you.** If none of the components is obviously pulling your PC down, there's no reason to spend money on improving the performance of a single part.

WEI does a surprisingly good job of giving you the big picture. If all the pieces work more or less harmoniously, and you still feel the need for speed, don't approach the problem piecemeal: wait until you can afford to buy a new machine.

✔ **When you're out to buy hardware — say, a new hard drive, or a video card, or even an entire new computer — the benchmark should help you compare among the products on offer.**

This is where WEI starts to break down. Part of the problem lies in the way the scores are calculated (see the next section). Part of it can be attributed to the historical problems with benchmarking.

✔ **Microsoft claims — and I remain skeptical — that the Windows Experience Index, in particular, can help you choose software.** If you're looking at a program that requires, say, a WEI rating of 4, and your hardware only comes in at 3.5, presumably the WEI can keep you from buying a product that runs like a slug.

 I'm skeptical because the examples I've seen work the other way: "Oh, Dad, Doom XVII only takes a WEI of 2.7, and we have a 2.8. Can we spend our rent money and splat more zombies?" In the end, I frequently get the feeling that Microsoft and its "partners" use the WEI to sell more stuff.

To see your computer's Windows Experience Index, follow these steps:

1. **Choose Start⇨Control Panel. Click the System and Maintenance link.**

2. **Under the System icon, click the link marked Check Your Computer's Windows Experience Index Base Score.**

Vista shows you the Performance Information and Tools dialog box shown in Figure 1-1.

• **Figure 1-1: Vista's benchmark of your computer's performance.**

3. **If you've changed hardware recently — or if you're looking at a computer in a dealer's showroom or considering buying one from a Friendly FlyByNight Fleamarket Fellow — click the link marked Update My Score.**

Why? Because Vista doesn't recalculate the Windows Experience Index score very often, and it may be possible to jimmy the score. Best to run an update (see the sidebar "WinSAT") and be sure that the score you see matches the hardware in the box.

If you run an update, the WinSAT program takes a few minutes, keeping you posted on the tests that it's running (see Figure 1-2). When it's done, your newly refreshed scores appear.

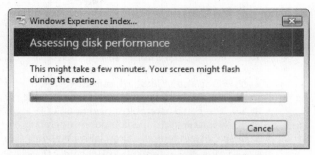

• **Figure 1-2: The Windows System Assessment Tool, WinSAT, updates all of your WEI scores.**

WinSAT

The Windows Experience Index amounts to little more than a pretty face painted onto a sophisticated, multitalented program called WinSAT, or the Windows System Assessment Tool. If you installed Vista from a DVD, WinSAT ran before you first logged on — when the aurora kept dancing on your screen. WinSAT results were used to determine whether Vista would first appear with the Aero Glass see-through interface running; less-capable video cards don't get Glass.

WinSAT also runs when certain kinds of hardware get installed — graphic card installers, in particular, are supposed to call WinSAT when the drivers are set up. When you tell Vista to Update My Score, WinSAT runs again.

Application installers can pluck numbers out of WinSAT while they run, modifying a program's options to take advantage of your computer's capabilities (or lack thereof).So the numbers you see in your Windows Experience Index may influence the features of the software installed on your computer.

Calculating the WEI

The Windows Experience Index consists of five component scores and an overall base score, which is simply the lowest of the five component scores. Microsoft figures — with no small amount of justification — that your PC's performance chain is only as strong as its weakest link. Yank the chain, and the slowest link bogs down the entire system.

In order to understand your overall score, you must therefore look at each component and struggle with the nuances.

Maxing out the WEI

 As Vista slid out the door, Microsoft decided to place an arbitrary upper limit on performance ratings: the day Vista hit the stands, *every* PC scored at least a 1, but the fastest, most capable, bestest components maxed out at 5.9. You could assemble a hive of 64,000 optically interlinked supercomputers operating at Bose Einstein temperatures, with petabytes of L2 cache and yottabytes of solid-state disk, and the self-aware über-computer would have to admit (no doubt in sheepish tones) that its Windows Experience Index doesn't exceed 5.9. It's a design requirement. Douglas Adams would be proud.

Microsoft promises that we can continue to count on the WEI because

- The WEI component score you get today will be the same WEI you get tomorrow. If you have a PC with a Gaming Graphics score of 4.8, it will always score 4.8.

- As technology improves, WEIs will be allowed to increase. By the year 2008, we should see WEIs of 6 or 7. Kind of like the open-ended Richter scale. In the year 2525 . . .

That said, there's no claim for scalability: a PC with a WEI of 7 won't necessarily run two (or ten) times faster than one with a WEI of 6.

Breaking down components

Vista includes terse descriptions of each of the five performance components in the Performance Information and Tools dialog box (refer to Figure 1-1). The method for calculating each of those five components goes way beyond wiggling your PC's fingers and toes — and the descriptions leave much to be desired.

Processor Component

Vista says that the **Processor Component** is rated by calculations per second, but that's only part of the story. In fact, WinSAT runs a battery of processor-intensive tests involving data compression and decompression, encryption and decryption (AES and SHA1), and encoding video. Then a secret formula gets applied to translate the results into a score between 1.0 and 5.9.

 Worth noting: Traditional CPU-intensive operations like, oh, running Fast Fourier Transforms or recalculating humongous Excel spreadsheets or festering automatic color calibrations in Adobe Illustrator aren't considered when coming up with the WEI processor score. If you spend a lot of time working with big spreadsheets, assembling book-size manuscripts, or doctoring photos for presentation to Congressional subcommittees and/or wayward spouses — to say nothing of searching for oil — your impression of processor speed may vary greatly from Vista's.

Memory (RAM) Component

The **Memory (RAM) Component** score supposedly reflects memory operations per second, but heaven help ya if you base a RAM-buying decision on that fallacious description.

Two competing RAM limitations are at work here: the speed at which Vista can shuffle data into and out of memory and the total amount of memory available for shuffles. It's hard to come up with a single number that encapsulates both aspects of RAM performance, so WinSAT basically punts. Here's how:

1. **WinSAT tests the throughput — the total number of megabytes per second — of large blocks of data going into and out of system memory.**

   A magic incantation translates the bandwidth in megabytes per second into a raw score between 1.0 and 5.9.

2. **Then WinSAT caps the score based on the total amount of memory available to the PC, minus any memory that's reserved for graphics. If you don't have "enough" memory, your memory speed score gets cut off at the knees.**

   The caps appear in Table 1-1.

TABLE 1-1: WEI CAPS FOR THE MEMORY (RAM) COMPONENT

If You Have This Much Memory (excluding memory reserved for graphics)	Your Memory Score Gets Cut Off At
256MB	2.0
512MB	2.9
768MB	3.9
Less than 1.5GB	4.5
1.5GB or more	Score isn't capped

Graphics Component

The **Graphics Component** WinSAT score determines whether Vista will try to run the Aero Glass interface automatically. It's a two-dimensional video-centric measurement. WinSAT runs the following three video bandwidth benchmarks, mashes the results together, and comes up with a score between 1.0 and 5.9:

- WinSAT simulates the Desktop Windows Manager — the program that controls the Aero Glass interface — at work, calculating the number of frames per second DWM.exe can push onto the desktop.

- It runs a Video Decoder test and measures how long your PC takes to display video.

- Finally, WinSAT measures video memory bandwidth in megabytes per second.

The graphics component score is a two-dimensional kind of test, with emphasis on playing video (including movies, TV, and the like) and the specific needs of Vista's Aero Glass interface.

Every recent graphics card supports the DirectX9 specification, which makes it faster for programs to interact with the screen, and WDDM, the Windows Display Driver Model, which provides a uniform way for programs to show things on the screen. If your graphics card doesn't have a DirectX9-compliant driver, WinSAT sets your Graphics Component score to 1.0. If it doesn't have WDDM, the highest score you can get is 1.9.

Gaming Graphics Component

More than anything else, the **Gaming Graphics Component** measures your video card's ability to handle 3D graphics. Internally, this benchmark is called the D3DScore — *D3D* being geek shorthand for *Direct3D,* Microsoft's proprietary set of commands for high-performance, three-dimensional picture rendering. WinSAT runs three different Direct3D benchmark tests:

- An alpha blending test that determines how quickly your graphics card can blend together two colors in a standard, semitransparent way.

- A straightforward calculation test that assesses the graphic card's computing power when working with shades.

- A shader texture test that measures the graphic card's ability to load textures.

Again, the three raw scores go into a blender, and the result is a score between 1.0 and 5.9.

The score can get clipped. It's set to 1.0 if the graphics card doesn't support the older Direct3D version 9.0 standard. If the graphics card can't handle the Pixel Shader 3.0 spec (en.wikipedia.org/wiki/Pixel_shader), the score maxes out at 4.9, no matter how fast the graphics card might be.

Any card that supports Direct3D 9.0, DirectX9, and WDDM (see the preceding section) receives at least a 2.0.

Primary Hard Disk Component

Surprisingly, the **Primary Hard Disk Component** doesn't look at the size of your hard disk, how much room is left, its fragmentation, caching, seek time, rotational latency, or anything else that you learned in hard disk school. Confronted by ultrasmart hard drives, caches, buffering policies, hardware optimizations, look-ahead, write-behind, and all sorts of confounding capabilities of hard drives and their drivers, Microsoft basically threw up its hands and gave up on any attempt to measure all-around disk performance.

WinSAT proceeds in a very simplistic way. It measures sequential read performance — which is to say, WinSAT jumps around your hard drive and reads the data on the drive, here and there, keeping track of the amount of data coming in and the time it takes to read.

That's it. No random reads or writes. Heck, it doesn't write at all.

WinSAT averages the ratings and converts the numbers into a score between 2.0 and 5.9. Yes, 2.0 is the slowest disk reading you're ever likely to see.

Assembling a base score

With five component scores under its belt, Vista picks the lowest score and presents that as your system's performance rating. The rating appears in the Performance Information and Tools dialog box (as in Figure 1-1), where it's identified as your Windows Experience Index base score. The same rating appears in the View Basic Information about Your Computer dialog box, which you can see by choosing Start, right-clicking Computer, and then choosing Properties (see Figure 1-3). In the View Basic Information dialog box, it's called the Rating.

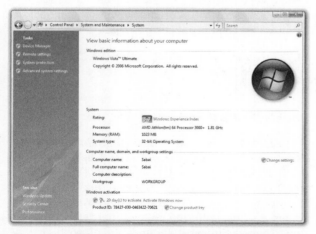

• **Figure 1-3:** The Vista System Rating is the same as the Windows Experience Index base score.

Analyzing the WEI

When you look behind the Windows Experience Index component scores, several idiosyncrasies stand out. In particular:

✔ For people who use Vista as a multimedia repository or as a host for games, the Processor Component score makes sense. But for those of us who rely on our PCs to get actual work done, the choice of benchmark programs leaves much to be desired. In particular, if you use your PC in some computer-intensive pursuit, the WEI processor score may not reflect your experiences in the slightest. On the other hand, if you while away most of your hours online, working with e-mail or Word documents, PowerPoint presentations, or garden-variety spreadsheets, you don't put much of a strain on your processor anyway, and the WEI processor benchmark number is largely irrelevant. Spending the money to raise your processor score may not save you much time at all.

✔ Adding more memory to a Vista PC makes sense, up to a point — say, 1GB if you use only a couple programs concurrently, or 2GB if you run Microsoft Outlook all day and a couple of additional big programs. The Memory Component score is entirely dependent on bus speed, with caps for lesser amounts of memory — and the caps aren't dependent on the memory's speed at all. Ultimately the score's an apples-and-oranges kind of mish-mash. How else to explain the fact that you can upgrade from 1.5GB to 4.0GB of memory on *any* computer and not nudge your score one iota?

✔ On the other hand, the Graphics Component score means a great deal to almost everyone who uses Vista day in and day out, precisely because it's closely linked to WDM, the program that draws on the screen.

✔ D3D component scores make a big difference for gamers, three-dimensional modelers, certain sophisticated graphic designers, some scientists and engineers — and almost nobody else.

✔ The disk component score is a joke. Drives are so sophisticated now that any attempt to benchmark their real-world performance is just as dependent on the assumptions made by the benchmarking software as the capabilities of the drive itself.

Analyzing component scores remains more of an art than a science, but differences of less than a point in any of the scores doesn't affect performance to the extent that I can feel it. If you put a PC with a base score of 5.1 next to a PC with a base score of 4.2 and try to slog through a normal day's work, you probably won't feel much of a difference. But if you put a 5.1 next to a 3.5, I bet you'd feel the difference in a New York minute.

With those caveats in mind, take a closer look at the Windows Experience Index in Figure 1-1 and see what the numbers really mean.

 The PC with the 3.7 WEI in Figure 1-1 (and 1-3) runs an AMD Athlon 64 3000+ processor, which is rated by AMD at 1.8 GHz. The Athlon only delivered a 3.7 on the WEI processor component benchmark — a number that drew down the base score rating for the entire PC. The memory component benchmark came in at 4.5, not because of the "memory operations per second," but because this computer has 1GB of memory (see Table 1-1). With a graphics benchmark of 4.7, this system performs quite nimbly. Because I don't use the PC for games, the gaming graphics score doesn't mean much, and the hard disk score means even less.

When I feel the urge to upgrade this computer, I will start by adding more memory. That won't boost the Windows Experience Index by much, but because I leave Outlook open all day long and use it frequently, more memory will make the PC run faster.

The disparity between the processor component score and the graphics component score — a difference of a full point — doesn't overly concern me because Microsoft's processor benchmark is so

heavily weighted toward compression, to the exclusion of other activities that I use far more frequently. When AMD makes a CPU with a WEI of 5.0 or so that'll work on my motherboard, I'll consider upgrading, but I won't lose any sleep over it — and I won't expect to notice much of a timesaving difference.

Other than memory and possibly a processor upgrade, that's about it. Unless I run out of hard disk space, I won't bother trying to upgrade any other part of this computer — the relatively well-balanced scores tell me that it isn't worth the time or the money. When I outgrow this computer, I'll hand it off to someone else in the family and buy a brand-new one.

Compare that PC with the one shown in Figure 1-4, with a WEI base score of 4.3.

• **Figure 1-4: This PC runs considerably faster than the one in Figure 1-1.**

This second PC uses an Intel Pentium 4, rated by Intel at 3.2 GHz. The computer feels much faster than the PC in Figure 1-1, a fact that I attribute to having 2GB of memory and running a faster video card. Once again, the laggard performer of the five components is the processor. Once again, that doesn't bother me.

I use this PC as my main production computer. The fast graphics component score translates into very snappy screen responsiveness — an important timesaving consideration for people like me who work with multiple windows open and frequently switch among them.

In spite of the low processor score, the components of this PC are very well matched for the kind of work that I (and most folks chained to an office desk) perform every day. It would be a waste of time and money to upgrade any of the major components individually.

Digging Deeper

Vista can show you a few more details about the WEI ratings. To see the More Details about My Computer dialog box shown in Figure 1-5, follow these steps:

• **Figure 1-5:** Details for the PC in Figure 1-4.

1. Choose Start, right-click Computer, and then choose Properties.

Vista shows you the View Basic Information about Your Computer dialog box (refer to Figure 1-3).

2. Click the link marked Windows Experience Index, which appears to the right of your system rating score.

The Performance Information and Tools dialog box appears, as in Figures 1-1 and 1-4.

If there's any reason to doubt the validity of the Windows Experience Index shown on the screen, click the Update My Score link to have Vista recalculate all five component scores.

3. Under the component column, click the link that says View and Print Details.

You see the More Details about My Computer dialog box, shown in Figure 1-5.

 Don't bother clicking the link to View Software for My Base Score Online. If you do, Microsoft takes you to Windows Marketplace (see Figure 1-6), a giant Microsoft advertising site designed primarily to separate you and the advertisers from feeelthy lucre. Don't be fooled: Software and hardware companies pay Big Bucks to advertise on Microsoft's site.

• **Figure 1-6:** Windows Marketplace, a Microsoft owned-and-operated advertising site. Avoid it.

The More Details about My Computer dialog box shows you a few more details about your WEI scores, including the type of processor and video card that you're using.

I talk about performance-enhancing tweaks in the next Technique, "Tracking Performance and Reliability."

If you're curious about your raw WEI scores, it's easy to see the log of the tests WinSAT has performed and how the benchmarks stack up. Here's how to look at the log:

1. **Choose Start⇨Computer.**

2. **Double-click your C: drive and then double-click to navigate to Windows⇨Performance⇨WinSAT⇨DataStore.**

   You see one or more XML files, as in Figure 1-7, containing WinSAT results, each with a filename that includes the date and time WinSAT was run.

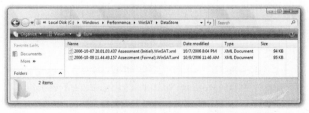

• **Figure 1-7:** Results from WinSAT runs, which update your WEI scores, appear in XML files in this folder.

 Can't see the .xml at the end of the file names, like in Figure 1-7? You need to tell Vista to show you filename extensions. I explain how to do that in Technique 15. Quick hint: Press the Alt key to bring up the menu, click Tools⇨Folder Options, and click the View tab. Under Advanced Settings, uncheck the box marked Hide Extensions for Known File Types. While you're there, consider choosing the option Show Hidden Files and Folders. Click OK.

3. **To see the results of your PC's first WinSAT run, which happened before you logged on for the first time, double-click the file with** (Initial) **in its name. To see the most recent**

results, double-click the last file in the list, which is also the result of the most recent WinSAT run.

Vista opens Internet Explorer and shows you the contents of the XML file.

 An *XML file* is a specific kind of text file that contains settings organized in a standard way that's easy for programs to recognize and digest. Values inside the XML file are set off with beginning and ending tags, which are stropped with < and > wedges. For example, your overall WEI system base score is listed in the WinSAT XML file as `<SystemScore> 3.8</SystemScore>`. Other XML values follow the same `<Tag>SomeValue</Tag>` form.

4. **Scroll down the WinSAT results (see Figure 1-8). When you're done, click "X" to exit Internet Explorer.**

• **Figure 1-8:** The full, raw results that get massaged to produce your Windows Experience Index.

You can find your WEI component ratings (formerly known as your System Performance Ratings) under the tag `<WinSPR>`. Perhaps surprisingly, as you can see in Figure 1-8, WinSAT maintains seven component scores, not the five that Vista shows you in the Performance

Information and Tools dialog box. You can also see your raw ratings for each piece of the component scores. That information may prove helpful if you're comparing machines, trying to figure out why one's slower than the other.

Now you know why it's important to have Vista update your scores, particularly if you're relying on WEI scores to buy a computer from someone you don't know. The raw values can be jimmied, and the raw score file could be compromised.

The Most Important Benchmark Score

With all the emphasis on benchmarking in Windows, I find it surprising that Microsoft doesn't even attempt to calculate a component score for the most important component of all: your Internet access speed.

As more and more of our working lives take place online, your PC's processing speed becomes less and less relevant. (Kind of like Windows itself, eh?) For most people, most of the time, a point or two difference in WEI scores doesn't count as a blip on the radar screen when compared to lightning fast, or abysmally slow, download times.

Just as there are myriad arguments for running certain kinds of CPU speed tests or hard disk access tests or pixel subshader blinder blender blaster

tests, there are also zillions of Internet speed tests, each of which has its adherents and detractors.

Personally, I use the DSLReports test, available free at www.dslreports.com/speedtest (see Figure 1-9). I always test by bouncing off the same location, and the reports produced are surprisingly consistent. If you ever wondered how much data your line can handle, this is the place to check.

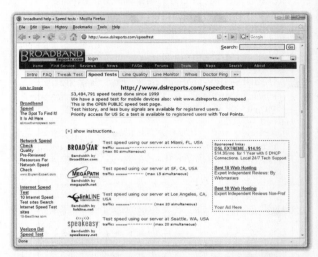

• **Figure 1-9: DSLReports features independent, reliable Internet line speed tests. Free.**

The folks at DSLReports run extensive broadband service comparisons, gripe lines, and well-informed forums. Next time you catch yourself swearing at your slow computer, run over to DSLReports and see if the problem lies with your line.

Technique 2

Tracking Performance and Reliability

Save Time By

✓ Knowing what's going on beneath the hood — and in the 'Hood

✓ Turning off the things you don't need

✓ Diagnosing little problems before they become big problems

Whereas previous versions of Windows hid performance data in dozens of obscure nooks and crannies, Vista brings them front and center. If you want to speed up your computer, the tools you need to highlight the laggards sit just a few clicks away.

This Technique shows you Vista's performance measurement tools and then steps you through the creation of a system health report. Although many of Vista's snazzy displays don't tell you much, a few key players can really help you speed up your system, particularly if you're encountering some sort of recurring problem.

Be careful. If you read on the Internet that you can speed up Vista by disabling some specific service or making some simple Registry change, take the advice with a grain of salt. Many people discover that they can axe some obscure piece of Vista and then somehow convince themselves (and try to convince others) that reducing Vista's startup time by a fraction of a second "speeds up" their machine or that lopping off a program that performs duties beyond the ken of mortals somehow makes their system "more secure." These same people seem mystified when Vista suddenly stops working, frequently for a very obscure reason.

 This much I can guarantee: If you take five minutes to disable a piece of Vista, and your system startup time decreases by a second or two, you've just wasted five minutes. And if your system crashes because of the change, well, life's too short. KnowhutImean?

Watching for Redliners

If you've ever come face to face with the Vista circle-chasing-its-tail cursor and watched and watched and watched as your system seemingly did absolutely nothing, there are things you can do that may make you feel better.

No, kicking your computer doesn't count.

Stuck or twisting (as in twisting in the wind) cursors generally reflect one (or more) of four preoccupations that commonly bedevil PC users:

 ✔ Vista is out to lunch.

 ✔ Your system is waiting for some data to come to it over the network or Internet.

 ✔ Your system is trying to bring in a massive amount of data from a hard drive, CD, or diskette.

 ✔ Something has your computer's processor redlined.

The first problem is a fact of life — like taxes, traffic, and bad hair days. I talk about the second and third problems (and their solutions) in various Techniques throughout this book. You can monitor (and at least identify, if not solve) the last problem by using the Technique in this section.

Trolling the Task Manager

The Task Manager's Performance tab (see Figure 2-1) shows you how hard your computer's processor is working and how much memory your system has grabbed. At first glance, the Task Manager looks mighty boring. Come to think of it, on second glance, it looks even *more* boring. But bear with me.

You can bring up the Task Manager in many ways:

 ✔ Click Start, type `taskmgr` in the Start Search text box, and press Enter.

 ✔ Hold down Ctrl and Alt and press Delete. That brings up a menu primarily related to locking the computer, but at the bottom of the list lies the option to Start Task Manager. Click that link and the Task Manager begins.

 ✔ Choose Start➪Control Panel➪System and Maintenance➪Performance Information and Tools. From the Performance Information and Tools dialog box (see Technique 1), on the left under Tasks, click the link at the bottom marked Advanced Tools. Then click Open Task Manager.

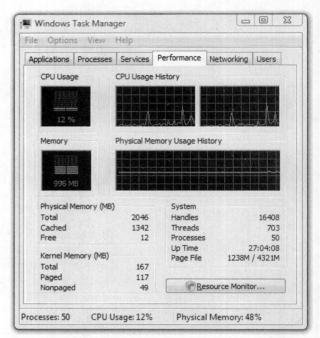

• **Figure 2-1: The Task Manager shows you how hard the computer is working and how much memory it takes.**

When the Task Manager is up and alive, click the Performance tab to watch your computer's CPU chug away, and follow the bobbing line that shows the percentage of memory being used.

 Usually, the Task Manager reports on CPU usage every two seconds. To increase the sampling rate to twice per second, choose View➪Update Speed➪High. To decrease it to once every four seconds, choose View➪ Update Speed➪Low.

 If you want to see the Task Manager's CPU history graph in considerably greater detail, you can double-click anywhere in the upper part of the dialog box. The Task Manager turns into a very simple box that you can move anywhere on the desktop or resize by dragging the edges or corners (see Figure 2-2). To bring the normal Task Manager back, double-click anywhere on the expanded box.

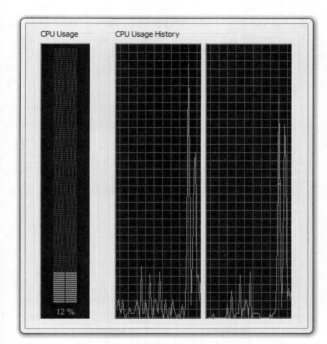

• **Figure 2-2:** The Task Manager's stripped-down look.

Bringing up the CPU Meter

The Task Manager's Performance tab runs in lock-step with the CPU Meter gadget on Vista's Sidebar (see Figure 2-3).

• **Figure 2-3:** Vista's Sidebar CPU Meter gadget, with CPU usage on the lower left and physical memory on the upper right.

If you don't yet have the CPU Meter gadget showing, follow the instructions in Technique 8 to put it on your desktop. Watching the CPU Meter gadget is considerably simpler (and even slightly more entertaining) than watching the Task Manager's bobbing green bars.

Starting with the Task Manager

Given a choice, the CPU Meter's visual display beats the Task Manager hands down. Unfortunately, you don't always have a choice. For those times that the CPU Meter gadget isn't visible (and if your machine freezes, it may be impossible to get the CPU Meter out in the open), you should consider putting the tiny-but-still-useful Task Manager icon in your notification area.

It's easy to tuck the Task Manager icon down under, if you don't mind futzing around with it a bit. Here's how:

1. **Start Task Manager in any convenient way.**

   Three viable options appear in the section, "Trolling the Task Manager."

2. **Choose Options and check the line marked Hide When Minimized.**

3. **Click the Minimize button (which looks like an underscore) in the upper-right corner.**

   When you minimize Task Manager in this way, it doesn't appear in the Vista taskbar. Instead, a bouncing green CPU utilization bar appears in the notification area, near the clock (see Figure 2-4).

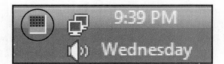

• **Figure 2-4:** Your CPU utilization appears in the notification area.

 Double-click the Task Manager icon in the notification area, and the full Task Manager appears.

After you've trained the Task Manager to sit in the notification area, it's easy to tell Vista that you want to start the Task Manager, minimized in your notification tray, every time you log on to your computer:

1. **Right-click Start and choose Open.**

Windows Explorer appears in the `Roaming\ Microsoft\Windows\Start Menu` folder.

2. **Double-click Programs and then double-click Startup.**

Windows Explorer moves to the `\Windows\ Start Menu\Programs\Startup` folder. Any program or shortcut you place in this folder runs when you log on to Windows.

3. **Right-click an empty place on the right and choose New➪Shortcut.**

Vista responds with the Create Shortcut Wizard, shown in Figure 2-5.

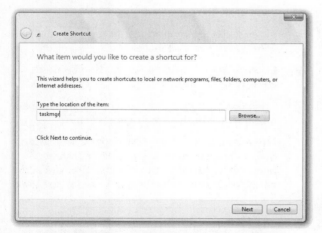

• **Figure 2-5:** Create a shortcut to `taskmgr`, **the Task Manager program.**

4. **In the box marked Type the Location of the Item, type** `taskmgr` **and then click Next.**

Vista responds with a dialog box that asks what name you want to give the shortcut.

5. **In the box marked Type a Name for This Shortcut, type something intelligent. Or at least intelligible. Then click Finish.**

I typed `Task Manager`. Not particularly creative, but it gets the job done.

Vista creates the new shortcut and puts it in the `\Start Menu\Programs\Startup` folder (see Figure 2-6).

• **Figure 2-6: This shortcut runs every time you log on to Windows.**

6. **Right-click the new Task Manager shortcut and choose Properties.**

Vista shows you the properties dialog box for the shortcut (see Figure 2-7).

7. **In the Run drop-down box, choose Minimized. Click OK, and then "X" out of Windows Explorer.**

The next time you log on to Windows, the Task Manager runs minimized, and the bobbing green bar appears in your notification area.

Interpreting the CPU monitors

Although some people like to keep an eye on their CPU utilization just to see how fast the grass grows, most people watch the zooming speedometer to see if something has gone really haywire. If your CPU usage goes up to 100% when you start a program and stays there for more than a few seconds, something is probably wrong — a lot of overhead from old, unused add-ons, for example, or maybe a startup file that's grown too big.

• **Figure 2-7: Have the Task Manager run minimized.**

 If the CPU usage pegs at 100% for more than a minute, when you've never had a problem before, Windows itself could be suspect. Microsoft has released several faulty patches that drive applications up to 100% CPU utilization for extended periods. If you suspect a bad patch, get online and ask — AskWoody.com is always a good starting place.

Monitoring Resources

The Task Manager's Performance tab (and its twin, the CPU Meter gadget) tracks demands on your processor and memory, as I describe in the preceding section. Vista also helps you look at other key resources and how they're going to Hades in a handbasket.

To bring up Vista's Resource Monitor the easy way, click Start, type perfmon /res (note that there's a space before the / and no space after), and press Enter. (Yes, there are a half-dozen other, more difficult ways to accomplish the same thing, including clicking the Resource Monitor button on the Task Manager's Performance tab, which you can see in Figure 2-1.) No matter how you get there, you see the Resource Overview report shown in Figure 2-8.

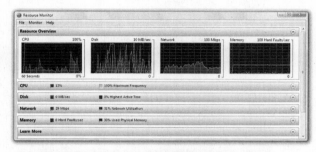

• **Figure 2-8: How Vista is handling your computer's resources.**

The Resource Monitor graphs at the top track four components and two indicators for each component. Each of the components has its own list with supporting details. Look for these:

✔ **CPU** tracks the current processor usage in green, much the same as the Task Manager and CPU Meter (see the preceding section). At the top of the graph is a blue line that shows the processor's maximum speed. That seems a bit odd (what, isn't it 100% all the time?) until you realize that laptops, in particular, sometimes throttle back their CPUs to reduce battery drain.

The CPU supporting list (Figure 2-9) shows running *processes* (programs or, a little more accurately, sub-programs), their *PID* (process identifier) numbers, a description of each process, the number of threads each process currently has active, and the percentage of CPU used by each process in the preceding 60 seconds. For example, in Figure 2-9, the Desktop Window Manager (dwm.exe) used 2.38% of the available CPU cycles in the minute prior to the report being shown.

Use this report if your system seems sluggish and you can't figure out which program is gobbling up all your processing power. Click the Average CPU column heading, and the sluggish one should float to the top of the list.

CPU	18%		100% Maximum Frequency			
Image		PID	Description	Threads	CPU	Average CPU
perfmon.exe		3880	Reliability and Performance Monitor	9	2	6.70
explorer.exe		1120	Windows Explorer	35	5	4.79
dwm.exe		2396	Desktop Window Manager	6	1	1.38
sidebar.exe		3000	Windows Sidebar	23	3	0.89
Snagit32.exe		3640	SnagIt 8	3	0	0.71
System		4	NT Kernel & System	111	0	0.57
SearchProtocolHost.exe		3488	Microsoft Windows Search Protocol Host	5	1	0.48
SearchIndexer.exe		340	Microsoft Windows Search Indexer	22	2	0.31
svchost.exe (LocalSystemNetworkRestricted)		1112	Host Process for Windows Services	36	0	0.23

• **Figure 2-9: The Resource Monitor lists which programs are taking over your computer.**

Note: The process list in the Resource Monitor differs from the process list in the Task Manager, so don't be surprised if you bring up the Task Manager, click the Processes tab, and see a whole bunch of processes that the Resource Monitor forgot. Microsoft doesn't explain why the lists are so different, but it appears as if the Task Manager tracks all running processes, whereas the Resource Monitor reports only on processes that are running at the moment each snapshot is taken.

✔ **Disk** shows you how much data is being written to and read from your hard drives. If you have more than one hard drive, the total amount of data being read and written for all drives appears here as the green line. The blue line keeps track of *highest active time percentage,* which is a snapshot of the amount of time the connection to the drive is kept busy. See Figure 2-10.

Disk	5 MB/sec		54% Highest Active Time				
Image		PID	File	Read (B/min)	Write (B/min)	IO Priority	Response Time (ms)
SearchProtocolHost.exe		3488	C:\Users\Woody\Des...	39,424	0	Background	148
SearchProtocolHost.exe		3488	C:\Users\Woody\Des...	33,792	0	Background	107
SearchProtocolHost.exe		3488	C:\Users\Woody\Des...	35,840	0	Background	105
SearchIndexer.exe		340	C:\ProgramData\Mic...	0	131,072	Background	102
SearchProtocolHost.exe		3488	C:\Users\Woody\Des...	33,280	0	Background	79
SearchIndexer.exe		340	C:\ProgramData\Mic...	0	131,072	Background	77
SearchIndexer.exe		340	C:\ProgramData\Mic...	0	131,072	Background	64
SearchIndexer.exe		340	C:\ProgramData\Mic...	0	131,072	Background	63
SearchProtocolHost.exe		3488	C:\Users\Woody\Des...	34,816	0	Background	63

• **Figure 2-10: Track the amount of data being written to and read from your hard drive(s).**

Use this report if your hard drive light keeps blinking and you don't know what's banging against your hard drive(s). Chances are good it's just the Vista indexer, `SearchIndexer.exe`, but if you find a process that you don't recognize, start getting concerned about malware.

✔ **Network** shows you how much data has traversed your network connection, in green, and the percentage of available bandwidth consumed, in blue (see Figure 2-11). If you have only one network connection, the green and blue lines move in lockstep.

Network	19 Mbps		20% Network Utilization			
Image		PID	Address	Send (B/min)	Receive (B/min)	Total (B/min)
System		4	SHUTTLEGRAY	268,486	164,249,561	164,518,047
svchost.exe (LocalService)		1320	ff02::c	0	34,356	34,356
svchost.exe (LocalService)		1320	239.255.255.250	17,178	8,571	25,749
svchost.exe (NetworkService)		1500	ff02::1:3	0	544	544
svchost.exe (NetworkService)		1500	224.0.0.252	272	0	272
svchost.exe (NetworkService)		1500	192.168.1.4	0	254	254
svchost.exe (NetworkService)		1500	192.168.1.1	136	0	136
System		4	239.255.255.250	100	0	100

• **Figure 2-11: Network activity appears here.**

Odd-looking network activity can be a sign of a worm or Trojan, but far more frequently, it's just some program doing what it's supposed to do. Don't be overly alarmed by unfamiliar addresses. In Figure 2-11, the address 224.0.0.252 may look suspicious, but it's just the address that Windows uses to look up names on your local network.

✔ **Memory** keeps track of *hard page faults* — the number of times Vista has to go out to your hard drive to bring in "virtual" memory (see Technique 4). The number of hard faults per second appears in green. The total amount of memory used appears in blue (see Figure 2-12).

Memory	0 Hard Faults/sec		30% Used Physical Memory				
Image		PID	Hard Faults/min	Commit (KB)	Working Set (KB)	Shareable (KB)	Private (KB)
svchost.exe (LocalSystemNetworkRestricted)		1112	0	48,416	49,072	7,364	41,708
explorer.exe		1120	13	41,428	55,300	27,572	27,728
sidebar.exe		3000	0	47,168	40,382	15,324	25,068
dwm.exe		2396	0	34,744	47,428	24,636	22,792
SearchIndexer.exe		340	8	44,668	26,476	7,668	18,808
perfmon.exe		3880	0	13,392	21,952	9,812	12,140
svchost.exe (netsvcs)		1124	0	20,448	25,036	13,548	11,488
svchost.exe (secsvcs)		928	0	12,700	15,224	6,896	8,328
svchost.exe (LocalServiceNoNetwork)		1668	0	12,432	11,588	5,160	6,428

• **Figure 2-12: The amount of memory in use, and the amount of virtual memory getting swapped in and out.**

In the best of all possible worlds, you should see very few hard faults — the green bar should appear very low on the graph. If your machine starts *thrashing* — generating hard faults like crazy — you're running out of memory. For temporary relief, if you have more than one hard drive, you can try to speed up your system's ability to handle faults by putting paging files on more than one hard drive:

follow the instructions in Technique 4. But in the long run, the only thing that'll reduce thrashing is more memory.

 If you use the Resource Monitor frequently, put a shortcut to it on your desktop. It's easy:

1. **Right-click an empty space on your desktop and choose New⇨Shortcut.**

Vista brings up the Create Shortcut Wizard (refer to Figure 2-5).

2. **In the box marked Type the Location of the Item, type** `perfmon /res` **and then click Next.**

Remember, there's a space in front of the / and no space afterward.

3. **In the box marked Type a Name for This Shortcut, type** `Resource Monitor` **or something similar and then click Finish.**

Use the new shortcut any time you want to bring up the Resource Monitor quickly.

Monitoring Performance Your Way

The Resource Monitor, as described in the preceding section, tracks four key performance indicators. In fact, Vista lets you build your own custom reports covering hundreds of different indicators.

To build your own report, follow these steps:

1. **Click Start, right-click Computer, and choose Manage.**

After you click through a User Account Control security box, Vista shows you the Microsoft Management Console.

2. **On the left, double-click Reliability and Performance, then double-click Monitoring Tools, and then double-click Performance Monitor.**

Vista shows you an empty Performance Monitor report.

3. **Click the Add icon (it looks like a green "+" sign).**

The Performance Monitor shows you the Add Counters dialog box, as in Figure 2-13.

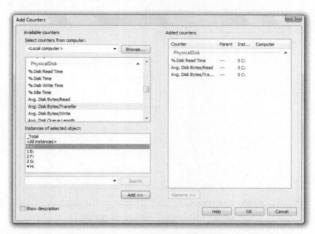

• **Figure 2-13: Choose your own performance indicators.**

4. **Scroll down the Available Counters list and, one by one, choose counters that interest you, choose the source of the counters (for example, just one drive, or all drives), and then click the Add button.**

The indicators you choose appear in the Added Counters box on the right. In Figure 2-13, I chose three Physical Disk performance indicators: % Disk Read Time, the Average Disk Bytes per Read, and the Average Disk Bytes per Transfer, all for the C: drive.

5. **Click OK.**

The Performance Monitor starts displaying the indicators you chose in a graph tracking from left to right, as in Figure 2-14.

 If you can find the right indicator, a custom report can pinpoint bottlenecks on your computer. Custom reports are particularly useful if you have a time-consuming task that you repeat often, say, an Excel report that gets generated every day or a high-volume disk transfer that runs once an hour. Looking at the processor performance or hard drive peculiarities may give you some insight that will help you speed up the problematic task.

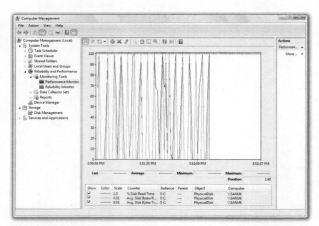

• **Figure 2-14:** A custom report showing the performance of an extended series of reads.

Reading the Reliability Report

Vista has a vastly oversimplified performance number called the System Stability Index that's tied to a useful, timesaving report called the Reliability Monitor. The Reliability Monitor itself scans Vista's Event Log and retrieves, massages, and presents information about system failures that may help you pinpoint problems and solve them.

Here's how to use the Reliability Monitor:

1. **Click Start, type** `perfmon /rel`, **and press Enter.**

There's a space in front of the / and no space afterward. Yes, you can get to the Reliability Monitor in a half-dozen different ways (for example, click Start, right-click Computer, choose Manage, double-click Reliability and Performance, double-click Monitoring Tools, and then click Reliability Monitor).

Vista shows you a Reliability Monitor report like that in Figure 2-15.

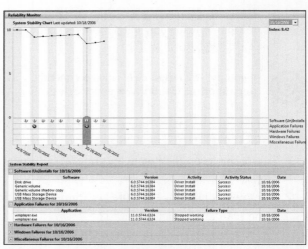

• **Figure 2-15:** The Vista Reliability Monitor keeps track of many untoward events in your PC's life.

2. **Look at the Index in the upper-right corner.**

That's your PC's System Stability Index. Don't take it too seriously, but if you have a 10, your computer hasn't encountered any problems recently, and if it's below a 7, consider hiring an exorcist.

The Stability Index is calculated by first assigning a stability rating to each day in the report and then constructing a weighted average, where more recent days weigh more heavily than older points. (Days when the computer is turned off don't count at all.) The running weighted average is what you see in the graph.

3. **Click a date with a red X under it.**

Red Xes indicate software failures — usually when a program hangs. Vista doesn't catch all your unexpected system failures, but it does manage to trap many of them. In Figure 2-15, Windows Media Player stopped working twice on the same day. That drove my stability rating down.

4. **Look for days with multiple problems that may be interrelated.**

For example, if you installed a new video driver on a particular date (or Vista, bless its pointed little head, installed one for you) and a cluster of programs started failing on the same date, that video driver rates as suspect number one.

5. Look for inflection points — days when your Stability Index started to get consistently better or consistently worse.

 Pronounced, extended changes in stability commonly point to a single cause, and that cause could be a new version of a program, a new driver, or hardware that has suddenly decided to join the dark side of the force.

6. When you're done with the Reliability Monitor, click "X" and revert your seat to its normal upright position.

Don't forget to lock the tray in front of you.

Generating a System Health Report

Vista has a prebuilt data collection program best known as a "Health Report." Although much of the information in the report duplicates other, more accessible reports listed in this Technique, you might want to run a Health Report from time to time. You'll find the volume of information gathered overwhelming.

Here's how to run a checkup:

1. Click Start, type `perfmon /report`, and press Enter.

There's a space in front of the / and no space afterward. As is the case with other Performance Monitor reports, you can get to the Health Report in a half-dozen different ways. (For example, click Start, right-click Computer, choose Properties, and click the link to the Windows Experience Index. From the WEI dialog box, on the left, click Advanced Tools and then click Generate a System Health Report.)

Vista gathers data for about a minute and then shows you the System Diagnostics Report shown in Figure 2-16.

2. Start with the Warnings: Click the down arrow to the right of the Warnings line and see if

Vista has identified any problems that cause you heartburn.

• **Figure 2-16: The System Diagnostics Report.**

For example, in Figure 2-17, the Warnings report of Basic System Checks gives the PC a clean bill of health.

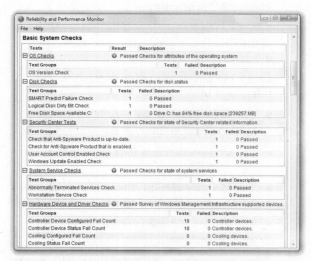

• **Figure 2-17: You should take multiple device failures into consideration if something goes bump in the night.**

3. **Skim lightly over the Performance section.**

The Resource Monitor (see "Monitoring Resources," earlier in this chapter) does a much better job of organizing and presenting the same information.

4. **If you have any questions about what software you're running, click the down arrow to the right of Software Configuration.**

The Software Configuration section contains details about the operating system, Security Center settings (which are better handled in the Security Center; see Part VIII in this book), System Services (which you shouldn't touch), and Startup Programs (which are better handled in Windows Defender; see Technique 3).

5. **If you want to know more about your hardware, click the down arrow to the right of Hardware Configuration.**

In particular, the System section includes details about all your drives. There are also sections on your Desktop Rating (better known as your Windows Experience Index; see Technique 1), your BIOS version, controllers, fans, motherboard, network adapters, video, and much more.

6. **Check out the CPU section for more details about your processor.**

Note that the Resource Monitor presents much of the same basic processor information in a much more digestible way.

7. **Check out any of the other sections you're interested in:**

► The Network section contains summary information about inbound and outbound traffic.

► The Disk section lists files causing the most disk activity.

► The Memory section shows lots of details about processes, paging, and the like.

► The Report Statistics section lists details about this specific Health Report.

8. **When you're done, "X" out of the Health Report.**

And you go back to Vista.

Slogging through the Event Log

Vista's Event Log isn't so much a log as a giant dumping ground. The primary problem with the Event Log stems from its size. Finding the source of a specific problem by scanning the entire Event Log goes beyond looking for a needle in a haystack. It's more like looking for a carbon molecule.

Sometimes, when Vista is bogged down, takes forever to start, and otherwise appears to be misbehaving, you have to look at the Event Log: No other diagnostic tool contains all the details.

Fortunately, Vista has a filter that you can use to narrow your search specifically to performance-related Event Log entries. Unfortunately, even with the filter, the sheer volume of entries — many of which mean nothing — will keep you, uh, challenged.

With that caveat, here's how to call up the performance-related entries in the Vista Event Log:

1. **Click Start, right-click Computer, choose Properties, and then click the link to the Windows Experience Index.**

2. **From the WEI dialog box, on the left, click Advanced Tools, and then click View Performance Details in Event Log.**

The Microsoft Management Console appears with an Event Log filter for "Diagnostics - Performance / Operational," as shown in Figure 2-18.

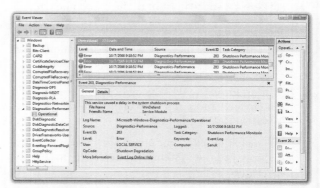

• **Figure 2-18:** The Event Log as seen through Vista's predefined Performance filter.

3. **In the Operational box, scroll down to any event that interests you and click it.**

Details of the event appear in the lower box. For example, in Figure 2-18, I clicked a Shutdown Performance Monitor "Error" entry and discovered that Windows Defender has been flagged as a laggard, slowing Vista's shutdown process.

Think about that for a minute. Microsoft's own Windows Defender generated an error in the Event Log because it didn't respond fast enough when Windows was trying to close. That should give you a good idea of the nature of many — dare I say almost all — of the Event Log entries.

4. **If you're curious about the details of the particular event, click the link at the bottom marked Event Log Online Help.**

If you're lucky, you see a Microsoft-generated Web page that describes the reason for the Event Log entry. You're just as likely to see a placeholder, though, with no additional information.

5. **When your eyes glaze over, click "X" to return to Windows.**

And marvel on the fact that this is the first entry for Vista's Advanced Tools dialog box, which you're invited to use "to get additional performance information."

Technique 3

Keeping Programs from Starting Automatically

Save Time By

- ✔ Taking down scummy junk
- ✔ Finding and deleting those annoying auto-starting programs
- ✔ Trapping auto-starting programs before they get into your system

I once visited a friend at a prestigious university known for its outstanding computer science faculty and courses. He took me over to his office PC and booted it. Windows came up with a notice that it had detected a bad driver and wouldn't load it.

I asked him about the notice.

"Oh that?" he said. "My PC has been doing that ever since I installed this CD burner. I just check the Don't Display This Message box and then click Cancel. When the notification box comes up by the clock that says the driver isn't being installed, I click the X over there."

Every time he boots Windows, he clicks three times in three different places, just to get his PC running. And this guy has an IQ that'd fry an egg.

There's something seriously wrong here.

Recognizing That You Have a Problem

If your PC runs a program that you don't want every time you start it, you have a problem. I don't care if the interloper is a cutesy greeting of the day, a vicious piece of won't-let-go advertising, a big-name antivirus program that keeps begging for money, or a direct connection to the XXX-rated Internet Search Page: If you got it, and you don't want it, you need to get rid of it. More than that, you need to make sure that similarly scummy programs don't have a chance to infect your PC again.

Far too many people think it's normal for Windows to hiccup on startup: Bad drivers are common, especially on older systems. (Drivers are small programs that control specific devices, such as printers and video cards.) Instant Messenger programs invite themselves to start every time you log on. The company that made your PC may have "helpfully" installed an antivirus system, DVD player, system cleaner, smiley icon bundle, media program, toothbrush recharger, or other piece of garbage that you don't want.

Even the big-name programs from major companies can be obnoxious. Have you ever tried to tell Yahoo! Messenger that you don't want it to run when you log onto your computer (see Figure 3-1)? Have you ever tried to remove all the vestiges of Norton Antivirus? Believe me, it ain't easy.

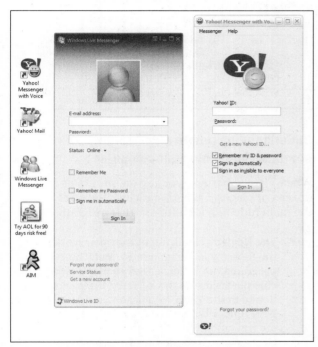

• **Figure 3-1: Windows Live Messenger and Yahoo! Messenger auto-start unless you turn them off. AOL Instant Messenger isn't quite so obnoxious.**

Each time you install a new application, you have a fair-to-middling chance the new application will launch some part of itself every time you start the computer, or it'll try to change your Internet Explorer home page, or it'll dangle a toolbar in IE or Firefox.

The application may also put an icon in the notification area (the box in the lower right of the Windows screen, next to the clock), and you may or may not be able to get rid of the program by using the application itself or the Control Panel's Add/Remove Programs feature. After six months or a year of operation, your machine could easily be launching two dozen programs every time it starts — and you may want or need only a few of them.

If you bought your PC with Windows preinstalled, every two-bit gewgaw the manufacturer threw in to get you to buy a product (or to collect royalties from a software vendor) is bound to automatically start something as well.

 Viruses and other pieces of malware can try to auto-start themselves by using Vista's features. The best way to stop them is with a program called StartupMonitor, which I discuss at the end of this Technique.

It has to stop. Literally. Although unneeded programs don't slow down your system perceptibly, having to wait for three different Instant Messengers to get kick-started every time Windows boots is a pain. Mostly, auto-starting programs make it tough to wade through the icons in the notification tray, pose some security risks, and can contribute, in often mysterious ways, to lock-ups, crashes, and all sorts of time-gobbling problems.

Finding and Eliminating Auto-Starting Programs

Sometimes, a computer suddenly starts doing something that you didn't tell it to do — such as putting a message on-screen, trying to connect to your network, running your video camera, or hanging an extra toolbar on Internet Explorer or Firefox. Or maybe you get a message about a driver that won't load, or one that would make the system unstable. In such cases, the most likely culprit is an auto-starting program. If your computer suddenly starts hanging or crashing, the cause may be an auto-starting program, too.

Many times, you can install auto-starting programs without knowing it. "Free" icon and game programs are notorious for installing many auto-starting programs — which many people call scumware. You may have accidentally installed an auto-starting program when a perfectly legitimate-looking Web site asked if it could install some sort of custom "download content."

If you have a particularly scummy program starting all by itself for no apparent reason, your first line of defense should be Webroot Spysweeper. I talk about Spysweeper extensively in Technique 47. It isn't free, but it's your best friend in the anti-scum field.

Ridding yourself of the auto-starting vermin is a three-step process.

1. **You have to find the programs that start when Windows starts.**

A little-known corner of Windows Defender makes that easy.

2. **You have to figure out whether the programs are good or bad.**

Not all auto-starting programs are bad. The ones listed in Table 3-1 appear on almost all systems.

3. **You need to unhook the bad ones so that they don't start by themselves. You might want to delete the programs, too.**

Again, Windows Defender comes to the rescue.

TABLE 3-1: COMMON AUTO-RUNNING PROGRAMS

Name	What It Means	What It Does
ehTray.exe	Media Center Tray Applet	Makes Media Center spring to life more quickly
userinit.exe	Microsoft Userinit Logon Application	Gets network connections going and starts the Windows shell
Explorer.exe	Windows Explorer	Starts the main Windows program you use all the time

Name	What It Means	What It Does
WMPNSCFG.exe	Windows Media Player network sharing service configuration application	Allows you to share media files across the network
Sidebar.exe	Windows Sidebar	Helps get the Sidebar going
WpcUmi.exe	Windows Parental Control Notifications	Implements Vista's Parental Controls restrictions
MSASCui.exe	Windows Defender	Always runs in the background

Understanding where auto-starting programs hook into your computer

When Vista starts and you log on, programs from dozens of places run automatically. Here are some of the main hideouts for auto-starting programs:

- **The Registry:** I talk about the inner workings of the Registry in Technique 56. Many auto-starting programs run because they're mentioned in specific places inside the Registry. Programs mentioned in the \Run, \RunOnce, and \RunOnceEx keys (under both \Windows and \WindowsNT) are run automatically every time Windows starts, as are those in the \Windows\Load and \System\Scripts keys, plus \Winlogon\ Userinit and \ShellServiceObject DelayLoad. If you go spelunking in your Registry looking for wayward auto-starting programs, you need to look at all those keys.

The Registry won't jump up and bite you, but if you go in and change things, make sure you know what you're doing. See Technique 56 for some hard-won advice.

- **Startup folders:** Vista automatically runs everything in the system's Startup folder (C:\ Program Data\Microsoft\Windows\ Start Menu\Programs\Startup) and your personal Startup folder (C:\Users\<usename>\ AppData\Roaming\Microsoft\Windows\ Start Menu\Programs\Startup) every time you log on.

✔ **Scheduled Tasks:** These get run, too, from the `C:\Windows\Tasks` folder.

✔ **Group Policy scripts:** If you're attached to a Big Corporate Network, the domain's network administrator can tell Windows to run even more programs when you log on.

If Vista has a definitive list of all the places auto-running programs can hide, I've never seen it. The official Windows documentation falls far short of the mark.

Detecting and deleting auto-starters

Tucked away deep in Windows Defender sits a remarkable program called Software Explorer that lets you see, and control, many of the programs that start automatically when you log on to Windows.

Here's how to use Software Explorer:

1. **Bring up Windows Defender by choosing Start➪All Programs➪Windows Defender.**

Windows Defender probably tells you that there are no creepy-crawlies on your PC (see Figure 3-2). Of course, Defender's definition of "unwanted" software may differ drastically from yours.

• **Figure 3-2: Windows Defender may report that you have no unwanted software, but you get to make the final decision.**

2. **Click the Tools icon at the top. Then, on the right, click the link to Software Explorer. In the Category drop-down box, choose Startup Programs.**

Windows Defender shows you a list of all the identified programs that run when you log on to Windows, as shown in Figure 3-3.

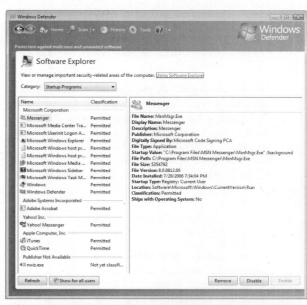

• **Figure 3-3: Startup programs that Vista could find, listed by manufacturer.**

3. **If you want to understand where the programs come from, right-click any program and choose Startup Type.**

Defender re-sorts the list based on where the auto-starting program hooks into your system, as shown in Figure 3-4. (See the earlier section, "Understanding where auto-starting programs hook into your computer," for details.)

In Figure 3-4, I have auto-starting programs that come from four sources:

▶ Shortcuts stored in my Startup folder, `C:\Users\<username>\AppData\Roaming\Microsoft\Windows\Start Menu\Programs\Startup`

▶ The All Users Startup folder, `C:\Program Data\Microsoft\Windows\Start Menu\Programs\Startup`

▶ The Current User `\Run` key in the Registry, `HKEY_CURRENT_USER\Software\Microsoft\Windows\CurrentVersion\Run`

▶ The Local Machine \Run key (which you can think of as the "all users" \Run key), HKEY_LOCAL_MACHINE\SOFTWARE\Microsoft\Windows\CurrentVersion\Run

If you go looking for the source of your auto-running programs, or if you're trying to figure out how a piece of scumware got hooked into Vista, the list in Figure 3-4 will tell you.

4. **To prevent a specific program from starting automatically, click once on the program and then, in the lower-right corner, click Disable. When Windows Defender asks if you are sure you want to disable the application, click Of Course, You Stupid Machine; That's Exactly What I Just Told You to Do. Or something like that.**

 If a program appears twice in the list — starting from two different locations, using two different hooks into Vista — you have to disable both locations to keep the program from running when you log on to Vista.

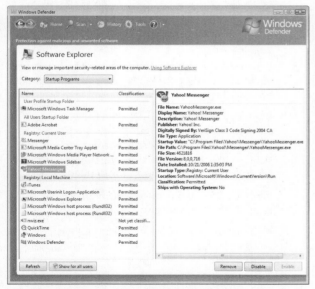

• **Figure 3-4:** My auto-starting programs, showing precisely how they hook into Vista.

 Don't click the Remove button and remove the program's auto-run hook completely. Disable it. That way, if you change your mind, you can always come back to Software Explorer and reverse your decision. Also, if you bump into an exotic form of malware, leaving the hook in (but disabling it) can help anti-scumware researchers figure out how it got into your PC in the first place.

In Figure 3-5, I disabled Windows Live Messenger (identified as Messenger; program name, ahem, MsnMsgr.exe), Yahoo! Messenger (which is an absolute bear to disable by using the program itself unless you have a Yahoo! ID), and the Media Center Tray Applet.

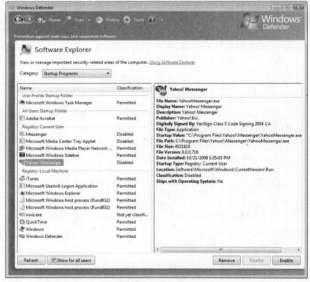

• **Figure 3-5:** Prevent a program from running when you log on to Windows by disabling it.

Note that the term *disable* doesn't mean the program itself gets disabled, deleted, detangled, or defanged. It only means that the program will not run automatically every time you log on to Windows.

Some auto-starting programs can't be disabled by Windows Defender. For example, in Figure 3-5, iTunes (which I only use to synch with my iPod) and QuickTime (which I avoid like the plague that it is) can't be disabled. Apple, the company that makes iTunes and QuickTime, has decreed that its auto-run components must launch every time you log on. If you want to get rid of the auto-starting program, you have to remove the program completely (use Start⇨Control Panel⇨ Uninstall a Program) or find a way from inside the program to turn off the auto-starting component. Good luck.

 The Microsoft Windows host process (Rundll32), as shown in Figure 3-6, is a "wrapper" program that's used to run other programs. If you see Rundll32 on the left side, you have to look at the Startup Value on the right to see what program actually runs. In Figure 3-6, the Rundll32 instance shown runs NvCpl.dll,NvStartup, which is the startup program for my NVIDIA video card.

5. **When you've finished disabling the program(s) you don't want to run (or identified the ones that can't be disabled in Windows Defender), click "X" to return to Vista.**

Don't forget to follow up on the programs that need to be clobbered by more direct means.

Getting rid of Microsoft Office's speech recognition

My vote for one of Office's most frustrating "features": speech recognition. For people with disabilities, it's a god-send. For many business users, it's insufferable. Worse, it's almost impossible to figure out how to turn it off if you ever have the misfortune to turn it on. The Office Help files are all wrong.

When you perform a "Full" installation of Office XP, you get speech recognition whether you like it or not. Microsoft showed some restraint in Office 2003 and 2007, where speech recognition only comes to haunt you if you specifically ask for it in a "Custom" install.

Unfortunately, disabling speech recognition isn't as easy as disabling the ctfmon.exe program in Windows Defender's Software Explorer. If you do try to get rid of this annoying auto-starting component of speech recognition, the next time one of the Office applications starts, it puts ctfmon.exe back on the auto-starting list. (Remember the old Office paper clip — the one that kept popping up, no matter how hard you tried to get rid of it? The sins of the father are visited on this son, methinks.)

To turn off ctfmon.exe for good, choose Start⇨Control Panel and under the Clock, Language, and Region icon, click the Change Keyboards or Other Input Methods link. Click the button marked Change Keyboards, and then click the Language Bar tab. Under Language Bar, click the Hidden button. Then click OK twice to get out. That has to be the most arcane setting ever.

Alternatively, you can uninstall speech recognition from Office XP itself, but that's an entirely different pain in the neck.

• **Figure 3-6: RundlI32 is used to run other programs, which you can identify on the right.**

Getting the Junk out of Internet Explorer and Firefox

So you installed Yahoo! Messenger (or your PC vendor did it for you), and now you have a stupid Yahoo! toolbar taking up space in Internet Explorer, or even in Firefox.

Who you gonna call? Scumbust . . . er, Timesavers!

Escaping the endless add-on cycle

When you open Internet Explorer, it traps many — but probably not all! — attempts by rogue IE add-ons to go behind your back and connect directly to the Internet. For example, if you install Yahoo! Messenger and then open Internet Explorer, you may see the warning dialog box shown in Figure 3-7.

• **Figure 3-7: No, I won't allow your scummy junk to phone home from Internet Explorer.**

 If you click Don't Allow, Internet Explorer pauses for a moment and then shows you precisely the same dialog box. Click Don't Allow (or "X" out of the box) and you get it again. And again. You can't get past the dialog box, and you can't "X" out of Internet Explorer while the dialog box is open. You're stuck between a rock and a hard place, a place I call Hoo!Hell.

Here's how to break the cycle:

1. Press Ctrl+Alt+Del and click Start Task Manager. In Windows Task Manager, click the Applications tab.

You see a list of running applications, as in Figure 3-8.

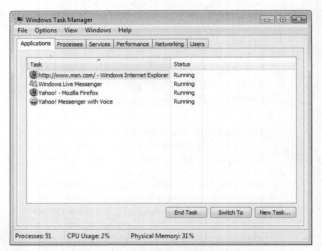

• **Figure 3-8: Shut down Windows Internet Explorer.**

2. Select the line for Windows Internet Explorer and click End Task.

Vista responds with a scary dialog box that says it cannot end the program because it is waiting for a response from you. Well, DUH!

3. Click End Now to chop the beast off at the knees and then "X" out of the Task Manager.

Once again, you see the dialog box in Figure 3-7.

4. Click Don't Allow. (You can check the box marked Do Not Show Me the Warning for This Program Again if you're superstitious, but it probably won't do anything.)

This time, the dialog box disappears.

5. Choose Start⇨All Programs⇨Accessories⇨ System Tools⇨Internet Explorer (No Add-ons).

Internet Explorer starts without running any add-ons, and you see the warnings in Figure 3-9.

• **Figure 3-9:** Start a clean copy of Internet Explorer.

6. In the Add-Ons Disabled dialog box, click Tools⇨Manage Add-ons⇨Enable or Disable Add-Ons.

7. In the box marked Show, choose Add-Ons That Have Been Used by Internet Explorer. Then click the Publisher column head to sort by publisher.

When you've jumped through all those hoops, you see a Manage Add-Ons dialog box that looks like the one in Figure 3-10.

• **Figure 3-10:** Get rid of offensive add-ons here.

8. One by one, click any suspect add-ons and then click Disable.

Even if you can delete an add-on (in particular, you can delete any listed with a Type of ActiveX Control), it's better to Disable. That way, if you change your mind, you can go back and Enable any unjustly accused add-ons, and if you run into something spectacularly unique, the people responsible for tracking down such things might want to be able to see what was there. Kinda like tarantulas on *CSI* or fuzzy green stuff on *House*. Know what I mean?

Since Yahoo! was causing my grief in Figure 3-7, I respond in kind by disabling everything from Yahoo!, per Figure 3-11.

• **Figure 3-11:** Yahoo! gets the heave-hoo!

9. Click OK three times, "X" out of Internet Explorer, and then start IE normally.

The scummy add-on will never darken IE's door again.

Removing rogue toolbars in Internet Explorer

So you installed AOL Instant Messenger — or any of a thousand other programs — and you forgot to tell the helpful, friendly installer that you don't want the helpful, friendly toolbar that comes along for the ride. Hey, we all slip up sometime — I got AOL-ified once, too (see Figure 3-12).

• **Figure 3-12: The AOL Toolbar helps you spend time with AOL, spend money with AOL — and it keeps tabs on everything you do.**

The problem with the AOL Toolbar, and so many others of its ilk, is that it won't *stay off:* If you right-click any toolbar and uncheck the line that says AOL Toolbar, the toolbar goes away for a while. But the minute you restart IE, the banished toolbar, like a bad penny, comes right back.

 Here's how to get rid of a rogue toolbar for good:

1. **Start Internet Explorer. Click the Tools icon and choose Manage Add-ons➪Enable or Disable Add-Ons.**

2. **In the box marked Show, choose Add-Ons Currently Loaded in Internet Explorer. Click the Name column heading.**

   You should see a list of add-ons, sorted by name, as in Figure 3-13.

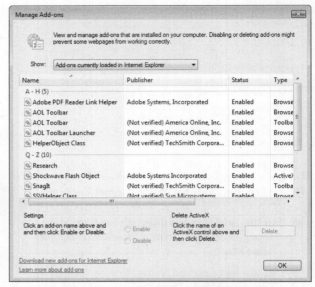

• **Figure 3-13: Your hunt for rogue toolbars starts here.**

3. **One by one, select any toolbars that you don't want, and any "helpers" that come along for the ride, and click Disable.**

   As in the preceding section, I recommend that you only Disable — don't Delete — if you have the option.

4. **When you're done slashing the unwanted critters, click OK twice, "X" out of Internet Explorer, and then restart Internet Explorer.**

   The unwanted toolbar's gone — and it won't come back again.

Removing rogue toolbars in Firefox

 Perhaps scummy programmers aren't as interested in subverting Firefox, or perhaps the Firefox design doesn't accommodate scum so readily, but whatever the reason, I've found very few problems with rogue toolbars in Firefox. Certainly, I've never seen anything in Firefox like the endless cycle of prompts such as the one described in the section, "Escaping the endless add-on cycle," earlier in this chapter.

Removing a less-than-senseless toolbar in Firefox is very easy: Right-click any empty space on a toolbar and uncheck the line next to the toolbar. For example, if you install Yahoo! Messenger and suddenly discover that Firefox has sprouted a Yahoo! toolbar, you just right-click an empty spot and remove the check mark next to the line that says Yahoo! Toolbar. That's all it takes. When you restart Firefox, the toolbar doesn't come back.

If you encounter a really obnoxious toolbar in Firefox, or if you want to get rid of all vestiges of a scummy install (say, the Yahoo! menu entry that gets planted with a Yahoo! Messenger installation), you can haul out the big guns. Here's how:

1. **Start Firefox and choose Tools⇨Add-Ons.**

Firefox responds with a list of add-ons, as shown in Figure 3-14.

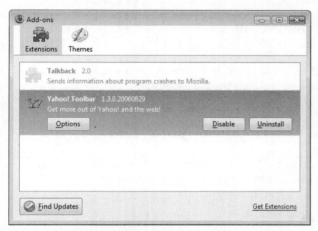

• **Figure 3-14:** Yahoo! darkens Firefox's door.

2. **Select the cantankerous add-on. Click the Disable button, "X" out of the Add-Ons dialog box, and restart Firefox.**

Poof. It's gone.

Firefox is really that simple.

Preventing New Auto-Starters

Now that you've gone to all that trouble of cleaning up your auto-starting programs, stopping new programs from adding their demon offspring to the auto-start lists is easy.

Mike Lin has a nifty free utility called StartupMonitor, which watches and warns you when intransigent applications try to tell Windows to auto-start programs. For example, Figure 3-15 shows you how StartupMonitor trapped Yahoo! Messenger's attempts to get itself hooked up to start automatically.

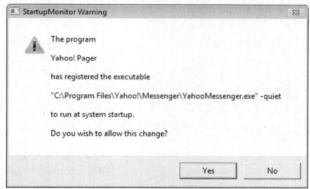

• **Figure 3-15:** Yahoo! Pager wants to run at startup, but you can block it if you have Mike Lin's StartupMonitor.

To use StartupMonitor, follow these steps:

1. **Download the file at www.mlin.net/ StartupMonitor.shtml.**

2. **Unzip it and run the StartupMonitor.msi program.**

That's all it takes. From that point onward, Startup Monitor keeps watch. I bet you'll be surprised by how many auto-starters it catches.

If you use and like Mike's programs, go to his Web site and leave him a tip. Mike wrote StartupMonitor a few years ago, while he was a student at MIT. Bright kid.

Technique 4

Getting Your Drives Up to Speed

Save Time By

- Understanding your drives and what they're up against
- Running defrags effectively, when necessary
- Changing or adding paging drives
- Using ReadyBoost to increase available memory when it makes sense

Once upon a time, cleaning and defragmenting hard drives rated right up there with washing the car or taking out the trash. Yeah, you had to do it eventually, but many other higher-priority things got in the way. Like sleeping.

We've come a long way.

Vista makes defragmenting easy. In fact, it's automatic — Vista runs defrags once a week whether you need them or not (and usually, you don't). In the not-so-good old days, running a defrag meant your PC went out to lunch for an hour or two or six. Vista defrag runs at low priority, both for your computer's processor and for demands on the hard drive, so if you're up at 1:00 on Wednesday morning when the defrag kicks in, you'll hardly notice that a defrag is in progress.

Vista has several additional disk-related timesaving tricks up its sleeve. This Technique takes you through the high points.

Cleaning and Defragging Your Hard Drive

No doubt you've heard of "defrag" or "defragging" or "defragmenting" your hard drive. But you might not know why it's important.

Understanding fragmentation

If you gloss over a few details, visualizing disk *fragmentation* is easy. Windows carves up a disk so it has lots of little spaces, like mailboxes. When Windows puts a file on the disk, it starts with the first open mailbox and pours the data from the file into the first box until the box is full. Then Windows goes on to the next available box, fills it up, and so on.

When you delete a file, Windows goes back and marks the boxes that contain the file as "available," freeing them up for more data. None of the data gets moved, however — the content in all the boxes stays put. Because new files are saved in the first available box, over time, the boxes turn into a patchwork quilt, with files scattered in boxes located all over the drive — fragmentation. Extensive fragmentation is bad because, when you open or want to use a file, Vista has to jump all over the disk to pull the pieces together.

When you *defragment* (or *defrag*) a hard drive, Windows rearranges the data on the drive so that each file is located in a single side-by-side block of mailboxes. With the files located contiguously, pulling data off the drive and into the computer takes less time.

In fact, deleting files in Windows is a bit more complicated than this mailbox analogy because deletion is a two-step process. When you delete a file in Vista, you don't delete the file or its data; in effect, you move the file into a special folder called the Recycle Bin. Vista doesn't actually delete a file — free up the file's mailboxes so other data can be stuffed into them — until you empty the Recycle Bin.

 If you clean your hard drive by deleting lots of files that you no longer need and then empty the Recycle Bin, you can free up thousands or hundreds of thousands of mailboxes all at the same time. That makes running a defrag all the more important *after* you clean up your disk.

Cleaning unnecessary files

If you want to make your hard drive work faster, start by cleaning out the files that you don't want or need. It's easier than you think.

Here's how to quickly delete unnecessary files from your hard drive:

1. **Double-click the Recycle Bin icon and make sure you don't want any of the files in there.**

If you do want to pull a file out of the Recycle Bin, select it and then click the Restore This Item icon at the top.

2. **Choose Start⇨Computer.**

3. **Right-click the drive you want to clean and choose Properties.**

Vista shows you the hard drive's Properties dialog box, as shown in Figure 4-1.

4. **Click the Disk Cleanup button.**

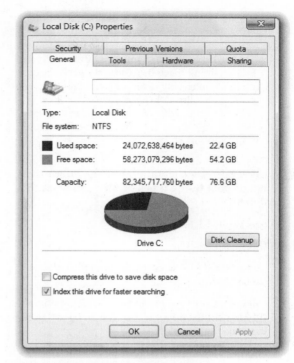

• **Figure 4-1: Properties for my C: drive.**

Vista asks if you want to clean up your files only, or files for all users on this computer.

5. **Click the Files from All Users on This Computer link.**

6. **Click Continue in the User Account Control dialog box; then wait as Vista gathers information about how much room can be saved.**

Finally, Vista brings up the Disk Cleanup dialog box.

7. **Click the More Options tab.**

Vista displays two key cleanup options, as shown in Figure 4-2.

8. **Click the lower Clean Up button, the one under System Restore and Shadow Copies.**

Vista asks if you're really sure that you want to delete all but the most recent restore point.

9. **If you're running Vista Home Basic or Home Premium and your system is working well**

(so it's unlikely that you will need an older restore point), click the Delete button.

On the other hand, if you have Vista Ultimate Edition, think twice (no, three times) before clicking Delete. By deleting your older restore points, you also get rid of Vista's "shadow copies" — the older versions of your data files. (Vista Home Basic and Vista Home Premium don't support shadow copies.)

10. **Click the Disk Cleanup tab. Then check the boxes next to the types of files you want to delete.**

See Table 4-1 for pointers.

11. **Click OK.**

Vista asks if you want to permanently delete these files.

12. **Click the Delete Files button, wait for Vista to finish, and then "X" out of the Properties dialog box.**

Your system should've reclaimed a lot of space — and I bet your hard drive looks like Swiss cheese, so go on to the next section and run a defrag.

• **Figure 4-2: Most people can give up a bunch of old restore points without losing much.**

TABLE 4-1: TYPES OF FILES YOU MAY WANT TO DELETE

Name	Recommendation	Description
Downloaded Program Files	Delete	Go ahead and delete all of your ActiveX and Java programs. If Internet Explorer or Firefox needs new copies, they can download them easily.
Temporary Internet Files	Delete	It'll slow down surfing to sites that you've already seen, but IE or Firefox can refresh the contents as needed.
Hibernation File Cleaner	Delete	Unless you've enabled it, Vista doesn't use hibernation; instead, it has "sleep mode." If you check this box, Vista deletes the hibernation file, which takes up as much room as you have in physical memory (1GB memory = 1GB hibernation file).
Recycle Bin	Delete	If you checked your Recycle Bin for any files you want to keep before running Disk Cleanup (it's Step #1), let Vista clean out the dross.
Temporary Files	Delete	Vista deletes .tmp files and files in the Temp folder if they are more than seven days old. No problem.
Thumbnails	Delete	Windows Explorer stores thumbnails of video and picture files, and some other types of files. Give 'em the heave-ho.
System Queued Windows Error Reporting Log	Keep	If (perhaps I should say "when") Vista crashes, it generates a log. Might as well hold onto them in case a tech needs them to figure out why Vista went bye-bye.

Cleaning and Defragging Your Hard Drive 43

Running a manual defrag

So you followed the instructions in the preceding section and deleted a humongous bunch of useless, old files. Now's a good time to run a manual defrag. Here's how:

1. **Choose Start⇨All Programs⇨Accessories⇨ System Tools⇨Disk Defragmenter.**

You have to click Continue to clear the User Account Control prompt, and then Vista shows you the Spartan Disk Defragmenter dialog box shown in Figure 4-3.

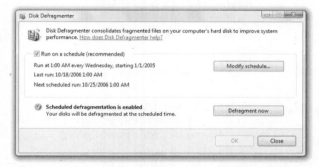

• **Figure 4-3: You can run a manual defrag any time you like.**

2. **Click the button marked Defragment Now.**

According to the dialog box that appears, Vista takes "from a few minutes to a few hours" to examine your hard drive, and, if it determines that a defrag is warranted, Vista defragments the drive.

 There is no status bar, no estimate of the remaining time, no report on how badly fragmented the drive might be — in fact, no information of any kind. The simple note that appears in the dialog box represents the whole shootin' match. If you want information, you have to run the defrag through the command line, as I describe in the next section.

 While the defrag is in progress, you can continue to use your computer in just about any way. You can even turn off or restart the computer with no ill effect — although the defrag will stop, and you have to restart it again manually.

When Vista finishes, it doesn't say anything. You just see the original Disk Defragmenter dialog box, as in Figure 4-3.

3. **Click Close.**

You return to Windows with a freshly defragged hard drive.

 Vista actually performs a *partial defrag* — it doesn't work hard enough to get all the pieces of all the files stuck into contiguous places on the hard drive. Instead, it only defragments chunks of less than 64MB. When it encounters a file larger than 64MB, any 64MB piece that's already defragmented isn't touched. Ends up that there's little, if any, benefit to bringing together pieces larger than 64MB because of the inherent delay in reading a spinning disk.

Defragmenting — the advanced course

Unless you change the settings (by using the Modify Schedule button in Figure 4-3), Vista runs a defrag automatically every Wednesday at 1:00 a.m. If your computer is turned off at 1:00, the defrag will start shortly after your computer comes back to life. The automatically scheduled defrag runs on all your hard drives.

 You can run an automatic defrag daily, weekly, or monthly, but few people need to run one more than once a week. I recommend that you leave Microsoft's default in place.

 If you want to dig deeper in de Disk Defragmenter (sorry, couldn't resist), you can run the program from the Vista command prompt. You might want to do so if you want to see whether your drive needs defragmenting or if you only want to defrag a single drive.

Here's how to run a manual defrag:

1. **Choose Start⇨All Programs⇨Accessories.**

2. **Right-click Command Prompt and choose Run as Administrator.**

Vista makes you click Continue in (yet another) User Account Control dialog box.

The command prompt comes up, as shown in Figure 4-4.

• **Figure 4-4:** The command prompt comes up in Administrator mode.

3. Type `defrag c: -a` to check the C: drive and see if it needs a defrag, or choose one of the other commands from Table 4-2. Press Enter.

Vista produces a report like the one in Figure 4-5.

• **Figure 4-5:** Check to see if you need to run a defrag on the C: drive.

4. You can type another command if you like. When you're done, "X" out of the command prompt.

If you run a defrag from the command prompt, it behaves precisely like a manual defrag run through the Vista interface. There's nothing inherently faster or safer about running a defrag from the command prompt.

TABLE 4-2: DEFRAG COMMANDS

This Command	Does This
`defrag d: -a`	Analyzes drive D: to see if it needs to be defragged
`defrag c: -w`	Runs a full defragmentation of drive C:, consolidating all files whether or not they're larger than 64MB

This Command	Does This
`defrag -c -v`	Defrags all the drives (that's what –c means) and produces a "verbose" (-v) detailed report
`defrag -c -i -v`	Defrags all the drives and produces a verbose report, but only runs when the computer is completely idle (that's what –i means)

 If you want to see the results of all the defrag runs on your computer, you need to look in the Microsoft Management Console. It's worth the effort to occasionally make sure that defrags are running as scheduled. Here's how:

1. Click Start, right-click Computer, and choose Manage.

The Microsoft Management Console (MMC) appears.

2. On the left, double-click to navigate down to System Tools⇨Task Scheduler⇨Task Scheduler Library⇨Microsoft⇨Windows⇨Defrag.

3. In the middle, click the History tab.

Vista shows you a list of all the events associated with Disk Defragmenter — including manual runs, automatic runs, rescheduling, and so on, as shown in Figure 4-6.

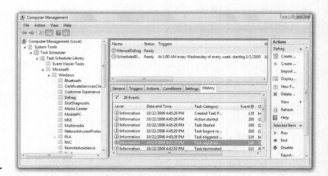

• **Figure 4-6:** All the defrag events.

4. To see the details about a particular defrag event, double-click it. Click Close to return to the MMC.

For example, in Figure 4-7, a scheduled defrag didn't run. If you see many error reports like this one, you should follow the instructions to get to the bottom of the problem.

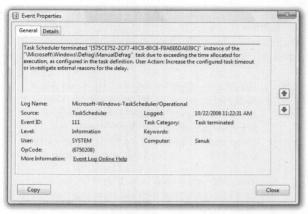

• **Figure 4-7: A scheduled Disk Defragmenter run took too long to start.**

5. When you're satisfied that defrags are running properly, "X" out of the Microsoft Management Console.

 Do you want more control over your defrag runs? Check out Diskeeper, the company that Microsoft turns to when it needs defrag help: `www.diskeeper.com`.

Expanding Paging Volumes

When Windows runs out of memory — the 256MB or 1GB that you have in your PC — Vista needs to shuffle things around quickly. That shuffling is called *paging*, and it's accomplished by copying blocks of memory out to your hard disk.

Think of it this way: Many different programs are running on your computer at the same time. Each needs memory in order to accomplish its tasks. When programs want more memory, they ask Windows to hand some over. When programs are finished with a chunk of memory, they hand it back to Windows. Your memory rapidly turns into a patchwork quilt of chunks,

with Windows taking care of parceling out chunks of memory when they're requested and returning them to the available pool when they're no longer needed.

Everything goes along swimmingly until Windows runs out of chunks of memory. Suddenly, a program wants more memory, but Windows has already handed out every single chunk. Windows solves the problem by taking a snapshot of a chunk of memory and tossing that snapshot to the hard drive. It then gives the chunk of memory to the program that requested it.

At some point, the program that originally had the chunk of memory wants it back. No problem. Windows runs out to the disk, retrieves the snapshot, sticks it in memory, and hands that chunk over to the old program. That's called a *hard page fault*. (I won't mention the fact that bringing the snapshot into memory may, itself, force Windows to take yet another snapshot and send it out to disk. And so on. But you get the picture.)

The snapshots of chunks of memory out on your disk are called *virtual memory*. Virtual memory sits in *paging files*.

 Here's where speed comes in. Windows works like crazy getting programs and their data into the computer. It also works like crazy keeping the virtual memory going. If your virtual memory sits on the same disk as your programs and data, Windows has to hop all over the disk to keep all the programs going. On the other hand, if your paging file sits on a hard disk that doesn't contain your programs, that helps solve the memory problem simply because Windows can run faster if it's juggling two different disks at the same time. The net result is that you should allow Windows to use all your fast hard drives for virtual memory (er, paging files), providing the drives have room available.

If the Resource Monitor (see Technique 2) tells you that you're getting a lot of hard page faults — say, more than a couple dozen hard faults per second — and you have two (or more) fast hard drives, you may be able to speed up your system significantly by allowing Vista to put paging files on both hard drives.

Here's how to spread the paging load:

1. **Click Start, right-click Computer, and choose Properties.**

   Vista shows you the View Basic Information about Your Computer dialog box (see Technique 1).

2. **On the left, under Tasks, click the Advanced System Settings link.**

   You have to click through a User Account Control security prompt, and then Vista brings up the System Properties dialog box, showing the Advanced tab.

3. **At the top, under Performance, click Settings.**

   You see the Performance Options dialog box.

4. **Click the Advanced tab, and then under the heading Virtual Memory, click the Change button.**

   Vista brings up the Virtual Memory dialog box.

5. **Uncheck the box marked Automatically Manage Paging File Size for All Drives.**

6. **Click any drive that doesn't currently have a paging file, click the button marked Custom Size, and type Initial and Maximum sizes for the unused drive.**

   Make the sizes similar to the sizes set for your C: drive.

7. **Click Set and then click OK three times to go back to Vista.**

   Your change takes effect immediately.

As long as you have space free on your hard drives, it doesn't hurt to have extra paging files set up in case you start running low on memory.

Changing Partitions on the Fly

Vista allows you to break off chunks of your hard drive and turn them into more-or-less autonomous *partitions*. To a first approximation anyway, each partition is treated like a different drive: Each partition has its own drive letter, and each can be formatted

independently of the others. You can put different operating systems in different partitions so, for example, one hard drive can hold both Vista and Windows XP, and you can choose between them when you start the computer.

Some learned sages insist that any sufficiently large hard drive should be divided into two or three partitions.

I say balderdash. Having a single hard drive broken up into a C: drive, a D: drive, and an E: drive only makes life more difficult. It doesn't improve performance, doesn't make things more secure, doesn't do anything but make it harder for you to find and manage your data.

Yes, there are exceptions. If you set up a computer to multiboot into different operating systems, you want a partition for each operating system, and you may need to set up different kinds of partitions depending on which OS you're using. But if you're serious about multibooting, you're better off installing virtual machines by using a product such as VMware (www.vmware.com) anyway. Partitioning for the sheer delight of it doesn't make any sense.

If you're stuck with partitions (some computer manufacturers still insist on partitioning hard drives in new PCs), or if somebody's convinced you that you need to use partitions, you should know that there's a fast, relatively easy way to change the size of the partitions on your hard drive, as long as Vista's in charge.

Here's how to resize your partitions:

1. **Click Start, right-click Computer, and choose Manage.**

   You will probably be required to click Continue in a User Account Control dialog box. The Microsoft Management Console appears.

2. **On the left, double-click Storage and then click Disk Management.**

   You see a schematic diagram of your disk drives and partitions, like the one in Figure 4-8.

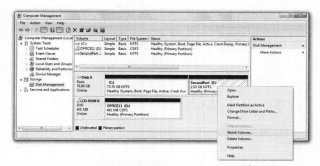

• **Figure 4-8: A diagram of your drives and partitions.**

3. To resize a partition, right-click the partition and choose either Extend Volume or Shrink Volume.

In order to extend a partition, you must have space available on the physical drive.

If you choose to Extend the partition, Vista launches the Extend Volume Wizard, which steps you through the rest of the process.

If you choose to Shrink the partition, Vista asks by how much with a dialog box like the one in Figure 4-9.

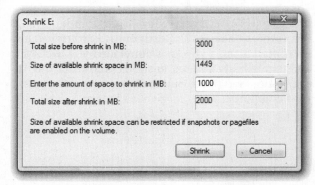

• **Figure 4-9: Specify how much you want to shrink.**

4. Type the amount you want to shrink and then click the Shrink button.

Vista shows the newly shrunken area as Unallocated (see Figure 4-10).

• **Figure 4-10: New partitions start out unallocated.**

5. To create a new partition in the unallocated area, right-click it and choose New Simple Volume; then follow the New Simple Volume Wizard.

6. When you're done, "X" out of the Microsoft Management Console.

What about Drive Accelerators?

Vista boasts three technologies that speed up your computer by judicious use of drives:

- **SuperFetch** keeps track of which applications are being used the most on your computer and tries to pre-load those applications so they're available before you need them. Vista handles SuperFetch automatically; you don't need to change anything.

- **ReadyDrive** takes advantage of "hybrid" hard drives — the drives with significant amounts of integrated flash memory — to boot faster, come back from "sleep" faster, and minimize battery drain. Vista handles ReadyDrive automatically, too.

- **ReadyBoost** helps PCs with limited amounts of memory by using a flash memory drive ("key drive" or "USB drive") to augment the functions of regular memory. Vista uses the flash memory as an adjunct to regular memory. Unlike the other two acceleration technologies, you have to make ReadyBoost work: You need to plug a key drive into a USB port, and when Vista asks if you want to use the key drive to speed up your computer, you need to give your permission.

If you have 1GB of memory on your computer, ReadyBoost won't do much. If you're limping along with 256MB or thereabouts, ReadyBoost is definitely worth the effort. If you're somewhere in between, and you have a fast USB drive handy, give it a shot. You may be pleasantly surprised.

Here's how to get ReadyBoost going:

1. **Plug a fast key drive (a USB drive or Flash Memory drive) into any handy USB port.**

   Older key drives tend to use slower memory. Given a choice, go for a newer key drive with faster memory access times.

   Vista brings up the AutoPlay dialog box.

2. **Choose Speed Up My System Using Windows ReadyBoost.**

   Vista shows you the key drive's Properties dialog box, on the ReadyBoost tab, as shown in Figure 4-11.

3. **Choose the Use This Device option and adjust the slider to reserve the indicated amount of space for ReadyBoost.**

   Any space that's left on the drive can be used for data — but the ReadyBoost part is off limits.

4. **Click OK.**

   ReadyBoost starts immediately. You can take the key drive out at any time without fear of clobbering anything.

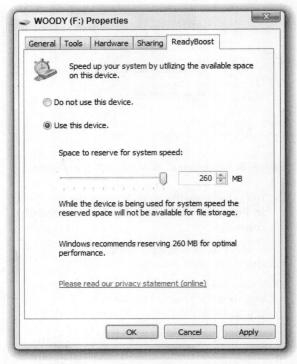

• **Figure 4-11: ReadyBoost appears as a property of the drive itself.**

Vista stores data on the ReadyBoost key drive in an encrypted form. If you lose the key drive, it would be exceptionally difficult for anyone to crack the encryption and figure out what you had running on your computer.

Technique 5

Making the Screen Run Faster

Save Time By

- Understanding video performance tradeoffs
- Eliminating Aero Glass if you don't need or want it
- Adjusting on-screen animations
- Recovering from clobbered video features

Windows Vista and Aero Glass: a match made in marketing heaven.

No doubt you've heard and read about Aero Glass — after all, Microsoft spent a fortune tying Vista and Aero Glass together in the minds and pocketbooks of computer consumers. A very large percentage of all Vista Home Basic users upgrade to Home Premium because they want to get Aero Glass. But when you get right down to it, do you know what *Aero* is? Or *Glass*?

In this Technique, I cut through the bafflegab and show you the pieces you can throw away. You can make your computer run faster by cutting out the glitter and fluff, and the speed-up can be considerable if you have a less-capable video card. Follow along as I show you how.

Understanding Aero Glass

To understand Aero Glass, you must first realize that *Aero* and *Glass* are two completely different display features. Each one imposes a significant overhead on your computer. If you can live without one or the other or both, you can speed up your computer's performance.

Running Aero

Microsoft calls Aero a *color scheme*, but that's like calling the Starship Enterprise a footlocker. Aero is a unique design — sometimes called a *shell* or maybe a *skin* — that defines the way windows look on your screen. The best way to understand Aero is to compare it with other window designs.

In Figure 5-1, you see Vista's Aero shell, the one that you probably have on your computer right now. It's quite distinctive in many ways, most noticeably because the control buttons in the upper-right corner of each window sit on the edge of the window; because the "X" button glows red when you hover your mouse over it; and because of the gray shadow around the window.

• **Figure 5-1: A Vista Aero window.**

If your computer doesn't have enough oomph (more specifically, if your graphic card doesn't have enough oomph), Vista won't run Aero. Instead, you're relegated to Vista Basic, which you can see in Figure 5-2.

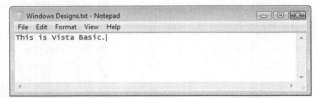

• **Figure 5-2: Vista Basic doesn't look much like Aero.**

Vista Basic doesn't look much at all like Aero: The control buttons sit farther down on the title bar; the "X" button doesn't glow red; and there's no five o'clock (much less three o'clock or nine o'clock) shadow.

Vista also supports the Windows Standard shell, shown in Figure 5-3, which is identical to what folks used to see in Windows 98, Windows 2000, and other less-mentionable versions.

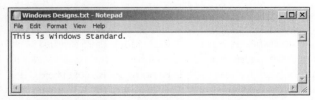

• **Figure 5-3: The Windows Standard design has a decidedly retro feel.**

If you're willing to live with the Vista Basic or Windows Standard shell, and you have a relatively sluggish video card, you can speed your computer's

window-handling considerably by switching yourself to a less-demanding shell.

Here's how to switch from Aero to one of the other shells:

1. **Right-click an empty spot on the desktop and choose Personalize.**

   Vista shows you the Personalize Appearance and Sounds dialog box.

2. **Click the Window Color and Appearance link.**

   Vista brings up the Window Color and Appearance dialog box, shown in Figure 5-4.

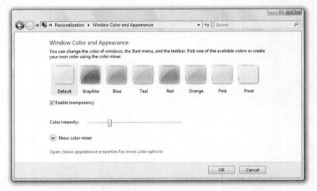

• **Figure 5-4: Control the Aero shell's appearance here.**

   Note: If you don't see the Window Color and Appearance dialog box, you aren't running the Aero shell. You may be incapable of running Aero because of your graphics card, memory, or video settings — or it may be because you got stuck with the Bait 'n' Switch, er, Home Basic version of Vista. If you don't see the options shown in Figure 5-4, and instead you see the classic Appearance Properties dialog box. Go on to Step 4.

3. **Click the Open Classic Appearance Properties for More Color Options link.**

   The wording here is a bit confusing, but in the end, you get the Appearance Settings dialog box shown in Figure 5-5.

• **Figure 5-5:** Change to non-Aero shells.

4. **Choose Windows Vista Basic, Windows Standard, or one of the other shells in the box marked Color Scheme. Then click OK and, when Vista comes back, "X" out of the Personalize Appearance and Sounds dialog box.**

Your new shell takes effect immediately.

 When the Aero shell is running, Vista makes full use of the Windows Display Manager. In particular:

▶ When you hover your mouse over a button in the Windows taskbar, Vista frequently displays the contents of the minimized program, as you can see in Figure 5-6.

▶ You can use "Flip 3D" (see Figure 5-7) to riffle through running programs by either holding down the Windows key and pressing Tab or by clicking the Switch Between Windows icon in the Quick Launch toolbar, next to the Start button.

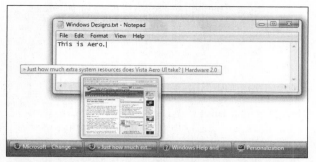

• **Figure 5-6:** One of the nice benefits of the Aero shell — you can see a thumbnail of programs in the taskbar.

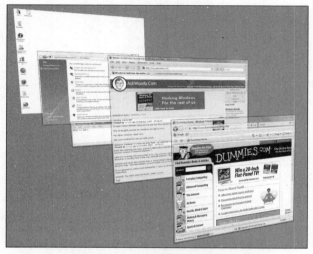

• **Figure 5-7:** Flip 3D works only if the Aero shell is running.

If you turn off the Aero shell, you lose both of those capabilities.

 How can you tell how much faster your computer runs without Aero? The short answer: you can't. Perhaps some day, somebody will come up with a benchmark that can say whether shifting from Aero to Windows Standard on your computer speeds up window handling by 10 percent or 50 percent, but I would take any such numbers with a grain of salt. The best approach is to simply try it. Change over to Vista Basic or Windows Standard and live with it for a few hours. If you yearn for the Aero interface, switch it back on.

Superimposing Glass

In Vista, *Glass* refers to a transparent (more accurately a translucent) effect that allows you to see through the border around windows on your desktop and look at a blurry version of whatever lies beneath. Most people find Glass worthwhile because it gives a visual clue about the contents of the window immediately below the one they're working with. (See Figure 5-8.)

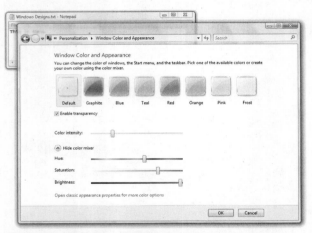

• **Figure 5-8:** The Glass effect lets you see through the border of the topmost window.

You can see the Glass effect only if you're running the Aero shell (see the preceding section). If you switch to any other shell, Glass doesn't exist: Borders around windows are opaque, and there's nothing you can do about it.

 The Glass effect puts significant demands on your graphics card by pushing the Direct3D pixel-shader feature hard. Just how much additional demand — and how much you can speed up things by disabling Glass — is something that you simply have to try.

Confusingly, you won't find a setting called "Glass" anywhere in Vista. Here's how to disable it:

1. Right-click an empty spot on the desktop and choose Personalize. Then click the Window Color and Appearance link.

If Aero is running, you get the Window Color and Appearance dialog box, shown in Figure 5-9.

2. Uncheck the box marked Enable Transparency.

The Glass effect disappears. You can see that the borders in Figure 5-9 are opaque.

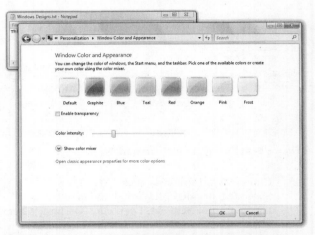

• **Figure 5-9:** With the Glass effect turned off, you can't see through the borders of windows.

3. Click OK and then "X" out of the Personalize Appearance and Sounds dialog box.

To bring Glass back, repeat the procedure, and in Step 2, check the Enable Transparency box.

 People frequently confuse the Aero shell with a particular set of colors. In fact, the colors offered by Vista in Figure 5-8 are simply pre-configured combinations of Hue, Saturation, and Brightness demonstrated in the Color Mixer part of the dialog box. You can change the color of the Aero shell by clicking one of the pre-established colors (Graphite, Blue, Teal, and so on), or you can mix your own by varying the Color Intensity, Hue, Saturation, and Brightness.

Tweaking the Display for Speed

Most Vista users think that Aero Glass consumes an inordinate amount of computer processing power. In my experience, that isn't the case: Your video card takes a performance hit, but your computer itself isn't as badly affected. As long as you have a moderately capable video card with 256MB or more of on-board memory, you probably won't notice much of a speed boost if you disable Glass, Aero, or both. If your video card isn't up to snuff, you may see slowdowns that can be alleviated by turning off Glass or Aero. The only way to find out for sure, though, is to give it a try.

If you aren't terribly concerned about Vista's appearance, however, there *is* a way to speed up the screen substantially, no matter what kind of video card you may have. You can, to a first approximation anyway, turn off virtually all the cute visual effects that make Vista so suave. But if you want to make your interface mean and lean, be careful to follow the instructions in this section. Vista still has bugs in it, and the bugs crop up on my machines whenever I try to get the display lead out.

Here's how to wring the most possible speed out of your display — and do it safely:

1. **First, back up your current display settings. To do so, right-click an empty location on your desktop and choose Properties. Then click the Theme link.**

You can save all your display settings by creating a restore point, if you like, but if you change something (such as installing a program) and then decide to go back to your original display settings, Vista can get mightily confused. I prefer to save the current display settings as a theme.

Vista shows you the Theme Settings dialog box.

2. **Click the Save As button.**

You see the Save As dialog box, shown in Figure 5-10.

• **Figure 5-10: Give your theme a name you can remember.**

3. **Type a name for your saved theme and click Save. Then "X" out of the Theme Settings dialog box and "X" out of the Personalize Appearance and Sounds dialog box.**

4. **Click Start, right-click Computer, and choose Properties. Then click the link to the Windows Experience Index.**

You see the Windows Experience Index. I discuss the WEI extensively in Technique 1.

5. **On the left, under Tasks, click the link to Adjust Visual Effects.**

After you click to Continue through a User Account Control warning, Vista presents you with a laundry list of visual effects — performance-sapping features that make it easier to interact with Vista but take up a lot of cycles in the process. See Figure 5-11.

• **Figure 5-11: These effects really do slow down your PC.**

6. **Choose the Adjust for Best Performance option and then click OK.**

Vista goes out to lunch for a second or two, and when it comes back, everything looks different (see Figure 5-12).

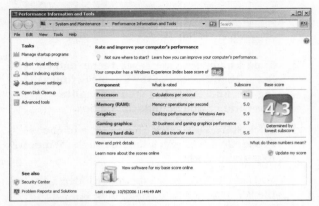

• **Figure 5-12: The Best Performance setting zaps out the Aero shell and much more.**

7. **Play with Vista for a while and see if you can stand it. You'll notice immediately that Vista is much, much snappier. But it's also much more dour.**

If you want to bring back your old display settings, don't bother going into the Visual Effects dialog box, as in Step 5. Resetting your visual effects to Adjust for Best Appearance or Let Windows Choose What's Best for My Computer, at least in my experience, doesn't reset all the visual effects. It's buggy. Thar be tygers here.

8. **If you decide to revert to your original settings, right-click an empty location on the desktop and choose Properties. Click the Theme link. Choose your original theme (which you set in Step 3) and click OK.**

You may need to log off and log back on again for the changes to take effect.

Reclaiming Automatically Zapped Visual Elements

From time to time, Vista decides that it can't handle Aero Glass anymore, displays a message to the effect that "some visual elements have been turned off," and disables some portion of the interface — commonly, it drops Glass, but occasionally it'll drop way back to the Vista Standard shell (see the section, "Understanding Aero Glass," earlier in this chapter).

If that happens to you, chances are good the program(s) you're running hasn't been tweaked to run well with Vista. You should check the program's support site to see if an update is available.

After the problem is cured or you quit the program, if Vista doesn't automatically switch itself back to Aero Glass, follow these steps to get yourself back where you should be:

1. **Right-click an empty spot on the desktop and choose Personalize. Then click the Window Color and Appearance link.**

Vista will show you one of two dialog boxes.

2. **If you see the Appearance Settings dialog box (Figure 5-5), select Windows Aero and then click OK. Then click the Windows Color and Appearance link again and proceed to Step 3.**

3. **When you see the Window Color and Appearance dialog box (Figure 5-8), check the box marked Enable Transparency and click OK.**

4. **"X" out of the Personalize Appearance and Sounds dialog box.**

Technique 6

Scheduling a Nightly Reboot

Maybe I'm superstitious, but I think my computer runs faster, or at least better, after it has been rebooted. There's something about a full restart that cleanses the beast's soul. I'm not talking about a piddling "sleep" or hibernation mode: trickling back on the PC's power may save electricity, but it does nothing to restore the psyche. I'm talking about a full-fledged, all-the-way-to-the-farm-and-back boot. You know, the kind you get when you pull the plug.

Unfortunately, I never remember to reboot until it's too late: something starts acting weird, or my PC starts behaving like it's stuck in a foot of mud, and I figure, "Aw heck, I should've rebooted this morning." Hindsight. 20/20. 'Nuff said.

That's why I was so tickled to discover that you can convince Vista to reboot itself, every night, and do so with a minimal amount of fuss and destruction. That's what this Technique is all about.

Hibernating with a Hot Key

Buried deep inside Vista lurks a little-known program called shutdown that shuts down your system quickly — in many cases, without asking whether you want to save any work in progress. shutdown has many interesting capabilities.

For example, if you want to set up a hot key that will hibernate your laptop — so you can go into hibernation without futzing with the mouse — it's quite easy using the shutdown command. First, you need to set up a shortcut that hibernates your computer. Then, you need to assign a hot key to run the shortcut.

Here's how to set up the shortcut:

1. **Right-click any empty location on your desktop.**

2. **Choose New⇨Shortcut.**

   The Create Shortcut Wizard appears (see Figure 6-1).

• **Figure 6-1: This shortcut points directly to the Windows program called** `shutdown`.

3. **In the Type the Location of the Item box, type** `shutdown /h` **and click Next.**

   It's important that you have a space before the slash and no space after the slash.

4. **In the Type a Name for this Shortcut box, give your shortcut a name.**

   Use something daring, like `Hibernate`.

5. **Click Finish.**

   Vista puts a new shortcut on your desktop.

6. **Right-click the shortcut and choose Properties.**

   Vista warns you that `shutdown` doesn't have any icons and that you have to choose one from the list or specify a file.

7. **Click OK.**

   You see the Change Icon dialog box shown in Figure 6-2.

8. **Pick an appropriate icon for the shortcut and double-click it.**

   I like the "off switch" icon in the lower-right corner of Figure 6-2.

9. **Click OK and your new, quick Hibernate shortcut appears on the desktop.**

• **Figure 6-2: Choose an icon that won't be confused with more prosaic icons on your desktop.**

To test the new Hibernate icon, get a couple of programs running and double-click the Hibernate icon. Vista should take just a second to darken the screen and a couple seconds more to complete the transition to hibernation.

 This isn't "sleep" mode. When your PC hibernates, there's no power consumption at all.

To bring your computer back, push the power button on your PC, and the Resuming Windows message appears. A moment later, you're ready to log on — and resume from precisely where you left off.

After you have the Hibernate shortcut working, here's how to hook it up with a hot key:

1. **Right-click the Hibernate shortcut and choose Properties.**

   Vista shows you the Properties dialog box.

2. **Click inside the box marked Shortcut Key.**

3. **Press the key combination that you would like to use in order to hibernate your computer.**

   For example, I held down the Ctrl key and pressed F11.

4. **Click OK.**

Some programs "swallow" hot keys, so you may have trouble getting a specific key combination to work when you're using one of the voracious programs. Most programs, though, let unusual key combinations get through to Vista.

Test your fast hibernation hot key: just press the key combination you established in Step 3 earlier. Bet you'll be impressed.

Using Other Shutdown Switches

The preceding section used a specific shutdown switch — the /h switch — to put your PC into hibernation. The shutdown command has many other switches, some of which can be useful. Table 6-1 lists the ones I find most useful.

TABLE 6-1: SWITCHES FOR THE SHUTDOWN COMMAND

Shutdown Switch	What It Does
/h	Puts the computer in hibernate mode.
/l	Logs off the current user, allowing very little time to save any unsaved work.
/r	Restarts the computer, allowing very little time to save.
/g	Restarts the computer, and then restarts any registered applications that were running when the system was shut down.
/t *nn*	Counts down a timer *nn* seconds before running the specific restart command. After *nn* seconds, the computer shuts down, without any additional time to save, and then restarts.
/c "*text*"	Displays whatever text you type between the quotation marks in a message box while the shutdown timer (/t *nn*) is in progress.
/p	Turns off the computer. Very little warning.

Generally the easiest way to work with these switches is by constructing a shortcut, by using the approach in the preceding section, and then either right-clicking the shortcut or assigning a hot key to the shortcut. Or (as you see in the next section), you can let the Vista Task Scheduler reboot your computer automatically at a specific time.

For example, you can use the steps at the beginning of the preceding section to create shortcuts to run

- ✔ shutdown /l, which logs you off and gives you only a few seconds to save.

- ✔ shutdown /p, which turns off the computer.

- ✔ shutdown /r /t 90 /c "Your computer will restart in 90 seconds", which displays a message saying as much for about 90 seconds and then restarts the computer.

Restarting Overnight

You can use the shutdown command, as described in the preceding section, in conjunction with Vista's Task Scheduler to perform a reboot at a specific time of day. The reboot takes the computer back to the Windows logon screen. When you log on in the morning, Vista restores most of the programs you were using to the point they were in when you shut down.

The operative word there: *most*.

This Technique doesn't use "sleep" or "hibernate" mode. It completely reboots the computer, from scratch, clearing out the cobwebs. Any programs that register themselves with Vista (including all the Microsoft Office programs, Internet Explorer 7, and Firefox 2) get restored to the point they were at before the reboot. Many other programs, particularly older programs (such as Wordpad and Paint), won't reappear. If you leave unsaved work open in those programs, when you come back after the automatic restart, any changes you made are lost. Forever. Don't say I didn't warn you, okay?

With that important warning, you can make Vista reboot overnight by telling Vista's Task Scheduler to run the correct `shutdown` command in the middle of the night. Here's how:

1. **Make sure your user account has a password.**

You can run scheduled tasks only for accounts with passwords. If you aren't sure whether you have a password, click Start➪Control Panel; then under the User Accounts and Family Safety icon, click the link to Add or Remove User Accounts. Click through the User Account Control dialog box, and your account will appear in the list; it should say `Password Protected`.

2. **Choose Start➪All Programs➪Accessories➪ System Tools➪Task Scheduler.**

After you click Continue on a User Account Control warning message, Vista shows you the Task Scheduler.

3. **On the right, under Actions, click the Create Task link.**

The Task Scheduler shows you the Create Task dialog box, as in Figure 6-3. This is a rather odd buzzard (that's another technical term) because it works like a wizard, but it doesn't behave like one. Follow along closely.

4. **In the box marked Name, type a name for the restarting job. (I used `Dummies Restart`.)**

• **Figure 6-3: Create a task to reboot your computer.**

5. **At the bottom, under Security Options, select the button marked Run Only When User Is Logged On (don't worry, the scheduled task will run even if the PC is in "sleep mode," as you will see in Step 11).**

6. **Check the box marked Run with Highest Privileges.**

7. **Click the Triggers tab. At the lower left, click New.**

The Task Scheduler brings up the New Trigger dialog box, shown in Figure 6-4.

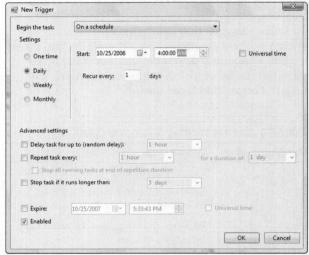

• **Figure 6-4: Set the reboot to run every day, early in the morning.**

8. **On the left, under Settings, click Daily. For a Start time, choose a time when you're not likely to be using the computer. Click OK.**

In Figure 6-4, I chose to run the reboot at 4:00 in the morning every day. It's unlikely that I'll be using the computer at 4:00. Vista's automatic defragger runs at 1:00 on Wednesday mornings (see Technique 4), so the reboot is unlikely to interfere with the defrag run.

9. **Click the Actions tab. At the lower left, click New.**

(See what I mean about this acting like a wizard?) You see the New Action dialog box.

10. **In the Program/Script box, type** shutdown, **and in the Add Arguments (Optional) box, type** /g /c "Rebooting the computer" **and then click OK.**

Vista displays a text box with the message Re-booting the computer while the shutdown is in progress. It's important that you have no spaces after the slashes, and a space in front of the second slash only. You can put any text you like between the quotes.

11. **Click the Conditions tab (see Figure 6-5). If you are using a desktop computer, or if you have a laptop that you keep plugged in all the time, in the Power area of the dialog box, check the box marked Wake the Computer to Run This Task. If you're running a laptop that isn't plugged in all the time, consider whether you want to run the task even if the computer isn't plugged into the wall and then make the change accordingly. Then click OK.**

The Task Scheduler displays a password prompt.

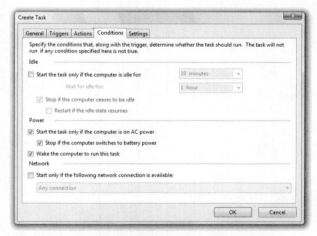

• **Figure 6-5: Make sure the computer wakes up, if need be.**

12. **Type your current password into the box and click OK.**

 This is tricky. The password you type into the prompt box must be valid *when the shutdown command runs*. So remember that if you change your password at any time in the future, you have to come back to the Task Scheduler and change the password here, too.

Your new task appears in the Active Tasks list at the bottom of the Task Scheduler (see Figure 6-6).

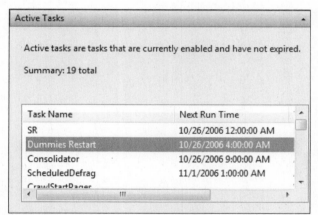

• **Figure 6-6: The new scheduled task appears.**

13. **"X" out of the Task Scheduler.**

14. **Restart your computer.**

It isn't supposed to work this way, but I've had trouble with scheduled tasks not "taking" until the computer is restarted.

From that point on, until you change your password, your computer will automatically reboot itself every morning.

Part II

Convincing Windows to Work Your Way

The 5th Wave   By Rich Tennant

UBER-USER DWAYNE GRANTZ CHALKS UP BEFORE PUTTING WINDOWS VISTA THROUGH ITS PACES.

Technique 7

Streamlining the Start Menu

Save Time By

- ✔ Supercharging the Start menu
- ✔ Sticking the programs *you* choose on the Start menu
- ✔ Organizing the All Programs menu (yes, really!)
- ✔ Turning the click-click-click Control Panel into a quick cascading menu

The Start menu: It's one place you go back to over and over again. Microsoft set up the Start menu so it works well for the average Vista user. Unfortunately, there's no such thing as an average Vista user (or, if there is, he or she certainly isn't reading this book!).

Changing the Start menu couldn't be simpler. Changing it to do the work you want, as quickly as you want it, presents an ongoing challenge. A pre-customization Start menu appears in Figure 7-1.

This Technique shows you the key tools at your disposal to mold the mother of all Windows menus. It's a great place to organize, consolidate, group, and simplify.

• **Figure 7-1: Duangkhae's Start menu before this Technique's makeover.**

Navigating the Start Menu

If you look closely at the Start menu in Figure 7-1, you can see that it's divided into different sections:

- ✔ In the upper-left, just above that really faint line, sit the programs, folders, or shortcuts that you want to get to quickly. These items are *pinned*, which means that, after you put 'em there, they stay put. Windows starts with Internet Explorer and Outlook (or Windows Mail) in the list, but if you install Firefox or a different e-mail program and choose it as your default, the usurper's icon replaces IE or Windows Mail.

  I pontificate on pinned programs, pieces, and places in "Pinning and Unpinning," later in this Technique.

- ✔ Below that, there's the Most Frequently Used list. They really aren't your most frequently used programs. Microsoft builds a bias into determining what's "frequent." Your best bet is to limit what Microsoft can do with this space and make more room for pinned items. See the sidebar, "Adapting the adaptive menu," later in this Technique.

- ✔ Then comes the All Programs submenu. It doesn't list all your programs — you didn't really think it was that simple, did you? But you can clean up this submenu to make it more useful. The details are in "Reining In the All Programs Submenu," later in this Technique.

- ✔ At the bottom, you see the Start Search box, which ties into Windows Explorer's search capabilities. See Technique 16 for details.

- ✔ On the right at the top, you see the name and icon of the current user. To change your icon — or, yes, even your name! — see Technique 40.

- ✔ All along the right side is a list of various locations and system programs that you can modify — to some extent — to reflect how you use Vista. See "Cascading to Save Time," later in this Technique.

- ✔ At the bottom right, you have buttons to put your computer in "sleep" state and to "lock" your computer — in other words, go to the Windows logon screen. The arrow points to options for shutting down and restarting, but you already knew that, right?

 A hierarchy of needs is at work on the Start menu. You'll save an enormous amount of time, every day, if you make the Start menu work your way. Put the programs you use many times a day on your Quick Launch toolbar (see Technique 12), pin the ones you need frequently in the upper-left corner of your Start menu, rearrange the structure of the All Programs submenu so that you can find infrequently used programs with some ease, and judiciously choose the entries for the right side of the Start menu.

To speed up the Start menu — and the rest of the Windows interface, for that matter — in another way that makes sense, check out the section about no-nonsense tweaking in Technique 5. Turn off the time-consuming animations that you don't want, and the Start menu speeds up.

Pinning and Unpinning

The upper-left corner of the Start menu, prime real estate on the Vista screen, awaits your beck and call. You can add items to the upper left — called *pinning* — or take them off — *unpinning* — with wild abandon. Put the area to work for you, not for Microsoft.

Unpinning your Web browser and e-mail program from the Start menu

Most people use their Web browsers (Internet Explorer or Firefox) and their e-mail programs (Outlook or Windows Mail or Windows Live Mail or . . .) so much that the browser and mail icons really should be on the Quick Launch toolbar, not pinned to the top of the Start menu. In Technique 12, I show you how to put icons for both your browser and your mail program on the Quick Launch toolbar.

There are several ways to remove both the browser and mail icons from the top of the Start menu — as long as you have an administrator account (see Technique 40). Here's the fastest:

1. **Choose Start, right-click your browser (at the top of the Start menu), and choose Remove from This List.**

2. **Choose Start, right-click your e-mail program (which should now be at the top of the Start menu), and choose Remove from This List.**

They're gone. Easy, eh? Don't forget to put both your Web browser and your e-mail program on the Quick Launch toolbar (see Technique 12).

Instead of pinning IE or Firefox to the Start menu, consider pinning two or three specific Web sites. That way when you want to launch IE or Firefox, you can click its icon on the Quick Launch toolbar, but if you want to go to a specific site — say, a news site you visit daily or to retrieve a stock quotation — you can use the Start menu. I show you how to pin in the next section.

Pinning what you like to the Start menu

The programs you use all the time really belong on the Quick Launch toolbar. That makes them easy to find. On the other hand, you don't want to put too many icons on the Quick Launch toolbar — they're tiny and hard to click — so programs (and documents and Web sites and . . .) that you use less frequently should be pinned to the Start menu.

You can pin just about anything to the upper-left corner of the Start menu quickly and easily. Here are the details:

1. **Locate the item that you want to pin to the Start menu.**

You can put programs, folders, documents, or shortcuts on the Start menu.

To find the item you're looking for, you can navigate to it by using Windows Explorer (Start⇨Computer, say, or Start⇨Network or Start⇨Documents). You can locate it on the Start⇨All Programs menu. Many of the icons in the Control Panel can be pinned; try Start⇨ Control Panel. Or you can use Windows Search (see Technique 16) to find what you want.

2. **Right-click the item. If you see an entry that says Pin to Start Menu, select it.**

Programs, shortcuts, the Start menu's All Programs entries (which are shortcuts), and many items in the Quick Launch toolbar (which are also, technically, shortcuts) have Pin to Start Menu options.

If you choose Pin to Start Menu, the item gets added to the upper-left corner of the Start menu, at the bottom of the list — which is to say, the new item goes immediately above the faint line dividing the upper and lower parts of the left side of the Start menu.

3. **If you right-click an item (folder, file, whatever) and don't see a Pin to Start Menu entry, left-click the item and drag it over the Start button. Hover there for a moment and the Start menu opens. Drop the item where you want it in the pinning area on the Start menu.**

You can see the results in Duangkhae's modified Start menu, shown in Figure 7-2, which includes a Word document, a Control Panel icon pointing to the Printers list, the Windows volume controller, a folder, a game, and several programs.

Here's one that'll amaze your friends and confound your enemies. Want to put the Vista sound volume control on your Start menu? It's easy if you know the trick. Make sure Windows Explorer is set up to show you hidden files and folders (see Technique 15). Navigate to `c:\Windows\System32\SndVol.exe`, right-click the file, and choose Pin to Start Menu.

• **Figure 7-2:** It takes only a few seconds to completely customize the Start menu.

Don't like the text you see on an item pinned to the Start menu? No problem. Right-click any item, choose Rename, and type the name you want to see.

You can pin Web pages to the Start menu, too, although it takes a little extra work. Here's how:

1. **Start your favorite Web browser and make sure it's restored — that is, click the box next to the "X" in the upper-right corner so the browser doesn't occupy the entire screen.**

2. **Navigate to the site that you want to put on your Start menu.**

3. **Click and drag the little icon to the left of the Web page's address (if the icon has a special design, some call it a *favicon*) from the address bar to the desktop.**

In Figure 7-3, you can see the little icon that I'm talking about. It looks like a bull's-eye, to the left of `http://www.dummies.com/WileyCDA/`. Drag that icon to the desktop, and Vista automatically creates a shortcut to the Web page.

• **Figure 7-3:** Drag the icon next to the URL onto the desktop, and Vista creates a shortcut.

4. **Click your newly minted Web page shortcut and drag it over the Start button. Hover for a moment, and the Start menu opens. Drop the shortcut anywhere you like on the pinning list.**

I have no idea why Microsoft makes pin-the-URL-on-the-Start-donkey a two-step process, but both Firefox and Internet Explorer require the intermediary step of creating a shortcut and then dragging it to the Start menu.

Duangkhae's final Start menu (at least, for today) appears in Figure 7-4. Notice the pinned link to the Dummies Home Page. Total time to put together the customized Start menu? About five minutes. Total time saved by not having to hunt and peck to find the documents, programs, Web sites, folders, and hardware settings that she changes frequently? Maybe 15 minutes a day.

Take control of your Start menu by filling up the pinned items area. Don't be bashful. Vista controls the Most Frequently Used list below the pinned items — and Windows has its own biases.

• **Figure 7-4: Duangkhae's final Start menu.**

As you add more items to the pinned area, Vista makes the Start menu taller and taller. When it reaches the top of the screen, Vista mercifully starts reducing the number of items that it salts in the lower part — the Most Frequently Used list or, as the propeller-heads call it, the *adaptive menu* (see the "Adapting the adaptive menu" sidebar). Don't let Vista railroad you into using the programs it prefers. Pin, pin, pin, and pin again, says I.

Adapting the adaptive menu

Microsoft calls the area below the pinned items on the Start menu the Most Frequently Used programs list.

Bunk.

There's a list of programs that *never* make it onto the list at `http://support.microsoft.com/?kbid=282066`. That's the official story. Here's the unofficial story: Windows salts the list with programs it wants you to try.

Instead of listing the most frequently used programs, Windows adapts the menu (in sometimes inscrutable ways!), taking into account how many times you use specific programs. In short, it's an adaptive menu — and there's precious little you can do to keep it from, uh, adapting. However, you can right-click any entry that offends you and click Remove from This List.

Reining In the All Programs Submenu

Every time you choose Start⇨All Programs, Windows reaches into four folders and assembles the entire tangled mess you see on-screen. (If you've been using your PC for more than a few months, I bet All Programs looks like the front page of *The New York Times*.) If you want to untangle and organize the mess, unfortunately, you have to understand where the things on the menu come from.

> Rearranging the All Programs menu rates as a high-payoff timesaving technique. If you've ever lost five minutes wading through All Programs' endless (and frequently meaningless) menus, you know why.

Where All Programs comes from

Items on the All Programs menu come from combining the contents of four folders:

- `C:\ProgramData\Microsoft\Windows\ Start Menu`

- `C:\ProgramData\Microsoft\Windows\ Start Menu\Programs`

- `C:\Users\<username>\AppData\Roaming\ Microsoft\Windows\Start Menu`

- `C:\Users\<username>\AppData\Roaming\ Microsoft\Windows\Start Menu\Programs`

So, for example, if you're logged on as the user Duangkhae, every time you choose Start⇨All Programs, the menu items you see come from the four folders, with \Duangkhae substituted for \<username> in the final two.

To look at these folders on your system quickly, right-click the Start menu and choose Explore. Vista opens Windows Explorer at your \<username>\AppData\Roaming\ Microsoft\Windows\Start Menu folder. If you right-click Start and choose Explore All Users, you're magically transported to \ProgramData\Microsoft\Windows\ Start Menu.

In Figure 7-5, you can see the contents of a very simple \ProgramData\Microsoft\Windows\Start Menu folder.

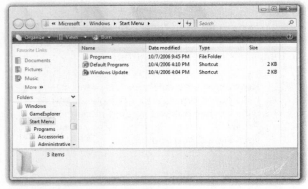

• **Figure 7-5:** A very simple \ProgramData\ Microsoft\Windows\Start Menu folder.

One level down, in \ProgramData\Microsoft\ Windows\Start Menu\Programs, though (see Figure 7-6), things start getting complicated. Microsoft put its advertisement — er, its shortcut for the Windows Live Messenger download — in the folder. Office 2007 puts a folder in there, too. (That sure beats Office 2000 and XP, which insist on cluttering this folder with lots of files.)

Duangkhae's Start Menu folder is empty except for a Programs folder, but her C:\Users\<username>\ AppData\Roaming\Microsoft\Windows\Start Menu\Programs folder looks like Figure 7-7 — a typical bare-bones Programs folder in Vista.

• **Figure 7-6: The** \Windows\Start Menu\Programs **folder, which applies to all users.**

• **Figure 7-7:** Duangkhae's Programs folder.

When Duangkhae chooses Start⇨All Programs, Windows combines those three folders (plus Duangkhae's \Start Menu, which is empty) to produce the All Programs menu you see in Figure 7-8. All the individual items appear in alphabetical order above the folders. Folders turn into submenus.

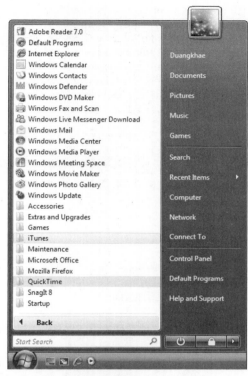

• **Figure 7-8:** Duangkhae's All Programs menu.

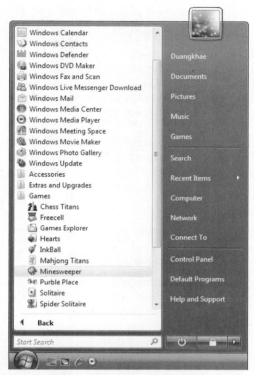

• **Figure 7-9:** Folders, such as the Games folder, turn into collapsible menus.

For example, the `C:\ProgramData\Microsoft\Windows\Start Menu\Programs\Games` folder in Figure 7-6 becomes the Games collapsible folder in Figure 7-9. Windows Live Messenger Download from the "All Users" Programs folder turns into the Windows Live Messenger Download item on the menu. Duangkhae's `\Start Menu\Programs\Windows Media Player` shortcut turns into the Windows Media Player item on the All Programs menu.

 Although it's certainly good for Microsoft's bottom line to put Windows Live Messenger Download and the gosh-spend-more-money-with-Microsoft Extras and Upgrades folder in your face every time you choose Start➪All Programs, there's no reason in the world why you should have to wade through all that garbage when you're trying to get some work done. Follow the steps in the next section to take back the All Programs real estate you paid for.

Rearranging the All Programs submenu

One of the truly significant improvements in Office 2003 was the removal of a whole lotta garbage from the All Programs menu. If you're still running Office 2000 or Office XP, you know what I mean: half a dozen programs scattered all over the All Programs menu getting in the way every time you want to get some work done.

 Lest you think I'm railing exclusively about Microsoft, I'm not. Many hardware manufacturers put really annoying little programs at the highest level of the All Programs menu, too. Most software manufacturers, though, got a clue long ago. They typically put their programs in a fly-out menu that occupies a minimum of space on All Programs.

Thankfully, Microsoft Office finally showed us some respect, starting with Office 2003, and more recently with Office 2007.

You need to be set up as a Computer Administrator in order to change the All Users folder. That's where you're likely to find the most junk that needs trimming.

Permit me to step you through the cleanup process that Duangkhae performed on her All Programs menu. (Duangkhae's a Computer Administrator, so she can finagle the All Users folder.) This is a real-life demonstration of the timesaving methods I talk about in this section that should give you a number of ideas for taking control of your own All Programs menu:

1. **Right-click Start and choose Explore.**

That put Duangkhae in her Start Menu folder, shown in Figure 7-10. There's nothing in there to gum up the All Programs menu. Whew.

• **Figure 7-10:** Duangkhae's clean Start Menu folder.

2. **Double-click the Programs folder and make any worthwhile changes here.**

Now you're getting to the garbage. (Duangkhae's original Programs folder appears in Figure 7-7.)

Duangkhae can't stand Windows Mail, doesn't use Windows Mail, and has no intention of ever even *typing* "Windows Mail." So she right-clicks the Windows Mail icon and chooses Delete. That deletes the shortcut to Windows Mail; regrettably, it doesn't delete Windows Mail itself.

She already pinned Windows Media player to the top of her Start menu, so it doesn't need to go here, either — right-click and delete. She has nothing in the Administrative Tools folder (that's why Administrative Tools doesn't appear on the All Programs menu), so the whole folder gets the right-click-and-delete heave-ho. The final result is shown in Figure 7-11.

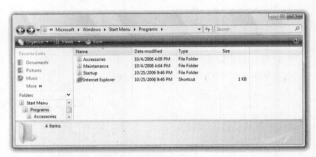

• **Figure 7-11:** Duangkhae's final `\Start Menu\ Programs` **folder.**

3. **Right-click Start and choose Explore All Users.**

Explore All Users put Duangkhae in the "All Users" Start Menu folder, which was shown in Figure 7-5. Nothing in there worth deleting.

4. **Double-click the Programs folder and slash and burn.**

Duangkhae started out with the Programs folder you see in Figure 7-6.

The Extras and Upgrades folder — which contains Microsoft's infamous link to the pay-you-pay-me Windows Marketplace, as well as other nifty Microsoft advertising locations, gets the right-click-and-delete treatment. (She had to click through, what, *three?* security messages to make the change.) Windows Live Messenger Download goes. She doesn't use Windows Calendar or Contacts, so they're out. She scans directly in various applications, so Fax and Scan goes. She refuses to use Vista's absolutely wretched DVD Maker. Finally, yet another Windows Mail icon, uh, bytes the dust.

If you have Office 2000 or XP (and a lot of you never came up with a good reason to pay for the newer versions), you'll undoubtedly see four Office application icons in the Programs folder. If you want to move them to a location on your All Programs menu that's a little less obnoxious, right-click the Microsoft Office Tools folder, choose Rename, and rename it MS Office. Then click and drag each of the four Office applications, in turn, into the newly renamed MS Office folder.

When she finishes, Duangkhae's considerably simpler Programs folder looks like Figure 7-12.

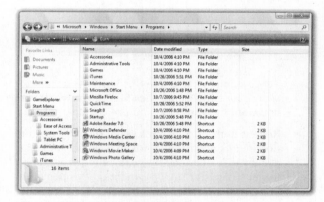

• **Figure 7-12: Get rid of the junk you don't ever use.**

5. "X" out of Windows Explorer.

6. Choose Start⇨All Programs and make sure the menu looks right.

Duangkhae's much simpler All Programs menu looks like Figure 7-13. When it comes to saving time, day in and day out, this All Programs menu runs rings around the original, Microsoft-built behemoth in Figure 7-8.

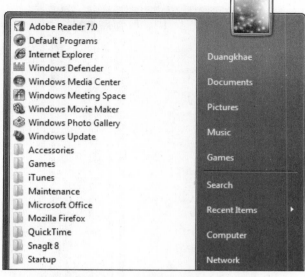

• **Figure 7-13: Duangkhae's final, timesaving All Programs menu.**

Cascading to Save Time

Figure 7-14 shows you what the Start menu looks like with all the available options selected, using small icons on the left.

 If you compare Figure 7-14 to Figure 7-4 (Duangkhae's original pinned Start Menu), you'll notice that you can add a lot more to the right side of the Start menu. In the sections that follow, you see what all your options are and then find out how to add what you want to this area of the Start menu.

Introducing the options

Here's what each entry does:

✔ **Duangkhae (the username):** Starts Windows Explorer based in the C:\Users\<username> folder. That folder contains folders for Contacts, the Desktop, Documents, Download (aha! *that's* where Internet Explorer puts its downloads!), Favorites, Links (both from IE), Music, Pictures, Saved Games, Searches, and Videos.

• **Figure 7-14: A fully decked-out Start menu.**

 For most people, the username entry is most useful for entree to the Downloads folder. The rest of it's largely redundant and a waste of time.

✔ **Documents, Pictures, Music:** Starts Windows Explorer based in the Documents, Pictures, or Music folders, all of which sit in the user's `C:\Users\<username>` folder.

✔ **Games:** Goes to a specially constructed, Explorer-like view that includes the contents of the `C:\Program Files\Microsoft Games` folder and, in some cases, other games that are properly registered with Vista. If you can't see your game here, the programmers who built the game didn't design it for Vista.

✔ **Favorites:** Starts Windows Explorer in the user's Favorites folder, which is maintained by Internet Explorer. If you use Firefox, this link doesn't mean anything.

✔ **Search:** Brings up the Explorer Search window, as in Figure 7-15.

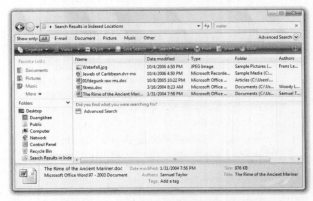

• **Figure 7-15: There's no reason to use the Search link to bring up this Explorer Search window.**

There's no reason to use this link. If you want to search for something, click Start, type whatever you want to search for, and press Enter.

✔ **Recent Items:** Brings up a list of recently opened documents and other kinds of files, occasionally accurate, maintained by Vista. Some programs forget to register the documents they open with Windows; those documents never appear in the list. In addition, Windows modifies the list to "hold onto" different kinds of files: If you open two graphics files, for example, and then two dozen documents, the graphics files still appear in this list.

✔ **Computer:** Starts Windows Explorer, showing your disk drives. From there, you can easily get into any of your hard drives, floppies, CDs, or other drives, or (if you have authorization) get to any user's Documents folder.

This link is also useful because you can right-click it and bring up the Microsoft Management Console (choose Manage) — I talk about MMC in Technique 2 — and the Control Panel's System dialog box (choose Properties), which I discuss in Technique 1 and many other locations throughout this book.

- ✔ **Network:** Starts Windows Explorer, showing computers, connected media devices, and other network-attached pieces of equipment.

- ✔ **Connect To:** Starts the Connect to a Network Wizard, which I describe in Technique 38.

- ✔ **Control Panel:** Brings up the Windows Control Panel.

- ✔ **Default Programs:** Brings up the Control Panel's Default Programs applet. This entry appears on the Start menu thanks to Microsoft's settlement with the European Union, requiring the Softies to make it easy to hook up non-Microsoft media players, Web browsers, e-mail, and Instant Messaging programs.

- ✔ **Administrative Tools:** Gives you quick access to the various management tools that control devices, users, performance, and the like. Also includes the Event Viewer, which tells you when there has been a problem.

- ✔ **Printers:** Lists available printers. Same as choosing Start⇨Control Panel⇨Hardware and Sound⇨ Printers.

- ✔ **Help and Support:** Brings up the Windows Help System (see Technique 52).

- ✔ **Run:** Opens the Windows command line, which allows you to type and run terse commands.

Choosing the options you want

Unfortunately, you can't click and drag anything onto the right side of the Start menu. It'd sure be nice if you could put the Public folder directly underneath Documents, for example, but you can't. Don't waste your time trying to find the correct magical incantation.

 However, you *can* click and drag any item from the right side of the Start menu onto the pinned list on the left. Go figger.

Vista gives you the option to turn many of the Start menu items into fly-out menus. For example, in

Figure 7-16, Duangkhae turns the Computer menu item into a fly-out menu, so the drives on her system appear as clickable entries.

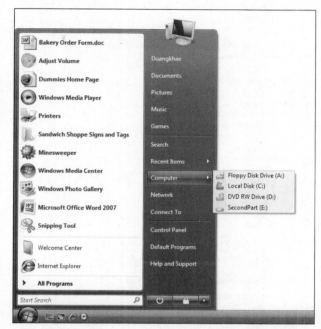

• **Figure 7-16:** Fly-out menus can make selecting items faster.

 Some menu items turn completely unwieldy when viewed as fly-outs. For example, if you have more than a few folders and documents in your Documents folder, turning the Documents menu item into a fly-out will make it very difficult to find the files you want.

You can turn ten of the items on the right side of the Start menu into fly-out menus: the User link, Documents, Pictures, Music, Games, Favorites, Recent Items (which can only appear as a fly-out menu), Computer, Control Panel, and Administrative Tools.

To choose which items you want to appear on the right side of the Start menu, and how you want them to look, follow these instructions:

1. **Right-click Start and choose Properties.**

2. **On the Start Menu tab, click Customize.**

You see the Customize Start Menu dialog box, shown in Figure 7-17.

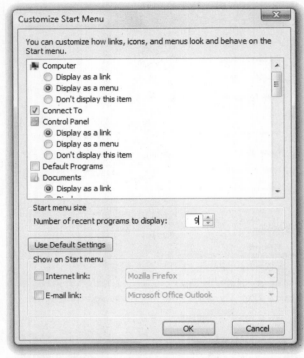

• **Figure 7-17:** This one dialog box controls the entire right side of the Start menu.

3. **Follow Duangkhae's advice in Table 7-1, or make whatever choices you like.**

You can always come back here if you change your mind.

4. **Click OK twice.**

Your changes take effect immediately.

Figure 7-18 shows you Duangkhae's final Start menu. She cut out all the marketing garbage and (finally) made Windows ready to rumble!

• **Figure 7-18:** Duangkhae's final Start menu.

TABLE 7-1: DUANGKHAE'S START MENU PICKS

Thumbs Up	Thumbs Down	Why
Computer		Having a fly-out menu to show all my drives saves time.
	Connect to	I have a permanently connected ADSL line. No fuss.
Control Panel		Keep it as a link — the menu's waaaaaaaay too long.
	Default Programs	Microsoft lost the lawsuit. I didn't.
Documents		Link only because a fly-out looks like *War and Peace*.

Thumbs Up	Thumbs Down	Why
Enable Context Menus and Dragging and Dropping		Lets you right-click on a Start menu entry and see a full array of options, as well as click and drag a file to one of the Start menu entries. It's weird to move, say, a document by dragging it to the Documents link on the Start menu, but if it works, why not?
	Favorites Menu	I don't use Internet Explorer. I can pin any important sites on the left side of the Start menu.
Games		I like it as a menu.
Help		Of course.
	Highlight newly installed programs	Putting a yellow highlight on newly installed programs just gets in the way. Axe it, I say.
Music		As a link, fer sure. But if you always get at your music from the Media Player or Media Center, you can turn this entry off.
Network		It's a handy, fast way to go looking on my home network.
Open menus when I pause on them		Sure. It's faster that way.
Personal folder		I only keep this one (as a link) because I need to get to my Downloads folder. (And, yes, I have Firefox download things into my Downloads folder.)
Pictures		Absolutely. As a link.
Printers		I switch printers fairly frequently. Sometimes I make the switch on the fly in the Print dialog box, but sometimes I want to switch everything over.
	Run	Who needs it? Click Start, type whatever you want to run, and press Enter.
	Search	Who needs it? Click Start, type whatever you want to search, and press Enter. Is there an echo in here?
Search Communications		This should be called "search e-mail messages." Of course, when I search, I want to search for e-mail messages. Sheesh.
	Search Favorites and History	This is an Internet Explorer–only setting, and I don't use IE.
Search Files		When I search, I want to search the entire index. Of course.
	Search programs	I never search for stuff inside program files.
Sort All Programs by Name		Might as well. That way I can scan through all the "Windows" stuff quickly and ignore it.
System Admin Tools		There are some very cool tools in here that I use from time to time. I put them on the All Programs menu and on the Start menu.
Use Large Icons		It's much easier and faster to "hit" big icons.

Technique 8

Building a Power Desktop

Save Time By

- ✔ Getting your desktop right (now)
- ✔ Working effectively with multiple programs
- ✔ Optimizing your new right-click menu
- ✔ Sorting out the Sidebar

D oes your desktop look like the cat licked it? Yeah, mine too (see Figure 8-1). The desktop is a horrible place to organize things. But it's a great place to stick stuff temporarily.

Or so I'm told. Hey, do as I say, not as I do, okay?

This Technique is more a set of rapid-fire mini-techniques. I step you through a handful of tricks for turning your desktop into the lean, mean face of your machine that it should be. I also explain what to avoid (useless icons) and what doesn't really hurt (screen savers). Finally, I show you some truly masterful, timesaving ways to make Vista work your way, building on several rarely seen (and in some cases completely undocumented) settings that you can use right now.

• **Figure 8-1:** My desktop has seen better days.

Desktop Brevity: The Soul of Wit

Your desktop is just like your kitchen table. It's where you put things for a short period of time; it's where you place files you don't want to forget about. At least, that's the conventional wisdom. When is enough enough? The problem, of course, is that when you place things on the desktop, even temporarily, you can easily forget to put those things where they rightly belong. Then your convenient kitchen table looks a little more like a heaping mess.

 If you ever want to hide all the icons on your desktop — not delete them, but just tuck them out of the way — right-click an empty spot on the desktop, choose View, and uncheck the line marked Show Desktop Icons. To bring them back, do the same thing, but check the line marked Show Desktop Icons.

 You can make all the icons on your desktop larger (or smaller) and the text underneath the icons larger (or smaller) by holding down the Ctrl key and twirling the wheel on your mouse. Seriously cool, eh?

Here are my five favorite, fast tips for tuning up a Vista desktop.

Adding key icons

I don't know about you, but I like to have icons sitting on the desktop for my computer and for the network. Although it's true that I can click Start⇨Computer or Start⇨Network and arrive at the same location, sometimes it's easier and faster to click on the desktop.

Here's the quick way to put those icons on the desktop:

1. **Right-click an empty part of the desktop and choose Personalize.**

The Personalize Appearance and Sounds dialog box appears.

2. **On the left, under Tasks, click Change Desktop Icons.**

Vista shows you the Desktop Icon Settings window, as shown in Figure 8-2.

• **Figure 8-2: Choose from a handful of built-in icons.**

3. **Check the boxes next to the icons you want.**

In my case, I check boxes for Computer and Network.

4. **Click OK.**

The icons appear on your desktop.

 Note that you can use this same approach if you ever want to hide the Recycle Bin. Just uncheck the box next to Recycle Bin in Figure 8-2.

Cleaning up old icons

Your desktop is a great place to park things for short periods of time, but a lousy place for organizing anything long term. Start by cleaning up the mess that's there right now.

 Windows XP had a program called the Desktop Cleanup Wizard that offered to clean unused or infrequently used icons off your desktop, placing them in a special folder called Unused Desktop Shortcuts. One little problem: the wizard didn't work very well. It frequently missed icons that hadn't been used at all, and it sometimes snagged icons that were quite handy. Vista doesn't have a Wizard of that ilk, but you can accomplish the same thing — much more accurately — by doing it yourself.

Here's how to identify and shuffle old stuff off your desktop:

1. **If this is your first time spiffing up your desktop, right-click a blank place on the desktop, choose New⇨Folder, and create a new folder called, oh, Aging or Merely Annoying Icons That Used to Be on My Desktop but Are Now Relegated to a Place Where I Can Find Them If I Really Need To.**

   Personally, I call the folder Old Stuff. Up to you.

2. **Click Start, and then click your username in the upper-right corner.**

   You see the contents of your user folder, as in Figure 8-3.

3. **Double-click the Desktop folder.**

   In Figure 8-3, the Desktop folder is at the upper right. It's a bit weird to think of the desktop — *your* desktop — as being a folder, but that's what it is.

   Windows Explorer shows you the contents of your Desktop folder, looking something like Figure 8-4.

   Note that some items that appear on your desktop aren't in the Desktop folder.

• **Figure 8-3: My user folder, the one called Woody.**

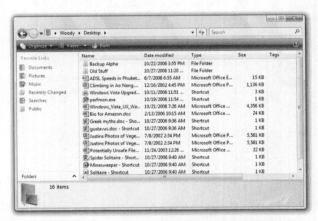

• **Figure 8-4: My desktop, as seen through Windows Explorer.**

4. **You want to see which items on the desktop (files, folders, shortcuts, whatever) haven't been accessed recently. To do so, right-click one of the column headers (such as Type or Size or Tags) and choose More.**

   Explorer shows you the Choose Details dialog box, shown in Figure 8-5.

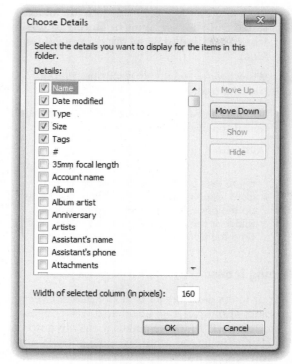

• **Figure 8-5:** Add Date Accessed to see what hasn't been used recently.

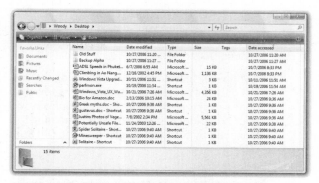

• **Figure 8-6:** Click to sort by age so you can see which items haven't been used in a long time.

5. Scroll down the list of column headings and check the box next to Date Accessed. Then click OK.

Although you may not be able to see it just yet, Date Accessed appears as one of the column headings in Windows Explorer.

6. Resize the column headings by clicking and dragging on the boxes around the headings until you can see the column marked Date Accessed. Then click the Date Accessed heading to sort the list by, uh, date accessed.

Folders appear at the top of the list. Don't let that confuse you. In the end, you should be able to see which items on the desktop have been used recently and which are as old as politicians' promises (see Figure 8-6).

7. Click and drag the old stuff into the folder called Old Stuff (or Aging or Merely Annoying Icons That Used to Be on My Desktop but Are Now Relegated to a Place Where I Can Find Them If I Really Need To, as the case may be). Then "X" out of the Desktop folder.

8. To see your new desktop, log off and log back on. (Choose Start, click the right wedge in the lower-right corner, and choose Log Off; then log back on again.)

When Vista comes back for air, all the things you moved into the Old Stuff folder no longer appear on your desktop.

9. BUT WAIT! You aren't done yet.

Vista also puts items (typically shortcuts) stored in the `C:\Users\Public\Public Desktop` folder on your desktop. Think of that folder as an "All Users" desktop folder. That's why you see shortcuts (and possibly other items) on your desktop even after you got rid of the junk in your Desktop folder, logged off, and logged back on again, using Steps 1 through 8.

You face a moment of truth about those remaining icons:

▶ If you're content to let the remaining icons continue to clutter the desktops of everybody who uses your computer (including yourself), you're done. Stop right here.

▶ If you want to delete the remaining icons from your desktop, and your desktop alone, just right-click each remaining icon in turn and choose Delete.

▶ If you want to put away the remaining icons, but only for yourself — so they still show up on the desktops of all the other people on your computer — click on each remaining icon, one by one, and drag it into the Old Stuff folder.

▶ If you want to put away the remaining icons on the desktops of all the people who use your computer, continue with the next step and stick the "All Users" icons into your Old Stuff folder. That way, the icons won't show up on any desktop, but you can bring them back if somebody really wants them.

10. So you decided to put some of the "All Users" icons in the Old Stuff deep-freeze, eh? Good. Click Start⇨Computer.

Windows Explorer shows you the drives on your computer. To get into the right folder, you have to tell Explorer to show you hidden folders.

11. Push the Alt key to bring up the menu. Click Tools⇨Folder Options⇨View. Under the line Hidden Files and Folders, select the option marked Show Hidden Files and Folders. Click OK.

12. Double-click the C: drive and then choose Users⇨Public⇨Public Desktop.

Explorer shows you the Public Desktop folder — you can think of it as the "All Users" Desktop folder — as in Figure 8-7.

• **Figure 8-7:** Desktop icons that appear for all the users on this computer.

13. Click and drag the old icons into the folder called Old Stuff (or Aging or Merely Annoying Icons That Used to Be on My . . . you get the idea).

14. When you're done, "X" out of the Public Desktop folder.

15. You may need to log off and log back on again for all the changes to take effect.

Cool, eh?

 If you ever want to restore one of the old icons, double-click the Old Stuff folder, bring up the original folder (either your Desktop folder or the "All Users" Desktop folder), and drag the icon back to where it came from.

Aligning icons

Are your icons dangling all over the place? Ever had a problem finding an icon because it was covered up by another one? Windows makes it easy to automatically align your icons — but a couple of tricks can save you even more time.

To quickly line up the icons on your desktop:

1. Right-click an empty part of the desktop.

2. Choose View, and if Align to Grid is not checked, check it. (See Figure 8-8.)

The icons are "snapped" to an invisible grid on the desktop.

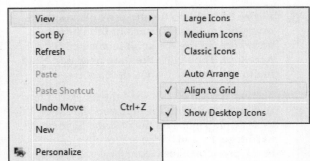

• **Figure 8-8:** Alignment options.

After the icons are aligned, I always uncheck Align to Grid because it allows me to put related icons next to each other without worrying whether Vista will jump in and rearrange everything. When my icons get so jumbled I can't work with them any more, I align them to the grid again. But in the interim, I want control over where they sit.

You can select groups of icons (by using Ctrl+click or Shift+click or by "lassoing" groups of them) and drag them all together. They stay aligned with each other after the move. These two very quick tricks can come in handy if you want to move a bunch of icons all at once.

Avoid the temptation to use any of the Sort By settings. Name, Size, Type, and Date Modified (see Figure 8-9) reorder your icons in often inscrutable ways. Leaving the Auto Arrange option checked (in Figure 8-8) sets one of the Sort By options (in Figure 8-9), which forces Windows to drag your icons back into line, no matter where you move them. After you jumble your icons using one of these Sort By settings, undoing the change is impossible.

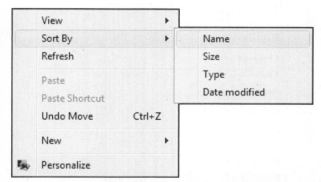

• **Figure 8-9: Sorting with these options can lead to strange results.**

Moving icons so you have more room on the desktop

To quickly force icons into the upper-left corner of the screen (and thereby free up space at the bottom and on the right), follow these steps:

1. Right-click an empty spot on the desktop and choose Personalize.

2. At the bottom, click the link to Display Settings.

3. Reduce your screen resolution. For example, if you're running at 1,024 x 768, choose 800 x 600.

4. Click Apply. When Vista asks whether you want to keep your new screen resolution, click Yes.

The icons move to the upper-left corner of the screen.

5. Right-click an empty place on the desktop, choose Personalize⇨Display Settings, and return your desktop to its original resolution. Click Apply.

Vista doesn't move the icons, so they stay in the upper-left corner.

To free up the entire right edge of the screen, pushing the icons aside, follow these steps:

1. Right-click an empty spot on the Windows taskbar and choose Properties.

2. Uncheck the Lock the Taskbar box and the Auto-Hide the Taskbar box. Click OK.

3. Click any unused part of the taskbar and drag it to the right edge.

After you have the taskbar in place, you can see that Windows moves all the icons out of the way.

4. Hover your mouse over the left edge of the taskbar until it turns into a double-headed arrow. Then click and drag the taskbar to the left, expanding it to fill as much of the screen as you like.

When you release the mouse button, the icons (and the Sidebar, if it's showing) get shoved out of the way.

5. Right-click an empty area on the taskbar, click Properties, and check the Auto-Hide the Taskbar box.

When the taskbar auto-hides itself, you'll be able to verify that all the icons have moved. Leave the Lock the Taskbar box unchecked.

6. **Click any unused part of the taskbar and drag it back to wherever it originated.**

None of the icons are disturbed.

7. **Right-click an empty spot on the taskbar and check the line marked Lock the Taskbar.**

The icons have all been pushed to the left.

Getting the most from the Sidebar

By now you've probably had a chance to play with the Vista Sidebar. Yes, Microsoft ripped off the idea from Konfabulator. Yes, Apple did, too. (See `www.konfabulator.com/cartoon/partOne.html`.) No doubt you already know that you can add more Gadgets — those little applications that run in the Sidebar — by clicking the "+" sign at the top of the Sidebar. At least, if you confine yourself to Microsoft-approved Gadgets, that's the easiest way to get them.

 Sidebar Gadgets are multiplying like rabbits: The best ones today will be also-rans tomorrow. Keep on top of the latest by running "Sidebar Gadgets" through Google.

A note on screen savers

Bottom line on screen savers: They don't do any good, but they don't do any harm as long as your energy-saving settings kick in properly. (Some PCs have a hard time reconciling specific screen savers with your power-shutoff settings. If in doubt, try turning off the screen saver.)

That said, one screen saver may save you some time. Then again, it may waste your time. Hard to say. If you have a (figurative) ton of digital pictures sitting on your PC, you should use them in the Vista My Pictures Slide Show screen saver. Windows cycles through all the pictures in a folder of your choosing, showing each picture on the screen. If your resolve is better than mine, you'll save time by not having to wade through all those folders. Of course, if you see a picture that you remember and dig into the file to take a longer look — well, sometimes saving time isn't everything, is it?

To crank up the Slide Show screen saver, right-click the desktop, choose Personalize, click the link for Screen Savers, and, in the Screen Saver drop-down box, choose Photos. Then it's an easy step to click Settings and reach for your favorite photos.

Generating One-Click E-Mail

Here's another quick trick I've never seen documented anywhere.

Say you have to e-mail a status report to the same people every day. You can create an icon on the desktop which, when double-clicked, starts your e-mail program (Outlook, Windows Mail, or some other client) and creates a new message all filled out and ready to go.

Setting up the e-mail

 Here's how to set up basic one-click e-mail:

1. **Right-click any empty spot on the desktop.**

2. **Choose New➪Shortcut.**

Windows responds with the Create Shortcut Wizard, shown in Figure 8-10.

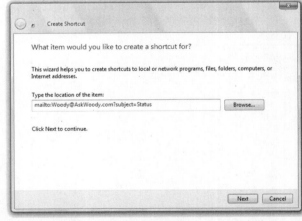

• **Figure 8-10:** Send an e-mail message with the Create Shortcut Wizard.

3. **In the Type the Location of the Item box, you need to type the e-mail recipient's address in a very specific way, using the `mailto:` command. It takes the form**

```
mailto:somebody@somewhere.com?
    subject=Something
```

For example, in Figure 8-10, I typed the following:

```
mailto:Woody@AskWoody.com?subject=
    Status
```

 The e-mail address immediately following the colon is the recipient of the message. The text to the right of the equal sign is the subject. For the moment (to get around a bug in the Create Shortcut Wizard), use only one word for the subject. In the next section, I show you how to type in any subject.

4. **Click Next.**

You see the Name the Shortcut dialog box shown in Figure 8-11.

• **Figure 8-11: Give the e-mail-creating shortcut a name.**

5. **In the Type a Name for This Shortcut box, type a label for the shortcut.**

In Figure 8-11, I typed

```
Status Report Message
```

6. **Click Finish.**

The shortcut icon appears on your desktop.

7. **Double-click the new icon.**

Your e-mail editor kicks in, creating a new e-mail message to the person whose information you entered in Step 3.

In my example, a new message to `Woody@ AskWoody.com` appears, with the subject `Status`, as in Figure 8-12. Because I have Outlook 2007 installed, Word 2007 appears as my e-mail editor.

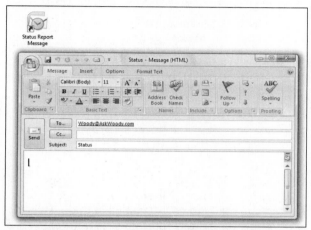

• **Figure 8-12: A very quick way to create new e-mail messages.**

8. **"X" out of the new e-mail message. No, you don't want to keep the draft.**

You can improve on this simple example by bypassing the Create Shortcut Wizard and editing the shortcut directly. I show you how in the next section.

 In addition to individual e-mail addresses, you can create a `mailto:` shortcut that sends a message to all the members of an Outlook Distribution List. To do so, follow the steps, but instead of entering a single e-mail address, use the name of the group. For example, if you have a Distribution List called `DepartmentHeads`, create a shortcut that says `mailto:DepartmentHeads`.

Improving one-click e-mail

But wait! There's more! After you create a shortcut that generates e-mail, you can go back and modify it, making the subject much more legible, sending copies or even blind copies. You can even specify text that's supposed to go in the message.

To look at it another way, it's easy to put a single icon on your desktop that, when double-clicked, creates an e-mail message that looks like, oh, maybe this:

```
To: myboss@myworkplace.com
Cc: herboss@myworkplace.com
From: woody@AskWoody.com
Subject: Status Report
We're on schedule. No problems
   to report. Looks like we won't
   have any difficulties making the
   end-of-month target. Will keep you
   posted. Let me know if you have any
   questions.
- Woody
```

When you double-click that icon, the message appears in Outlook or Windows Mail, properly formatted and ready to go. All you need to do is click Send, and your status report goes out. ***Note:*** Unfortunately, this technique doesn't work with Gmail, Windows Live Mail, or other online mail programs. Yet.

To embellish the one-click e-mail icon you constructed in the preceding section, follow these steps:

1. **Right-click a `mailto:` shortcut that was created by following the steps in the preceding section.**

2. **Choose Properties⇨Web Document.**

You see a Properties dialog box like the one in Figure 8-13.

3. **In the URL box, use any combination of the symbols and fields in Tables 8-1 and 8-2 to create the message you want.**

In Figure 8-13, I typed this:

```
mailto:BillG@Microsoft.com?cc=Steve
   B@Microsoft.com&subject=Can you
   confirm?&body=Bill - %0B%0BI
   just heard that Microsoft is
   going to sell off the Windows
   Division.%0B%0BTrue?%0B%0B-
   Woody
```

4. **Click OK.**

5. **Double-click the new shortcut.**

Your pre-fabricated message appears, ready to edit if you so desire. See Figure 8-14.

• **Figure 8-13:** Create an entire message by using simple commands.

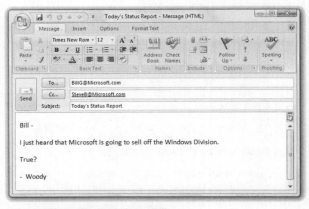

• **Figure 8-14:** Say it ain't so, Bill.

6. In your e-mail program, click Send to send the message.

It's that fast and easy.

When constructing subject and body fields, keep these points in mind:

✔ Spaces and most punctuation marks pose no problem at all.

✔ The character %0B generates a carriage return inside the body of the message.

✔ The e-mail message you generate goes straight into your e-mail program. So, for example, if you have an automatic entry that turns billg into BillG@Microsoft.com, you only need to use billg in the shortcut's URL box.

Also check out Tables 8-1 and 8-2 to see what other codes mean.

 After you create this icon on the desktop, you can easily pin it to the Start menu or move it down to the Quick Launch toolbar by simply clicking it and dragging.

TABLE 8-1: E-MAIL SHORTCUT SEPARATORS

Symbol	Meaning
;	Separates multiple e-mail addresses
?	Appears after the mailto:xxx field, before any other fields
&	Marks the end of one field and the beginning of the next

TABLE 8-2: E-MAIL SHORTCUT FIELDS

Field	Meaning
mailto:	To: address(es) follow
cc=	cc: addresses follow
bcc=	bcc: addresses follow
subject=	Subject field
body=	Text inside the message

For example, to send a message to tom, dick, and harry@bogus.com, a copy to woody@bogus.com, and a blind copy to daboss@bogus.com, with the subject Free Beer, and a message body of Tomorrow only., you would use this shortcut:

```
mailto:tom@bogus.com;dick@bogus.com;h
   arry@bogus.com?subject=Free
   Beer&cc=woody@
   bogus.com&bcc=daboss@bogus.com&body=
   Tomorrow only.
```

Or if you wanted to send a message to woody@khunwoody.com, with a copy to sales@khunwoody.com, subject Complaint, and a two-line body that says Dear Sir:/Why can't you make garlic bagels?, you could use the %0B (that's the number "0") line break character to come up with:

```
mailto:woody@khunwoody.com?cc=sales@
   khunwoody.com&subject=Complaint&
   body=Dear Sir:%0B%0BWhy can't you
   make garlic bagels?
```

Opening Multiple Documents at Once

If you find yourself commonly opening the same group of documents using a single program, some programs (including the Office programs) allow you to set up a single shortcut that opens all the documents at once. It doesn't work all the time — as you will see, there are size limitations — but for people who always open the same group of files, this can be an enormous timesaver.

Here's how to set up a single shortcut to have a program open multiple documents at once (for example, to have Excel 2007 open three spreadsheets):

1. Choose Start➪Computer, double-click Program Files, and navigate to the folder containing the program in question.

Usually it's easy to figure out which application folder you need after you're looking at the list in the Program Files folder. In this case, because I'm looking for an Office 2007 program, I click Start➪

Computer➪Program Files➪Microsoft Office➪ Office 12. If I were looking for an Office 2003 program, I would look in Microsoft Office➪Office 11; Office XP is in Microsoft Office➪Office 10.

2. **Find the program you want to start (for a list of the Office programs, see Table 8-3). Right-click the program and choose Send To➪Desktop (Create Shortcut).**

You have a shortcut to the program on your desktop.

3. **Choose Start➪Documents and navigate to the first document that you want to open with the program.**

4. **Right-click the document and choose Send To➪ Desktop (Create Shortcut).**

A shortcut appears on your desktop that points to the document.

5. **Repeat Step 4 for each document that you wish to open.**

At this point, you have a shortcut for the program on the desktop and separate shortcuts for each document. In Figure 8-15, I have a shortcut for Excel, plus shortcuts for three spreadsheets.

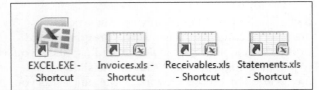

EXCEL.EXE - Shortcut   Invoices.xls - Shortcut   Receivables.xls - Shortcut   Statements.xls - Shortcut

• **Figure 8-15: Shortcuts for Excel and three spreadsheets.**

6. **Right-click the program's shortcut icon and choose Properties.**

Windows shows you the Properties dialog box for the program (such as the one in Figure 8-16).

In this example, the Target box says

```
C:\Program Files\Microsoft Office\
    Office12\EXCEL.EXE
```

 For no apparent reason, the Target box is limited to 259 characters.

7. **With your cursor inside the Target box, press End and then press the spacebar.**

That puts a space at the end of the Target box and leaves your cursor precisely where it needs to be.

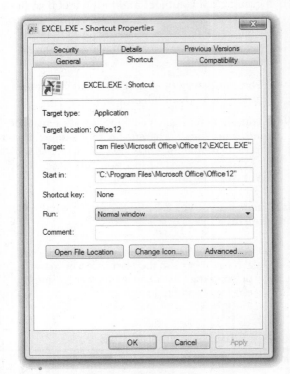

• **Figure 8-16: Build on the Target box.**

8. **Right-click the shortcut to one of the documents you wish to open and choose Properties.**

You see the Properties dialog box for the shortcut, as in Figure 8-17. Note that the location of the document is highlighted in the Target box.

9. **Immediately press Ctrl+C.**

That copies the full name of the document onto the Windows Clipboard.

10. **Click Cancel and return to the program's Properties dialog box.**

11. In the Target box, with your cursor positioned at the end of the text, type " and then press Ctrl+V and type " again; then press the spacebar.

That pastes the full name of the first document, surrounded by quotes, into the Target box. (If the filename already has quotes, you don't need to type in a second pair.) The cursor is in position for you to enter the next document name.

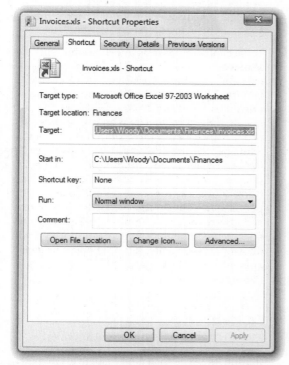

• Figure 8-17: The full name of the document (including its location) is in the Target box.

12. Repeat Steps 8 through 11 for each of the documents you wish to open.

When you're done, the Target box looks something like this: `C:\Program Files\Microsoft Office\Office12\EXCEL.EXE" "C:\Users\Woody\Documents\Finances\Invoices.xls" "C:\Users\Woody\Documents\`

`Finances\Receivables.xls" "C:\Users\Woody\Documents\Finances\Statements.xls"`

If you run out of room in the Target box (that is, if a filename gets truncated), change the Start In box to point to the folder that contains one or more of your documents. For example, if you change the program shortcut's Start In box to `C:\Users\Woody\Documents\Finance`, then the filename in the Target box can be simply `Invoices.xls`.

This may take some jiggling, but a little perseverance now results in a shortcut that you can use over and over again.

13. When you finish with the Target box, click OK.

14. Test the shortcut by double-clicking it.

Your chosen program should spring to life with all the indicated documents loaded and ready to rumble.

 Don't forget that you can move this shortcut from the desktop to the Quick Launch toolbar (see Technique 12), or you can pin it to the Start menu (see Technique 7). You can place it in the Startup folder so it opens whenever you log on to Vista. Or you can delete it, just to keep your desktop tidy.

TABLE 8-3: MICROSOFT OFFICE PROGRAM NAMES

Application	File
Excel	`Excel.exe`
InfoPath	`InfoPath.exe`
Access	`MSAccess.exe`
Publisher	`MSPub.exe`
Office Picture Manager	`OIS.exe`
Outlook	`Outlook.exe`
PowerPoint	`Powerpnt.exe`
Word	`Winword.exe`

Arranging Multiple Windows Side by Side

You can arrange multiple windows on your desktop very quickly and easily. You can tile them side by side (vertically) or from top to bottom (horizontally). Here's how:

1. **Make sure both the windows are open and thus have icons that appear on the Windows taskbar.**

2. **On the taskbar, click one window's icon; then hold down the Ctrl key and click the other window's icon.**

3. **Right-click one of the selected icons and choose Show Windows Stacked or Show Windows Side by Side.**

   The selected windows are tiled, as shown in Figure 8-18.

• **Figure 8-18: These windows are tiled side by side.**

Shooting a Picture of Your Desktop

Sooner or later — probably sooner — you'll want to take a picture of your desktop. You might want to do this for a lot of reasons — some more socially acceptable than others:

✔ To get all the details of an error message.

✔ To show a friend how to do something or to show them what went wrong.

✔ To bypass print restrictions. Some demo versions of programs allow you to open files but not print them. The easy, fast workaround is to take a screen shot and print the screen. Of course, if you use the program, you should buy it — and a printout of a screen shot is a very poor substitute for a genuine printed document. But if you're in a pinch, this works.

✔ To circumvent onerous Information Rights Management restrictions. If you haven't bumped into IRM yet, don't worry, you will. The IRM features built into Office 2003 and 2007 and supported by Windows 2003 Server allow the author of a document to specify who can open, edit, print, copy, or even forward that document. Some people see IRM as a step forward in allowing companies to control their documents. Other people (present company included) see it as a horrendous way for some people to make other peoples' lives miserable — particularly when somebody screws up granting permissions for a specific document that you need to use. If you're allowed to view a file, but not copy it or give it to someone else, taking a shot of the screen is almost as good.

Quick pictures are a snap with Vista:

1. **Line up the picture that you want to take.**

   Setting up the screen shot is an art unto itself, but it helps if you use a high screen resolution and take great care to make sure the overlapping windows don't obscure anything important.

 If you want to get rid of all the icons on the desktop, right-click an empty place, choose View, and uncheck the box next to Show Desktop Icons.

2. **Choose Start⇨All Programs⇨Accessories⇨ Snipping Tool.**

   The screen colors wash out as the Snipping Tool appears (see Figure 8-19).

3. To take a rectangular screen shot, click and drag the cursor around the part of the screen that you want to capture. Alternatively, if you want to shoot a window, the full screen, or a free-form area corresponding to your mouse meanderings, click the down-arrow next to the New button and choose your poison. Then click and drag around the area you want to snip.

• **Figure 8-19: Taking screen shots is easy with the Snipping Tool.**

When you release the mouse button (or click on a window, or on the whole screen), the Snipping Tool comes back with an editing window that looks like Figure 8-20.

4. Use the editing tools — draw with the pen, paint with the highlighter, or erase with the eraser — and when you're done, click the appropriate icon to save, copy, or mail the picture.

You can save in JPG, GIF, HTML, or PNG format.

Purists will be interested to know that the Snipping Tool removes the gray cast around windows, fills in the rounded edges, and, by default, puts a red border around the captured screen shot.

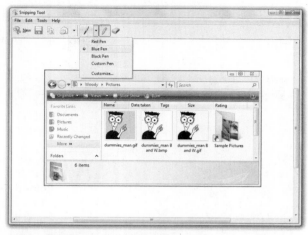

• **Figure 8-20: Edit your figure here.**

The old Windows screen shot keyboard shortcuts work in Vista. To take a snapshot of the entire screen and place it on the Windows Clipboard, press the PrtScr (or the Print Screen) key on your keyboard; to shoot the active window or dialog box — the one that's "on top" — press Alt+PrtScr. When the shots are on the Clipboard, you can use Word or Paint or Outlook or almost any other program to paste them into a document or file — you can even paste them into an online e-mail program like Gmail or Yahoo! Mail.

 If you have a friend who wants some help but has a hard time explaining exactly what he's doing, have him start a Word document. Tell your friend how to use this technique to snap screen shots and have him paste a sequence of shots into the document as he goes along.

Just so you know, the Snipping Tool has lots of limitations. The shots in this book were taken with SnagIt (www.techsmith.com), a program that provides many more capabilities — including the ability to number files sequentially as they're shot. It takes better-looking shots, too.

Technique 9

Tricking Out the Taskbar

Save Time By

- ✔ Making the Windows taskbar work your way
- ✔ Jumping to important Web sites quickly
- ✔ Putting any folder on the taskbar
- ✔ Creating a custom pop-up menu for the taskbar

When you're trying to save time, the taskbar (shown in Figure 9-1) takes the cake: That little strip at the bottom of your screen is the one place you can get to quickly, easily, from any place in Windows, at any time.

To look at it a different way, the taskbar is, quite literally, where you go before you venture over to the Start menu.

Microsoft realizes the taskbar's supremacy in the timesaving pantheon, and because of that, provides us Windows customers myriad settings for tweaking, mashing, and mangling the bar. Unfortunately, many of those settings get in the way of saving time. This Technique presents the ones you should consider if you want to make Windows work more effectively for you.

Figure 9-1: The familiar Vista taskbar.

Customizing the Taskbar

Vista gives you many built-in ways to change the taskbar.

Making the taskbar taller

One taskbar tweak rates as a no-brainer. If you haven't already changed your taskbar so it's two (or even three) lines tall, do so now:

1. **Right-click an empty part of the taskbar and uncheck Lock the Taskbar.**

   Before you can change the taskbar, you have to unlock it. When it's unlocked, you can see a pattern of dots immediately to the right of the Start button (see Figure 9-2).

• **Figure 9-2:** An unlocked taskbar.

2. **Hover the mouse pointer over the top of the taskbar until you see the double-headed arrow.**

3. **Click and drag upward to make the taskbar taller.**

If you're running at relatively low resolution, you probably want the taskbar to be two lines tall. At higher resolutions, on better monitors, three can help.

4. **Right-click the taskbar again and check Lock the Taskbar.**

Your taskbar now looks something like the one in Figure 9-3. Note that the area on the right — called the *notification area* — now shows the date as well as the time.

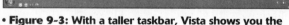

• **Figure 9-3:** With a taller taskbar, Vista shows you the date, too.

 When the taskbar is unlocked, you can move it to the top, left, or right side of the screen by clicking in an unused area on the taskbar and dragging it. Because it's relatively easy to move — and most people don't want to move it — I recommend that you leave the taskbar locked unless you specifically need to unlock it.

Beyond that one no-brainer — making the taskbar at least two lines tall — I recommend the timesaving settings in the next section for every Vista user.

Changing taskbar settings in one fell swoop

Are you ready to change your taskbar? Good. It should be changed, and as you can see in Table 9-1, there's no dearth of timesaving options.

Follow these steps to take the training wheels off the taskbar:

1. **Right-click an empty place on the taskbar and choose Properties⇨Taskbar.**

Windows shows you the Taskbar and Start Menu Properties dialog box, with the Taskbar tab showing (see Figure 9-4).

• **Figure 9-4:** Setting taskbar options is as easy as checking and unchecking boxes.

2. **To enable the features you want, check the appropriate boxes (refer to Table 9-1).**

Personally, I check all of them and recommend that you do, too.

3. **Click the Notification Area tab.**

You see the Notification Area settings, shown in Figure 9-5.

4. **To control the notification area, follow Table 9-2 to check the boxes you like.**

5. **Click OK.**

Your changes take effect immediately.

As with so many parts of Windows, there's no one "right" setting or group of settings. Duangkhae and I disagree on two key points: auto-hiding and locking. She wants to see the taskbar all the time; I want it out of the way. She likes to leave the taskbar unlocked so she can rearrange things at will; I like to keep myself from accidentally dragging it all over Gates's Half Acre. You say "potato;" I say "potatoe."

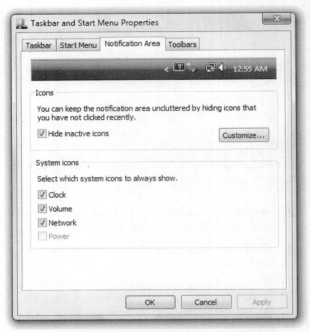

• **Figure 9-5: Set up the notification area the way you want, too.**

TABLE 9-1: TASKBAR OPTIONS

Name	What It Does	Timesaving Bonus Info
Lock the Taskbar	Keeps you from accidentally doing something stupid, such as dragging the taskbar to the top of the screen. When the taskbar is unlocked, you can see a bunch of dots to the right of the Start button.	I keep the taskbar locked all the time. Duangkhae prefers to keep hers unlocked, so (among other things) new icons on the Quick Launch toolbar always show up.
Auto-Hide the Taskbar	Keeps the taskbar out of the way until you roll your mouse to the bottom of the screen (or to the side, if you moved the taskbar). As soon as you're through using the taskbar, it disappears.	I always auto-hide the taskbar to maximize my available screen real estate. Duangkhae, on the other hand, likes to keep hers showing so she can switch programs without "bouncing" the mouse against the bottom of the screen.
Keep the Taskbar on Top of Other Windows	If deselected, floats the taskbar up and down like any other window.	If you don't check this box, you may have trouble finding the taskbar. It's hard to imagine why anybody would float the taskbar.

(continued)

TABLE 9-1 *(continued)*

Group Similar	When Windows runs out of room on the taskbar, it looks to see if any one program has more than one button on the taskbar. If so, Windows groups the buttons for a single program together. For example, you may have four Excel windows grouped together under one taskbar button, and that button says you have four Excel windows. (Rocket science, eh?)	You do have some control over the way Windows combines buttons. See "Grouping Windows" later in this Technique.
Show Quick Launch	Puts the Quick Launch toolbar on the taskbar, to the right of the Start button (refer to Figure 9-3).	The Quick Launch toolbar is the best location for your most heavily used programs, documents, Web pages, and the like. See Technique 12 for important details.
Show Window Previews (Thumbnails)	If you have Vista Aero working (see Technique 5), and you check this box, whenever you hover your mouse over a taskbar button, Vista shows you a thumbnail preview of whatever is running, as in Figure 9-6.	This is one of the great features in Vista Aero. A big timesaver.

TABLE 9-2: NOTIFICATION AREA OPTIONS

Name	What It Does	Timesaving Bonus Info
Hide Inactive Icons	If a program isn't running, its icon is hidden.	I always have problems with too many icons, not too few. Keep this box checked — and if you find an obnoxious program like QuickTime that insists on showing its icon whether you want it or not, click the Customize button and tell it to stay hidden all the time.
Clock	Shows the clock, which is synchronized automatically with an ultra-accurate clock (either the National Institute of Standards and Technology clock — widely regarded as the premiere clock in all the world — or Microsoft's mirrored version of that same clock).	Let's be honest — your Windows clock is the most accurate one in your house or office. No, Microsoft doesn't use its clock to spy on you, but if you're concerned, switch over to the NIST clock by clicking on the time in the notification area, choosing Change Date and Time Settings, clicking the Internet Time tab, and clicking Change Settings.
Volume	Puts the computer's volume control in your notification area.	Why not?
Network	Shows a network icon in the notification area that'll tell you if your network's connected.	If you want to have the icon flash whenever there's data traveling to or from your computer, right-click the icon and check the line marked Turn On Activity Animation.

• **Figure 9-6:** Make sure you have Vista show you thumbnail previews of programs in the taskbar.

Grouping Windows

Each time you start a program, and sometimes when you open a document or open a new Web page, Windows puts a button down on the taskbar. Sooner or later, you have so many programs running simultaneously that the taskbar runs out of room.

When that happens, Windows looks at the Group Similar Taskbar Buttons setting on the Taskbar and Start Menu Properties dialog box (refer to Table 9-1).

If you don't allow Windows to group similar buttons (which is to say, all the buttons associated with one specific program), the buttons keep getting smaller and smaller until you can't see much at all (as in Figure 9-7).

• **Figure 9-7: If you get too many windows, you can't see much.**

On the other hand, if you do allow Windows to group similar buttons — if you have checked the Group Similar Taskbar Buttons box — Windows tries to figure out which program is being used the least and groups buttons for that program. You can then click the group button and see and select from a list of all the open documents (see Figure 9-8).

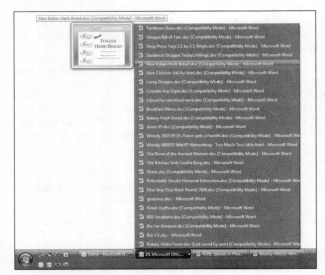

• **Figure 9-8: Least-used programs get grouped first.**

If you start even more programs or open more documents, Windows groups together another set of buttons, and so on.

The timesaving problem: When buttons are grouped, they're harder to find and slower to use. If you commonly have many programs, documents, or Web pages open simultaneously, it can take a lot of time to switch among them.

Both Internet Explorer and Firefox support tabbed browsing. When you open Web pages in tabs, they don't add more buttons to the taskbar.

Some applications have tools for switching among open documents. All the Microsoft Office applications, for example, allow you to switch among open documents. In Office 2000, XP, and 2003, you choose Window on the main menu and then pick the document from a list. In Office 2007, click the View tab and then use the Switch Windows drop-down list (see Figure 9-9).

• **Figure 9-9: Switching among windows in Word 2007 without using the taskbar.**

In Office XP, 2003, and 2007, most of the applications (Word, Excel, PowerPoint, and Access) can be told to put only one button on the taskbar. If you tell your Office application to use this option, you then use the application's own internal mechanism for switching among open documents. The difference can be substantial.

To tell any Office XP or Office 2003 application (except Outlook) that it should use only one taskbar button, follow these steps:

1. **Start the application.**

2. **Choose Tools⇨Options⇨View.**

   The application shows you an Options dialog box.

3. **In the Show area, uncheck the Windows in Taskbar box.**

4. **Click OK.**

To tell Outlook 2002 or 2003 to use only one taskbar button, right-click the Outlook icon in the notification area (next to the clock) and check the Hide When Minimized line.

To do the same thing in Office 2007 applications:

1. **Click the Start icon in the upper-left corner and choose Options (Word Options, Excel Options, and so on).**

2. **On the left, click Advanced.**

   In Figure 9-10, for example, you see the Advanced pane of the Word Options dialog box.

• **Figure 9-10: Tell Word 2007 that you want it to use only one button in the taskbar, no matter how many documents are open.**

3. **In the Display section, uncheck the box marked Show All Windows in the Taskbar.**

4. **Click OK.**

Changes take effect immediately.

Blitzing the Address Bar

People on the move should activate another buried treasure available on the taskbar: a full-fledged rendition of the Firefox/Internet Explorer/Windows Explorer Address bar.

Before your eyes glaze over, realize that the Address bar lets you type or paste

- ✔ **Web addresses (but you already guessed that).** You can use most of the tricks for quickly typing Web addresses, which I discuss in Technique 18, including pressing Ctrl+Enter to put `http://www.` in front of what you type and `.com` after.

- ✔ **Any command that you would use in the Search (or Start⇨Run) command box,** including `regedit`, `calc` (to bring up the Windows calculator), `winword` (to start Word), `ping`, `mspaint`, `msconfig`, and many more.

- ✔ **The name of a folder.** Press Enter, and Windows Explorer appears, starting at that folder.

- ✔ **The name of a document** (generally, you have to include the full path). Windows starts the appropriate program and opens the document.

- ✔ **search followed by any text.** Windows fires up your preferred Web browser and starts a search using your chosen search engine, such as Google (which I discuss in Technique 19).

 Because of a very bad design decision at Microsoft that limits where you can put the Address bar, in order to take full advantage of the Address bar, you probably need to expand the taskbar so that it occupies three lines. If your screen resolution is 1,024 x 768 or higher and you auto-hide the taskbar, that shouldn't be an insurmountable problem. Auto-hiding becomes more and more important as you add features to the taskbar.

Unfortunately, Vista doesn't let you put the Quick Launch toolbar and the Address bar just anywhere. The Windows Media Player mini-player also gets shoehorned into an unrecoverable chunk of taskbar real estate. It's a very bad design restriction, but there doesn't appear to be any way around it. I've come to the conclusion, after lots of trying, that the best way to arrange things is with the Quick Launch toolbar on the left and the Address bar on the right, on the lowest level of the taskbar. You can try rearranging things differently, but I bet you come to the same conclusion.

Here's how to put a lean, clean Address bar on your taskbar and snuggle it up against your Quick Launch toolbar:

1. Follow the instructions in the section, "Making the taskbar taller," to make your taskbar at least two (and probably three) lines tall. Leave the taskbar unlocked (right-click an empty spot on the taskbar and uncheck the line marked Lock the Taskbar).

The familiar dots of the Quick Launch toolbar's resizing handle should be visible immediately to the right of the Start button.

2. Right-click any open area on the taskbar and choose Toolbars➪Address.

The Address bar appears on the right, near the notification area (see Figure 9-11).

• **Figure 9-11: The Address bar takes up a lot of room, hogging the entire right side of the taskbar**

3. This part's tricky. Click on or just below the word *Address*. The cursor should turn into a four-headed arrow. Then click and drag the Address bar all the way to the left, dropping it just below the Quick Launch toolbar. See Figure 9-12.

I talk about the Quick Launch toolbar in Technique 12.

• **Figure 9-12: First, move the Address bar underneath the Quick Launch icons.**

4. Next, click immediately to the right of the resizing dots on the Quick Launch toolbar. The cursor should turn into a four-headed arrow. Click and drag the Quick Launch toolbar down, as in Figure 9-13.

• **Figure 9-13: Drag the Quick Launch toolbar down, so it's on the same level as the Address bar.**

If you have the Quick Launch toolbar and Address bar arranged as they are in Figure 9-13, they will take up the minimum amount of space possible on Vista's taskbar.

5. With everything in place, right-click the word *Address* and uncheck the line that says Show Title.

That removes the word *Address* from the left side of the Address bar.

6. Right-click an empty part of the taskbar and check the line marked Lock the Taskbar.

Your slim 'n' quick taskbar should look like the one in Figure 9-14.

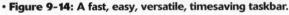

• **Figure 9-14: A fast, easy, versatile, timesaving taskbar.**

 If you ever need to rearrange the Address bar, make the Quick Launch area larger, or generally futz with the layout of this taskbar, unlock it, but remember to show the word *Address* by right-clicking the Address bar and checking the line Show Title. Once the word *Address* appears, it's comparatively easy to grab the Address bar and move it around.

Navigating from the Taskbar

This technique isn't for everyone. It's for those of you who frequently need to navigate around a hornet's nest of folders and don't want to do the navigating from inside a specific program (such as Word or Excel). Instead, you can put a pop-up menu — a new toolbar, in Windows parlance — on the taskbar. This toolbar whisks you directly to a folder, and from that point, subfolders turn into submenus. You can navigate through the folder maze to individual files. For example, in Figure 9-15, I put a shortcut to my `Documents\Articles` folder on the taskbar. Digging into that folder is as easy as clicking a toolbar button.

• **Figure 9-15:** My Articles folder on the taskbar.

 Most people don't need the extra cascading toolbar: You can navigate through your program's usual File⇨Open menu with no problem, or click Start⇨Documents and you're on your way. For most of us, this fancy custom toolbar just takes up room on the Windows taskbar — where space is in short supply anyway. But if you have a bunch of folders that you navigate frequently, it can really save a lot of time.

To put a new toolbar on the Windows taskbar:

1. Right-click any unused part of the taskbar and choose Toolbars⇨New Toolbar.

You see the New Toolbar dialog box shown in Figure 9-16.

• **Figure 9-16:** Choose the root folder for the taskbar.

2. Navigate to the folder you want as the root of the pop-up menu and click Select Folder.

The contents of this folder will appear on your new toolbar. Figure 9-15 shows the result of my placing the Articles folder on my taskbar.

3. If you want to try to relocate the toolbar, make sure the taskbar is unlocked (right-click an empty part of the taskbar and uncheck the line marked Lock the Taskbar). Then click and drag your new toolbar wherever you want.

If you play with it a bit, you see that Vista restricts the placement and sizing of the toolbar quite drastically.

4. When you're happy with the result, right-click an unused spot on the taskbar and check Lock the Taskbar.

Try using the new toolbar a bit and see if you get used to it.

 If you change your mind and want to get rid of the new toolbar, right-click an open place on the taskbar, choose Toolbars, and uncheck the line that mentions the new toolbar.

Technique

10

Using Built-In Keyboard Shortcuts

Save Time By

✔ Picking and choosing the keyboard shortcuts you need most

✔ Finding the right shortcut quickly

Vista abounds with shortcut key combinations. Did you know that holding down the Alt, Shift, F1, End, and Print Screen keys simultaneously brings up a secret picture of Bill Gates wearing a T-shirt that says, "Hey-Hey! No-No! Open Source Has Gotta Go!"?

Naw. Just joking.

Arguably the most important key combination is Ctrl+Alt+Del — the combination that's used to bring up the Lock This Computer menu (see Figure 10-1).

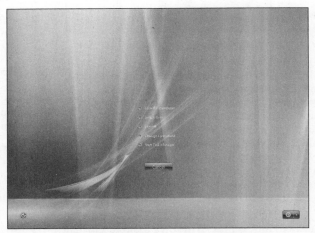

• **Figure 10-1: The secret handshake that brings up Task Manager — Ctrl+Alt+Del.**

Unless Vista is hopelessly hammered, that three-finger salute (or is it a Vulcan Mind Meld?) gives you access, almost all the time, to the Windows Task Manager. If you memorize just one keyboard shortcut, it should be Ctrl+Alt+Del.

From the Lock This Computer menu (Figure 10-1), click the link to Start Task Manager. That brings up a list of running programs, shown in Figure 10-2, from which you can halt programs that are misbehaving. (I talk about other features of the Windows Task Manager in Technique 2.)

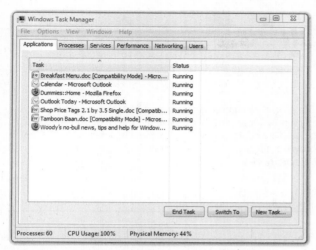

• **Figure 10-2: The next time your computer freezes, remember to press Ctrl+Alt+Del and then click Start Task Manager so you can manually end tasks that have gone astray.**

This Technique makes it easy and fast for you to find the shortcuts you need. Training your fingers is up to you.

Shortcuts Everybody Needs

I have a very short list of shortcut key combinations that every single Vista user needs to memorize. They work in practically every Windows program ever made. Table 10-1 shows you the Big Three

shortcut keys that go back to the ancient days of personal computing, and, man, do they come in handy.

Tattoo these to the inside of your eyelids.

TABLE 10-1: SHORTCUT KEYS EVERY VISTA USER MUST KNOW

Key	What It Does
Ctrl+C	Copies the selected items to the Clipboard
Ctrl+X	Cuts the selected items to the Clipboard
Ctrl+V	Pastes the contents of the Clipboard at the current cursor location

There's a handful of additional shortcut keys (see Table 10-2) that are recognized in *almost* every program — and, usually, in Windows itself.

 In most applications, you can press Alt+ underlined letter in a menu item (for example, the "F" in File), and the menu behaves as if you clicked it. Fast-touch typists find this approach useful because it saves them from moving their fingers to the mouse.

Office 2007, bless its pointed little head, no longer shows underlines on menu items (heck, it doesn't even show menus!), but all of the old Office 2003 shortcuts work (including Alt+F+X for File⇨Exit). The new, improved Office 2007 interface puts boxes around the shortcut keys when you press Alt. Progress, eh?

TABLE 10-2: OTHER USEFUL KEYBOARD SHORTCUTS

Key	What It Does
Ctrl+A	Selects everything.
Ctrl+Z	Undoes the last thing you did.
Ctrl+click	Selects items one by one: Click something to select it; then hold down the Ctrl key and click something else. Both things are selected. To select more, hold down the Ctrl key again and select another one. To deselect items that you have selected, hold down the Ctrl key and click the thing you want to get rid of.
Shift+click	Similar to Ctrl+click, except this action selects everything in between. Say you're working on a list of files. Click the first file to select it. Hold down the Shift key and click another file. Every file between the first one and the last one is selected.

(continued)

TABLE 10-1 *(continued)*

Key	What It Does
Tab	Goes to the next item (in, say, a dialog box, or to fill in a form on the Web). Just to confuse things, if you want to move from tab to tab in a tabbed dialog box, press Ctrl+Tab.
Shift+Tab	Goes to the previous item.
Alt+F, Alt+X, and then Enter	In most (but not all!) applications, this combination starts an orderly shutdown of the application. If your screen suddenly goes black — perhaps a power outage? — and you need to bail out quickly, hold down the Alt key, press F and release it, wait a second, press X and release it, release the Alt key, wait a few more seconds, and press Enter to save whatever file you've been working on. Press Enter a few more times for good measure, and you're usually okay.
F1	Finds you some Help.
F5	Refreshes (in other words, goes back out and checks things all over again). In Word, F5 is Find/Replace.

Important Windows Key Combinations

Sometimes Windows goes out to lunch, and you need a key combination to get it back. Other times, the shortest distance between two points, er, programs is a simple key combination. You'll use the keyboard shortcuts in Table 10-3 over and over again.

TABLE 10-3: IMPORTANT WINDOWS COMMANDS

Key	What It Does	Timesaving Bonus Info
Ctrl+Alt+Del	The infamous three-finger salute brings up the screen that lets you get to the Windows Task Manager. When Windows freezes tighter 'n' a drum, this is the way out.	Doing the Ctrl+Alt+Del combination twice no longer results in an automatic reboot of Windows.
Alt+Tab or Windows+Tab	Once known as the "CoolSwitch," holding down the Alt key and repeatedly pressing Tab cycles through all running programs. (With the Windows key, it's known as Flip 3D.)	This approach can be faster than using the taskbar if you don't have many programs running. It's also convenient if your machine freezes and you want to see if any other programs are available.
Shift	Holding down the Shift key when you insert a CD temporarily overrides Vista's attempts to run, play, copy, or otherwise automatically do something with the inserted CD.	If you need to insert the Windows installation CD to retrieve a file, hold down the Shift key while you slide in the CD so you don't have to close out of the installer's starting screen.
Shift+Delete	Permanently deletes an item — it isn't placed in the Recycle Bin.	Windows asks if you're sure you want to delete the file.

Key	What It Does	Timesaving Bonus Info
Ctrl+drag	Hold down the Ctrl key while you drag an item, and you make a copy.	I tend to use a right-click drag because it gives more options, and it's just one less key combination I need to memorize.
Windows key or Ctrl+Esc	Brings up the Start menu.	Easy way to exit Windows if your mouse freezes.
Windows+M or Windows+D	Minimizes all open windows so that you can see your desktop immediately.	After you get that key combination down, you can take the desktop icon off the Quick Launch toolbar to give way to another shortcut.

A Grab Bag of Application Shortcuts

These key combinations can be incredibly useful for some people — but probably rate as real duds for most of us. Scan Table 10-4 and try the ones that look good in your favorite programs.

TABLE 10-4: MISCELLANEOUS COMMANDS FOR ALMOST EVERY PROGRAM

Key	What It Does	Timesaving Bonus Info
Esc	Stops whatever is happening.	If you get to the point where you really need it, chances are good Esc won't work. But it's great for closing open dialog boxes and closing drop-down or pop-up menus.
Alt+F4	Closes the current program.	I use Alt+F, X, Enter (refer to Table 10-2) because it seems to work in more programs, but your mileage may vary. In programs for which the Alt+F4 option works, it saves you a step.
Home	Moves the cursor to the beginning of the current line or list.	Ctrl+Home moves the cursor to the beginning of the document.
End	Moves the cursor to the end of the current line or list.	Ctrl+End moves the cursor to the end of the document.
Ctrl+B	Bold (usually toggles bold on or off — if it was off, this shortcut turns it on, and vice versa).	If you're typing, and your text suddenly turns bold, press Ctrl+B to turn off the bold.
Ctrl+I	Italic (usually a toggle).	Same as the bold eliminator (see earlier entry).
Ctrl+U	Underline (usually a toggle, too).	Same as bold and italic.

Odds 'n' (Sometimes Useful) Ends

Some of the keyboard shortcuts in Table 10-5 don't amount to much more than parlor tricks. But if you need to do something over and over again, memorizing one or two of these is worthwhile.

Finally, Table 10-6 contains a mercifully short list of shortcuts that may help if you spend a lot of time navigating through Windows Explorer (say, when you choose Start⇨Computer or Start⇨Documents). A great collection of Firefox and Internet Explorer keyboard shortcuts is in Technique 18.

TABLE 10-5: WINDOWS SHORTCUTS THAT MIGHT COME IN HANDY

Key	What It Does	Timesaving Bonus Info
Windows+E	Opens Windows Explorer, starting at the Computer window, showing your drives	Beats Start⇨Computer when you don't want to dive for the mouse.
Windows+F	Same as Start⇨Search	In earlier versions of Windows, Search used to be called Find — thus, F.
Windows+R	Same as Start⇨Run	Many people find it faster to start Word by pressing Windows+R and then typing **winword** instead of click-click-clicking.
Shift+F10	Same as right-clicking	Shows the context menu at the current cursor location.
Windows+L	Brings up the welcome screen	This is a good boss key. If the boss is coming, hit Windows+L and your game of Solitaire (or anything else) disappears. To get it back, just log on.

TABLE 10-6: WINDOWS EXPLORER SHORTCUTS

Key	What It Does
F2	Lets you rename the selected folder or file.
F3	Brings up the Search window.
F11	Toggles Windows Explorer into (or out of) full-screen mode.

Technique 11

Making Your Own Keyboard Shortcuts

Save Time By

✔ Creating your own hot keys to run programs, open files, or bring up Web pages

✔ Running a PowerPoint presentation by pressing one hot key

✔ Starting an e-mail message with a hot key

✔ Using ActiveWords — the hot key capability that Vista should have

All the Techniques in this part help you use the Windows desktop efficiently and effectively. There's one additional desktop technique you should add to your timesaving arsenal: the ability to designate your own *hot key* (Vista calls it a *shortcut key*) to start a program, bring up a Web page, or open a folder or file.

Unfortunately, for reasons known only to the folks in Redmond, the Vista custom hot key capability has many limitations. I tell you about those limitations — and how to work around many of them, of course! — in this Technique.

At the end of this Technique, I talk about an extraordinary shareware product called ActiveWords, which gives Windows outstanding hot key capabilities.

Putting Custom Hot Keys to Work for You

Windows has had a hot key capability since the heady days of Windows 95. The basic idea is pretty simple: You tell Windows that you want to use a specific key combination to run a particular program or to bring up a Web page, document, or spreadsheet. For example, you might make Ctrl+Alt+G bring up the Google Web site, or have Shift+F9 create a new invoice.

Hot keys are particularly handy in the following scenarios:

✔ You run the same program many times a day.

✔ You create a new document based on the same template many times a day.

✔ You update a document many times a day.

✔ You perform any of the preceding actions, and diving for the mouse is a pain in the neck.

Hot keys save most people enormous amounts of time. Maybe you run a consulting business, or maybe you're an attorney. Whatever you use Vista to do, you can come up with a hot key that saves you time. In fact, you might even want to set up hot keys for your time-management program. If you have a small business, setting up a hot key to create a new invoice or sales slip can hack lots of time off the click-click-click routine.

Knowing What You Can't Do with Hot Keys

Hot keys have some strange limitations, many of which aren't documented anywhere. Here's a short list of the most confounding restrictions:

- **You can assign a hot key only to a shortcut.** There's no way to assign a hot key directly to a program, document, or folder. But it's easy to assign a hot key to a *shortcut* to a program, document, or folder. Go figger. (Note that items on the Start menu and in the Quick Launch toolbar are generally shortcuts.)

- **You can assign a shortcut key to an icon on the Quick Launch toolbar, but it won't work.** Alas, you may think you have a shortcut key assigned, but the shortcut key won't work. I have no idea why.

- **Vista recognizes only hot keys that are attached to shortcuts that are on the Start menu, on the desktop, or stuck inside folders on the desktop.** For example, you can add a hot key to a shortcut that's buried in a subfolder of your Documents folder, but it won't work.

These restrictions lead to some senseless hoop-jumping when you set up a hot key (see the next section).

 After you have the hot key up and working, it keeps on working — in many cases, to the point of overriding a hot key that previously existed inside the program you're using.

For example, if you're using a program that recognizes Shift+F11 as a specific command, but you've told Windows that you want Shift+F11 to run the calculator, every time you press Shift+F11, Windows probably trumps the running program, and the calculator takes over (although I've seen a few situations where the program wins).

Creating and Organizing Hot Keys

From your point of view, you press a hot key, and a program runs (perhaps with a document open or a Web page loaded). Simple.

From the computer's point of view, pressing a hot key isn't so simple. Windows has to watch what you're typing and jump in whenever it detects something that could be a hot key combination — primarily odd combinations of Ctrl and Alt keys or Shift and function keys (such as F1). When Windows sees you press one of those strange key combinations, it goes out and looks for shortcuts that have that particular key combination listed as the shortcut's hot key. If Windows finds a shortcut, and that particular hot key is associated with the shortcut, Windows runs the shortcut.

For example, say you set up a shortcut to the Windows Calculator and put that shortcut inside a folder on your desktop. You tell Windows that Ctrl+Alt+C is the hot key for this particular shortcut. Windows watches as you use the keyboard. When you press Ctrl+Alt+C, Windows recognizes that as a possible hot key combination. It then looks in a handful of places for shortcuts with that combination. One of the places Windows looks is inside all the folders on the desktop. So sooner or later, Windows finds that you have a shortcut to the Windows Calculator with Ctrl+Alt+C as its hot key. Ba-da-bing ba-da-boom, Windows runs the Calculator.

Generally, you have to jump through a few different hoops in order to get a hot key working:

✔ If a suitable shortcut doesn't already exist, you have to create one.

✔ You need to change the properties of the shortcut to reflect the specific hot key that you've chosen.

✔ You have to organize your hot keys. Well, you don't have to. But if you want to save time, you should.

 Theoretically, shortcuts with hot keys can go anywhere on the desktop or inside any folder that sits on the desktop. I've found that it's much easier to find things if I put all the shortcuts with hot keys inside a single folder on the desktop. That way, if I ever wonder what hot keys I'm using, I can look inside the folder and check out the properties for each shortcut. It's also a good way to make sure I don't accidentally delete a shortcut with a hot key.

If you haven't yet created a folder devoted to hot key shortcuts, it's easy:

1. **Right-click an empty part of the Windows desktop and choose New⇨Folder.**

2. **Type** Hot Key Shortcuts **(see Figure 11-1) and press Enter.**

You now have a central hot key repository.

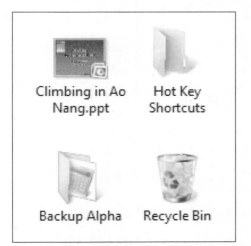

Climbing in Ao Nang.ppt

Hot Key Shortcuts

Backup Alpha

Recycle Bin

• **Figure 11-1:** Create a new folder to hold your hot key shortcuts.

Setting up a proper shortcut — one that can support a hot key — can be very easy or ridiculously difficult. I run you through the gamut in the following sections.

Starting a program with a hot key

If you want to establish a hot key for any program on the Start⇨All Programs menu, the method is quite simple:

1. **If you don't already have a Hot Key Shortcuts folder on your desktop, follow the steps in "Creating and Organizing Hot Keys" to do so. Double-click the Hot Key Shortcuts folder to open it.**

Although Windows doesn't absolutely require you to set up a special folder for hot key shortcuts, you end up saving more than a few gray hairs by creating the folder. It's so much easier if you put shortcuts to all files, folders, and programs that contain hot keys in one place. That way, you can quickly locate them and find out the properties of the shortcut in case you forget the hot key.

2. **Choose Start⇨All Programs and navigate to the program that you want to launch with a hot key (but don't actually launch the program).**

For example, if you want to set up Ctrl+Alt+C to start the Windows Calculator, choose Start⇨ All Programs⇨Accessories⇨Calculator but don't actually open the Calculator.

3. **Right-click the program and choose Send To⇨Desktop (Create Shortcut).**

That puts a shortcut to the program on your desktop.

4. **Drag the newly created shortcut into your Hot Key Shortcuts folder.**

5. **In the Hot Key Shortcuts folder, right-click the newly created shortcut and choose Properties. Click the Shortcut tab.**

Figure 11-2 shows you the Properties dialog box for the shortcut to the Windows Calculator.

6. **Click in the Shortcut Key box.**

• **Figure 11-2: No hot key has been assigned for this shortcut.**

 If you press the Backspace key at this point, the Shortcut Key reverts to None. That's how you get rid of a hot key that's already assigned.

7. **Press the key or keyboard combination that you want to use as a hot key.**

By default, Windows uses Ctrl+Alt for most keyboard shortcuts. Simply type the letter that you want to associate with Ctrl+Alt, and Windows fills in the rest for you without any extra fuss or muss.

 Windows recognizes several odd combinations and a bunch of very common ones (including all the function keys), but to avoid confusion and conflict with the programs you commonly use, I recommend that you stick to the list in Table 11-1.

8. **Click OK.**

After you click through zero, one, or two security messages, your hot key becomes, uh, hot.

9. **Press your new hot key combination.**

If you didn't get the results you expected, you chose a hot key combination in Step 7 that's already being used. For example, if you already have Ctrl+Alt+P set up to launch Windows Paint, and you try to assign Ctrl+Alt+P to a different program, as soon as you press Ctrl+Alt+P, Paint starts running. There's no way to use Ctrl+Alt+P a second time.

10. **If another program suddenly appears when you type a keyboard shortcut, choose a different key combination for this program or change the other program's hot key (in both cases by right-clicking on the offender and choosing Properties — see, I told you it was easier if all your hot key shortcuts are in one place).**

If at first you don't succeed, try, try . . . oh whatever.

 Some combinations just don't seem to work on some machines. I have a PC that refuses to recognize Shift+F12, for example. You may encounter similar problems.

TABLE 11-1: RECOMMENDED VISTA HOT KEYS

Use This	Plus This	Example
Ctrl+Alt	Any letter, A thru Z	Ctrl+Alt+A
Ctrl+Alt	Any number, 0 thru 9	Ctrl+Alt+1
Ctrl+Shift	Any letter or number	Ctrl+Shift+1
Alt+Shift	Any letter or number	Alt+Shift+1
Shift	Any function key	Shift+F2
Ctrl	Any function key	Ctrl+F2
Alt	Any function key	Alt+F2

Opening a folder with a hot key

It's relatively easy to set up a hot key that starts Windows Explorer with a specific folder open and ready to go. Here's how:

1. **If you don't already have a Hot Key Shortcuts folder on your desktop, follow the steps in "Creating and Organizing Hot Keys" to do so. Double-click the Hot Key Shortcuts folder to open it.**

2. **Navigate to the folder that you want to spring to life with a hot key.**

You might click, oh, Start⇨Documents and find a folder named Books.

3. **Right-click the anointed folder and choose Send To⇨Desktop (Create Shortcut).**

Vista creates a shortcut on your desktop with the original folder's name; in this example, the shortcut is called Books-Shortcut.

4. **Drag the newly created shortcut into your Hot Key Shortcuts folder.**

5. **Right-click the shortcut and choose Properties.**

Vista opens the Properties dialog box for the shortcut and puts you on the Shortcut tab (see Figure 11-3).

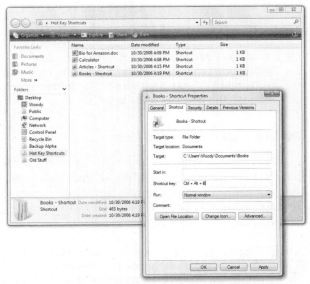

• **Figure 11-3: The hot key gets set in the shortcut's Properties dialog box, on the Shortcut tab.**

6. **Click in the box marked Shortcut Key and press the key or key combination that you want to use as a hot key.**

I recommend that you pick from the list in Table 11-1. In Figure 11-3, I typed B; Vista interprets that as Ctrl+Alt+B.

7. **Click OK.**

Again, you may hit zero, one, or two security messages. Click through them to give your short-cut key combination the hots.

8. **Press your new hot key combination.**

If you didn't get the results you expected, you chose a hot key combination that's already being used.

9. **If another program, folder, or file appears when you type the keyboard shortcut, choose a different key combination for this folder or change the interloper's hot key.**

Surfing to a Web site with a hot key

It's easy to set up a hot key that launches your pre-ferred Web browser and runs out to retrieve a spe-cific page. You're well on your way to saving yourself time.

To open Firefox or Internet Explorer at a specific Web address with the touch of a key, follow these quick steps:

1. **If you don't already have a Hot Key Shortcuts folder set up on your desktop, follow the steps in "Creating and Organizing Hot Keys" to do so. Double-click the Hot Key Shortcuts folder to open it.**

Standard operating procedure by now, eh?

2. **Start your favorite browser and navigate to the site you want to have under hot key control.**

In Figure 11-4, I started Firefox and navigated to www.askwoody.com.

• **Figure 11-4: Creating a shortcut to AskWoody.com.**

3. Click immediately to the left of the Web address — the URL — and drag that little icon into the Hot Key Shortcuts folder.

Vista creates a shortcut to that specific Web site and puts the shortcut in the folder. In Figure 11-4, I dragged the icon that says "AW" to the Hot Key Shortcuts folder.

4. Right-click the new shortcut and choose Properties.

Vista shows you the Properties dialog box for the shortcut, open to the Web Document tab, as in Figure 11-5.

5. Click in the Shortcut Key box and press the key or key combination that you want to use as a hot key.

Again, I recommend that you pick from the list in Table 11-1. In Figure 11-5, I typed A; Vista interprets that as Ctrl+Alt+A.

6. Click OK.

Again you may hit zero, one, or two security messages. Click through them to hottify your shortcut key. Or something like that.

• **Figure 11-5: Set the hot key in the shortcut's Properties dialog box.**

7. Press your new hot key combination.

If you didn't get the results you expected, you chose a hot key combination that's already being used.

8. If another program, folder, or file appears when you type the keyboard shortcut, choose a different key combination for this folder or change the bad guy's hot key.

Sending e-mail with a hot key

If you've been following the instructions for hot keys that start programs, open folders, or visit Web sites, I bet you can guess how this one works. What may surprise you is how much flexibility you have with creating new e-mail messages.

You can set up a hot key that, when pressed, fires up your e-mail program and starts a fresh new message addressed to whomever you wish, with a predefined subject, and with text according to your specification. You can have one key combination to start an e-mail message to your boss, another combination for a message to your mom, and a third for your stockbroker, each with its own custom subjects and body text, ready for you to edit — very slick. And the approach works for most major e-mail programs, including Outlook and Windows Mail (although it doesn't work for online mail programs like Gmail, Yahoo! Mail, or Hotma . . . er, Windows Live Mail). Give it a try and see if it works on your machine.

 If you want to see what I'm talking about, consider this: Flip forward a couple of pages in this book and take a look at Figure 11-10. You can generate an e-mail message like that with one key combination; in this case, I created that entire message by pressing Ctrl+Alt+S. The message is fully editable — you can change anything you like prior to clicking the Send button.

This trick can be a real godsend to people who send many e-mail messages to the same person in one day. I won't mention your boss by name.

Here's the basic approach:

1. **If you don't already have a Hot Key Shortcuts folder set up on your desktop, follow the steps in "Creating and Organizing Hot Keys" to do so. Double-click the Hot Key Shortcuts folder to open it.**

Is there an echo in here?

2. **Right-click an empty place inside the Hot Key Shortcuts folder and choose New➪Shortcut.**

The Create Shortcut Wizard appears (see Figure 11-6).

3. **In the Type the Location of the Item box, type** mailto: **followed by the e-mail recipient's address and the beginning of a subject line, like this:**

```
mailto:somebody@somewhere.com?
   subject=Something
```

For example, in Figure 11-6, I typed this:

```
mailto:DaBoss@mycompany.com?
   subject=Status
```

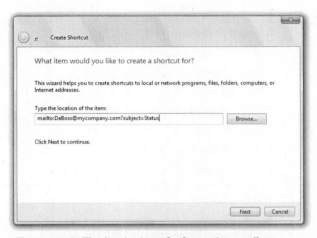

• **Figure 11-6: The beginning of a fantastic e-mail message.**

 The e-mail address immediately following the colon is the recipient of the message. The text to the right of the equal sign is the subject. There's a bug in the Create a Shortcut Wizard that prevents you from using more than one word in the subject, but you can work around that (and put together a dozen more supremely cool things) by following the instructions in Technique 8.

4. **Click Next.**

You see the Name the Shortcut dialog box shown in Figure 11-7.

• **Figure 11-7: Give the e-mail-creating shortcut a name.**

5. **In the Type a Name for This Shortcut box, type a label for the shortcut.**

In Figure 11-7, I typed

`Status Report for DaBoss`

6. **Click Finish.**

The shortcut icon appears in the Hot Key Shortcuts folder.

7. **Double-click the new icon.**

Your e-mail editor kicks in, creating a new e-mail message to the person whose information you entered in Step 3.

In my example, a new message to `DaBoss@ mycompany.com` appears, with the subject `Status`, as shown in Figure 11-8. Because I have Outlook 2007 installed, Word 2007 appears as my e-mail editor.

• **Figure 11-9: Set the hot key in the shortcut's Properties dialog box.**

10. **Click in the box marked Shortcut Key and press the key or key combination that you want to use as a hot key.**

Again, I recommend that you pick from the list in Table 11-1. In Figure 11-9, I typed S (for Status Report, don'tcha know?); Vista interprets that as Ctrl+Alt+S.

11. **Click OK.**

Again, you may run into zero, one, or two security messages. Click through them to short your key . . . or key your shorts . . . I'm running out of verbs here.

12. **Press your new hot key combination.**

If you didn't get the results you expected, you chose a hot key combination that's already being used.

13. **If a program, folder, or file appears when you press the keyboard shortcut, choose a different key combination for this e-mail message or change the competitor's hot key.**

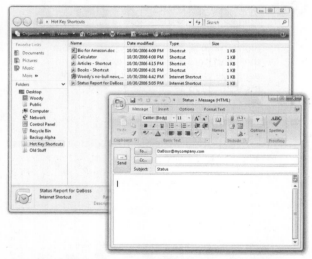

• **Figure 11-8: First stab at a status report e-mail with a single hot key combination.**

8. **"X" out of the new e-mail message. No, you don't want to keep the draft.**

9. **Right-click the new shortcut and choose Properties.**

Vista shows you the Properties dialog box for the shortcut, already open to the Web Document tab, as shown in Figure 11-9.

14. **Now for the fun part. Flip over to Technique 8 and look at the section about improving one-click e-mail. You can add CC lists, BCCs, expand the subject, specify text for the message — even include %0B paragraph marks.**

In Figure 11-10, I used this command:

```
mailto:DaBoss@mycompany.com?
   subject=Today's Status Report&
   body=Boss -%0B%0BWe're on
   schedule. Everything is going
   fine. %0B%0BShould be able to
   hit our next deadline.%0B%0BLet
   me know if you have any
   questions.%0B%0B- Woody
```

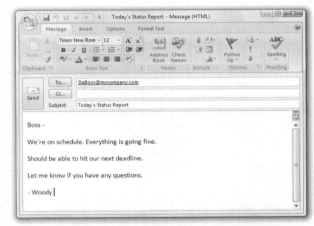

• **Figure 11-10:** One key combination is all it takes to lie to . . . that is, update my boss.

 Any time I want to send a Status Report to DaBoss, I press Ctrl+Alt+S, wait a few seconds, and it's there. I change a word or two and click Send. That's all she wrote. Magic.

Opening a file with a hot key

Hot keys for documents work in two ways, both of which can be major timesavers for people who work with the same document over and over again:

✔ If the document isn't already open, pressing the hot key starts the program associated with the document and then opens the document.

✔ If the document is already open, pressing the hot key directs Windows to find the document and move it to the top of the heap so that it appears on top of all other open documents.

That's a dynamite, useful combination.

 Here's the fastest, easiest way I know to make a Windows application open a specific file when you press the magical hot key:

1. **If you don't already have a Hot Key Shortcuts folder set up on your desktop, follow the steps in "Creating and Organizing Hot Keys" to do so. Double-click the Hot Key Shortcuts folder to open it.**

Yada yada yada.

2. **Navigate to the document whose destiny you want to control with a hot key.**

In this case, I chose Start➪Documents➪Time Sheets and found an Excel 2007 spreadsheet called `Big Client.xlsx`.

3. **Right-click the document and choose Send To➪Desktop (Create Shortcut).**

Vista creates a shortcut on your desktop with the original file's name; in this example, the shortcut is called `Big Client.xlsx - Shortcut`.

4. **Drag the newly created shortcut into your Hot Key Shortcuts folder.**

5. **Right-click the shortcut and choose Properties.**

Vista opens the Properties dialog box for the shortcut and puts you on the Shortcut tab (see Figure 11-11).

6. **Click in the Shortcut Key box and press the key or key combination that you want to use as a hot key.**

Again, I recommend that you pick from the list in Table 11-1. In Figure 11-11, I typed `T` (for Time Sheet — sometimes my mind works in mysterious ways); Vista interprets that as Ctrl+Alt+T.

• **Figure 11-11: A shortcut to a document acts like most other shortcuts.**

7. **Click OK.**

Again, you may hit zero, one, or two, or two hundred and two security messages. Click through them to cut your key some shorts. You know what I mean.

8. **Press your new hot key combination.**

If you didn't get the results you expected, you chose a hot key combination that's already being used.

9. **If another program, folder, or file appears when you type the keyboard shortcut, choose a different key combination for this folder or change the (in)appropriate hot key.**

Running presentations with a hot key

There are many tricks for making hot keys work effectively. As an example, in this section, I show you how to set up Vista so that pressing Ctrl+Alt+P runs a specific PowerPoint presentation. That could come in handy if you use a portable computer for making presentations, and you don't want to go to the hassle of hooking up the mouse just to start the presentation.

Say you have a PowerPoint show called `Great Show.pps` (or, if you use Office 2007, `Great Show.ppsx`) in a folder called `\Documents\Presentations`. Here's how to tell Windows that you want to run the presentation every time you press Ctrl+Alt+P.

This tip works great if you have the presentation on a USB flash drive, as long as you know which drive letter corresponds to the card. Just make the shortcut point to the presentation on the flash drive.

If you're going to use a hot key to launch a PowerPoint presentation, take a few extra minutes to save the presentation as a show: Go into PowerPoint, open the presentation (which has a `.ppt` or `.pptx` extension), choose File➪Save As (or Office➪Save As in PowerPoint 2007), and choose PowerPoint Show (*.pps) in the Save As File Type box. With the presentation saved as a show, you can't accidentally modify it while you're standing at the podium talking!

To set up the hot key, start by putting a shortcut to the presentation in the Hot Key Shortcuts folder. There are many ways to do that, but here's a quick one that uses PowerPoint itself:

1. **If you don't already have a Hot Key Shortcuts folder set up on your desktop, follow the steps in "Creating and Organizing Hot Keys" to do so. Double-click the Hot Key Shortcuts folder to open it.**

Cough. Cough.

2. **Start PowerPoint. Click File➪Open (or, in PowerPoint 2007, click the Office button and choose Open).**

In Figure 11-12, you see the Open dialog box in PowerPoint 2007.

• **Figure 11-12:** Another way to skin the shortcut cat.

3. **Right-click the presentation you want to adorn with a hot key and choose Send To⇨Desktop (Create Shortcut).**

Vista creates a shortcut on your desktop with the file's name; in this example, the shortcut is called `Great Show.pps -Shortcut`.

4. **"X" out of the Open dialog box. Then "X" out of PowerPoint. You have what you want from Office. Drag the newly created shortcut into your Hot Key Shortcuts folder.**

5. **Right-click the shortcut and choose Properties.**

Vista opens the Properties dialog box for the shortcut and puts you on the Shortcut tab (see Figure 11-13).

6. **Click in the box marked Shortcut Key and press the key or key combination that you want to use as a hot key.**

Again, I recommend that you pick from the list in Table 11-1. In Figure 11-13, I typed `P`; Vista interprets that as Ctrl+Alt+P.

7. **Click OK.**

• **Figure 11-13:** Shortcut to your Great Show (TM).

Again, you may run into zero, one, negative one, or two to the power of two to the second security messages. Click through them to give your key combination short shrift. Or long shrift, I s'pose.

8. **Press your new hot key combination.**

If you didn't get the results you expected, you chose a hot key combination that's already being used.

9. **If another program, folder, file, Web page, e-mail message, or UFO appears when you press the keyboard shortcut, choose a different key combination for this presentation or change ET's hot key.**

Undoing hot keys

Windows hot keys work great — most of the time. Occasionally (as I mention several times in this Technique), their behavior is odd, more than odd, or downright bizarre.

Sometimes, you can find solutions to these anomalies. Case in point: A friend of mine reassigned a key combination that she uses for formatting in Word. Instead of formatting text, she changed Ctrl+Shift+F10 so it started the Pinball game. After playing Pinball a few times, she decided she wanted Ctrl+Shift+F10 back for her work in Word. Cool. She reassigned the hot key to format text again and . . . Ctrl+Shift+F10 still brought up Pinball.

She tried everything she could think of to dislodge the Ctrl+Shift+F10 key combination, and nothing worked — until she restarted Windows. Then, miraculously, everything went back to normal: Ctrl+Shift+F10 did its formatting thing in Word. Pinball didn't enter the picture.

 If you have trouble getting a hot key assignment "unstuck," try restarting Windows. It shouldn't be necessary, but sometimes it is.

 You can easily "unassign" an assigned hot key combination: Open the Properties dialog box's Shortcut tab, click in the Shortcut Key box, and press Backspace.

Hot keys are powerful, useful timesavers — when they work right. They don't always work right.

Using ActiveWords for Expanded Hot Keys

If you have read the majority of this Technique (and Technique 10, as well), you have some idea of the enormous timesaving power available through Windows' native hot keys. Now I introduce you to a product that takes hot keys into a new dimension.

It's called ActiveWords, and the concept couldn't be simpler. Instead of limiting your hot keys to odd key combinations, ActiveWords lets you type just about anything and then press F8, and whatever command you associate with the active word takes effect.

For example, you can set up ActiveWords so that typing `myadd` and pressing F8 "types" your name and address wherever the cursor happens to be. You can also make custom *triggers* — so instead of pressing F8, you might trigger ActiveWords when you press the spacebar twice.

More than that, you can have it bring up programs: Typing `calc` and then pressing F8 might bring up the Windows Calculator; typing `xl` and pressing F8 could start Excel.

Ah, but there's more:

- ✔ Typing `bbc` and pressing F8 can start Internet Explorer and bring up the BBC Web site.

- ✔ Typing `mb` and pressing F8 might start an e-mail message to `billg@microsoft.com`.

- ✔ Typing `inv` and pressing F8 could start Excel using your invoice template to create a new invoice.

- ✔ Typing `lthd` and pressing F8 might bring up Word with a new letter, based on your letterhead.

- ✔ Typing `Mxyzptlk` and pressing F8 could call Superman . . . well, you get the idea.

ActiveWords Plus, `www.activewords.com`, ain't cheap — it costs $49.95 for individuals — but you can use your copy on all the PCs that you have, and you get a 60-day free trial.

Part III

Packing Programs and Files

The 5th Wave   By Rich Tennant

"Needlepoint my foot! These are Word fonts.
What I can't figure out is how you got the
pillow cases into your printer."

Technique 12

Launching Your Most-Used Programs Quickly

Save Time By

✔ Customizing your Quick Launch toolbar

✔ Identifying Quick Launch programs instantly

✔ Opening documents and starting new documents in a flash

A re you tired of the Start⇨All Programs⇨Blah⇨Blah⇨Blah hunt-and-click routine? Do you have a small handful of programs you run every day? Man, have I got a toolbar for you!

The Quick Launch toolbar contains small icons that let you open programs quickly. In its initial state, it holds little icons for showing the desktop, for the "Flip 3D" window switcher, and, if you've run the programs at least once, for Internet Explorer, Outlook or Windows Mail, Windows Media Player, and a few more programs (the company that manufactured your PC may have jimmied the mix a bit).

This Technique and Technique 8 go hand-in-hand. You can tackle them in either order, as long as you go through them both.

Using the Quick Launch Toolbar

The Windows Quick Launch toolbar sits immediately to the right of the Start button on the Windows taskbar (see Figure 12-1). It's a very convenient place to put your own icons so that launching programs — or even opening frequently used documents — is just a click away.

• Fi e 12-1: The programs available directly from my Quick Launch toolbar.

 Quick Launch has a hidden, little-known advantage. In addition to its convenient location, every item on the Quick Launch toolbar gets blessed with an automatically assigned hot key. Press the Windows button on your keyboard and press 1, and Vista "clicks" the first icon on the Quick Launch toolbar. Windows+2 launches the second icon, and so on.

After many years of kicking and futzing with the Windows desktop, I've settled on a simple hierarchy that really streamlines Windows, and in my opinion, the Quick Launch toolbar stands at the top of the timesaving food chain. Here's how to organize Windows for maximum efficiency, based on how frequently you use specific programs, folders, and so on:

- Put programs and documents that you use several times a day on the Quick Launch toolbar. Each gets its own automatically generated hot key (Windows+1, Windows+2, and so on). You should assign your own shortcut keys to these frequently used programs and documents, as well. (Take a look at Technique 11.)

- Put programs, folders, and documents that you use at least once a day on the Start menu. (Check out Technique 7.)

- Use the Windows desktop as a temporary parking area and clean it up as frequently as you possibly can. (Technique 8 can help.)

 Following those three guidelines ensures that the programs, documents, and folders you use most are the easiest ones to find.

Making the Quick Launch Toolbar Appear

If you can't see the Quick Launch toolbar next to the Start button on your Windows taskbar, that's because you turned it off! Here's what you need to do:

1. **Right-click any open spot on the Windows taskbar.**

2. **Choose Toolbars⇨Quick Launch.**

Adding Programs to the Quick Launch Toolbar

There's no need to settle for Windows' bone-stock Quick Launch toolbar. Any program that you want to get at quickly deserves to be there. Here's how to add your frequently used programs to the toolbar:

1. **Navigate to the program you want to put on the Quick Launch toolbar.**

   Most commonly, you'll want to click Start or Start⇨All Programs and work your way to the program in question.

2. **Click the program and drag it to the Quick Launch toolbar.**

   An I-beam appears where the new Quick Launch icon will go (see Figure 12-2).

• **Figure 12-2: The I-beam tells you where the icon will go.**

 To remove a program from the Quick Launch toolbar, right-click it and choose Delete. That does not delete the program from your computer; it only deletes the icon on the toolbar.

Making Room for More Programs on the Quick Launch Toolbar

It won't take long before you run out of room for Quick Launch icons. Although keeping the number of icons manageable is important so that you can readily remember what each one does, in my experience, feelings of claustrophobia rapidly overcome deficiencies in long-term memory.

Give your icons more elbow room:

1. **Right-click any open spot on the Windows taskbar.**

2. **Uncheck the line that says Lock the Taskbar.**

   A domino pattern of dots appears, marking the edges of the Quick Launch toolbar (see Figure 12-3).

• **Figure 12-3: Drag the dots to resize the Quick Launch toolbar.**

3. **Drag the dots left or right to make the Quick Launch toolbar area bigger or smaller.**

   If you can remember what all the icons mean, or you take the time to make the Screen Tips meaningful (see the following section, "Changing Quick Launch Screen Tips"), there's no reason to be stingy with Quick Launch real estate. Personally, I drag the entire Windows taskbar up so it occupies two or even three rows (see Technique 9) and leave plenty of extra room for Quick Launch icons.

4. **When the Quick Launch toolbar is the right size for you and in the location you want, right-click any unused part of the Windows taskbar and check the line that says Lock the Taskbar.**

 My son, Justin, leaves the taskbar unlocked all the time so it's easier and faster to rearrange things. If you find yourself adapting to many different working situations on any given day, this may be the most efficient approach.

Make sure you read through Technique 9 for a bunch of hard-hitting taskbar timesaving tips.

Changing Quick Launch Screen Tips

When you hover your mouse pointer over an icon on the Quick Launch toolbar, a Screen Tip appears directly above the icon. Although Windows uses lots of Screen Tips that are frequently more of a bother than a help, the Quick Launch Screen Tips can be very helpful, particularly if you have more than a few Quick Launch icons, and even moreso if several of the icons look the same.

 Unfortunately, many companies (and I won't mention Microsoft by name) put ridiculously long essays in their Screen Tips. The Screen Tip for Word 2003, for example, reads (I kid you not): `Microsoft Word / Create and edit text and graphics in letters, reports, Web pages, or e-mail messages by using Microsoft Office Word.` In Word 2007, Microsoft took a brevity pill and reduced that multiple-mouthful to `Microsoft Office Word 2007 / Create and edit professional-looking documents such as letters, papers, reports, and booklets by using Microsoft Office Word.` Oh, wait a sec. I guess the Word 2007 version is *longer* than the Word 2003 rambling. Nothing like a quick and snappy Screen Tip to increase your efficiency, eh?

Depending on the way you created your Quick Launch icons — or the way they were created for you — you might have such illuminating Screen Tips as `Shortcut to capture32.exe` or `CorelDRAW 10 Launch CorelDRAW 10`, which, no doubt, originated in Corel's Department of Redundancy Department.

You might think that you could right-click a Quick Launch icon, choose Rename and, uh, rename the icon. Nope. Taking control of the ridiculously long Screen Tip involves a convoluted process:

1. **Right-click the icon and choose Properties.**

Vista creates the Screen Tip on the fly by combining the name at the top of the Properties dialog box's Shortcut tab with the Comment at the bottom. Figure 12-4, for example, shows you the stock Word 2007 properties. Windows combines "Microsoft Office Word 2007" at the top with "Create and edit professional-looking . . ." from the Comment section.

• **Figure 12-4: The Screen Tip comes from a combination of the Shortcut and the Comment text.**

2. **Unless you really want to see the verbiage in the Comments box every time you hover over a Quick Launch icon, delete everything in the Comments box.**

Good riddance. Bad rubbish. You know the tune.

3. **Click the General tab at the top of the Properties dialog box.**

The General tab for the Word icon looks like Figure 12-5.

4. **Type whatever you want to appear as the Screen Tip in the top box on the General tab.**

In Figure 12-5, I changed "Microsoft Office Word 2007" into "Word." Short and sweet, don't you think?

• **Figure 12-5: This is where the Quick Launch toolbar picks up the text "Microsoft Office Word 2007."**

5. Click OK.

Your Screen Tip should be a bit more palatable — and usable.

Opening Documents Quickly

Do you have a document that you open every day — or even several times a day? If so, adding the document to the Quick Launch toolbar can save you all sorts of time. Here's how to add a document to the Quick Launch toolbar:

1. **Locate the file you want to put on the Quick Launch toolbar.**

You can use Windows Explorer or File➪Open from inside most applications.

 Surprisingly, this quick tip doesn't work if you try to grab the file from Windows' Start➪Recent Items list. It also doesn't work if you try to grab documents in the Office applications' Recent Documents list.

2. **Click the file and drag it to the Quick Launch toolbar.**

If you have the taskbar set to auto-hide, sometimes you have to "bump" your cursor against the bottom of the screen a couple times.

An I-beam appears where the icon will go.

3. **Release the mouse button.**

Voilà! Next time you want to open the document, click on it in the Quick Launch toolbar.

Opening Web Pages Quickly

You can create a Quick Launch toolbar icon that opens a specific Web page in many different ways.

Here's my favorite, fast way:

1. **Start your favorite browser and navigate to the site you want to put on your Quick Launch toolbar.**

In Figure 12-6, I started Firefox and navigated to www.dummies.com.

• **Figure 12-6: Creating a shortcut to Dummies.com.**

2. **Click immediately to the left of the Web address — the URL — and drag that little icon onto the Quick Launch toolbar.**

In Figure 12-6, I clicked the icon that looks like a bull's-eye and dragged it to the Quick Launch toolbar. Vista shows an I-beam where the icon goes.

3. **Release the mouse button.**

You have a new icon in the Quick Launch toolbar. Click it, and your favorite browser will kick in, load the page, and show it to you.

Adding a Blank E-Mail Message to the Quick Launch Toolbar

In Technique 8, I show how to put an icon on your desktop which, when clicked, generates a full-fledged e-mail message, complete with mailing address, CCs, subject, boilerplate text, and a request for donations through PayPal. (Okay, okay, the PayPal part is a bit hard to put together.)

You can use the same method to create a Quick Launch icon that starts a blank e-mail message addressed to whomever you wish, saying whatever you like. Follow these steps:

1. **Use the method described in Technique 8 to construct a desktop shortcut that creates the message you want to send.**

2. **When you're happy with the way the shortcut works, click it and drag it to the Quick Launch toolbar.**

It comes through without a hitch. The next time you want to create a new e-mail message — whether or not your e-mail program is running — click that Quick Launch icon, and the message appears. Make whatever changes you wish, click Send, and the message is ready to roll.

Technique 13

Making Programs Run Your Way

Save Time By

✔ Running the programs you choose whenever Windows starts

✔ Setting up programs so every user on the computer can run them

✔ Making programs start your way — right away

Vista is nothing without programs. Hey, I'm not saying Windows isn't nice, but your work (and play!) gets done inside programs — word processors, e-mail programs, spreadsheets, *Warcraft XIX: The Prequel* . . . you get the idea.

Windows has all sorts of hooks for making programs run in a specific way — and gotchas to trap the unwary. Windows is the ooze that all the programs have to play in. And if they play well, you can push and nudge Vista to control the programs themselves. You don't have to write a program. You don't need to be a Computer Science grad. All you need is a little gumption and good ol'-fashioned ingenuity.

This Technique contains three program-controlling tips that you can use right now to save time and take control of your PC.

Twiddling program controls is a two-way street: The same methods that allow scumware programs to start automatically on your PC can be used for good, to start the programs you want. In Technique 3, I show you how to turn off auto-starting programs. In this Technique, I show you how to save time by making the program(s) you use most often start up with Windows.

Running a Program When Windows Starts

Many Vista users run some specific program every time they get on their computers. Personally, I run Outlook and the Task Manager every time. (I describe how to get Task Manager going in Technique 2.) Duangkhae likes to get Firefox, Windows Media Player, and the Calculator cranked up every time she logs on. Odd combination, that.

Here's how to tell Windows to run a specific program each time Windows starts:

1. **Right-click the Start button.**

You can run the program whenever you log on to your PC, or you can run the program no matter who logs on to the PC.

2. **Choose Explore to run the program when you log on. Choose Explore All Users to run the program regardless of which user logs on.**

Windows Explorer opens to the Start Menu folder.

3. **Double-click your way down to Start Menu⇨ Programs⇨Startup.**

Chances are good that your Startup folder is empty, as in Figure 13-1. (Why? Because most programs — and your computer manufacturer — install their annoying auto-starting components in the "All Users" Startup folder, so everyone who logs onto the computer gets the same treatment!)

• **Figure 13-1:** An empty Startup folder.

Any shortcut that sits in the Startup folder runs whenever this particular user signs on to the PC.

4. **Starting back in Windows itself, navigate to the program you want to start automatically.**

If a shortcut is already on the Quick Launch toolbar (see Technique 12), you have all you need. Otherwise, go through the Start⇨All Programs route. Say you want to start Windows Media Player every time you log on. In that case, you choose Start⇨All Programs and then hover your mouse (but don't click) over Windows Media Player.

5. **Right-click the program and choose Send To⇨ Desktop (Create Shortcut).**

You might think that it would be safe to drag the All Programs shortcut into the Startup folder, but it isn't: Sometimes Vista copies the shortcut into the Startup folder, but sometimes Vista moves it. The safest approach is to create a shortcut on the desktop.

You may need to click through a security dialog box, but ultimately Vista creates a shortcut to the program and places it on the desktop.

6. **Click and drag the newly created shortcut into the Startup folder.**

7. **Repeat Steps 4 through 6 for any other programs that you want to start automatically.**

Duangkhae's Startup folder, complete with shortcuts to Windows Media Player, the Vista Calculator, and Firefox, appears in Figure 13-2.

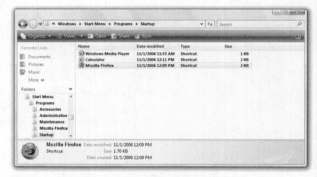

• **Figure 13-2:** Drag programs you want to start automatically into the Startup folder.

8. **"X" out of the Startup folder.**

9. **Log off (click Start, click the right wedge at the bottom-left corner of the Start menu, and choose Log Off). Then log back on again.**

The programs that you placed in the Startup folder run. (See Figure 13-3.)

You can place as many programs as you like in the Startup folder.

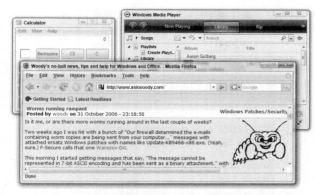

• **Figure 13-3:** Duangkhae's designated Startup programs run automatically when she logs on.

Allowing Other Users to Run Your Programs

Tell me if you've heard this one before:

Justin installed one of *The Sims* games on the family-room PC, and he took me through a quick demo. Cool stuff. I was interested in the, ahem, mathematical simulation capabilities, so one day, while he was at school, I logged on to the PC in the family room, chose Start⇨All Programs, and . . . no Sims.

Huh?

Turns out that Justin had installed *The Sims* for one user only — it doesn't show up on the Start⇨ All Programs menu for anybody but Justin.

Many older programs install themselves for the current user only. More recent ones frequently give you the option of installing for just one user or for all users. If you have the option, unless you have a very compelling reason to do otherwise, always install for all users.

I could go into Windows Explorer and look for *The Sims,* but that's a pain in the neck. In the end, I put

shortcuts for *The Sims* on everybody's Start⇨ All Programs menu. Here's how:

1. **Log on as the user who can get to the program.**

In this case, Justin logged on as himself.

2. **Right-click Start and choose Open. On the right, double-click the Programs folder.**

You end up in the `Start Menu\Programs` folder for the user who's logged on.

3. **Find the folder that contains the programs you installed.**

The folder that contains the *The Sims* is called Maxis (see Figure 13-4). That's the name of the company that makes *The Sims*.

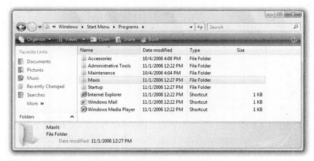

• **Figure 13-4:** Find the folder in the `Start Menu\ Programs` **folder that contains the shortcuts you want.**

You may have to click and search a bit to find the folder you need, but make sure you get the main folder — the one that contains all the shortcuts.

4. **Right-click the folder and choose Copy.**

Now you need to move over to the "All Users" Programs folder.

5. **Right-click Start and choose Open All Users.**

Windows Explorer shows you the Start Menu folder for "All Users."

6. **Double-click the Programs folder.**

That puts you in the "All Users" Programs folder.

7. Right-click a blank spot on the right side of the Explorer window and choose Paste. Then "X" out of Windows Explorer.

You may need to jump through a security dialog hoop, but in the end, the program shortcut folder (in this case, to the folder Maxis) appears in the `Start Menu\Programs` folder, as shown in Figure 13-5.

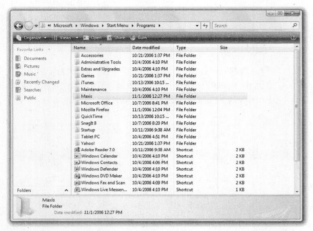

• **Figure 13-5:** Placing the Maxis folder here ensures that it appears on the Start Menu for all users.

8. "X" out of Windows Explorer.

By virtue of its location in that folder, Maxis appears on the Start⇨All Programs menus for every user.

Bringing Back Word's Last Document

Many programs use *command line switches* — little directives that tell the program what to do when it starts. All the Office applications have various command line switches — most of which are widely ignored and rarely used.

One of the most useful Office command line switches tells Word that it should open the last-used document when it starts.

You can use that switch to put an icon on your desktop that, when double-clicked, starts Word with the last-used document open, ready for you to dig in.

Here's how to use a command line switch to tell Word to open with the last document you were working on:

1. Right-click any open spot on the desktop and choose New⇨Shortcut.

The Create Shortcut Wizard appears, as in Figure 13-6.

• **Figure 13-6:** Start here to create a shortcut that will start Word with its last document open.

2. Click the Browse button and locate `winword.exe` — the program better known as Word.

Unfortunately, finding programs can be a challenge in and of itself. For example, Word's location varies depending on which version of Word you use. Use Table 13-1 as a start.

To find out which version of a specific Office application you're using, start the application (Word, Outlook, Excel, PowerPoint, and so on) and choose Help⇨About and the product name. For Word, you choose Help⇨About Microsoft Word; for Excel, it's Help⇨About Microsoft Excel, and so on. Office 2007 and later versions don't have a Help menu item.

If you don't see "Help" along the menu bar at the top of the screen, click the ? Help icon in the upper right and choose What's New. The dialog box tells you which version is running.

3. **When you find `winword.exe`, click it once and then click OK.**

The Create Shortcut dialog box looks similar to Figure 13-7.

• **Figure 13-7: The location of** `winword.exe` **for Office 2007/Word 2007.**

4. **Press the End key.**

You're taken to the end of the long line in the Type the Location of the Item box, which points to `winword.exe`.

5. **In the text box after `winword.exe`, type a space, type `/mfile1`, and then press Enter.**

That's space, slash, the text `mfile`, and the number 1 with no spaces after the slash or before the 1. The net result looks like Figure 13-8:

```
"C:\Program Files\Microsoft Office\
    Office12\WINWORD.EXE" /mfile1
```

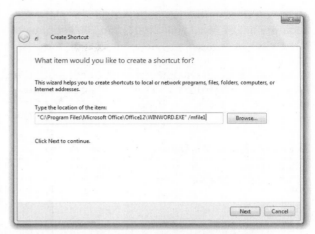

• **Figure 13-8: The secret incantation that tells Word to open its most recently used file.**

The `/m` command is a Word command line switch that tells Word to run a built-in program (also known as a macro). In this case, the `file1` macro simply opens the last-used file — or, more accurately, the first file in Word's most-recently-used list.

6. **Click Next.**

The Create Shortcut Wizard asks you to provide a name for the shortcut.

7. **Type a name for the shortcut and click the Finish button.**

I call this shortcut Last Word Doc, but you can call it Gefilte Fish if you like. You end up with a new shortcut on your desktop.

8. **Double-click the new shortcut.**

Word opens the last-used document, ready for edits.

If you commonly start Word and want to open the last-used document, put a copy of this new shortcut on your Quick Launch toolbar, or even on the Start menu. Usually, you want to leave the old Word shortcut in place so you can quickly decide whether to open Word normally or open the last-used document.

Microsoft finally (finally!) published a complete and accurate list of Word 2000, 2002, and 2003 command line switches at `support.microsoft.com/kb/210565`. (Pardon me if I sound excited. I've been complaining about the lousy switch documentation for a decade.) Word 2007's command line switches are at `office.microsoft.com/en-us/word/` `HP101640101033.aspx`. Excel's command line switches appear at `support.microsoft.com/kb/291288`. Outlook's Help has a list of all the command line switches: search Help for `select` (which is a switch). PowerPoint command line switches (for the Viewer, too) are at `support.microsoft.com/kb/830040`.

TABLE 13-1: PLACES YOU USUALLY FIND WINWORD.EXE

Version of Office	Default Location
Office 97/Word 97	`C:\Program Files\Microsoft Office\Office\winword.exe`
Office 2000/Word 2000	`C:\Program Files\Microsoft Office\Office\winword.exe`
Office XP/Word 2002	`C:\Program Files\Microsoft Office\Office10\WINWORD.EXE`
Office 2003/Word 2003	`C:\Program Files\Microsoft Office\OFFICE11\WINWORD.EXE`
Office 2007/Word 2007	`C:\Program Files\Microsoft Office\Office12\WINWORD.EXE`

Technique 14

Removing and Reinstalling Programs

Into every program's life a little rain must fall. For some programs, it's a gentle mist. For others, it's a monsoon-borne torrent. There are many good reasons for getting rid of programs that are causing you problems. Even programs that you use all the time — Outlook and Word come to mind — occasionally become unstable and need to be uninstalled and reinstalled, when the Repair feature doesn't work.

The rub comes when removing a program and reinstalling it doesn't fix things: Lingering problems — which are usually in the Registry, but sometimes in a "bad" file — can keep reinstalled programs misbehaving just as badly after the makeover as before, coughing up messages like the one shown in Figure 14-1.

Here are the tips you need to oust the offal — quickly, reliably, the first time.

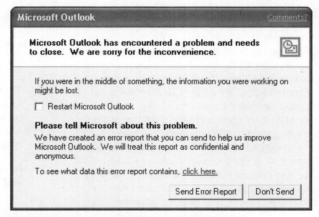

• **Figure 14-1:** Outlook has encountered a problem.

Removing Programs Thoroughly

Sometimes, the only way you can get a program to work again is by removing and then reinstalling it. And sometimes you just want to get rid of the stupid thing — forever.

You can use a few tricks to save yourself a bunch of time. To truly remove a program, follow these steps:

1. **Choose Start⇨Control Panel and, under the Programs icon, click the link marked Uninstall a Program.**

Windows shows you the Uninstall or Change a Program dialog box, shown in Figure 14-2.

• **Figure 14-2: All well-behaved installers leave an entry here.**

2. **Click the program you want to remove.**

Some older programs don't jump through the right hoops to "register" their uninstallers with Vista. If you're trying to uninstall a program, and it isn't on the Uninstall or Change a Program list in Figure 14-2, don't panic. Chances are good the program has its own uninstaller, and you can get to it by choosing Start⇨All Programs and navigating to the program. You should see an entry to Uninstall the program nearby. Failing that, go to the manufacturer's Web page and complain loudly. Nowadays, the only programs that don't have uninstallers are scummy programs that deserve your ire.

3. **If a Repair button appears, consider trying to repair the program.**

Sometimes, running a repair at this point can fix a problem, assuming you want to keep the program. If the repair works, it's much less time-consuming (and hair-raising) than a complete uninstall followed by a reinstall. Give it a try.

Some programs (notably, all the modern versions of Microsoft Office) include an option to change the components of the program that are installed. If you click the Change button, you have an opportunity to bring in new features or lop off old ones that you don't want. The choices are vast. For example, in Figure 14-3, the options for Excel include an Analysis ToolPak and Euro Currency Tools.

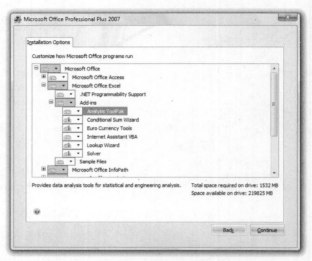

• **Figure 14-3: Microsoft Office Change options are not for the faint of heart.**

4. **If you want to remove the program, click the Uninstall button. When Vista asks if you're sure you want to uninstall the program, click Yes You Stupid Machine, That's What I Just Told You to Do.**

You may have to jump through several security dialog boxes.

5. **Some programs (see Figure 14-4) require you to restart your computer in order to remove all vestiges. If so, answer in the affirmative.**

It's always best to reboot immediately. If you continue to try to work, Vista's left in a potentially unstable state, and you might get clobbered unexpectedly. Take the time to reboot.

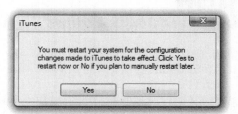

• **Figure 14-4:** Don't put it off — reboot immediately if at all possible.

Cleaning Up before a Reinstall

Sometimes removing a program and reinstalling it isn't sufficient; the program continues to cause problems in the same way it did before you went through this mind-numbing process. In some cases, pieces of the old program are left behind, even if the uninstaller tells you that it got everything.

If you believe that remnants of an old program are hampering your attempts to get it to reinstall correctly, try this:

1. **Use Add or Remove Programs, as described earlier in this Technique, to remove the program.**

That should always be your approach of first resort.

2. **Even if the uninstaller tells you that it got everything, if you're having problems with vestiges of old programs sticking around, choose Start, type** `regedit`**, and press Enter.**

Click through a security box, and the Vista Registry Editor appears.

 I talk about the Registry Editor extensively in Technique 56.

3. **Inside the Registry Editor, search for the name of the program by choosing Edit⇨Find (see Figure 14-5).**

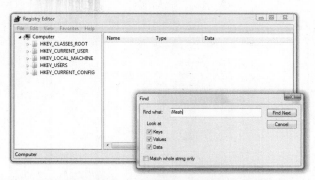

• **Figure 14-5:** Searching the Registry for vestiges of iMesh.

Make sure all three boxes — Keys, Values, and Data — are checked. You might not be able to find the precise program name, but you may be able to find something similar to it, or possibly the manufacturer's name.

4. **Keep searching (use the F3 key or the Find Next button) until you find a major entry for the program.**

Usually, you can find a major entry for the program itself, as opposed to minor entries for certain kinds of documents or filename extensions. At first, you should eliminate any major entries. If that doesn't work, you may have to go back and pluck off the smaller entries, one at a time.

5. **If you find an entry that seems to include lots of settings for the program, right-click it and choose Export.**

In Figure 14-6, I found a few entries for iMesh — and they're still in the Registry after I ran the iMesh uninstaller.

When you right-click and choose Export, the Export Registry File dialog box appears, as in Figure 14-6.

6. **Use the Export Registry File dialog box to put the contents of this key on your desktop. Give the exported Registry key a filename that you can remember and click Save.**

The desktop is a good place to stick the entries because you won't need to keep them very long.

• **Figure 14-6:** Always export any registry entries before nuking them — just in case.

7. **In the Registry Editor, click the offending key and press Delete. When the Registry Editor asks if you want to permanently delete the key, click Yes. Then "X" out of the Registry Editor.**

That removes all the old information about this specific Registry entry from your computer — and may help knock loose whatever was preventing the reinstallation from working correctly.

8. **Reinstall the program that's been giving you problems.**

You'll probably insert a CD or double-click a downloaded file.

Chances are very good that going through the additional step of scouring the Registry to remove all the old, potentially bad settings makes the program work right.

9. **If the reinstalled version of the program still doesn't work, double-click the Registry key on your desktop to put the Registry back the way you found it.**

That doesn't fix the problem. But it does mean any changes you made to the Registry are undone.

Adding Windows Components

If you didn't install all the pieces of Vista — or if the PC manufacturer didn't before it shipped your PC to you — then you might find references to a program you just don't have. Perhaps you can't find one of the Windows games, or you read about the Windows Calculator or WordPad and you can't find those on your PC.

If you ever think that parts of Windows haven't been installed, grab your Vista CD and follow these steps:

1. **Choose Start➪Control Panel➪Programs.**

2. **Under the Programs and Features icon, click the link marked Turn Windows Features On or Off.**

You have to click through another User Account Control security dialog box, and Vista goes out to lunch for a while, but when it comes back, you see the Windows Features dialog box shown in Figure 14-7, which enables you to turn features on or off.

• **Figure 14-7:** Vista manages its own version of the Uninstall or Change a Program dialog box.

3. **Select check boxes to add or remove components.**

4. **Click OK when you're done.**

Removing Windows Patches

So you got a bad patch from Microsoft?

Hey, join the club. Line forms at the end of the block.

 If you have Automatic Update turned off (more precisely, turned to "Notify"), as I discuss in Technique 44, and you're cautious about applying Vista patches only when you're confident that they'll do more good than harm, you shouldn't be forced to remove a Windows update very frequently. On the other hand, if you let Microsoft patch your machine automatically, you may be forced to uninstall a patch much more often than you would like.

Usually, you find out about bad patches (or the bad side effects of patches) through the news or by searching for specific problems you may encounter. Google can help you uncover all sorts of problems. I cover bad patches extensively — almost daily, it seems — at www.AskWoody.com. The SANS Internet Storm Center, http://isc.sans.org, also keeps on top of the latest problems.

If you know you have a bad patch, and you want to remove it, you need to know the patch's Knowledge Base number, or KB number. Armed with the KB number, you can scan the list of patches that have been applied to your PC, with or without your knowledge or consent, and get rid of the offender rather easily. Here's how:

1. **Choose Start⇨Control Panel and click the Programs link.**

    Vista shows you the Programs dialog box, as in Figure 14-8.

2. **If you want to delete a bad update, click View Installed Updates.**

• **Figure 14-8: To back out a bad patch, click View Installed Updates.**

Vista shows you the Uninstall an Update dialog box, shown in Figure 14-9. (What happened to the "View Installed Updates" terminology? I guess the marketing guys didn't get down this deep in the dialog boxes!)

• **Figure 14-9: Windows patches are listed by Knowledge Base article number.**

3. **Click the patch that's causing you heartburn.**

    An Uninstall button should appear. If it doesn't, you're outta luck — Microsoft won't allow you to uninstall the patch.

4. **Click Uninstall.**

    You may have to reboot to make your change "take."

Using Non-Microsoft Replacements

As part of one Microsoft antitrust settlement, the programmers in Redmond modified Windows XP to make it much easier to use non-Microsoft products for browsing the Web, reading e-mail, sending instant messages, and playing media files. The sins of the father are visited on the Vista son.

Top choices for alternatives include the following:

- **Firefox** (www.getfirefox.com): I use Firefox instead of Internet Explorer whenever humanly possible, and I recommend that you do, too. Firefox doesn't have the kind of security exposures that are inherent in IE. I like its interface better. And, most of all, it ain't Microsoft. See Technique 18.

- **Trillian** (www.trillian.cc): Until Google comes up with a good alternative, I'll use the only polyglot instant messenger worthy of the name: Trillian talks to Windows Live Messenger, Yahoo! Messenger, AOL Instant Messenger, and many others. Not as flashy as Windows Live Messenger, but far more useful. See Technique 21.

- **iTunes** (www.apple.com/itunes): I'm no fan of Apple, and I've sworn at QuickTime for years. But iTunes (which, admittedly, runs with QuickTime) actually works as a media player, has a decent interface, and, most of all, doesn't help Microsoft further entrench its music file formats. I use Windows Media Player most of the time but don't hesitate to flip over to iTunes when the mood strikes or my iPod needs feeding. And I wouldn't touch any of Microsoft's or Apple's online music stores with ten 10-foot poles. See Technique 25.

- **Any mail program except Windows Mail** (www.gmail.com): I use Outlook 2003 (or sometimes 2007) on my desktop and Google's Gmail online. I'll begrudgingly hop onto Windows Live Mail or

Yahoo! Mail if pressed into service. But for the life of me, I can't stand Windows Mail.

Your PC manufacturer may have set up non-Microsoft programs for you as your default instant messenger or media player. They aren't necessarily better. Make up your own mind — don't feel compelled to use the manufacturer's choices.

If your PC manufacturer installed different (non-Microsoft) messaging or media-playing software for you, and you want Microsoft's applications, downloading and installing the latest versions of the Microsoft applications is as simple as visiting http://windowsupdate.microsoft.com. Or you can venture into Microsoft's rapid-development front by looking at http://ideas.live.com.

To make your own choices for default programs:

1. **Install the alternative program, start it, and if it asks, allow it to become your default program for Internet access, e-mail, messaging, and/or media.**

Some programs are smart enough to replace the Microsoft equivalents all by themselves, but you may need to manually kick some of them in the seat of the pants. (That's another one of those technical terms.)

If you've installed a Web browser or e-mail application, click Start and see if it appears at the top of the Start menu. If it doesn't, your new program hasn't yet taken over. Continue with these steps.

2. **Choose Start➪All Programs➪Default Programs.**

Vista brings up its default program chooser, shown in Figure 14-10.

3. **Down at the bottom, click Set Program Access and Computer Defaults.**

You have to click through another User Account Control security box.

• **Figure 14-10:** Override Microsoft's (and perhaps your computer manufacturer's) biases here.

4. Click the down-arrow to the right of the word Custom.

You finally arrive at the Set Program Access and Computer Defaults dialog box, shown in Figure 14-11.

5. Use the buttons on the left to set your default programs. Don't bother unchecking any of the boxes on the right — you may need to get at some of the more unsavory programs from time to time. Yes, even Windows Mail.

6. When you're happy with your choices, click OK.

Your changes take effect immediately. Your new program(s) appear everywhere that Microsoft's built-in programs used to appear. They have to. The judge ordered it.

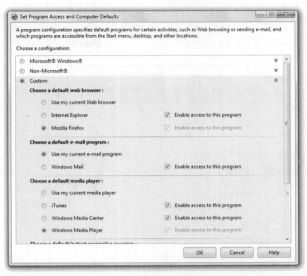

• **Figure 14-11:** It's easy to get out of the Microsoft rut for Web browsers, e-mail packages, messaging, playing media files, and your version of Java.

 Don't worry. The old Microsoft programs are still there — and they should still work just fine. When you make this change, the Microsoft programs simply won't appear as your default Web browser, media player, e-mail program, and the like.

Technique 15

Exploring Effectively

Save Time By

- Coaxing Windows into showing all your files — the first time
- Finding things quickly and reliably in Windows Explorer
- Navigating the Open and Save As dialog boxes quickly

Windows Explorer provides the lens by which you see all the files and folders on your computer. It was designed to look good and feel comfortable for first-time users: When you choose Start⇨Documents for the first time, Microsoft wants you to be able to look around and get warm and fuzzy vibes all over.

But if you want to save time, you need to take off the training wheels.

Underneath Explorer's docile exterior beats the heart of a powerful, adroit assistant. You need to push it here and poke it there, but if you spend a few minutes to apply the suggestions in this Technique, you can emerge with a world-class file handler that saves you time, day after day.

Even if you never use Explorer, and you don't have time to go through this entire Technique, please read the first section, which describes how (and why!) to make Windows show you filename extensions. It's the single most important tip in the whole book.

If you want to apply the changes I describe in this Technique, be sure to follow the tips in the Technique in order; you may get unexpected results if you apply the tips at the end before you apply the tips at the beginning. Take a few minutes right now to work through these timesaving customizations. Start with the first procedure in this Technique and make Windows show you filename extensions. Then continue from there.

Making Windows Show Filename Extensions

Yes, this is the most important tip in the entire book. If you let Explorer hide filename extensions, you vastly increase your chances of being zapped by a virus or a worm. Microsoft executives — people who should know better — have been bitten by Explorer's intransigence. Don't let it bite you.

Every computer program since the dawn of time (okay, so maybe I'm exaggerating a little bit) puts a handful of letters on the end of each file's name to identify which program goes with the file. For example, Microsoft Word files are branded with .doc (or, starting with Word 2007, .docx); WordPerfect files usually get .wpd; Excel has .xls and, more recently, .xlsx; Adobe Acrobat uses .pdf (you've heard of PDF files, right?); Windows Remote Assistance uses .msrcincident. (No, I don't make this stuff up.)

If you save a file in WordPerfect and call it ByeByeBallmer, WordPerfect automatically converts the name to ByeByeBallmer.wpd.

The stuff that goes on the end of the filename is called a *filename extension.* Although the extension is commonly three letters long, there are in fact no hard-and-fast rules.

 Certain generic types of files are inexorably bound to their extensions: .jpg files are JPEGs (pronounced "jay-pegs"), .gif files are GIFs ("jiffs" or, rarely, "giffs"), .pcx files are PCXs, and I bet you can guess what .mp3 files are called.

Somebody sitting in a dark cave in Redmond decided that filename extensions were too confusing for the average user. As a result, Vista's Explorer hides filename extensions from you. They're still there, and they can definitely bite you in the posterior if you aren't careful. Renaming files can be enormously complicated if you can't see the extension (try renaming some.doc to some.txt and you'll see what I mean).

Most importantly, a very large percentage of the worms that come attached to e-mail messages take advantage of this blind spot to propagate: the MyDoom variant with an attached file called readme.log.cmd (which is a .cmd — command — file; double-click it and run it, and you get infected). The Warezov files like Update-KB9468-x86.exe. cSspy.exe. A&A--1.COM. rpst.exe. Then there are the classics: Fizzer, Klez, BugBear, Nimda, Goner,

Irok, Happy99, ExploreZip, the Anna Kournikova virus, Frethem, Freelink, Myparty, Badtrans, Magistr, Navidad, Bubbleboy. ILOVEYOU, too.

 Recent versions of Outlook and Windows Mail show you the filename extension for any file you receive simply because so many people got bitten so badly by this lousy design decision. Microsoft's original intention — to hide the "confusing" filename extension from novice users — now leads to an even-more-confusing situation in which novices see filename extensions on inbound files but don't see the extensions on files currently residing on their computers. You may or may not see filename extensions on files included in ZIPs attached to inbound messages. It's an unholy mess.

Do us both a favor. Take off the training wheels and make Vista show you filename extensions. That way you'll never waste time second-guessing what a file's really called or how to work extensions that need changing. This one quick procedure will pay for the cost of this book, all by itself:

1. **Double-click any folder to open it, or choose Start⇨Computer.**

Windows Explorer appears.

2. **Press the Alt key. Then choose Tools⇨ Folder Options⇨View.**

You see the Folder Options dialog box, shown in Figure 15-1.

3. **Uncheck the Hide Extensions for Known File Types check box.**

Remarkably, unchecking this check box doesn't just force Windows to show you filename extensions inside Explorer itself. The setting actually ripples all the way through Windows and every application.

4. **If you want to continue with the other settings in this Technique, leave the Folder Options dialog box open. Otherwise, click OK.**

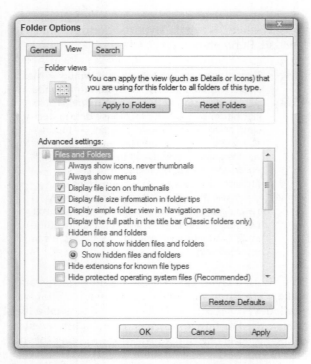

• **Figure 15-1: Make Vista show you filename extensions.**

Customizing Explorer for Speed

I don't know why, but every time I get into Windows Explorer — by choosing Start⇨Computer or Start⇨ Documents or via some more devious means, such as right-clicking the Start menu — I'm always in a hurry. Many of the standard settings in Explorer drive me nuts: Scrolling through dozens of identical pictures of folders, for example, makes me see red.

 If you ever want to jump quickly to the end of a whole bunch of files or folders, press Ctrl+End. To go back to the top, press Ctrl+Home.

You can make a handful of changes to Explorer that greatly simplify and speed up the way you work. Most of the changes are simply cosmetic, but when you strip away some of Windows' happy face, it's a whole lot easier to get to the meat.

In the next few sections, I take you through the customizations that I find most beneficial — most timesaving, if you will. Unfortunately, you must apply all the changes in the order presented here. Changing one setting sometimes clobbers others.

 Here are a few of my favorite Explorer timesaving tips:

✔ There's a sneaky way to make sure folders and files you use all the time "rise to the top" in folder lists. Put an underscore at the front of the folder's or file's name. For example, if you always want to see your company's Human Resources folder at the top of every list, call it _Human Resources. You can use any symbol or punctuation mark, in fact.

✔ You can use a dozen different ways to name folders (and files) so they stay in order. Using numbers at the beginning of the folder's name works well: 00 Admin, 01 Copy Edit, 02 Tech Edit, and so on.

✔ If you identify folders by date, use the Year - Month - Day format so they'll appear in the proper order. So, for example, use 2007 09 Invoices, 2007 09 Statements, 2007 10 Invoices, 2007 10 Statements, and so on.

Seeing all your files and folders

Windows has this nasty habit of hiding files from you. As long as you're beyond the abject beginner phase — and you know enough to refrain from deleting files with names like cmd.exe or shell32.dll — there's no reason in the world why you can't see all the files on your computer.

Make Windows show you all your files and folders:

1. **If the Folder Options dialog box is not currently visible, choose Start⇨Computer, press Alt, then choose Tools⇨Folder Options⇨View.**

You see the Folder Options dialog box, like the one shown earlier in Figure 15-1.

2. **Click the Show Hidden Files and Folders radio button.**

These are files and folders with the so-called "hidden attribute" set.

3. **Uncheck the Hide Protected Operating System Files (Recommended) check box.**

 If you make "Protected Operating System Files" visible, you're going to see some strange files and shortcuts that most mortals never encounter. For example, as you will see later in Figure 15-4, there are shortcuts inside your Documents folder called My Music, My Pictures, and My Videos — all of which are designed to improve compatibility with programs designed for Windows XP (which may be looking for, say, My Music inside the Documents folder). If such oddities mystify you unnecessarily, by all means keep this box checked. But if you want to see the truth, the whole truth, and nothing but the Vista truth, uncheck the box and dive right in.

When you uncheck the Hide Protected Operating System Files (Recommended) box, Windows tosses up a warning saying that you shouldn't mess around with system files and asks whether you're sure you want to make them visible.

4. **Click Yes, dear.**

Your Folder Options dialog box now looks like the one shown in Figure 15-1.

5. **Click OK to make your folder options changes permanent; then "X" out of Windows Explorer.**

Your changes take effect immediately.

Seeing pathnames in Explorer

Windows Explorer lets you traverse folders within folders within folders, buried so deep you may never get out. But it doesn't give you one simple place to look that tells you precisely where you are. The "cookie crumb" navigation bar inside Explorer (so called because it acts like it's leaving behind a trail of *Hansel and Gretel* cookie crumbs, er, bread crumbs, gingerbread crumbs, whatever) lets you click any of the right-wedges and navigate to different folders. But all too often, particularly when you're navigating deep within a complicated folder structure, the cookie crumb list doesn't go back far enough.

There are three tricks to orienteering within Explorer:

✔ **Don't forget to use the Folders list.** On the left, underneath the Favorite Links list, sits an option called Folders. Sometimes (as is the case in Figure 15-2) the Folders list on the left can give you more navigation options than the cookie crumb navigation bar at the top. When digging deep into nested folders, though, you have to expand the width of the Folders list so much you may not be able to see the files anymore!

• **Figure 15-2: The Folders list on the left can tell you more about where you're located.**

✔ **Try a cookie . . . crumb.** Sometimes, if you aren't buried too deep in sub-sub-sub-folders, simply clicking inside the cookie crumb navigation bar will convince Vista to divulge the precise location of the current folder (see Figure 15-3).

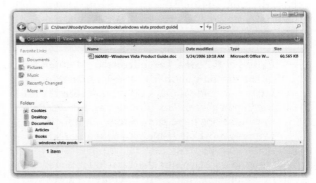

• **Figure 15-3: Sometimes clicking inside the navigation bar gives you a full pathname for the current folder.**

➤ **Make your own path.** But when you're buried deep, there's only one sure-fire way to find out precisely where you're located. Bring up the folder in question in the main (right-hand) part of Windows Explorer. (This trick doesn't work in the Folders or Favorite Links section on the left.) Hold down the Shift key. Right-click the folder that you need to reconnoiter and choose Copy as Path. That puts the full pathname for the folder you right-clicked in the Windows Clipboard. You can then open Notepad or any sufficiently malleable word processor and paste the pathname where you can see it.

 Advanced Vista users who like to play with the command prompt (you know, the old DOS-like C:\> command line) will be happy to know that it's possible to bring up a C: prompt based in any folder at all, without struggling with Vista's enormous pathnames. To open a C: prompt based in a specific folder, hold down the Shift key, right-click the folder, and choose Open Command Window Here. Vista brings up the command prompt, based in the selected folder.

Choosing the Right View

Explorer offers you many options for viewing your folders and files, and you can change the view in each individual folder. To switch among views, open the folder you want to change, click Views, and choose from one of these:

➤ **Extra Large Icons, Large Icons,** or **Medium Icons** all display a thumbnail of the document, providing the document has a thumbnail stored with the file. In general, picture files and PowerPoint presentations have embedded thumbnails, whereas most other file types do not. As this book went to press, several companies were working on programs that scan common kinds of documents (like Word documents and Excel spreadsheets), create a thumbnail, and embed the thumbnail in the file. We cover the latest programs at www.AskWoody.com.

 If you're using any of the three icon views to rummage through picture files, try using Photo Gallery instead (choose Start➪ All Programs➪Windows Photo Gallery). Bet you find the Photo Gallery is both easier to use and much faster.

➤ **Small Icons** aren't thumbnails at all, but pictures that vary depending on the file's filename extension (see "Making Windows Show Filename Extensions," earlier in this Technique).

➤ **List** lists only filenames, showing icons that vary according to filename extension. The horizontal scroll bar (which only lets you scan from left to right) and the lack of any information about the files makes this a limited view. Not very useful.

➤ **Details** view, on the other hand, ranks as the timesaving view of choice in almost all situations. It shows you important information about your files and folders, and you can customize the information in no time at all (see the next section, "Working with Details view").

➤ **Tiles** is best known as the view for the Computer folder. Tiles take up a lot of room and don't give you much benefit in return.

 If you want to whoosh quickly through all the Views choices, hold down the Ctrl key and roll your mouse's wheel. Amazing.

If you're tired of Windows Explorer's glamorous face, and you're ready to get down to work, here's a sparse overview of what you gotta do:

1. Modify Details view in your Documents folder to show you the specific details that you can use.

2. When you're happy with the details that appear, apply that set of details to all similar folders.

3. If you commonly use Windows Explorer instead of Picture Gallery to look at pictures, go back and change the settings of specific folders — primarily media folders — to use other views.

In the next section, I show you what to do in more, uh, detail.

Working with Details view

Here's how to customize the Details view so it shows you the details you want to see:

1. **Choose Start⇨Documents.**

For most people, the Documents folder is a good place to try out different details. If you generally store documents somewhere else (such as, oh, on a network drive), start in that folder instead.

2. **Choose Views⇨Details.**

Windows Explorer switches to Details view (see Figure 15-4).

• **Figure 15-4: The standard Details view.**

3. **Right-click one of the column headings (such as Name) and click More.**

The Choose Details dialog box appears (shown in Figure 15-5).

4. **Check the boxes next to the details you want to see.**

Think of these details as values you can sort by: name, size, or date. When you want to get the right file, fast, the first time, the details lead the way.

 You rarely look for a file based on the Type column, simply because the column contains such bizarre names. If I'm looking for a Word `.doc`

file, my natural inclination is to scan for `.doc` or, at worst, W. To me, it's completely counter-intuitive to look under M — for "Microsoft Word Document" — right next to the `.xls` Excel spreadsheets and `.ppt` PowerPoint presentations. Still, I include the File Type column in the details that I use, and suggest you do, too. Once in a blue moon, it helps. When all else fails, look at the icon on the left.

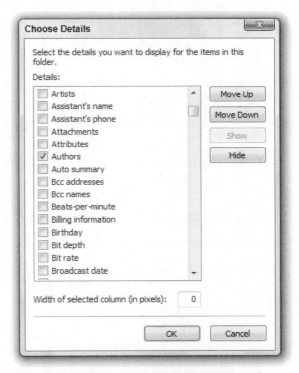

• **Figure 15-5: Pick details that will help you drill down quickly.**

5. **Use the Move Up and Move Down buttons to arrange the details in the order that helps you find files (or folders or programs) the fastest.**

Personally, when I'm looking for a file, I look for Name, Size, Date Accessed, and Date Modified, in that order. Occasionally, I'll look for Author and Type, so I include those, too. In Figure 15-6, you can see how I set up my Details view to help me find what I want quickly.

• **Figure 15-6: The details that work best for me — in order.**

 See the box at the bottom that says Width of Selected Column (in Pixels)? Don't bother with it. I show you a much better way to set the width in the next few steps.

6. **Click OK.**

Windows Explorer comes back with your chosen details, in the sequence you specified (see Figure 15-7).

7. **Click and drag the vertical bars separating the column headings to make the columns wider or narrower.**

 If you double-click directly on the bar, Explorer automatically adjusts the width to accommodate the widest entry in the column.

• **Figure 15-7: Explorer is set up for quick, powerful scanning.**

Alternatively, you can hold down the Ctrl and Alt keys and press the + sign on the number pad, and every column adjusts to accommodate the widest entry.

8. **Adjust the columns until they feel right.**

If you've never used Details view columns to sort a list of files, you should try it now. If you click the Date Modified column heading, for example, Explorer sorts the entire list, with folders on top and files on the bottom, by the date the file (or folder) was last modified, oldest date first. Click Date Modified again, and Explorer reverses the sort order, with newest date first and the folders at the bottom. When you're done, click Name to set the sort order back to normal.

When you're satisfied with the list of details, you're ready to tell Explorer to use these specific details in all its similar folders.

9. **Press the Alt key, then choose Tools⇨ Folder Options⇨View.**

You see the Folder Options dialog box (refer to Figure 15-1).

10. **Click the Apply to Folders button.**

Explorer warns you about the consequences of your actions and asks if you want all folders of this type to match this folder's settings. (See the section "Setting Folders' Behaviors," later in this Technique.)

11. **Click Yes. Then click OK in the Folder Options dialog box to clear it out of the way.**

Effective immediately, all document folders show the details you chose, in the order you specified.

Sorting files by group

Windows Explorer includes a rudimentary capability for grouping files together. If you group by name, for example, Explorer breaks the alphabetized list into five groups: 0 through 9, *A* through *H, I* through *P, Q* through *Z,* and "Other" (for files that start with non-alphanumeric characters). Click the down-arrow to the right of the Name column heading and choose Group (see Figure 15-8). Explorer puts a big 0-9 above the files whose names start with numbers, an A-H above the files whose names start with *A* through *H,* and so on.

• **Figure 15-8: Vista's uninspiring ability to group by letters of the alphabet.**

When Microsoft puts on demos of Vista's "advanced" capabilities, this particular feature draws *oooohs* and *aaaaahs* and applause. Yawn.

I've found one situation, though, where showing files in groups can help speed up my scanning — and it involves the File Type column, which I begrudgingly included in the discussion of Details view earlier in this Technique, specifically so this timesaving trick works:

1. **Open a folder in Details view.**

Your Documents folder would be a prime suspect. This trick works particularly well if you're looking at a folder with several different kinds of files.

2. **Click the Type column header.**

The list of files gets sorted by file Type.

3. **Click the down-arrow next to the column heading Type and choose Group.**

Explorer breaks up the list visually, based on file type (see Figure 15-9). Although the specific file type itself may be a bit obscure, the fact that you can look at groups of files of similar type frequently makes it easier to pinpoint the file you want.

• **Figure 15-9: Viewing by Type can make it easier to rummage around long lists of files.**

Setting Folders' Behaviors

As mentioned in the section, "Working with Details view," earlier in this Technique, you can tell Vista to apply your specific details settings to all your folders "of this type."

Soooooo . . . what is "this type"? Good question.

Based on the contents of a folder, Vista decides what kind of *template* to apply to the folder. There are five different templates: Documents, Pictures and Videos, Music Details, Music Icons, and All Items (which you can think of as "All Other"). Each folder's template determines what kind of picture appears on the folder's icon when you look at the folder in Windows Explorer, and which details appear in Explorer's Details view.

You can use the procedure in the "Working with Details view" section to change the Details view settings for a specific folder template. When you change the Details view settings for, say, the Documents template, every "Documents" folder inherits the settings.

The template also determines when the Slide Show button appears in Windows Explorer: If you open a "Pictures and Videos" folder, Explorer slaps a Slide Show button on its toolbar. For example, in Figure 15-10, Vista has incorrectly assigned the All Items template to a folder full of photographs. As a result, when I open the folder, there is no Slide Show button on the toolbar near the top of the window.

• **Figure 15-10:** A folder full of photographs incorrectly assigned to the All Items template.

 You can waste a lot of time futzing with these settings, but every time-conscious Windows user needs to know two things:

✔ If you can't get the Slide Show icon to appear on a folder's toolbar, you need to change the folder's template to Pictures and Videos.

✔ You can put your own picture on a folder to help you move through folders quickly and visually. The picture you choose appears in Extra Large Icons, Large Icons, Medium Icons, and Tiles views.

To change a folder's behavior:

1. **Use Windows Explorer to open the folder.**

2. **Right-click any blank area inside the folder and choose Customize This Folder.**

The folder's Properties dialog box appears with the Customize tab showing (see Figure 15-11).

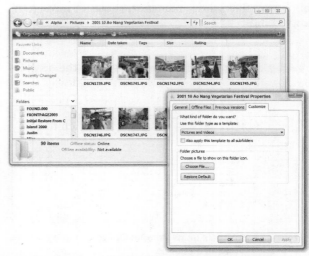

• **Figure 15-11:** Assign the folder to the Pictures and Videos template, and suddenly the Slide Show button appears.

 Not all folders have Customize This Folder as a right-click option. Sometimes, you can change the folder's template by right-clicking and choosing Properties⇨Customize. Sometimes, for reasons known only to Microsoft, you can't even do that — no Customize tab is in the folder's Properties dialog box.

3. **Choose a template from the Use This Folder Type as a Template box.**

In particular, if you want to see the Slide Show button, you must choose Pictures and Videos.

4. **If you want to put a picture on the folder, click Choose File and find the picture you want.**

The picture appears when you view the folder itself in Extra Large Icons, Large Icons, Medium Icons, or Tiles view.

5. **Click OK.**

The toolbar inside the folder changes immediately. If you're in Details view, the template's details also appear.

Copying Files Quickly

If you copy files into the same location over and over again, you can save time by putting the destination on the right-click Send To menu. That way, you select the file(s) or folder(s) you want to copy, right-click, choose Send To, and the destination you want appears. In Figure 15-12, I use this approach to copy the Resume.docx file to the Public Documents folder.

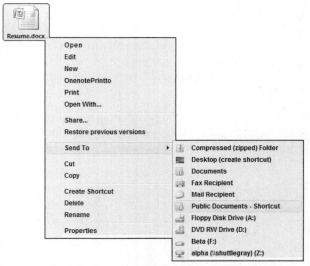

• **Figure 15-12: Copying files and folders is a right-click away.**

Here's how to put your commonly used folder on the Send To menu:

1. **In Windows Explorer, locate the folder you want to copy things into.**

In this example, I clicked Start➪Computer. Then, on the left, under Favorite Links, I clicked the Public folder. On the right, I can see the Public Documents folder (Figure 15-13).

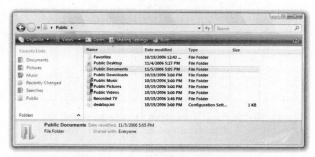

• **Figure 15-13: Navigate to the folder you commonly copy into.**

2. **Right-click the folder and choose Copy.**

3. **Right-click the Start button and choose Explore.**

That puts you in the Windows Start Menu folder, which is very close to where you want to be.

4. **On the left, under Folders, click the SendTo folder. It's located immediately above the Start Menu folder.**

That's a very slick, quick way to get into the SendTo folder. See Figure 15-14.

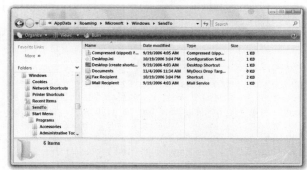

• **Figure 15-14: The fast way into your SendTo folder.**

5. **Right-click a blank spot in the SendTo folder and click Paste Shortcut.**

That puts a shortcut to the Public Documents folder inside your SendTo folder, per Figure 15-15.

• **Figure 15-15:** Paste a shortcut to your intended destination inside the SendTo folder.

6. **"X" out of both copies of Windows Explorer.**

When you right-click a file or folder, your chosen destination appears in the Send To listing (refer to Figure 15-12).

Sometimes you don't want to copy a file, but you do need to copy the file's name, including the full path to get to the file. If you know the trick, it's easy: Hold down the Shift key, right-click the file, and choose Copy as Path. The fully qualified filename, including its path and surrounding quotes (such as, `"C:\Users\Woody\Documents\MyDoc.doc"`), gets copied to the Windows Clipboard. From the Clipboard, you can paste it into a document, a command line, a shortcut, or any other place that needs a fully qualified filename.

Zipping

Zipped (or *compressed*) folders contain files that have been squished down in size. That may sound a bit odd, but the technology has been around for many years. A very large percentage of all the files available on the Internet, for example, are zipped. Zipping involves scanning a file to determine what chunks are duplicated and then replacing the duplicated entries with much smaller pointers. For example, you

could scan "How much wood would a woodchuck chuck if a woodchuck could chuck wood?" and perform the substitution <1>=" wood"<2>="chuck". The resulting phrase, "How much<1> would a<1><2><2>if a<1><2>could <2><1>?" is considerably smaller than the original. Wood.

In practice, file compression methods are much more complex, but you can probably understand why a typical text file can be compressed to half of its original size.

Vista makes it easy to zip a file and stick it in a special kind of folder called a zipped (or compressed) folder. Simply select the file or files that you want to zip, right-click, and choose Send To⇨Compressed (zipped) Folder. Although Windows goes to great lengths to hide the fact from you, the compressed folder is actually a file with a `.zip` filename extension. If you send the folder to a friend, attaching it to an e-mail message, your friend receives a `.zip` file.

Changing Filename Associations

From time to time, really obnoxious programs take over your filename associations. One day, you double-click `.bmp` files, and they open in the Windows Photo Gallery, as they should. The next day, they open with Billy Bob's Giffy-Bumpy Deluxe Pro.

What happened?

Chances are good that you recently installed a new program and, whether you gave your permission or not, that program took over the `.bmp` filename extension.

You can easily see which program is associated with a specific filename extension and change the association, too, should Billy Bob's Giffy-Bumpy Deluxe Pro take over:

1. **Choose Start⇨Control Panel. Click the Programs icon. Then, under Default Programs, click the link that says Make a File Type Always Open in a Specific Program.**

Vista takes a year or two to scan all the file associations (which is to say, the programs associated with specific filename extensions) and then presents you with the list in Figure 15-16.

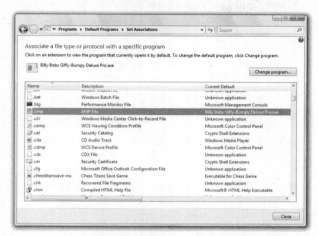

• **Figure 15-16: Bill Bob's Giffy-Bumpy Deluxe Pro.exe has hijacked the** `.bmp` **filename extension.**

2. Click the filename extension that's been shanghaied and then click the Change Program button.

Vista shows you the Open With dialog box, as in Figure 15-17.

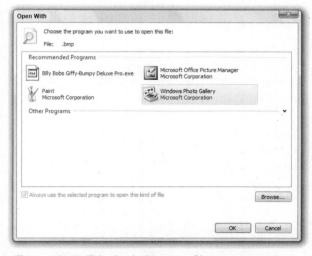

• **Figure 15-17: Take back the** `.bmp` **filename extension.**

3. Select the program you want to associate with this filename extension and then click OK.

If the program you want isn't listed, click the Browse button and find it.

4. "X" out of the Set Associations dialog box and "X" out of Control Panel.

Go ahead and test your new filename association by double-clicking a file with that extension.

Renaming Files En Masse

Do you have a bunch of files with such scintillating names as IMG_0671.JPG, IMG_0672.JPG, and so on?

You could rename these files individually, but chances are that you have better things to do, like watching grass grow. Vista has a limited ability to rename groups of files like that:

1. Select the files you wish to rename.

You can Ctrl+click to select individual (noncontiguous) files, or click at the beginning of a bunch, hold down the Shift key, and click the last of the bunch (see Figure 15-18).

• **Figure 15-18: Select a group of files.**

2. Right-click the first of the bunch, choose Rename, and type in a name that identifies the whole bunch.

In Figure 15-18, I right-clicked the `IMG_0671.JPG` file, chose Rename, and typed `Sandwich Shoppe Patong`.

3. **Press Enter.**

Explorer renames the first file `Sandwich Shoppe Patong.JPG`, as expected. It calls the second one `Sandwich Shoppe Patong (2).JPG`, then `Sandwich Shoppe Patong (3).JPG`, and so on. See Figure 15-19.

No, there's no way in Vista to change this very rigid naming convention. But any identification at all is better than `IMG_0671.JPG`, eh?

 You can undo the naming, one file at a time, by pressing Ctrl+Z.

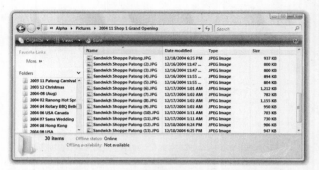

• **Figure 15-19: Giving multiple files user-friendly names.**

There are many free utilities that will rename groups of files. One of my favorites: MRename, from a Croatian by the name of Rajko. Get it at `http://fly.srk.fer.hr/~rajko/MRename/`.

Technique 16

Finding the Files You Want Fast

Save Time By

- ✔ Understanding search options and limitations
- ✔ Searching intelligently
- ✔ Recycling searches

The hardest part about searching in Vista? Understanding what in the %$#@! is going on.

Time and time again, you'll discover that Vista hasn't found what you thought it should find — only to find out that, by golly, Vista search works the way Microsoft thinks it should work, no matter what *you* think.

This Technique focuses on the high-payback choices you can make to speed up your searching. I'm not talking about making the Vista search engine work faster. I'm talking about setting up Vista search so that it finds what you want it to find, correctly, the first time. Believe me, that isn't easy.

If you don't understand Vista's search, you aren't alone. Many of us swear at the poorly designed feature every day. There's a reason why Vista search seems so haphazard: Microsoft cobbled it together at the last minute. When the Vista Gods first designed the operating system that became Vista, it included a wondrous new file system with built-in search capabilities. As the devil met the details, Microsoft found itself lopping off big pieces of the new "Windows File System," trying to stick the remaining chunks together with chewing gum and baling wire. WinFS finally died late in the Vista development cycle, but Microsoft kept hacking off pieces of the corpse, trying desperately to find a small subset of features that would work. Major modifications and realignments in search occurred all the way to the very last beta test releases.

The Vista search you see now is a vastly scaled-back hodgepodge, a pastiche of the original vision, consisting of the pieces that Microsoft could ship out the door in time to meet its deadline. It's a "version 1.0" system in the pejorative sense of the term. I wouldn't even call it half-baked.

Welcome to your search world.

If you follow the nostrums in this Technique and you still find Vista search somewhat, uh, lacking, take solace in one fact: It's only a matter of time before somebody will do it better. Vista's anemic search capabilities are ripe for the plucking, and you can bet that there will be lots of far more capable competitors on the market soon — and they'll get better every week.

 To understand Vista's search foibles, it helps if you can see all your filenames. You may get a "hit" on a filename extension that you can't even see and waste a lot of time scratching your head trying to discern something that Vista doesn't even show you. Make sure you follow the steps in Technique 15 and make Windows show you filename extensions.

The Cardinal Rule of Searching

 The Cardinal Rule: If you know where the file you desire might be located, navigate to the folder before you start the search. For example, if you know that the file you want is inside the `\Documents\Invoices` folder, go to that folder before you type the search argument(s) in the Search bar.

Corollary I: If you're searching for an e-mail message, search from inside your e-mail program. That effectively restricts the scope of the search.

Corollary II: If you're searching for a picture or video, use the Photo Gallery (Start⇨All Programs⇨ Windows Photo Gallery).

Corollary III: If you're searching for a song, use Windows Media Player (Start⇨All Programs⇨ Windows Media Player).

Building an Index

At the heart of Vista's search feature sits the index. Much like the index to this book, the Vista index stores references to your computer's contents.

If you're looking for information about the Quick Launch toolbar, check the index in the back of the book and you're directed to pages x, y, and z (and this page, too, for that matter). Similarly, if you tell the Start menu's Search bar to look for the word *water*, Vista consults its index and knows more-or-less immediately that your computer has a handful of matching entries, as you can see in Figure 16-1. (I talk about the Start menu's Search bar in a later section, "Searching from the Start.")

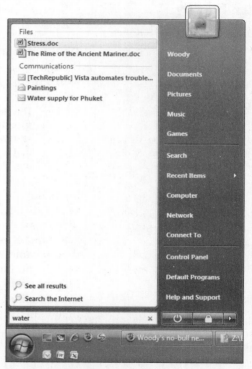

• **Figure 16-1: A Start menu search for the word** *water.*

Vista's index doesn't include every item from every file on your computer: You wouldn't want to index, oh, the text of Windows warning messages, or the patterns of bits inside picture or music files.

On the other hand, you *do* want the indexer to look at files that you're likely to go searching for. Scanning the index takes seconds. Scanning your unindexed files — going through them, character by painful character — can take hours. Or years.

Thus, the indexing dilemma: what should Vista incorporate into the index, and what can be safely left aside?

You have control over both processes:

✔ You can tell Vista to look in specific locations for files that it should index.

✔ You can tell Vista that it should or should not index specific filename extensions.

The rest of this section goes into the details.

Inside the index

When Vista builds and maintains its index, it keeps track of the files going into and being removed from specific locations on your computer. When a file gets added or removed from one of the locations that the indexer tracks, Vista looks to see if the file type (which is to say, if the filename extension for the file) is on the list of file types that the indexer is supposed to index. Then, and only then, is the file added to the index.

Building an index takes time, and maintaining an index can put quite a strain on your computer. Vista has things rigged so the indexer only kicks in when the computer's idle. But if Vista is busy indexing when you want to start typing, it takes a second or two to clear the indexer out of the way and start responding to your key taps.

Setting index file type options

Vista's indexer keeps track of filenames, various file properties (such as the day it was created or modified or viewed), most other *metadata* that gets assigned to the file (author, tags, star rating, artist), and in some cases, the contents of the file itself.

 Although the indexer includes information about zip files, it doesn't index the contents of the zip files. So if what you're searching for is zipped, you're outta luck. Bet you've been bitten by that one.

Vista indexes files based on their filename extensions. (Yet another reason to show filename extensions, eh?) For each filename extension that Vista recognizes, you can tell the indexer to:

✔ Ignore all the files with that particular filename extension. The ignored files, their filenames, properties, other metadata, and contents never make it into the index.

✔ Only index the filename, the file property information, and other metadata.

✔ Index the filename, information, other metadata, and the contents of the file. In order to index the contents, Vista must have a program — a *filter* — available to look inside that particular kind of file and retrieve its contents.

You can't pick and choose the specific file information and other metadata that gets indexed: it's an all-or-nothing kind of thing.

 By and large, Vista's choices for indexing make a lot of sense. In particular, if you install Adobe Acrobat or Adobe Reader to look at PDF files, Vista takes advantage of the Adobe filter to index the contents of all the PDF files in the areas of your hard drive that get indexed (see the next section, "Adding locations to the index"). RSS feeds get indexed, too, as do Rich Text Format (RTF) files and the titles of pages in Internet Explorer's Favorites and History folders.

If there's a particular kind of file that you don't want to index, or if you want to tell Vista to index only the file information and other metadata for a particular type of file, ignoring the contents, making a change is easy. Here's how:

1. **Choose Start➪Control Panel and click the System and Maintenance link. Then click the Indexing Options link.**

You see the Indexing Options dialog box shown in Figure 16-2.

2. **Click the Advanced button, click through the pesky User Account Control dialog box, and then click the File Types tab.**

Vista shows you the File Types tab of the Advanced Options dialog box, as shown in Figure 16-3.

• **Figure 16-2:** Vista gives you a brief overview of its indexing activities.

• **Figure 16-3:** Indexing options listed by filename extension.

If you have Adobe's Acrobat or Reader installed, PDF files are set up to have both the file properties and the contents indexed.

3. **If you want to stop indexing a particular kind of file, uncheck the box next to the filename extension.**

 If you elect to remove a filename extension from the indexing list, Vista goes back and rebuilds the entire index. Although in theory the re-indexing should take place in the background without interrupting your work, in practice, you will find that your machine frequently slows down to a crawl. Remove a file type from the index only when you're ready to take a very, very long break.

4. **Click the filename extension for the type of file you want to have indexed differently. At the bottom, choose either Index Properties Only or Index Properties and File Contents.**

 You can't take all these entries seriously. For example, if you click the RTF entry, Vista doesn't indicate which of the two indexing options are in force. If you have an RTF file handy (or create one using Word), you can verify that Vista does, in fact, index the contents of the file. But this dialog box doesn't tell you.

5. **When you're done, click OK and then click Close to close the Indexing Options dialog box.**

New items are indexed immediately. Give or take a minute or two.

Adding locations to the index

Vista's indexer doesn't even look at a file unless it's in one of the locations that you've chosen — or, more frequently, one of the locations that's been chosen for you.

A typical Vista user running Microsoft Office 2007 has four folders tagged for indexing (they're shown in Figure 16-2):

✔ **Outlook files:** Outlook 2007 (and later versions) works with Vista to extract information from your e-mail and put it in the index. Outlook also uses the Vista index whenever you search for e-mail from inside Outlook.

When Outlook extracts information for the indexer, it looks inside *everything* — including messages in your Junk E-Mail folder. If you don't want your junk to show up in a search, you have to go into Outlook, click on the folder you want to search, and use Outlook's Instant Search feature to look for the messages you want — and ignore the junk in the Junk E-mail folder. If you have to search for messages from Vista, first delete your Junk Mail folder in Outlook. Hard to believe, but Vista indexes all of your junk. This one, ahem, *feature* alone does more to gum up Vista's search capabilities than all the other problems combined.

Some other mail programs, including Windows Mail, have this two-way indexing capability. Many do not. If you're curious about your specific e-mail program, contact the manufacturer and see if they have a Vista indexer–savvy version available.

Note that e-mail indexing works only if the mail sits on your computer. If you use Gmail or Hotma . . . er, Windows Live Mail or Yahoo! Mail or AOL Mail, Vista's indexing doesn't help one whit.

✔ **Offline Files:** If you're connected to a Big Corporate Network, you can set up files and folders to be available offline — which is to say, to sync with a network copy of the file or folder whenever you connect to your network — by right-clicking the file or folder and choosing Always Available Offline. By default, Vista indexes files in Offline folders.

✔ **Start Menu:** Actually, Vista indexes the file names (but not the contents) of all the files in the "All Users" Start Menu folder (`c:\Program Data\Microsoft\Windows\Start Menu`) and all the individual users' Start Menu folders

(`C:\Users\<username>\AppData\Roaming\Microsoft\Windows\Start Menu`).

Why index the names of files in the Start menus? That way, Vista's search engine will pick up the programs and systems that you expect it to find.

✔ **Users:** Everything in the `C:\Users` folder gets indexed — everybody's Documents, Pictures, Music, Desktop, Downloads, and Videos folders, and a whole bunch more.

"Normal" privacy protection pertains. For example, if you search for text, Vista only returns matches on your documents — not on the contents of all the files of all the users on your computer.

Want to add more folders to the index? That's a common situation for advanced users, who might store indexable files in locations other than Documents.

Nope, you can't index a networked drive or folder. The Vista indexer only works on drives (including USB drives) that are connected directly to the computer.

So now that you know a little more about what's indexed by default and what folders you can and can't index, here's how to twiddle the Vista index's settings:

1. **Wait until you can leave your computer alone for a few hours. Or overnight.**

2. **Choose Start➪Control Panel. Click the System and Maintenance link. Then click the Indexing Options link.**

   Vista shows you the Indexing Options dialog box (refer to Figure 16-2).

3. **Click the Modify button.**

   Vista shows you a stunted list of indexed locations that doesn't even include all the places listed in the Indexing Options dialog box. Harumph.

4. **Click the Show All Locations button.**

You have to click through yet another pesky User Account Control dialog box, but in the end, you see the Indexed Locations dialog box, shown in Figure 16-4.

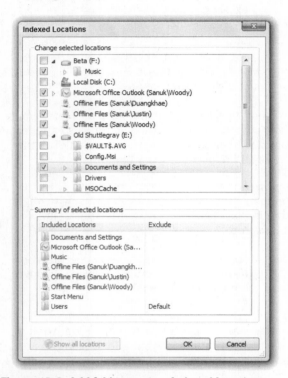

• **Figure 16-4: Add folders to your Indexed Locations.**

5. **If you want to have Vista index the files in a specific location, navigate to the location and click the box next to the folder (or drive) in question.**

In Figure 16-4, I added the \Music folder on my Beta (F:) drive and the \Documents and Settings folder on an old Windows XP drive called Shuttlegray (E:).

Don't index an entire drive unless you're willing to take an enormous performance hit — *for little or no benefit.* On the rare occasions that you need to search an entire drive (in order to, oh, find a system file that isn't in the Start Menu), you can tell Vista to go outside the index.

6. **Click OK.**

Vista wheezes and moans (see Figure 16-5) and indexes the locations you picked.

• **Figure 16-5: The notice should say "User speed is reduced due to indexing activity."**

7. **When you get tired of looking at the indexing pilgrim's progress, "X" out of the Indexing Options dialog box.**

Your new index should be ready in an hour or day or week or two. But when it's done, you will be able to find lost information in seconds.

Judicious choice of indexed folders can save you an enormous amount of time, day in and day out.

Rebuilding or moving the index

Once in a very blue moon, Vista's index just doesn't work. I don't know why, but internally the beast just turns belly-up. Rebuilding the index is easy. Guessing when it *needs* to be rebuilt is another story altogether.

It would be very glib and easy to say that you should rebuild the index whenever it fails to turn up a file that you know is there: You search for the word *mxyzptlk* and you know it's in a file, somewhere, but Vista comes up empty. When that happens, you might be tempted to rebuild the index. Unfortunately, life's rarely so simple. There are lots of reasons why the search could've come up empty-handed. Perhaps the word was misspelled in the original document. Perhaps it's been moved to a location that isn't in the indexer's purview. Maybe it's been zipped inside an archive. Maybe the document itself got scrambled. Maybe . . . just maybe . . . Mr. Mxyzptlk zapped Superman and used his magical digital rights key to lock the document remotely. Naw. Never happens.

I don't have any solid advice for determining when you need to rebuild the index, except when search just stops working altogether, or its oversights are so extended and gross that you know something has to be wrong under the hood.

On the other hand, you might want to move the index to a new, faster drive. That part's easy, too.

If you need to rebuild or move the index, follow these steps:

1. **Wait until you don't need your computer for a long, long time.**

2. **Choose Start⇨Control Panel. Click the System and Maintenance link. Then click the Indexing Options link.**

    Vista shows you the Indexing Options dialog box (refer to Figure 16-2).

3. **Click the Advanced button.**

    After you click through yet another User Account Control dialog box, Vista brings up the Index Settings tab on the Advanced Options dialog box (see Figure 16-6).

The Index Settings tab has one very confusing entry that shouldn't occupy more than a nanosecond of your time. The check box that says Index Encrypted Files doesn't really index the contents of encrypted files on your computer. There's no way the Vista indexer can reach into encrypted files, much less index them. That check box should say Index Encrypted Offline Files but Watch Out for Your Network Admin Who's Likely to Really Hit the Roof If He Finds Out That You Chose to Index Encrypted Corporate Files without Company Permission.

• **Figure 16-6:** Rebuild or move the index here.

'Nuff said.

4. **To delete the current index file and rebuild it in a new location, click the Select New button (which ought to say "Browse," like every other Vista "Browse" button), choose where you want to stick the new index, and click OK.**

5. **To rebuild the index, click the Rebuild button.**

6. **Go out to a very long lunch.**

    By the time you get back, your system might be re-indexed.

Engaging Your Brain Before the Search

All the search engines in the world can't help until you have your act together. You can save a lot of time and frustration by following these suggestions:

- ✔ **Visualize exactly what you want.** Don't search for *lightning* if you're looking for *lightning bug*.

- ✔ **Know your tools.** The Vista search engine works in mysterious ways, but you can increase your chances of finding what you want quickly if you know Vista's foibles.

- ✔ **Narrow down the search ahead of time.** It's easy to get massive lists of files that match specific search criteria. But if you're looking for a file that you last opened a few days ago, why search all files?

- ✔ **Stay flexible.** If you keep typing the same search string, you keep getting back the same answers — guaranteed. Any idea how many different ways you can spell "Shakespeare" — correctly?

- ✔ **Use every trick in the book.** This book, of course.

Searching from the Start

When you click Vista's Start button, you can immediately type into the Start Search bar and have Vista look for the text you type.

At least, that's the theory. The reality is considerably more complex and doesn't appear to be documented anywhere. As best I can tell, here's what really happens:

- ✔ When you type the first character, Vista looks in the Start Menu folders and in the Internet Explorer Favorites and History folders for matches. The "hits" from the Start Menu folders appear in a section marked Programs (see Figure 16-7). The hits from Favorites and History appear in a section marked Favorites and History.

For example, if you type an a, you immediately see all the programs that have "a" in their names, and you also see such luminary sites as MSN Autos and Microsoft At Home — whether you've ever ventured to those sites or not.

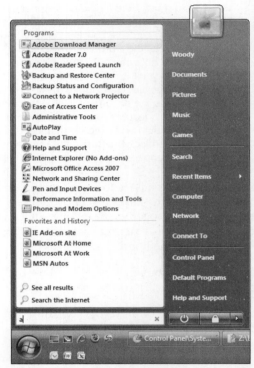

• **Figure 16-7: Type the first letter, and you see only programs and Microsoft's salted list of "Favorites."**

- ✔ When you type the second character, Vista brings in Files (which includes documents, pictures, and music) and Communications (which is a combination of all the RSS feeds and e-mail items, including everything in your Junk E-Mail folder). If you have a lot of junk e-mail, you will no doubt find that it dominates your search.

 If there are more hits than will fit in the Start menu area, you have no way to see them. You can't scroll down, and there's no indication that the Search bar found more than it is displaying.

✔ The Start Search bar doesn't recognize wildcards (say, * or ? representing unknown characters) or any of the keywords that Advanced Search uses (see the section, "Searching Advanced," later in this Technique).

You can change the way the Start Search bar behaves, but only in a limited way. Here's how:

1. **Right-click the Start button and choose Properties.**

Vista shows you the Taskbar and Start Menu Properties dialog box.

2. **At the top, next to Start Menu, click the Customize button.**

Vista shows you the Customize Start Menu dialog box, shown in Figure 16-8.

I discuss the Customize Start Menu dialog box at length in Technique 7.

3. **Consult Table 16-1 to see if you want to uncheck any of the Search-related boxes. If you do, uncheck the appropriate box.**

4. **Click OK twice.**

Your changes take effect immediately.

 Note that these changes to the Start Menu Properties dialog box affect the way *only* the Start Search bar acts. Changes here have no effect on other kinds of searches in Vista.

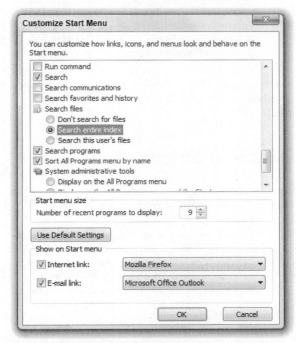

• **Figure 16-8:** Change the Start Search bar's behavior here.

TABLE 16-1: CUSTOMIZING THE START SEARCH BAR

This Customize Entry	Means This	Timesaving Recommendation
Search	Uncheck this box, and no Start Search bar appears.	Although the Start Search bar is very limited, you might as well keep it available.
Search Communications	Have the Start Search bar look for e-mail messages and RSS feeds.	Consider unchecking this box if the volume of junk e-mail on display (or its nature in general) offends you.
Search Favorites and History	The Start Search bar should look in Internet Explorer's Favorites and History folders.	Basically useless unless you're tied to IE and don't mind looking at Microsoft's MSN ads. Zap it.
Search Files	Controls whether the Start Search bar looks for files and, if so, whether only your files (which is to say, files in your Users\ <username> folder) get searched, or whether all files in the index get searched.	Might as well look at the entire index.
Search Programs	Tells the Start Search bar that it should look in the Start Menu folders.	Might as well pick up matches from the Start menu.

If you type in the Start Search bar and press Enter, Vista's reaction depends on the results that you can see at that point. If the results include any programs, when you press Enter, Vista runs the top program on the list. If the results don't include any programs, pressing Enter throws you into a simple search, covering everything in the Vista search index (see the next section for details).

You can also start a simple search by clicking the magnifying glass icon and link that says See All Results.

Searching Simply

Every Windows Explorer window includes a Search bar in the upper-right corner.

 If you type something in the Search bar, Vista initiates a search, looking at all the indexed items in indexed files in the current folder and all its subfolders. That's a very limited search. Make sure you understand Vista's predilections before you accept a simple search result as conclusive!

If you haven't changed any of Vista's default search parameters, Vista performs a simple search in a very straightforward way:

✔ **Vista looks only at files in the current folder and its subfolders.**

 If you have a shortcut in one of the folders, even if it's a shortcut to another folder, Vista *does not* follow the shortcut.

✔ **With one exception, Vista looks at filenames whether the files are in the index or not.** As long as the text you seek is part of a filename, Vista will find the file.

 The exception? It's complicated. If you start your search outside a system folder, Vista doesn't look at filenames inside system folders. For example, if you search for `winword`

from the C: drive (which is to say, click Start⇨ Computer, double-click the C: drive, and type `winword` in the Search bar), Vista won't find anything. But if you start the same search inside `C:\Program Files`, Vista *does* find `winword.exe` (the program that runs Word). To make things even more complicated, if you type `winword` into the Start menu's Start Search bar, Vista finds the shortcut to Word that's in your Start menu. Now you know why I say the hardest part about Vista search is understanding what the %$#@! is going on. . . .

See the section, "Adding locations to the index," earlier in this Technique, to see how Vista indexes certain files but ignores others.

✔ **Except for filenames (which are always included in the search), Vista looks only at entries in the index.** Depending on the file type (in other words, depending on the filename extension), Vista may have indexed all the contents of the files, or it may have indexed only the filename, information, and other metadata. See the section "Setting index file type options," earlier in this Technique, for details.

In Figure 16-9, I searched for the term `bake` in all the files in my Documents folder.

• **Figure 16-9:** A simple search that adheres to very strict rules.

 The cookie crumb navigation bar in the upper-left corner tells you which indexed files are being considered in the search. In Figure 16-9, the notice Search Results in Documents should tell you that the index for your entire computer has not been searched. Only the files in your Documents folder are even considered.

You can also perform a simple search by typing in the Start menu's Start Search bar and clicking See All Results or by pressing Enter if Vista doesn't find a program that matches the search. The simple search so instituted covers all the indexed items on your computer, so the overall result is the same as clicking Start⇨Computer and then typing the search criteria in the Computer dialog box's Search bar. See the preceding section, "Searching from the Start," for details.

If you click the link at the bottom of the search results, the one that says Advanced Search, Vista sets things up for an Advanced Search. See the section, "Searching Advanced," later in this Technique, for details.

Modifying a simple search

After you perform a simple search, you can narrow down the search results by clicking the Search Tools button and choosing Search Pane. In many cases, though, narrowing down the search using the Search Pane doesn't really accomplish anything. Permit me to demonstrate.

In Figure 16-10, I chose Start⇨Computer, searched for the term `bake`, clicked the Search Tools button, and chose Search Pane. That brought up the bar marked Show Only at the top of the dialog box, with the All button selected.

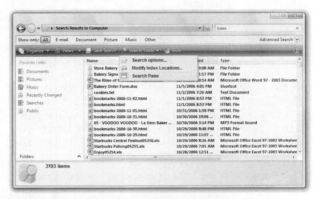

• **Figure 16-10: Bringing up the Search Pane.**

In the Search Pane, you can choose from the following types of files:

- **All** searches for all the indexed file types.

- **E-mail** includes indexed e-mail messages and the contents of RSS feeds.

- **Document** includes indexed Word and text documents, Excel spreadsheets, PowerPoint presentations, Adobe PDF files, Web pages (HTML files), and XML files.

- **Picture** includes all the standard indexed picture file types (JPG, GIF, TIF, PNG, and so on), even if the picture is of an album cover and is sitting in a music folder.

- **Music** includes all the standard indexed music file types (MP3, WAV, and those types that the software manufacturers control) plus playlists.

- **Other** includes indexed folders, JavaScripts, shortcuts, Windows theme files, setup information (INF) files, and even program (DLL) files if they're sitting in indexed locations.

Why is search so confusing?

If you find yourself in the middle of a simple search and you can't figure out why clicking the Picture button doesn't bring up pictures (D'OH!), or if search's other arcane activities leave you befuddled, it might help to understand how search evolved.

Originally, Vista's search engine was designed to revolve around a giant index called a *Library*. The Library would have sublibraries, one for Documents, one for Pictures, one for Music, and so on. As originally conceived, the physical location of a file didn't matter — you could stick a John Philip Sousa music file in your \Documents\Letters to Mom folder, and Vista wouldn't mind a bit. The interface you see in Vista today — the buttons for Documents and Pictures and so on — was designed to make the physical location of a file completely irrelevant.

Unfortunately, as the Vista development team dug deeper into the offal, they discovered that (1) people relied on the location of files to help organize things; (2) people didn't trust Windows to keep track of everything correctly; and (3) the developers didn't have time to make everything work the way they wanted before Vista shipped. They also found out that normal people (which is to say, people with lives) don't use tags, could care less about metadata, and wouldn't take the time to keep the index fields manicured.

The search features you see are a result of shoe-horning this location-independent Library concept back into the good old Windows folder structure. (Or should I say the ancient DOS directory structure?) Perhaps some day we'll get a full relational database to keep track of our files, and the logical/illogical folder structure of our disks won't matter. But for now, it's still location, location, location.

 Many people are mystified when they search a Documents folder, bring up the Search Pane, click Picture or Music or E-mail, and don't see any results. There's a reason why. If you click Start⇨Documents and then run a simple search from the Documents Search bar, Vista only returns results in the Documents folder and its subfolders. If you then bring up the Search Pane and click, oh, the Picture button, Vista continues to restrict itself to results in the Documents folder. Because most people stick pictures in their Pictures folder, and because the Pictures folder isn't underneath the Documents folder, Vista doesn't even look at the pictures.

Searching with OR and AND

Vista has limited Boolean search capabilities. They're hard to use and error-prone — and they have a nasty habit of highlighting the bugs in Vista's search engine.

 As we went to press, there was a persistent rumor from the Vista search development team that Microsoft may release a Search PowerToy. If you find yourself constructing moderately complex searches (that is, searches involving Boolean operators), go to Google (www.google.com) and search for Vista Search PowerToy. I also keep on top of **PowerToys** at my site, www.AskWoody.com.

One nice side effect of using a Search PowerToy, should one ever become available: The folks who build the PowerToy know enough about the inner workings of Vista search so that they can work around the bugs. If you do any sophisticated searching, that fact alone makes it worth the effort to download and install the PowerToy.

If you type two different words in the Search bar, Vista finds files that match both words. For example, in Figure 16-9, I searched on the word bake. If I search on the words bake sandwich, Vista finds those files that contain both the word bake and the word sandwich, as shown in Figure 16-11.

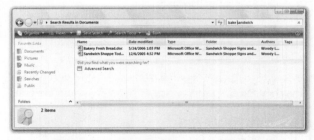

• **Figure 16-11:** Searching the Documents folder for files with the words bake **and** sandwich.

Your inner geek may recognize that as an "AND" search criteria: bake sandwich is the same thing as bake AND sandwich. (Note that Vista search MAKES YOU CAPITALIZE weird things; you have to capitalize AND.)

You can also perform OR searches. Figure 16-12 shows the results of a `bake OR sandwich` search. Vista retrieves all the index entries in the Documents folder that contain reference to either `bake` or `sandwich`. (Yes, OR must be capitalized.) Not exactly rocket science, but it may save you some time.

• **Figure 16-12: Searching the Documents folder for files with either the word `bake` or the word `sandwich`.**

Predictably, you can combine AND and OR with parentheses and NOT to further guide Vista's search. For example, in Figure 16-13, I searched for files that contain either the words `bake` and `bread` or the words `sandwich` and `bread`. In Vista-speak, that's `(bake OR sandwich) AND bread`.

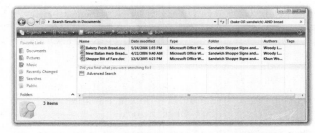

• **Figure 16-13: A more complex search combining criteria.**

Remember that, when you search for Office documents, the words can appear inside the documents, or they can be part of the filename, the author name, one of the tags, or any other piece of information or metadata.

 Vista's search engine recognizes other commands, but it's easiest to use them (and see how they work) by using Advanced Search. See the section "Searching Advanced" for details.

Changing Simple Search parameters

 You can change Vista's Simple Search parameters, but if you do anything, you're bound to slow down searches enormously — and probably won't find what you're looking for anyway. Make sure you understand the time-sapping consequences of any changes before applying them.

Here's how to change the default Simple Search settings:

1. **Run a Simple Search.**

You can use the Start menu's Start Search bar or the Search bar in any Windows Explorer window.

2. **Click the Search Tools button and then select Search Options.**

Vista shows you the Folder Options dialog box's Search tab, as in Figure 16-14.

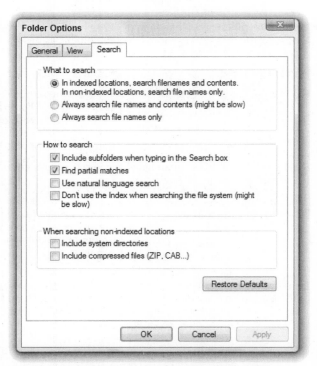

• **Figure 16-14: One of the most confusing dialog boxes in all of Vista-dumb.**

3. Use the tips in Table 16-2 to make any changes to Vista's search options.

 Altering the settings here can make all your searches painfully slow.

4. When you're happy with the results, click OK.

The settings apply to any new simple searches you may make.

TABLE 16-2: SEARCH OPTIONS

Setting	What It Means	Timesaving Tip
In indexed locations, search file-names and contents. In non-indexed locations, search file names only	Vista may or may not search filenames, depending on where you base your search. See the exception in "Searching Simply," earlier in this Technique.	This is the setting you probably want — although it isn't described correctly in the dialog box.
Always search file names and contents (might be slow)	Ignore the index and crawl through the contents of every file in the current folder and subfolders.	*Slow* isn't the right term. Try *glacial*. If you use this option more than once, modify the index by using the method described in "Adding locations to the index," earlier in this Technique.
Always search file names only	Look exclusively at filenames. Ignore file properties and other metadata.	This is the Windows XP approach. If you can live with it, results appear much faster, but most people need (and are willing to wait for) the full text search.
Include subfolders when typing in the Search box	Vista looks in the current folder and subfolders, as described elsewhere in this Technique.	Leave it checked.
Find Partial Matches	Match anywhere in the word.	Leave it checked.
Use Natural Language Search	You can type search strings in a less-structured way. For example, if you check this box, you can type by Woody and Vista will retrieve everything with "Woody" listed as author.	If you check this box, you can still use "regular" searches, but sometimes Vista gets confused. I leave it unchecked. AND I talk funny.
Don't use the Index when searching the file system (might be slow)	Ignore the index entirely.	You can use this setting if you think your index is broken, but otherwise don't check the box.
Include system directories	Include system folders when searching for filenames (see the complicated exception described under "Searching Simply").	If you commonly search for system files, and you don't want to navigate to c:\Windows or c:\Program Files before initiating every search, this setting can help.
Include compressed files (ZIP, CAB, ...)	Look at the filenames of the files inside compressed (ZIP and CAB) files, which are normally ignored by the indexer.	Check it if you like, but realize that there's a performance hit when Vista scans the files inside zips — and also realize that Vista won't look at the contents of the files; you only get to search for filenames.

Searching Advanced

At the bottom of every simple search dialog box is a link that says Did You Find What You Were Searching For? Advanced Search. Click the link and you enter a new, confusing world (see Figure 16-15).

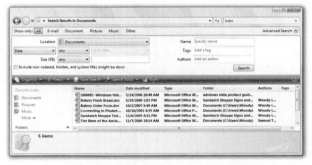

• **Figure 16-15:** Advanced Search — not for the faint-hearted.

From the Advanced Search pane (at the top of the dialog box), you can use a few tools to help build search criteria. As you build the search criteria, they appear in the Search box, in the upper-right corner.

For example, in Figure 16-15, I searched for the word `bake` in my Documents folder. Say I want to modify the search so Vista finds files in the Documents folder that contain the word `bake`, as before, but I only want to see the files for which `Woody` appears in the Author field. Here's how to put together the search:

1. **Start by performing a simple search. Click the Advanced Search link at the bottom of the results list.**

   You see the Advanced Search pane, shown in Figure 16-15.

2. **To search for a specific author, click in the Authors box and type the name of the author or a part of the name of the author.**

In this case, I clicked in the Authors box and typed `Woody`.

3. **Directly below the Authors box, click the Search button.**

   Two things happen very quickly. First, Vista amends the Search bar in the upper-right corner so it says `bake author:(Woody)`. Then, Vista runs out and performs this modified search.

   You can see the results in Figure 16-16.

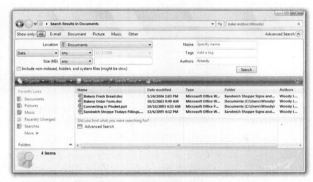

• **Figure 16-16:** Modifying the search so it looks for a specific author.

4. **You can change the location of the search by choosing something new in the Location drop-down box. Or you can further refine the search by working with the Date, Size, Name (which means filename), and Tags boxes. Or you can click in the Search box and delete some or all of the search criteria and try again.**

   The Advanced Search pane covers a weird combination of settings that control how the search is performed (Show Only, Location, and the Include Non-Indexed check box) with tools that help you build a search string in the Search box (Date, Size, Name, Tags, Authors). See Table 16-3 for a bit of much-needed enlightenment.

TABLE 16-3: ADVANCED SEARCH ARGUMENTS

Entry	What It Means	Timesaving Tip
Show Only (All, E-Mail, and so on)	Creates a `Show Only:` entry in the Search bar. Limits the results to specific kinds of files, based on filename extensions. See the discussion under "Modifying a simple search," earlier in this Technique.	This setting frequently conflicts with the Location box; don't get confused.
Location	Lets you choose a specific drive or folder as the "base" for the search.	To get the best search results, always drill down as low as you can go before starting the search. See "The Cardinal Rule of Searching" at the beginning of this Technique.
Date (meaning Date Modified)	Creates a `date:>xx/xx/xxxx` entry in the Search bar. Restricts the search to files last modified on the date specified.	Although the Advanced Search pane won't let you do it, you can manually type a pair of date restrictions in the Search bar. For example, `date:>2/1/2007 date:<3/31/2007` will return files modified between February 1 and March 31, 2007.
Size (meaning Size in Kilobytes)	Creates a `size:>xx,xxxxKB` entry in the Search bar. Restricts the search to files of the indicated size.	Almost never useful in real-world situations.
Name (meaning Filename)	Creates a `name:` entry in the Search bar. Search restricted to files that match the string or partial string specified here.	You can use wildcards. See the sidebar, "Using search wildcards," earlier in this Technique.
Tags	Creates a `tag:(xxx)` entry in the Search bar. Search restricted to files with tags that match the string or partial string specified here.	Tags are notoriously unreliable.
Authors	Creates an `author:(xxx)` entry in the Search bar. Restricts the search to files with an "Author" tag that matches the string or partial string specified here. Not case-sensitive ("woody" matches "Woody").	Author tags aren't as unreliable as other tags because the Microsoft Office applications reliably mark files with the registered author.
Include non-indexed, hidden, and system files (might be slow)	Overrides the settings in the Search Options dialog box (see the section, "Changing Simple Search parameters," earlier in this Technique).	You get all the files in one slow fell swoop.

If you're curious about the kinds of search strings that you can type into the Search box, play with the Advanced Search pane until you see how they're put together. The general format looks like this:

```
searchstring Show Only:Document
   date:=2/28/2007 author:(Doyle)
   size:=10,000KB name:somefilename
   tag:(atag)
```

Note that the date can look like `date:<2/28/2007` (meaning the date modified is before February 28, 2007) or `date:>2-28-2007` (modified after February 28, 2007). The size can look like `size:<10,000KB` (the size of the file is less than 10,000,000 bytes) or `size:>10,000KB` (more than 10,000,000 bytes).

After you know what the search string is supposed to look like, you can type the string directly into the Search box. You don't need the Advanced Search pane at all.

You'd be forgiven if you thought of this approach to search as, er, half-baked. It's speedy, though, so I couldn't call it half-fast. The combination of inconsistent, weird notation (why does `date` use `:=` and `author` use `:( )`?), a "pane" that confuses the living bewilickers out of nominally normal people, a completely senseless means of accessing the advanced search functions (you have to run a simple search before you can bring up an advanced search?), and bugs galore tells me that Microsoft rushed this version 1.0 product out the door.

Don't lose any sleep over it, okay?

Saving and Reusing Searches

Windows Vista lets you store search definitions (essentially the contents of the Search bar, plus the root location for the search and the types of files it covers) and rerun the searches at will. Much has been made about this capability — the marketeers love it. Few will find it worth the effort.

It's important to realize that Vista doesn't store search *results*. If it took five minutes to run the original search, and your configuration hasn't changed substantially, it'll take five minutes to rerun the search.

Saving a search is easy:

1. Run a simple or advanced search using any of the methods in this Technique.

2. When the search is done, click the button marked Save Search.

Vista responds with a plain-vanilla Save As dialog box, which offers to save the search in the Searches folder, with a file type `*.search-ms` (see Figure 16-17).

3. Type a name for the search and click Save.

• **Figure 16-17: Saving the search shown in Figure 16-10.**

Vista saves the contents of the Search bar, plus the settings that define the search — what folder you're searching from, whether you restricted the search to specific types of files (All, Documents, E-Mail, and so on), and whether you checked the box that makes Vista search non-indexed, hidden, and system files. That's it.

4. If you ever want to rerun the search, open Windows Explorer (by, say, choosing Start➪Computer or Start➪Documents), click the Searches link on the left, and then double-click the saved search.

Vista reruns the search. Ho-hum.

If you've ever heard of Search Folders (for example, the Search Folders feature in Outlook 2003), Vista doesn't have Search Folders. In a Search Folder situation, the contents of the folders are updated on the fly. Vista doesn't update anything on the fly. It's all static, time-consuming, and boring.

If you commonly construct and run complex searches, one Vista search feature may prove useful. You can build a search that's based on another search. That could save you time if, for example, you have a handful of different searches that look for different tags for files all written by the same author. In that case, you would first build a search for documents written by the author. Then you would construct sub-searches based on the original search, each of which looks for the specific tags of interest.

Here's how:

1. **Build and save a search using any of the tricks in this Technique. Leave the Advanced Search pane open.**

2. **In the Advanced Search pane, click the down-arrow next to Location and select Choose Search Locations (see Figure 16-18).**

• **Figure 16-18:** Build a search based on another search by using Choose Search Locations.

Vista responds with a dialog box called Choose Search Locations (see Figure 16-19).

3. **Navigate to the search that you want to base the new search on, check the box next to it, and click OK.**

Vista returns to the Advanced Search pane. This time, the Location drop-down list names the saved search that you selected.

4. **Construct your new search in the usual way and then save it.**

The new search takes the result of the original search and modifies it.

• **Figure 16-19:** Pick the search that forms the foundation of the new search.

Finding Files That Got Lost

Wish I had a nickel for every time someone asks me why Windows stole some files. The story always goes like this: "Woody, I used to have a whole bunch of important files in Documents\ Someplace, and now they're gone! What did Vista do with them?"

Oy.

When you discover that your files are lost, save yourself a lot of time and headaches and remember that there are only four possibilities:

✔ You moved them somewhere (Probability: 90 percent).

✔ You deleted them, and they're still available (Probability: 9 percent).

✔ You permanently deleted them and it will be difficult, but probably not impossible, to get them back (Probability: less than 1 percent).

✔ Little green men broke into your office in the middle of the night and ate them (Probability: varies).

First, don't panic

If you suddenly discover that some of your files are "lost," here's the fastest, most reliable way to get them back:

1. **Don't panic.**

Douglas Adams's sage advice pertains.

2. **Don't create any new files or delete any existing ones.**

Do not choose this particular moment to defragment your hard drive. Even when you "permanently" delete a file, all the data remains on your disk until it is overwritten.

3. **Open Windows Explorer (Start⇨Documents or Start⇨Computer) and look at the folders near the one that used to contain the "lost" files.**

Chances are very good that you accidentally moved the files while you were in Explorer. Accidentally dragging a bunch of files to a nearby folder is easy. If you go back to the scene of the crime, you may be able to retrace what went wrong.

4. **Run Search to find one of the lost files.**

Don't bother trying to find all the lost files at the same time. Just look for one of them. With a little luck, you can remember one lost file's name, or part of a name, or some of the data inside.

5. **If you find one of the lost files, right-click the filename and choose Open File Location (refer to Figure 16-20).**

• **Figure 16-20:** Find a whole bunch of lost files by locating just one of them.

6. **If the files (or file) are in a regular, everyday folder, select them, right-click, and choose Cut. Navigate back to where they belong. Right-click and choose Paste.**

7. **If you find the lost files in the Recycle Bin, select them and click the button marked Restore the Selected Items.**

If that doesn't work, take a chill break and then continue with the next section.

Second, get determined

If you can't find the files with a simple search, it's time to haul out the big guns. Or at least the bigger guns:

1. **Go to your desktop and double-click the Recycle Bin icon.**

Windows brings up the contents of the Recycle Bin, as shown in Figure 16-21. Any files that you deleted are probably in the Recycle Bin.

2. **Scan the Recycle Bin for your lost file.**

You've already tried searching, but maybe you didn't spell the name exactly right — the Achilles heel of searches. A little bit of eyeballing might turn up the culprit. Usually it's fastest to look at the most recently deleted items first. To do so, click the Date Deleted column heading.

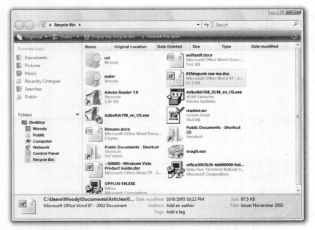

• **Figure 16-21: Look through the Recycle Bin.**

3. **If you find the lost files, select them and click the button marked Restore This Item (or These Items).**

4. **If that still doesn't work, shut your machine down and go buy a file recovery program.**

Even if you've "permanently" deleted a file, its remnants remain and can frequently be put back together. Norton Utilities has long been the product of choice for undeleting files, but there are dozens of competitors, all of which basically do the same thing. It's important that you follow the instructions precisely in order to maximize your chances of getting your file back.

5. **If you still can't find the file, and there aren't any suspicious green men lurking about, and you're willing to spend many hundreds of dollars getting your data back, look for a data recovery company.**

These folks can scan every bit on your hard drive and bring seemingly lost files back from the dead. Here's the best way to find a data recovery company, short of a recommendation from a satisfied customer: Go to Google (www.google.com) and search on the phrase data recovery services.

Technique 17

Listing Files Quickly

Save Time By

- Listing all the files in a folder with one click
- Sorting files by filename extension
- Printing a list of files automatically

How many times have you wanted to get your hands on a list of all the files in a folder? Amazingly, there's no way to do it in Vista. Never has been. It's one of the gaping holes left in Windows Explorer — right up there with sorting files by filename extension, which is another important thing you can't do, for love or money.

This Technique presents three variations on the "list filenames" (or "print directory") theme. When you're done with the Technique, you'll be able to right-click any folder and do any of the following:

- **Create a list of all the files in the selected folder:** The list you create is poured into a file, which is automatically opened in Notepad. From there, you can search, look at, print, or copy the information into Excel, Word, or any other program, to do with what you will.

- **List files in the selected folder by filename extension:** The list is the same as the one above, only it's sorted by the `.doc`, `.xls`, and `.exe` filename extensions that control so much of your files' destinies. The trick I explain in this Technique is the only way I know (short of writing a very hairy macro) to generate a list of all files in a folder sorted by the filename extension.

 Make sure you have Vista show you filename extensions by following the steps in Technique 15.

- **Print file listing:** The list you create is sent to the printer. The list is then automatically deleted, all with one click.

I also let you in on a couple of additional undocumented tricks.

Cool stuff.

You need an administrator account (or the user ID and password for an administrator) to get these programs working. No other qualifications necessary.

You'll find life in general (and this Technique in particular) much less mystifying if you have Vista show you filename extensions. If you can't see the `.doc` or `.txt` or `.jpg` at the end of filenames, follow the instructions at the beginning of Technique 15 to have Vista reveal all.

 Barry Simon and I originally came up with several of these tricks in *The Mother of All Windows 95 Books*, a dozen years ago. Microsoft still hasn't caught up.

Showing Directory Listings

Follow the steps in this section to create a new entry for the right-click menu on every folder. When you're done, if you right-click a folder, you see that the context menu includes a List Files in This Folder entry, as shown in Figure 17-1.

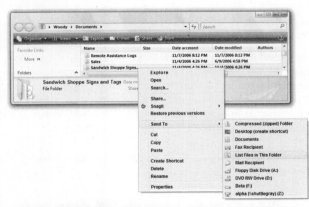

• **Figure 17-1:** Listing all the files in a folder is a right-click away.

Click Send To⇨List Files in This Folder, and Notepad appears with a sorted list of all the files and their sizes, as shown in Figure 17-2. Okay, so it's not pretty, but it's better than anything that Windows currently allows you to do.

• **Figure 17-2:** A list of all the files in the selected folder, ready for you to search, print, or copy into another program.

Here's what you see in the list:

- ✔ The date the file was created.

- ✔ The size of the file (the number of bytes).

- ✔ The name of the file, including the filename extension: The third file in the list in Figure 17-2 is `Closed for electrical work.doc`.

The list includes only normal files and folders; hidden system files, for example, don't appear.

Writing a program to show directory listings

Here's how you write the two-line program that creates the list:

1. **Right-click an empty spot on your desktop and choose New⇨Text Document.**

   Vista creates a new document called `New Text Document.txt`.

2. **Immediately overwrite the name that Windows created by deleting the old name, typing** `List Files in This Folder.bat`, **and pressing Enter.**

   Don't forget to delete the `.txt` at the end of the original filename.

   Vista warns you that if you change a filename extension, the file may become unusable. Of course, Vista neglects to mention that in this case, if you change the filename extension, the file suddenly becomes *usable*, but *c'est la vie.*

3. **Click Yes, I Want to Change the Filename Extension, Turkey.**

If you forget and do something else before typing the file's new name, just right-click New Text Document.txt, choose Rename, and type List Files in This Folder.bat.

You now have an empty text file called List Files in This Folder.bat on your desktop.

4. **Choose Start➪Computer.**

5. **Double-click the C: drive and then double-click Program Files.**

6. **Click and drag List Files in This Folder.bat from your desktop into the Program Files folder. It's easier if you make sure that List Files in This Folder.bat goes into the Program Files folder and not some other folder, so take a little time and make sure you drop it directly into the Program Files folder.**

Vista responds with a scary-looking dialog box that tells you Destination Folder Access Denied (see Figure 17-3).

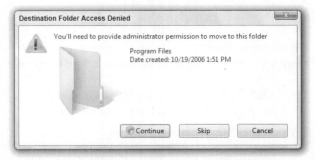

• **Figure 17-3:** Hey, it's my computer, and I'll put my programs in my Program Files folder if I want to.

7. **Scoff at the admonition and click Continue. When Vista comes at you again with a User Account Control dialog box, click Fie Upon You**

and Your Worthless Ilk! Continue, I Command You! Or something like that.

Vista, sensing your superior intelligence, acquiesces and moves List Files in This Folder.bat into the Program Files folder, as in Figure 17-4.

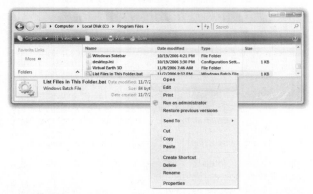

• **Figure 17-4:** List Files in This Folder.bat in the folder where it belongs.

8. **Right-click List Files in This Folder.bat and choose Edit.**

Notepad appears with List Files in This Folder.bat open and ready for mangling. Er, editing.

9. **Type this two-line program into Notepad:**

```
dir %1 /o:gn /n /-p > "%temp%\List
   Files.tmp"
start notepad "%temp%\List
   Files.tmp"
```

Make sure that you don't press Enter at any point, except immediately before the word start. See Figure 17-5 for an exact rendition. An explanation of all the strange commands is in the sidebar, "Understanding what all those funny characters mean."

• **Figure 17-5:** The two-line program that runs List Files in This Folder.

10. **Choose File⇨Exit to leave Notepad.**

Be sure you save the changes. And leave Windows Explorer open. You'll need it in the next section.

Understanding what all those funny characters mean

Here's a handy babel fish for all that programming tom-foolery. Strip away the funny stuff, and you get this gem:

```
dir %1 > "%temp%\List Files.tmp"
```

That command tells Windows to put a list of everything in the current ("%1") directory into a file called List Files.tmp, which is located in the temporary folder. Then

```
start notepad "%temp%\List Files.tmp"
```

simply starts Notepad and feeds it List Files.tmp from the temporary folder.

Everything else is embellishment. The switch

```
/o:gn
```

tells Windows to put the folders first and to sort by file-name. (No, I have no idea why "put folders first" is g. Programmers are trained not to ask such insightful questions.) The switch /n tells Windows to put the filename on the right. (n stands for "new." Don't ask.) Finally, /-p tells Windows to override another switch, which can force the whole command to hang when the file gets too large. I told you not to ask.

Feel like a programmer now? Great. Choose Start⇨All Programs⇨Accessories⇨Command Prompt and type dir /? the first chance you get. That shows you all the options you have available for the dir command. I use several of them in this Technique.

Adding the program to the right-click menu

If you followed the steps in the previous section, you now have a program that lists all the files in a folder. That's all well and good, but if you want to access the program quickly (and, therefore, save time), the next step is to hook the program into the right-click Send To menu. You do that by sticking a shortcut to the program in Vista's SendTo folder. Piece o' cake.

Follow these steps:

1. **You left Windows Explorer open in the last section, so you can see List Files in This Folder.bat, as in Figure 17-4, right? Good. Right-click List Files in This Folder.bat and choose Send To⇨Desktop (Create Shortcut).**

That puts a shortcut to List Files in This Folder.bat on your desktop. You're going to need it momentarily.

2. **Right-click the Start button and choose Explore.**

That puts you in the Windows Start Menu folder, which is very close to where you want to be.

3. **On the left, under Folders, click the SendTo folder. It's located immediately above the Start Menu folder.**

Bingo. You took the back entrance to the SendTo folder. See Figure 17-6.

• **Figure 17-6: Move the shortcut into your SendTo folder.**

4. **Click and drag the List Files in This Folder.bat shortcut into the SendTo folder.**

5. **Right-click the newly relocated shortcut to List Files in This Folder.bat and choose Properties. Then click the General tab.**

Vista shows you the Properties dialog box.

6. **In the box at the top, delete the junk that says .bat - Shortcut. Then click OK.**

You're left with the simple command List Files in This Folder, as in Figure 17-7.

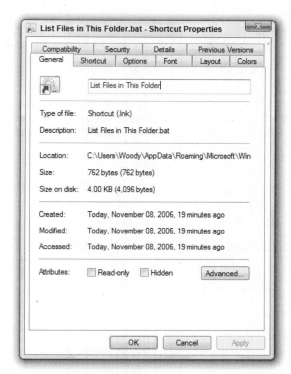

List Files in This Folder.bat - Shortcut Properties

Compatibility	Security	Details		Previous Versions
General	Shortcut	Options	Font	Layout	Colors

List Files in This Folder

Type of file: Shortcut (.lnk)

Description: List Files in This Folder.bat

Location: C:\Users\Woody\AppData\Roaming\Microsoft\Win

Size: 762 bytes (762 bytes)

Size on disk: 4.00 KB (4,096 bytes)

Created: Today, November 08, 2006, 19 minutes ago

Modified: Today, November 08, 2006, 19 minutes ago

Accessed: Today, November 08, 2006, 19 minutes ago

Attributes: ☐ Read-only   ☐ Hidden   [Advanced...]

[OK]   [Cancel]   [Apply]

• **Figure 17-7: A good, legible shortcut to List Files in This Folder.**

7. "X" out of any open copies of Windows Explorer.

8. Test your new file lister. Use Windows Explorer to go just about anywhere (try, oh, Start⇨ Documents). Right-click a folder and choose Send To⇨List Files in This Folder.

Notepad should appear with a listing similar to the one in Figure 17-2.

As you will soon discover, List Files in This Folder is a very fast program that works on shared network drives, too. There's no fluff, no undue overhead. I've often wondered why Microsoft doesn't build that time-saver into Windows. Oh well. Maybe in Windows 2014.

Embellishing the File Listings

If you followed the instructions in the preceding section, you have a program called List Files in This Folder that attaches itself to the normal Vista right-click Send To menu. It cranks up Notepad and fills a text file with a simple listing of all the files in the folder that you right-clicked. (If you right-click a file and choose List Files in This Folder, you only see the current file. But I bet you already tried that, eh?)

There are two minor variations on the file-listing theme that I use all the time:

✔ **List Files in This Folder by Extension,** which presents the same text list of files, but sorted alphabetically by filename extension.

✔ **Print Files in This Folder,** which generates the same list as List Files in This Folder, prints the list on the default printer, and then deletes the list.

I show you how to build both variations in this section. I bet you can think up your own combinations, too.

Listing files by filename extension

I'm still fuming that Windows Explorer doesn't let me sort files by filename extension — the usually-three-or-more letters at the end of a filename — and I've been complaining about it, in print, since the days of Windows 3.1.

Until Microsoft gets a clue, at least you can generate a list of files by filename extension. It isn't anywhere near as effective as, say, clicking a column heading in Explorer. But if you can find the file you're looking for in the generated list, it's reasonably easy to go back to Explorer and find it.

You can build a program that does the trick by using a copy of List Files in This Folder.bat, which I discuss in the preceding section.

The instructions here are horribly convoluted because Notepad won't let you modify a file in the Program Files folder and then save it with a different name, even if you use an administrator account. Ridiculous, but true.

Here's the fastest way I know to get the job done:

1. **Choose Start⇨Computer. Double-click the C: drive, and then double-click Program Files.**

You should see List Files in This Folder.bat down near the bottom of the list.

2. **Right-click List Files in This Folder.bat and choose Copy. Then right-click on your desktop (*not* in the Program Files folder) and choose Paste to make a copy of the file.**

Leave Windows Explorer open with the Program Files folder showing. You will need it shortly. Vista should have a file on your desktop called List Files in This Folder.bat.

3. **Right-click the List Files in This Folder.bat file, choose Rename, and rename the file List Files in This Folder by Extension.bat. Press Enter.**

Bet you'll never guess what we're going to do with that file, eh?

4. **Right-click List Files in This Folder by Extension.bat and choose Edit.**

Notepad opens with your original file listing program showing (refer to Figure 17-5, earlier in this Technique).

5. **Change the original program so it looks like this:**

```
dir %1 /o:ge /x /-p > "%temp%\List
   Files.tmp"
start notepad "%temp%\List
   Files.tmp"
```

There are only two tiny changes from the original — the switch /o:gn gets turned into /o:ge and /n turns into an /x.

6. **Choose File⇨Exit. Be sure to save changes.**

7. **Click and drag List Files in This Folder by Extension.bat from your desktop into the Program Files folder.**

Take care to make sure the .bat file ends up in the Program Files folder and not in some subfolder.

Once again, Vista responds with its obnoxious Destination Folder Access Denied message (refer to Figure 17-3, earlier in this Technique).

8. **Click Continue, and then in the resulting User Account Control message, click Continue again.**

That's what Vista calls Security. You end up with List Files in This Folder by Extension.bat in your Program Files folder, per Figure 17-8.

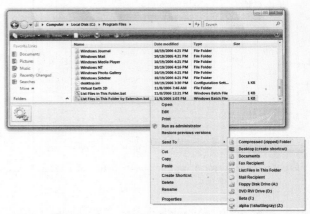

• **Figure 17-8:** List Files in This Folder by Extension.bat **goes into your Program Files folder.**

9. **Right-click List Files in This Folder by Extension.bat and choose Send To⇨Desktop (Create Shortcut).**

That puts a shortcut to List Files in This Folder by Extension.bat on your desktop. You're going to need it momentarily. Raise your hand if these instructions are starting to sound familiar.

10. **Right-click the Start button and choose Explore.**

That puts you in the Windows Start Menu folder.

11. On the left, under **Folders**, click the **SendTo** folder. (Refer to Figure 17-6, earlier in this Technique.)

It's located immediately above the Start Menu folder.

12. Drag the `List Files in This Folder by Extension.bat` shortcut into the SendTo folder.

13. Right-click the shortcut to `List Files in This Folder by Extension.bat` and choose **Properties➪General**.

Vista shows you the Properties dialog box's General tab.

14. In the box at the top, delete `.bat - Shortcut.` Then click **OK**.

You're left with the simple command `List Files in This Folder by Extension`, as in Figure 17-9.

• **Figure 17-9:** A short and sweet description of List Files in This Folder by Extension.

15. "X" out of any open copies of Windows Explorer.

16. Test your new program. Right-click a folder of your choice and choose **Send To➪List Files in This Folder by Extension**.

Notepad should appear with a listing similar to the one shown in Figure 17-10.

• **Figure 17-10:** Files and folders listed by filename extension.

 I set up this program to show you old-fashioned short (so-called "8 plus 3") file-names in a column just before the real file-names. I did that to make it easier to scan for filename extensions — a big timesaver. If you'd rather drop the short filenames, perhaps to minimize confusion for people who don't understand short filenames, replace the `/x` switch with `/n` in the first line of the program.

Printing a file list automatically

 You can manually print lists of files that are created by the programs mentioned in this Technique. Simply create a list and then choose File➪Print in Notepad.

But this book is about saving time. Sometimes all you want to do is just right-click a folder and print the contents.

Here's how to build a "Send To" program that creates and prints the List Files in This Folder list on your default printer. You might want to take a moment and make sure that you have a default printer specified. Choose Start⇨Control Panel; then, under the Hardware and Sound icon, click the Printer link. Your default printer has a check mark next to it.

If you've gone through the steps in the preceding section, you already know the basics. Here's a very abbreviated description:

1. **Choose Start⇨Computer⇨C:⇨Program Files. Copy** List Files in This Folder.bat **onto your desktop.**

2. **Right-click the** List Files in This Folder.bat **file, rename the file** Print Files in This Folder.bat**. Right-click** Print Files in This Folder.bat **and choose Edit.**

3. **Change the original program to look like this:**

    ```
    dir %1 /o:gn /n /-p > "%temp%\List
        Files.tmp"
    start /w notepad /p "%temp%\List
        Files.tmp"
    del "%temp%\List Files.tmp"
    ```

4. **Choose File⇨Exit. Save changes.**

5. **Click and drag** Print Files in This Folder.bat **from your desktop into the Program Files folder. Click Continue through both obnoxious security prompts.**

6. **Right-click** Print Files in This Folder.bat **and choose Send To⇨Desktop (Create Shortcut).**

7. **Right-click the Start button, choose Explore, and then click SendTo (immediately above the Start Menu folder on the left). Drag the shortcut to** Print Files in This Folder.bat **into the SendTo folder.**

8. **Right-click the shortcut to** List Files in This Folder by Extension.bat **and pick Rename. Delete the** .bat - Shortcut **part.**

9. **Test the printing program by right-clicking any folder and choosing Send To⇨Print Files in This Folder.**

This program takes longer than the others because Notepad takes forever to print.

For a complete list of switches for the start command, choose Start, type cmd, and press Enter. Then type start /?. The /w switch, for example, tells Windows to wait until Notepad finishes printing before going on to the next command line, which deletes the temporary file. Printing in Notepad is so slow that, if you don't tell Vista to wait, the file gets deleted before Notepad has a chance to print it!

 If you created all three of the programs described in this Technique, your right-click Send To menu should look like the one in Figure 17-11. If you ever need to look at file listings, this Technique should save you gobs of time.

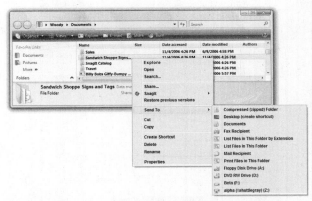

• **Figure 17-11: The three file listing programs described in this Technique.**

 You can mix and match any of the switches discussed in this Technique. Many valid, useful, timesaving combinations are a great help in specific situations. For example, you may want to print "8+3" filenames, or create a listing in Notepad, print it, but not delete it. The best way to see what you can do (short of taking a course on old-fashioned DOS commands) is by consulting the list of switches, as I describe in the preceding sections.

Part IV

Making the Most of the Internet

The 5th Wave · By Rich Tennant

"Look at this, Mother! I customized the browser so I can navigate the Web the way I want to."

Technique 18

Customizing Internet Explorer and Firefox

Save Time By

✔ Making the most of IE *and* the most of Firefox

✔ Using timesaving methods to bypass browser inanities

✔ Adopting RSS to bring in the news you need, fast

✔ Understanding the privacy consequences of antiphishing

✔ Tweaking and twisting IE and Firefox

More than any other product, Internet Explorer reflects Microsoft's odd and tortured approach to the Web. After ignoring the Internet, by and large, for many years, Microsoft released the first version of Internet Explorer in 1995 as an add-on to Windows 95. In 1996, Microsoft built Internet Explorer version 3 into Windows itself, violating antitrust laws and using monopolistic tactics to overwhelm Netscape Navigator. That isn't my opinion. That's proven fact, attested to by court decisions all over the world.

Having illegally driven its competitor from a starting position to the back of the bench, Microsoft made almost no improvements to Internet Explorer between August 2001 and October 2006, when the 'Softies finally released Internet Explorer 7. IE has become the single largest conduit for viruses, trojans, spyware, and junkware in the history of computing, with major security patches appearing almost every month. Microsoft didn't make any money from IE, had no incentive to improve it, and you and I suffered.

And then there was Firefox. Dave Hyatt, Blake Ross (who was a sophomore at Stanford at the time), and hundreds of volunteers took on Microsoft, producing a fast, small, free alternative that quickly grabbed a significant share of the browser market. Microsoft responded by incorporating many Firefox features into Internet Explorer 7, which you now see in Vista.

This Technique shows you, perhaps surprisingly, how to use *both* Internet Explorer and Firefox, taking advantage of each product's strengths without forcing you to learn two different ways of working. If you follow along here, you'll see how to save time in your day-to-day surfing and protect yourself from the big, bad Internet, simultaneously.

It's a jungle out there.

Using IE and Firefox Together

Many people think that you have to choose between Internet Explorer and Firefox.

Ain't so.

Internet Explorer is baked into Vista. You don't have any choice. You can scrape off the first layer, install a competing browser, and pretend that IE isn't pulling the strings behind the scenes, but many parts of Vista and Microsoft Office use pieces of IE to accomplish myriad tasks.

You're stuck with Internet Explorer, or at least the vestiges of Internet Explorer, even if you never double-click the swirling "e" icon.

That poses a major Problem (with a capital *P*) because, in spite of Microsoft's extreme efforts to overcome its holey code base, IE continues to be the target of choice for Internet mayhem makers. In the first two weeks after IE 7's release, four widely publicized IE security holes appeared. Two of them amounted to little more than parlor tricks. But two of them used IE to grab Windows XP systems by the throat. Vista isn't as easily subverted as Windows XP. But IE's congenital defects remain for all to see, the ghosts of Windows' past.

That's why I strongly recommend that you take a two-pronged approach to fast, safe Web surfing:

✓ **Keep Internet Explorer updated.** Go through the steps in the next section to "harden" IE — make it much less vulnerable to attack. Then let it lie dormant. Don't *use* Internet Explorer unless you absolutely have to. (Some sites, notably the Microsoft Update site, require IE. There's one other good reason for using IE momentarily, which I describe in the section, "Feeding on RSS," later in this Technique.)

✓ **Download, install, tweak, learn, and use the latest version of Firefox.**

Hardening IE and using Firefox isn't a panacea. Firefox has lots of security holes, to be sure. But if you want to save time — and sleep at night — it's the best combination I know.

If your company requires you to use Internet Explorer, talk to somebody with clout. There are good technical reasons why some companies are

stuck with IE — most have to do with very adept Microsoft salespeople who convince the powers-that-be to use products and create applications that demand IE. Even if you're stuck with IE some of the time — there may be an intranet application that doesn't work with Firefox, for example — you probably aren't stuck with IE all the time. Check it out. And tell the people who pay the bills that they're backing a dark horse indeed.

Hardening Internet Explorer

Microsoft extols the new, enhanced security on offer in IE 7, the version of Internet Explorer included in Vista. Of course, the 'Softies have been doing that for years: Internet Explorer 3.01 sported three advanced security levels that rode herd on *ActiveX controls,* the programs on Web sites that IE can run, sometimes to deleterious effect. IE 4 introduced *Security Zones,* which figure prominently in IE 7, ten years later. It remains to be seen if the cracking community will be able to break IE 7 with the dexterity and alacrity applied to IE 6. One thing's for sure. It couldn't get much worse.

The primary culprits:

✓ **ActiveX** (formerly known as Object Linking and Embedding, or OLE) is used, *inter alia,* to stick movies and other multimedia files in Web pages. A very large percentage of IE security breaches occur when an ActiveX program (or *control*) is used in ways that IE's designers never intended. Firefox doesn't recognize ActiveX — and, I'm assured in the strongest possible language, never will.

✓ **Scripting,** whether by JavaScript or VBScript, uses IE to run programs that sit inside Web pages. Firefox does support JavaScript, but in a different way than IE.

✓ **.NET Framework** ("dot net framework") is a big collection of program pieces that Web site designers can stitch together to create programs. Firefox doesn't do .NET.

✔ **XAML** (Extensible Application Markup Language, pronounced "ZAM-uhl") works with .NET Framework to simplify the design of visually complex Web pages.

None of these technologies is bad, in and of itself, but all of them present an invitation to malware writers intent on breaking into your system.

 You may be thinking to yourself, "Hey, why do I care? I don't surf to weird Web sites. The warez guys and crackers don't draw me in. I'm not going to get stung." Unfortunately, "bad" Web sites are just part of the problem.

✔ Many "good" Web sites have, in the past, hosted advertisements that harbored malicious code. The ads get pulled in from a pool supplied by a vendor, and if one of the ads gets modified surreptitiously, a perfectly legitimate Web site can start planting malware on your machine.

✔ Some "good" Web sites have been altered — hacked — by slimeballs who stick destructive programs on otherwise legitimate pages. Unless the people who maintain the page are on the lookout, hacked pages can go undetected for a long time.

✔ Internet Explorer works behind the scenes, and it can be subverted in seemingly innocuous ways by a formatted e-mail message or a particular kind of downloaded file.

 The solution? Harden IE so it doesn't process potentially problematic Web pages (or e-mail messages) unless you give your explicit permission. If you harden IE by using the following steps, you'll also "break" some features, even if you never use IE as your Web browser. For example, some cool things that are supposed to happen when you open a formatted e-mail message just might not happen. It's the price you pay for progress.

 When you start running Internet Explorer, you may be asked if you want to enable IE's antiphishing protection. If you don't intend to use IE as a Web browser, go ahead and enable

antiphishing. But if there's a chance you might use IE much at all, read the details in the section, "Choosing Antiphishing Technology," later in this chapter before you commit yourself. There's more to antiphishing than meets the eye.

Here's how to make Internet Explorer 7 considerably less vulnerable to attack:

1. **Start Internet Explorer. Choose Tools➪Internet Options and click the Security tab.**

You see the IE security settings shown in Figure 18-1. In particular, the Internet icon should be selected (to indicate that you're working on security settings for the "Internet Zone" — which includes almost all your Internet interactions). The Security Level for This Zone should say Medium-High, and the box marked Enable Protected Mode (Requires Restarting Internet Explorer) should be checked.

• **Figure 18-1: Work with the Internet Zone.**

2. **Click the Custom Level button.**

IE shows you the Security Settings - Internet Zone dialog box, as shown in Figure 18-2.

• **Figure 18-2: Use the recommended settings in Table 18-1.**

3. **Follow the recommendations in Table 18-1 to make the changes that will effectively lock down IE's Internet Zone.**

4. **When you finish making all those changes, click OK. When IE asks if you're sure, click Yes.**

You return to the Internet Options dialog box shown in Figure 18-1.

Congratulations. Almost all the Web sites you visit will be subjected to this stringent set of restrictions. Occasionally, though, you will need to open up Internet Explorer to let some sites through. A prime example: `microsoft.com` itself.

 Take a few moments right now to familiarize yourself with the procedure for relaxing these lockdown rules on sites that can be trusted. `Microsoft.com` is a good example of a site that can be trusted (no matter what you may think of the company) because it's one of the most heavily protected sites on the Internet.

5. **Click the green "check mark" icon for Trusted Sites.**

You see the Trusted Sites version of the Internet Options security dialog box, as shown in Figure 18-3.

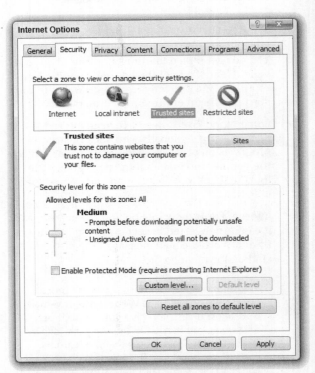

• **Figure 18-3: When you add a site to the Trusted Sites list, IE's built-in Medium security settings apply.**

Note that Trusted Sites are automatically assigned to the Medium security category, which is less stringent than the default Internet sites setting (Medium-High) and much less stringent than your custom locked-down Internet sites settings.

6. **Click the Sites button.**

IE shows you the Trusted Sites dialog box, shown in Figure 18-4.

• **Figure 18-4: Add trusted sites here.**

7. **In the top box, type** `http://microsoft.com`. **Uncheck the box marked Require Server Verification (https://) for All Sites in This Zone. Then click Add and then Close.**

You have just instructed Internet Explorer to relax its security settings for any Web pages that end in `microsoft.com`, even if they aren't secure sites (indicated by the `https://` prefix).

8. **Click OK to exit the Internet Options dialog box.**

Your changes to Internet Explorer take effect immediately.

With Internet Explorer hardened and security restrictions on `microsoft.com` relaxed, you're ready to install and start using Firefox. See the next section.

TABLE 18-1: INTERNET ZONE LOCKDOWN SETTINGS

Change This Setting	Recommended Lockdown Value
Loose XAML	Disable
XAML Browser Applications	Disable
XPS Documents	Disable
Run Components Not Signed with Authenticode	Disable
Binary and Script Behaviors	Disable
Run ActiveX Controls and Plug-Ins	Disable
Script ActiveX Controls Marked Safe for Scripting	Disable
Font Downloads	Disable
Enable .NET Framework Setup	Disable
Allow META REFRESH	Disable
Allow Web Pages to Use Restricted Protocols for Active Content	Disable
Display Mixed Content	Disable
Drag and Drop or Copy and Paste Files	Disable
Installation of Desktop Items	Disable
Launching Applications and Unsafe Files	Disable
Launching Programs and Files in an IFRAME	Disable
Navigate Sub-Frames across Different Domains	Disable
Software Channel Permissions	High Safety
Submit Non-Encrypted Form Data	Disable
Userdata Persistence	Disable
Websites in Less Privileged Web Content Zone Can Navigate into This Zone	Disable
Active Scripting	Disable
Allow Programmatic Clipboard Access	Disable
Scripting of Java Applets	Disable

Tweaking Firefox

I hope you follow my recommendation (see "Using IE and Firefox Together" at the beginning of this chapter) to update and harden IE (see "Hardening Internet Explorer") and then download, install, tweak, learn, and use Firefox.

You can install Firefox without disturbing Internet Explorer at all — they co-exist peacefully — and you can run either, or both, at any time.

To get Firefox, start Internet Explorer and go to www.getfirefox.com. Click the line that says Free Download. Follow the instructions on the page to download and install the latest version of Firefox. It'll take you just a few minutes: Compared to IE, Firefox rates as a bantam weight.

When you first start Firefox, it asks if you want to make it your default browser. I suggest you check the box marked Always Perform This Check When Starting Firefox and click Yes. That makes Firefox your browser of choice in almost all situations, except when Vista insists that you use Internet Explorer (for example, when checking for Windows or Office updates).

Getting used to tabs

Try using tabs for a few minutes. I guarantee you'll get hooked. I find tabs to be most useful when I'm working on several different topics at once. I crank up a brand-new copy of Firefox to handle each topic — say, one copy of Firefox for breaking software stories, another to follow the bugs and patches of the day (see Figure 18-5), and yet another for news and local events. Inside each copy of Firefox, I add or delete tabs as new information appears or as I follow a train of thought. To switch topics, I switch copies of Firefox. But to ping-pong around within one topic, I tab-tab-tab. Speeds up my surfing enormously.

• **Figure 18-5:** Use tabs to move among related topics, as I do with this collection of security sites.

My favorite tabbing timesavers:

✔ If you've used tabs for more than a few minutes, you probably already know that Ctrl+T opens a new tab and puts the cursor up in the address bar, ready for you to type a URL. But did you know that Ctrl+W closes the current tab? Or that, in Firefox, Ctrl+Shift+T reopens the tab you just closed?

✔ You probably know that holding down the Ctrl key while clicking a link opens the clicked page on a new tab. But did you know that clicking the "middle" button — the scroll wheel on most mice — does the same thing? Or that clicking the "middle" button on a tab title closes the tab?

✔ You can type a URL in the address bar and then press Alt+Enter, and the Web site you typed appears in a new tab. Similarly, typing a search term in the Search bar and pressing Alt+Enter runs the search in a new tab. (Those tricks work in Internet Explorer, too.)

Aside from learning how to use tabs — and going through a refresher course on keyboard shortcuts, which I provide in the section "Using important shortcuts," later in this Technique — there are two tweaks that I recommend for every Firefox user:

✔ Many people complain that it's hard to tell in Firefox which tab has been chosen: The highlighting of the chosen tab doesn't stand out well enough from the others. In the next section, I show you a way to make the selected tab more obvious.

✔ Firefox puts only a handful of tabs on the screen before sticking left- and right-arrows on the ends, so you can scroll through the tabs. I far prefer allowing Firefox to make the tabs very small before sticking the scroll arrows on the screen. It's easy to make the switch.

Mozilla, the company that makes Firefox, lists more than 200 tweaks that you can readily make to Firefox (http://kb.mozillazine.org/category:preferences). I make only two.

Put the Close button on the active tab

If you take a close squint at Figure 18-5, you can see why people complain about the lackluster highlighting Firefox applies to selected tabs. If it weren't for a slightly darker "X" close button on the right edge of the middle tab, you probably wouldn't know that, in fact, the middle tab is selected.

You can tell Firefox that you want to see an "X" close button only on the currently selected tab. I find that an excellent timesaving choice for two reasons:

✔ It's easier to see at a glance which tab is selected.

✔ It's harder to accidentally click and close the wrong tab.

Make Firefox rearrange its "X" close buttons:

1. **Start Firefox.**

2. **In the Address bar, type** about:config **and press Enter.**

You see an enormous array of preferences, as shown in Figure 18-6.

3. **Double-click on the line marked** browser.tabs.closeButtons.

Firefox shows you an Enter Integer Value dialog box like the one in Figure 18-7.

4. **Type a** 0 **(which is to say, the number zero) in the box if you want Firefox to show the red "X" button only on the active tab. Or choose one of the options in Table 18-2.**

5. **Click OK.**

Your change takes effect immediately (see Figure 18-8).

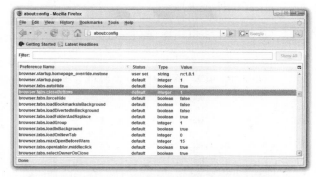

• **Figure 18-6: A few of Firefox's 200+ easily changed preferences.**

• **Figure 18-7: Change the setting here.**

• **Figure 18-8: Note how only the center tab — the active one — has an "X."**

TABLE 18-2: FIREFOX "X" CLOSE BUTTON PREFERENCES

This Entry	Causes This Behavior
0 (zero)	"X" appears only on the currently active tab.
1 (one)	"X"s appear on all the tabs, and the "X" on the active tab is red and bold.
2	No "X"s appear on any tabs.
3	One "X" appears to the right of all the tabs.

Squeeze more tabs on the screen

Your results may vary, but I get more work done, faster, if I can see all my tabs at once. I'm willing to let Firefox squeeeeze them down so they're pretty darn tiny to avoid having right and left scroll arrows stuck on the sides of the tabs, as you can see (just barely!) in Figure 18-9.

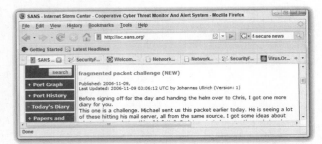

• **Figure 18-9:** When you get a lot of tabs, scroll arrows appear to the left and right of the tabs.

To make Firefox squeeze in all the tabs that're fit to print:

1. **Start Firefox.**

2. **In the Address bar, type** `about:config` **and press Enter.**

   You see the preferences shown earlier in Figure 18-6.

3. **Double-click the line marked** `browser.tabs.tabMinWidth`.

   Firefox shows you an Enter Integer Value dialog box like the one in Figure 18-7.

4. **Type a** 0 **(the number zero) in the box to make Firefox squeeze down tab sizes as much as it can.**

5. **Click OK.**

   If the tabs get too narrow for you, try increasing `browser.tabs.tabMinWidth` to 10. Fiddle with it until you're happy.

Speeding Up Your Browser

The best way to speed up your browser — whether it's Firefox or IE — is to get a faster Internet connection. Moving up to a fast broadband connection will do more than all the browser speed-up tips in all the books in the universe. The second best way is to adapt your browser to your way of working. Or vice versa.

If you look around on the Web, you'll find dozens — hundreds — of shop-worn tips on how to speed up Firefox or IE. One minor problem: Most of the methods don't work, and those that do work have unintended consequences.

In this section, I step you through speed-up techniques that actually save time. They all entail a change in the way your browser works, and you may not like their side effects. That's why I give you instructions on how to undo each specific tweak, so you can return Firefox (or IE) to its original state.

Note: If you want to try to speed up Vista's Internet connection in general, you may be able to see some improvement by tweaking your TCP stack. Vista's completely new IPv6 stack has been the source of much controversy, and it's still in its early years, so some manual improvements may be possible. Don't expect to turn your dSLug line into a whipper-snapper, but if you're up to a bit of heavy-duty spelunking, look at the tips on the DSL Reports site, `www.dslreports.com/tweaks`.

By the by, DSL Reports is a great source of information about Internet service providers and school-of-hard-knocks advice about keeping your line alive. Highly recommended.

Choosing a fast home page

Your *home page* is the place you go when you start your browser.

Firefox starts itself on Google's main page. That's a downright classy home page, a decent choice for many people. There's no place like Google.

Microsoft stacks the Internet Explorer deck on new Vista installations; if you install Vista on a clean machine, Internet Explorer always starts by running out to www.msn.com, Microsoft's MSN main page. There, you'll find just oodles of ways to spend mo' money.

If you bought your computer with Vista preinstalled, your home page may have been set to the manufacturer's site, to the MSN site, or to some other equally advertisement-laden corner of the Internet.

 Web site owners pay PC manufacturers for shepherding you to their home pages. The folks with the sites are betting on the chance that you won't change the home page to something more to your liking. The number of hits increases exponentially, as does the small chance that you'll actually buy something. Ka-ching.

Getting stuck with a big, slow home page rates as a first-class time sink, which you should change immediately. If you want Firefox to come up with no page at all — a blank page — every time it's started, here's how:

1. **Start Firefox.**

You *did* follow my instructions in "Using IE and Firefox Together" at the beginning of this chapter, didn't you?

2. **Choose Tools⇨Options.**

Firefox shows you its main Options page, as in Figure 18-10.

• **Figure 18-10:** Control Firefox's starting page here.

3. **To make Firefox start as quickly as possible, in the box next to When Firefox Starts, choose Show a Blank Page. Then click OK.**

 Before you do, though, remember that Google has a sparse interface and generally opens very quickly.

4. **On the other hand, if you always want Firefox to retrieve a specific page or set of pages — thus saving you the time and hassle of navigating to those pages — click the Use Bookmark button. In the Set Home Page dialog box (see Figure 18-11), choose a single page or a folder to open multiple pages. Then click OK.**

Your changes take effect the next time Firefox starts.

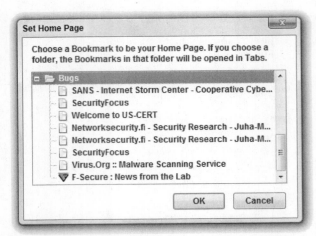

• **Figure 18-11:** Firefox can pull up a single page or group of pages every time it starts, if that'll save you time.

If you use Internet Explorer as your browser, you can similarly set the home page, or tell IE to start with a bunch of pages open in tabs. The mechanics are a little bit different from Firefox:

1. **Start Internet Explorer.**

2. **If you want IE to start every time with more than one page open, navigate to each of the pages you desire, with each on its own tab.**

3. **Choose Tools⇨Internet Options.**

You see the Internet Options dialog box shown in Figure 18-12.

4. **To use all the currently open pages, click the button marked Use Current. Or you can have IE open with a blank page by choosing Use Blank. Or you can always go back to MSN. Make your choice and click OK.**

If you choose Use Default, you deserve it. Harumph.

 Some unscrupulous Web pages may hijack your home page by tricking you into clicking something that takes over this setting. If you start your browser one day and a strange Web page appears, follow the preceding steps to get your home page back.

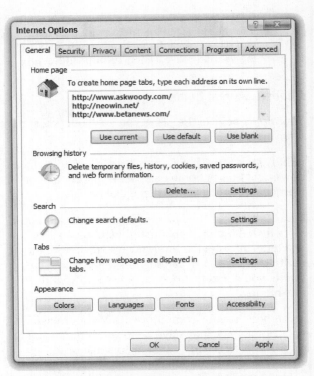

• **Figure 18-12:** IE gets the same job done with a clunkier set of choices.

Showing placeholder pictures

Most of the time, pictures add a lot to Web pages (just take a look at Figure 18-13 if you don't believe me). In fact, you'll frequently have a hard time figuring out what a Web page is supposed to be showing you if you can't see the images.

• **Figure 18-13:** Pictures make the text-heavy Internet more colorful.

Other times, though, you need only the text, thank you very much. In times like these, you can save tons of time by telling Firefox (or Internet Explorer) to forget about the pictures and simply show boxes where the pictures should go (see Figure 18-14).

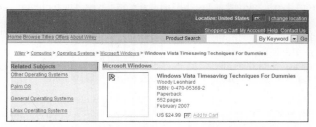

• **Figure 18-14: The same page as the one in Figure 18-13, without the pictures.**

 Savvy Web site designers put pieces of text underneath their pictures, so if you visit a well-designed site, you can get the gist of what's going on without seeing the pictures themselves.

Here's how to tell Firefox that you don't want to see pictures:

1. **Start Firefox.**

2. **Choose Tools⇨Options. Click the Content icon.**

Firefox shows you its Content options, per Figure 18-15.

3. **Uncheck the box marked Load Images Automatically.**

4. **Click OK.**

The setting takes effect on the next page you view.

If you ever want to see a picture, right-click the placeholder box and choose View Image.

To make Internet Explorer stop showing pictures, choose Tools⇨Internet Options⇨Advanced. Under the Multimedia heading, uncheck the box marked Show Pictures and click OK.

• **Figure 18-15: A sleek approach to removing content.**

Bumping up the cache

Web browsers cache Web pages — that is, they save Web pages and pictures on your PC as they go along and, whenever possible, pull pages and pictures from your PC instead of retrieving them from the Web again.

In spite of what you may have read in those breathless pieces of spam (Did YOU know that YOUR computer has COPIES of EVERY PICTURE you've SEEN on the INTERNET?), caching is a good thing. It speeds up your Web surfing enormously, especially if you tend to come back to the same page — or view related pages with the same graphics — over and over again.

With your browser cache, as with any cache, the question boils down to how much room on your hard drive you're willing to give up in exchange for shaving a few seconds off the time it takes for the computer to do its thing. In addition, both Firefox and IE allow you to specify how frequently the browser should check for updated pages. The settings are summarized in Table 18-3.

TABLE 18-3: BROWSER CACHE REFRESH SETTINGS

Firefox Level	IE Level	What It Means
0	Every Time I Start IE	When you view a page, the browser checks to see whether a copy was put in the cache on the current day, during the current session. (One "session" lasts from the time you start the browser until you close the last open window.) If the current day and session doesn't have a cached page, the browser retrieves a copy from the Web.
1	Every Time I Visit the Web page	When you view a page, the browser checks whether a copy of the page is cached. If a copy is in the cache, the browser then looks to see if the page available on the Web has the same date stamp as the one in the cache. If they match, the browser doesn't download the page, and the cached version comes up lickety-split.
2	Never	You only get what's in the cache. The first time you go to a Web page, it's put in the cache, but after that, you have to hit the Refresh icon or press F5 to update it.
3	Automatically	The browser starts by using the "Every Time I Visit the Webpage" method — but it keeps track of the pages you visit and how frequently they change. Using a formula that's different in Firefox and IE, the browser figures out which pages that you view change a lot, and which change very little, and thus decides whether or not to look for a new copy on the Web.

Evaluating and resizing your Firefox cache, and adjusting the refresh rate, couldn't be simpler:

1. **In the Firefox address bar, type** `about:cache` **and press Enter.**

Firefox shows you a cache utilization report like the one in Figure 18-16.

• **Figure 18-16:** Firefox's report on cache availability and usage.

The number you're most concerned about is labeled Disk Cache Device. (The Memory Cache Device is Firefox's in-memory storage space. In my experience, tweaking the memory cache doesn't help speed things up much at all.) The Maximum Storage Size is the number of KB (abbreviated KiB) set aside for Firefox's cache. The cache is physically stored in files with random names in the location given as the Cache Directory. The Storage in Use number tells you how much disk space is currently being used for Firefox's cache.

2. **Press Ctrl+T to start a new tab; then type** `about:config` **and press Enter.**

Firefox brings up its config file, as shown in Figure 18-17.

• **Figure 18-17:** Change the size of your cache here.

3. Take a look at how much cache space you're using (the `about:cache` Storage in Use number) and compare that with the maximum allotted for your cache (Maximum Storage Size). The amount you use should be considerably less than the maximum — say, oh, half. If you want to try to speed things up by making the cache bigger, go to the `about:config` page, double-click `browser.cache.disk.capacity`, and type in a new number for the allocated storage size.

4. If you want to change the refresh frequency, per Table 18-3, double-click `browser.cache.check_doc_frequency` and make your change.

5. When you're done, click OK.

Give the cache a few hours to expand and then see if you've sped things up. If you haven't, repeat Steps 1 through 3 and set the `browser.cache.disk.capacity` back to `50000`.

Internet Explorer is easier to change but doesn't give you nearly as much information about how your cache is being used. Here's how to jiggle the settings:

1. In Internet Explorer, choose Tools⇨Internet Options.

2. On the General tab, in the area marked Browsing History, click the button marked Settings.

You see the Temporary Internet Files and History Settings dialog box, shown in Figure 18-18.

3. Make any changes, based primarily on Table 18-3.

4. Click OK twice to get back to IE.

Try things for a while and see if IE's faster. If not, set the size back to 50MB and the refresh to Automatic.

• **Figure 18-18:** IE doesn't tell you much, but it does let you fiddle.

Speeding Up Yourself

You can tweak and tumble and thwack your browser upside the head, but (apart from installing a faster Internet connection) your largest online speed gains, by far, will come from you learning how to use your browser better.

Al Roboform

Don't know about you, but I have a couple thousand online accounts, all of which require usernames and passwords. Okay, okay. Many dozens. But it sure feels like thousands.

(continued)

A product called AI Roboform works with both Firefox and IE, storing and retrieving usernames and passwords with a click or two. You have to remember your AI Roboform password, but after you clear that hurdle, the program takes care of the rest. You can stick the AI Roboform password database on a key drive and take it with you. You can install AI Roboform on a key drive, so it's completely self-contained. Take the key drive with you when you log on from a public computer, and you'll foil keyloggers — you never type your online passwords, so a logger can't log it. How many logs would a keylogger log if a keylogger could log logs? Hmmmm . . .

More than a mere password regurgitator, it'll even generate "tough" passwords for you and keep track of them, so you don't have to dream up your own unique passwords for every site that demands one — and the passwords that Roboform provides are far more random than anything you or I could conceive. Super secure. Super easy.

There are very few "must have" utilities in the online world. This is one of them. The free limited version stores up to ten passwords. Unlimited RoboForm Pro costs $29.95. Check out `www.roboform.com` for more info.

Feeding on RSS

 RSS takes the timesaving cake. Of all the Web developments in the past five years, *Really Simple Syndication* (which goes by several other appellations) has to be among the best. RSS speeds up your online life by delivering the news you want as soon as it's available.

Here's how RSS works:

1. **You find an RSS-speaking Web site with news that won't make you snooze.**

I use the term "news" loosely. One of my favorite RSS sites delivers a "How to" article every day — How to Look Like a Zombie at Halloween, How to Tan Between Your Toes, that kind of stuff (www.wikihow.com). All the major news sites have RSS feeds these days — the big network news organizations, sure, but also important places like Slashdot.org (news for nerds), neowin.net (where unprofessional journalism looks better), and bink.nu (hi, Bink). I'm also partial to comedycentral.com (joke of the day), quotationspage.com (quote of the day), and amidabuddha.org (Buddhist thought of the day).

2. **You "subscribe" to the RSS feed.**

The *feed* delivers the news. You *subscribe* to the feed. It's a lot like subscribing to a newspaper, except you don't have to call the circulation department and wait ten minutes to fork over your credit card number.

Subscribing through either Firefox or IE is fast, easy, and free. A click or two and you're done.

3. **You figure out how (and where) you want to read the news.**

I talk about three different methods that I recommend and use every day later in this section.

4. **Sit back and relax. The news comes to you.**

Nope, you don't have to go out in the rain to fetch the paper, or argue with the delivery guy about paying your six-month-old bill. You don't lift a finger, and you don't pay a thing. When you feel like looking at the headlines, you take a gander. See something you like? Click it, and the full article comes up. Fast. Sweet.

Finding RSS-speaking sites is easy. You can use Google to search for such sites, but if you just watch as you go about your daily surfing, you'll bump into them.

Subscribing in Firefox

In Firefox, you can tell when you've stumbled upon an RSS-speaking site by the orange icon on the address bar, like the one to the right of the http://www.neowin.net address in Figure 18-19.

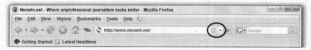

• **Figure 18-19: Many RSS-capable sites show the orange "broadcast" icon on the address bar. Others have orange boxes with the letters RSS or, less frequently, XML.**

When you've found a site that speaks RSS, subscribing to the feed couldn't be simpler:

1. **Click the orange "broadcast" icon. (Or you can click the RSS or XML box.) If more than one feed presents itself, choose the feed you want.**

For example, in Figure 18-20, I want to subscribe to Neowin's Main News Feed. Their Software, Gamer, and Forum news items aren't of any particular interest to me.

• **Figure 18-20: Pick the feed you like.**

2. **Firefox responds by showing you a handful of the latest news items (see Figure 18-21). If you like what you see and want to subscribe to the feed, click the Subscribe Now button.**

When you "Subscribe to this feed using Live Bookmarks" — horrible terminology, that — you're telling Firefox that you want it to put a clickable button to the right of the Getting Started and Latest Headlines buttons.

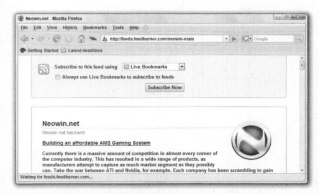

• **Figure 18-21: The easiest approach is to use Live Bookmarks.**

3. **Firefox asks you to type a name for the new Live Bookmark. Type something appropriate and click OK.**

I typed `Neowin` as the name of the Live Bookmark and clicked OK. The result (shown in Figure 18-22) is a new button to the right of the Getting Started and Latest Headline buttons.

• **Figure 18-22: The new Neowin Live Bookmark button coughs up the latest news from Neowin.net with just a click.**

4. **Whenever you want to see the latest news from Neowin, click the Neowin Live Bookmark button.**

Quick as a wink, Firefox hops out to the Neowin RSS feed and presents the results as the drop-down list you see in Figure 18-22. Click a link, and Firefox moves to the page with that news item.

 You may have wondered about Firefox's "Latest Headlines" button. In fact, that's a Live Bookmark that's attached to the BBC's RSS news feed. You can see the source of the news items that appear on the button — the source of the RSS feed — by going to `http://bbc.co.uk`.

Subscribing in IE

Subscribing to an RSS feed in Internet Explorer is almost as easy:

1. **Surf to the site with the RSS feed.**

In Figure 18-23, I use Internet Explorer to go to www.neowin.net.

• **Figure 18-23:** Subscribing to the same Neowin feed with Internet Explorer.

2. **Click the arrow next to the orange "broadcast" feed sign and pick the feed you like.**

Internet Explorer shows you a list of the current RSS "news" items, similar to the one in Firefox, except IE has additional tools for displaying and sorting the RSS items. See Figure 18-24.

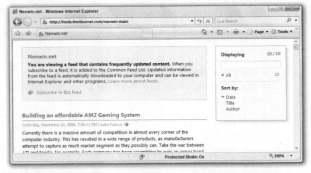

• **Figure 18-24:** Internet Explorer's ability to manipulate RSS items beats Firefox's.

If you want to look at the "raw" RSS feed information (as opposed to jumping over to the source Web site), IE's RSS viewing tools beat Firefox's hands down. In addition to sorting, you can mark an entire feed as "read" so you don't look at the feed items again. That may be a compelling reason for you to use IE. Occasionally.

3. **Click the link marked Subscribe to This Feed.**

IE asks you to give the feed a name and recommends that you create the feed in a Favorites folder called Feeds.

4. **Type a name for your feed and click Subscribe.**

5. **When you want to see the feed from a particular site, click the "Star" icon on the left and choose Feeds, as shown in Figure 18-25.**

IE doesn't have Live Bookmarks, like Firefox, so getting at the feeds is considerably more difficult.

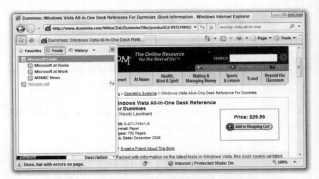

• **Figure 18-25:** Click the star and then Feeds to peruse RSS feeds you've set up in IE.

Viewing the news

There are three different ways to look at RSS feeds that I recommend and use every day:

✔ **Google home page:** Google doesn't tap into Firefox or Internet Explorer's RSS feeds. Instead, you have to set up your custom home page using Google's own RSS subscription engine. But, hey, this is Google, which means it's easy, it's customizable, it works right the first time, and it doesn't have a lot of bells and whistles, but it's fast. My customized Google home page rates as my RSS reader of choice, and I use it all day, every day (Figure 18-26). To set up your own, go to www.Google.com and click the link marked Personalized Home. Then, on the right, click Add Stuff. You can customize each feed (click the Edit link), click and drag the individual blocks anywhere you like — even create multiple tabs.

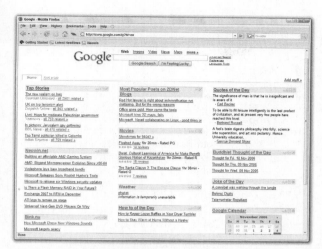

• **Figure 18-26:** My RSS feed reader of choice, cleverly disguised as a customized Google home page.

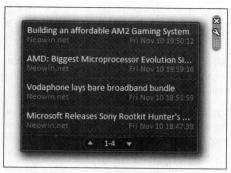

• **Figure 18-27:** The Vista Sidebar gadget that views RSS feeds from Internet Explorer.

✔ **Firefox Live Bookmarks:** When I'm ready for a jolt of news, and I know where I want to look, I click the Live Bookmark button for the site I want to peruse. It isn't fancy. (Unlike Internet Explorer's Feeds folder, for example, I can't sort by date, title, or author in Firefox.) But it gets the news in my face, on my terms, when I want it.

✔ **Vista Sidebar Gadgets:** As of this writing, only one reliable RSS news reader works in the Vista Sidebar, and it's the one from Microsoft that ships with Vista (see Figure 18-27). (See Technique 8 for details about the Sidebar.) You can view any single RSS feed with the Gadget; if you want to view more than one RSS feed, you have to bring up more than one Gadget. Being a Microsoft product, it only works with IE — you have to subscribe to an RSS feed in Internet Explorer before the feed appears as an option in the Gadget: Click the little icon that looks like a wrench to select which feed gets monitored.

To see more text — the Gadget sitting on the Sidebar is squintingly tiny — click and drag the Gadget onto the desktop. Once on the desktop, you can't resize it, but at least you'll be able to read more of the news items.

No doubt by the time you read this, there will be many Gadgets that work with Firefox and/or work independently of any browser. Check Google or AskWoody.com for the latest.

From time to time, I like to see full details of all my feeds in Firefox. For that task, I use a little add-on called Sage. (You can see Sage's little leaflike icon to the left of the address bar in Figure 18-26.) Sage has all the industrial-strength qualities of Internet Explorer's RSS feed reader, but it works in Firefox. To get your own copy, start Firefox, click Tools↪ Add-Ons, click the link that says Get Extensions, and search for Sage RSS.

Using important shortcuts

After RSS feeds, the second most important way to speed up your surfing is by learning and using various shortcuts that Firefox and IE support.

Here are seven timesaving shortcuts that every browser user should know:

✔ **Ctrl+T:** Starts a new tab.

✔ **Ctrl+F:** Opens a Find box you can use to find specific text on the current page.

✔ **Ctrl+Enter:** If you type the middle part of an address in the address bar — say, `wiley` — and then press Ctrl+Enter, both Firefox and IE immediately put an `http://www.` on the front and a

.com on the back. Type `wiley` and press Ctrl+Enter, and your browser immediately knows to look for `http://www.wiley.com`.

- **Alt+Enter:** If you type in the Search bar and press Alt+Enter, your browser opens the search results in a new tab.

- **Ctrl+F5:** If you think that the Web page is "stuck" — it isn't being updated properly, perhaps because it's been put in the cache on your PC — pressing Ctrl+F5 forces your browser to go out and get the latest copy of the current page. In theory, the key combination even blasts past copies that are cached with your Internet service provider (which can be a real headache if your ISP is slow to update cached pages).

- **Ctrl+click:** When you click a link, sometimes you want to leave the old page in place while you look at the new page — for example, if you're going through Google and want to look at several search-results pages at the same time. To force either Firefox or IE to open a Web page in a new tab, hold down Ctrl while you click the link. Cool timesaving variation: center-click on a link (on most mice, that means click the scroll wheel) to open the clicked page on a new tab.

- **Center-click (scroll wheel click) on a tab title:** Closes the tab.

 Put a sticker on your monitor with those seven shortcuts until they become ingrained in your fingers' little gray cells.

The rest of the shortcuts (see Table 18-4) are gravy. They can save you some time if you fear rodents or if you repeat some specific action many times in a day. But I wouldn't lose a lot of sleep over them.

TABLE 18-4: WORTHWHILE BROWSER SHORTCUTS

Press This	And Your Browser Does This
F5	Refreshes the current page (same as clicking the Refresh button), but if you really want to refresh the current page and bypass your Internet service provider's cache, press Ctrl+F5.

Press This	And Your Browser Does This
F11	Full Screen Mode — eliminates all but the Standard Button bar. Return to normal by pressing F11 again.
Ctrl+mouse wheel	Increases or decreases the size of the font on the current page. This doesn't work on all Web pages.
Ctrl+D	Adds the current page to the bottom of your Bookmarks or Favorites list, which is probably the last place you want to put it.
Ctrl+H	Brings up the History pane.
Ctrl+K	Jumps to the Search bar. (In Internet Explorer, it's Ctrl+E.)
Esc	Stops loading the current page.
Home	Goes to the top of the page.
End	Goes to the bottom of the page.
Page Down or spacebar	Scrolls down one screen. If your cursor is in a text box, pressing the spacebar doesn't work.
Page Up or Shift+↑	Scrolls up one screen.
Alt+← or Backspace	Same as clicking the Back button.
Alt+→	Same as clicking the Forward button.

Unhijacking the Back button

Have you ever surfed to a Web page and noticed that the Back button suddenly doesn't work? You can click the Back arrow over and over again, and you never get off the page. I think Dante reserved the sixth ring of Hell for Web sites that hijack the Back button. Or at least he should've.

 Unfortunately, you can't do anything to prevent the hijacking. But you can do something to bypass it.

If you click the down arrow to the right of the Back button (in Internet Explorer, it's to the right of the Forward button), a list of the sites you have recently visited appears. Even if the Web page commandeers your Back button, it can't wipe out your history. Click the down-arrow and move back to someplace safe.

Creating custom shortcuts from the Address bar

When most people first start using browsers, they think they have to type in the full URL, or Web address, and they worry that upper- and lowercase letters matter. So they type something like

    http://www.Wiley.com

Pretty soon, most people figure out that you don't need the `http://`, and that lowercase and upper-case are all the same on the new frontier. Most Web page designers are savvy enough to make the www part optional, too. (If you hit a site that requires the www, complain to the Webmaster!) So both of these work fine:

    www.wiley.com or even wiley.com

 If you read the section, "Using important shortcuts," earlier in this Technique, you have probably hit the first stage of enlightenment: You know that typing `wiley` and pressing Ctrl+Enter takes you to the same place.

Are you ready for the next step?

Both Firefox and Internet Explorer let you click and drag shortcuts from the address bar onto a separate bar just below the address bar — Firefox calls it a Bookmarks toolbar; IE calls it simply Links.

 Here's how you can create a custom shortcut:

1. **Make sure the shortcut bar is showing.**

In Firefox, you can probably see the Bookmarks toolbar; it has buttons for Getting Started and Latest Headlines, plus any RSS feeds you may have added (see "Feeding on RSS," earlier in this Technique). In IE, you may not be able to see the Links toolbar; it says Links (see Figure 18-28).

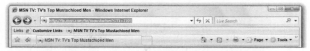

• **Figure 18-28: The Internet Explorer Links toolbar.**

2. **If you can't see the appropriate toolbar, right-click an empty place on one of the toolbars and check the box for the toolbar in question.**

In Firefox, you would check the box next to the line that says Bookmarks toolbar.

3. **Navigate to the Web site you want to enshrine with its own shortcut.**

4. **Click and drag the icon at the far left end of the address bar onto the shortcut toolbar.**

In Figure 18-28, that's the tiny icon with a circle and a right-facing wedge. When the icon's on the shortcut toolbar, click it to go to the site in question.

You can use a similar procedure to drag a shortcut onto the Vista desktop. See Technique 8 for several examples.

Keeping Your Browser Under Control

Firefox and Internet Explorer go out of the way to help you, and in some cases, they simply go too far. Although the features may save you some time, they also leave you exposed in various ways. This section shows you how to turn off some of those "helpful" features.

Removing "saved" passwords and usernames

Back when you first started using your browser, it asked you if you wanted the program to remember your passwords so you wouldn't need to type them in again. Chances are pretty good you let Firefox and/or IE have its way. They may be storing your passwords even now.

Firefox has an inherently safer way of storing and accessing passwords, if you enable it. The Master Password feature requires you to type in a password before Firefox will automatically fill in individual passwords for you. It's a worthwhile feature, but it doesn't hold a candle to AI Roboform (see the sidebar earlier in this Technique).

Internet Explorer, on the other hand, happily fills in passwords for anybody who can log on with your name on your PC. Although it's true that anyone who can sit down at your machine can, ultimately, pull just about anything off of it (with the exception of BitLocker-encrypted data, at least), the IE approach leaves you vulnerable to anybody who happens to sit down in front of your PC while you're away for just a minute.

 Don't let either browser hold onto your passwords. Period. If you have a bunch of passwords that you don't remember, log on to each site, in turn, change your password, and write down the new password. Then go through these steps to give Firefox and/or IE a severe case of amnesia.

Here's how to clear your passwords out of Firefox and make sure it doesn't store any more:

1. Choose Tools➪Clear Private Data.

2. Make sure the Saved Passwords box is checked.

3. Click Clear Private Data Now.

4. Choose Tools➪Options and click the Security icon.

5. Clear the check box that says Remember Passwords for Sites.

6. Click OK.

And in Internet Explorer:

1. Choose Tools➪Internet Options.

   IE shows you the Internet Options dialog box.

2. On the General tab, under Browsing History, click Delete.

IE brings up the Delete Browsing History dialog box.

3. Under the Passwords heading, click Delete Passwords.

4. IE asks if you're sure. Click Yes.

5. Back in the Internet Options dialog box, click the Content tab.

6. In the AutoComplete section, click Settings.

   IE brings up the AutoComplete Settings dialog box, shown in Figure 18-29.

• Figure 18-29: Tell IE that it shouldn't try to remember usernames or passwords.

7. Uncheck the box marked User Names and Passwords on Forms.

 In general, to save time, you want to have IE remember the Web addresses that you type. But you may not want to leave that trail of information sitting around either.

8. Click OK twice to return to Internet Explorer.

   Your change takes effect immediately.

 If you want to delete some AutoComplete entries (such as your credit card numbers) but want to use others (such as your name and address), there's a way. The next time you fill out a form on the Web and you see some data you don't want IE to remember, select what's inside the box that's coming up with your sensitive data and then press Delete. That gets rid of it.

Checking for add-ons and parasites

A *parasite* is a program that's been installed, usually without your knowledge, and usually through Internet Explorer, that doesn't benefit you in any way. An *add-on* is a program that's been installed, usually without your knowledge, that may or may not be of any benefit.

See the difference?

Okay. I'm joking. A little bit.

Typically, you get parasites when you download and install a free software package. Sometimes, you install the parasite as a byproduct of installing a program that you really want, after clicking Yes to a warning that's longer than the Declaration of Independence. Or maybe the Tax Code. Frequently, the good program's installer has a tiny notice buried in the End User License Agreement (EULA) that says you grant your permission for the parasite to be installed.

 Both Firefox and Internet Explorer give you the tools to see what's gotten into your browser. You may have a hard time discerning which programs are good and which are bad, but at least you can see what's under the hood.

In Firefox, click Tools➪Add-Ons. You can click the Options button to find out more about the add-on, and click Disable or Uninstall if you don't like the smell of things.

In Internet Explorer, choose Tools➪Manage Add-ons➪ Enable or Disable Add-ons. From that point, you can see which add-ons are currently running and, by choosing to show add-ons that have been used by Internet Explorer, a list of all the add-ons that have ever been run. Click a specific add-on and choose Enable or Disable in the settings box to turn off the suspect ones.

Choosing Antiphishing Technology

Firefox and Internet Explorer take radically different approaches to antiphishing — the art and science of preventing you from entering personal information into Web sites that aren't what they appear to be. When Internet Explorer encounters a site that seems to be trying to steal data from you, it puts up a big warning like the one in Figure 18-30.

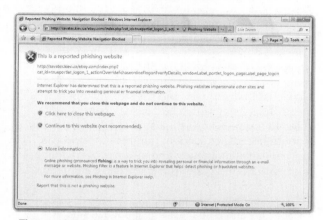

• **Figure 18-30: Internet Explorer's antiphishing warning.**

Firefox's warning is a little more, uh, colloquial, but equally startling: "Suspected Web Forgery / This page has been reported as a web forgery designed to trick users into sharing personal or financial information. Entering any personal information on this page may result in identity theft or other fraud."

 You might think enabling full antiphishing capabilities in either Firefox or Internet Explorer would be a no-brainer. Alas, that's not the case. The approach used by Internet Explorer, in particular, has all sorts of negative privacy implications. If you enable IE's antiphishing filter, Microsoft keeps records about you and every single Web site that you visit. Think about that for a second.

The Internet Explorer approach

Lest you believe that Microsoft wants to assemble a master database of everybody on the Internet and all the sites they visit (cue the creepy take-over-the-world laugh), consider the nature of the problem. Phishing sites go up and come down in the blink of an electronic eye. The most convincing sites might only be up for a day. Maybe not even that long.

All a good phisher needs is a handful of folks who believe they're answering a real eBay message (what, you bought a non-existent laptop and didn't pay for it?), or a Wells Fargo message (gosh, they need your password to unblock that imaginary account again?). The best phishing scams — the ones most likely to succeed — move quickly: a phishing site goes up, spam goes out, a couple thousand unsuspecting bank customers log on, and the site disappears. Meanwhile, a guy with a bad case of halitosis sits glued to a screen in Kazbukistan and grabs dozens, if not hundreds, of account numbers, passwords, mothers' maiden names, and all sorts of ancillary information. He's gone with a key drive and a burp.

Any effective antiphishing tool needs to identify and raise the alarm about bad sites in a matter of hours, or even minutes. While Firefox and IE can (and do) identify bogus sites by their phishiness, nailing a site conclusively requires human evaluation. The Internet's a big place. Hundreds of thousands of sites go up every day. Unless lots and lots of people are looking for phishing sites — and unless their efforts are made available quickly to anyone visiting a potential phishing site — we might as well cut bait.

That's the crux of the problem. An antiphishing tool that guards against new attacks has to coordinate the observations and feedback from millions of people, shooting the results to potential victims very quickly.

The only way that can happen on your computer is if your Web browser consults an up-to-the-minute database of phishing sites each and every time you move to a new site. And the only way that can happen is if your Web browser sends the address of the site you're about to visit to that giant database before you open the site. Because of the way the Web works, when you contact that database with a notice that you're about to open a Web page, you leave behind an IP address. If you're more-or-less permanently connected to the Internet with a broadband line, that IP address identifies you more-or-less uniquely.

If you turn on the antiphishing filter in Internet Explorer, that giant database belongs to Microsoft, and a log of every Web site you visit, complete with your IP address, gets added to Microsoft's compilation of information about you. Except for a few pre-ordained "safe" sites, Microsoft receives notification about every single site you visit. Every single time. Making matters worse: Internet Explorer won't even perform a heuristic analysis on the site you're about to visit — trying to determine its phishiness — unless you turn on the phishing filter. So if you want any antiphishing protection from IE, you have to agree to send your entire Web-surfing history to the folks in Redmond.

To turn on IE antiphishing:

1. **Click Tools⇨Phishing Filter⇨Turn on Automatic Website Checking.**

IE responds with the Microsoft Phishing Filter dialog box, shown in Figure 18-31.

2. **If you understand the implications of what you're doing, click the option marked Turn On Automatic Phishing Filter (Recommended) and click OK.**

That starts the heuristic analysis of sites and ensures that Microsoft receives copies of almost all your Web-surfing history.

At least now you know the rest of the story.

• **Figure 18-31: Does this dialog box remind you that Microsoft keeps a complete log of your surfing history?**

The Firefox approach(es)

Firefox takes a kinder, less intrusive — but not necessarily better — approach. Unlike Internet Explorer, Firefox doesn't pester you to sign up for antiphishing services. Instead, Firefox periodically downloads a blacklist to your computer — a list of known and suspected phishing sites that the browser blocks. Firefox also scans each page as you open it and tries to determine its phishiness. But, by default, Firefox does not send Web pages to a big blacklist database, and it therefore doesn't keep track of every site you visit. That's the antiphishing protection you receive automatically in Firefox.

If you want more up-to-date protection, Firefox gives you the option, but you're never pestered.

You have to know where to look in order to sign up for Firefox's Microsoft-style database approach. Moreover, the database isn't run by Firefox. It's from Google. So if you turn on the advanced antiphishing capability in Firefox, you aren't giving Firefox a complete list of your browsing history. You're giving it to Google.

Here's how to switch Firefox over to the more advanced, but more intrusive, approach:

1. **Choose Tools⇨Options.**

2. **Click the Security icon.**

3. **At the top, click the button that says Check by Asking Google about Each Site I Visit.**

Firefox tosses up a crystal-clear warning (see Figure 18-32) about how you're giving up your privacy. "If you choose to check with Google about each site you visit, Google will receive the URLs of pages you visit for evaluation. . . . Google will receive standard log information, including a cookie, as part of this process." Straight talk. Admirable.

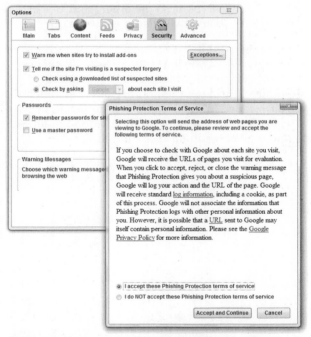

• **Figure 18-32: Firefox's privacy warning. Heed it well.**

4. **To sign up, click the button marked I Accept these Phishing Protection Terms of Service and click Accept and Continue. Then click OK to go back to Firefox.**

The next site you visit will be checked against Google's database — and a record of your visit to that site will be deposited in Google's records. (Why do I keep hearing that creepy take-over-the-world laugh?)

Comparing the two

Microsoft's dialog box (Figure 18-31) states that "some website addresses will be sent to Microsoft to be checked," and that's literally true. Internet Explorer strips some potentially identifiable information from the URL before it hits the Microsoft database. For example, if you surf to `www.someplace.isp/results.aspx?id=somename&password=blah`, IE strips away the stuff after the question mark and hits the database with `www.someplace.isp/results.aspx`. Firefox, on the other hand, doesn't promise to strip anything before it goes to Google.

IE maintains a whitelist of "safe sites" that's updated frequently. When you surf to a new site, IE checks the site against the whitelist, and against a list of sites currently in your temporary Internet folder. If the site you're going to isn't on either list, IE phones home and checks, leaving your IP address and URL in that big Microsoft database in the sky.

 Technically, in my experience and as of this writing, there's no doubt that IE identifies more phishing sites, sooner, than Firefox. IE beats Firefox both with the "heuristic" analysis (where a site hasn't yet been officially pegged as a phishery) and in the lookup analysis (where a site was definitely flagged as being phishy).

So which approach is best?

Tough question. It depends on how much you value your privacy; whether you trust Microsoft (or Google) to keep your private information private; and whether you believe that Microsoft (or Google) can or will defend its privacy policies against lawsuits, governmental actions, crackers, and the wayward actions of individual employees.

Personally, I use Firefox with the default antiphishing settings. I realize that I'm not getting the best protection, and if Google's antiphishing filter gets better, I'll be tempted to switch.

On the other hand, I set my dad up with Internet Explorer's full phishing filter and have him use IE specifically because of its superior antiphishing technology. It's a bitter pill to swallow, but unless the phishing problem abates, that's the safest approach for him.

19

Technique

Saving Time with Google

Save Time By

- ✔ Making your Web searches work right — the first time
- ✔ Playing Google like a violin
- ✔ Digging in the newsgroups

E ven though everybody says that Google is the best search engine, not everybody knows just how great Google is. Some of the engine's most timesaving parts are also its best-kept secrets. That's a shame, really, because folks who spend time searching the Web for information can save a lot of effort if they know how to use Google effectively. And folks who don't spend time searching the Web for things should.

Google's shotgun approach can be augmented by very precise searching, both with Google and with other search engines, if you know precisely what you're looking for. Firefox and Internet Explorer put boxes up in the upper-right corner that connect directly to a search engine, giving quick access to Web-based searches whenever you like. Both make it easy to add new search engines or modify existing ones.

This Technique has the potential to save you more time than all the other Techniques in this book put together — especially if you spend a lot of time doing online research. If you can learn to search for answers quickly and thoroughly — and cut through the garbage on the Web just as quickly and thoroughly — you can't help but save time in everything you do.

Using Google Effectively

If you use Firefox and you haven't changed anything, Google already appears as your default search engine. You can tell by the boxed "G" in the Search bar in the upper-right corner.

On the other hand, if you use Internet Explorer (see my recommendations against doing so in Technique 18), you probably have Windows Live Search listed as your default search engine. If you want to change IE over to use Google instead of Microsoft's proprietary search engine, follow these quick steps:

1. **Click the down-arrow on the right edge of the Search bar and select Find More Providers.**

Internet Explorer takes you to a page of pre-approved search engines, as in Figure 19-1.

• **Figure 19-1: Switch Internet Explorer to Google through this Web page.**

2. **On the left, click the link to Google.**

   IE brings up the Add Search Provider dialog box.

3. **Check the box marked Make This My Default Search Provider and then click Add Provider.**

   Google makes an appearance as IE's search provider.

Just to make sure we're on the same page, start your favorite Web browser, type your name in the Search bar with quotes around it — say, `"woody leonhard"` — and press Enter. You should see a Google search-results page listing your name, as in Figure 19-2.

• **Figure 19-2: Bet you didn't know your name was so popular, eh?**

With Google immediately at hand from your browser's Search bar, you're ready to get down to business.

No discussion of Google is complete without a mention of the customizable Google home page. I use mine as my number-one source of news of all types — RSS feeds, in the parlance. To understand how the home page works, and to set yours up, refer to Technique 18.

PageRank

Ever wonder how Google decides which search matches appear at the top of the list? You aren't alone. A lot of people have devoted a whole lot of effort, time, and money to getting their pages put at the top of the Google hit list.

Eight years ago, Google (then called BackRub) amounted to little more than a simple idea: If a lot of Web sites point to a particular Web page, chances are good that the page being pointed to contains information that many people would find interesting.

Stanford grad students Larry Page and Sergey Brinn, BackRub's founders, scrimped together enough money to build a working prototype in a Stanford dorm room. By 1998, the (ahem!) PageRank system was generating a lot of interest on campus: Students could actually find the stuff they wanted without slogging through endless lists of categories. In September, 1998, Page and Brinn opened a real office with a cool US $1,000,000 initial capital. Truth be told, the "office" was in a garage, which came with a washing machine, dryer, and hot tub. They blew all the money on computers.

The original PageRank system, subject of much scholarly discussion, tried to assign a number predicting the relevance of a page to a specific query. Originally, the PageRank was calculated by counting the number of links *to* a page and attempting to assess how "good" those links might be. Over time, the PageRank has become clouded in mystery, and for good reason: Raising your PageRank by a point or two can make a big difference in where your page appears on a Google hit list, and that translates into big bucks.

Saving time with search terms

Obviously, you should choose your search terms precisely. Pick words that will appear on any page that matches what you're looking for: Don't use *Compaq* when you want *Compaq S710*. That's true of any search engine.

Beyond the obvious, the Google search engine has certain peculiarities that you can exploit (these peculiarities hold true whether you're using Google in your browser's Search bar or you venture directly to www.google.com):

✔ The first words you use get more weight than the latter words. If you look for `phuket diving` you get a different list than the one for `diving phuket`. The former list emphasizes Web sites about Phuket that include a mention of diving; the latter includes diving pages that mention Phuket.

✔ Google shows you only those pages that include *all* the search terms. The simplest way to narrow down a search that returns too many results is to add more specific words to the end of your search term. For example, if `phuket diving` returns too many pages, try `phuket diving beginners`. In programmer's parlance, the terms are "anded" together.

If you type in more than ten words, Google ignores the ones after the tenth.

 Google ignores a surprisingly large number of short words (such as *who, how, where, to,* and *is*) as well as single-digit numbers. The results page tells you whether it ignored certain words.

✔ You can use OR to tell Google that you want the search to include two or more terms — but you have to capitalize OR. For example, `phuket OR samui OR similans diving` returns diving pages that focus on Phuket, Samui, or the Similans.

✔ If you want to limit the search to a specific phrase, use quotes. For example, `diving phuket "day trip"` is more limiting than `diving phuket day trip` because with the former, the precise phrase `day trip` has to appear on the page.

✔ Exclude pages from the results by putting a hyphen in front of the words you don't want. For example, if you want to find pages about diving in Phuket, but you don't want to associate with lowly snorkelers, try `diving phuket -snorkeling`.

 You can combine search tricks. If you're looking for overnight diving, try `diving phuket -"day trip"` to get the best results.

✔ Google supports wildcard searches in a very limited way. The * stands for a single word. So you can't search for `div*` and expect to find both diver and diving. But if you search for, oh, `email * * wellsfargo.com`, you'll find a lot of e-mail addresses. (That second * matches the @ sign in an address. Try it.)

✔ Just like the points in *Who's Line Is It Anyway?*, capitalization doesn't matter. Search for `diving phuket` or `diving Phuket` — either search returns the same results.

 There are lots of little tricks that may come in handy, depending on what you seek. I put these on a sticky note and tape them next to my monitor. Really.

✔ Google has a built-in units converter. The word "in" triggers the converter. Try `10 meters in feet` or `350 degrees F in centigrade` (or `350 f in c`) or `20 dollars in baht` or (believe me, this is impressive) `.89 euros per liter in dollars per gallon`.

✔ To calculate, just type the equation `1234*5678` or `3/pi`. No, Google doesn't solve partial differentials or simultaneous equations. Yet.

✔ To find a list of alternate (and frequently interesting) definitions for a word, type `define`, as in `define booty`.

✔ You can get movie reviews and local show times by typing `movie` and then the name of the movie. Like, oh, `movie borat`.

✔ Or try quick questions for quick facts: `height of mt everest` or `length of mississippi river` or `currency in singapore`.

✔ FedEx, U.S. Postal Service, and UPS tracking numbers, UPC codes, U.S. area codes — just type in the number. For example, if you type in an area code, Google not only tells you where the area code covers, it offers to show you a map!

When you're in a hurry, those can make a difference.

Using Advanced Search

If you need to narrow down your searches — in other words, if you want Google to do the sifting instead of doing it yourself — you should become acquainted with Google's Advanced Search capabilities. Here's a whirlwind tour:

1. **Run your search and, if it doesn't have what you want, click the Advanced Search link to the right of the Google Search button.**

Google brings up its Advanced Search page (see Figure 19-3).

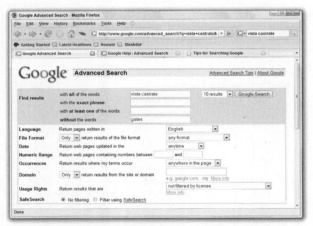

• **Figure 19-3:** Advanced Search lets you narrow down your Google search quickly and easily.

2. **Fill in the top part of the page with your search terms.**

In Figure 19-3, I refine my search by asking for pages that don't include the word gates.

Anything you can do in the top part of this page can also be done with the shorthand tricks mentioned in the preceding section. If you find yourself using the top part of the page frequently, save yourself some time and brush up on the tricks (such as OR, -, and " ") that I mention in "Saving time with search terms," earlier in this Technique.

3. **In the bottom part of the Advanced Search page, further refine your search by matching on**

▶ The identified source language of the page (not always accurate).

▶ A specific filename extension (such as .pdf or .doc).

 This setting is generally used for finding downloadable files — not Web pages.

▶ When the page was last updated (although this information, too, is not always accurate).

▶ If the page contains numerals between two given values.

▶ Whether the search terms appear in the URL, the title, or links to the Web page.

▶ The domain name, such as AskWoody.com.

You can also tell Google whether it should look for pages with specific licensing allowances (not widely implemented) or use its offensive-page filter, called SafeSearch, on this specific search.

4. **Press Enter.**

The results of your advanced search appear in a standard Google search results window.

You can find more details about Google Advanced Search on the Google Advanced Search page, www.google.com/help/refinesearch.html.

Posting on the Newsgroups

One of Google's most important (but largely unknown and underutilized) gems is the ongoing archive of Usenet newsgroup postings. For many, many years, the Usenet newsgroups on the Internet served as a vital person-to-person link, with hundreds of millions of absolutely uncensored messages on every conceivable topic.

You may know newsgroups for their extensive collections of pictures, movies, songs, and other media. I talk about those in Technique 20. You may not know that the original reason for the newsgroups — providing a way for people to communicate with each other about a bewildering number of topics — is still alive and well.

Google, being Google, has indexed the messages, built a credible viewer that shows you who replied to what message and when, and even assembled a very serviceable front-end so that you can post your own messages on the groups.

When you perform a standard Google search, frequently you will find the results of a Google Groups search at the bottom of the search results page. Feel free to click the offered links and see what other people are saying!

To search for a message in the massive Google newsgroups archive:

1. **Start your favorite browser and go to** `http://groups.google.com`.

Google shows you the Google Groups search page.

2. **Type your search terms in the box and press Enter.**

Google returns a list of all the messages that meet your criteria (see Figure 19-4).

The results are normally presented to you in order of Google's calculated relevance. You may find it more enlightening to click the Sort By Date line at the top of the results list.

3. **You almost always want to see the entire thread (the message itself, with all the messages that came before it and after it), so click the underlined link at the top of a message that interests you.**

Google shows you the thread (the list of messages, who posted them, and an indication of who they responded to) on the left. Messages appear on the right. (See Figure 19-5.)

• **Figure 19-4: An enormous wealth of sometimes-accurate information awaits in the newsgroups.**

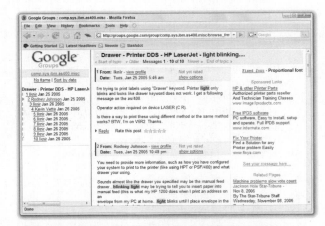

• **Figure 19-5: Google Groups shows fully threaded messages.**

4. **To reply to a message, locate and click a Reply link.**

Generally, you can post on threads that are no more than 60 days old. You may need to sign up for a Google account, which takes only a few seconds. As soon as you're signed up, you see a Posting form.

5. **Type your message in the space provided and click Post.**

Your message appears on the group in short order.

That's how hard it is to talk to anyone, on any subject, anywhere in the world.

Finding Images, News, and More

Google has several specialized search engines, and the number seems to grow every week. Many times, when you perform a standard, everyday Google search, results from one or more of these specialized search engines appear at the top of the results page.

I use these specialized Google engines most frequently:

✔ **Images** at `images.google.com` contains an enormous collection of pictures, gathered from all over the Internet (see Figure 19-6). You can easily modify the results based on the size (think quality) of the picture, and you can invoke or banish Google's nanny, SafeSearch. Click Advanced Image Search for more details.

• **Figure 19-6:** Google Images finds pictures from every corner of the Web.

 Windows Live Search has a decent alternative to Google Images at `images.live.com` (which you can use with either Firefox or Internet Explorer). If you can't find the pic you want with Google, try searching Microsoft's collection. You can also drop by Flickr (`www.flickr.com`) to see photos submitted by hundreds of thousands of people.

✔ **News** at `news.google.com` aggregates news reports from 4,500 English-language newspapers, wire agencies, and the like, all over the world. It's completely automated: no human intervention required. That's good and bad. It's good because you get to see a cross section of how the news is being reported in many different places. It's bad because the automatic distiller ain't perfect.

I like searching Google News because it doesn't try to "spin" a topic, and the biases that show through tend to be biases shared by English-speaking people worldwide. You can sign up for news alerts via e-mail or SMS, and there's an RSS feed, so you don't need to search for the news — it can find you.

Almost every major newspaper in the world these days includes a search engine that you can use to find articles. Most are free. Some cost two arms and three legs.

✔ **Newsgroups** at `groups.google.com` combines, indexes, and makes it easy to see the Usenet newsgroup feeds going back many years. See the preceding section, "Posting on the Newsgroups," for details on how to search the newsgroups.

To keep on top of the latest specialized search engines, go to `www.google.com` and click the link More⇨Even More.

Refining Browser Choices

Firefox, straight out of the box, uses Google as its default search engine. It also sticks several search engines that I never use in the drop-down list next to the "G in the box" (see Figure 19-7).

• **Figure 19-7:** Loads of Firefox search engines I never use.

On the other hand, there are several kinds of searches I perform all the time: Google images, news, and groups; I like to search Wikipedia for encyclopedia-style references; and I frequently find myself banging my head against the microsoft.com site, usually looking for Knowledge Base articles.

 It's easy to take Firefox's selection of search engines and mangle them to work the way you work. Just follow these steps:

1. **In Firefox, click the down-wedge to the right of the "G in a box" on the Search bar.**

You see a list similar to the one in Figure 19-7.

2. **Choose Manage Search Engines.**

Firefox shows you the Manage Search Engine List dialog box, shown in Figure 19-8.

3. **Click each search engine that you don't want, one by one, and click Remove.**

Firefox cleans up its act.

4. **Click the link at the bottom that says Get More Search Engines.**

Firefox takes you to a page full of search engine add-ons.

• **Figure 19-8:** Get rid of recalcitrant search engines here.

5. **If you find any additional search engines that strike your fancy, click the appropriate link. When you're ready to get serious, scroll way down the page and click the link that says Browse Through More Search Engines at mycroft.mozdev.org.**

You go to the Sherlock and OpenSearch Search Engine Plugins page, shown in Figure 19-9.

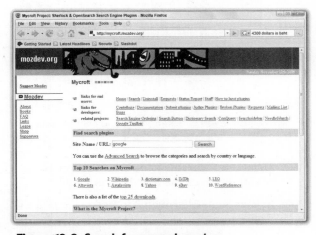

• **Figure 19-9:** Search for a search engine.

Mycroft is an open source project that makes search plug-ins for Firefox. Apple's search engine project was called Sherlock. Mycroft, as I'm sure you know, was Sherlock Holmes's older and decidedly less obsessive brother. Smarter, too, by all accounts. OpenSearch may not sound as hip, but OpenSearch plug-ins work with both Firefox and Internet Explorer.

6. **In the Site Name/URL box, type** `google` **and click Search.**

You should find a list of more than 500 plug-ins for Firefox that use Google, in various ways, to enhance the Firefox Search bar.

7. **Pick each Google-related engine that you want by clicking the link next to the search icon.**

Personally, I use the *A9 Google Images* search tool by Sefan Hittler, *Google Groups* by James Baca, and *Google News by Date* by Daniel S.

When you click a link, Firefox puts up a message box (see Figure 19-10) that asks if you want to add the search engine to the list in the Search bar. The message is a bit confusing because it has a box that says Start Using It Right Away. The box should say something like Make This Your New Default Search Engine.

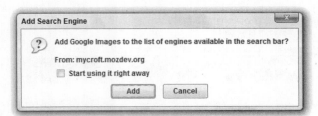

• **Figure 19-10:** If you check the box, you change your default search engine.

8. **To add the search engine to the Search bar's list, don't check the box, but click Add.**

9. **Repeat Steps 6 through 8 to find other search engines.**

For example, I search on `wikipedia` and pick up the *Wikipedia (3rd Party - Google)* engine from Thomas Guignard. (That engine searches Wikipedia but returns results in the

familiar Google style.) I search on `microsoft` and pick up the *Microsoft - KB* engine from John Forrest, which searches the Microsoft Knowledge Base.

10. **If you want to move the search engines around, so your most frequently used engines appear near the top of the list, click the down-arrow next to the "G in the box" and choose Manage Search Engines.**

The Manage Search Engine List dialog box (refer to Figure 19-8) is pretty self-explanatory.

11. **When you have attained search engine nirvana, click OK.**

Firefox goes back to its usual cheery self.

There's an über-search-engine called Dogpile (www.dogpile.com) that combines search results from several engines. I explain how to hook up Dogpile with Firefox in *Windows Vista All-In-One Desk Reference For Dummies*.

Changing search engines in Internet Explorer is easy, too. Click the down-wedge on the right end of the Search bar and choose Find More Providers. You see the Web page in Figure 19-11.

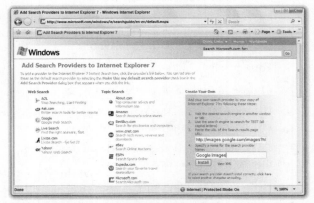

• **Figure 19-11:** Internet Explorer's search engine manager.

Internet Explorer has an interesting approach to rolling your own search engines — you can add just about any search to the drop-down search engine list. Follow the instructions on the page.

Downloading from the Newsgroups

N o doubt you've heard that you can download pirated music, commercial software, and pictures of dubious repute "from the newsgroups." But did you know that you can also download perfectly legal, absolutely genuine files, like live recordings from the Grateful Dead, the Allman Brothers, the Dave Matthews Band, and Blues Traveler? That there are hundreds of thousands of 100-percent legal songs, pictures, movies — freely distributed, public-domain demos, trailers, and much more — on the newsgroups?

If you're tired of the hassles of file-sharing programs and slow Web sites, go back to the future with one of the oldest — and newest — technologies on the Web.

In this Technique, I show you everything you need to know about newsgroups — and give you a discount from my favorite newsgroups company to get you started.

Understanding Newsgroups

Internet newsgroups predate the World Wide Web by an eternity, in Internet years. Heck, newsgroups were around long before e-mail became common. Hard to believe, but true.

In 1980, a group of grad students at Duke University figured out a way to package discussions and send them out all over the world by using a new-fangled communication medium called the Internet. During most of the past few decades, Usenet newsgroups (as they're properly called) carried mind-numbing discussions about bits and bytes, lengthy discourses about the virtues of various kinds of automatic transmissions, cookie recipes, and egomaniacal flames from people who didn't have the slightest idea what they were talking about.

Not much about that part has changed. It's a democratic medium, after all.

The part that's changed? The tools.

Working with newsgroup limitations

Those grad students at Duke were interested in exchanging relatively short text messages. Then, as now, newsgroup messages were severely limited in size: say, 200,000 characters of text (200KB). That's a whole lotta typing, but it isn't much at all if you're digitizing a song or a photo.

A few hardy souls discovered that they could send pictures using the newsgroup mechanism, back in the early days. If you open a picture file in, say, Notepad, and copy the contents of the file into a text message, someone receiving the message could copy the body of the message into a file on their computer, rename it, and open the reconstituted file with a picture viewer like Paint.

 Don't laugh. I did it.

Now consider how the problem scales up in size. Say that a single message can hold 200KB. If you want to send a 400KB picture, you need to use two messages.

The person on the other end has to copy the data from the first message into a new file and the data from the second message onto the end of that same file, save it, and then open it. That's a lot of work.

If you want to send a 2MB picture, the size of a typical electronic camera shot these days, you have to break it into ten messages and send each one. Your correspondent has to retrieve all ten messages and stitch them together into one big file.

If your garage band just put together a 60MB music video, all your adoring fans have to copy and paste 300 messages. I don't even want to think about a 4GB full-length DVD. What? 20,000 messages to show off your trip to the Bahamas?

 In January 2005, Usenet postings, worldwide, hovered around 1,500,000,000,000 characters a day. That's 1.5 terabytes: 1.5 trillion characters. Every *day*. By January 2007, we're looking at 4TB per day — the volume has nearly tripled in two years.

Sounds like a job for a computer, doesn't it?

Spreading messages around

There are more than 100,000 active newsgroups right now. You can start your own, if you like. Google Groups (groups.google.com) makes it relatively painless.

Messages posted on newsgroups get stored on servers all over the world. A newsgroup post raving about the best burgers in Biloxi may end up on servers in Birmingham, Boston, Bridgewater, Berlin, Bogota, and Bhutan. Well, okay . . . Bhutan doesn't have a Usenet server. Yet.

Almost every Internet service provider grants you access to a newsgroup computer connected to Usenet (see the sidebar "What's a Usenet?"). These free newsgroup feeds generally hold only a very tiny fraction of all the newsgroups on the Internet. If you want to see the Microsoft tech support newsgroups, for example, you can probably get into them for free from your ISP. Few people bother anymore.

Why? Google's taken over the market for mainstream text newsgroup postings. Google Groups gives you easy access to a huge number of newsgroups. Google figured out a way to take newsgroup messages and make them available on the World Wide Web. As a result, a very large percentage of the people who post and read text messages nowadays work through Google. There are plenty of complaints about Google and its handling of newsgroups, but it's fast and easy — and it's free.

 I talk about Google Groups in Technique 19.

Mainstream text newsgroups — the kind that Google supports — are only part of the newsgroup picture. There are plenty of offbeat (and off-color) text newsgroups that Google wouldn't touch with a ten-foot pole. And there are tens of thousands of newsgroups that specialize in transferring files — pictures, music, computer programs, Aunt Gertrude's cross-stitch patterns — that don't do Google.

Geeks call the file-bearing newsgroups (and the files they contain) *binaries*. Guess it sounds better than trinaries. Binaries account for more than 90 percent of the volume of data on Usenet.

Legally speaking

Just because something's posted on a newsgroup doesn't mean it's in the public domain. Quite the contrary, in many cases.

 While newsgroups contain enormous quantities of completely legal, legitimate material, they also contain enormous quantities of copyrighted, pirated, and otherwise illegal, immoral, or fattening content.

The Internet's a Wild West kind of place, and Usenet newsgroups sit somewhere on the other side of the OK Corral. On the one hand, Usenet access companies actively discourage the posting and downloading of copyrighted and illegal material. On the other hand, the sheer volume of data posted — 4 trillion characters a day, for heaven's sake — makes it

clearly impossible to monitor what's going up and what's coming down.

More than that, Usenet spans the globe. What may be illegal in Kansas City might be completely legit in Kazakhstan. Or vice versa.

 Downloading a copyrighted album of music and playing it is clearly illegal. Downloading and installing a bootleg copy of Vista is similarly illegal — and probably won't get you anywhere, given all the activation hurdles. Downloading government-created material (such as, oh, photographs of the moon) may be legal, and it may not. If you have any questions about the legality of something you want to download, ask your attorney. Perhaps she has downloaded it already.

For interesting, multifaceted coverage of online copyright issues, see www.benedict.com.

Using Newsgroups

So you understand the repercussions of your actions, and you still want to dive into the binaries newsgroups?

Good.

 In this section, I explain in general how files get broken into smaller chunks so they can be shoehorned into the newsgroups, and how you reassemble the files after you've downloaded them. Then I show you, step by step, how to get connected to the newsgroups, download a file, and bring it back to life.

I demonstrate how to do all of that by using Giganews to access the newsgroups, NewsLeecher to find and download the file, and the free Salami's RarSlave to bring the original file back. Giganews and NewsLeecher have many competitors, but I've used both for quite some time; they're not expensive, and they work well.

Take a look at the last section in this Technique before you order anything.

Breaking up and posting files

About the second or third time you try to reassemble a file by hand, you'll understand why the advent of programs that break apart files and put them back together has made such a difference in the way newsgroups work.

You, personally, aren't going to put a file on a newsgroup anytime soon. But if you want to understand how to put a big file back together, you need to understand how it gets taken apart.

People who put big files on the Internet run programs that usually work like this:

1. **The big file gets fed into the program, which compresses the file.**

You're probably accustomed to zip files as the compressed form of choice, but by far the most common form of compression on the newsgroups is a format called RAR. Don't worry. You don't need to deal with the RAR files directly.

2. **The compression program squeezes the big file down and breaks it into *parts*, typically 15MB in size.**

Why 15MB? Historical reasons, mostly. From time to time, one of the parts goes missing — it doesn't get transferred over Usenet, so you might not be able to download it, or even see it. If the person who posted the file discovers that one of the parts has gone missing, he or she can repost it without a lot of hassle — 15MB isn't too big, and it isn't too small.

3. **After the big file is broken into parts, additional files get added to the front and back.**

At the beginning, the program puts an NZB file, which is like a packing list, detailing all the files that have been generated. At the end there are PAR2 (short for "parity") files that let your computer reassemble the original big file, even if some of the pieces go missing.

 Missing data is still a problem with all the newsgroups. Automatically generated NZB and PAR2 files go a long way toward covering up these nasty little potholes.

4. **All the files are assembled and posted on the newsgroup.**

The names of the files can be confusing at times, but a good poster will identify all the files that are needed to reassemble the original big file by numbering them in sequence (see Figure 20-1). The filenames look something like this:

```
MyFavoriteMovie -[03/79]-
description.part01.rar
MyFavoriteMovie -[04/79]-
description.part02.rar
```

• **Figure 20-1: A list of files on the newsgroups that match the term** `caligari`.

The `[03/79]` means this is the fourth file in a bunch of 80 files that you need to download in order to get everything associated with the big file. (Frequently, the numbers start at zero — for example, the files are numbered `[00/79]` through `[79/79]`.) If one of the 80 `[xx/79]` files is missing, chances are good you won't be able to reassemble the big file.

The `part01`, `part02`, and so on refer to the compressed parts from the original big file. If the poster did her job right, you never have to look at these numbers. Just make sure you get all the files listed in `[xx/yy]` sequence.

On the other hand, if the poster isn't quite up to snuff, you may not see the `[xx/yy]` sequence numbers at all. In that case, you may have to make sure you get all the parts of the file by looking at the `partxx` numbers.

The big file I use as an example in this Technique, *The Cabinet of Dr. Caligari*, runs about 1GB — less than a quarter of the size of a plain-vanilla DVD. *Caligari* comes from a kinder, gentler, less-pixel-intensive and silent age: An hour of HD programming can easily exceed the size of a DVD. The person who posted *Caligari* broke it into parts of 15MB each. With the extra files tacked on the beginning and end, the movie weighs in at 80 parts (numbered [00/79] through [79/79]). Most of those parts take up 64 text "messages" on the newsgroup. So sending *Caligari* through the newsgroup involves a bit under 5,000 individual messages.

Wow.

Of course, you aren't putting any big files on the newsgroups, so you don't have to worry about the mechanics. But you do have to understand where those [xx/yy] numbers come from, and if you're unlucky, you need to understand the partxx numbers, too.

Assembling files

Posting big files on the newsgroups is a pain in the neck. By comparison, downloading and reassembling them isn't difficult at all — if you have the tools.

Here's how the assembly process works:

1. **You find the item you want to download.**

This is the hardest part of the process. If you have a newsgroup search program (see my upcoming discussion of NewsLeecher), you can search for specific terms like caligari or fractal or grateful dead concert tapes.

 Don't know what to search for? There's a list of classic, free (mostly public domain) movies at http://emol.org/movies/freemovies. html. **Good stuff.**

2. **You download all the associated files.**

If you have a newsgroup search program, this usually entails marking all the parts of the big file (by looking at the [xx/yy] numbers) and telling the program to download all the files you've marked.

Downloading can take a minute, a day, or a week. The files end up on your hard drive.

3. **You run a program that reassembles the big file.**

This used to be very difficult, but now it takes just a click.

When the program finishes, you have the big file, assembled and ready to run (see Figure 20-2).

• **Figure 20-2: The Cabinet of Dr. Caligari, to go.**

Connecting to a news server

The Usenet's a huge place. With 4 trillion characters of new data added daily, it's no wonder that most *news servers* — companies that deliver the bits — only try to keep up with a fraction of all the newsgroups. The vast majority of free or low-cost news servers that you might encounter pare down the list of newsgroups that they make available, and older posts on those newsgroups don't hang around very long.

On the other hand, some companies specialize in keeping up with nearly all the Usenet traffic, nearly all the time. You might imagine that they have some serious storage, uh, challenges.

 If you decide that the free news server offered by your Internet service provider doesn't cut the mustard, you should look at five qualities when looking for a new news server:

✔ **Speed:** If your news server can't push the bits out the door, you'll waste enormous amounts of time waiting for the files to arrive. Think Godot in slo-mo.

✔ **Completion:** Newsgroup postings aren't an exact science, and dropped file parts are all too common. A news server's completion rate measures what percentage of the little files that make up big files are actually available at any given moment.

✔ **Retention:** How long does posted data hang around? Good news servers have enough room to store 30 days' worth of binaries (posted files). Great news servers hang onto 90 days' data.

✔ **Reliability:** A news server that isn't serving news is like a politician who isn't politicking. Er. Wait a sec. That isn't exactly what I meant, but . . .

✔ **Censorship:** If your news server doesn't carry the newsgroups you want, you might as well hang it all up and try again.

 I, personally, use Giganews. It's fast. They claim 99%+ completion. Binaries stick around for 90 days or more. They have an amazing up-time record. And they carry 110,000+ newsgroups, including almost everything you can imagine, and most things you can't. They aren't cheap — at this writing, an unlimited download plan costs about $25 per month. Take a look at the sidebar at the end of this chapter for an offer from Giganews that'll reduce the bite a bit.

Giganews has lots of competition. There's a lengthy list of alternatives, including subscribers' evaluations and comments, at www.slyck.com/ng.php?page=2.

Here's how to get yourself set up with newsgroup access through Giganews:

1. **Using your favorite browser, go to www.giganews.com.**

You see a sign-up page like the one in Figure 20-3.

2. **Click the package you'd like to use.**

At least for the first few months, you'll probably want an unlimited use package.

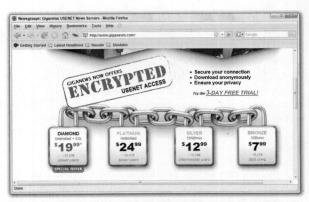

• **Figure 20-3: Sign up for Giganews here. Competitors' sites are similar.**

3. **Complete the forms, fork over your credit card number, and wait.**

Within a few minutes, you will receive an e-mail message with your username, password, and the Web address of the news service's server. Save that message.

 Note, in particular, that there's no specific software you have to download or install. What you need is permission to tap into the news server's computers and the user ID and password that will get you in.

It's really that easy.

Setting up a good news reader

Unlike news services, which tend to sit in the background and either work or don't work, your *news reader* — the program that downloads files and helps you reassemble them — becomes part of your daily routine. That's why it's worth taking some time to look at the major news readers on offer.

Here's what you should consider when choosing a news reader:

✔ **Do you like it?** Seriously. Can you understand how it hangs together? Many news readers are either very simple or laid out so poorly it's hard to figure out where to start.

✔ **Does it handle NZB and PAR2 files automatically?** Many news readers these days do. NZB and PAR2 make reassembling a big file infinitely easier.

✔ **Can it scan for files quickly?** You should be able to type in a wildcard search and get a list of all hits on all newsgroups within a few seconds.

✔ **Can it use multiple bots?** Most news servers let you access their computers with more than one *bot* simultaneously.

 It sounds like bad science fiction, but in this case, a *bot* is an independent download program running on your machine. If you can run five or ten download programs at the same time, you'll speed up your download times significantly.

Personally, I use NewsLeecher and recommend it in spite of its shortcomings. At this writing, NewsLeecher and SuperSearch (the NewsLeecher feature that lets you search for files quickly) run $29.99 a year. If you want to look at alternatives, there's a long list at www.slyck.com/ng.php?page=3.

Here's how to set up NewsLeecher and download your first file:

1. Start your favorite browser and head to www.newsleecher.com.

The NewsLeecher main page appears, as in Figure 20-4.

• **Figure 20-4: Download NewsLeecher here.**

2. Download the free demo version or go ahead and buy the full-fledged version.

3. Follow the instructions to install NewsLeecher.

4. Double-click the NewsLeecher logo on the desktop to start NewsLeecher. Then click the tab marked Manager.

NewsLeecher opens the Manager tab, as in Figure 20-5, which is where connections are managed.

• **Figure 20-5: Connect NewsLeecher to your news server.**

5. Click the Add button.

You see the Server Setup dialog box, shown in Figure 20-6.

6. From your news server notification message (see "Connecting to a news server," earlier in this Technique), type in the server address, the number of connections, your username, and your password. Type a nickname for the server that will be easy for you to remember and then click OK.

You return to the main NewsLeecher window (refer to Figure 20-5).

7. Click the SuperSearch Service tab.

NewsLeecher brings up its search dialog box.

• **Figure 20-6:** Tell NewsLeecher all the details about your news server.

8. In the drop-down Max Days box, choose 90 to tell SuperSearch to ignore files more than 90 days old. In the Search For box, type whatever you'd like to search for. Then click Go.

In Figure 20-7, I searched for `caligari`. The dear old doctor's cabinet is still shaking.

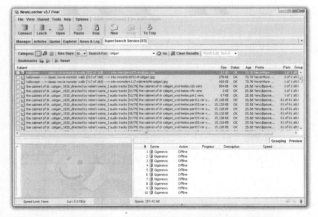

• **Figure 20-7:** Calling Dr. Caligari. Calling Dr. Caligari.

9. Click the first file that you want to download, hold down the Shift key, scroll to the last file in the bunch, and click it. That should select all the files you want to download.

10. Right-click anywhere in the selected group of files and choose Leech➪Leech.

In this case, *The Cabinet of Dr. Caligari* comes in 80 files, numbered [00/79] through [79/79]. I select the bunch, right-click, and tell NewsLeecher to, uh, Leech (Figure 20-8).

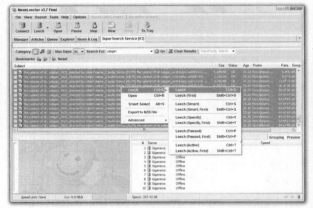

• **Figure 20-8:** Select the files you want to download and then Leech.

 NewsLeecher doesn't start leeching right away. You have to connect to the news server first — a fact that many first-timers puzzle over for a long, long time.

11. In the upper-left corner, click the Connect button.

If you typed in your news server information correctly, the bottom part of NewsLeecher springs to life (Figure 20-9), showing you the progress as your files slowly download.

12. If you're curious, click the Queue tab to see which files are waiting for download, or the Explorer tab to see which files have come down already. If you think there's a problem, click the News & Log tab and look for red entries, which warn you of untoward events.

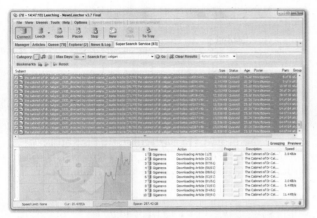

• **Figure 20-9: NewsLeecher shows you detailed progress on your download.**

Eventually, all the files come down, and all the servers (the "bots") report that they are Offline (Connect on Demand), as you can see in Figure 20-10.

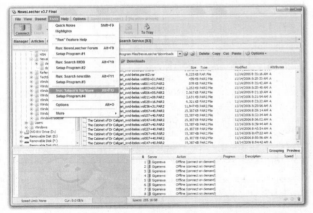

• **Figure 20-10: When the bots report that they are offline, the files have been downloaded.**

13. **Run NewsLeecher's tool to repair any downloaded files that aren't quite right and to reassemble the compressed RAR files.**

This part of NewsLeecher was in a state of flux as this book went to press. If all goes as planned, by the time you read this, NewsLeecher will have a built-in feature called Repair'n'Extract. If you can

find it, run it. If you can't find Repair'n'Extract, choose Tools and run Salami's RarSlave (see Figure 20-10). Either program should repair any broken downloaded files and then reassemble them from their RAR file constituents.

Why do you need to repair the downloaded files? Accept it as a simple fact of life that bits get scrambled on newsgroups. If everything were perfect, you'd never have a messed up file, but with 4 trillion bytes of new data floating around every day, bits get flipped all the time. The PAR2 files that come along for the ride, tacked to the end of most big files, contain redundant information that helps restore files that get scrambled along the long and winding road that leads to your drive.

Repair'n'Extract and RarSlave work similarly. They scan each downloaded file, using internal check numbers to see if the files that you received are exactly the same as the ones that were sent. If there's a discrepancy, either program rummages through the PAR2 files to see if the original file can be restored to its original state. Almost always, the wayward bits can be corrected. When the files are in perfect condition, either Repair'n'Extract or RarSlave will "unzip" the files, re-creating the big file that was originally posted.

RarSlave is a free, independent program that has to be installed separately from NewsLeecher. If you can't find Repair'n'Extract and you click Tools➪Run: Salami's RarSlave, the RarSlave program may run immediately (see Figure 20-11). If nothing happens, you need to download and install RarSlave. The easiest way to do that is to go to `filesplit. org`. They enjoy redesigning this site, but at the time of writing, you just click the RarSlave link on the left (under Menu); then click the Download link, click the You Can Find the Latest Build of RarSlave Here link, and follow the instructions.

Your fully reassembled file appears in NewsLeecher's download folder (refer to Figure 20-2).

• **Figure 20-11:** RarSlave, if you need it, pops up in a command window.

14. **Using Windows Explorer or the NewsLeecher Explorer tab, double-click the reassembled file and enjoy! (See Figure 20-12.)**

• **Figure 20-12:** Doctor Caligari, right on cue.

You may have trouble finding the folder that contains your reassembled big file; if you have any questions, go to the NewsLeecher support site at www.newsleecher.com/?id=support for the latest Vista news.

If you downloaded a movie, you may need to install a *codec* — a file that helps Windows Media Player decipher that particular kind of file — before you can see the movie. (In particular, this rendition of *The Cabinet of Dr. Caligari* requires the XviD codec, which is free and works quite well.) I talk about codecs in Technique 26.

Some wags say I look like Dr. Caligari when I get up in the morning. Bah.

Special offer for Timesaving Techniques readers

In a surprisingly short amount of time, newsgroup access has become a key part of many Windows users' computing life. It's fair to say that I couldn't have written this book without Giganews.

The folks at Giganews have put together a special deal for those who own a copy of *Windows Vista Timesaving Techniques For Dummies*. If you aren't already a subscriber to Giganews, you automatically qualify for a discount on your first month of service. Go to giganews.com/?a=vistatimesavingtechniquesfordummies and choose your preferred package. The Diamond package comes with a $10 discount. If you use that link, you'll receive $8 off the first month of the Platinum package, or $5 off the Silver or Bronze package.

With Giganews' free three-day trial, what do you have to lose?

Technique 21

Instant Messaging with Microsoft and Trillian

Windows Live Messenger. AOL Instant Messenger. Yahoo! Messenger. Even Google Talk and Trillian. I hate 'em. Talk about a time sink. All my friends feel free to just start chatting with me every five minutes. It's worse than having a compulsion to answer your phone every time it rings. You know, before caller ID?

Blech.

Ever wondered about the difference between Windows Live Messenger and MSN Messenger — or the old Windows Messenger in Windows XP? There is a difference. Heck, sometimes some of them won't even talk to each other.

This Technique steps you through the shady history of Windows-based messaging, culminating in the ultimate MIM (that's Microsoft Instant Messenger), Windows Live Messenger. Then I try to help you sort through all the OM (Other Messengers) and help you find TOM (The One Messenger) that's best for you. I step you through installing both Windows Live Messenger and Trillian, give a few pointers about using them, and then — the most important step of all — I show you how to turn the %$#@! things off. Or at least tone them down.

It's a noisy, pushy, cacophonous world.

Saving or Shooting the Messenger?

 Before you dig into this Technique, permit me to save you some time:

✔ If you're absolutely convinced that you don't want to run instant messaging — and believe me, I sympathize — skip this Technique completely. Don't download any messengers. And don't feel guilty.

✔ If you and all your IMing friends use Windows Live Messenger or the latest version of Yahoo! Messenger, and you don't mind being bombarded relentlessly with intrusive, distracting advertising, download and install Live Messenger. I show you how in the section, "Using Windows Live Messenger."

✔ But if any of your friends use Windows Live Messenger, Yahoo! Messenger of any vintage, AOL Instant Messenger (AIM), MSN Messenger, or the ancient Windows XP–based Windows Messenger, try Trillian. See the section, "Using Trillian," later in this chapter.

✔ If you and your IMing friends are willing to try something different — something that'll be around a long time — try a Jabber-speaking messaging system like Google Talk (see the sidebar). (The $25 Trillian Pro talks to Google, too.)

✔ If you decide to run Windows Live Messenger, use the advice in this Technique to minimize your exposure to spam, messenger-based attacks, and simple intrusions on your privacy. You'll be glad you did.

As of this writing, if you run Windows Live Messenger, you can converse only with other people who are running Windows Live Messenger, the latest version of Yahoo! Messenger, or Trillian. Some people have good reason to stick with Windows Live Messenger — some companies, for example, take advantage of specific Windows Live Messenger features. But the vast unwashed masses, present company included, prefer a polyglot instant messenger such as Trillian, even if Trillian doesn't have a "feature" that makes the screen shake. Oy.

Choosing a Messenger

If you or your messaging buddies are stuck in the MSN Messenger or Yahoo! Messenger mold, Windows Live Messenger is your only choice.

I wouldn't recommend Yahoo! Messenger to anyone. Why? Yahoo! has this infuriating habit of sticking other things in with the Yahoo! Messenger installer. Trying to get Yahoo! Messenger put on a machine without hauling in a ton of garbage is like trying to dry-dock the QE II without dragging along any seaweed. No thank you.

By comparison, Windows Live Messenger isn't a bed of roses. At its most irritating level, this version of MSN Messenger, er, Windows Live Messenger, is just like the last one, only moreso. Every nook and cranny is filled with advertising and come-ons. You can pay to join `Match.com`. You can buy music at Rhapsody. You can "find great deals on eBay." You can "get the latest scoop on Xbox and Xbox Live Gaming" or learn about your credit score or find a job or post a resumé or . . . Golly. How thoughtful.

Although Windows Live Messenger has a few neat capabilities, in the final analysis, I think that "open" networks such as Jabber (via Google Talk) and polyglot systems (such as Trillian) will win, sooner or later.

Maybe Microsoft and Yahoo! can come up with compelling reasons for people to sign on for their advertising-laden proprietary services. I certainly haven't seen anything that would convince me.

The triumph of the open network

Google Talk (`talk.google.com`) employs a variant of the almost-sorta-open Jabber network protocol. At least in theory, any company can build a Jabber-compliant Messenger and have it hook into the Jabber network without any problems. It's kind of like what Microsoft tried to do with AOL Instant Messenger, many years ago.

Nowadays, there's a lot of money being made with IM. Until recently, the IM software manufacturers guarded their turf jealously and heatedly, without the slightest concern for their customers being able to communicate. Quite the contrary now. The fact that Microsoft and Yahoo! found middle ground and started (literally and figuratively) talking to each other shows that there's some sanity returning to the market. And more money to be made.

Perhaps Microsoft/Yahoo! will end up dominating the IM market and shut out everyone else, but I rather doubt it. IM users are a fickle lot. As soon as they find a way to talk to everybody, all the time, they'll shun Microsoft and Yahoo! and their closed network. I hope.

Using Windows Live Messenger

So you've decided to give Windows Live Messenger a whirl. Fair enough.

It isn't hard to get started. And if you take a few minutes now and do it right, you can save yourself a bunch of time down the line.

Messaging in a Microsoft World

Over the past decade, Microsoft has used the names "MSN Messenger," "Windows Messenger" (presumably Windows Dead Messenger), ".NET Messenger," and now "Windows Live Messenger," all applied to essentially the same product, its derivatives, and its plumbing. You're to be forgiven if you don't get the names straight.

In the beginning . . .

The original MSN Messenger (also called, confusingly, "MSN") first appeared in July 1999. Microsoft designed it to be fully compatible with AOL Instant Messenger, so MSN Messenger users could talk to AIM users, and vice versa. For a few weeks, all the Microsoft and AOL Messaging world came together. AOL had a cow, changed a few bits, and knocked MSN off the AOL network. Lawsuits ensued. When the lawyers got through with the wrangling, AOL had its network, Microsoft had a different one, and Yahoo! had another. Later, Google Talk came out with Jabber, an (arguably) open network. Trillian talked to all of them, to a greater or lesser extent.

Then Microsoft started playing footsie with Yahoo!, and both Microsoft and Yahoo! released products that talk to each other. (Even though the latest versions may have trouble talking to earlier versions of their own programs.) Google bought part of AOL. Trillian got knocked out of a couple of

networks, but has been fighting valiantly to get back into the ring.

What a mess.

And in the end . . .

Microsoft doesn't even ship a messaging product with Vista. Why? Messengers change too quickly. The first Windows Live Messenger, version 8.0.0787, appeared on July 22, 2006. Two days later, we got version 8.0.0792. Three and a half months after that, WLM was up to version 8.1, and there were at least a dozen minor version changes in between. If Microsoft put a Messenger in the box — which is to say, in the shrink-wrapped Vista box — it'd be obsolete before anyone bought the box, much less took it home.

That's why Microsoft gives you many, uh, *opportunities* to "Go online to connect and share," as you may have noted in the Vista Welcome Center (see Figure 21-1).

• **Figure 21-1: The Welcome Center really wants you to download more Microsoft products.**

Click the Welcome Center link, and you end up on Microsoft's Live site (Figure 21-2), with an offer to sign up for Windows Live Mail (see Technique 22) or Windows Live Spaces (for an alternative, try `Blogger.com`), or to download and install Windows Live Messenger.

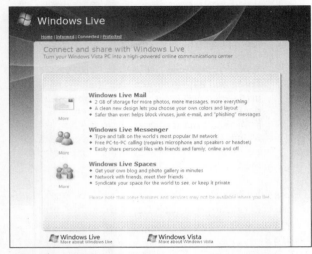

• **Figure 21-2: Three Windows Live products share the limelight.**

Installing WLM

First, download and install Windows Live Messenger:

1. **Start your favorite browser and go to** `http://messenger.live.com`.

Or, if you like, you can click the invitation in the Vista Welcome Center and then click the Windows Live Messenger More link in Figure 21-2.

2. **Click the button marked Get It Free. Download the installer file and run it.**

The Windows Live Messenger Setup Wizard appears.

3. **Click Next. Click to Accept the terms of use.**

The installer asks about settings, as in Figure 21-3.

4. **Choose your "additional features and settings" wisely. (See Table 21-1 for timesaving tips.) Then click Next.**

You have to click through a User Account Control box, but in the end, Windows Live Messenger appears on your desktop.

5. **When the wizard shows you its final pane, click Close.**

The installer may continue. Don't be alarmed.

• **Figure 21-3: Be careful what you ask for — you just might get it.**

6. **Don't log in yet. Click the small down-wedge to the left of the "_" minimize icon and then choose Tools⇨Options (see Figure 21-4).**

WLM brings up the Options dialog box.

7. **On the left, click General.**

You see the General Options dialog box, shown in Figure 21-5.

8. **Uncheck as many boxes as you can and click OK.**

That keeps WLM out of your face as much as possible, for now.

9. **Don't log in yet. See the next section for details.**

TABLE 21-1: A WINDOWS LIVE MESSENGER SETUP TRANSLATOR

What It Says	Timesaving Tip	What It Means
Windows Live Messenger Shortcuts	Check	You can easily delete the Messenger shortcuts you don't use.
Windows Live Sign-In Assistant	Uncheck	As of this writing, the Live Sign-In Assistant, which is supposed to help you juggle multiple Windows Live IDs, isn't working very well. Maybe later.
MSN Home	Uncheck	What, you *want* to make msn.com your home page? Sheesh. See Technique 18.
Windows Live Toolbar	Uncheck	You already have a Search bar. You don't need another advertising opportunity from Microsoft.
Rhapsody Music Service	Uncheck	As part of an anti-trust settlement, Microsoft gets a bounty for every sucker they can sign up for Rhapsody. You gotta be kidding.

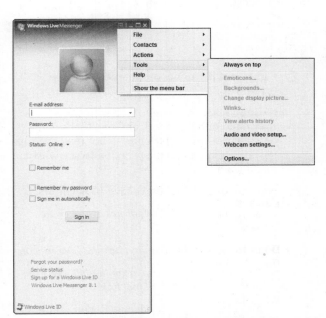

• **Figure 21-4:** The WLM menu appears under a tiny downward-pointing wedge in the upper-right corner.

• **Figure 21-5:** Uncheck boxes to keep WLM from making a pest of itself.

Getting the skinny on user IDs

If you plan well, you can minimize Messenger's intrusiveness — and save yourself tons of time down the road. The trick lies in acquiring multiple free user IDs, passing out those IDs to the right people, and logging on with the correct ID at the right time.

 The best moment to put the plan into action is right now, before you log on to Windows Live Messenger for the first time.

To save time, I recommend using more than one user ID for all your messaging needs. For example, I have three IDs that I use exclusively for Messenger,

Hotmail (er, Windows Live Mail), and all the other Microsoft Passport–rigged (er, Windows Live ID–rigged) applications. Here's a list of user ID–related things you can do to keep meaningless messaging to a minimum:

- **Choose a user ID for fun time:** Ideally, this ID is one that you don't mind sharing with the rest of the world. For example, I don't mind sharing with you, dear reader, that my fun-time ID is AskWoody@hotmail.com. I use it on alternate Wednesday mornings between 3:00 and 3:15, which are my allotted fun-time hours. Everybody knows about that ID. Now you do, too.

- **Choose a user ID for travel time:** Don't broadcast this ID. For example, try something like WoodyOnTheRoad@hotmail.com to minimize the amount of e-mail traffic coming in. Only a few people have the ID that I really use for this purpose. I encourage them to use it when they want to send e-mail to me or to chat with me when I'm on the road.

- **Choose a user ID for first-tier friends:** From SomeOtherID@hotmail.com to NoneofYourBeeswax@hotmail.com, this user ID is the one you hand out only to immediate family, close friends, and any essential work colleagues. That's the ID you use when you want to get some work done. No, you can't have it.

You might've noticed that I don't use my regular e-mail address, woody@AskWoody.com, for Windows Live Messenger. I have many reasons why, but the fundamental sticking point is that I refuse to let my real IDs be assimilated by The Borg . . . er, I refuse to put my real IDs in the Passport database.

Making Messenger forget your password

Have you already told Windows Live Messenger to sign you in automatically? Now that you understand how to use multiple accounts with Messenger, do you regret that choice?

Yeah. I know what you mean. Been there. Done that. Got the scars — or the arrows in the back.

If you have a Messenger ID that's set to sign in automatically, you can switch it back to manual: Choose Start⇨ Control Panel⇨User Accounts and Family Safety⇨User Accounts. In the upper-left corner, click Manage Your Network Passwords. Click the account that you want to return to manual control and click Remove.

Setting up your Messenger account

It's none of Microsoft's business what IDs you use. If you need a Passport to run Messenger — or to participate in Office 2007 collaboration, or open a locked Office document, or use any other piece of Microsoft software that you've already bought and paid for — I say use one of Bill's free IDs, thank you very much.

Here's how:

1. Figure out if you need one, two, or three (or more) IDs.

Most people can do quite well with two — one they hand out in general, and one that's given to only a close circle of friends — but read the suggestions in the preceding section to see why you might want three.

2. Sign up for free Windows Live ID accounts.

a. *Start your favorite Web browser and go to* www.live.com.

b. *In the upper-right corner, click the Sign In icon.*

c. *On the Sign In page, over on the left, click the Sign Up for Windows Live! link.*

You see the Do You Have an E-mail Address page shown in Figure 21-6. Things may get confusing until you realize that Windows Live ID, Passport account, MSN ID, MSN Hotmail ID, MSN Hotmail e-mail address, MSN Messenger account, Hotmail address, Windows Live Mail ID, and Microsoft ID *are all the same thing.* Besides, you probably don't want to use any of your existing accounts. Might as well start with a clean IM slate.

• **Figure 21-6:** Sign up for new, free Hotmail e-mail addresses.

3. Choose No, Sign Me Up for a Free MSN Hotmail E-mail Address (or Windows Live Mail E-mail Address or Windows Live ID or whatever the box says this week) and click Continue.

Microsoft's `Passport.net` site steps you through the process of creating a new address.

4. Type as little information as possible.

Alternatively, you *could* sign up as William Gates III, One Microsoft Way, Redmond, WA 98052, born October 28, 1955 — but don't be too surprised if the Web site just ignores what you've entered.

5. Be sure to click the Check Availability button to make sure you get a Hotmail address that hasn't been used.

In Figure 21-7, Duangkhae verified that the address `DuangkhaeT@hotmail.com` is still available.

6. Make sure you read the entire terms of service agreement and click I Accept.

Hint: It's only slightly longer and a little more complex than the instructions for Form 1040.

If everything worked okay, you get a message that says your account is ready to go.

7. Repeat Steps 2 through 6 for each new account that you need.

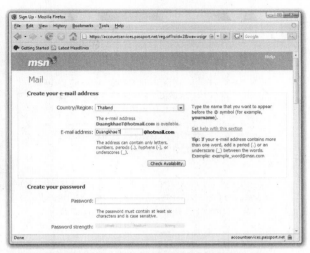

• **Figure 21-7:** Choose a name that hasn't been used before. Good luck.

 You have to log on to Hotmail (er, Windows Live Mail) or Windows Live Messenger at least once shortly after you create the IDs, and then once a month thereafter, to keep the IDs alive.

8. Start Messenger.

You can do that by choosing Start⇨All Programs⇨Windows Live Messenger or by double-clicking the bubble boy icon in the notification area (near the clock). If you just finished the steps in the preceding section, Windows Live Messenger is already on-screen.

9. Fill in the Passport sign-in box with your "give it to anybody" Messenger ID and your password, select the check boxes for features you want to use, and click Sign In.

You have to be careful with how much control you turn over to WLM. Here are a few guidelines:

▶ If you're using a computer in a public place, don't check any of the boxes.

▶ If you're at home or in a relatively secure office, check the Remember Me box and think about checking the Remember My Password box (see below).

▶ Do *not* check the Sign Me In Automatically box.

If you check the Remember My Password box, anybody who can get onto your computer can start a Windows Live Messenger session and pretend to be you. If your computer's located in a room that's reasonably secure, or if you have a password on your Vista account, checking the box makes it easier to use Vista, but it isn't terribly secure. If you don't have a password on your Vista user account, think twice — three times — before you check this box.

You don't want WLM to sign you in automatically because you want to make it easy to use different IDs, depending on how busy you are.

10. **Click the Sign In box.**

The Windows Live Messenger main window and welcome wagon . . . er, welcome window appear, as in Figure 21-8.

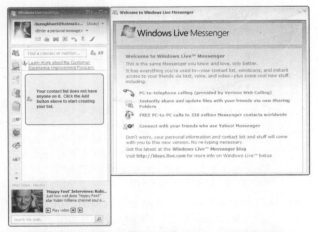

• **Figure 21-8: WLM's main window. Avoid the temptation to spend all your money immediately, okay?**

11. **Immediately click your e-mail address in the upper-left corner and choose Options.**

I guess you could click Create a Dynamic Display Picture and spend money with some of Microsoft's "partners," creating a cute display picture that you'll share with a million other people. But Options is a more, uh, staid course.

WLM shows you its Personal Options dialog box, as in Figure 21-9.

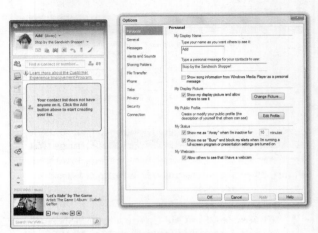

• **Figure 21-9: Adjust the information for all to see.**

WLM gives you many options. Figure 21-9 shows you how Duangkhae decided to present her persona to the public.

12. **Customize your personal settings to your heart's content.**

▶ Fill out the name and message boxes.

▶ Click Change Picture and pick your favorite pic (oh, golly gee, there's that chance to spend more money on cute display pictures again!).

▶ If you want to put your personal information in Microsoft's giant database (or you want to goof around a bit), click Edit Profile and show Microsoft what a character you are. Bonus points for originality.

13. **When you're done, click the General line at the left.**

WLM shows you the General tab. Er, line. Uh, box. Whatever.

14. **Adjust the General Options until you're happy with them (refer to Figure 21-5).**

Some people can't get off the phone. Some people always run Windows Live Messenger when Vista starts. Same-same. The Windows Live Today box is, to a first approximation, yet another attempt to shanghai your browser start page — except if you check this box, you get Windows Live Today as a pop-up. The Quality Improvement Program gives Microsoft permission to keep track of what you do on the Internet. And so on.

Windows Live Messenger has a potful of useful settings — and a whole bunch of settings that can eat into your time. Figure 21-5 shows you Duangkhae's suggestions for saving time and keeping your sanity (though she selected Show Display Pictures from Others, too) — but still using Messenger when you absolutely have to.

15. **Click the line marked Privacy on the left.**

WLM brings up the Privacy dialog box, shown in Figure 21-10. Think of the Privacy dialog box as a "cloaking device" — you can tell WLM who should be able to see you, and under what circumstances.

• **Figure 21-10: Relaxed privacy settings *only* for your "give it to anybody" Messenger ID.**

 16a. **If you're using your "give it to anybody" Messenger ID, in the Privacy dialog box, click the button marked Allow.**

That moves "All Others" onto the Allow List.

16b. **If you're using any other Messenger ID, make sure that the box marked Only People on My Allow List Can See My Status and Send Me Messages is checked.**

If you follow this advice, anyone who has your "give it to anybody" Messenger ID can see when you're online. That's good. But if you only allow contact with your Allow List for your other Messenger IDs, you can pick and choose specifically who can see you when you're logged on with one of your less promiscuous IDs.

17. **Click OK.**

You return to the WLM main window.

 At this point, if you have the IDs of your friends who are Messenger-enabled with either Windows Live Messenger or the latest Yahoo! Messenger, you're ready to start adding contacts.

Adding contacts

Contacts are people you can contact readily: Messenger knows about them, notifies you when they're signed in to Messenger, and lets you start a conversation with them by simply double-clicking their names.

The Contacts list is not restrictive; anybody on the Contacts list who has your Messenger ID can start a conversation with you when you're online (unless you specifically block them — refer to Step 15 in the preceding section).

Messenger contacts aren't the same as Outlook or Windows Mail or Windows Live Mail (Hotmail) contacts. They're completely separate entities, although from time to time you're given the opportunity to merge the lists.

After you've followed the steps in the preceding section to get Windows Live Messenger going, you should set up your Contacts list. Here's how:

1. **In Windows Live Messenger, to the right of the box that says Find a Contact or Number, click the Bubble Boy with a Plus Sign icon (patent pending).**

    The Add a Contact Wizard appears. See Figure 21-11.

• **Figure 21-11: Add BillG to your Contacts list.**

2. **Fill in information about the contact. You need either an IM address or a mobile phone number — everything else is optional.**

    If you check the box marked Subscribe to Updates for This Contact, whenever the contact changes information in his or her contact card, that change gets reflected in your contact information.

    You can also put text in the Personal Invitation text box to make the invitation in the next step a little less, uh, impersonal.

3. **Click Add Contact.**

 When you click Add Contact, Windows Live Messenger sends a message to your new contact using the text that you typed in the Personal Invitation text box as a message. Your new contact can either accept or reject you. Summarily. And there's nothing you can do about it.

4. **Repeat Steps 1 through 3 for all the people you want to put in your Contacts list (see Figure 21-12).**

    Remember that these people will generally be able to bug you any time they want.

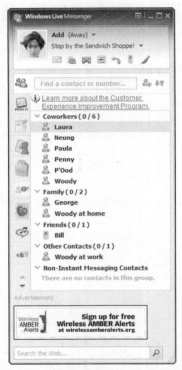

• **Figure 21-12: Duangkhae's short 'n' sweet Contacts list.**

As soon as you've set up your "give it to anybody" Messenger ID, choose File⇨Sign Out on the main WLM pane (use the tiny down-wedge in the upper-right corner) and then repeat Steps 1 through 4 for each of your tightly held IDs.

Making contact

When one of your contacts logs on, the contact's "bubble boy" icon turns green. To initiate a conversation with the person, double-click his or her name in the Messenger main window, and a Conversation dialog box appears.

Then you can pick up on the conversation:

1. **Just type.**

    Whatever you type appears in the box at the bottom of the Conversation dialog box.

    You can edit what you've typed by clicking and pressing the usual keys: arrows, Delete, and so on. You also can cut, copy, and paste text down in the box at the bottom of the dialog box.

2. **When you're ready to send what you've typed, press Enter or click the Send button.**

3. **To put a cute smiley face in your message, type** :) **or** :D. **Better, try** (A) **for an angel,** (6) **for a devil,** (b) **for a mug of beer, or** :[**for a very cool bat. If you must, click the Emoticons button and choose from a bunch of icons or winks. (See Figure 21-13.)**

    Golly gee, you can even go online and buy *more* emoticons and winks.

4. **When you're done with the conversation, click the "X" button to leave the Conversation dialog box.**

    Messenger returns you to the Messenger main window.

5. **If you don't want to allow anyone to contact you, click the down arrow next to your name and choose Appear Offline.**

    One guess how often I do *that*.

The first time you close a Conversation dialog box, WLM gives you the option of keeping transcripts of all your conversations (see Figure 21-14). If you ever want to change your mind — either start keeping

records, or stop keeping them — on the main Messenger pane, click the little down-wedge in the upper-right corner, choose Tools⇨Options, and click the Messages line on the left.

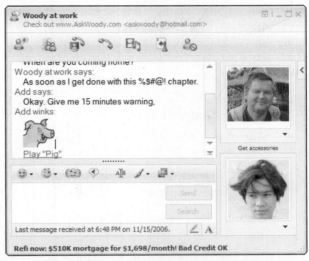

• **Figure 21-13:** The text, the pictures, the emoticons, the winks . . . they're all right here.

• **Figure 21-14:** To save or not to save? It depends on your circumstances.

Messenger records are usually kept in `c:\Users\<username>\Documents\My Received Files`.

Using the fancier features

After you establish a conversation, you may have some success with Windows Live Messenger's more advanced features. These icons appear at the top of the Conversation window (refer to Figure 21-13):

✔ **Invite:** Click here to invite other contacts to join the current conversation.

✔ **Share files:** Click the second icon and WLM opens a Sharing Folders window like the one in Figure 21-15. Figure out which folder should hold the files that you want to share with the contact and then start copying files into the contact's folder.

• **Figure 21-15:** Create a folder for each contact that you want to share with and then drag files into the folder.

✔ **Start or Stop a Video Call:** Both you and your correspondent have to be using WLM to initiate a video call. Run through the brief setup routine and then click Start Camera. You see a notification that a request has been sent. If your correspondent accepts the notification, and you both have cameras, you can see her and she can see you.

✔ **Call a Contact:** Either by computer (free; similar to Skype) or by phone (thanks to Verizon; extra-cost option).

✔ **Share Fun Activities:** And expect to pay for them.

✔ **Games:** Takes you to MSN Games. They're not the most, uh, challenging games around, but they're moderately amusing. And, golly, you have lots of opportunities to buy more things from Microsoft.

✔ **Block this Contact:** Turns things off, right away.

Using Trillian

Does Microsoft's incessant advertising — emblazoned in every nook and cranny of Windows Live Messenger — get to you?

 Yeah, me too.

If you gotta have Windows Live Messenger, you gotta have it. But if you have just a little bit of say-so in your instant messaging pursuits, you owe it to yourself to try Trillian.

Trillian Basic is free for the downloading — and it sports no ads, no spyware, no scum. And it won't pester you to death with ads for Microsoft products. Trillian Pro sets you back $25. The Pro version talks to Google Talk, and it includes major upgrades and full technical support by e-mail for a year.

Weighing Trillian against the competition

Trillian boasts four major advantages over Windows Live Messenger:

- ✔ Most of the time, it communicates with anyone who uses Windows Live Messenger, Windows Messenger (you know, the old, Dead Messenger), MSN Messenger, AOL Instant Messenger, or Yahoo! Messenger. It also works with ICQ and IRC (bonus points if you have ever heard of those pioneering instant messaging programs). The extra-cost Trillian Pro also speaks Google Talk. With Trillian, no matter which IM network you're using, you set things up once, you learn one way of doing things, and Trillian does all the heavy lifting.

- ✔ Trillian doesn't constantly bug you about signing on, or signing up, for anything. The Trillian folks aren't trying to accumulate the world's largest user database.

- ✔ It doesn't slam nonstop obnoxious advertising in your face. The makers of Trillian don't have other products to sell you.

- ✔ And, most of all, it ain't Microsoft.

Installing Trillian

Downloading Trillian is like falling off a log:

1. **Crank up your favorite Web browser and head to www.ceruleanstudios.com.**

2. **Download Trillian Basic.**

   Trillian Basic is the free version.

3. **Double-click the downloaded file to run the installer.**

   Take the defaults. Installation goes very quickly.

4. **When the installer finishes, click Launch. If you're using the free version, click the Trillian Basic button.**

5. **Go through the First Time Wizard, pick a screen name and icon, and let the wizard finish.**

   Trillian downloads the files it needs, looks for and installs patches, and presents itself to you, ready for business (see Figure 21-16).

Using Trillian

If you just finished installing Trillian, using the steps in the preceding section, it's ready to rumble. If you are coming back to your computer, double-click the two-headed Trillian icon on your desktop and stand back.

• **Figure 21-16:** Trillian Basic, ready to go.

Your first step on the road to Trillian enlightenment involves setting up your Connections — the IDs that you want to use for each IM network. To do so:

1. **Choose Trillian⇨Connections⇨Manage My Connections.**

Trillian brings up the Identities & Connections dialog box, shown in Figure 21-17.

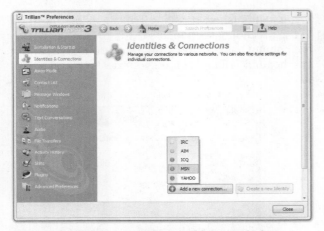

• **Figure 21-17: Set up your messaging networks here.**

2. **Click the button marked Add a New Connection and choose your first IM network.**

In Figure 21-17, I chose MSN.

Trillian has you fill in your MSN Passport (a.k.a. Windows Live ID, Hotmail account, and so on — they're all the same thing), as in Figure 21-18.

3. **Fill in your Windows Live ID and password and then click Connect.**

 If Trillian has trouble connecting to your chosen network, you see a notification in the lower-right corner of the screen. Click the notification to retry the connection.

4. **Click Close.**

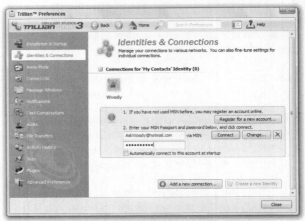

• **Figure 21-18: Enter your logon ID and password.**

Trillian probably picked up your Contacts list, per Figure 21-19.

• **Figure 21-19: Trillian is smart enough to grab any Contacts list you may have waiting online.**

Trillian can connect to only one messaging network at a time. You can tell which network you're connected to by the colored dot just below your name. In Figure 21-19, although it's hard to see, the fourth dot glows. The fourth dot represents the MSN/Windows Live network.

You can right-click a dot and choose Show Status Window for Trillian to display a blow-by-blow account of all the connection activities.

To connect to a contact, simply double-click the contact's name. Your conversation proceeds much like it does with Windows Live Messenger — without the ads, without the stupid come-ons, without the click-click-click that leaves you in a position where you have to spend more money or give up on your pursuit. In Figure 21-20, I carry on a complete conversation with Duangkhae, who's stuck using Windows Live Messenger.

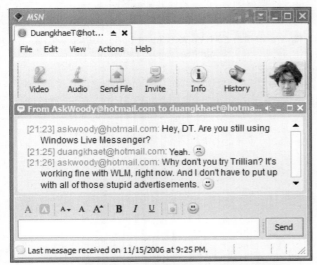

• **Figure 21-20: Duangkhae logged off and immediately installed Trillian.**

If Trillian didn't get all your contacts, or you want to add some more, it's easy:

1. **Choose Trillian⇨Add Contact or Group.**

Trillian starts the Contact Wizard.

2. **Make sure the Add Contacts or Groups button is selected and click Next.**

Trillian brings up the group and medium list shown in Figure 21-21.

• **Figure 21-21: Each contact is assigned to a Contact list, a Group within the list, and a "Medium" — the Messaging network.**

3. Unless you plan on adding large numbers of contacts, keep the Destination list on the left simple by not touching anything. On the right, choose the IM network for your first contact. Click Add.

Trillian invites you to type in the Messaging name of your next contact (Figure 21-22).

4. Repeat Step 3 for all your contacts. When you're done, click Done.

Trillian comes back with all your contacts.

 Try Trillian for a while. Bet you'll like it. Don't forget the long list of additional features available if you decide to upgrade to the full Trillian Pro: separate Buddy lists for each IM network; groups of Buddies; autocorrect spell checking; tabbed chat windows; more and better skins. A most impressive product.

• **Figure 21-22:** Each contact must be identified with a single Messaging network.

22 Technique

Using Windows Live Mail Desktop — Or Not

Save Time By

✔ Choosing a good e-mail program

✔ Installing and Using Windows Live Desktop Mail

✔ Windows Mail — a last resort

As we went to press, Windows Live Mail Desktop was a bloated, buggy, snarly, half-fast application that took unwanted and unwarranted liberties with your system (such as enabling Microsoft Update without asking) and didn't work worth two hoots an' a holler.

 By the time you read this, Windows Live Mail Desktop may have settled down a bit, but it's definitely a version 1.0 product. Beware.

If you bought a computer with Windows Vista and Microsoft Office 2007 Home & Student Edition pre-installed, you're stuck between a rock and a hard place. As you've undoubtedly discovered, Office 2007 Home & Student doesn't include Office's venerable Outlook e-mail program. That means you're left to wander in the e-mail wilderness, looking for a decent e-mail application. (The geeks call such programs e-mail *clients* for reasons that still evade me.)

Even if you have one of the better-endowed Office 2007 editions, you may decide that Office Outlook is just too much — too big, too slow, too hard to figure out, and way too hard to take with you when you travel.

The e-mail world abounds with choices, most of which don't come from Microsoft. This Technique takes you through your e-mailing options and helps you pick the right one. If you end up with Windows Live Mail Desktop, or even Windows Mail, this Technique points out the minefields so you can get up and limping quickly.

Counting Microsoft's E-Mail Programs

Last time I looked, Microsoft offered four completely *different* e-mail programs:

✔ **Outlook,** the program in Microsoft Office, stands out as the granddaddy of e-mail programs. It's enormous. It's convoluted. It's expensive. Its pieces don't hang together very well. It doesn't travel well unless you have a corporate VPN (Virtual Private Network). But most of the corporate world, and many normal folks (including yours truly), depend on it every day. There are hundreds of versions of Outlook used by hundreds of millions of people every day.

✔ **Windows Mail** is a very slightly warmed-over version of Windows XP's Outlook Express, with two new features of note: junk mail filtering (which works surprisingly well) and an antiphishing filter (which is kind of tacked onto the junk mail filter). Windows Mail also has automatic indexing and fast searching, but those are inherited from Vista itself.

 Outlook Express, uh, Windows Mail, hasn't changed much in the past ten years. Why? Microsoft doesn't make any money from it — no advertising spaces to sell, no buy-this-buy-that links. It's legacy software in the most pejorative sense of the term, and it's been slowly dying on the vine for a decade. Microsoft would much rather have you buy a copy of Outlook or sign up for Windows Live Mail or Windows Live Mail Desktop, which offer money-making links at every turn. Hard, cold fact of life.

✔ **Windows Live Mail,** formerly Hotmail, once owned the online e-mail market. Every few months, Microsoft comes out with a facelift (or, more recently, a name change), each time promising that the new, improved Hotmail — er, Windows Live Mail — works "just like Outlook!"

In fact, Windows Live Mail doesn't work anything at all like Outlook. It can't. Windows Live Mail stores all your messages on Microsoft's giant servers — none of it ever comes down to your desktop unless you use a separate program to reach into Windows Live Mail and pull mail down to your computer. Which brings me to . . .

✔ **Windows Live Mail Desktop** connects to Windows Live Mail and many other mail sources, including traditional Internet e-mail computers (so-called *POP3 servers*) and the other big-name online mail services, like AOL Mail, Yahoo! Mail, and Google's Gmail. Windows Live Mail Desktop pulls mail down and stores it on your computer. It also includes a bunch of features that you may

never use, such as RSS feeds (which are much easier to handle in Firefox, per Technique 18, or with the Vista Sidebar gadget).

None of those four programs bears even a slight resemblance to the other three. And when you go on beyond Microsoft, a great big world of e-mail awaits.

Choosing an E-Mail Program

With so many choices, what's a Windows wonk to do?

When you choose your own e-mail program, keep these points in mind:

✔ If you don't want to carry your mail with you, use one of the many Web-based e-mail services. Internet access is cheap, easy, and generally reliable all over the world. Recently, Google's **Gmail** (mail.google.com), and **Yahoo! Mail** (mail.yahoo.com) have garnered the best reviews. **Hotmail** (er, **Windows Live Mail**, www.hotmail.com or mail.live.com) and, perhaps surprisingly, **AOL Mail** (discover.aol.com) cover all the bases. It seems like the feature set and promotions change every week, so check each Web site to see what's best for you.

 Don't like the incessant advertising that inexorably comes with those products? Take a look at **Fastmail** (fastmail.fm), a very inexpensive but sometimes overworked (status.fastmail.fm) e-mail program that's staying afloat in an advertising-laden sea.

✔ If you've been using Outlook Express in Windows XP, and you need to import a bunch of old messages, and you don't particularly want to learn anything new, **Windows Mail** is for you. See "Mauling Windows Mail," later in this chapter, for a few pointers.

On the other hand, if you're ready to get out of the OE/Windows Mail rut, many decent desktop alternatives exist.

✔ In my experience, people who rely on e-mail, and who want to keep their mail on their own computer, ultimately gravitate to **Outlook.** I know that's a heretical observation, but it's true. Outlook 2003 and 2007 combine excellent spam filtering and so-so antiphishing technology with the kind of industrial strength that many e-mail addicts need. It's also surprisingly easy to use — at least, the common e-mail actions are easy to find and run. The big downside? Outlook's expensive.

 If you decide you want Outlook, keep several points in mind. Many companies get licenses for Outlook that come along for the ride when they buy Microsoft's Exchange Server; your company may have a license for Outlook that's already been paid for, and you may be able to finagle a copy for your personal use. If you have to buy a copy of Outlook, read up on the differences between Outlook 2003 and Outlook 2007. You may find that Outlook 2003 has everything you need, for a fraction of the 2007 price.

✔ Want to store mail on your own computer, but don't want to shell out the (considerable!) bucks for Outlook? Follow the steps in this chapter to install Windows Live Mail Desktop. In spite of its snarly origins, you may find that it rings your chimes, and new versions will likely appear at very frequent intervals. "Live" products work on very short development cycles. Hey, it can only get better, right?

Many Windows Live Mail Desktop options parallel those for Windows Mail. Take a look at their respective options dialog boxes side by side, and you will find that the major difference is that Windows Mail uses 9-point Arial for composed messages, whereas Windows Live Mail Desktop uses 10-point Verdana.

Okay, I'm joking a bit. But only a bit.

 If you decide to use Windows Live Desktop Mail, make sure you go through the timesaving tips in the "Mauling Windows Mail" section of this Technique, too. Many of the tips that apply to the old, boring Windows Mail also apply to the new, snazzy (and almost barely functional) Windows Live Mail Desktop.

Starting Windows Live Mail Desktop

Here's a walkthrough of the installation and use of a late beta test version of Windows Live Mail Desktop. The final should be very similar:

1. **Locate and download Windows Live Mail Desktop.**

   The home base of Windows Live Mail Desktop will change, but for now, start at `http://ideas.live.com` and click through to download.

2. **Run the installation file.**

   It's probably called `Install_WLMail.exe`.

   The installer runs a setup wizard.

3. **Click Next, taking all the defaults, until you get to the Windows Live ID window (see Figure 22-1).**

4. **Enter a valid Windows Live ID (also known as a Hotmail account, a Passport ID, an MSN ID, and myriad other names).**

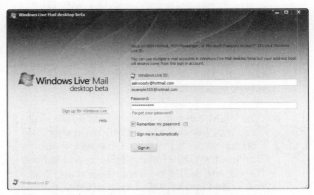

• Figure 22-1: Give WLMD a Windows Live ID to use when it starts.

WLMD uses the Windows Live ID that you provide to store your address book, contacts, and the like. If you have a Hotmail, er, Windows Live Mail account set up with this ID, WLMD is smart enough to connect the dots and retrieve mail from that account.

If you don't have a Windows Live ID, or you want to create a new one, see Technique 21 for the painless and quick details.

WLMD initiates a second wizard that starts by inviting you to customize the program.

5. **Click Next, and the installer offers to import your Outlook Express accounts and settings (see Figure 22-2).**

• **Figure 22-2:** "Outlook Express" is the old, obsolete name for Windows Mail.

Of course, you're using Vista, so Outlook Express is actually called "Windows Mail," but what the heck.

6. **Check the box if you want to import your old Windows Mail accounts, settings, and folders, and then click Next.**

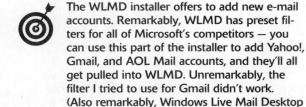

The WLMD installer offers to add new e-mail accounts. Remarkably, WLMD has preset filters for all of Microsoft's competitors — you can use this part of the installer to add Yahoo!, Gmail, and AOL Mail accounts, and they'll all get pulled into WLMD. Unremarkably, the filter I tried to use for Gmail didn't work. (Also remarkably, Windows Live Mail Desktop calls Windows Live Mail "Hotmail" — six of one, half-a-dozen of the other.)

7. **If you have e-mail accounts other than the one you entered in Step 4, and you want WLMD to accumulate mail from those accounts, click the**

button marked Add an E-Mail Account and click Next.

No need to add the primary account that you entered in Step 3.

WLMD asks you for information about your e-mail account. (See Figure 22-3).

• **Figure 22-3:** Enter information for other e-mail accounts here.

8. **Type the information for each account that you want to enter, in turn, and click Next. When you're done, in the following window, click Finish.**

WLMD offers to merge contacts from Vista and Outlook, as in Figure 22-4.

This is a remarkable feat, which Microsoft has yet to perfect. If and/or when Microsoft gets it to work, you will be able to merge your contact information from Windows Live Messenger, Windows Live Mail (née Hotmail/MSN Hotmail), Vista (including Windows Mail née Outlook Express), and any version of Office Outlook *and* keep the accumulated mess updated automatically by using Windows Live Messenger's automatic update feature (see Technique 21). Yes, I can hear the loud guffaw from the back of the room all the way out here. It's a noble effort. Let's hope that Microsoft succeeds some day.

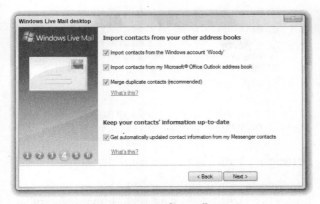

• **Figure 22-4: Merge contacts from all over.**

9. Check all the boxes — hey, there's no harm in trying — and click Next.

WLMD offers to bring in RSS feeds from anyone in any of your Contacts lists who has a blog on Windows Live Spaces. (For details on RSS feeds, see Technique 18.)

10. Check the box that says Subscribe to Feeds from Your Contacts' Blogs on Spaces. Then click Next.

In its final step, the installer offers to sign you up for the Customer Experience Improvement Program.

11. Personally, I never sign up for the CEIP, but this is a noble effort, and you might feel differently. Choose the option you like and click Finish.

Windows Live Mail Desktop asks if it can be set as your default e-mail program.

12. If you're ready to take the plunge and make WLMD your main e-mail program, go ahead and click Yes. Personally, I'm going to wait a year or two, so I click No.

WLMD takes a few minutes to locate your mail and merge your contacts and then appears in its four-pane glory, as in Figure 22-5.

13. Click around and explore a bit.

The Active Search pane, on the right, goes a bit off the deep end at times (see Figure 22-5), but its digital heart is in the right place.

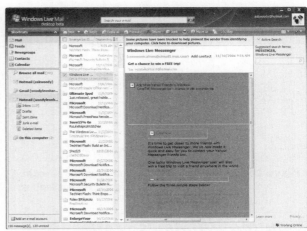

• **Figure 22-5: WLMD pulls in mail from all over. Note this message from Microsoft, which has had pictures blocked.**

The Feeds icon, on the left, brings in all the feeds that you have authorized through Internet Explorer. As you can see in Figure 22-6, the interface is a bit clunky, but it works.

• **Figure 22-6: RSS feeds come in from Internet Explorer and your contact's Spaces blogs.**

The Search box at the very top works like greased lightning (see Figure 22-7).

14. When you're done, click the down-wedge just below and to the left of your picture. Then choose File⇒Exit.

If you click the red "X," WLMD keeps running, watching for incoming mail.

 Come back again in a year.

• **Figure 22-7:** A very fast search on the word `Rolex` in my Hotmail, er, Windows Live Mail inbox.

Mauling Windows Mail

You should go through these timesaving steps *even if you use Windows Live Mail Desktop.* The similarities between Windows Live Mail Desktop and Windows Mail are extensive.

If you have a bunch of old Outlook Express messages that you need to keep, or you just don't trust those online Web-based e-mail companies — or Internet access where you work is too slow or unreliable — Windows Mail may be your best choice.

I talk about Windows Mail extensively in *Windows Vista All-In-One Desktop Reference For Dummies.* It's a good place to start if you're trying to get Windows Mail to work.

You may like the Windows Mail interface for working with Microsoft tech support newsgroups, but I like the Google Groups interface better. With Google Groups, you have instant search access to many newsgroups that aren't part of the official Microsoft offerings. Microsoft *MVP*s (Most Valuable Players — read *tech guru volunteers*) help guide the Microsoft newsgroups, but there are lots of knowledgeable people outside the Microsoft fold who know just as much and help just as frequently. For details about Google Groups, see Technique 20.

I'm also partial to my own tech support haven, the Lounge. Drop by `www.AskWoody.com` and click the tab that says Ask a Question. Any question. Our WMVPs (Woody's MVPs — catchy name, eh?) will give it a shot. Half a million posts are just a click away.

In the rest of this section, I list my favorite Windows Mail timesaving tips.

Arranging Your Windows Mail desktop

Windows Mail, out of the box (see Figure 22-8), presents a streamlined view of your main mailing needs.

• **Figure 22-8:** Right out of the box, Windows Mail looks pretty good.

There's one additional bar, called the Views bar, that doesn't take up any extra room and provides another worthwhile filter. To make it appear:

1. **Choose View⇨Layout.**

You see the Window Layout Properties dialog box.

2. **Check the box next to Views Bar.**

3. **Click OK.**

The Views bar appears in the upper right, just below the Search bar. Click it, and you can tell

Windows Mail to hide the messages that you've read or the ones you've marked to ignore (see Figure 22-9).

• **Figure 22-9: The Views bar can help when you're scanning for messages.**

Where did my contacts go?

Windows XP's Outlook Express included a Contacts application, and contacts were visible on the Outlook Express window.

They're gone now. Vista has its own contacts manager, of sorts. If you try to get into your Contacts from Windows Mail, you're automatically rerouted to the Vista Contacts application — which is a bit, uh, underwhelming.

Making Windows Mail wait to send and receive

As soon as Windows Mail starts, it looks for mail. If you haven't changed the out-of-the-box settings, Windows Mail continues to check for mail every 30 minutes, whether you want it to or not.

By default, Windows Mail is set up to send messages the moment you finish composing and click the Send button. Wish I had a nickel for every time I've sent out a message and immediately wished I could take it back. E-mail messages, like computer geeks, get better with age. At least, that's what I tell my significant other.

I think it's much better to force Windows Mail to wait until you click the Send/Receive button

before either receiving or sending any mail. Here's how:

1. **Choose Tools⇨Options⇨General.**

You see the Options dialog box.

2. **Uncheck the Send and Receive Messages at Startup box and uncheck the Check for New Messages Every . . . Minutes box.**

3. **Click the Send tab.**

Windows Mail shows you the Send settings in Figure 22-10.

• **Figure 22-10: Disable automatic sending.**

4. **Uncheck the Send Messages Immediately box.**

5. **If you use a dial-up Internet connection, click the Connection tab and check the Hang Up after Sending and Receiving box.**

That'll free up your phone line so you can use the, uh, phone.

6. **Click OK.**

Your changes take effect immediately.

Dealing with read receipts

When people send you a message, they can request a read receipt. As soon as you open or preview a message with a read receipt requested, you get the dialog box shown in Figure 22-11. These receipts are yet another time-consuming pain in the neck.

• **Figure 22-11: The sender wants to know if you got the message — another big waste of time.**

If you click Yes, Windows Mail automatically generates a message back to the sender.

Generally, read receipts do nothing but waste your (and the sender's) time. If you receive a message with a read receipt, are you any more likely to respond to it? No way. If you receive a read receipt, do you know that your intended recipient actually saw the message? Well, no — at least, not unless you're absolutely certain you got the right e-mail address, and that nobody else reads the recipient's mail.

You can deal with read receipts in two easy ways. One is to always send a receipt; the other is to never send a receipt. My personal predilection is to never send a receipt because I don't want to encourage people to use the blasted things!

If you ask Windows Mail to always send a receipt or never send a receipt, at least you can bypass that time-consuming dialog box. To make a permanent yes-or-no decision:

1. **Choose Tools⇨Options⇨Receipts.**

Windows Mail shows you the Receipts tab.

2. **Click the Never Send a Read Receipt radio button (or, if you must, click Always Send a Read Receipt).**

3. **Click OK.**

A pox upon you and your kin if you check the box that says Request a Read Receipt for All Sent Messages.

Using signatures the smart way

Most people sign their e-mail messages, typically with their name and e-mail address, and perhaps a line (or two or ten) of additional . . . stuff.

Here's the easiest way to create a signature for your messages:

1. **If you want a plain text signature, start Notepad (Start⇨All Programs⇨Accessories⇨Notepad).**

If you want a formatted signature, start any program (such as Word) that's capable of creating an HTML file.

I have a plain text signature, so in Figure 22-12, I open Notepad.

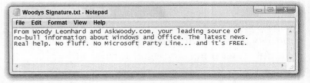

• **Figure 22-12: My signature.**

2. **Create the signature that you want to use and save the file in a convenient location as either a .txt (text) or .html (formatted) file, and then exit the application (Notepad or Word, for example).**

In this example, I saved the file as Woodys signature.txt.

3. **In Windows Mail, choose Tools⇨Options⇨ Signatures.**

Windows Mail shows you the Options dialog box with the Signatures tab displayed. The first time you see this dialog box, everything is grayed out. Not to worry. Follow along, Pilgrim.

4. **Click the New button (at the top), click the File button (down below), and then click Browse. Find and select the signature file you created in Step 2 and click Open.**

5. **Check the Add Signatures to All Outgoing Messages box.**

The Options dialog box looks like the one shown in Figure 22-13.

• **Figure 22-13:** Tell Windows Mail to use your signature for new messages.

6. **Click OK.**

7. **Test your signature by clicking the Create Mail icon in Windows Mail.**

Your signature appears at the bottom of the new message (see Figure 22-14). If you use the method I describe in Technique 8 to create one-click e-mails, the message gets added to them, too.

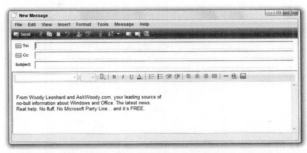

• **Figure 22-14:** New messages — even replies — have your signature at the bottom.

Dealing with e-mail attachment security

Windows Mail blocks — that is, it refuses to show you — any inbound e-mail file attachment with a name that ends with certain "dangerous" filename extensions (see `support.microsoft.com/ ?kbid=291369` for the complete list).

 Of course, the concept of a "dangerous" filename extension is laughable. Up until September 2004, the `.jpg` filename extension was considered "safe." Then somebody discovered that it was possible to stick a killer program inside a JPEG picture file, and a filename extension that was once considered innocuous became, overnight, one of the world's Ten Most Wanted. Conversely, Microsoft doesn't block `.doc` Word documents or `.xls` Excel spreadsheets or `.ppt` PowerPoint files, even though all of them have been used quite recently to carry "0day," previously unknown, viruses. Danger is in the eye of the beholder, eh?

If you can exercise a tiny amount of caution when handling files attached to e-mail messages, and if you have an antivirus program that's worth its salt, there's no reason to have Windows Mail block your inbound files. Here's how to override the setting:

1. Choose Tools⇨Options⇨Security.

You see the Security tab.

2. Uncheck the Do Not Allow Attachments to Be Saved or Opened That Could Potentially Be a Virus box.

3. Click OK.

Windows Mail no longer blocks attached files.

Of course, you should never, ever, ever open or run a file attached to an e-mail message unless you know the person who sent it to you, and you know that they actually did send it to you. If you have any doubt, send them a message and confirm that they sent you the file before you open it. If you get confirmation, save the file and run your favorite antivirus package on it before you open it.

Technique

23

Zapping Junk Mail

Save Time By

✔ Avoiding spammers' traps

✔ Staying off e-mail lists

✔ Getting rid of junk mail — accurately

I downloaded 455 e-mail messages this morning; 418 of them were spam. Sound familiar?

Don't get me wrong. I really do want to buy an amazing printer cartridge that never runs out of antigravity ink, refinance my house with the lowest rates in 499 years, increase my bust size by 17 inches in just two weeks, and help Mr. Mungwabe get his $10,368,475,890 out of Nidibia. I'm a New Age kind of guy. But I'd rather not be reminded about my shortcomings every day. And I don't have an extra $100,000.49 to guarantee Mr. Mungwabe's wire transfer.

E-mail is a unique timesaving medium — quite possibly the most effective timesaving communication device since the advent of the telephone. But it has its own set of potential pitfalls. And the continuing onslaught of spam threatens to kill the golden goose. This Technique is a crash course in spam — because if you understand the beast, you're better prepared to fight it — and contains some school-of-hard-knocks advice about e-mail.

Understanding Spam

Spam — unwanted commercial e-mail messages that tout everything from IQ-building enzymes to calisthenics with barnyard animals — makes me furious. I bet you have a few choice words about it, too.

E-mail set the advertising world on its ear by lowering the bar for direct marketing: Instead of spending thousands or tens of thousands of dollars for a mass mailing campaign via snail mail, an advertiser can send millions of messages for less than $100. You don't have to find very many suckers to make back your investment. And there's one born every minute.

Everybody gets spam. Few take the time to understand how and why spammers construct messages the way they do. Figure 23-1 shows a particularly well-crafted piece of unwanted e-mail that didn't get caught by Microsoft's Windows Live Mail spam filter (particularly surprising because it's an ad for an iPod). Although the message came from a bonafide CAN-SPAM-complying "direct e-mail marketing list vendor," and the product on offer is 100-percent legitimate, the message shows all sorts of scummy traits:

• **Figure 23-1:** Anatomy of a spam message.

✔ The subject doesn't have any trigger words. Many spam filters look in the Subject line for trigger words (keywords) such as *mortgage*. Some words are easily disguised; that's why you see a lot of spam with a subject of, oh, \/iagra, or a message from Shed25 with a subject of LbsIn30Days.

✔ A unique identifier is buried in the message. In this case, you can bet that the spammer's database has my e-mail address linked to ID:exc93kk.4i3. If I reply to the message and include a copy of the original, the spammer knows that I got the message. Compare this to Web Beacons, described a little later in the Technique.

✔ The message starts with a perfectly good word (COMPLIMENTARY). That's used to trip up spam filters, which would go bananas if they encountered a word like FREE.

✔ Almost everything in the ad is a picture — not text. If you have a spam filter that looks at text, there's nothing to look at! Moreover, you can bet that the sender was using a Web Beacon (see the upcoming "Lurking in Web Beacons" section).

✔ While the return address of the sender indicates the message was sent by a "direct e-mail marketing list vendor" (how do you spell *spam?*), the top of the message says that it's from Dos Now Media. The CAN-SPAM compliance section, at the bottom of the message, says that it was sent by "Dos Now Media, Encinitas, CA 92024." Two problems.

▶ When I try to go to DosNowMedia.com, Firefox tells me there's no such site (Figure 23-2).

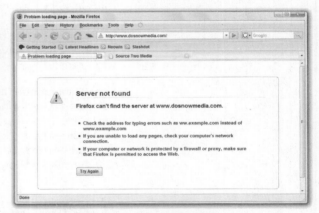

• **Figure 23-2:** The spam lists a dead Web site.

▶ When I look for Dos Now Media in Encinitas, California, using Google and other search tools, I can't find any record of the company. On the other hand, I did see that Utah's Consumer Protection Agency just fined *Dos Media Now* in Encinitas, California, for sending e-mail "touting gambling, alcohol, and pornography to children." Must be a coincidence, right?

✔ All the links in the body of the message (which I discovered by looking at the source code for the message — *never* by clicking through on the message) point me to the BlackJack Ballroom Casino site, per Figure 23-3.

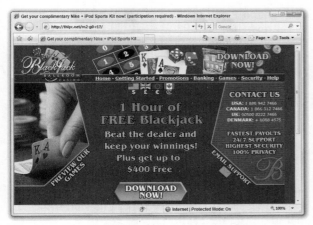

• **Figure 23-3:** Click to participate in the survey, and you get surveyed, all right.

✔ The opt-out parts of the message, which are required by the CAN-SPAM Act, are all pictures, and they all point to a Universal Unsubscribe site purporting to be from "Incentive Leader" (see Figure 23-4). One little problem. The Web address at the top of Figure 23-4 is registered to the same "direct e-mail marketing list vendor" that apparently sent the message — it isn't registered to Incentive Leader. I would sooner stick my hand in a pickle grinder than type my e-mail address in their Unsubscribe box.

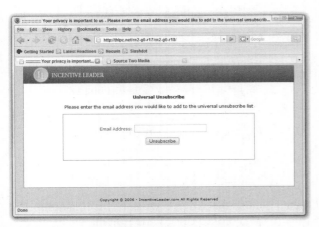

• **Figure 23-4:** Would you trust this company to unsubscribe you? Really?

If you ever wondered why it's hard to make spam-zappers that catch the bad mail but let through the good, this example should give you a few ideas.

The *Controlling the Assault of Non-Solicited Pornography And Marketing* (CAN-SPAM) Act of 2003 was supposed to put a crimp on this kind of spam, but I've seen more of it now than before the Act went into effect. Some estimates say the number of spam messages more than doubled in the year following enactment of CAN-SPAM. I'd say that's a conservative estimate. Somewhere between 75 percent and 90 percent of all the e-mail on the Internet at this moment qualifies as unsolicited, unwanted junk. Several proposals for limiting spam — and putting technical teeth into the mix — have failed, ultimately because the folks floating the proposals know that spammers can get around them in a matter of days. Hours. Frankly, I'm not optimistic about the future of e-mail.

Outlook 2003 and 2007, Windows Mail, Windows Live Mail, and Windows Live Mail Desktop all have spam filters. So do Gmail, Yahoo! Mail, AOL Mail, and all the other major online e-mail sites. None of them catches all the spam, all the time. Be wary.

Before we leave the subject, permit me to stand on my soapbox once again. Whenever election time rolls around in the United States, I get hit with a barrage of political spam, especially from my old home state of Colorado. I haven't lived in Colorado for six years, but that doesn't stop the spammeisters. Or the politicians. The all-time low came when a candidate for state Attorney General kept sending me requests for donations, thinly disguised as clever campaign brochures. I can't *believe* that the people who should be protecting us from the blight of spam are among the worst offenders.

If a politician starts spamming you, write to him or her and let 'em have it with both barrels. They're engaging in unsolicited commercial e-mail (the trigger term for CAN-SPAM) just as surely as Dos Now

Media. They're wading in the same murky water and dealing with the same scummy mailing list managers. The only difference between a spamming politician and a spamming casino operator . . . come to think of it, is there *any* difference between the two?

Phishing Phor Phun and Prophit

Phishing — sending out e-mail messages that try to convince you to divulge personal information — has become breathtakingly clever. Phishers generally rely on spam databases to send out millions of messages. The messages frequently look like real notices from banks, credit card companies, online auction houses (see Figure 23-5), and the like. Most phishing messages tell you that you have to log on to a Web site because your account has a problem, or you should click on a link to resolve some difficulty.

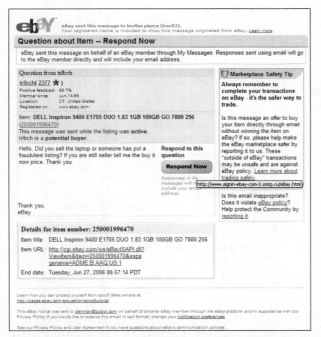

• **Figure 23-5: A phishing message that looks like a mix-up from eBay.**

Typically, phishers try to trick you into logging onto a Web site that they control. While you may think that you're clicking a link in the message to, say, the eBay Web site, the real link buried behind the text actually goes to some Web site that was set up just hours before you received the message (in Figure 23-5, click Respond Now and you end up at a site in Russia, `smtp.ru`). You're asked to provide an account number and password and sometimes other forms of identification. The phisher watches what's being typed into the fake Web site, absconds with your financial information, and then uses it to pull money out of your bank account, con you into something stupid, or do any of the myriad things that identity thieves do.

How do these guys (and they're almost always guys) make any money at it? The numbers. Say someone sends out a million phishing messages purporting to be from Wells Fargo. Maybe 5 percent of those people have eBay accounts. Maybe 10 percent of the people with accounts are gullible enough to provide their logon information. Do the math. A million messages nets five thousand suckers gleefully typing their logon IDs and passwords into an ersatz Web site.

 Smart phishers move quickly. That's how they stay ahead of the law. A well-organized phisher can milk hundreds of thousands of dollars in less than 12 hours, and all of it can be done online: setting up the bogus Web site; sending out the phishing messages to a spam e-mail list; waiting for naïve folks to respond; then using the acquired information to drain the victims' accounts. Frequently, the only trail left behind for law enforcement is at the end, where the money from the victim has to make its way to the perpetrator. It's massive fraud, conducted on Internet time.

Office Outlook 2003 and 2007, Windows Mail, Windows Live Mail, Windows Live Mail Desktop, Gmail, Yahoo! Mail, AOL Mail, and all the other Web-based e-mail companies have antiphishing filters, but they're tacked onto the spam (er, junk e-mail) filters and aren't nearly as effective as the spam catchers.

For the most part, phishing is a two-part exercise: first, you're lured by an e-mail message (which may get intercepted by your e-mail program before you see it); second, you have to go to the bogus site and enter your data. Both Firefox 2 and Internet Explorer 7 have antiphishing options, but all the alternatives have severe problems. See Technique 18 for the low-down on choosing antiphishing technology.

Avoiding Spammeisters and Phishers

The first step every Windows user needs to take: minimize your chances of being added to a spam list.

Where do spammeisters get your e-mail address? More often than not, they buy it on a CD that holds millions of addresses, as shown in Figure 23-6. Note how the people offering the e-mail addresses suggest you buy a CD, make copies, and resell them for twice the price! Honor among thieves, I guess.

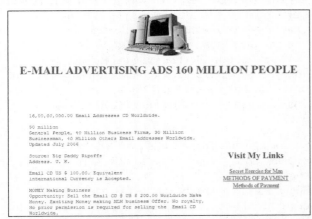

• **Figure 23-6: 160 million addresses for $100. This is a real ad.**

E-mail address compilation CDs cost next to nothing, and if 98 percent of the addresses on the CD are out of date, the remaining 2 percent still represent a huge number of marks. Er, potential customers.

The spammeisters who go out and harvest original new addresses can be quite devious. The worst ones work in cahoots with virus/worm writers, who put spam address–spewing routines into their programs. If you get infected with one of those critters, every e-mail address on your computer gets harvested and sent to the bad guy's address trap. He sells those millions of harvested addresses for a princely sum.

Many times, spam list creators just guess: If woody@AskWoody.com is a good address, maybe AskWoody@AskWoody.com is also good — or woody@microsoft.com, for that matter. (No, I haven't joined the Dark Side.)

Lurking in Web Beacons

One of the most common, old-fashioned methods for verifying e-mail addresses employs a method called Web Beacons. (You may have heard of them referred to as Web Bugs.) Web Beacons work by using a link to a picture inside a message (instead of a copy of the picture itself) that looks something like this:

```
<img src="http://ogy.cc/trm/botyi_
    01.gif">
```

When Outlook or Windows Mail or Windows Live Mail or Gmail (or whatever e-mail reader you use) sees a code like that, it knows that it needs to reach out to http://ogy.cc/trm and pick up the picture called botyi_01.gif. Using a link makes the message much smaller, but it takes longer for you to view the message because you have to wait while your e-mail program picks up the picture.

Unfortunately, unscrupulous companies can use linked pictures to determine if a specific e-mail message has been viewed and thus verify your e-mail address. To see how it works, look at the message in Figure 23-7.

The message in Figure 23-7 looks like a typical piece of scum spam, but what you can't see can hurt you.

• **Figure 23-7: A typical obnoxious piece of spam.**

If I choose File➪Save As, save the message as an EML file, and then open that EML file with Notepad, the HTML working behind the scenes appears and divulges the full story. One of the pictures gets pulled from an oddly-named source, which you can see in Figure 23-8. The source for the image is

```
http://redirect.virtumundo.com/bt?m=
    368782&e=woody@askwoody.com
```

• **Figure 23-8: The code sitting behind one of the pictures in Figure 23-7.**

If I had opened, or even previewed, the pictures in that Beacon-enhanced message, my e-mail program would go out to `redirect.virtumundo.com/bt` and retrieve a picture there, but leave behind my e-mail address!

Even more appalling, if my e-mail program had gone out and retrieved the picture, the folks at `virtumundo.com` would not only have confirmation that somebody is reading messages sent to `woody@AskWoody.com`, they would also be able to tie my e-mail address to my Web (so-called "IP") address. Because I have a broadband connection, and my IP address doesn't change, `virtumundo.com` would be able to associate my e-mail address with *any* Web access I make.

Scary, eh?

Fortunately, Windows Mail blocked the pictures in the message to "help prevent the sender from identifying your computer" and stuck the message in the Junk E-mail folder. Many times, that admonition and the picture blocking are merely a pain in the neck. This time, it saved me from being stung by a Web Beacon.

As an added flourish, the picture in Figure 23-7 has an on-screen height of 1 and a width of 1, as you can verify in the HTML code listing in Figure 23-8. That means your e-mail program retrieves the picture and puts it on the screen, but it's so small you can't see it. Your information goes to `virtumundo.com`, you get a picture back, but Outlook (or Hotmail or . . .) doesn't even display the picture. That makes this `<img>` tag a so-called *Invisible Web Beacon*. Slick.

Surmising what happened is easy. The people at `virtumundo.com` got a list of e-mail addresses somewhere. They sent out messages like the one in Figure 23-7 to everyone on the list, each message customized to include the victim's e-mail address in the body of the Web Beacon. Then they gathered e-mail addresses on their Web server, as unsuspecting people opened (or even previewed) their scummy mail. Ka-ching!

Oh. Did I mention? The list of unscrupulous companies that have used Web Beacons includes a few you probably know: Barnes & Noble, cooking.com, and eToys, among many others, including Microsoft, back in the days before anyone knew what Web Beacons were.

Unfortunately, Web Beacons have become so common that almost every e-mail user gets one (or many) every day. Fortunately, e-mail programs are keeping up. Unless you change things, Office's Outlook 2003, 2007, Windows Mail, Windows Live Mail, Windows Live Mail Desktop, Gmail, Yahoo! Mail, and AOL Mail all block Web Beacons. Yes, you have to click to retrieve the pictures embedded in messages. Yes, it's worth the effort.

Crawling and Trawling

Giant Web spiders scan millions of Web pages every day, seeking valid e-mail addresses. If your e-mail address is on the Web anywhere — even if it's hidden from view, behind some kind of link on your personal home page, for example — one of the Web crawlers can pick it up.

The crawlers go through all the newsgroups, too, every night. If you post on a newsgroup, make sure you use a return address that can't be automatically lifted. If you want people to be able to send you e-mail, try a combination that's legible to humans but a real stumper for spiders: woody@AskWoody. DeleteThisBeforeSending.com for example.

Some unscrupulous online greeting card companies make most (if not all!) of their profits by skimming From and To e-mail addresses from people sending cards. If you send an online greeting card, stick to one of the bigger, better-known companies and check their privacy policy before you send.

Unsubscribing — Not!

Most vexing: If you follow the instructions to unsubscribe or stop receiving mailings from some spam houses, the company can use the information you provide to confirm that it has your up-to-date, working e-mail address! It's one of the abiding ironies of the CAN-SPAM Act: Every unsolicited e-mail message is supposed to have an opt-out link, so opt-out links are "normal" and expected, so more people click the links, verifying the legitimacy of their addresses.

The spam at the beginning of this Technique has an opt-out clause (actually, two) that goes to the Web page shown in Figure 23-4. That page is notable because it doesn't include any mention of the e-mail address that received the spam. You have to type in your address. And if you accidentally provide an address that the spammer doesn't have already, there's no telling how the address will be used.

The moral of the story: Don't try to unsubscribe unless you're looking at a bonafide message from a big-name company and you know that you personally asked for a subscription in the first place. If you find yourself face to face with a form that asks for your e-mail address, think twice before you give it away. Can't win, can't get ahead, can't even get out of the game.

Fighting Back

Spam isn't a black-and-white problem. There are plenty of shades of gray, and zealots (like me) need to temper their anti-spam rabidity with some common sense. That said, spam is probably your number-one computer time sink — if it isn't yet, it will be soon, unless you get sucked in by instant messaging.

So what can you do about spam?

Taking spam action

I wish everyone would follow these simple rules about spam:

- ✔ **Don't ever, ever, ever respond to spam.**

 If someone sends you an unsolicited offer to make you look 20 years younger, or add inches here, or take off inches there, don't reply. Don't click the Take Me Off Your List button. Don't click any links. If you respond to one piece of spam in any way, I guarantee you'll end up on a gold list somewhere and pay for your transgression over and over again. Moreover, if you respond, you only encourage these cretins to keep pestering all of us. Give them the silent treatment.

 The only exception: established, credible companies. If you click the link to get off the Eddie Bauer direct mail list, rest assured that you're taken off. Just be super certain it's the real Eddie Bauer you're dealing with and not some spammer posing as Eddie Bauer.

- ✔ **Tell your friends about Rule #1.**

- ✔ **Spammeisters are the scum of the earth. Treat them accordingly.**

 I know highly experienced and intelligent people who see a piece of spam about something that interests them, and they figure that once — just this once — they'll click through and look at the details. Don't do it.

- ✔ **Get mad. And get even.**

 Don't bother trying to spam the spammers. Sending copious huge e-mail files to the return address on a piece of spam doesn't work. Spamming a spammer is just as illegal, and the return address might really belong to some unsuspecting wonk. Like me.

 Legislation against spammers deserves all the support we can muster, as long as the legislation doesn't make matters worse. Sue a few of them, just for practice. Throw the vermin in jail. And the politician-spammers? They deserve all the embarrassment you can heap upon them.

It may not reduce the volume of spam, but it'll sure make me feel better. Lots of resources are on the Web, particularly at `spam.abuse.net`, Spamhaus (`spamhaus.org`), and the Antispyware Coalition, `www.antispywarecoalition.org`.

Biting the phishers

As spammers' evil twins, phishers deserve all the disdain their scummy brothers receive and more. I hate to belabor the obvious, but

- ✔ **Don't fill out any form you receive in a message.**

 I don't care if the message claims that all your credit cards are about to be shredded, the Federal Reserve needs to know about your bank account, and the government of Ubistanibia will fall if you don't provide your podiatrist's aunt's maiden name. Send any message asking for any personal information straight to the bit bucket.

- ✔ **If you click a link in an e-mail message, assume that you're not in Kansas anymore.**

 You may think that clicking a proffered link will take you to `citibank.com` or `paypal.com`, but they won't. Guaranteed. Companies that legitimately require your response won't send you mail with a link. If you need to fix your Citibank card, go to Firefox and type `www.citibank.com`. Or pick up the phone and call the bank.

- ✔ **Check your accounts often.**

 Check any account that has online access every few days. If you see something that doesn't look right, contact the folks who manage your account (but never by clicking an e-mail link) and yell, real loud, right away.

- ✔ **Book 'em, Dan-O.**

 Phishing takes place in real time. If you enable antiphishing features in Firefox or Internet Explorer (see Technique 18), zealously report any site that looks questionable.

 If you get a suspicious-looking e-mail message that asks you to click through and provide personal information, forward a copy of it to the

Anti-Phishing Working Group (`reportphishing@ antiphishing.com`) and the U.S. Federal Trade Commission (`spam@uce.gov`). Don't delete the message. Keep it in a safe place because investigators may want to examine it.

The experts also suggest that you forward a copy of the phishing message to the company that's being clobbered. I once did that, forwarding a copy of a very clever phishing message to PayPal, `spoof@paypal.com`. What a joke! The folks there thought I was trying to report a compromised account. It took more than a week to get it all straightened out — a complete waste of time for all involved. (What's the old saying? "No good deed goes unpunished"?) You may have better luck than I, but I wouldn't bother trying to alert the company involved.

Don't add to the problem

If you forward messages that look like this:

```
For each person you send this email
   to, you will be given $5. For every
   person they give it to, you will be
   given an additional $3. For every
   person they send it to you will
   receive $1. Microsoft will tally
   all the emails produced under
   your name over a two week period
   and then email you with more
   instructions...
```

you're part of the problem. If it sounds too good to be true, it is. Check out `www.snopes.com` for more information.

Technique 24

Surfing Anonymously

If you read Technique 18, you know that you can use Firefox or Internet Explorer to warn you about phishing sites. But in order to receive the protection, you have to leave behind a trail of every Web site that you visit, and that trail can probably be traced directly to you. Turn on antiphishing in IE, and Microsoft accumulates a big database that includes records for most of the sites that you visit. In the case of Firefox, if you turn on advanced antiphishing, the records go to Google. Either way, you have good reason to be alarmed about your privacy.

If you read Technique 23, you know that Web sites can use Web Beacons to gather information about your e-mail address — most alarmingly, if you allow your e-mail program to show you the pictures inside an e-mail, the company that sent you the e-mail can associate your e-mail address with your Web address (your so-called *IP address*), and they can sell either or both. After the connection has been made, any Web surfing records (which always contain IP addresses) can be traced back to your e-mail address, give or take a waffle or two.

The situation's worse in other countries. One Yahoo! executive admitted to *The Washington Post* in late 2005 that his company gave the government of China records that were used to convict journalist Shi Tao. Although the precise details have never been published, to the best of my knowledge, it's apparent that Shi Tao signed up for a Yahoo! Mail account using an IP address that could be traced back to him. Surfing anonymously might have kept him out of a Chinese jail. A slightly less-compliant Yahoo! might've done the same.

Whether you want to get the best antiphishing technology without leaving your life history in Redmond, send whistle-blower messages without being traced, daze and confuse your company's Internet monitoring programs, or blast through your school's firewall to go to the places you want to go, you need to know how to surf anonymously.

This Technique explains how to do it thoroughly — and quickly.

Understanding Anonymous Surfing

It all comes down to IP addresses.

If you have an always-on Internet connection, you have an IP address that never changes. Even if your ADSL connection drops every ten minutes, when you reconnect, you probably get the same IP address. The IP address is unique — no two computers connected to the Internet at the same time have the same IP address. And you leave behind your IP address every time you go to a Web site, interact with an e-mail server, or connect to your Internet service provider.

Seeing your IP address is easy:

1. **Start your favorite Internet browser and go to all-nettools.com/toolbox.**

AllNetTools dishes out many pieces of information about networks — looking up Web site owners, tracing your packets as they wend their way through the Web, and much more. If you don't already have the site bookmarked, do it.

2. **Near the bottom of the page, under the heading Proxy Test, click the button marked Check.**

Your IP address appears, along with an extensive list of routing information. (See Figure 24-1.)

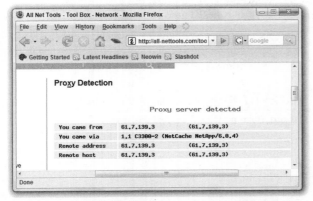

• **Figure 24-1: AllNetTools will hunt down your IP address and try to blast through any anonymizing tricks.**

When you visit a Web site, you leave more than your IP address behind. To see an eye-opening list of all the baggage that goes along when you surf, hit the site www.plinko.net/404/supersleuth.asp. The report looks like Figure 24-2, except it goes on for pages.

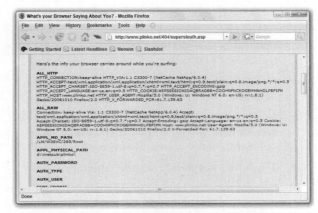

• **Figure 24-2: Bet you never knew how much junk you leave behind when you hit a Web page.**

If you're serious about anonymous Web surfing, you want to make sure that the sites you visit can't see your IP address. That much is a given. But anonymizing goes beyond simple IP address masking. You may also be interested in

- Going around a firewall if, for instance, the firewall at work won't let you log on to Hotmail.

- Making life as difficult as possible for anyone who tries to snoop on the data you're sending or receiving.

- Eliminating a backtrack path, so it's impossible to find you even if all the records of the masking computers are available.

- Preventing your Internet service provider from snooping.

If all this starts sounding a bit too much like guys in white lab coats trying to act like James Bond, remember that anonymous surfing plays an important role if you

✔ Want to level the playing field against spammers and phishers who have your IP address nailed.

✔ Can't get to a specific Web site and want to know if your Web address is being blocked.

✔ Want to use advanced antiphishing features, but don't want to leave your history in Microsoft's (or Google's) vaults.

✔ Need to use a truly anonymous online e-mail address.

✔ Don't want your Internet service provider to know where you go and what you do. In some countries, that can be a life-or-death proposition.

✔ Think that somebody may be tapping your line.

✔ Don't want your boss to know that you're looking around for a new job. Or playing interactive bridge.

Ain't nobody's business but your own.

Using Anonymous Sites and Toolbars

The simplest kind of anonymous surfing involves a special kind of Web site called an *anonymizing site* (also called a proxy server or public proxy server). To a first approximation, the interaction goes like this:

1. You log on to the anonymizing site.

2. You tell the anonymizing site which Web page you want to visit.

3. The anonymizing site goes out to the Web site you requested, retrieves the page, and sends it back to you.

That way, your only interaction is with the anonymizing site. You don't actually go to the "forbidden" site; the anonymizing site does it for you.

More advanced anonymizing sites intercept the pages coming back and jigger the hot links inside the pages so you can click on a hot link and be routed back through the anonymizing site.

If you want to try an anonymizing site:

1. **Start your favorite Web browser and go to one of the sites listed in Table 24-1.**

In Figure 24-3, I went to ShySurfer.com.

• **Figure 24-3: Using the free anonymizing site** ShySurfer.com.

2. **Use the site to go to www.plinko.net/404/ supersleuth.asp.**

3. **Read the results of Plinko's Supersleuth to see if your identity is well concealed.**

As you can see in Figure 24-4, the report comes up clean — there's no reference to any of the "real" details shown in Figure 24-2.

TABLE 24-1: A SAMPLING OF FREE ANONYMIZING SITES

Anonymize.net	Proxify.com
Anonymouse.org	ShySurfer.com
Guardster.com	The-cloak.com/anonymous-surfing-home.html
Merletn.org/uk/ anonymizer	

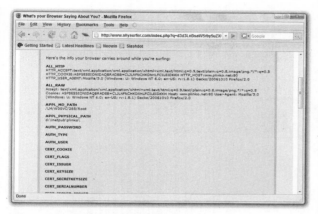

• **Figure 24-4:** A clean bill of health.

Working through an anonymizing site is inherently slower than going the direct route. If response times get to the point that they're annoying, use a different site, try one of the pay sites connected to the free sites (for example, `the-cloak.com` has a highly regarded extra-cost service that runs 1.7 cents per megabyte) or consider one of the other approaches in this Technique.

Most anonymizing sites support secure communication (SSL — the kind of secure access you commonly see on the Internet). Secure connections prevent your ISP or eavesdroppers from knowing where you've been or what you've downloaded or uploaded. Giganews, the giant newsgroup service I describe in Technique 20, also supports SSL encryption for precisely the same reason.

Anonymous toolbars work like anonymizing Web sites, but they add the convenience of operating through a toolbar that's attached to your Web browser. Here are the best toolbars I've found:

✔ For Internet Explorer, try Amplusnet's Anonymous Browsing Toolbar, which has a free 40-day evaluation period and costs $9.95. See www.amplusnet.com/products/anonymousbrowsing/overview.asp.

✔ Firefox has a free Anonymization Toolbar from Anonymization.Net Service (see Figure 24-5). To install it, start Firefox, choose Tools➪Add-Ons, click the link to Get Extensions, and then search for Anonymization.

• **Figure 24-5:** A very easy-to-use Firefox Anonymization toolbar.

If you're using an anonymizing site or toolbar, and you click one of your Bookmarks (or Favorites in IE), the browser takes over and goes straight to the location, bypassing your anonymizing intermediary. Not being able to use Bookmarks (Favorites) is one of the big downsides to using anonymizing sites and toolbars.

The Achilles heel with Web anonymizing? The anonymizing service itself. Although all the sites claim they don't keep records of your activities, those records *could* be kept, and could be used to determine where you've been. It's hard to say what might happen if, say, a large corporation and a high-power legal team decided to track down the source of blogged news leaks about its secret projects.

Hooking into Anonymous Proxy Servers

If you want your Bookmarks back — or you don't like the speed hit associated with Web anonymizers — try the next step up: *anonymous proxy servers.* When you strip away the technical gobbledygook, the idea's pretty simple. You need to hook your browser up so it automatically goes through an intermediary — a *proxy* — which, in turn, connects to the Internet.

The main difference between anonymizing Web sites and anonymous proxy servers is in the way they handle incoming and outgoing traffic.

 Hold on a second. **Before you go charging out and changing IE or Firefox to any old anonymous proxy server that catches your fancy, be very circumspect. The folks who run anonymous proxy servers are notorious for watching and capturing traffic that comes their way. That includes your bank account ID and password. You need to know who you're dealing with. When using an anonymous proxy server, make triply sure that you use encrypted sites for sensitive information, and don't send any private info out in e-mail.**

Here's how to hook Firefox into a "high anonymous" proxy server (that's the most secure kind) in a reliable way:

1. **Start Firefox. Choose Tools⇨Add-Ons and click the link to Get Extensions.**

Firefox goes to its Add-Ons Web site.

2. **In the box at the bottom, where it says Find More Add-Ons, type** switchproxy **and click Search.**

3. **Click the link to the SwitchProxy Tool, and then click the Install Now link. When Firefox bring up its Software Installation dialog box, click Install Now.**

Firefox brings up the Add-Ons Installation dialog box.

4. **Click Restart Firefox (don't worry, all your current pages will return).**

When Firefox returns, you see the SwitchProxy toolbar, shown in Figure 24-6.

• **Figure 24-6: The SwitchProxy toolbar for Firefox.**

5. **Go to** www.publicproxyservers.com/page1.html.

You see a very recent list of free proxy servers, as in Figure 24-7.

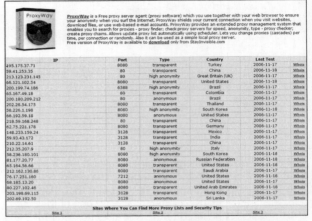

• **Figure 24-7: One of many frequently updated lists of free proxy servers.**

 Many pages listing free proxy servers advertise a product called ProxyWay (you can see it in Figure 24-7). The free version of ProxyWay has received good reviews. Unfortunately, as we went to press, it had some stability problems with Vista. If you don't want to hunt around for up-to-the-minute lists of free proxy servers, consider installing ProxyWay from www.proxyway.com.

6. **Pick one of the "high anonymity" servers on the list. Select the IP address on the left, and remember the port number. Press Ctrl+C to copy the IP address into the Windows Clipboard. Then, on the new SwitchProxy toolbar, click Add.**

SwitchProxy asks you to select a proxy configuration type.

7. **Click the button marked Standard and then click Next.**

SwitchProxy shows you the Proxy Info dialog box shown in Figure 24-8.

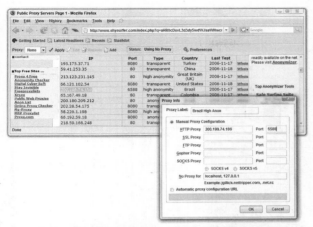

• **Figure 24-8:** Enter the high anonymity proxy server information here.

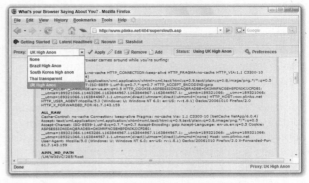

• **Figure 24-9:** Connecting to a proxy server through the proxy toolbar.

8. **Enter the proxy information and click OK.**

▶ Type a name for the Proxy Label.

▶ Click inside the HTTP Proxy box and press Ctrl+V to copy the IP address into the box.

▶ Type the port name that you can see on the Web page into the Port box in the Proxy Info dialog box.

SwitchProxy goes back to its main page.

9. **Repeat Steps 6 through 8 for all the high anonymity servers on the list, and any other servers that catch your eye.**

It doesn't hurt to have a few extras.

10. **To switch to one of your chosen public proxy servers, choose it from the Proxy drop-down box and then click the Apply icon.**

Wait a few seconds for the Status box to reflect which proxy server you're using.

In Figure 24-9, I switched to the UK High Anon server and clicked Apply. After a few seconds, Firefox comes back with the SwitchProxy Status box indicating that it's using the UK High Anon proxy.

11. **Test your connection by going to (what else?) www.plinko.net/404/supersleuth.asp to make sure none of your real information "leaks."**

12. **Anytime you want to change servers, pick the new server from the drop-down list and click the Apply icon.**

 When you no longer wish to surf anonymously, make sure you choose None from the drop-down list and click Apply.

 Free public servers go up and down all the time. If one doesn't work, another will. That's the beauty of SwitchProxy — it's very fast and easy.

Just make sure you don't send any financial information over the Internet unless it's on a secure site and therefore impenetrable to the proxy server, okay?

Routing the Onion Way

Tor, short for *The Onion Ring*, began as a U.S. Naval Research Laboratory project that was (and is) used by intelligence gathering and law enforcement agencies all over the world; it was used during a recent U.S. Navy deployment in the Middle East. It's now considered the premiere anonymizing software in all the world, although it's still admittedly experimental, sometimes slow, and prone to down time.

The Electronic Frontier Foundation picked up the Tor project and its two principal originators, Roger Dingledine and Nick Mathewson, in October 2004. Although EFF still hosts the Tor effort, the organization is largely composed of volunteers, and they actively seek donations at http://tor.eff.org.

Tor uses "onion routing" to implement anonymous routing along its entire network — you're not only anonymous at the beginning and end of the network, but there's effectively no way to track your requests through the Internet.

 Neither anonymous sites nor anonymous proxy servers can protect you from detailed traffic analysis. For example, if someone can get their hands on transmission logs at a particular anonymizing site, they could check to see when you interacted with the site and if, milliseconds later, the site interacted with, oh, a bank site or a blogging site. If the interloper sees a couple of interactions, they just might be coincidence. But if you use the anonymizing site long enough, it becomes quite clear that you're the one going from Point A to Point B.

Onion routing scrambles the interactions by introducing Points C, D, E, and maybe an F or two or three, skipping your traffic like a stone on water. None of the servers along the way knows anything about what you're doing: They only know which server sent them a particular packet and which server it should be sent to.

There's a very good detailed (and comprehensible!) description of the technology on the Tor Overview page, http://tor.eff.org/overview.html.en.

Here's how to get Tor working with Firefox:

1. Go to tor.eff.org/download.html.en and download the latest Tor & Privoxy & Vidalia package.

It comes in a file called vidalia-bundle-0.1.1.25-0.0.x.exe or something similar.

2. Double-click the downloaded .exe file and run the installation wizard (see Figure 24-10), taking all the defaults.

• **Figure 24–10: The Tor setup wizard.**

3. At the end of the installation wizard, click Finish to run Tor.

Tor runs Privoxy, shows you a cryptic single line about loading a configuration file, and then sits there. Go ahead and minimize the window. Privoxy reduces itself to a blue "P" in the notification area, near the clock.

4. Start Firefox. Choose Tools⇨Add-Ons and then click the link to Get Extensions. At the bottom of the Firefox extensions page, search for the add-on called FoxTor.

5. On the FoxTor page, click Install Now.

Firefox shows you the Software Installation dialog box.

6. Click Install Now.

When the installer finishes, you see an Add-On dialog box that instructs you to restart Firefox.

7. Click the button marked Restart Firefox.

Don't worry about any open sites — they'll come back. Click to Close tabs if you have any open browser windows with tabs.

When Firefox comes back, you see a small fox icon in the lower-left corner (see Figure 24-11).

• **Figure 24-11: When Tor is not running, the fox is "unmasked." Turn on Tor, and it grows a brown paper bag.**

8. Click the fox icon in the lower-left corner.

FoxTor takes a few seconds, and when it's hooked you into the Tor network, the fox is masked.

9. Anytime you want to disconnect from Tor — and for "normal" browsing, you should — just click the masked Fox and wait for him (her?) to unmask.

If you use Tor, consider donating money or bandwidth to the Tor effort. See `tor.eff.org/docs/tor-doc-server.html.en` for details on turning your computer into a Tor server.

If you like Tor, consider trying the Java Anonymous Proxy project, or JAP Anon for short. Undertaken by the Technical University of Dresden and the University of Regensburg, JAP Anon (`http://anon.inf.tu-dresden.de/index_en.html`) is a long-standing open source effort to bring anonymity and privacy protection to the masses. The project uses a technique called "server mixes" that, increasingly, operates in conjunction with Tor. While the current stable version of JAP Anon crawls along at a snail's pace, the new AN.ON servers make JAP quite sprightly. Follow the instructions at `anon.inf.tu-dresden.de/PaymentTest_en.html` to download the free "developer version" of JAP Anon and get onto the AN.ON network.

Part V

Cranking Up Your Audio

The 5th Wave   By Rich Tennant

MIXING THE FIRST "RUDE AUDIENCE" CD

"I laid down a general shuffling sound, over dubbed with periodic coughing, some muted talking files, and an awesome ringing cell phone loop."

25

Technique

Fighting for Your Musical Rights

Save Time By

- ✔ Choosing the right music (and video) for your needs
- ✔ Cutting through the marketing hype
- ✔ Using the songs and videos you pay for, anywhere

Did you get caught in the "Plays for Sure" inanities? Microsoft spent more than a hundred million dollars on its "Plays for Sure" advertising campaign, extolling the virtues of a raft of small music players, Microsoft-proprietary WMA audio files, and a bevy of big-name audio (and video) online stores.

You heard the punch line, right?

Three years after it spent gazillions of bucks reassuring the world that Microsoft's music "plays for sure" on the music players you want to buy, Microsoft released the all-new iPod-poseur called Zune. But, uh, well, er . . . none of the music you bought that "plays for sure" can play on a Microsoft Zune.

For sure.

What's Going On Here?

Microsoft leapt into the online music business with the unveiling of MSN Music (http://music.msn.com) in October 2004. Since then, it has launched URGE (with MTV), which ties into Windows Media Player 11 (see Technique 26) and the Zune Music Store, Zune.net. In November 2006, it shut down MSN Music, redirecting shoppers to Zune and the Real Rhapsody site.

If you have a rusty old calculator sitting around, do the math. No matter how you slice it, even if Microsoft sells a million songs a day, the company can never turn a decent profit on the music. No way. Probably won't break even. Ever. Microsoft may be a lot of things, but it ain't dumb. Why the foray into a line of business that, in analysts' wildest dreams, couldn't possibly contribute more than 0.01 percent to the company's bottom line?

In my opinion, Microsoft saw that it was losing the audio/video file format wars to Apple's astoundingly successful iPod/iTunes effort. The 'Softies want to make the WMA and WMV file formats industry standards, and they decided that an online music store would help stem the Apple tide. A decade from now, Microsoft wants to collect a royalty on every song and every movie sold. It can't do that unless you and I and all the other Windows consumers shift to Microsoft's WMA and WMV format. That's why Microsoft is willing to spend tens — probably hundreds — of millions of dollars to sink Apple's AAC/FairPlay file format, and herd us all over to the WMA/WMV fold.

Real — the company behind Real Audio — used to promote its own file format, but it has pretty much given up. In October 2005, Real and Microsoft reached an agreement. Microsoft agreed to pay $460,000,000 in cash to RealNetworks to settle antitrust allegations and $301,000,000 more to "support Real's music and game efforts." Microsoft gets a credit against that $301,000,000 for every sucker, er, customer it can deliver to Real.

That leaves Microsoft and Apple to duke it out for the hearts and minds and pocketbooks of Windows users everywhere.

Behind it all lurks the specter of copy protection — er, excuse me, Digital Rights Management (DRM). Microsoft and Apple both want to hold the keys that lock up audio and video files, preventing you and me from copying them at will. That's why I'm an unabashed fan of the MP3 audio format, which — in spite of its manifest shortcomings — can't be copy protected.

Besides, MP3 music can be played on any portable audio player. Yes, the iPod plays MP3. Yes, the Zune plays MP3. It's the only "plays for sure" format.

What You Need to Know about CRAP

Digital Rights Management doesn't add any value for the artist, label (who are selling DRM-free music every day — the Compact Disc), or consumer[;] the only people it adds value to are the technology companies who are interested in locking consumers to a particular technology platform.

— Ian Rogers, Yahoo! Music

ZDNet Executive Editor David Berlind hit the nail on the head when he called all that copy-protected music CRAP — Content Restriction, Annulment, and Protection (http://blogs.zdnet.com/BTL/?p=2428). You can call it "Digital Rights Management" if you want, but the bottom line is clear: Don't buy CRAP.

In one corner, we have Microsoft. In the other, Apple. Each employs its own version of CRAP. Apple uses a copy-protection method known as AAC with FairPlay encryption, M4A files. Microsoft uses copy-protected WMA files. Which is superior? Who cares? It's all a bunch of . . . ah, don't make me say it.

Comparing Music Formats

There are many ways to convert a sound into a string of bits. Almost all the methods you'll encounter are *lossy* — they don't pretend to be 100 percent accurate reproductions of the original. The major formats are the following:

✔ **CD Audio,** the original mainstream digitizing technique, rates as the baseline against which all other encoding methods are measured. Usually. Top-quality. Big files.

- **MP3** doesn't get much respect among audio-philes, but at the 128-Kbps recording rate, the sound fidelity is good, and files run about one-tenth the size of CD Audio. At 320 Kbps, quality is very good, but the files more than double in size. MP3 is by far the most popular audio compression technique in the world today.

 Once upon a time, when you ripped a CD — pulled music off an audio CD and stuck it on your computer — you always ripped into MP3 format. It isn't the coolest format — no Dolby 5.1, for example — but it works, and it works well. If you have a machine that plays digital music — an old PC, an ancient portable audio player (there's a reason they're called "MP3 players"), a 400GB iPod, or a Zune Ultimate — it can understand MP3.

- **WMA,** Microsoft's proprietary format, started out as a rather lackluster offering, rarely outper-forming MP3 in double-blind listening tests. The new WMA 10 Pro format, however, appears to produce slightly better recording quality than MP3 at the same recording rate.

- **AAC,** Apple's format, has always held a technolog-ical edge over the other mainstream competitors: It produces somewhat better quality in some-what smaller files. When Apple sells music at the iTunes store, it encrypts the file using a technique called *FairPlay.*

Everybody and his brother have tried to introduce a format that's better than MP3, and almost all of them have succeeded, technically. But none of them even approached MP3's colossal share of the market and minds of the world's music consumers — until Microsoft and Apple launched their CRAP formats.

WMA (Microsoft audio) and WMV (Microsoft video) files are proprietary formats: Microsoft owns them, lock, stock, and digital barrel. Microsoft wants you to use the WMA format. It wants to see WMA sup-plant MP3 as the audio file format of choice, for all computer users, everywhere. Microsoft has plenty of reasons for wanting to control the format of digi-tal media — and almost all of them are spelled with dollar ign.

Similarly, Apple wants you to buy music that will play only on an iPod. Anything and everything you buy from the iTunes Music Store can play only on a computer running Apple's QuickTime, or on an iPod. That's it. If you buy Apple's CRAP music or videos, you're locked in to Apple's hardware and software.

 Worse yet, the restrictions on using CRAP music or video can change — unilaterally. With no notification to you or anybody else. No consent required. No consent requested. If Apple suddenly decides that you should be able to "burn" a list of songs onto a CD only three times, the magic of CRAP, er, DRM, allows Apple to reach into your computer and make that restriction come true. It's scary.

Making Your Own MP3s

So you have a whole bunch of iTunes music files (in AAC/FairPlay format) or WMA files that you bought from one of the many online music stores. And you've suddenly discovered that those files have copy restrictions on them — typically, you can copy the files to at most five PCs or burn them onto audio CDs a limited number of times.

Cracking the CRAP

Every month or so, somebody comes out with a new method for cracking Microsoft's and/or Apple's proprietary digital formats. Both companies have a lot riding on their formats, so they fight back. Hard. With legions of lawyers.

But in at least a few cases, wily crackers, working alone, have figured out how to poke one or the other of the giants in the eye. If you watch the major news sites (including AskWoody.com), you'll bump into a few fascinating examples.

Is it legal to strip Digital Rights Management encryption from files that you bought? Microsoft and Apple say no, absolutely not. Individual legal experts aren't quite so sure, particularly if you're taking off CRAP licenses so that you can play the music you bought on machines that you own.

Stay tuned. The debates are going to get thick.

I don't know about you, but that really gets my goat. You paid for the music. You aren't allowed to send out a hundred thousand copies of the songs to your closest friends, of course. But you should be able to play them on your PCs or download them to your music player as many times as you want, or burn them daily for the next hundred years, I figure.

Guess what? You can. Even if your music has the worst copy-protection (uh, DRM) restrictions in the world, you can convert that AAC or WMA file to an unprotected MP3, and pretty easily. The quality isn't anything to write home about, and it takes time. But it can be done. Follow these steps:

1. Burn the tracks onto a typical, everyday audio CD.

   I give detailed instructions in Technique 26. If you use iTunes, follow the instructions on the Burn tab.

2. Stick the CD back in your PC and rip the songs to MP3 format.

   Instructions for doing so with Vista's Windows Media Player are described in Technique 27. If you have iTunes, follow the Rip tab.

 It's really that easy. Some loss in quality occurs unless you have very-high-quality audio files to begin with (in which case, you should rip with an MP3 rate that's slightly lower than the original recording rate). But the resulting files aren't copy protected and aren't protectable. And they play on any machine, anywhere.

Sorting through the Stores

If you really, really want to spend your money on music that can't be freed from Microsoft's or Apple's ever-changing restrictions, make sure you shop around a bit. When you go looking for an online music store, here's what you should consider:

✔ **What is the price?**

✔ **What kind of restrictions do you have to endure?** If you "rent" a library, do you need to reconnect your MP3 player to your computer every month to prevent the music from self-destructing? (Visualize the intro to any *Mission Impossible* movie.)

✔ **Can you find the kinds of music you want to buy quickly and easily?** Hey, any site has the latest release from Eminem, but not many cover Buckwheat Zydeco. And finding new bands such as Buckwheat can be a daunting task.

✔ **Can you download the music without a hassle?** You can access Apple's iTunes Music Store only through the iTunes media player (which is a very good media player; see Technique 26).

✔ **What are the format and quality of the songs on offer?** If you have a tremendous computer audio setup, looking for WMA Pro Lossless may be worthwhile. But for most of us whose audio budgets don't approach the national debt, any of the major download sites works fine.

✔ **Oh, did I mention? What's the price?**

 To date, the online music stores differ very little, except for the price — and with the inevitable price wars coming, there's no reason to get locked into a single service. For most people, the difference between a WMA VBR recording of U2's latest album and a 192-Kbps AAC recording doesn't amount to a hill of beans. Play the field. Go for price.

Got the URGE?

Microsoft and MTV created URGE, the online music store built into Vista's Windows Media Player (yes, you can change the store, but most people don't — see Technique 26 for the way to avoid it entirely). It's easy to buy music from URGE — you don't have to leave Windows Media Player. But before you buy any music from URGE, make sure that you understand the CRAP, er, Digital Rights Management restrictions that apply (see the figure):

"We shall (and you agree we are permitted to) transmit and arrange for automatic installation of any and all updates, modifications, and/or even full re-installations of the Software to address security, digital rights management, interoperability, and/or performance issues. . . . The Software also includes automated features that collect information that uniquely allows the Software to automatically identify your computer and your system, the version of the Software in use and to manage some or all of the digital rights associated with Content. These features may be remotely activated in order to update security components used by the Software, including, without limitation, portions of the Windows Media Player associated with your use of URGE. These updates, modifications, re-installations and other modifications to the Software can occur periodically or when necessary and without any notice to you."

That's what the URGE license says. Really. (Or, at least, said. Heaven knows how it has changed by now.) Are you sure you want to buy anything from URGE?

 In the final analysis, the only songs that "play for sure" are plain, old-fashioned MP3 files. Don't let Microsoft's marketing palaver sway you. Don't heed the Apple siren call. As long as they're copy protected, files that "play for sure" often don't.

26

Technique

Using Windows Media Player

Save Time By

✔ Getting Windows Media Player's settings right

✔ Customizing and controlling the beast

✔ Putting the volume control where you can reach it quickly

Microsoft has come a long way from Windows Media Player 8 (WMP 8), which shipped with the original version of Windows XP. For one thing, the old version automatically kept track of what you played and sent Microsoft these great little notices with details about your audio and video proclivities, complete with a "branding" number that uniquely identified your PC. In the latest version, Microsoft tries to convince you that allowing Mama Microsoft to keep track of your playing and viewing habits is to, er, enhance your personal experience. Yeah, that's the ticket.

To Microsoft's credit, the version that ships with Windows Vista, Windows Media Player 11, gives you plenty of opportunity to protect your privacy, if you know which check boxes to uncheck. I don't credit Microsoft's largesse: The company has lost a lot of credibility — and more than a couple of court cases — over privacy-infringing shenanigans in Media Player.

If you choose correctly, you can even avoid installing the (huge) URGE support package, thus dodging Microsoft's attempt to gang up with MTV and outsell Apple's iTunes. Hey, you can waste your time with URGE if you like — but make sure that you understand where the URGE-ies are coming from (see the sidebar "Got the URGE?" in Technique 25). This technique gets you up and running WMP 11 quickly and with a minimum of hassle — now and in the future.

Getting the Right Media Player

Windows Media Player ain't the only game in town.

If you grow weary of WMP's in-yer-face advertising and obnoxious Microsoft-file-format bias, you have plenty of good alternatives. Two stand out — iTunes and Winamp:

✔ **Apple's iTunes** (www.apple.com/itunes), based on the QuickTime platform (a buggy program I've been railing about for years), has a good interface. So good, in fact, that Microsoft, uh, borrowed many of its elements when it designed WMP 11. iTunes makes printing CD case inserts easy. It even allows you to convert songs from Microsoft's WMA format to Apple's AAC format, as long as the WMAs aren't copy protected. And if you own an iPod (I love mine — all of 'em!), you have to use iTunes or Winamp to get songs transferred from your PC to your iPod (see Technique 30). iTunes is free.

✔ **Nullsoft's Winamp** (www.winamp.com) includes several innovative capabilities, including Winamp Remote, which lets you use a Web browser anywhere in the world to create a list of all the media files on your computer at home and "stream" the songs or movies to your current location. Winamp Dashboard helps you locate music that you might want to play and keep on top of improvements to Winamp. A full-featured free version of Winamp is available. For $9.99, you get faster CD burning and ripping and the ability to rip into MP3 format (an important capability that is free in both Windows Media Player and iTunes).

 Nowadays, I use Windows Media Player (without URGE, thank you very much) for most of my media mangling. But I load iTunes with the music that I want on my Pod. I keep swearing that if QuickTime locks up on me one more time, I'll switch to Winamp for Pod feeding. It could happen.

 If you decide to go with Windows Media Player, make sure that you get the latest version. Microsoft updates it about as often as *Survivor* changes locations. Historically, the updates have not been distributed automatically via Microsoft Update. Check to see whether a new version is available by choosing Start⇨All Programs⇨Windows Update.

Running WMP for the First Time

If you haven't yet run Windows Media Player, it's easy to get started on the right foot. Follow these steps:

1. **Choose Start⇨All Programs⇨Windows Media Player.**

Note that we're working with Windows Media Player here, not Windows Media Center (which is more widely focused on video, TV, and the "10-foot interface" that works well with a TV remote).

The WMP 11 setup wizard appears, as shown in Figure 26-1.

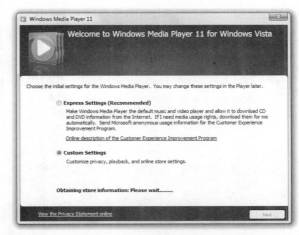

• **Figure 26-1:** To set privacy options right the first time — and avoid waking URGE — select the Custom Settings option.

2. **Select the Custom Settings option, and click the Next button.**

The Privacy Options dialog box appears, per Figure 26-2.

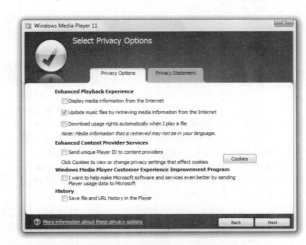

• **Figure 26-2:** Don't let WMP get too intrusive.

3. **Consult Table 26-1 for an English translation of the options on offer, check the boxes you really want to use, and click the Next button.**

WMP asks whether you want to add a shortcut to the desktop and/or the Quick Launch toolbar.

4. Check the box to add an icon to the Quick Launch toolbar; then click the Next button.

 WMP asks whether it can take control of all your music and video files (see Figure 26-3). Actually, WMP is asking whether it can be associated with the filename extensions for a couple dozen audio and video file types — every extension that WMP understands.

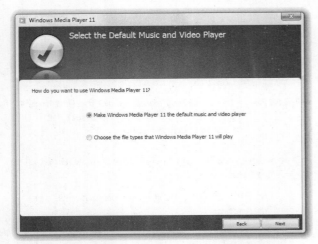

• **Figure 26-3:** I let WMP take over all the filename extensions that it can understand.

5. I usually let WMP take control of all the audio and video filename extensions, and selectively reassign individual extensions to specific programs by hand. (For example, I may assign MP3 files to Winamp or MPG files to WinVideo. Maybe.) If you feel comfortable with that approach, select the Make Windows Media Player 11 the Default Music and Video Player option and click the Next button.

If you don't feel comfortable with that approach, select the Choose the File Types That Windows Media Player 11 Will Play option and click the Next button. At that point, you can manually sift through a couple dozen filename extensions.

WMP asks you to choose an online store, as shown in Figure 26-4.

6. You can select the option that says Golly Gee, I'd Really Like to Stare at My Computer for the Next Half-Hour while You Download This Wonderful Media-Purchasing Opportunity for Me. Or, you can select the Don't Set Up a Store Now option and click the Finish button.

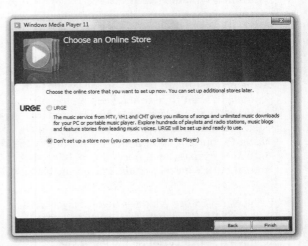

• **Figure 26-4:** Hey, at least Microsoft asks for permission.

 If you don't choose to set up URGE, Windows Media Player appears rather quickly. It scans the preordained disk locations for music and video files and presents them to you in the WMP Library, as shown in Figure 26-5.

 I talk about setting up alternative folders for the WMP Library in Technique 27.

• **Figure 26-5:** Windows Media Player reporting for duty.

TABLE 26-1: WMP PRIVACY OPTIONS

What It Says	What It Really Means	Timesaving Tip
Display Media Information from the Internet	Every time you play a song or watch a video, WMP goes out to a Web site owned by a Microsoft "partner" (possibly www. windowsmedia.com, which is 100-percent owned by Microsoft), retrieves information about the song or video . . . and then offers to sell the CD or DVD to you! In the process of retrieving the information, you leave behind personally identifiable information, adding more observations about your personal activities to Microsoft's collection.	Checking this box is foolish, fattening, and immoral. And it wastes time with every song or video you play.
Update Music Files by Retrieving Media Information from the Internet	When you add music to your Library or rip a CD, WMP goes out to the "partner" database, retrieves the album info, and then changes the "metadata" associated with identified files, adding missing information from Microsoft's giant database.	I don't like the lost privacy, but I do use the feature because it saves a lot of time.
Download Usage Rights Automatically When I Play a File	When you try to play a song or video, if the file has usage restrictions (see the discussion of CRAP music in Technique 25), WMP automatically contacts the owner of the file (no, you don't own the file) and requests permission to play it.	I don't check this box for two reasons. First, if I have a file that needs permission, I want to know about it up-front so that I can delete the lousy thing. Second, this approach could be shanghaied to bring malware into my PC. An earlier version of this "feature" had that precise problem — see http:// securitytracker.com/alerts/ 2005/May/1013945.html for details.
Send Unique Player ID to Content Providers	Whenever WMP phones home to Microsoft, or contacts any "partner," you give your permission to send MS or the partner a number that uniquely identifies your computer.	You gotta be kidding. Microsoft lost a court case over this one: It can't turn this switch on by default, so it tries to convince you to turn it on. It's bad enough that Redmond gets my IP address, which is mighty darn close to a unique identifier.
I Want to Help Make Microsoft Software and Services etc., etc.	This option signs you up for the Customer Experience Improvement Program.	It's hard to fathom how Microsoft can call individual ID tracking a Customer Experience Improvement Program — especially after the court cases — but here it is, in the flesh. People wonder why I'm so cynical. . . .
Save File and URL History in the Player	WMP saves detailed logs of every song or video that you play, even if you play it (stream it) from the Internet.	Leave the box unchecked. The history logs don't help much, and they're certainly an enticing target for anyone who's interested in your browsing history.

Making Media Player Improvements

It's important that you take a minute to get WMP's privacy settings straight. Even if you went through the first-time instructions in the preceding section, run through these quickly — Microsoft "forgot" to put one privacy setting on the setup screen, and it doesn't hurt to double-check and ensure that everything's working in your favor. Follow these steps to get your privacy settings right:

1. While running Windows Media Player, hold down Alt (that brings up the menu) and choose Tools➪Options.

WMP opens its Options dialog box.

2. Click the Privacy tab.

You see the privacy options (see Figure 26-6), which closely mirror the options that you set when you first ran WMP.

3. Follow the guidelines in Table 26-1 to set WMP's privacy options.

Two additional settings appear in this dialog box:

▶ **Automatically Check If Protected Files Need to Be Refreshed:** This option comes into play if you "rent" music on the Internet. I don't rent music — heck, I don't rent water, either — but if I did, I'd want to be advised every time WMP reaches out to check on the rental status, and possibly charge my credit card. Uncheck the box unless the warnings bother you incessantly.

▶ **Set Clock on Devices Automatically:** This option ensures that your MP3 player's clock is synchronized with your computer's — this is of primary importance to folks who rent music on the Internet and transfer the rented files to an MP3 player. Keep this box checked unless you have an overwhelming need to change it.

4. Click the OK button.

Your new privacy settings take effect immediately.

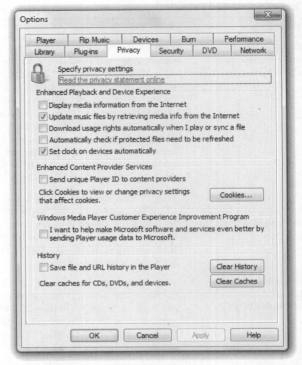

• **Figure 26-6:** Watch out for your privacy — nobody else will do it for you.

After you have Media Player's privacy-busting antennas clipped, you should go into WMP and make a handful of key changes. They'll save you no end of frustration and headache in the long run. Here's what every WMP user should do:

1. While running Windows Media Player, hold down Alt and choose Tools➪Options.

You see the WMP Options dialog box.

2. Click the Rip Music tab.

WMP shows you its Rip Music settings (per Figure 26-7).

Ripping is the process of pulling music off an audio CD and converting it into a computer file, thus making it more readily usable on a PC. I talk about ripping in Technique 27.

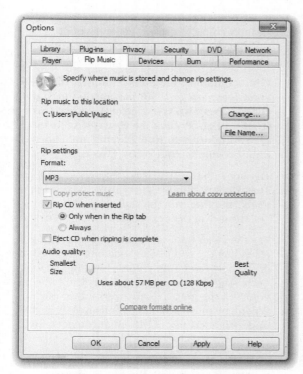

• **Figure 26-7: Make sure that you rip to MP3 format.**

3. If you want to store your ripped music in a Public folder (which makes it available to others on your computer and your network), click the Change button, navigate to your `Public\Public Music` **folder, and click the OK button.**

4. In the Rip Settings Format drop-down box, tell WMP that you want to rip your music into MP3 files.

 You will notice that, ahem, immediately after selecting MP3 as your ripping format of choice, the check box that says Copy Protect Music goes gray. You can't protect MP3 music — can't turn it into CRAP, for love or money.

Congratulate yourself. You just made one of the most important timesaving changes possible in all of Vista-dom.

 If you choose to rip into the WMA format, and the Copy Protect Music box is checked, every time you rip an audio track, WMP marks the file so that it can be played only on the machine that ripped it — or (depending on the restrictions in place at the moment and Microsoft's whim) a limited number of times on other machines. If you've ever tried to play a WMA file that was created on a different PC and it wouldn't work, now you know why.

5. Click the Devices tab.

WMP shows you a list of all the music-related hardware in your computer.

6. Choose the DVD or CD drive that you use to rip music and click the Properties button.

You see a DVD (or CD) Properties dialog box like the one shown in Figure 26-8.

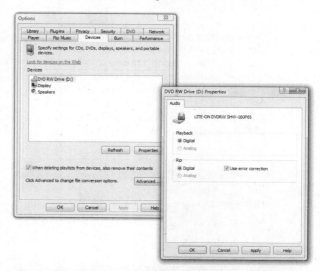

• **Figure 26-8: Make your DVD or CD drive try its best to recover scratchy songs.**

7. Check the box marked Use Error Correction.

With this box checked, WMP will mercilessly bother the DVD/CD drive when it detects a "skip" in the ripped song — you know, the zijjing and screeping that you hear when you have a dirty CD. Checking this box is no guarantee that your CDs will rip perfectly. But if you have a marginally scratched CD, at least WMP will try hard to recover the original music as best it can.

8. **Click the OK button.**

Your changes take effect immediately.

Running WMP

If you've never used Windows Media Player before, start by going through the steps in the preceding section. Then try playing a CD. Follow these steps:

1. **Pop a music CD into your CD drive.**

2. **If Vista tosses up a dialog box asking what you want to do, select the Play Audio CD Using Windows Media Player option and click the OK button.**

 WMP springs to life, as shown in Figure 26-9. If you told WMP that it's okay to update music files by retrieving media info from the Internet (see the preceding section), chances are good that WMP reached out to one of Microsoft's "partners" and correctly retrieved the name of the album, the artist, the names of the tracks, and album art.

• **Figure 26-9:** A view of WMP playing Rick Wakeman's classic electronic album *Six Wives of Henry VIII*.

If you hover your cursor over the picture of the album's cover, Microsoft will even offer to sell you the CD you just stuck in the drive. Thoughtful, huh?

3. **WMP contains a number of audio settings —** *enhancements* **in WMP parlance — including control over SRS WOW effects. To leaf through what's on offer, click the teensy-tiny down arrow underneath Now Playing and choose Enhancements➪SRS WOW Effects.**

To play with the SRS WOW settings, click the Turn On link, choose the type of speakers you're using, and then run the sliders up and down. Tell the guy in the next cubicle to put a sock in it.

Try the other enhancements — cross fading (blending the end of one song into the beginning of the next) and auto volume leveling (so that each song plays at approximately the same base volume), the graphic equalizer, and so on. When you're tired of it, click the little X in the upper-right corner of the enhancement's box.

4. **If you're looking for those far-out** *visualizations* **— the abstract patterns that move in concert with the music, more or less — click the down arrow under Now Playing and choose Visualizations, and then pick the visualization you want to see.**

All together now: "Grooooovy."

5. **Click the Minimize button in the upper-right corner (the one that looks like an underline).**

WMP asks whether you want to put the WMP toolbar — it's more like a mini-player — on the Windows taskbar.

6. **Click the Yes button, and the mini-player appears immediately to the left of the system tray (see Figure 26-10).**

 That's a good place for it. To bring back the full WMP, click the tiny icon in the far lower right that looks like two overlapping Windows windows.

• **Figure 26-10: Windows Media Player can reduce itself to a mini-player on the taskbar.**

Controlling WMP from the Keyboard

While you can use the on-screen controls for playing and pausing, many people find using the keyboard controls easier — especially if the mini-player is on the Windows taskbar. Check out Table 26-2.

 One particularly good key to remember: F7 immediately turns off the sound — but only if WMP is the active window.

TABLE 26-2: WINDOWS MEDIA PLAYER SHORTCUT KEYS

This Key	Does This
F7	Turns off the sound
F8	Decreases the volume
F9	Increases the volume
Ctrl+P	Plays/pauses the track
Ctrl+S	Stops the track
Ctrl+B	Goes back one track
Ctrl+F	Goes forward one track

Working with Codecs

Some people I know get all weak in the intellectual knees when they hear the term *codec*. You don't need to get spooked — it's nothing magical, and codecs won't take over your computer.

A *codec* (short for *coder-decoder* or *compressor-decompressor*) is a small program that converts data from one form to another — kind of a media Babelfish, if you recall the *Hitchhiker's Guide to the Galaxy*. Codecs are important in the Windows Media Player world because you need a codec to translate different kinds of media files into data that WMP can understand.

 Unfortunately, filename extensions don't tell the whole codec story. For example, the WMA files on your computer aren't all necessarily constructed the same way; they might be completely different, internally. Looking at a WMA file, you wouldn't necessarily know whether it was created using Microsoft's old WMA 7 format, the WMA 9.2 format (which is the default codec used in Windows Media Player 11), or the WMA Pro 10 format (the super-fancy one). It's up to Windows Media Player (or Winamp, which also plays WMA files) to look inside the file and decide which format was used to create the file. After the determination has been made, WMP (or Winamp) hauls in the right codec to decipher the file. You don't need to lift a finger.

Sometimes, though, Windows Media Player doesn't have the correct codec on hand to play a particular file. The AVI file I download in Technique 20 — `The Cabinet of Dr Caligari_xvid-belos.avi` — was constructed using a particular kind of video-encoding technique called DivX. (Actually, there are several different kinds of DivX files, but you get what I mean.)

 When you try to play a media file that WMP doesn't understand, WMP helps you find the codec.

The following steps describe how WMP located the codec to play `The Cabinet of Dr Caligari_ xvid-belos.avi`:

1. Double-click a video or audio file.

In this case, I double-click `The Cabinet of Dr Caligari_xvid-belos.avi`. WMP can't find the codec necessary to play this kind of DivX video, so it shows me the message displayed in Figure 26-11.

• **Figure 26-11:** WMP asks for help in finding the codec necessary to play the file.

2. Click the Web Help button.

Windows Media Player fires up Internet Explorer and connects to a Web site that specifically identifies the missing codec (see Figure 26-12). It needs the Xvid MPEG-4 (Xvid) codec.

• **Figure 26-12:** Microsoft's Web site correctly identifies the precise codec that's needed.

3. Click the WMPlugins.com link.

The WMPlugins Web site — which is owned by Microsoft — gives you a link to the Xvid codec, as shown in Figure 26-13.

• **Figure 26-13:** Microsoft's site points to a (free) codec.

4. Click the link to the codec download site.

In this case, click the Xvid Codec Download Site link.

Microsoft shows a disclaimer on the screen, saying that Microsoft is helping you leave a Microsoft site and that the site you're going to — the one with the codec — isn't associated with Microsoft.

5. Click the link that says Gee Microsoft, It Would Sure Be Nice If You Made a DivX Codec Available to Your Paying Customers, but Because You Don't, I Agree That You Can't be Held Responsible.

WMPlugins transports you to the download site — in this case, `www.xvidmovies.com` (see Figure 26-14).

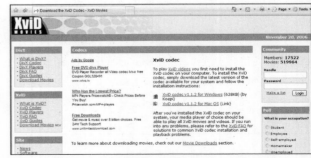

• **Figure 26-14:** The kind folks at XviD Movies make their codec available free.

6. **Click the link to download the codec.**

In Figure 26-14, the link is called XviD Codec v1.1.2 for Windows (by Koepi). Thank Koepi for me, wouldja?

Internet Explorer goes through the usual file download routine.

7. **When the download is done, click the Run button.**

You may have to click through some scary-looking dialog boxes saying that the publisher couldn't be verified and allowing the installer to run. Eventually, you get to the codec's setup wizard or something similar.

8. **Follow the installer's instructions. If it tells you to close all other applications, you can click the red *X* to exit the umpteen Internet Explorer windows. Then go back to Windows Media Player and click the Close button on the original codec notice (refer to Figure 26-11), and then click the red *X* to exit Windows Media Player.**

Ultimately, the codec gets installed.

9. **If you closed Windows Media Player, double-click the video or audio file again.**

This time, The Cabinet of Dr Caligari_ xvid-belos.avi plays like a champ (see Figure 26-15).

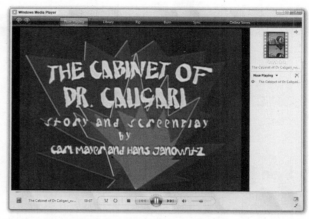

• **Figure 26-15:** The doctor is in.

If you ever want to see a list of all the codecs installed on your computer, choose Start⇨All Programs⇨ Accessories⇨System Tools⇨System Information. In the System Information dialog box that appears (see Figure 26-16), on the left, double-click to navigate down to System Summary⇨Components⇨Multimedia and then click either Audio Codecs or Video Codecs.

• **Figure 26-16:** A complete list of codecs installed on your PC.

27 Technique

No-Nonsense Music Gathering

Save Time By

- ✔ Adding music on your PC to the Media Library — fast
- ✔ Managing playlists so that you hear what you want, right now
- ✔ Ripping (pulling tracks from audio CDs) the right way, the first time
- ✔ Looking for music in all the right places

Hey, if you're a teenager, getting into things is part of your job description. Windows Media Player is full of nooks and crannies and interesting and fun places where you can poke and prod (and find out a lot about computers!) for hours on end.

On the other hand, if you just want to get the %$#@! thing to work, all those little fun places get in the way.

If you own an MP3 player, uh, iPod, er, personal media device, you might be suffering a little sticker shock. That fancy new iPod set you back a couple hundred bucks or so. But putting music on it? Whoa. Twenty thousand songs at 99 cents *each?* There has to be a better way.

This technique shows you how to get songs and video clips into Windows Media Player, and how to organize them so that you can push a button or two and listen to something you really want to listen to. Now.

Adding Music to the Media Library

Whether you intentionally downloaded them or not, whether you want them or not, your PC already overflows with audio files: grunts and squawks and bleeps and moans, with a few worthwhile songs here or there. If you have a home- or small-office network, and your son has been ripping CDs since he fell off the turnip truck, you may have a few more tunes sitting around.

 Your first step in gathering music? Catalog what you already have. In WMP-speak, that's called "adding items to the Media Library."

WMP is set up to search your personal folders and your computer's Public folders for music and videos. If you have more than one user on your computer, and these users aren't knowledgeable enough (or sharing enough) to stick their music and video files in the Public folders, your copy of Windows Media Player doesn't know squat about them. Moreover, if you store music or videos on a separate drive, or on your network, WMP hasn't a clue.

It takes a while to scan all your drives — and even longer to scan network drives — but when you're done, you can get at all the music and videos on your computer through WMP itself, rather than have to search manually for songs or videos on your hard drive.

To have WMP monitor unusual locations for audio and video files, follow these steps:

1. **Start Windows Media Player.**

If you can't find it immediately, choose Start➪ All Programs➪Windows Media Player.

2. **If you want to retrieve album covers, artist names, and song titles for all the music on your computer, click the little down arrow underneath the Library button and choose More Options. Click the Privacy tab and select the Update My Music Files by Retrieving Media Info from the Internet check box, and then click the OK button.**

Be aware that selecting this check box gives Microsoft a detailed list of all the music on your computer, along with your IP address to boot. Check out Technique 26 for more information.

3. **Click the little down arrow underneath the Library button and choose Add to Library. If you see an Advanced Options button, click it.**

You see a dialog box like the one shown in Figure 27-1.

 If you've run Windows Media Center at any point in the past, the `C:\Users\Public\ Recorded TV` folder appears as a manually added folder, at the top of the list. That's where it came from.

4. **Select the My Folders and Those of Others That I Can Access option.**

If you have an administrator account, checking this box forces WMP to monitor other users' folders.

• **Figure 27-1: Point Windows Media Player to different locations for real-time monitoring.**

5. **Check the box marked Add Volume-Leveling Values for All Files (Slow).**

 You know how TV commercials blare out louder than the normal TV programs? (At least it seems that way.) The Add Volume-Leveling Values for All Files (Slow) box tells Windows Media Player to scan each track as it's added to the Library and adjust the overall volume control for the track so that it isn't too soft or too loud. Choosing this leveling option significantly slows the processing of each file as Windows Media Player puts it in the Library. But it also means that you won't have to go diving for the volume control when some boorish audio or video track wants to play at an astoundingly high level.

6. **If you want to add a folder that isn't on the list, click the Add button.**

WMP shows you the Add Folder dialog box (see Figure 27-2). Choose the folder you want to add to Windows Media Player's "watch list" and then click the OK button.

• **Figure 27-2: Add folders from anywhere on your computer or your network.**

7. **When you've added all the locations you want to add, click the OK button.**

Windows Media Player scans the selected locations and apprises you of its progress with the Add to Library by Searching Computer message box, shown in Figure 27-3.

• **Figure 27-3: Windows Media Player scans all the media files.**

If you told Windows Media Player to add volume-leveling values (Step 5) or to retrieve media info from the Internet (Step 2), it can take hours to scan all your music. Days.

8. **When you get tired of looking at the message, click the Close button.**

Windows Media Player's scan continues in the background, and it will begin again anytime you add or delete a file in the selected locations.

The scanner does not look inside compressed folders or zip files.

Ripping CDs You Own

When the topic turns to ripping CDs — the process of pulling songs off audio CDs and putting them on your computer — the first question that inevitably arises is one of ethics.

Ripping ethics

I'm not talking about the ethics of ripping a song and giving the file to another person. There's no question about the ethics of illegally pirating music. You can make copies of music on CDs that you bought for your own private use. People try to hem and haw and weasel their way around the legalities, but their justifications are self-serving. The bottom line's pretty simple. In the United States, you can make copies of any music that you bought to do any of the following:

✔ Keep a backup for your own private use.

✔ Change the format (for example, so that you can download it to a small music player) for your own private use.

✔ Rearrange the order in which the music is played (commonly via a playlist) for your own private use.

✔ Make compilations of your favorite songs for your own private use. Do you see a pattern here?

 You also can loan the original CD to a friend, and your friend can listen to it. But your friend can't make a copy of the CD.

That's it. The ethics and legalities of pirating are quite straightforward. If you have any questions, ask your lawyer how she rips her music.

The real ethics question is whether you trust Microsoft or Apple to control the future format of your music. If enough people use Microsoft's proprietary WMA format or Apple's AAC format, the Big Boys will have a great deal of influence on the future direction of digital music and video.

Choosing a file format and sampling rate

Not so very long ago (he says, stroking his long, white virtual beard), the vast majority of computer-legible music existed in so-called MP3 format. You can learn about the whole sorry story of CRAP music in Technique 25.

Microsoft and Apple have their own music formats, called WMA and AAC, respectively. As of this writing, MP3, WMA, and AAC are locked in a celebrity death match duel (trial?) for the hearts and minds of Windows users. If Microsoft or Apple wins, the victor will likely rule the creation and distribution of music and video files well into the next decade. If lowly MP3 wins, Big Software loses — and the major record labels and video companies will find other ways to distribute their wares electronically.

 Yes, I know that AAC isn't a proprietary format — it doesn't belong to Apple — per se. Apple grafted a copy-protection, er, Digital Rights Management scheme called FairPlay onto AAC, and the Apple AAC + FairPlay combination is proprietary. When you download music from the iTunes store, you get AAC (for the music) + FairPlay (to keep you from giving the song to your 100,000 closest friends).

WMA was built, from the ground up, to protect the people who sell music. AAC started out as an open standard, but FairPlay turns the screws. MP3, on the other hand, sprang from the halcyon days when nobody cared much about Digital Rights Management. You can't copy-protect an MP3 file.

The choice of file format isn't entirely a political decision. There are technical considerations, too: After all, the name of the game is high-quality music. Each of the music formats has, in effect, a low-quality recording level, a couple of high-quality levels, and several levels in between. The recording level is called a *sampling rate*. Rates are measured in Kbps, or thousands of bits per second.

As you might expect, all these technical factors have an effect on how many songs you can squeeze into a portable music player (what many call an *MP3 player*) and on how good the music sounds when you play it. See Table 27-1 for a heads-up comparison.

That said, WMA and AAC have MP3 beat all to pieces in one area: surround sound. If you have a 5.1 surround-sound system built into your computer, don't bother with MP3. And be careful not to stub your toe on that $1,000 subwoofer, okay?

 If you have an outstanding audio setup and you love classical music, use 192 Kbps or higher, rather than 128 Kbps. If you want quality above compatibility, be sure to look at the Vorbis OGG format (www.vorbis.com). You can't play it on anything, but it sure sounds sweet! Okay, okay. I exaggerated a little bit. In fact, more and more products support OGG every day. You can even get an OGG codec for Windows Media Player (see Technique 26 for the lowdown on codecs).

Windows Media Player, right out of the box, includes a very good MP3 codec — a piece of software that lets you convert audio CDs into MP3 computer files and play MP3s till the cows moo home.

TABLE 27-1: WOODY'S TAKE ON THE FORMAT CONUNDRUM

Format	Sampling Rate	Hassle Factor	Music Quality	Number of Songs on a 2GB Player	Comments
MP3	64 Kbps	Low	Blech	1,000 or so	Good enough for playing on blah computer speakers.
MP3	128 Kbps	Low	Very Good	500	Woody's Choice Award Winner — if you want to keep Microsoft and Apple from taking over the music-distribution business.
AAC	128 Kbps	Medium	Best of the bunch	600	Apple's AAC-to-WMA converter helps, particularly because so few AAC players exist (other than the iPod and variants, of course).
WMA	128 Kbps	High	Excellent	500	A decent choice if you plan to play music only on your PC, or if you have a small music player that can handle WMA. But realize that you're helping Microsoft take over electronic music file formats.

The ballad of the MP3 codec

Back when Microsoft first released Windows XP and WMP 8, a hue and cry arose from many corners, saying that Microsoft failed to ship an MP3 codec because it didn't want people to use MP3. Not so, insisted the 'Softies: Most people didn't rip CDs, so they didn't need an MP3 codec. And, oh, the licensing fees! Adding MP3 support would be enormously expensive. Why should everyone pay extra for something only a few people want?

Yeah, right. MS wanted to get the WMA format on firm footing, and it wasn't about to put MP3 support in Media Player.

Fast-forward three years, and MS started to include a free MP3 codec in every copy of WMP 10. No wailing about licensing fees. No charge. You know why Microsoft did it? Because its competitors had free MP3 codecs, and every WMP review mentioned that fact. Microsoft was forced to keep up with the Joneses. Sometimes competition works, eh?

Ripping from A to Z

Ripping a CD is easy. The whole process takes five minutes or less for a typical album, and you can do it while you're working on something else.

If you followed the steps in Technique 26, you're ready to rip. Otherwise, you need to check a couple of settings. Here's how:

1. **Start Windows Media Player.**

   Choose Start➪All Programs➪Windows Media Player if no shortcuts are hanging around.

2. **Click the little down arrow under the Rip button and choose More Options.**

   You see the Rip Music tab of the Options dialog box, as shown in Figure 27-4.

3. **If you haven't already done so, choose MP3 from the Format drop-down box. And if you want to rip quickly, all the time, make sure that Rip CD When Inserted is checked and that the Only When in the Rip Tab option is selected.**

 You can change these settings quickly by working directly with the menu that appears when you click the little down arrow under the Rip button. You might want to do so if you have a particular album that you want to rip at a higher sampling rate, for example.

4. **Click the Library tab. If you haven't done so already, select the Retrieve Additional Information from the Internet check box.**

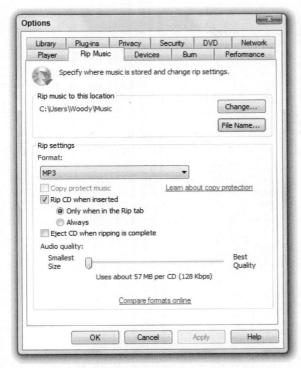

• **Figure 27-4:** Make sure that your rip options are right.

 Selecting this check box ensures that Microsoft will know about every single CD that you rip. But, hey, it's your music — and having the album information tagged automatically onto the tracks saves a lot of time and frustration. Check out Technique 26 for more information.

5. **Click the Devices tab.**

WMP shows you a list of all the media-related pieces of hardware on your system.

6. **Click your CD or DVD drive, and then choose Properties.**

WMP shows you a Properties dialog box like the one shown in Figure 27-5.

7. **Make sure that the Use Error Correction box is checked, and then click the OK button twice.**

• **Figure 27-5:** Properties for the drive you use to rip music.

This step ensures that WMP tries its utmost to retrieve all the music from scratchy, dirty old CDs. You know — the kind you like.

8. **Click the Rip button. Then insert the CD you want to rip into your drive.**

9. **Sit back and grab a latte. You don't need to lift a finger.**

Windows Media Player starts playing the CD and simultaneously rips your CD into MP3 files, complete with the album cover, song titles, and artist — all the information that's fit to print (see Figure 27-6). When the ripping's done, the music continues.

To rip another CD, go back to Step 8. It's that easy.

• **Figure 27-6:** Ripping *The Six Wives of Henry VIII*.

Looking for Music in All the Right Places

When you start worrying about filling up that 20,000-track iPod with 99-cent music, keep a few things in mind:

- ✔ MP3s will always play in any Windows-based media player, and in any portable music player. Why? Because any company crazy enough to manufacture a small music player that won't take MP3s will be out of business in a week. Okay, I'm exaggerating — some companies are stupid (and rich) enough to try. But you're smart enough to avoid their products, right?

- ✔ The best way to get music that "plays for sure" is to make sure that you get MP3s. You can always rip an audio CD and turn it into MP3s: Audio CDs are the electronic music world's universal donors.

- ✔ eMusic (www.emusic.com) has an enormous, legal MP3 collection — as we went to press, it had 1,800,000 songs from a wide array of artists, although it doesn't carry anything from EMI, Sony BMG, Universal, or Warner (the "Big Four" that run 75 percent of the music market). eMusic offers monthly subscriptions, starting at $9.99 for 30 downloads.

- ✔ If you venture to one of the not-legal-in-the-U.S. MP3 download sites (http://AllOfMP3.com, www.MP3Sugar.com, or http://MusicMP3.com), keep in mind that none of the money you spend goes back to the artists who created the music. Nor does it go to the conglomerates that control much of the music-distribution system around the world.

Happy hunting. . . .

Creating Your Own Music CDs and DVDs

Save Time By

- Understanding what you can — and can't — do with a CD or DVD writer
- Burning CDs and DVDs the right way, the first time
- Troubleshooting common problems

If you have a CD or DVD drive and you've never *burned* a CD or DVD — that is, written data to a CD — you're in for a treat. Windows Media Player truly makes burning audio CDs simpler than ever. In fact, the toughest part of the job is deciding what kind of CD to burn. There are a few tricks and a couple of potential traps — Microsoft's licensing of its copy-protected WMA files can drive you nuts. But I bet you'll be surprised at how fast and easy burning a CD can be.

Talk about saving time! If you fumble around in your car swapping CDs at 70 miles per hour (or even gently gliding from CD to CD on that big six-disc changer), you're a great candidate for burning your own mixes, getting more songs on a single CD, eliminating the lousy tracks from an otherwise-good album, or otherwise pulling together the music you want to hear without all the junk in between. It's cheap. It's easy. And now, with WMP, it's fast.

This technique shows you all you need to know.

 I don't cover burning video DVDs in this technique, and I'll tell ya why: The Vista product for burning video DVDs, called Windows DVD Maker, isn't worth your time or effort. Okay, I'll waffle a little bit. If you put together a movie in Windows Movie Maker (see Technique 35) and you just want to get the movie onto a DVD that Great Aunt Gertrude can stick in her DVD player, Windows DVD Maker can do the job. Barely. Windows DVD Maker rates as the single most woe-fully underpowered DVD burner on the market: It's hard to figure out, illogical, and buggy, and I've hit lots of situations in which it just doesn't work right. Definitely a Microsoft "version 1.0" product.

 If you need to burn a video on DVD, don't waste your time with Windows DVD Maker. Spring for a real DVD-burning package such as Nero (www.nero.com). When you install Nero, don't let it take over all your filename associations — the Windows Media Player interface is much better for playing CDs and DVDs. But the very first time you burn a real video DVD, Nero will pay for itself.

Choosing the Type of CD/DVD to Burn

If you look on store shelves, you see 74-minute CD-RWs, 80-minute CD-Rs, 90-minute CD-Rs, 120-minute DVD-Rs — and heaven-knows-what-all from this manufacturer and that. How do you know what works in your CD burner?

Heh, heh, heh. That's a trick question. Chances are mighty good that your burner — if you bought it in the past couple of years, anyway — can handle all those types of CDs. With aplomb.

Almost all CD (and DVD) burners can run the full gamut of CD-Rs, CD-RWs, DVD-Rs (I should say DVD plus-or-minus Rs), and DVD-RWs. Here's the lowdown:

- **CD-R (CD-Recordable) and DVD-R:** Record with these discs multiple times — in multiple sessions — but each time, the new stuff appends to the end of the disc. You can't erase and reuse the space occupied by the old stuff.

- **CD-RW (CD-Recordable/Writeable) and DVD-RW:** Record with these discs multiple times, adding and deleting files, with space from the deleted files being recycled.

 The differences between DVD-R, DVD-RW, DVD+R, and DVD+RW get a touch more complex, but the folks who make DVD burners decided quite some time ago that they should handle all the formats and do so without bothering you with any details. It's a rare DVD burner these days that can't handle everything.

In addition, Vista allows you to burn CDs and DVDs in two different formats:

- **Mastered** (or ISO), the older format, is compatible with more CD and DVD players and older versions of Windows. When Vista burns a mastered CD or DVD, it has to preprocess the files and then burn them all at one time.

- **Live File System** (or UDF), the newer format, is compatible with many DVD players, but not so many CD players. Live File System CDs and DVDs can't be read by versions of Windows prior to Windows XP (although XP deciphers them, no problem). When Vista first learns that you want to use Live File System on a CD or DVD, it has to format the disc. After the disc has been formatted, you can add or delete files, much the same as with a giant floppy disk.

 I hate it when Microsoft says that Live File System discs act like USB flash drives. They don't. Vista can access any location in a flash drive immediately: It's a random-access storage medium. Live File System CDs and DVDs act like giant floppy drives: Vista can hop around the disc a bit, but when the data comes out, it comes out sequentially. It gets laid down sequentially, too.

Mostly, it isn't a question of what your burner can handle. The question you need to ask is "What works in your CD or DVD player?"

There's the rub. You can record on almost any kind of CD with fairly recent CD writers, and using audio DVDs is like falling off a log. But can your CD player play what the burner has burned? The following list clarifies that question:

- Older CD players play only songs in the first recording session on a CD-R. If you want to make sure that your music will play on any CD player, you must opt for audio CD burning on a Mastered CD. And you get only one chance to put all the music you want on the CD.

- Later CD players play multiple recording sessions on CD-Rs and/or recordings on CD-RWs. Such players often have inscriptions that say "CD-R" or "CD-RW" and maybe even "multisession."

- Some CD players can play any kind of audio CD-R or CD-RW, and they can also play MP3 files (or even — gasp! — WMA files) directly. The best of them can also handle DVDs with any kind of file.

This I know from brutal first-hand experience: It's hard to tell by reading a CD player's manual exactly what it can play. Your best bet is to sacrifice a few CDs and try different approaches. If an approach fails, don't throw away the CD. The next CD player you buy can probably handle it.

Picking Songs and Burning the CD

To pick songs that you want to burn on a CD, follow these steps:

1. **Start Windows Media Player and click the Burn button.**

If you see no handy icon to start WMP, choose Start➪All Programs➪Windows Media Player.

You will save yourself many headaches if you don't try to burn any copy-protected Microsoft-proprietary-format WMA files on a CD. If you accidentally ripped audio files in copy-protected WMA format, go back and rip them again. See Technique 27 for details.

2. **Click the tiny down arrow below the Burn button (see Figure 28-1) and choose one of the following:**

• **Figure 28-1:** What kind of CD do you want to burn?

▶ **Audio CD:** Creates a traditional audio CD — the kind you can play in any CD player. You can

fit, oh, 15 to 20 songs on a typical audio CD. There's no such thing as an Audio DVD.

▶ **Data CD or DVD:** Copies files such as the music files from your PC (say, MP3 files, or possibly WMAs or AACs) directly onto a CD or DVD. Using this option, you can fit hundreds of songs on a CD, and thousands on a DVD — but you'd better have a CD or DVD player that can handle MP3s (or possibly WMAs or AACs).

 I've had no end of problems with CDs and DVDs that don't last very long. I've discovered that by recording them at a slower speed — something less than the fastest-rated speed for the DVD drive — they last longer. If you've hit the same problem, click the tiny down arrow below the Burn button and choose More Options (see Figure 28-2). In the drop-down box next to Burn Speed, choose Medium or Slow. Then click the OK button.

• **Figure 28-2:** Slow your burner to create higher-quality CDs and DVDs.

3. **Stick a blank CD or DVD in your drive.**

This is where Vista gets in the way, and you can be easily confused. Windows Media Player recognizes the inserted CD and, in the upper-right corner of the WMP window, tells you what kind of disc you inserted. At the same time, Vista discovers that a blank CD is in the drive and sticks its nose into the fray, displaying the AutoPlay dialog box you see in Figure 28-3.

• **Figure 28-3: So, do you go with Windows Media Player or with Vista? Do you feel lucky, punk?**

I always click the red *X* to exit the AutoPlay dialog box, and I suggest you do the same. It leads to less confusion.

4. **Find a bunch of songs that you want to burn — say, by bringing up an album or a playlist or by running a search.**

5. **Select songs by clicking them, by Ctrl+clicking individual songs, or by Shift+clicking a group of songs.**

In Figure 28-4, I click the artist name — Earl Scruggs — and all the songs in the album are selected.

6. **Right-click one of the selected songs and choose Add to Burn List. Alternatively, you can drag the songs to the Burn List playlist on the right, or you can click the Burn 'Earl Scruggs' link.**

Burn Earl Scruggs? Poor Earl.

• **Figure 28-4: Pickin' Scruggs flatt.**

Windows Media Player creates a new Burn List and adds the songs you selected to the list. Earl's entire Classic Bluegrass Live album, which I have in MP3 format, takes up about one-tenth of a CD — 634MB remain on a 702MB disc.

7. **Keep dragging songs over to the Burn List until your clicking finger gets tired or you run out of room on the CD.**

If you run out of room, WMP draws a line on the burn list and inserts a marker that says Next Disc (see Figure 28-5). At that point, you can right-click individual songs and choose Remove from List. Or, you can keep adding songs to fill out the second CD. Or the third . . .

Click and drag individual tracks to change the order in which they appear. Futz and finagle all you like. Ultimately, you are ready to burn the CD or DVD.

8. **Click the Start Burn button, below the Burn List playlist.**

WMP starts burning the disc (see Figure 28-6). Go grab a good book — or clean your poor, neglected mouse. It takes several minutes to burn a typical audio CD, and a half-hour or more to burn a fully loaded DVD (especially if you took my advice in Step 2 and slowed things down a bit). Fast burners are popular for a reason, eh?

• **Figure 28-5: One CD or many, WMP makes it easy.**

WMP puts a 2-second gap between each song. You can't change it. If you rip and burn an audio CD that plays songs back to back with no gap (I won't mention Nine Inch Nails by name), you hear an unexpected gap. That isn't an error or a bad track on the CD. It's just the way WMP does things.

• **Figure 28-6: Sit back and relax. The burn will be over sooner or later.**

When WMP is done, your computer ejects the CD from the drive.

9. **Take your new CD to whatever player you intend to play it in, and make sure that it works.**

Do it now, while it's easy to burn with different settings. As described at the beginning of this technique, compatibility problems with older CD players aren't unusual.

 If you want to erase a CD-RW or DVD-RW, way over on the left side, underneath the URGE icon, right-click the name of the disc and then choose Erase Disk. WMP looks at the CD or DVD, figures out whether it contains only music files, and, if so, erases all the files from the CD-RW or DVD-RW. If your CD or DVD contains other kinds of files (which is to say, any files other than standard audio "CDA" files, or MP3, WMA, or WAV files), WMP doesn't erase them.

29

Technique

Picking Up Podcasts

Save Time By

- ✔ Finding podcasts you want to hear
- ✔ Subscribing and keeping up
- ✔ Knowing the pitfalls when making your own podcast

L et's be clear about something that confuses the bewilickers out of most people: Podcasts have absolutely nothing to do with iPods. Apple would like you to believe that iPods and podcasts go together like mashed peas and honey or kid-leather gloves and hobnailed boots. (Don't ask.) Microsoft hardly even acknowledges the term. But even though the word originated as a mash-up of *iPod* and *broadcast,* a podcast isn't really a broadcast, and it doesn't require an iPod.

At this point, only iTunes and Winamp (see Technique 26) and a handful of lesser-known audio programs support the automatic downloading of podcasts. Microsoft has this thing about the letters *p-o-d.* That shouldn't deter you from listening to podcasts. In fact, it's one of the best reasons to switch to iTunes or Winamp.

 I talk about podcasting primarily from an iTunes point of view in my book *Windows Vista All-in-One Desk Reference For Dummies* (published by Wiley). If you have an iPod and/or use iTunes, that's a good starting point.

In this Technique, I focus on hooking up to podcasts directly — by playing them straight off the Internet in Firefox or Internet Explorer, and keeping updated via Really Simple Syndication (RSS) feeds. If you have iTunes or Winamp, this Technique can help you find podcasts quickly and directly, without tackling the iTunes maze. If you don't have and don't want iTunes, this Technique shows you how to go it alone without feeling like a second-class pod-citizen. Too much.

Understanding Podcasts

At its most basic, a podcast is just an audio file. You can play it, copy it, move it to your Zune, or delete it the same way that you play, copy, move, or delete any other audio file.

Two peculiarities differentiate podcasts from, say, the latest MP3 from DJ Cool or a Rachmaninov concerto:

✔ Podcasts are usually serialized — people who create podcasts publish them on a more-or-less regular basis.

✔ If you have iTunes or Winamp, most of the time you can *subscribe* to a series of podcasts, so you don't have to download each one — iTunes and Winamp can watch and automatically download new podcasts, possibly syncing them to an MP3 player. Alternatively, you can subscribe to an RSS feed that keeps you alerted when new podcasts from a specific source become available. When you see a new podcast that you want to hear, you click through to the Web site and play it immediately on your PC. (I talk about RSS feeds and how to view them in Technique 18.)

In short, podcasts combine the immediacy of a blog with the added dimension of sound. The glue that holds it all together? RSS.

Finding Worthwhile Podcasts

If you have Apple's free music player, iTunes (www.itunes.com; see Technique 30), you've no doubt encountered iTunes support for podcasting (see Figure 29-1).

• **Figure 29-1: iTunes has podcasting support built in.**

In iTunes, on the left, double-click Podcasts and the iTunes store pummels you with a plethora of podcasts, many of which are free (see Figure 29-2).

• **Figure 29-2: Podcasts galore from iTunes, including commercial news programs, NPR, Stanford lectures, and much more.**

Many times while wending your way around the Web, you'll stumble upon podcasts that interest you. For example, for many years, I've subscribed to a newsletter called Lockergnome (www.lockergnome.com). Chris Pirillo, "Mr. Lockergnome," tackles a bunch of geeky topics in unique ways. Chris was one of the first big-name podcast proponents, with podcasts appearing sporadically since Christmas 2004. Every issue of his newsletter has a link to his podcasts.

 If you take a look at Chris's approach, you see how podcasts can be short and sweet, and how finding good podcasts can go very quickly. You don't need to wade through the iTunes list (although "The Chris Pirillo Show" *is* available through iTunes). You can go straight to the source.

Here's how Chris does podcasts:

1. **Fire up your favorite Web browser and go to** www.thechrispirilloshow.com, **or click the podcast link in any of Chris's Lockergnome newsletters.**

Chris's podcasting page appears, as shown in Figure 29-3.

• **Figure 29-3:** The Lockergnome podcast.

2. **To listen to the latest podcast, click the Listen Now icon in the lower-left corner.**

Chris's Web page plays the podcast. No download. No iPod. No subscription.

3. **Scroll down to earlier podcasts, or click the Archive list to access any program Chris has produced over the years.**

4. **If you have iTunes and you want to subscribe to "The Chris Pirillo Show," click the Add to iTunes link in the upper-right corner.**

Firefox brings up a dialog box that asks your permission to run iTunes, handing it the subscribe request for Podcast number 73330048, which just happens to be "The Chris Pirillo Show." Click the Launch Application button and iTunes appears, ready to have you subscribe to Chris's show. Click the Subscribe button, and new editions of "The Chris Pirillo Show" appear automatically in iTunes. (See *Windows Vista All-in-One Desk Reference For Dummies* for more details.)

5. **If you want to subscribe to "The Chris Pirillo Show" RSS feed, click the little orange RSS "broadcast" feed icon on the far right.**

Firefox brings up its RSS feed subscription page, as in Figure 29-4. If you subscribe to the RSS

feed, you can easily watch to see when Chris posts new podcasts on his site. For more details about how Firefox and Internet Explorer handle RSS feeds, see Technique 18.

That's all you need to do. Sit back and when Chris has a new show, you'll either get it downloaded automatically through iTunes or be notified via RSS. Very slick.

• **Figure 29-4:** No need for iTunes — you can watch for new shows via RSS feed.

If you're looking for podcasts to fill that daily commute, by all means look at the 3,000-entry iTunes Music Store podcast listing. But also consider using one of these specialized search sites:

✔ **Podcast Alley** (http://podcastalley.com; see Figure 29-5) includes a viewer- (listener-?) generated Top 10 list of the most popular podcasts of the month.

✔ **BlinkX** (http://blinkx.com), **Podscope** (http://podscope.com), and **Podzinger** (http://podzinger.com) all "listen" to podcasts or the audio portion of posted videos, and try to analyze the content and present it in a text-searchable form. My results have not been outstanding, but it's an interesting concept that will only get better.

• **Figure 29-5:** Podcast Alley keeps you on top of the latest.

✔ **Singingfish** (http://search.singingfish. com) has the best interface in the business (see Figure 29-6). Emphasis is on well-known and sorta-well-known celebrities.

✔ **Yahoo! Podcasts** (http://podcasts.yahoo. com) turns up a lot of interesting podcasts that don't seem to be indexed anywhere else.

• **Figure 29-6:** The Singingfish interface makes it easy to rummage through lots of podcasts.

Rolling Your Own Podcast Quickly

The mechanics of creating your own podcast aren't beyond the reach of any budding radio personality. I cover the basics in *Windows Vista All-in-One Desk Reference For Dummies.* You can find a detailed "getting started" checklist at http://reviews.cnet.com/4520- 11293_7-6246557-1.html. And you'll find the advanced course in *Podcasting For Dummies,* by Tee Morris, Evo Terra, Dawn Miceli, and Drew Domkus (published by Wiley).

If you want to save time getting up to speed on creating your own podcast, you should do the following:

✔ **Watch the podgrunt video at** http:// gruntmedia.com/podgrunt_main.html. It's a good, quick visual overview of how podcasting hangs together, from a business perspective.

✔ **Tie your podcast to a blog.** If you have a blog entry devoted to each podcast, you create an easy "landing strip" for anyone who bumps into your podcast while otherwise employed on the Internet. Fill the blog entry with keywords that can be picked up by indexing engines and write copy that sizzles.

✔ **Minimize your expectations for making money podcasting.** Yes, some people do; the vast majority do not. Podcasts either support another income-producing product or activity, or the podcast is offered gratis, as a public service.

✔ **Check Google for podcasting support.** Podcasters are everywhere. Find them with your favorite search engine(s).

✔ **Take advantage of others' expertise and experience.** You might want to subscribe to a podcasting newsletter such as Weekly Podcast Tips (http://weeklypodcasttips.com) or The Podcasting Underground (www. podcastingunderground.com).

✔ **Know the legalities.** Podcasting can run you afoul of many different legal pitfalls. Be mindful of the fact that incorporating music into your 'cast has legal implications, and you can't simply read copyrighted material. Start by looking at

```
http://wiki.creativecommons.org/
Welcome_To_The_Podcasting_Legal_Guide.
```

Happy podcasting!

30 Technique

Transferring Music to iPods and MP3 Players

Save Time By

- ✔ Choosing an MP3 player — what counts, what doesn't
- ✔ Copying songs to an MP3 player (or video player) quickly and accurately

CDs are neat, but when it comes to saving time, MP3 players are better. No need to shuffle and scratch those shiny round discs. No need to fumble with all those moving parts. (Tell the truth — when's the last time you tore the top off a CD player?) And, man, the capacity on the new MP3 players boggles my mind. It's as though you could keep the songs going for a month and never hear the same one twice (or come pretty close).

Vista's Windows Media Player makes it drop-dead simple to copy music from your PC to most plain-vanilla MP3 players. You have to watch out for a few gotchas, but by and large, the entire process goes along with click (and occasional drag) precision. Similarly, copying video onto personal video players rates as fall-off-a-log simple, providing that the video player works with Windows Media Player.

iPods are another story altogether. If you have an iPod, you need to use iTunes (www.itunes.com) or Winamp (www.winamp.com) to get music off your PC and onto your iPod. Yes, you can transfer MP3 files. You don't need to buy your iPod music from the iTunes Store. See Technique 25 for a discussion of the various music formats and Technique 27 for ways to gather MP3s like roses in May.

As far as the mechanics go, copying files to an MP3 player is every bit as easy — and at least twice as fast — as copying to a CD-R or DVD-R drive (see Technique 28).

This Technique tells you how to avoid the gotchas and how to getcha goin' in no time.

Choosing an MP3 Player

People frequently ask me what to look for when they're shopping for an MP3 player. The answer is simple: If you want cool, get an iPod. If you want functional, don't worry about the brand and go for memory. If you want to keep paying for your initial mistake over and over again, find something that locks you into a dead-end proprietary format, such as Microsoft's Zune or the "Plays for Sure" fiasco.

I own iPods, and I love 'em. I use iTunes to put music on the iPods, but I may go back to Winamp one of these days. I don't buy songs from the iTunes store and recommend that you avoid the big-name conglomerates, too.

iPods have several problems. They're congenital and are described as follows:

✔ **You can't use Windows Media Player to put music on an iPod.** Microsoft doesn't touch anything with a "Pod" in it. That leaves you — and me — with an uncomfortable decision. I cope by using Windows Media Player for all my media stuff but hauling in iTunes when I need to pump the Pod. It's a messy solution. I talk about it at length in my book *Windows Vista All-in-One Desk Reference For Dummies* (Wiley).

✔ **You can't add music from two different computers to the same iPod.** At least, you can't with iTunes. But you can with Winamp, using an add-in called mlipod. See www.mlipod.com.

✔ **You can't transfer music from your iPod to your PC.** I should say that you can't transfer music from your iPod to your PC unless you know the trick. See Technique 31 for details.

✔ **You can't play Microsoft's proprietary WMA music files on an iPod.** Is that *really* a problem? Debatable. iTunes automatically converts non-protected WMA files into AAC files, which your iPod can play. But if you paid for a WMA file, you're up a creek. Of course, if you buy a song from the iTunes store, it won't play on any MP3 player other than an iPod. The lesson? Don't buy CRAP music. See Technique 25.

✔ **When you plug your Pod into your PC, all your music may disappear.** That's because iTunes, by default, "syncs" music with the iPod as soon as it's plugged in. "Sync" is a euphemism: In fact, iTunes looks at each song on your iPod, and if you don't have a copy of the same song on your PC's hard drive, it deletes the copy on your Pod. Bummer. See Technique 31 for very precise instructions on how to disable Autosync.

Whether you want to pay for the very cool iPod approach, or you're going for a bare-bones grunt-and-play MP3 player, you need to look at memory.

A song recorded in MP3 format at 128 Kbps (the setting I recommended in Technique 27) takes 1 to 2MB per minute — so a tiny, cheap 256MB MP3 player holds a little under 3 hours of music. The 2GB iPod nano realistically holds about 20 hours of MP3 music. A 20GB player holds about 200 to 300 hours of music.

Figure out how much memory you need — and whether you have to buy memory cards — and make that the controlling factor when you buy a player.

Everything else falls into the bit bucket. All players do the following:

✔ Support ID3 (or WMA) tags so that you can see the names of the songs on the player.

✔ Accommodate the latest, greatest, most thunderous earphones or headphones.

✔ Work with millions of different kinds of speaker systems, holders, belt clips, armbands, and navel spikes. Piercing not included.

✔ Use USB connections. These connections are good enough, unless you want to transfer a dozen CDs of music every night of your life (in which case, you might want to use FireWire).

Before you plunk down your credit card, make sure that you can understand the MP3 player's controls. Some MP3 players have such incredibly inscrutable buttons and on-screen commands that it's hard to believe they were designed to be used by humans.

iPods break all the rules, and I think that's great. I love my iPod, although I use my cheap Nomad MuVo, too. If you plan to get an iPod, don't sweat the small stuff. Stick with MP3 files so that Apple can't pull the rug out from under you — in other words, avoid the iTunes store — but other than that, go Apple all the way.

Copying Files to an MP3 Player

If you have an iPod, copying files to your Pod with iTunes is like falling off a log. You can find a thorough, accurate tutorial at www.apple.com/support/ipod/tutorial. Take the tutorial before you plug in the Pod and you'll be syncing in no time. I have more advanced information about updating the iPod's internal software and navigating rather complex problems in *Windows Vista All-in-One Desk Reference For Dummies* (Wiley).

The method of copying songs to an MP3 player is virtually identical to the one in Technique 28 for burning CDs.

 You can save yourself a lot of headaches if you make sure that you copy only MP3 files — or WMA files without copy protection — to your MP3 player. Some older MP3 players won't play WMA files. Protected WMAs require a digital license, which may be granted only ten times (you can copy the file ten times, but the eleventh time, you can't copy it). If you download a WMA song from a record company's Web site — or if you buy a WMA version of a song from one of Microsoft's "partners" — Microsoft or the record company determines how, when, or whether you can put the WMA file on your MP3 player. MP3 files have no such limitations. In fact, you'll find no hooks inside MP3 files to allow anything of the sort. With MP3, what you see is what you get. Read Technique 25 for more details about CRAP music and why you should stick to MP3s.

The easiest way to find legit MP3s? Buy the CD and rip it using the method I describe in Technique 27.

Follow these steps to get songs from Vista's Windows Media Library onto your MP3 player:

1. **Plug your MP3 player into your PC's USB port and turn on the player.**

Vista responds with an AutoPlay dialog box like the one shown in Figure 30-1.

• **Figure 30-1: Vista recognizes your MP3 player.**

2. **Click the Play Using Windows Media Player icon.**

Windows Media Player appears and starts playing the music on your MP3 player.

3. **Click the Sync button near the upper-right corner of the dialog box that appears.**

Windows Media Player shows you the MP3 player that's currently plugged in — the picture in the upper-right corner and an entry among the libraries on the left — and gives you an idea of how much room is left on the player. In Figure 30-2, you can see that I have 0 MB remaining on my MuVo. Yikes!

• **Figure 30-2:** Not a whole lotta room left on this puppy.

4. If you don't have enough room to hold the music you want to put on the player — or if you want to wipe out everything and start all over again — double-click the name of the MP3 player on the left and choose Songs (or possibly Artist or Album).

WMP shows you a list of the songs on the MP3 player, as shown in Figure 30-3.

• **Figure 30-3:** It's easy to remove songs from the player.

You can also use the Search box to find unwanted songs.

5. If you want to copy any specific songs or albums to your computer, don't bother trying to do it in Windows Media Player. Instead, choose Start➪Computer, double-click the drive letter for your MP3 player (you may have to hunt around a bit), and then click and drag the songs from the MP3 player to your computer. It's that easy.

Make sure that you have backup copies prior to deleting songs on the MP3 player.

6. When you find an album, song, artist, or whatever that you don't want on the player anymore, right-click it and choose Delete.

Windows Media Player asks whether you're sure that you want to delete the selected items.

7. Click OK.

WMP deletes the files on the MP3 player. They're gone.

8. When you're done deleting, double-click one of the categories on the left, under Library.

Time to go hunting for new music for the MP3 player.

9. Click and drag songs, albums, artists, or whatever from the Library on the left to the Sync List on the right.

When you have too much for your MP3 player, the indicator at the top says Filled (after Sync), as shown in Figure 30-4.

• **Figure 30-4:** Drag items to the Sync List.

Note that you can move items in the Sync List, right-click and remove them from the list, and basically do everything that you can do with playlists in Windows Media Player.

10. When you're happy with the items in the Sync List, click the Start Sync button.

WMP copies the items you place on the Sync List onto the MP3 player.

Any items that didn't make the cut are indicated by a Status notice saying `Did Not Fit on Device`, as shown in Figure 30-5.

When WMP finishes, it tells you that you can now remove your MP3 player.

11. **Pull the plug. Click the red X to exit Windows Media Player.**

You're ready to hip. And hop. Simultaneously.

• **Figure 30-5:** If you have too much to fit, WMP tells you that the songs didn't get copied.

Getting Music Off Your iPod

Technique 31

Save Time By

- ✔ Copying music files from your iPod back onto your PC
- ✔ Recovering "metadata" quickly and easily

iTunes and Winamp make it drop-dead simple to copy MP3 and AAC music from your PC to your iPod. You have to watch out for a few gotchas, but by and large, the entire process goes along with click (and occasional drag) precision. I cover the details in my book *Windows Vista All-in-One Desk Reference For Dummies* (Wiley).

But try to copy music from the iPod back to your PC — man, you'd think that you were trying to raise Lazarus.

iTunes won't help. Apple doesn't want you to copy music the other way. There's no money in it.

So what happens if, say, your hard drive dies, and all your music is stuck on your iPod? What if you need to send your iPod into the shop and you're not sure whether it'll come back the same way it went in? Apple lets you copy purchased iTunes music onto a backup hard drive. Why won't it let you do the same thing with music on your Pod? Why, indeed.

This Technique steps you through copying files from your iPod back onto your PC, and then reassembling all the details — artist, album name, and so on — that the iPod buries.

 I believe that this is the first time these instructions — for bringing files back from an iPod, and then reconstructing the filenames and folder structure — have ever appeared in print.

Disabling the iPod's Automatic Sync Feature

You need to take a precautionary step if you're trying to take songs off an iPod using a computer that's already been synced to the iPod.

If you've never synced your iPod with the computer that you're using to copy the iPod's music, you can skip down to the next section. But if you have synced with the current computer, or if you're not absolutely sure whether you have, follow these steps *before* you try to retrieve any music from your iPod. You need to make sure that iTunes won't automatically come in and wipe out what's on your iPod before you copy the music off — in other words, you need to disable Automatic Sync.

There's a trick. iTunes won't let you set iPod options unless an iPod is plugged into your computer. But if you have Autosync turned on, plugging your iPod into the computer could lead to all the songs in your iPod getting zapped. Catch-22. Fortunately, it's easy to work around. Follow these steps:

1. **Choose Start⊏>Music. If you've run iTunes on this computer and you haven't messed around with its default folder locations, you see a folder called iTunes, as shown in Figure 31-1.**

The iTunes folder contains all the weird info that controls iTunes and its behavior with your iPod.

• **Figure 31-1: If you've used iTunes on this computer, you have an iTunes folder in your Music folder.**

2. **Click the iTunes folder and drag it onto your desktop.**

Not to worry. You drag it back at the end of this section.

3. **Start iTunes. DON'T PANIC.**

None of your songs show up in the iTunes Library. That's okay. The Library is stored in the iTunes folder, which you've temporarily placed on your desktop, hidden from iTunes.

4. **Plug in your iPod.**

5. **If you get an AutoPlay notification, click the red X to exit AutoPlay.**

iTunes presents you with a notification that your iPod is linked to another iTunes music library (see Figure 31-2). That may or may not be true. By moving the iTunes folder in Step 2, you've severed the link between your iPod and this computer.

• **Figure 31-2: Be careful to click the No button.**

6. **In the Linked to Another iTunes Music Library message box, click the No button.**

That ensures that your Pod won't be synced. This time.

iTunes comes up with the iPod selected and shows you all the music on the Pod. You see the Display iPod Options icon (it looks like an iPod) down near the lower-right corner of the iTunes window.

7. **Click the Display iPod Options icon, found in the lower-right corner.**

iTunes brings up the iPod options dialog box shown in Figure 31-3, with the Music subtab selected.

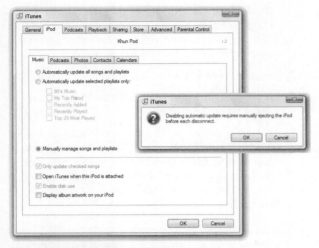

• **Figure 31-3: Disable automatic syncing here.**

8. **Uncheck the Open iTunes When This iPod Is Attached box. Then select the Manually Manage Songs and Playlists option.**

iTunes warns you sternly that you have to manually eject the iPod before each disconnect.

9. **Click OK twice.**

You return to iTunes.

10. **Go back to Vista's desktop and click and drag the iTunes folder back into your Music folder.**

Be careful to drop the iTunes folder inside the Music folder, *not* inside one of the other folders in the Music folder. If you did it right, Windows Explorer warns you that the destination already contains a folder named iTunes.

11. **Click Yes. You do want to merge the old iTunes folder with the new one.**

Vista asks whether you want to remove and replace a newer file with an older one (see Figure 31-4). Usually, that's a sure sign that you've goofed — in most cases, you want to keep the newer file — but in this case, yes, you do want to dump the new file and use the old one.

12. **Check the Do This for the Next 1 Conflicts box and then click the Move and Replace icon.**

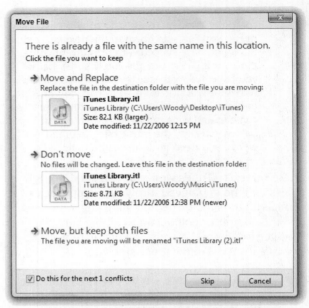

• **Figure 31-4: Get rid of the new files and copy the old ones.**

Vista overwrites the new files and replaces them with the older ones — the ones that contain your Library.

13. **Start iTunes and confirm that your old library is in place. If you're the paranoid type, click the iPod icon at the bottom and make sure that the Manually Manage Songs and Playlists option is selected and that the Open iTunes When This iPod Is Attached box is unchecked (refer to Figure 31-3).**

14. **Shut down iTunes and unplug your iPod.**

You can stop holding your breath now.

Copying iPod Music to Your PC

At the risk of repeating myself, if there's any chance that your iPod has ever been attached to the computer that you want to use to copy its music, you *must* follow the steps in the preceding section.

Here's how to get the music out of your iPod and into your PC:

1. **Make sure that iTunes isn't running and then unplug your iPod.**

2. **Choose Start⇨Music.**

   Windows Explorer shows you the Music folder.

3. **Press Alt and then choose Tools⇨Folder Options. Click the View tab. Select the Show Hidden Files and Folders option. (While you're here, if you haven't done so already, uncheck the Hide Extensions for Known File Types box.) Click OK.**

   That forces Vista to show you hidden files and folders; the folders on your iPod are marked hidden.

4. **Plug your iPod into your PC.**

   The standard Vista AutoPlay notification should appear.

5. **Click the Open Folder to View Files Using Windows Explorer link.**

   Explorer comes up with a list of the folders on the iPod, as shown in Figure 31-5.

• **Figure 31-5: The folders on your iPod. No, your music isn't in the Music folder!**

   The iPod has a very convoluted storage system.

6. **Double-click iPod_Control. Then click the Music folder and drag and drop it onto your desktop.**

This new Music folder contains a bunch of oddly named folders, probably called F00, F01, and so on. Each of those folders contains music files — but they, too, have odd names.

7. **Just to keep from getting confused, right-click the new Music folder on your desktop, choose Rename, and rename it to, oh, Music from iPod.**

8. **You can unplug your iPod now.**

   The songs are back on your PC. You don't need the iPod anymore.

 If you go poking around that Music from iPod folder (see Figure 31-6), you discover that all the songs from your iPod are there, but the files have weird names like JDAT.mp3, and they're all scattered around in various folders, willy-nilly.

• **Figure 31-6: All the music is there — somewhere.**

In the next section, I show you how to bring back the original filenames and folder structure by using The Devil Ye Ken.

Restoring Missing Information

So you followed the nostrums in the preceding section and you now have a folder on your desktop called Music from iPod, which contains a whole bunch of songs, all jumbled — the way they actually exist on your iPod.

Even though your files look as though they've gone through a wringer — in fact, they have — you can probably bring back all the original filenames (or at least the track numbers and song names), the folder structure, and all the tags such as artist and album — the whole nine yards. Here's how to do it:

1. **Start iTunes.**

The Devil Ye Ken, eh?

2. **Choose Edit⇨Preferences, and then click the Advanced tab.**

The iTunes Preferences dialog box appears, with the Advanced tab active (see Figure 31-7).

• **Figure 31-7: The options that tell iTunes to unscramble the mess it put on your iPod.**

3. **Select the Keep iTunes Music Folder Organized and the Copy Files to iTunes Music Folder When Adding to Library check boxes. Then click OK.**

You might want to keep a record of the original settings for both of those check boxes. That way, you can restore them to their original values when you're done reconstituting the iPod files.

You go back to iTunes.

4. **Click the Music from iPod folder and drag it onto the iTunes window.**

Most of the time, that adds the music in the Music from iPod folder to the iTunes Library. In some cases, however, iTunes doesn't respond the way it's supposed to. If you can't get the music added to the Library the easy way, you have the following two harder ways to accomplish the same thing:

▶ Choose File⇨Add Folder to Library. Then navigate to the \Desktop\Music from iPod folder (see Figure 31-8). Click the OK button.

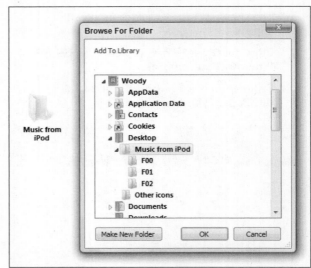

• **Figure 31-8: Have iTunes add the Music from iPod folder to its library.**

▶ Go through each of the folders in the Music from iPod folder (in Figure 31-8, that would be F00, F01, and F02). Open each folder, press Ctrl+A to select all the songs in the folder, and then click and drag the selected songs from the folder to the iTunes window.

It may take awhile, depending on iTunes's buggy behavior, but in the end, all your songs get copied to the iTunes library.

5. **Choose Start⇨Music, double-click the iTunes folder, and then double-click the iTunes Music folder.**

Lo and behold, all your original music is there, neatly filed in the proper folders, with filenames set to track numbers followed by song names (see Figure 31-9). Astounding.

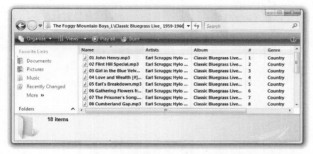

• **Figure 31-9:** iTunes puts the songs back in order, sets up the proper folder structure, and brands each file with the track number and song name.

6. **If you like, you can click and drag the music folders out of iTunes's clutches and put them anywhere you like — most likely in your Public Music folder or in your own Music folder.**

Treat them just as you would any other music file.

7. **To clean up after yourself, delete the Music from iPod folder on your desktop.**

You don't need it anymore.

8. **To return iTunes to its original settings, choose Edit⇨Preferences, click the Advanced tab, and consider deselecting the Keep iTunes Music Folder Organized and the Copy Files to iTunes Music Folder When Adding to Library check boxes.**

Restore them to the state they were in at Step 3, earlier in this list. If you really *want* iTunes to take control of your music and make a lot of redundant copies of your songs, heck, you can leave both boxes checked.

Amazing how iTunes can be shanghaied to help you unscramble the songs you put on your iPod, eh?

Part VI

Having Fun and Saving Time with Visual Media

The 5th Wave   By Rich Tennant

COSMETIC SURGERY

"This time, just for fun, let's see what you'd look like with bat ears and squash for a nose."

Technique 32

Organizing the Photo Gallery

Save Time By

- ✔ Getting the pics you want into the Photo Gallery
- ✔ Adjusting Photo Gallery Settings
- ✔ Scanning directly into the Gallery

When the subject turns to Vista's Photo Gallery, Microsoft's hype machine (patent pending) rolls into high gear.

We're treated to happy talk about "digital memories" meant to mask some of Photo Gallery's shortcomings — "digital memories" being a euphemism for "Photo Gallery handles JPG, BMP, MPG, AVI, PNG, and TIF files, but it won't even bother with GIF, PCX, or even Microsoft's own WMF format files."

We're assured that support for the super-detailed camera RAW format is on its way, and that wireless picture transfer is coming, too. Someday.

The value of the Photo Gallery Search bar is directly proportional to the capability of Vista's search engine, which has been clipped to such a point that . . . ah, don't get me started. I rant about Vista's search engine in Technique 16.

The reality of Photo Gallery: It's a moderately capable photo organizer with a few touch-up features that work reasonably well. Its primary redeeming social grace? It's built into Vista.

This Technique shows you how to make Photo Gallery more useful — saving you a ton of time in the process — and how to take advantage of a couple of buried features that rarely see light of day.

For more information about importing digital photos into the Photo Gallery, see Technique 34.

Coping with Photo Gallery Limitations

The first time I started the Photo Gallery, I nearly gave up. In its default configuration, the Vista Photo Gallery (Figure 32-1)

- ✔ **Shows pictures in your Pictures folder, Videos folder, and the Public Pictures and Videos folders.** That's it. You can add more folders to the

Gallery, but the rules for deleting folders are a bit, uh, convoluted. See the next section for details.

✔ **Shows thumbnails,** but you can't choose what size of thumbnail you want to see. If you roll your mouse over the thumbnails, the computer hesitates for a second or two, grabbing your mouse in the process, and displays an *enlarged thumbnail* of whatever picture you happened to be over at the moment (see the thumbnail with a thyroid dithorder in Figure 32-1).

If the picture has been rotated, sometimes the rotated picture appears enlarged, but sometimes you see the original, unrotated pic. Photo Gallery takes a long time to catch up.

✔ **Groups pictures by year.** By year? Well, sorta by year. If all your pics are properly tagged with the year in which they were taken or created, you get 'em by year. But if you have any scans of old family pictures, they'll probably be filed under the date they were scanned. At least you can see that Microsoft reached back to 2004 for its stock photos, stored in the Public Photos folder.

✔ **Doesn't show your GIF pictures,** or any older pictures in PCX or WMF (Windows Metafile) format, much less videos in MOV format.

Fortunately, you can solve — or at least mitigate — some facets of the first three problems. The last is a congenital defect without cure.

Futzing with the Photo Gallery

Here's how to correct some of the problems listed in the preceding section:

1. **Choose Start⇨All Programs⇨Windows Photo Gallery to start Photo Gallery.**

   You see the main screen like the one in Figure 32-1.

   If you enjoy seeing all your year 2006 photos in one blob, I admire your visual scanning ability. But if you're like most of us, you want to see your pics by folder.

2. **Find the heading above one of the groups of pictures — in Figure 32-1, the heading says 2004 - 152 items — right-click the heading, and choose Group By⇨Folder.**

   Photo Gallery sorts the list of pictures by folder, as in Figure 32-2.

• **Figure 32-1: Some of Photo Gallery's more annoying, time-soaking habits can be changed.**

• **Figure 32-2: Pictures sorted by folder, but Photo Gallery still slows down things by slowly showing enlarged thumbnails.**

I've heard that some people own computers so fast that they can hover over thumbnails and have the enlargements appear without hesitation. I don't *believe* it, but I've heard it. If you have a computer that costs less than a minute of advertising time during the Super Bowl, you probably hate the time-swallowing stutter.

3. To get rid of the enlarged thumbnails, choose File➪Options, and in the Windows Photo Gallery Options dialog box, uncheck the box marked Show Picture and Video Previews in Tooltips. Then click OK.

The thumbnails no longer grow enlarged when you hover your mouse. With the enlarged thumbnails disabled, Photo Gallery shows you the details of a photo when you hover your mouse over it (per Figure 32-3), a much faster process.

• **Figure 32-3:** Get rid of the enlarged thumbnails and speed up the Photo Gallery appreciably.

If you have your photos stored someplace other than your Pictures or Public Pictures folder, and you don't mind waiting an hour or two to have them indexed, you can tell Photo Gallery to include them in the mix.

4. To add other folders to the Photo Gallery, Choose File➪Add Folder to Gallery. In the Add Folder to Gallery dialog box (see Figure 32-4), choose the folder that you want to add and click OK.

• **Figure 32-4:** Tell Photo Gallery to start monitoring all the pictures going into and out of a specific folder.

If you have folders anywhere on your network, such as a public or shared folder, you can add those folders to the Photo Gallery in the same way you add a folder on your local hard drive, no problem.

You can also add a folder by clicking on it and dragging it into the Photo Gallery.

5. Photo Gallery advises that it might run slower while your pictures are being indexed. Click OK.

When Photo Gallery comes back, it shows the folder you added on the left, under the Folders list (see Figure 32-5). The contents of the added folder appear on the right, along with all the other pictures in Photo Gallery.

6. To tell Windows Photo Gallery that you no longer want it to monitor the contents of a folder, right-click the folder in the Folders list and choose Remove from Gallery.

• Figure 32-5: The new folder (in this case, on a network drive) appears in the Folders list.

Photo Gallery shows you a message that says that the pictures and videos in the folder will not be deleted. All you're doing is removing the folder from Photo Gallery's watch list.

7. **Click Yes in the message box, and the folder gets removed from the Folders list and is thus taken off the watch list.**

 For reasons known only to Microsoft, deleting a subfolder of an added folder in the Photo Gallery's Folders list deletes the files instead of merely removing the folder from the Photo Gallery's watch list. It's complicated. Here's what happens:

Say you have a folder called Products, with three subfolders called Bagels, Cakes, and Cookies. In Windows Photo Gallery, you click File↪Add Folder to Gallery and add the Products folder to Photo Gallery's Folders list. The result looks like Figure 32-6.

If you right-click the Products folder and choose Remove from Gallery, Photo Gallery tells you that it's removing the folder from its watch list, but not removing the files. That's great.

But if you right-click the Cookies folder (or the Bagels folder or the Cakes folder), there's no Remove from Gallery option. If you choose the Delete option, which does appear, Vista deletes the folder — pictures and all!

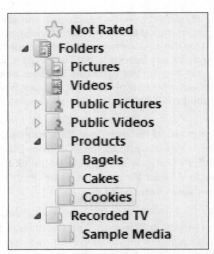

• Figure 32-6: The Products folder with three subfolders in Photo Gallery's Folders list.

 Fortunately, if you catch the mistake in time, you can retrieve the deleted folder and files from the Recycle Bin. But if you aren't careful, you could end up losing all your pictures — and any other files that happen to be in the deleted folder.

Scanning into the Gallery

If you have a scanner, you may be saddled with the software that came with the scanner. No offense to HP or its competitors, but I have yet to meet a scanning package that does what I want it to do — scan quickly, easily, and reliably, where I can pick the destination for the scan in a couple of clicks, with the whole process going fast, without a lot of bells and whistles.

 I rarely want to do OCR (optical character recognition) or stick multiple scans in a single file. I don't want the gamma correction or fine-tuning adjustments. Just copy the page and stick it in a file, thank you very much.

Here's the fast, easy way to get a page scanned into your computer:

1. **Choose Start➪All Programs➪Windows Photo Gallery.**

You see the main Photo Gallery page.

2. **Inside Photo Gallery, click the File icon and then choose Import from Scanner or Camera.**

You see the Import Pictures and Videos dialog box, sporting an icon for your scanner.

3. **Click your scanner icon, if it isn't already selected, and click the Import button.**

Photo Gallery shows you the New Scan dialog box, shown in Figure 32-7.

• **Figure 32-7: Photo Gallery scanning is a piece of cake.**

4. **Stick the page you want to scan into your scanner and click Preview.**

The scanner hums and screeches, softly of course, and a picture of the page appears on-screen.

5. **If you want to zoom in on a specific location, click and drag the resizing handles at the corners.**

In Figure 32-7, I zoom in on a newspaper photo I want to scan.

You can change the file type if you like — the resolution, too — but if you're just going to view the picture on-screen, 200 dpi JPEGs look fine.

6. **Click Scan.**

The scanner hums again. Then Photo Gallery invites you to tag the picture, as in Figure 32-8.

• **Figure 32-8: Photo Gallery uses the digital camera importing rules to assign folder and file names, based on the tag you type.**

7. **Type any tags that you feel may help retrieve the scan at a future date. Then click Import.**

That's it. Your tagged scan gets placed in a folder that's named according to the rules for importing digital photos and given a filename, also in accord with those rules (see Technique 34). Tags are assigned (see Figure 32-9), and you're ready to scan again.

• **Figure 32-9: Scanning goes very quickly with Photo Gallery.**

Technique 33

Touching Up Photos Quickly

Save Time By

- ✔ Getting the red out — quickly
- ✔ Cropping and rotating on a dime
- ✔ Getting and setting the blues
- ✔ Understanding (and working around) the bizarre "Revert" capability

So you followed the tricks in the preceding Technique, and now you're looking at an absolute *ton* of pictures.

Half the portraits contain one or more people who look like they've been frying with the devil, their pupils so red they radiate malevolence. Some of the rolling countrysides look like they've been bombed with yellow mush. And those gorgeous detail shots appear as tiny blobs in a vast sea of gunk.

And that's just last year's Easter vacation.

It's time to take a few minutes and clean up your act. Really, Windows Photo Gallery's tools are easy to use — and they're easy to find, too.

I think Windows Photo Gallery's nicest feature is its ultra-handy, if highly limited, grab-bag of photo touch-up tools. Don't expect Adobe Photoshop in a can, or even a decent clone of IrfanView (www.irfanview.com; see the sidebar in this Technique). But if your needs are few, and time's at a premium, Photo Gallery's good enough.

Usually.

This Technique steps you through the Photo Gallery's touch-up tools. It shows you how to get in and out of them with a minimum of fuss. It also explains how to get back your originals, should you make a teensy, tiny mistake — like turning the boss's face green. This "Revert" function works in a weird way that may bite you some day. I talk about that, too.

Changing Pics

Making straightforward changes to a picture in the Photo Gallery couldn't be simpler. You get the best results if you apply the edits to your picture in the order they appear in Photo Gallery:

1. **Choose Start➪All Programs➪Windows Photo Gallery.**

Photo Gallery appears, as in Figure 33-1.

• **Figure 33-1: Windows Photo Gallery, as it appears with the modifications in Technique 32.**

2. **Locate the picture you want to edit and double-click it.**

The picture appears with a tag-editing pane, as in Figure 33-2.

• **Figure 33-2: Most important: Make a backup copy.**

3. **Immediately click the File icon and choose Make a Copy.**

Photo Gallery has an automatic backup and "Revert" capability that behaves in a very strange way, which I describe in the next section. Because of the stupid, er, obtuse way that Photo Gallery handles backups, I strongly recommend that you create your own backup before you make any changes to a picture.

In addition, I like to have a copy of the original hanging around so I can see if the changes I'm imposing make the picture look better or worse.

When you choose Make a Copy, Photo Gallery shows you the Make a Copy dialog box, shown in Figure 33-3.

• **Figure 33-3: Give the backup a name that you will identify immediately.**

4. **Type a name for the backup file that you will instantly recognize and click Save.**

In Figure 33-3, I backed up the file 002.jpg and gave it the name 002.Backup.jpg. I like naming backup files that way because it's crystal-clear which file has been backed up and because when I look at a sorted list of files in the folder, 002.jpg and 002.Backup.jpg appear next to each other. The next time I edit 002.jpg, I can name my backup 002.Backup2.jpg, then 002.Backup3.jpg, and so on.

5. **Click Start, navigate to the backup file you just saved, and double-click it.**

That brings up your backup — a "reference" copy that you can eyeball while you make changes. The backup copy appears in a Photo Gallery window without a pane on the right.

6. **Drag the picture you're going to work on above the backup and then click the Fix icon at the top.**

You should be able to see the backup, reference copy underneath, and the file you're going to change on top. Photo Gallery lists its (small) group of editing tools on the right, as in Figure 33-4.

• **Figure 33-4:** Watch the backup reference copy while you make changes.

7. **Click Auto Adjust.**

Photo Gallery attempts to adjust the Exposure and Color settings simultaneously. Sometimes it does a good job. Most of the time, it's just a change for change's sake.

8. **If you don't like the Auto Adjust or don't see how it changed anything worthwhile, click the Revert button at the bottom.**

9. **Click Adjust Exposure and slide the Brightness and Contrast controls.**

Brightness changes the entire picture equally, making everything lighter or darker. Contrast makes the dark parts darker and the bright parts brighter. (*Hint:* Don't overdo the Contrast adjustment.) Keep an eye on the backup reference copy, and if you don't like the changes, click the Undo button.

10. **Click Adjust Color and slide the Temperature, Tint, and Saturation controls around.**

Again, watch the backup copy, and if you don't like the change, click Undo.

The Temperature control changes blues to reds and vice-versa. Tint adjusts the green and red. Saturation makes the color intensity increase or decrease.

11. **If you want to crop the picture, click Crop Picture. If you want to crop to a specific aspect ratio, choose the one you want from the Proportion drop-down box. Click and drag the handles around the cropping area and, when you have the crop the way you like, click Apply.**

Photo Gallery crops the picture, then expands it to fill the pane on the left. Figure 33-5 shows the selected area that will grow to fill the entire window.

• **Figure 33-5:** Cropping results in resizing the picture.

This is the only adjustment that requires you to click an Apply button. All the other changes in the Photo Gallery editor take place immediately — although you can Undo them.

12. **To fix red eye, click Fix Red Eye (d'oh!) and drag a box around each red pupil to show Photo Gallery which eyes need fixin'.**

There are several tricks to getting a good handle on red eye:

▶ Scroll your mouse wheel to zoom in on the eye you want to zap. (Or click the magnifying glass.) Then, to move the picture around and center the eye in the pane, hold down the Alt key while you drag the picture.

▶ Every time you drag a rectangle around the red part of the eye and release it, Photo Gallery tries to darken the area in a natural way. You can draw a rectangle around the same area multiple times, and the area will get darker with each try.

▶ Don't overdo it. You can zoom in too close. You can apply too much darkening. Make the rectangle as small as you can. Go gently.

▶ Don't forget that you have an Undo button!

13. **When you're done, click the Back to Gallery link in the upper-left corner.**

Your changes are all applied. (See Figure 33-6.)

• **Figure 33-6: Do the changes make the picture look better? You be the judge.**

IrfanView — A better way

If Vista's Photo Gallery and its tiny set of tools don't do everything you need, take a look at IrfanView, www.irfanview.com. I've been using it for years. Although it doesn't cover all the bases that, say, Photoshop does, it doesn't cost as much as Photoshop, either. In fact, for personal (home) use or for educational or nonprofit use, it's absolutely free. Or step up to the commercial version for $10. (Nope, I didn't drop a zero.) The commercial version is identical to the free version. Irfan's a remarkable guy.

Whether you need to emboss, sharpen, blur, or apply any of a zillion effects — or if you need to work with GIFs (much less animated GIFs), multipage TIFs, QuickTime MOVs, Macromedia Flash SWF files, or any of dozens of others — IrfanView does it with aplomb.

IrfanView doesn't integrate into Vista as well as Photo Gallery does. It feels like an application, not a part of the operating system. But it's still far more capable than Photo Gallery in so many ways — and the price is right!

Bringing Back the Old Version

I don't trust Photo Gallery's built-in "Revert" feature. You can see the Revert button at the bottom of Figure 33-4.

In theory, clicking the Revert button lets you, uh, revert to the original version of an edited picture. If you think about that for a second, your brain probably starts twisting in knots. At least mine does.

Two big questions:

▶ **How does Photo Gallery decide which version is "original"?** If I knock out the red eye in a picture and come back a month or a year later and crop it, is the "original" picture the one with the red eye, or the one without?

▶ **What happens if I revert a picture and then decide that I don't like the reversion?** Can I undo the change or (forgive me if your brain hiccups here) revert the revert?

Like so many convoluted Microsoft inventions, the Revert feature is steeped in good intentions, but implemented in a way that'll leave your head spinning — and gobble up hours of your time, should you ever hit a problem.

Here's what really happens:

1. Whenever you change a picture by using Photo Gallery's tools, Photo Gallery looks to see if it has stored an "original" of the picture.

The "originals" are stored in a bizarre, hidden folder called `c:\Users\<username>\AppData\Local\Microsoft\Windows Photo Gallery\Original Images`. They have long ID strings attached to the front of the filenames.

2. If there's no original stored, before the first change is applied, Photo Gallery sticks a copy of the original in that bizarre hidden folder.

For example, in Figure 33-7, my original picture, called `002.JPG`, got stored in `c:\Users\Woody\AppData\Local\Microsoft\Windows Photo Gallery\Original Images` with the filename `{ACE49601-7F66-4FE9-875A-A399029B568C}-002.JPG`.

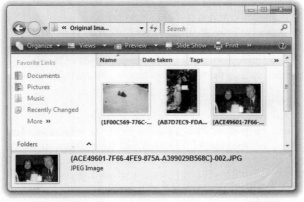

• **Figure 33-7: So that's where they hid my Restore file.**

3. Whenever you open a picture in the Photo Gallery and click the Fix button, Photo Gallery goes out to that bizarre hidden folder and sees if there's an "original" stored away. If there is, the Revert button is enabled.

Note that, after Photo Gallery has placed a copy of the file in that hidden folder, it doesn't update the original.

4. If at any point you click the Revert button, Photo Gallery copies the original in that hidden folder over the top of the picture you're working on.

It *doesn't* delete the original in the hidden folder.

 Microsoft realized that this particular approach incurs a lot of overhead: If you ever edit a picture, even a tiny edit, Photo Gallery keeps a copy of the original file in this hidden folder forever. In an attempt to mitigate the deleterious effect of this rather strange design decision, Photo Gallery allows you to set a rather confusing option.

You can see the confusing option by going into the main Photo Gallery window, clicking the File button, and choosing Options. In the middle of the Options tab, under Original Pictures (see Figure 33-8), you are given the option to move the files in this `c:\Users\<username>\AppData\Local\Microsoft\Windows Photo Gallery\Original Images` folder to the Recycle Bin after a day, a week, a month, six months, or a year.

When the file is moved to the Recycle Bin, Photo Gallery starts all over with a clean slate: It behaves as if the file in its original location is the original file.

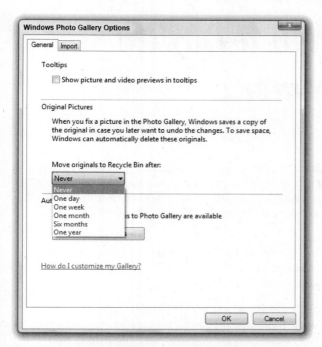

• **Figure 33-8:** The option to move originals was designed with good intentions, but may lead to a confusing array of backups (or lack thereof).

The strange design decision can also lead to an unexpected, time-hogging result. If you back up your Pictures and Public Pictures folders, but not your `c:\Users\<username>\ AppData\Local\Microsoft\Windows Photo Gallery\Original Images` folder, and your hard drive dies, you may find yourself wondering why in the world your restored pictures no longer have the Restore button available.

Now you know why I recommend that you maintain your own backups before you start editing pictures. Even if you have Vista Ultimate and its shadow copies working on your side, an extra precautionary backup won't hurt.

Technique 34

Managing Pictures from a Digital Camera

Save Time By

✔ Using Vista's built-in tools to copy, name, and delete pictures

✔ Reaching inside your camera with Windows Explorer

✔ Storing Windows files inside your camera

You probably think of your digital camera as an incredibly smart picture-taking machine. If it's built into your mobile phone or PDA, hey, it's gotta be smart. But you may not realize that it includes a reasonably capable computer — one that Vista is uniquely capable of manipulating.

Did you know that some cameras let you use their memory almost as easily as an external hard drive on your PC? Talk about a fast way to transfer files when no network is in sight!

Because Vista and the Photo Gallery work with digital cameras so well, you probably won't want to use your camera manufacturer's software. I don't. When I fill up my camera's memory card with pictures, I whip out a USB cable, plug the camera into the PC, click a couple times, type in a general description of the pictures (such as "Add's Birthday Party" or "Justin's Diving Trip"), and press Enter. Then Windows does everything else. It's truly breathtaking to see all those pictures move from the camera to the PC and have Windows handle all the details.

This Technique takes you quickly through the ins and outs of digital photography from a Vista point of view. And the last section includes a truly memorable way to use your camera as a portable storage device.

 One key bit of advice. Don't delete pictures while they're on your camera. Wait until you copy them onto your PC. Two reasons: You might be able to figure out a way to resurrect the picture when you see it on a bigger screen, and it's a whole lot easier to delete the wrong picture while working with the camera's controls. There's a point in the importing process where it's easy and fast to cull bad pics. I show you where in the next section.

Transferring Pictures to Your PC Automatically

You have a digital camera, right? Maybe a camera phone, or a PDA that takes pictures? One with a USB or FireWire attachment? Good. Glad I caught you in time.

 Don't install the software that came with your camera. Chances are good that your camera's software only gums up Vista and the Windows Photo Gallery.

If you've already installed the software, uninstall it. Choose Start⇨Control Panel⇨Add or Remove Programs, pick your camera manufacturer's software from the list, and click Remove.

At the very least, you should give the Vista native software a try before you trust your camera manufacturer to write Really Great Software. (Yes, my tongue is planted in my cheek.)

Here's the best way to connect a digital camera to a Vista computer, even if it's the first time you've ever hitched your camera up to a computer:

1. **Turn off the camera but leave your PC on.**

2. **Plug the USB (or FireWire) cable into the PC; then plug the cable into the camera.**

3. **Turn on the camera.**

Some cameras require you to flip them over to "PC Mode" or something equally obtuse, but most cameras recognize immediately that they're plugged into a, uh, Superior Intelligence. (Okay, that part's debatable. Especially if you're using a Hasselblad.) I think it's akin to recognizing you're hooked into The Borg.

If you've never plugged this specific camera into this specific computer, 99 times out of 100 (maybe more), Vista identifies the camera and

automatically installs the "driver" software that's necessary to communicate with it. You should see the notification shown in Figure 34-1.

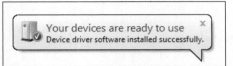

• **Figure 34-1: Camera is recognized and ready to rumble.**

 If Vista doesn't recognize your camera right off the bat, *don't* bother installing the software that came with the camera. Instead, consult Table 34-1, go to the Web site for your camera manufacturer, and look on the site specifically for the Vista driver for your camera. Each site is different, but all have search capabilities. Follow the manufacturer's instructions to install the driver only — don't bother with any other software they may have.

Sometimes you really do want to install the camera manufacturer's software because it can manipulate settings inside the camera that aren't readily changed from controls on the camera. (I've also had no end of problems trying to get phone cameras to download their pictures without the manufacturer's software.) If you're in that boat — and you really need to change something inside your camera — you don't have much choice. Most camera manufacturers create software that works on almost any computer — at least as far back as Windows 98. It's very difficult to build a program that runs on Windows 98, takes advantage of the features in Vista, and stays stable for any length of time. *Caveat photographor.*

Vista's AutoPlay notification box appears, as in Figure 34-2.

4. **Click the link marked Import Pictures Using Windows (which actually means Import Pictures Using Photo Gallery's importer).**

Vista asks you to tag the pictures, per Figure 34-3.

• **Figure 34-2:** It's easy to import your pictures *en masse*.

• **Figure 34-4:** Default import settings.

• **Figure 34-3:** Don't tag the pictures just yet.

5. Click the Options link.

The importer brings up its Import Settings dialog box, as in Figure 34-4.

6. Consult Table 34-2 for a description of the various (alas, limited) options in the Import Settings dialog box and make the changes you feel are appropriate. Click OK.

As we went to press, there were rumors that Microsoft would release a TweakPhotoGallery application or something with a similar name. You can bet that the shortcomings in the Import Settings dialog box — particularly the inflexibility in choosing folder and file names — will figure prominently on Vista customers' wish lists. Watch www.askwoody.com for the latest developments.

If you change any of the current settings in the Import Settings dialog box, the importer has to restart. Ho-hum. You get to click OK and wait a few seconds.

7. If you selected the Prompt for a Tag on Import check box, type a descriptive tag in the Tag These Pictures box that appears (see Figure 34-5) and click Import.

The importer brings in the pictures, one by one, as in Figure 34-6.

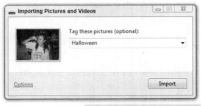

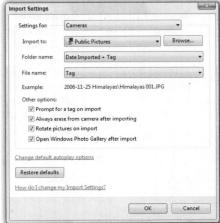

• **Figure 34-5:** My timesaving settings for importing Halloween pictures.

• **Figure 34-6:** Import in progress.

 You may uncheck the Erase After Importing box at any time to prevent Vista from erasing the imported pictures from your camera.

If you accidentally delete pictures on the camera, don't fret. There's a cheap, easy way to bring deleted pictures back. See Technique 36 for details.

Vista copies the files into the folder you specified in the Import Settings dialog box, using the current date and the tag you typed as a folder name, and the tag and a sequential number for the filename. When it's done, if you so specified, Vista deletes the pictures from your camera. Then Photo Gallery appears, opened to a specific saved search that's called Recently Imported. Not surprisingly, that saved search includes the pictures you just imported.

Having typed `Halloween` as a tag, and with the options specified in Figure 34-5, Vista brings in the pictures, and Photo Gallery opens to the folder `C:\Users\Public\Pictures\ 2006-11-25 Halloween`, showing you the files `Halloween 001.jpg`, `Halloween 002.jpg`, `Halloween 003.jpg`, and so on. Each of those files has a tag of `Halloween`, as shown in Figure 34-7.

• **Figure 34-7:** All your imported pictures, ready to edit.

 Seem a bit redundant redundant redundant? Yeah, I think so too too too. But that's how the importer works: Unless you pick something odd in the Import Options dialog box, the tag is used three times on each picture: as part of the folder name, as the filename (with a sequential number attached), and as a tag. I guess Microsoft wanted to make sure that when you go searching for Halloween shots, you're gonna find 'em.

8. Now's the time to delete bad pictures, edit the good ones, and get rid of red eye everywhere. Start by double-clicking the first picture of the imported set.

Photo Gallery brings up the first picture, as in Figure 34-8.

• **Figure 34-8:** Edit each picture quickly and easily.

9. Decide what to do with the good, the bad, and the ugly:

▶ If you took a bad shot, click the "X" at the bottom to delete the pic.

▶ If it's a good one, and you're more industrious than I, you can add tags or a caption by clicking on the right.

▶ Far more likely, you'll want to crop the picture or remove red eye. To do so, click the Fix icon at the top and follow the instructions in Technique 33.

10. When you're done with one picture, click the right-facing "play" button and move on to the next picture.

11. After all the pictures have been culled and edited, click the square Slideshow button at the bottom, sit back, and enjoy!

 With all your options set, the next time you want to import pics, it'll only take a few minutes: Plug in the camera, click Import Pictures, type a tag, click Import — and you're done.

TABLE 34-1: CAMERA MANUFACTURERS' WEB SITES

Manufacturer	U.S. Web Site
Canon	www.usa.canon.com
Casio	www.casio.com
Fuji	www.fujifilm.com
Kodak	www.kodak.com
Logitech	www.logitech.com
Nikon	www.nikonusa.com
Olympus	www.olympusamerica.com
Panasonic	www.panasonic.com/ consumer_electronics
Sony	www.sony.com

TABLE 34-2: VISTA'S IMPORT SETTINGS

What It Says	What It Means	Timesaving Tip
Settings For	Vista stores three different sets of settings, for Cameras, CDs/DVDs, and Scanners.	Most people never use the CD/DVD settings.
Import To	The place that will contain the folder you're about to create and fill with imported pictures.	Unless you need to keep the pictures away from prying eyes, import them into the Public\Pictures folder.
Folder Name	The name of the folder that's created to hold the imported pictures.	Unfortunately, the choices are very limited. If you put a Date at the beginning, it's easier to sort the folders consistently. I reluctantly use the default, Date Imported + the tag that you type into the Import dialog box (Figure 34-3).

What It Says	What It Means	Timesaving Tip
File Name	The first part of the filename for the imported files. A three-digit sequential number gets attached to the end, followed by the filename extension for the type of file you're importing.	Again, choices are extremely limited, and I reluctantly use the default, which is just the tag that you type into the Import dialog box.
Prompt for a Tag on Import	Makes Vista show a dialog box like the one in Figure 34-3. The tag you type is attached to each file and probably used for both the filename and the folder name.	This is the only way you have to put identifiable information on imported pictures. Check the box.
Always Erase from Camera after Importing	After all of the pictures have been transferred from the camera to the PC, and everything worked okay, Vista reaches out and erases the pictures on the camera.	A big timesaver. Check the box.
Rotate Pictures on Import	If your camera has a sensor that puts rotation information on your pictures, Photo Gallery reads the sensor information and automatically rotates the picture if you had the camera rotated when you took the picture.	Check it; you'll be pleasantly surprised if your camera supports the feature. Many do.
Open Windows Photo Gallery after Import	Photo Gallery opens, pointing to the Recently Imported search folder.	A nice, fast way to check and cull bad shots. Unless, of course, all your shots are perfect, all the time.

Using a Camera's Memory Card as a Storage Device on Your PC

How many times have you wanted to carry a file around when you travel, but you didn't want to fuss with a USB flash drive or a CD?

Have you ever run out of room on a hard drive and didn't know where to stick a few files while you cleaned out the junk?

 Guess what. If you attach your camera to your PC with its USB or FireWire cable, you may be able to use the memory inside the camera in precisely the same way that you use a key drive or a hard drive. Most people have a lot of memory inside their cameras. Few realize they can save time and money by using it as portable memory for their computer.

Many digital cameras can handle plain old everyday files. They're easy to get to, as long as you have a USB cable and a Vista computer. And they work the same way as regular Windows files: Double-click a Word document that's stored inside a digital camera, and Word comes up with the document loaded and ready to go; copy a PowerPoint presentation or an MP3 music file from your desktop to your camera's CompactFlash card and take it with you, inside your camera, when you travel.

 With 1GB (and larger) camera memory cards readily available and rapidly growing cheaper, consider using your camera's memory as another kind of external hard drive, particularly if you don't want to spend money for a USB flash drive or if you're traveling and the camera's coming along with you anyway.

The next time you want to show a PowerPoint presentation to a client, ask if you can plug in your camera. Your audience may forget your presentation by lunchtime, but it'll take a year for anyone to forget your storage medium.

Here's the quick way to get Windows files into and out of your digital camera — assuming that the camera triggers Vista's AutoPlay routine (most do, most of the time):

1. **Turn off the camera, but leave your PC on.**

2. **Plug the USB (or FireWire) cable into the PC; then plug the cable into the camera.**

3. **Turn on the camera.**

Vista's AutoPlay kicks in with the dialog box shown in Figure 34-9.

• **Figure 34-9:** Treat your camera like a key drive.

4. **Click the link marked Open Folder to View Files Using Windows Explorer.**

Windows Explorer opens the drive, just like a USB key drive, and shows you the folders inside. Depending on the make and model of camera, you may see two or more folders. In Figure 34-10, taken with a Panasonic camera, you see folders called DCIM (for holding photos) and MISC (for holding everything else).

• **Figure 34-10:** Inside your camera are folders and files that you can access just like any other drive.

5. **Take a look around inside your camera and try to find a folder that isn't being used by pictures. Navigate to that folder.**

In the case of this Panasonic camera, where the DCIM folder holds photos, I navigate to the MISC folder.

6. **Go out and find the file(s) you want to store on your camera.**

7. **Click the file you want to copy into your camera, drag it to the camera's folder, and drop it.**

Your copied file appears in the camera's folder.

8. **Give it a go: If you copied a document, spreadsheet, presentation, or any kind of graphic file, double-click it.**

Windows behaves in precisely the same way as if the file were inside your computer or on your network.

One less piece of gear for the modern road warrior to schlep — and now you have an excuse to take your camera no matter where you go.

35 Technique

Editing Your Home Movies

Vista's Windows Movie Maker 6 (in reality, a minor upgrade to Windows Movie Maker 2.1 — go figger) does a good job of handling home movies and minor video editing tasks.

Movie Maker's bag of tricks runneth over with more than 130 styles of titles ready for you to stick in your movies, more than 60 transitions, and almost 50 other effects. In addition, the Auto Movie Generator can make serviceable movies from a handful of clips with just a click.

Windows Movie Maker makes great demands on your hardware, particularly if you create long movies (er, "projects") and/or if you try to edit a movie and stick it back on your digital camera. For big movies, you need big iron. Symptoms of iron deficiency include unexplained freezes and hangs, video getting out of synch with the audio, color splotches or black bands, and video-induced narcolepsy. (Okay, that last one is more a side effect of editing ten hours of raw vacation videos down to nine and a half hours of sheer boredom.) To handle big movies, you need to have a fast hard drive with lots of free space.

In this Technique, I step you through the basics of assembling a movie, with an emphasis on skipping the parts you don't need. Then I show you how to get the movie out of your computer so you can actually use it.

Understanding the Limitations of WMM

Let's save a whole lotta time, right up front. These are the answers to questions about Windows Movie Maker that I hear every day:

✔ No, you can't buy or rent a DVD movie and use Vista to copy it onto your hard drive. Sorry. Microsoft's basic take on the matter is that copying a DVD to your hard drive is illegal. Period. End of discussion. But, yes, there are plenty of companies that make DVD movie-ripping software. Most DVD movie-ripping software will also burn DVDs. Google is your friend.

✔ No, you can't use Windows Movie Maker to edit or burn "protected" recorded television shows or broadcast movies, like the ones on HBO and Cinemax.

✔ Yes, you can use Windows Movie Maker to squeeze those horrendously huge DVR-MS recorded TV files that you created in Windows Media Center (at, oh, 3 to 4GB of space per hour of TV) into not-exactly-svelte WMV files (say, 400 to 500MB per hour) that will play on any modern Windows PC. You can't perform the slimming act with protected TV shows, but you can with most recorded TV, and you can also do it with the VOB files produced by some digital camcorders.

The only problem? Squeezing down an hour-long recorded TV program can take two hours, even on a moderately fast PC.

✔ No, Windows Movie Maker isn't as buggy as it used to be. Although Microsoft calls it Windows Movie Maker 6, in fact the Movie Maker in Vista is Microsoft's third attempt at getting it right.

✔ Yes, there are much more capable video editors around. iMovie from Apple, for one, runs rings around WMM. Roxio Easy Media Creator, Adobe Production Studio, and Ulead's VideoStudio all work well with Vista and give you tons of options that WMM can't touch.

In theory, Windows Movie Maker works with many kinds of files — AVI, MPG, WMV, and DVR-MS video files; MP3 and WMA sound files; and BMP, GIF, JPG, PNG, TIF, and WMF still picture files. (Remarkably, because Windows Photo Gallery won't touch BMPs.) Of course, Microsoft doesn't support Apple's video or audio formats.

In practice, I've had a heap of trouble with non-Microsoft codecs for AVI files. For example, the DivX codec I describe in Technique 26 — the one that Microsoft's Web site recommends — doesn't work with WMM.

On the plus side, WMM works directly and simply with your digital video (DV) camera. You can also plug in a microphone and record a voice-over. You, too, can be a Big Voice Video Announcer. . . .

Importing and Combining Clips

Start to build a movie from a bunch of clips or stills (er, picture files) and then follow these steps to put the clips together:

1. **Choose Start⇨All Programs⇨Windows Movie Maker.**

The main Movie Maker screen appears (see Figure 35-1).

• **Figure 35-1: Windows Movie Maker 6.**

2. **In the upper left, click the Import Media icon.**

You get the Import Media Items dialog box, as shown in Figure 35-2.

3. **Choose one or more video files or still picture files. (You can use Ctrl+click or Shift+click to pick more than one.) Click Import.**

WMM opens the file(s) you specified and places them in the assembly area in the middle of the screen (see Figure 35-3).

• **Figure 35-2:** Choose from available clips.

• **Figure 35-3:** The clips are ready for assembly.

4. Click the clip that you want to appear at the beginning of the movie and drag it down to the first spot on the storyboard near the bottom of the screen.

You're starting to assemble the movie by using a storyboard — a sequence of beginning still pictures in each clip that can help you organize the movie (as shown in Figure 35-4).

• **Figure 35-4:** The storyboard starts to take shape across the bottom of the screen.

5. Click and drag each clip into place on the storyboard (as shown in Figure 35-5). Don't like the sequence? You also can click and drag to rearrange clips on the storyboard.

• **Figure 35-5:** Build the clip collection in the correct order.

6. See how the clips play next to each other by clicking the Play button.

If need be, rearrange the clips by clicking and dragging them into place until you feel comfortable with the sequence.

7. **This is a good point to save your work. Choose File⇨Save Project, give your project a name, and click Save.**

A *project* isn't a movie. A project is the glue that holds a movie together — pointers to clips, instructions for putting them together, transitions, and other effects — but it isn't a movie and can't be played like a movie.

The AutoMovie Generator

You can create a movie from still photos with just a couple of clicks. Use Windows Movie Maker's Tasks list to import a bunch of pictures. When you have all the pictures gathered, click the AutoMovie icon.

WMM takes you through simple steps that let you specify the transitions, add music, insert titles, and the like. It only takes a few minutes to produce a superior slide show — one that runs just like a movie.

Trimming Clips

After you block out the clips, as I describe in the preceding section, I suggest that you trim away the parts at the beginning and end of each clip. You don't have to follow this advice, but you'll discover that the beginnings and endings of clips (invariably) don't work out.

When you *trim* a clip, you're just telling Windows Movie Maker to skip over part of the beginning or end of the clip. Nothing in the clip is actually removed — the clip isn't altered in any way.

Trimmin's easy. Just follow these steps:

1. **Open a project.**

If you're continuing from the preceding section, you already have a project underway.

2. **At the bottom of the project window, click the down wedge next to Storyboard and select Timeline.**

WMM replaces the storyboard at the bottom with a *timeline* — a representation of what the movie will show with the timing noted above the clips in the storyboard (as shown in Figure 35-6).

• **Figure 35-6:** The movie's timeline.

3. **Click between clips (or at the beginning of the first clip or the end of the last clip), and your cursor turns into a thick, red, two-headed arrow.**

4. **Click and drag the double-headed arrow to tell WMM how much of the beginning or end of the clip you want to leave out of the final movie.**

It takes a little practice to do this part right. If you drag around long enough, you'll get a feel for what's happening.

5. **Check what you've done by clicking once inside a clip and then clicking the Play button to see what's left after the clip is trimmed.**

6. **This is a good time to save, so choose File⇨ Save Project.**

Using Transitions and Effects

With the clips blocked out and trimmed, your next job is to set up transitions between the clips that help tell the story. Mechanically, WMM makes that very easy. Aesthetically, well, that's a fade of a different color.

Here's how I apply transitions and effects:

1. **Start Windows Movie Maker and open the project.**

   If you're continuing from the preceding section, you're in the right place.

2. **At the bottom of the project's window, click the down wedge to the right of Timeline and select Storyboard.**

   It's easier to work with transitions if you can see the storyboard (see Figure 35-7).

• Figure 35-7: The storyboard has slots for transitions between each clip.

3. **If you want a video effect — that is, if you want to alter or distort an entire clip in a specific way — click the Effects link on the left. Drag the desired effect (see Figure 35-8) from the center pane onto the clip that you want to distort.**

   It's unlikely that you'll want to add such an effect, but if you do, you can make the clip look pixelated, brown-toned, or cracked and old, or you can add slow-motion effects.

The effects are varied and fun, but I bet you get tired of them quickly. Figure 35-8 shows the effect of a pan from upper left to lower right.

• Figure 35-8: Effects distort the image, rotate it, pan or zoom, or make the clip run faster or in slow-mo.

 Effects are cumulative: If you drag the Sepia effect and the Watercolor effect onto a clip, it shows up watercolored (I call it blotched) and in sepia color. To get rid of one or more effects, right-click the clip and choose Video Effects. Use caution with effects because if you don't like them, you have to waste time clicking the Undo button, removing them one by one.

4. **If you want transitions between the clips, click the Transitions link on the left. Then click and drag the transition you want to the gray box between the clips.**

 The two transitions I rate as least jarring are Fade and Wipe — two well-established methods for moving between clips. If you're in a hurry, those are the ones to check first.

5. **Check transitions and effects by clicking a clip and clicking the Play button.**

6. **Now's a good time to save your work. Choose File⇨Save Project.**

Note that you're saving the project — not a movie. The project contains pointers to the clips, with instructions for putting the clips together, trimming them, fades, and the like. I talk about saving the entire movie — turning it into a file that can be played — at the end of this Technique. For now, save the project.

Adding Titles and Credits

Every movie can benefit from titles. Some justify adding credits. I don't know how many hours I've wasted composing titles in Word (such as, oh, "County Kilkenny" and "County Cork" and "Dublin"), printing those titles out on sheets of paper, filming the printouts, and cutting the titles in with my home movies. Don't laugh. Not many years ago, that was state-of-the-art.

Windows Movie Maker makes it easy and quick to show titles, both in plain colored boxes and superimposed on your clips.

To get titles working, follow these steps:

1. **If you aren't continuing from the preceding section, start Windows Movie Maker and open a project.**

2. **On the left, click the Titles and Credits link.**

Windows Movie Maker offers you four places to put the title: at the beginning of the movie, before any clip, superimposed on top of the video in any clip, or at the end of the movie (commonly called "credits").

3. **Click Title at the Beginning and supply the bits to your opening title.**

WMM has you fill out a template, which translates into a very short title clip (as shown in Figure 35-9). You can change fonts and the way

the title fades by clicking the Change the Text Font and Color option and the Change the Title Animation option, respectively.

• **Figure 35-9: The intro title is generated automatically from text you type.**

4. **When you're satisfied with the edits to your title, click the Add Title button.**

The title appears as the first clip in the storyline, as in Figure 35-10.

• **Figure 35-10: The title gets turned into its own clip and placed at the beginning of the storyline.**

5. **Repeat the same process for any other titles you wish to add or for credits at the end of the movie.**

6. **Choose File⇨Save Project.**

Again, remember that the project is not a movie. To save a real, live movie, see the next section.

Saving the Movie

On the left side of the screen, Windows Movie Maker offers you five different general methods for publishing your movie. You can publish to

✔ **This computer** and create a file (either an AVI file or a WMV file) that can be played on this or any other computer.

✔ A **DVD** that plays in any DVD player (including one connected to a TV). Windows Movie Maker doesn't burn the DVD. Instead, it saves the project and hands it off to Windows DVD Maker, which is a very rudimentary program that's only available in Vista Home Premium and Ultimate editions.

 I don't cover Windows DVD Maker in this book because it has few options — and I haven't found any of them that save any time. Quite the contrary, actually.

✔ A **Recordable CD** that makes a file in precisely the same way as the **This computer** option, but then burns the file on a CD.

 There's no reason to use this option. You have a lot more flexibility if you choose **This computer**, create that AVI or WMV file, and then burn the file on a CD or DVD.

✔ **E-mail** to automatically create an AVI file, attach it to a message, and leave you with the message ready to address and send.

This is another useless option. Far better to use the **This computer** option and then attach the file to your own e-mail message.

✔ **Digital video camera.** WMM prompts you to connect your camcorder, so Windows Movie Maker can put the file in your camera. WMM displays a message that says Cue Your Tape, at which point you need to fast forward or rewind your camera to the location you want for the movie and then click Next.

Here's how to create an AVI or WMV file containing your movie:

1. **If you aren't continuing from the preceding section, start Windows Movie Maker and open a project.**

2. **On the left, under Publish To, click the This Computer link.**

WMM asks you to give the file a name and specify a place to put it (see Figure 35-11).

• **Figure 35-11: Type a filename and pick a location.**

3. **Type a name, navigate to a location, and click Next.**

Windows Movie Maker asks you to choose the file format (see Figure 35-12). Yes, I know that the dialog box says Settings, but what you're really choosing is the type of file and the quality of the output.

4. Consult Table 35-1 and pick a reasonable format. Then click Publish.

WMM takes anywhere from a few minutes to a few centuries and ultimately churns out your file.

5. When WMM is done, click Finish in the wizard's last dialog box and watch your movie.

After you have the file, you can burn it on a CD or DVD, e-mail it, or print it out and turn it into confetti. Hmmm. Not a bad idea. . . . The medium is the message, eh?

• **Figure 35-12:** Pick a file format and encoding method.

TABLE 35-1: MOVIE "SETTINGS"

What It Says	What It Means	Timesaving Tip
Best Quality for Playback on My Computer (Recommended)	Uses Microsoft's proprietary WMV format in a high-quality variable bit rate but a very low resolution (320 x 240 pixels)	Good for a decent rendering of a typical TV movie.
DV-AVI (NTSC)	High quality, but huge file	Use AVI if you might want to copy the file back into a DV recorder or if you really don't like to use Microsoft's proprietary format.
Windows Media Portable Device	Small files at 640 x 480 pixels	Good for MP3 player screens (including Video iPods and Zunes), but that's about it.
Windows Media VHS Quality	Basically the same as the format for Portable Devices	Why bother?
DVD and HD versions	High- to very high-quality pictures that may well be more detailed than your source file can support	If you have high-quality source material and don't mind waiting for WMM to do its thing, pick the resolution closest to the TV or computer monitor that you're going to use.

36 Technique

Doing More with Your Pics and Videos

Save Time By

- ✔ Using your own pictures for your Windows desktop or as a screen saver
- ✔ Making big picture files smaller
- ✔ Retrieving deleted pictures from your digital camera

Have you ever deleted a picture on your digital camera accidentally? Did you know that the easiest way to get that picture back (if it's possible at all) is by running an undelete program *on your PC?*

Yes, you read that right. You can undelete a picture on your camera from your PC. It's easy, it's cheap, and it's so fast you won't believe it.

 If you're running out of room on your hard drive and the problem is too many pictures, don't waste your time with compressing and selectively deleting the files you no longer want. Instead, simply move a big bunch of pictures to CD. They'll last a long time — maybe even longer than your hard drive — and the whole procedure takes just a few minutes.

You may already know that you can view all the pictures in a folder as a slide show — just click the Slide Show icon in the Windows Explorer window. But you can also

- ✔ Burn a DVD with a slide show that plays on any TV with a DVD player.

- ✔ Use all the pictures in a folder — or even a bunch of folders — for a screen saver. The screen saver randomly picks a picture, shows it on the screen for a while, and then moves on to another randomly chosen picture.

 As we went to press, Microsoft appeared almost ready to release a new version of its venerable Image Resizer PowerToy — a program that makes it right-click simple to reduce the size of giant picture files with only a slight reduction in quality. With more and more digital cameras churning out ever-larger pictures (3MB? 6MB?), everybody needs to figure out a way to trim the flab from the pictures they want to send as e-mail attachments or upload to Web sites. It isn't clear as of this writing whether Microsoft will make the Image Resizer PowerToy available as a free download, as it has for many years, or if it will become part of an extra-cost bundle, possibly as a Vista Ultimate bonus.

If Microsoft wants you to pay to slim pictures, I have a much better, free alternative.

I show you how to do all that and more in this Technique.

Putting Your Pic on the Desktop

Do you have a favorite picture that you would like to use as your Vista wallpaper, er, desktop background?

Here's the fastest way to do it:

1. **Choose Start➪Computer and navigate to the picture you want to put on your desktop.**

2. **Right-click the picture and choose Set As Desktop Background.**

Plus or minus a lopped-off ear or dropped chin (see Figure 36-1), your desktop looks much like the picture you chose.

• **Figure 36-1:** Vista's PIX engine adjusts a chosen picture and reshoots it before using it as wallpaper.

 There's a reason why your picture may appear incorrectly chopped off or otherwise indisposed: When you right-click a picture and choose Set as Desktop Background, Vista's PIX graphic display program takes the picture and makes a new JPG image from it. The picture may be cropped a bit or a border might

be added. Unlike earlier versions of Windows, which had a nasty habit of stretching the picture in unflattering ways, Vista maintains the aspect ratio of the picture, although it may cut off pieces that you don't want cut.

3. **If you don't like the appearance of the wallpaper, right-click any open spot on the Windows desktop and choose Personalize; then click the Desktop Background link.**

You see the Desktop Background dialog box, as shown in Figure 36-2. Note that the Picture Location drop-down box points to the modified picture that the PIX engine created — it's in the folder `C:\Users\<`*username*`>\AppData\ Roaming\Microsoft\Windows Photo Gallery`, and the picture is called `Windows Photo Gallery Wallpaper.jpg`. (If you choose a different picture, the old one gets deleted.)

• **Figure 36-2:** The artificially created wallpaper appears as your desktop background.

If you don't like the wallpaper that's currently on the screen, you don't want the picture that's in this dialog box — the picture in the dialog box is the one that Vista is currently using on the desktop.

4. Click the Browse button and go find the original picture or an alternative.

5. Click the picture you want to use as wallpaper and then choose one of the three positioning methods mentioned at the bottom of the dialog box:

> ▶ *Stretched:* The picture is distorted to fit the screen.

> ▶ *Tiled:* The picture is repeated at its current resolution and set on the screen like a checkerboard.

> ▶ *Centered:* The picture appears in the center of the desktop, with no modifications to size or shape.

6. Click OK.

In Figure 36-3, I chose the original picture and had Vista center it.

• **Figure 36-3: A much better rendition — the chin isn't cut off.**

If you choose to center the picture, you can click the Change Background Color link at the bottom to specify the color of the desktop that surrounds the picture.

 You can also set the wallpaper from inside Firefox or Internet Explorer: When you find a picture you want to use, right-click it and choose Set as Desktop Background. IE automatically uses the centering settings that were last in force in the Desktop Background dialog box (Figure 36-3). Firefox delivers a small dialog box that lets you change the settings.

Using Your Pictures and Videos for a Screen Saver Slide Show

I talk about this nifty (and little-known) Vista feature in Technique 8. Here's the whole story on the Photos screen saver.

Vista has a built-in screen saver that automatically cycles through all the pictures in a folder. If you know the trick, it'll also cycle through the videos and/or recorded TV shows in a folder. In fact, the Vista Photos screen saver can cycle through all the pictures and videos and TV shows in a folder and all its subfolders. I don't know about you, but on my PC, that can be one heckuvalotta pictures!

 This feature rates as one of my favorites because old pictures tend to get buried. You shoot them, look at 'em once or twice, and never see 'em again. But if you use this screen saver, everything old is new again — even those really, really bad shots of Aunt Mildred — which, come to think of it, could be a good thing or a bad thing.

To use your pictures and/or videos and/or recorded TV shows for a screen saver slide show, follow these steps:

1. Right-click any empty spot on the desktop, and choose Personalize.

2. Click the Screen Saver link.

The Screen Saver tab of the Display Properties dialog box appears.

3. **In the Screen Saver drop-down box, choose Photos. Then click Settings.**

You see the Photos Screen Saver Settings dialog box, shown in Figure 36-4.

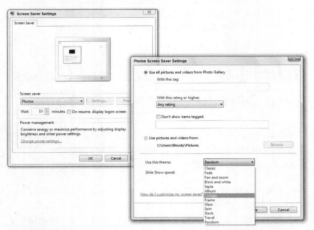

• **Figure 36-4: Choose any theme other than Classic if you want to see videos and recorded TV.**

4. **At the top, choose the location of the pictures, videos, and/or recorded TV shows that you want to use for the screen saver.**

 If you use the Photo Gallery, remember that the Photo Gallery doesn't include any GIF pictures, although it does include BMP and TIF files (see Technique 32).

5. **At the bottom, choose the theme and speed.**

 The only theme that doesn't play videos and recorded TV is the Classic theme. Choose any other theme, and the Photo screen saver shows your videos and recorded TV shows in sequence along with the other pictures.

If you want to see the effect of various themes in particular, click Preview; Vista shows you a preview of the screen saver.

6. **Click Save.**

7. **When you're happy with the results, click OK.**

Your custom Photo screen saver will kick in after the allotted waiting time.

Burning Pictures on a CD

Do you have about a hundred gajillion pictures on your PC eating up hard disk space?

Yeah. I thought so.

If you have a CD-R, CD-RW, DVD-R, DVD+R, DVD-RW, or DVD+RW drive, or even an old wax wind-up gramophone with a brass bell, burning those pictures onto a CD or DVD, where they'll last for many years (decades if your discs are of the highest quality), is very easy. A CD or DVD certainly lasts longer than your hard drive, providing you don't gum it up with one of those sticky CD labels (see Fred Langa's experiences at www.informationweek.com/ story/showArticle.jhtml?articleID=15800263 &pgno=2).

 I talk about backing up files in Technique 53, but photos and music tend to accumulate — and demand backup — at a different rate than, oh, documents or spreadsheets.

Unless you have a very high-resolution camera, a CD can hold a couple hundred photos, whereas a DVD can hold more than a thousand.

Burning pictures couldn't be simpler, particularly if you run through the Windows Photo Gallery:

1. **Stick a blank CD or DVD in your drive.**

No doubt you see a Vista AutoPlay advisory. "X" out of it.

2. **Choose Start⇨All Programs⇨Windows Photo Gallery.**

Your latest pictures appear. If you set up Windows Photo Gallery in the way I describe in Technique 32, they appear as in Figure 36-5.

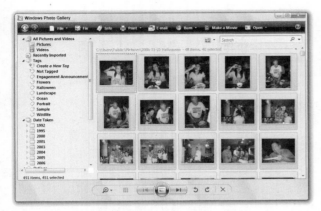

• **Figure 36-5: Burn from the Photo Gallery.**

3. **Select a handful of pictures that you want to burn.**

    For example, you might want to burn the folder that appears at the top of the Photo Gallery list. If so, click the folder name above the pictures.

4. **At the top, click the Burn icon and then choose Data Disc.**

    You see the Burn a Disc dialog box, shown in Figure 36-6.

• **Figure 36-6: Burn pictures on a Live File System (UDF) disc.**

5. **Type a name for the disc. Unless you absolutely have to be able to view the pictures on a Windows 2000 or Windows 98 (or earlier) PC, click the button marked Live File System and then click Next.**

    Vista takes a minute or two to format the disc and then copies the pictures you chose to the disc.

6. **When Vista finishes copying the pictures to the CD or DVD, go back to Step 3 and burn another bunch of pictures.**

7. **When you're tired of burning pictures, push the eject button on the drive.**

    Vista finishes off the disc — prepares it so it can be read on other computers — and, sooner or later, ejects the disc.

8. **Immediately try to look at the files to make sure your copies look okay.**

    You can put the CD back in the computer that you've been using or take it to another computer.

9. **If the pictures look good, take a CD labeling marker and write a description on the top of the CD (not the shiny side).**

    Store the CD in a cool, dry place, and it should last a long time.

Burning a Slide Show on a CD

If you followed the instructions in the preceding section, you have a CD (or DVD) filled with pictures. Plop that CD into any computer that runs Windows XP or Vista, and you can use the many Windows features to look at the pictures, copy them, and so on. In particular, viewing all the pictures in a folder as a slide show is easy — just open the folder in Windows Explorer and choose View➪As Slide Show in Windows XP, or click the Slide Show button in Vista.

But what about your friends who don't have Windows XP or Vista? If you send the CD to people who don't have XP or Vista installed, they can open the files, or (on most versions of Windows) view thumbnails of the pics. But they'll have a devil of a time watching the pictures as a slide show — a feature that older versions of Windows simply don't have.

And if they don't have a computer at all . . . . what then?

Fortunately, if you have the foresight, you can burn a DVD as a TV show — a slide show that runs when you plop the DVD in a simple DVD player. This technique is quick, efficient, and surprisingly easy to perform after you figure out what to do.

Here's the fast way to make a DVD slide show:

1. **Stick a blank DVD in your DVD writer.**

Vista responds with its usual AutoPlay offerings.

2. **"X" out of the AutoPlay message.**

3. **Choose Start➪All Programs➪Windows Photo Gallery.**

Your latest pictures appear. If you set up Windows Photo Gallery in the way I describe in Technique 32, they appear as in Figure 36-5, in the previous section.

4. **Select all the pictures and videos that you want to put in the slide show.**

You can select more than a thousand "normal" digital camera pics and put them on a single DVD. Don't worry if you select too many; you won't break Vista.

5. **Click the Burn button at the top and then choose Video DVD.**

Windows Photo Gallery starts the Windows DVD Maker and feeds it all the files you've selected (see Figure 36-7).

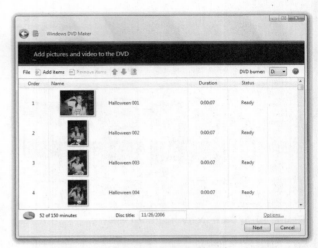

• **Figure 36-7: Photo and video files get fed to the DVD Maker directly.**

6. **If you want to change the slide show to make it play widescreen (16:9 aspect ratio), or if you want to make it play in a continuous loop, click the Options link, set those options, and click OK.**

7. **Click Next.**

Windows DVD Maker gives you a few very simple styles for the form of the opening screen, as shown in Figure 36-8.

• **Figure 36-8: Set the opening menu style.**

8. Click the button marked Slide Show.

Windows DVD Maker allows you to add music to the slide show, as well as make changes to the timing and the method for making the transition from one slide to the next (see Figure 36-9).

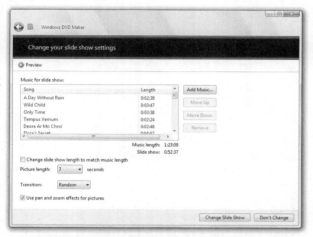

• **Figure 36-9:** Very straightforward effects are easy to apply.

9. Click the Add Music button and add whatever music you like. Change the transition scheme. Check the box if you would like to add "Ken Burns effect" pan and zoom to the show.

Ken Burns is the visual genius who first used the pan-and-zoom slide show effect in his 1990 documentary miniseries on the American Civil War.

10. Click Change Slide Show.

You go back to the main Windows DVD Maker window, as in Figure 36-8.

11. When you're happy with your choices, click Burn.

The Windows DVD Maker can take an eternity to create the DVD, but when it's done, you have a genuine, playable DVD.

Recovering Deleted Pictures from Your Camera

Tell me whether this has ever happened to you . . .

I just clicked the wrong button on my digital camera and deleted all the pictures I'd stored. I thought I had selected just one file, but my not-so-nimble fingers were working in preprogrammed mode, far faster than my brain. The net result: an entire Compact Flash memory card wiped out.

 Surprisingly, the fastest, easiest, bestest way to undelete files on your digital camera is through your PC.

Lots of programs on the market claim to resurrect dearly departed digital image files from your camera. I'm sure most of them work (although I've bumped into several that don't, at least on my cameras).

But I've only hit one company that has the guts to let you download its software and use it to bring back two pictures for free. If you want to undelete more, you have to pay $39.95 for the program. But the two-shot demo version of File-Rescue Plus doesn't cost a thing. It's cost effective and saves time, too. Hard to beat.

Here's how to test drive File-Rescue Plus:

1. Fire up your favorite Web browser and head to `www.softwareshelf.com`.

2. Find the link to download the trial version of File-Rescue Plus and click it. Then download and install the English (or other language) workstation version of File-Rescue Plus.

There's a very short and sweet setup wizard.

3. Connect the camera that contains the recently deceased picture(s) and turn it on.

If Vista's AutoPlay detects the camera, "X" out of the AutoPlay message.

4. **Choose Start➪All Programs➪Software Shelf➪File-Rescue Plus to start File-Rescue Plus.**

The program asks you to select a drive (as shown in Figure 36-10).

• **Figure 36-10: You want to scan for deleted pictures.**

5. **Choose the drive that corresponds to your digital camera and then click Scan.**

If you aren't sure which drive to use, choose Start➪My Computer and look for your camera.

File-Rescue Plus runs a quick scan and shows you the results.

6. **In the QuickScan Results message, click Close.**

File-Rescue Plus shows you the results of its scan, as in Figure 36-11.

7. **Choose a picture that you want to see and then click the Recover button at the bottom.**

File-Rescue Plus advises that you should save to a different disk than the one you're recovering and asks you to specify a location for the recovered files (see Figure 36-12).

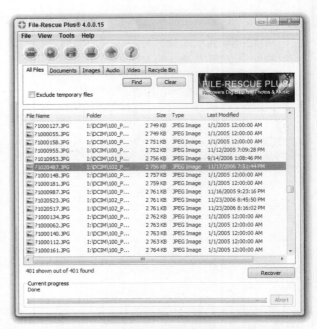

• **Figure 36-11: File-Rescue Plus has found all or part of many, many files on the camera.**

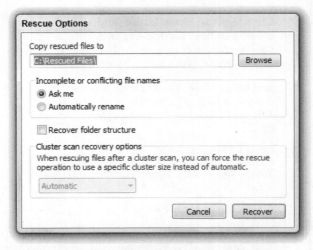

• **Figure 36-12: Don't stick recovered files back in the camera!**

8. **Choose a good location *not* on your camera for the recovered file and then click Recover.**

File-Rescue Plus tells you the results of the reconstruction effort.

9. **Click Close.**

10. **Use Windows Explorer to go to the location you specified in Step 8.**

There's your recovered picture (see Figure 36-13).

The first time I saw File-Rescue Plus bring back a deleted photo inside a camera, I could hardly believe my eyes.

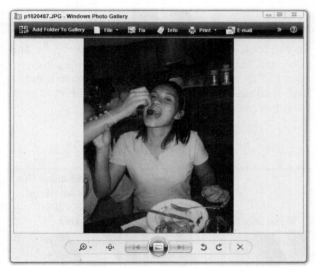

• **Figure 36-13: File-Rescue Plus brings 'em back from the bit bucket.**

Decreasing Picture Download Times

So you have one of those umpteen-gazillion-pixel cameras? Used to be that 3 megapixels was about as far as a camera could go. Now I'm beginning to wonder if we'll ever see a limit, really.

No doubt you know that more pixels means better-quality pictures (although sooner or later the lens quality sets the upper limit). After all, that's why you shelled out the bucks for a good camera. But the ramifications of all those pixels may not have struck you until you tried to e-mail a picture.

Just one picture can blow someone's e-mail account size limit: Most e-mail accounts have strict limits on the amount of space allotted to each user. Free e-mail accounts rarely accommodate more than a handful of high-quality pictures. Go beyond the limit, and messages get bounced. Gazillions of pixels translates into gazillions of bits. And the bits all take time, time, time to transmit over the Internet.

If you're sending a proof of the next cover of *National Geographic,* hey, use all the pixels you can stand. But if you're just trying to send the grandkids a pic of your new rose garden, all those bits only get in the way. This Technique shows you how to find the middle path between humongous file sizes and grainy little snapshots.

Understanding digital pic file sizes

High-resolution digital pictures take an enormous amount of space. But what does it all mean?

A pixel is a dot, give or take a semantic hair or two. If you have a 3.1-megapixel camera, it takes pictures that measure 2,048 dots across by 1,536 dots high.

 Chances are good that your camera has settings that save pictures in lower resolutions: 1,600 x 1,200 pixels, 1,280 x 960, 1,024 x 768, 800 x 600, and 640 x 480 are all possibilities that just happen to correspond to standard Windows screen resolutions. Your camera probably gives these settings truly illuminating names, such as Hi, Med, and Lo.

Before the camera stores the picture on disk, it uses a compression method — typically JPEG — to reduce the size of the file.

When you take a shot with a camera that uses 2,048 x 1,536 dots and you ask for pictures at 1,600 x 1,200 dots, the compression kicks in, and you end up with a file that's about 750,000 bytes in size, give or take 10,000 or 20,000 bytes. Variations occur because some shots compress more readily than others: A picture of the Pillsbury Dough Boy in a blinding winter snow compresses down to a smaller file than, say, a shot of Eminem's hair at the same resolution.

Table 36-1 gives you an idea of the size of files you can expect from common picture dimensions and how you can expect to use them.

When you reduce the resolution of a picture, you make it a little fuzzier — but a whole lot smaller, and thus easier to ship over the Internet.

Put another way, if you have a friend with 2MB left on her free e-mail account, and you e-mail her just one high-resolution shot from your 3.1-megapixel camera, you take up more than half of her storage allotment. You can't send her two.

But if you convert the high-resolution picture to 640 x 480 — which is fine for viewing on a computer screen — the file size goes down to 30 to 40K, and you can send her, oh, 50 pictures without blowing her account out of the water.

 Even if you can send a half-dozen 3.1-megapixel pictures to, say, your lawyer, if he doesn't have a fast line, you tie up his Internet connection for 30 minutes. I don't know how much your lawyer charges for a half hour of staring at Outlook downloading files, but mine wasn't too amused the last time that happened.

Changing the resolution of pictures

So you took a bunch of high-resolution pictures, and you used Technique 34 to pull the pictures onto your PC. Or at least that's what I do. I like to have high-resolution pictures hanging around just in case I want to make big prints.

TABLE 36-1: CAMERA RESOLUTION AND JPG FILE SIZES

This Resolution	Produces JPEG Files about This Size	So This Many Pictures Fit on a 1GB Memory Card	These Shots Are Suitable For	And Take about This Long to Download on a Good 56K Dialup Line
2400 x 1800	1.6MB	80	High-quality enlargements — virtually indistinguishable from (and possibly better than!) 35mm film	5 minutes
2048 x 1536	1.2MB	100	10 x 12 prints	4 minutes
1600 x 1200	0.8MB	160	8 x 10 prints	2.5 minutes
1280 x 960	0.5MB	250	5 x 7 prints	1.5 minutes
1024 x 768	0.4MB	300	4 x 6 prints (or very high-quality shots for documents)	1 minute
800 x 600	0.2MB	500	Wallet-size prints (or good-quality Web graphics)	30 seconds
640 x 480	0.1MB	1,000	Decent Web graphics (or viewing informal pictures on a computer monitor)	15 seconds

But now the time has come to send some of those pictures over the Internet — birthday pictures to Grandma, say, or product pictures to a client. Maybe you want to post on Flickr and you're getting close to the maximum size.

 Here's what you should *not* do: You should not send those huge files out over the Internet. Unless you know for a fact that your correspondent can handle big, big e-mailed files, you do her a huge disservice by clogging her inbox with stuff she doesn't need.

If you're sending a photo of your house to a real estate broker so it can be printed in a four-color glossy brochure, that's one thing. But if you just want to show your sister how the snow's piled up around the house, you're bound by Internet ethics to resize the image before you send it.

For many years, Microsoft has distributed a free resizing tool — the Image Resizer PowerToy — that works simply with a right-click: You right-click a picture, choose the image size you want, and the PowerToy creates a new picture according to your specs and puts it in the same folder as the original. As we went to press, though, it wasn't clear whether the Image Resizer PowerToy would be made available free or if it would be part of an extra-cost bundle.

Harumph.

There are many, many free image resizing tools on the market. You can find a good one by visiting www.tucows.com and searching for the term *image resize*.

 Personally, I use IrfanView for resizing. It takes a couple of extra clicks — there's no right-click-and-go option — but it does a very good job of high-quality reduction. And it's free. Here's how to use IrfanView to reduce the size of photos:

1. Get your favorite browser fired up and go to **www.irfanview.com. Click the link to download the current version and then install it.**

There's a very simple installation wizard; take all the defaults — no need to make IrfanView your default picture file handler unless you really want to.

2. Choose Start⇨Pictures and navigate to the picture you want to resize. Right-click the picture and choose Open With⇨IrfanView.

Your picture appears in IrfanView, as in Figure 36-14.

• **Figure 36-14: Open the picture you want to resize.**

3. Choose Image⇨Resize/Resample.

IrfanView shows you the Resize/Resample Image dialog box in Figure 36-15.

In the Resize/Resample Image dialog box, you can type in a new size in pixels or inches, you can scale by a specific percentage, or you can choose from many standard scaling options.

• **Figure 36-15: Choose from a wide array of resizing options.**

4. **Pick the resizing option you want. (Leave the box marked Preserve Aspect Ratio if you don't want IrfanView to stretch the picture.) Then click OK.**

IrfanView resizes *but does not save* the image.

5. **Choose File⇨Save As to give the resized file a new name.**

6. **Repeat Steps 2 through 5 for any other images you want to resize. When you're done, "X" out of IrfanView.**

It takes a little longer to go through IrfanView than the Image Resizer PowerToy, but you have much more control over the final product.

37 Technique

Posting Pics on Flickr and MySpace

By now I bet you have a 200GB hard drive stuffed with photos and videos that you've taken over the past five years — and I bet about three people have seen, oh, maybe 2 percent of all of them. It's hard to get your family to sit still long enough to drag out the pics — and even harder to keep their interest long enough to leaf through the collection between New Year and Aunt Gertrude's birthday, much less all the way to Valentine's Day.

Hey, *you* know you have good pics. *I* know you have good pics. Why don't you show the world that you have good pics?

With the advent of almost-infinite disk space, free online "social media sites" have taken the world by storm. You may be a frequent visitor to Flickr, MySpace, or YouTube. You may twitter at Twitter (or at least gaggle) or share bean-sprout-eating tips at Five Limes. You may just barely know that sites like that exist. Even if you don't buy into the electronic popularity contests at Technorati or the bookmarking gang mentality at del.icio.us, you should take advantage of the technology and the connectivity to convince (perhaps coerce?) your friends and family to take a gander at your pics.

In this Technique, I take you on a whirlwind tour of Flickr, the site that's kind of rolled over the photo-posting world, and drop by MySpace to show you what's happening. I also touch briefly on Yahoo! Groups because they're a great resource for clubs, small organizations, and even workgroups at the office.

Mostly, in this Technique, I want to show you some of the many ways to get your shots shared, noticed, and appreciated. Quickly. It's easy.

Sharing with Flickr

Think of Flickr (www.flickr.com) as a giant photo-sharing community with a serious blogging problem and a streak of critique thrown in for good measure. Feel free to drop by my Flickr site, www.flickr.com/photos/woodyleonhard (see Figure 37-1).

• **Figure 37-1:** My friend Flickr.

Yahoo! (which bought Vancouver-based Flickr in 2005) says it's a "deep" application, and I would have to agree. At Flickr, you can

- ✔ **Upload photos directly from your camera-phone to your site.** As long as your phone can send e-mail, it's easy — you send the pic attached to a message to an address that's specific to your site.

- ✔ **Send pics directly from Flickr to your blog,** whether you're using the blogging sites from Blogger (www.blogger.com), Typepad (www.sixapart.com/typepad), or LiveJournal (www.livejournal.com), or even if you have your own site and you use Movable Type (www.sixapart.com/movabletype).

- ✔ **Work with groups.** Flickr is built around groups — whether they're informal groups in your contacts list or invitation-only groups formed for a specific purpose. You can form a group for your family reunion, for example, and

have everyone upload their pictures as the reunion is under way. That sure beats everyone hunkering around a laptop, sequentially slogging through each participant's shots.

- ✔ **Find fascinating photos.** From Vintage Advertisements (see Figure 37-2) to Logos to Jersey Street Art to shots taken at 8:50 a.m. local time (no, I'm not kidding) and many places in between, Flickr's linked photo pools, tied to groups, range from mundane to exquisite.

- ✔ **Brainstorm.** Pick a tag, any tag, and run with it.

• **Figure 37-2:** A small selection of shots in the Vintage Advertising group.

Here's how to get going with Flickr:

1. **Get your favorite browser going and head to www.flickr.com. (See Figure 37-3.)**

2. **If you already have a Yahoo! ID, click the link in the upper right to sign in, otherwise click Sign Up and get a Yahoo! ID.**

   If you sign up, Yahoo! (er, Flickr) sends you an e-mail message that you have to respond to in order to get the Yahoo! ID.

• **Figure 37-3: The Flickr main site.**

After you've passed the Yahoo! account hurdle, Flickr asks you to choose a Screen Name.

3. **Type a screen name that you can live with and click Sign In.**

Flickr tells you that you're all set and invites you to upload your first photo (see Figure 37-4).

• **Figure 37-4: No beating around the bush; Flickr takes you straight to the upload page.**

4. **Click the link marked Upload Your First Photo.**

Flickr presents you with the Photo Upload page, shown in Figure 37-5.

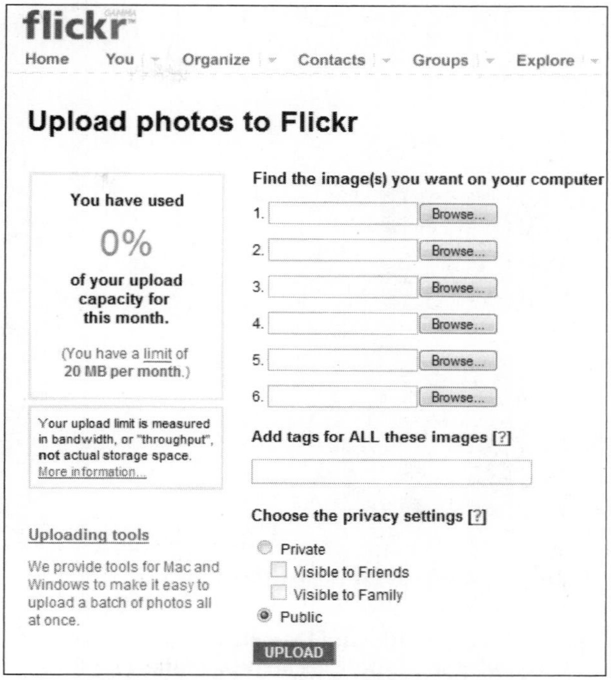

• **Figure 37-5: Upload your first pictures to Flickr.**

5. **Select your first pictures to upload and click Upload:**

a. Click the top Browse button and then go out on your computer, find a picture you want to upload, and click Open.

b. Then click the next Browse button, find another picture, and so on.

c. If you can think of a tag that goes along with all the pictures, type it in the Add Tags box.

d. If you want the pictures to be visible to anyone, select the Public option.

Depending on the speed of your Internet connection and how badly bogged down Yahoo!'s servers are, uploading can take many minutes. Chill. Grab a latte. When you come back, you have the beginning of a Flickr site, as shown in Figure 37-6.

• **Figure 37-6:** Duankghae's first Flickr site.

6. Fill in the Title and Description and make a good stab at the Tags so other folks can find your pics. Then click Save.

Flickr takes you to your home page, as in Figure 37-7.

• **Figure 37-7:** In a matter of minutes, pictures are ready for viewing.

To replace the placeholder picture next to Your Photos, you need a 48-by-48-pixel picture to go there.

7. Use the method described at the end of Technique 36 to make a 48-by-48-pixel picture of yourself (probably using the free IrfanView). Then click the down-arrow to the right of You and choose Your Profile.

Flickr presents you with a fledgling profile page like the one in Figure 37-8.

• **Figure 37-8:** Change your picture here.

8. On the right, click the Your Buddy Icon link.

You see an upload page for your picture, er, your buddy icon.

9. On the right, click Browse. Then navigate to your 48-by-48-pixel picture and click Open. Then click the Upload button.

Flickr confirms that it received your new picture.

10. In the upper left, click You.

Your new icon appears in the upper left, as in Figure 37-9.

Before you go gallivanting off exploring Flickr, there's one more change you should make. I strongly suggest that you set up your own Web address for your Flickr site.

11. Click the down-wedge to the right of You and choose Your Account. Scroll way down and look on the right side. Click the link that says Set Up Your URL.

• **Figure 37-9: Your main page is complete.**

Flickr invites you to create your own, permanent Flickr address (see Figure 37-10).

• **Figure 37-10: Create your own Flickr URL.**

You can't change your permanent Flickr URL, but you can create a new Yahoo! ID and move all your pictures over to the new ID.

12. **Type a likely name in the box and click Preview.**

If you chose a name that doesn't already exist, Flickr warns you once again that it can't be changed later.

13. **Click OK, Lock It In.**

You now have a permanent URL for your Flickr site, which you can hand out like candy at Halloween.

There are many places to go in Flickr — it's an engaging, complex site with a lot of good tools and fun people and great pics. One of the first things you should do is invite your friends to come see your site. Just click the down-wedge to the right of Contacts and choose Invite Your Friends. Follow the instructions and you'll soon have thousands of gawkers. Or at least maybe your Aunt Gertrude will drop by to look at her own birthday pictures.

14. **Explore!**

Click the button marked Explore and take it away. . . .

Gabbing in MySpace

While Flickr can be described as a photo place with a blogging problem, MySpace seems more like a place to hang out and blog and drop a photo off on the way out. Get the difference?

MySpace has branched into many different services in the past couple of years. Once a wildly popular blogging space known best for its adolescent behavior (and complexity), it has turned into a meeting-and-greeting place with music (for sale, of course; see Figure 37-11), videos (hey, YouTube did it), a matchmaking service, classified ads, and the kitchen sink.

• **Figure 37-11: MySpace covers a whole lotta bases.**

When you join MySpace, you're invited to blog, upload pictures, use the MySpace services for e-mail and instant messaging, and meet and greet to your heart's content.

You can find a very thorough tour of MySpace at `collect.myspace.com/misc/tour_1.html` (see Figure 37-12). If MySpace sounds like your kind of space, take the tour and follow the instructions there to get started.

To get the most out of MySpace, take a look at *MySpace For Dummies,* by Ryan Hupfer, Mitch Maxson, and Ryan Williams (also from Wiley).

• **Figure 37-12: The MySpace tour tells you what you need to know to get started.**

Going for the Yahoo! Groups

Before I finish this Technique about spreading your pictures far and wide, I want to mention an old-fashioned service that's ideal if you have a small circle of friends who want to post pictures and send messages within the group. I've seen it used for many years by family groups, volunteer organizations, even clubs in schools.

Yahoo! Groups are easy to set up, and you can make them private so new members have to be approved by the group moderator. Members of the group can

send e-mail to each other, and the mail can go to any address — it isn't limited to yahoo.com addresses. Members can post pictures, which are visible by other members of the group. They can also share files. You can even post a group calendar.

Setting up a group is very easy:

1. **Fire up your Web browser and go to `groups.yahoo.com`.**

2. **Click the Start Your Own Group link.**

3. **Just fill out the simple application form (see Figure 37-13), and your group will be ready in minutes.**

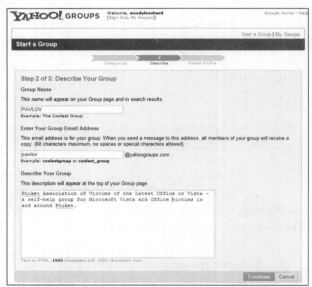

• **Figure 37-13: Setting up your own Yahoo! group is fast and easy.**

The groups don't scale well — closed groups with more than a few dozen members can take a great deal of time to administer. They aren't ultra-secure, so don't plan on setting up a Yahoo! Group to handle your next hostile takeover. But they do provide an excellent way to share photos and messages within a small circle.

Part VII

Networking at the Speed of Light

The 5th Wave   By Rich Tennant

"That's it! We're getting a wireless network for the house."

38 Technique

Installing a Small Network

Save Time By

- ✔ Buying the right equipment — the first time
- ✔ Understanding IP addresses
- ✔ Getting your network up in no time

I f you have two or more computers in your office or in your home — or even in your home office — they should be networked. Whether you want to share a printer or a single Internet connection (over a single phone line or cable TV box) or if you just need to transfer a few files every once in a while, a small peer-to-peer network — what Microsoft calls a *workgroup* — fits the bill. You can throw away your floppies. Stop running up and down the stairs. Whatever weird machinations and incantations you've endured to swap stuff between computers have become a thing of the past. And . . . oh, man, the games!

As long as one of your computers uses Vista and the others run Windows 98 or later, setting up a network is fast, cheap, and easy — and almost always painless.

This Technique steps you through the process of putting your first network together. If you're not sure about the technical bafflegab, I fill you in on the terms you need to know — and studiously ignore the stuff you don't.

Most of the time, assembling a network is like falling off a log — if you get the right equipment and put it together in the correct sequence. All it takes is a credit card and a decent computer shop.

For those unusual occasions when your network doesn't come together right the first time, there's always the Pizza Solution, a time-honored tradition in the industry. Ask your friends and colleagues, and find the best computer guru available — he or she could be a buttoned-down, three-piece kind, but far more likely you'll end up with a gangly high school or college student, or a marginally intelligible oaf like me. Invite him or her over for pizza. Beer, too, if you aren't violating any child labor laws. Plan on spending about an hour. If you can't figure it out in an hour, dump all the stuff (including at least two PCs) in your SUV, haul it back to the computer shop, and have the shop put it together.

Life's too short, eh?

Putting the Pieces Together

Most discussions of Windows networking tend to get bogged down in questions of cable types and hub specifications, IP addresses, and DHCP servers. Bah.

 Here's the straight, timesaving scoop. You have four different ways to string a network together.

You can choose from any of the following ways to assemble your network:

✔ If you're networking two PCs, you can use a crossover cable. This process is cheap and fast, and if you ever need to add more PCs, you just throw the crossover cable away. If you want to go that way, walk into your nearest computer store and say, "crossover cable." The folks should have you on your way in two minutes.

✔ Go wireless. You need an 802.11b or 802.11g card or USB antenna in each PC (your notebook may have one already) plus an 802.11b or g base station. The base station usually plugs directly into the Internet or into an existing wired network (in which case, it's called a *wireless access point*).

Don't you love these obfuscating buzzwords? The 802.11b technology is a particular way for computers to talk to each other over radio channels. It's very similar to the method used by 2.4-GHz telephones — another obfuscating buzzword. The 802.11g technology is faster, smarter, and better than 802.11b. Given a choice, always go for 802.11g.

 Other kinds of wireless networks are gradually appearing, with names like 802.11a and 802.11n, which seems poised to make some inroads if the standards organizations ever manage to settle on a definitive specification. Don't be overly impressed by the technology; each has advantages and disadvantages — in particular, 802.11n, in day-to-day use, isn't *that* much better than 802.11g. Just make sure that the base station and the cards (or internal circuitry) in each of your computers use the same flavor.

✔ If the computers you want to connect are sitting on the same desk, consider using a traditional hard-wired Ethernet network. It's cheap and easy to set up, and you don't have to worry about radio interference. You need a network card in each of the PCs, a cheap box (variously called a hub, switch, or router) that interconnects the PCs, and enough network cable to hook each PC to the hub.

Ethernet is an ancient technology, predating Windows itself, that still works very well. The terminology can drive you nuts, but 10 Base-T, 100 Base-T, 10/100 Base-T, 1000 Base-T, gigabit, 10/100/1000 Mbps, Category 5, Category 6, Category 5E, UTP, TPE (Twisted Pair Ethernet), and RJ-45 all refer to Ethernet-related stuff.

✔ The best and worst of both worlds come with running two networks — one wired and the other wireless — and connecting the two together. Nowadays, if you have a fast cable, ADSL, or satellite connection, the easiest and fastest way to work in both worlds involves a wireless broadband router. You plug one side of the box into your fast Internet connection, run local-area network (LAN) cables from the router to nearby PCs, and use wireless cards for any other computer on your network. In many cases, your Internet service provider can supply the box and have you going in no time.

Although wireless networks run at a fraction of the speed of hard-wired Ethernet networks (give or take a waffle or two), the speed of a network comes into play only if you're pumping massive amounts of data through it. Someday, when your TV runs directly off the Internet, that'll be important. Right now, it's just marketing hype.

Choosing the right hardware

If you're worried about getting the right hardware, here's a bit of school-of-hard-knocks advice. For hard-wired Ethernet networks, get cheap, get generic. For wireless networks, don't skimp; get everything from the same manufacturer — and make sure that you can return the components if they don't work.

My quick buying guides for network components are as follows:

- ✔ **Wireless base stations/cards:** These are changing so fast that any recommendation I make today will be useless tomorrow, except for one: Don't try to mix and match. Get one package and stick with it. Or throw it away and get another one. Keep on top of the latest developments in wireless technology by visiting www.practicallynetworked.com.

- ✔ **Network cards (also known as NICs, or network interface cards):** Chances are pretty good that any newer PC you own already has a place to plug in a network cable. (Hint: Look for something like a wide telephone jack on the back of your PC.) If you need a card for a desktop PC and you have an extra card slot available, get a generic NIC (for less than $20) and install it yourself. Installing cards isn't nearly as difficult as it used to be, and most cards deal with Vista quite well. For a portable computer — or if you're too intimidated to install a card — get a USB Ethernet adapter ($20) or PC-card Ethernet adapter ($40).

- ✔ **Cable:** You can spend a lot, but I'm not convinced that the more expensive ones are any better than the cheaper ones. Look for generic, 8-wire Category 5 cable with telephone-like (RJ-45) connectors on the ends. Buy cables that are long enough to stretch from each PC to the hub.

- ✔ **Hubs/switches/routers:** A simple $50 eight-port hub is more than most small offices and homes will ever need. If you intend to get a new one, spend a few extra bucks and get one that supports 802.11g wireless access.

 If you have a fast Internet connection from the phone company or cable company, see how much the company wants for a wireless router. Timesaving bonus: The company can install it and have you going in no time.

Pulling cable through your office or house

Don't. If you have to drill into walls to run Ethernet cables, you're far better off going with 802.11g wireless technology. Running cables may look easy, but it isn't. If you kink the cable, it may work right for the first day or two. But then it may go all to Hades when you get your first major rainfall or the temperature gets too high or too low.

Typically, 802.11g goes through two or three thick concrete walls, and/or up to a couple hundred feet of relatively unobstructed territory. In case you need to go farther, all the major wireless manufacturers sell range extenders that relay the signal.

Locating the hardware

In general, it doesn't matter much where you put any of your wired network's components. A wired hub — even if it's a fancy, switched, gold-plated residential gateway — can easily go in a closet. With one exception, a printer works just as well whether it's attached to the PC in your office or the PC in your living room. The exception? If the printer is attached to a PC that falls into sleep mode, you can't use it from other computers on the network.

Wireless is a horse of a different color. If you want wireless coverage to extend through several rooms, it helps to put the base station in the middle. Because 802.11b and g use the same 2.4-GHz frequency employed by most cordless phones, keeping the base station away from a cordless phone station is a good idea. Finally, wireless manufacturers recommend that you not place a base station right next to a wall. Reflections can cut down the efficacy of the base station.

The only significant limitation you're bound to encounter is the 100-meter (330-foot) limit on the total length of all the Ethernet cables connecting to a single hub. If that becomes a bother, just go wireless. It's that simple.

Preparing for Vista Networking

Vista almost always identifies a functioning (or even semifunctioning) network and sets up the software correctly the first time. The settings won't be right — as I discuss later in this Technique — but the hardware almost always works — the first time.

Before you try to get Vista to recognize your new network, it's your responsibility to make sure that the hardware is working. For traditional hard–wired Ethernet systems, or simple crossover cable-based two-PC networks, follow these steps:

1. **Turn off every PC in the network.**

2. **Disconnect the Ethernet cable from the back of every PC.**

3. **One by one, turn on each PC.**

4. **Make sure that Vista boots without rejecting the network card and that the machine itself — along with all its peripherals — is working.**

   If Windows needs drivers, it tells you. If Windows tells you that a network card is unplugged, great! That means that everything is working fine.

5. **Again, turn off every PC in the network.**

6. **Connect the Ethernet cables on each PC, and double-check to make sure that the cables are connected on the hub.**

7. **One by one, turn on each PC.**

   Verify that the light on the hub comes on — that means the PC is talking to the hub — and watch the network card to make sure that its light is blinking, too.

   If the lights don't come on, go back and check the card and the cable.

8. **Turn off everything — the PCs, the hub, and the routers if you have any.**

   You want all the machines off so that you can wake them up, one by one. (Bringing them back one by one can help you minimize — or at least

isolate — problems with something called an IP address. See the section "Understanding Addresses," later in this Technique.)

For wireless networks, you can follow the same basic steps, but you have to consult your manufacturer's manuals to make sure that the PCs and base station are talking to each other.

Cranking Up Vista Networking

Everything on the network is turned off, right? You know that the hardware's working. You know the cables are connected. But it's all turned off. Good.

 Here's the best way to get Vista to recognize your network the right way the first time:

1. **Turn on whatever you have that's connected to the Internet and wait a minute.**

   Whether it's a modem with a power switch, a router, a residential gateway, a hardware firewall, or a miniature paisley homing pigeon, turn it on first. Something called a DHCP server (the box that assigns network addresses; see the section "Understanding Addresses," later in this Technique) may need to get itself started.

    If you have an internal modem — one without a power switch — skip this step. It gets turned on when you turn the PC on.

2. **If you have a hub/switch/router and it has a power switch (not all of them do), turn it on. If you have a wireless base station, turn it on, too. Wait another minute.**

   If you have two DHCP servers in your network (see the section "Understanding Addresses"), you have to give them both time to scratch each other's eyeballs out, stomp on them, and otherwise resolve their differences. It's an IP jungle out there.

3. Turn on all the PCs in the network. Turn on their peripherals, too — especially printers.

If you have anything that you don't normally use, leave it off. In particular, if you have a portable computer with an internal modem that you don't intend to share with the network, don't plug it into the phone jack.

4. Pick a Vista PC at random.

If you have a network with a mixture of Vista PCs and earlier-generation-Windows PCs, start with the Vista PCs. They're much easier to set up.

5. In the system tray, at the lower right, next to the clock, click the network activity icon — the one that looks like two monitors with a blue beach ball (see Figure 38-1) — and click the Network and Sharing Center link.

• **Figure 38-1:** The networking monitor icon.

Depending on how you set up your PC (or how the folks who sold you the PC set it up for you), the Network and Sharing Center that you see may or may not have the settings shown in Figure 38-2.

6. On the right, click the Customize link.

Vista brings up the Set Network Location dialog box, as shown in Figure 38-3.

• **Figure 38-2:** Typical Network and Sharing settings for a PC fresh out of the box.

• **Figure 38-3:** Basic network settings.

7. If you already have a network, type the network's name in the indicated box. If you're setting up a brand-new network, pick a name (something simple, please) and type it into the box.

8. Choose the Location Type that best describes your network.

If you are setting up a home or home-office network, you probably want Private.

"Public" and "Private" are just shorthand for a bunch of security settings that Vista applies. Don't get too hung up on the definition: You have a chance to fine-tune the security settings in Step 11.

9. Click the Next button.

You may have to click to continue through a User Account Control security dialog box. When Vista comes back, it confirms that it has successfully made the changes.

10. Click the Close button.

Vista returns to the Network and Sharing Center (see Figure 38-4), updating your Sharing and Discovery settings to conform to the Public or Private choice that you made in Step 8.

11. One by one, click the down arrows to the right of Network Discovery, File Sharing, Public Folder Sharing, Printer Sharing, Password Protected Sharing, and Media Sharing.

Refer to the handy list in Table 38-1. If you don't agree with any of the settings that have been made based on Vista's pre-defined settings for your Location Type, change them.

• **Figure 38-4:** Sharing and Discovery settings get modified to match your Location Type.

Vista has a horribly convoluted, poorly documented, overlapping set of Sharing and Discovery settings, but hey, that's what we have to work with. Stick with my recommendations for home and home-office networks, and you'll be fine.

TABLE 38-1: SHARING AND DISCOVERY SETTINGS

What It Says	What It Means	Timesaving Tip
Network Discovery	You can see other computers on the network, and they can see you.	That's why you set up the network, isn't it?
File Sharing	Files in shared folders can be seen by other people on the network.	That's why you set up the network . . . oh, never mind.
Public Folder Sharing	No matter what you do, other people on this computer can get to the Public folders. (That's why they're public, eh?) This is the place where you tell Vista whether people on the network can see (read only) or change (read/write/delete) files in the Public folders.	I usually allow full read/write/delete access, but beware: If someone on the network deletes a file in your shared folder, it doesn't go into the Recycle Bin. It disappears. Exercise some caution.
Printer Sharing	If for some reason you told Vista to share a printer but you turn this off, you didn't share the printer. Make sense? No, I didn't think so.	Leave it on. That's why you share printers, isn't it?

What It Says	What It Means	Timesaving Tip
Password Protected Sharing	An ultra-confusing setting. If it's set to On, people who try to get into your Public or shared folders or to use your shared hardware have to provide a logon ID and password *that's valid on this computer.* Overrides all the previous settings.	In a home or home-office environment, leave it off. Password-protect individual files if you need to.
Media Sharing	Allow other people on the network to get at the music, pictures, and videos in the Public folders.	Why on earth would you set it to Off?

I leave my home and home-office networks wide open, per Figure 38-5.

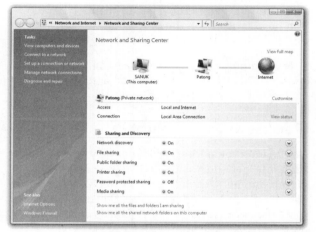

• **Figure 38-5: Profile of a wide-open PC, like what I run at home and in my home office.**

12. **When you're happy with your settings, click the red *X* to exit the Network and Sharing Center.**

    You're fully loaded and ready for bear.

Checking the Pieces

After you have all the PCs on your network connected and their Sharing and Discovery settings modified, you should check to be sure that the computers can see each other.

To do that on a Vista computer, follow these steps:

1. **Choose Start⇨Network.**

   Windows Explorer shows you all the computers that are available on the network, with separate entries for shared media, as shown in Figure 38-6.

• **Figure 38-6: All the computers on the network.**

2. **If you can't see one or more computers on the network, go to the "missing" computer and verify that its Discovery and Sharing settings match your expectations.**

   Use the steps in the preceding section.

3. **If you still can't see one or more computers on the network, but you can remember the name of a computer that you can't see, click once in the Address bar (where it says *Network* in Figure 38-6), type two backslashes and the name of the computer, and then press Enter.**

   With a little luck, you can get at the shared folders and devices on the computer via this manual method. Vista may show you the name(s) of the computer(s) in the Folders list on the left side of the window, per Figure 38-7, even if it doesn't include icons for the computers in the "enumerated" section on the right.

• **Figure 38-7: A networking bug in Vista: Computers on the left don't appear on the right.**

If you can get the computers to come up manually by typing in their names, but they don't appear in the "enumerated" list, you're looking at a bug in Vista. Someday Microsoft may fix it.

 If worse comes to worst and you need to get to computers on your network that don't appear in the Start➪Network list, you can tell Vista to make an unused drive letter (such as Z) refer to the inaccessible drive. To do so, when you're in Windows Explorer, hold down Tab and then choose Tools➪Map Network Drive. Vista takes you through the steps.

You aren't really *mapping a drive* — you're assigning a drive letter on your computer to a shared network folder — but in the end, you can get at your missing-in-action computer by using a drive letter on your PC.

 Wireless networks are particularly vulnerable to intruders. Most wireless networks, installed precisely according to manufacturers' instructions, have little or no security enabled. This means that a neighbor or passerby may, in certain circumstances, be able to tap into your network. If you have a wireless network, follow the advice in Technique 39.

Understanding Addresses

If your network goes bump in the night, and you aren't suffering from the missing-in-action enumeration bug I describe in the preceding section, your problem can probably be traced back to addresses.

Every computer on a network has to have an *address*. That's how computers on a network talk to each other — they use addresses.

IP addresses on the Internet

On the Internet, addresses take a very specific form: Each Internet address (called an IP address) is a set of four numbers, each between 0 and 255. For example, the IP address 208.215.179.139 just happens to be the address of the *For Dummies* server, `www.dummies.com`. The address for `www.microsoft.com` is 207.46.134.222.

 Perhaps obviously, no two computers can have the same IP address. If two computers had the same address, communication would get horribly messed up — not unlike the way it would be with two different people having the same telephone number or the same street address.

If you dial in to the Internet, every time you dial your Internet service provider, you're assigned an IP address, right there on the spot. Your computer picks up its IP address as part of the logon process.

If you have a permanent connection to the Internet — typically with a residential gateway, cable modem, DSL router, and so on — you get an IP address, and it's yours to keep as long as you continue to use your current Internet service provider.

IP addresses on your local network

Now comes the part where most people get confused.

Every computer on your office or home network has to have an address, too. That's how computers on the network talk to each other. The confusion arises because these local IP addresses look just like Internet IP addresses. The 192.168.0.1 address is the most common local IP address on a plain-vanilla peer-to-peer small network. Most (but not all!) small networks have one computer with the address 192.168.0.1. Most (but not all!) computers on a small network have addresses that look like this: 192.168.0.x, where x is a number between 1 and 254.

Don't let the similarity in numbers fool you. IP addresses on the Internet work on the Internet. IP addresses on your home or office network work on your local network. IP addresses on your neighbor's home or office network work on her local network. Ne'er the twain — er, train — shall meet.

Just as in the case of the Internet, no two computers on your local network can have the same local IP address. That begs the obvious question: Who assigns them?

Assigning local IP addresses

Each network connection (such as a network interface card or wireless adapter) must have an IP address. You have two ways to assign local IP addresses:

- You can type them yourself.
- You can let one — and only one — box assign them.

I use the term *box* generically here because several different kinds of assignors automatically assign local IP addresses:

- If you have Vista Internet Connection Sharing enabled on a PC, that PC assigns local IP addresses.
- If you have a residential gateway, router, DSL router, cable modem, wireless broadband router, Dynamic Address Translator, or some other Internet box attached to your network, that box may insist on assigning local IP addresses.

Confusingly, more than one box can try to assign addresses. That's when the bits hit the fan.

If you want your local IP addresses assigned automatically, one of the boxes has to be the designated top dog — and the others have to be told to keep their mutts, er, mitts off. If you have more than one box trying to assign local IP addresses on your network at the same time, you will have pandemonium.

See what I mean? It's all about addresses.

Static local IP addresses are ones you dole out by yourself and type by hand. Every time you reboot a PC with a static local IP address, it comes back with the same static local IP address.

Dynamic local IP addresses are assigned by a box called a DHCP server. Every time you reboot a PC with a dynamic local IP address, the PC asks the network's DHCP server to assign it an address.

Sometimes the only way you can get a network to work is by manually assigning static local IP addresses. Think of it as the last refuge of those whose networks are so messed up that the boxes can't be trusted to assign addresses dynamically. Frequently, hardware manufacturers recommend that you dig into each computer and assign its IP address by hand — an approach you should greet with some fear and trepidation because it indicates that you're near the end of the rope. Here's how to switch between static and dynamic local IP addresses and change a static address manually:

1. **In the notification area, down near the clock, click the network activity icon — the one that looks like two monitors and a blue beach ball (refer to Figure 38-1). Click the Network and Sharing Center link.**

Vista brings up the Network and Sharing Center, which looks something like that shown back in Figure 38-5.

2. **On the right, click the View Status link.**

You see the Local Area Connection Status dialog box, like the one shown in Figure 38-8.

• **Figure 38-8: Operating statistics for your network card.**

3. **Click the Properties button. Then click the Continue button on the User Account Control message.**

Vista brings up the Local Area Connection Properties dialog box for your network card (or wireless adapter), as shown in Figure 38-9.

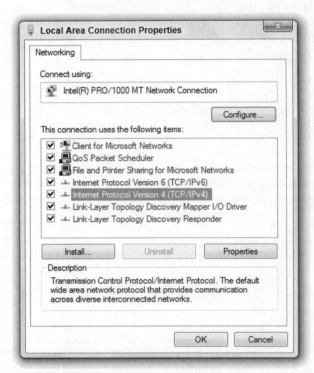

• **Figure 38-9: A list of the settings for your network card.**

4. **Click the Internet Protocol Version 4 (TCP/IPv4) line and then click the Properties button.**

You finally drill down to the dialog box that lets you assign IP addresses manually, as shown in Figure 38-10.

5. **If there's any way your computer can connect to the network with an automatically obtained IP address, choose that option here and skip to Step 9.**

Using an automatically assigned, dynamic IP address eliminates volumes of problems.

• **Figure 38-10: Give yourself a static IP address here.**

6. If you have absolutely no other choice and you know what address will work (the one in Figure 38-10 probably *won't work* for you), select the Use the Following IP Address option and type your static IP address in the four boxes.

7. Type in your Subnet mask (which is almost always 255.255.255.0).

8. If you can't rely on a server to set your IP address automatically, you can't get an automatically assigned DNS server address. (A DNS server is a computer that translates addresses you can understand, such as www.dummies. com, into addresses that the Internet can understand, such as 208.215.179.139.) Type the address of your DNS server.

9. Click the OK button twice, click the Close button once, and then click the red *X* to exit the Network and Sharing Center.

You may be able to verify whether the changed setting works immediately, but I always reboot the computer to be sure that the new IP address "takes."

More time has been wasted in this dialog box than in all the other networking dialog boxes combined.

The Move to IPv6

Right now, most of the addresses you see on the Internet consist of four groups of digits — 208.215.179.139 or 192.168.0.0.

Slowly, over the coming years, the Internet will be shifting to addresses with six groups of digits. The new addressing scheme is called *IPv6*.

There are lots of good reasons for shifting to IPv6, but the overarching reason is that the Internet is running out of telephone numbers, er, IP addresses. Just as phone companies have had to switch to ten-digit dialing, the switch to IPv6 is vital, controversial, and a pain in the, uh, neck.

Technique

39

Securing Your Wireless Network

Save Time By

✔ Using the Wireless Router or Access Point Setup Wizard the right way

✔ Getting your network secure in no time

The most important part of installing a wireless network comes after the network is up. You have to protect it against random intrusions, in spite of all the weird techy terminology. If you don't, your next-door neighbor will be able to get onto your network any time.

That may not sound like a Real Big Deal — and if you trust everyone passing within a hundred yards of your house, it may not be. But you have to consider the possibility that someone could, quite easily, sit in a car parked down the block, log on to your network, reach into your PC, and install a keylogger — a program that watches as you type and then sends full records to a clandestine Web site. Or, the self-same critter in his car could send a hundred thousand bogus e-mail messages using your Internet connection. Or something considerably less savory. It's happened, many times, in quiet suburban neighborhoods just like yours.

 Twenty years ago, you might've gotten away with not locking your front door. Nowadays, in some parts of the world, you still can. But for the vast majority of people in the vast majority of locations, locking up your wireless router has become a top priority. Sad, but true.

My first encounter with wireless networking really drove home the point. A friend of mine came over to the house and helped me put together a wireless network — a Linksys WRT54G wireless broadband router tied into an ADSL line. We had it up and running in no time flat, thanks largely to the old Windows XP Network Setup Wizard (which doesn't hold a candle to the automatic setup in Vista). My friend started downloading a big file, using his portable computer and its built-in wireless chip.

One thing led to another; my friend got a phone call and had to leave. As he was walking near the beach, a hundred meters or so away from the house, he sat down, pulled out his portable, and opened it. With absolutely no effort on his part, Vista connected to my wireless home network, found its way onto the Internet, and continued downloading the file.

Scary, eh?

If you have a wireless network and you haven't taken the necessary steps to secure it, anybody can get onto your network with essentially no effort. He can use your Internet connection and — most alarmingly — go snooping all over your network, just as if he were sitting in your office, plugged into your router.

Securing your wireless network is vitally important.

Running the Wireless Router Setup Wizard

The plumbing for wireless network support in Vista runs deep. One of the best features is the wizard that helps you plug up your wireless network. You need a USB flash drive, or a USB flash card reader, and a free USB port on every computer attached to the wireless network.

 If your wireless broadband router, wireless access point, or other wireless base station has a USB port and it supports Windows Smart Network Key (another meaningless marketing term), you're in luck: The wizard can configure your entire network in a matter of minutes. If your router doesn't support WSNK, not to worry — entering the requisite codes by hand is pretty easy.

 The fastest way to "lock down" a wireless network involves working with a PC that's plugged into the router. (If you use a PC with a wireless connection, you have to make the security changes to your router and then reconnect the wireless PC when it gets booted out for not having the proper security settings!)

Here's the fast way to get your wireless network secure:

1. **Plug your PC into the network.**

Even if you normally use a wireless connection, this lockdown runs much faster and easier if you're connected to the router with a wire.

2. **Choose Start, right-click Network, and select Properties.**

You see the Network and Sharing Center.

3. **On the left, under Tasks, click the Set Up a Connection or Network link.**

Vista asks you to choose a connection option, as shown in Figure 39-1.

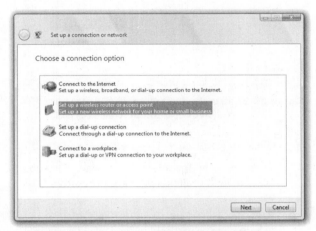

• **Figure 39-1: Choose from Vista's networking setup wizards.**

4. **Click the Set Up a Wireless Router or Access Point link; then click the Next button.**

Yes, you should click that link even if you already have a router set up (see Technique 38). This is the way to go if you want to "lock down" your router.

Vista shows you the first step, Set Up a Home or Small Business Network, in the Wireless Router Setup Wizard.

5. **Click the Next button.**

Vista reaches out onto your network (which you've already set up) and tries to communicate directly with your router. Usually it fails, and you see the second step in the wizard, as shown in Figure 39-2.

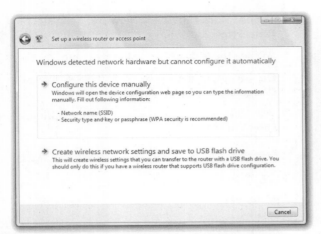

• **Figure 39-2:** Vista tried to talk to your router but couldn't get through. That's normal.

6. **Click the Configure This Device Manually link.**

   Vista opens your router's login page. The screen you see next depends on which router you're using.

7. **Type your router's password and click the Log In button.**

   At this point, the details vary depending on which router you're using. You may have to consult your user manual (blech), but clicking around a bit will probably unveil the settings you need to change.

8. **At a minimum, you need to do the following:**

   ▶ **Change the router's Service Set Identifier (SSID).** Your router ships with a preset SSID, most commonly Linksys, Default, 3Com, NETGEAR, WLAN, or wireless. Change the SSID to something other than the manufacturer's default (see Figure 39-3, in which I'm using the 3Com OfficeConnect ADSL router).

   ▶ **Stop broadcasting the SSID.** That won't keep out determined hackers, but it will prevent casual computer users from stumbling onto your network.

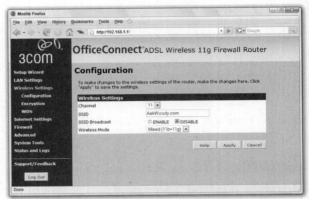

• **Figure 39-3:** Change the router's name — its SSID — and don't broadcast it.

   ▶ **Enable WPA (or WPA-PSK) encryption.** That's the strongest form of security available in most routers these days, and it's pretty hard (but not impossible) to crack. You'll have to provide a passphrase (in Figure 39-4 it's called a Pre-shared Key). Don't forget the passphrase.

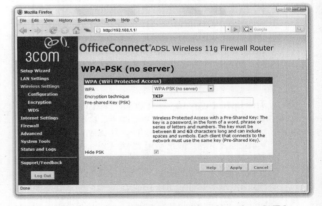

• **Figure 39-4:** Don't settle for anything less than WPA encryption.

   If you need more information about WPA encryption, see *Wireless Home Networking For Dummies,* 2nd Edition, by Danny Briere, Pat Hurley, and Edward Ferris (published by Wiley).

▶ **Change your router's password.** If you use the default password, you're not only leaving out the welcome mat but also stringing neon lights and shouting "Crack me!"

▶ **Save your changes.** Every router is different, but if you log out before you click Apply (or Set or whatever), your changes won't "take" and you'll have to do it all over again.

 Don't forget to write down your new SSID and WPA passphrase. You will need them in Steps 12 and 13.

9. **After you've made the changes *and saved them,* log out of the router, typically by clicking the Log Out or Log Off button.**

If you can't find a Log Out or Log Off button, click the red *X* to exit your browser.

Vista returns to the wizard at the point shown in Figure 39-2.

10. **If you're working on a computer with a wireless connection, your computer gets booted off the network at this point, and you need to reconnect.**

As soon as you change the router's settings, the wireless connection disconnects, and you have to get reconnected. I talk about how to do that in my book *Windows Vista All-in-One Desk Reference For Dummies* (published by Wiley). Basically, you need to go through the manual wireless network discovery steps.

11. **If you're working on a computer that's attached to the router with a wire, click the Create Wireless Network Settings and Save to USB Flash Drive link.**

The wizard asks you to give your network a name.

 This is a bit confusing. The wizard wants you to type in the name of the router — not the name of the network. (You can see the name of your network in the Network and Sharing Center.)

12. **Type the name — the SSID — that you entered into the router in Step 8; then click the Next button (see Figure 39-5).**

• **Figure 39-5: Enter the name you typed into the router.**

The wizard asks you to enter the network's passphrase.

13. **Type the passphrase ("Pre-shared Key") that you typed into the router in Step 8, and then click the Next button.**

You have to click the Continue button to get through another User Account Control dialog box, after which the wizard asks about your File and Printer Sharing Options, as shown in Figure 39-6.

14. **For now, choose whichever general options look best to you and then click the Next button.**

(You find much more detail about these options in Technique 41. Don't worry. You can always go back and change the Sharing and Discovery settings.)

The wizard now asks you to put a USB drive in the computer.

15. **Insert a USB drive. If an AutoPlay notification appears, click the red *X* to exit AutoPlay. Make sure that the Save Settings To box shows your USB drive; then click the Next button.**

• **Figure 39-6:** These choices map, loosely, into the Network and Sharing window's Sharing and Discovery settings.

The wizard creates a folder on the USB drive called SMRTNTKY, stuffs it with the settings for your router, and then sets up an Autorun.inf file on the drive so that the installer will run automatically when you insert the USB drive in any Windows computer.

The wizard then gives you instructions for moving the router settings to any Windows XP or Vista computer (see Figure 39-7).

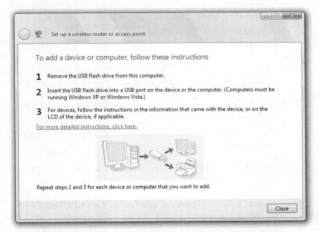

• **Figure 39-7:** Abbreviated instructions for moving these settings to other computers on your network.

16. **Click the For More Detailed Instructions, Click Here link.**

Vista brings up a WordPad document with the details shown in Figure 39-8. I suggest that you print the document. The pertinent details are also stored on the USB drive, in a file called \SMRTNTKY\MessageB.txt.

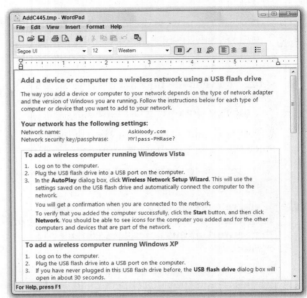

• **Figure 39-8:** Print these instructions for future reference.

17. **Back in the wizard, click the Close button.**

You're ready to take the USB drive to other computers on your network and spread the settings.

Congratulations. Your router is locked down, and you're a few steps away from getting your wireless network put back together.

Propagating Changes

Armed with the USB drive that you made in the preceding section, it's time to get all the wireless computers on your network brought up to speed.

Be of good cheer. The Wireless Network Setup Wizard does all the heavy lifting. If you're running Vista on your wireless PC, it's pretty easy. Follow these steps:

1. **Use the steps in the preceding section to create a USB drive with your wireless settings.**

2. **Insert the USB drive in a PC with a wireless connection that you want to hook into your new, improved, WPA-protected, stealthy (at least, SSID-nonbroadcasting) network.**

Vista identifies the drive and presents you with the AutoPlay notification shown in Figure 39-9.

• **Figure 39-9: Your new network settings are a click away.**

If you don't see the AutoPlay notification, choose Start⇨Computer and double-click the USB drive.

3. **Click the Wireless Network Setup Wizard icon.**

The wizard asks whether you want to hook this computer up to the wireless network that you established in the preceding section, per Figure 39-10.

• **Figure 39-10: The wizard identifies your "stealthy" network.**

4. **Select the Save This Network for All Users of This Computer option and then click the OK button.**

You have to click through yet another User Account Control message.

The wizard comes back and tells you rather cryptically that all is well (see Figure 39-11).

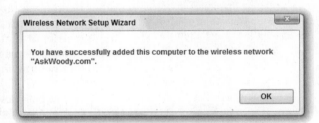

• **Figure 39-11: The Wireless Network Setup Wizard worked.**

5. **Click the OK button.**

You can start using the new wireless connection immediately.

6. **Repeat Steps 2 through 5 for every additional wireless computer on your network.**

It's that quick and easy.

The end result: a very secure wireless network that works like a-ringin' a bell!

Technique 40

Adding and Configuring a New User

Save Time By

✔ Setting up new users on your computer quickly and correctly

✔ Choosing security settings that are right for you

✔ Understanding the crucial difference between accounts

✔ Avoiding the bogus information you see in print about the Guest account

If you're connected to a Big Corporate Network (BCN), skip this Technique entirely. The network administrator controls all the user capabilities on a BCN. The only way you can change anything about users on a BCN is by convincing or cajoling the network administrator into changing things. Bribery may work. Calling him the "Network Admini" is not recommended.

On the other hand, if your computer sits by itself in a corner, or if you have a peer-to-peer workgroup network, setting up accounts for each person who uses the computer can be a worthwhile, timesaving endeavor.

Depending on how you set up accounts and your willingness to temper other people's ability to make substantial changes to your computer, Vista may help you keep prying eyes from viewing your files. Even if you don't restrict other users' access to the computer, simply having one account for each user can go a long way toward keeping people from accidentally bumping into each other.

 It all boils down to a question of how much flexibility you want to give other people who use your computer, and how much security you're willing to sacrifice in return. The decisions aren't easy.

This Technique tells you what you need to know about user accounts. It also gives you the straight story about many topics that have been garbled in the press and online: Much of what you may have read about Guest accounts and the Administrator account is accurate for Windows 2000 but completely wrong for Vista. This Technique sets the record straight.

Grasping User Accounts

Every Vista computer has at least three accounts:

✔ **"The" Administrator account:** It's hidden. Unless you jump through extraordinary hoops, you will never see "The" Administrator account. Microsoft hid it for a reason — you'll only get confused if you try to play with "The" Administrator account. "The" Administrator can perform some actions that other accounts can't. Many of those actions have to do with resuscitating a nearly dead Windows installation. Under normal circumstances, you have no need to use Administrator — indeed, Windows goes to great lengths to hide it from you. My advice: Don't worry about it. I won't even mention it in the rest of this Technique. But be aware that such a beast exists.

✔ **"The" Guest account:** It's hidden, too, but not buried nearly as deep as "The" Administrator account. You can turn on "The" Guest account quite simply. As its name implies, "The" Guest account is a good account for your friends and guests to use if they want to borrow your computer. It's suitably defanged and declawed. Behind the scenes, it accomplishes myriad tasks, besides serving as poster boy for hobbled user accounts.

✔ **An account that was set up when Vista first started:** This account probably has your name on it. If the people who put together your computer decided to run the full Vista installation for you, the account may have a name like "Satisfied Dell Customer" or "Disgruntled Aggies Fan" or "OEM Lackey." More likely, when you first turned on your computer, it prompted you to create a new account and asked you to enter a name — such as, oh, "Disgruntled Aggies Fan." You know what I mean. Especially if you're an Aggie.

You have two good reasons for adding more accounts to your computer:

✔ **Security:** If you put a password on your account, and you don't hand out that password, and you give new users fairly limited abilities to change things on the computer (see the next section), you can keep the new users out of your files. At least, it's fairly difficult for them to get into your files.

✔ **Convenience:** Having separate accounts for each person who uses a computer can be enormously convenient. It's also a good way to keep neophytes from accidentally clobbering other users. Many a time-consuming tragedy has been averted this way.

Recognizing account types

Vista, set up on a Big Corporate Network (a client-server domain network), inherits all the account security restrictions imposed by the server. Nothing in this Technique applies to PCs running on a BCN. To do anything, you have to contact your network administrator.

In all other circumstances, Vista has the following two built-in types of users:

✔ **Standard:** A person using this type of account can run most programs that are already installed on the computer, including programs on USB drives; use hardware that's already installed on the computer; work with her own files — and the files in the Public folders, if those have been made available (see Technique 41); change her own password; and make minor changes to the computer (such as setting the desktop background or adding gadgets to the Sidebar).

✔ **Administrator:** A person using this type of account can install programs and change them, add new hardware, get at any files on the computer (except for a few weird system files that require some extra effort), and make changes that affect other users of the computer. A person with an Administrator account can create new accounts and delete existing accounts — even change the password for password-protected accounts.

For more details, see the next section.

If you are using a Standard account and you want to do something that requires an Administrator account, Vista prompts you with a dialog box like the one shown in Figure 40-1. You must supply the password for an Administrator account before you're allowed to perform the Administrator-level activity.

Every computer has to have at least one Administrator account. Otherwise you couldn't install programs or create new accounts, much less make changes to the computer itself (such as, oh, set the clock).

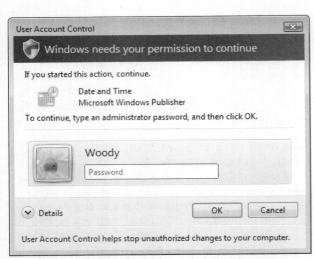

• **Figure 40-1:** The hurdle for Standard accounts trying to perform Administrator-level tasks.

Microsoft recommends that you create Standard accounts for other people who use your computer, and that you use a Standard account from day to day as well. The reason? If you accidentally kick-start a virus or Trojan or some other piece of sniveling scumware, the malware "inherits" your security clearance. If you're running only a Standard account, the scummy program can do only, uh, Standard things. It's good advice. I've never known anybody to follow it. The fact is that most people who use Vista much at all find Standard accounts overly restrictive.

"The" Guest account is a special kind of Standard account that you can turn on (make it visible on the Vista Welcome screen) or turn off (not make it visible on the Welcome screen). Whether you turn it on or off, it's still there. People who use "The" Guest account can't give it a password, but they can do everything else a Standard user can.

By the way, all Administrator accounts are created equal. Just because your account was the first Administrator account doesn't give you any special privileges. All Standard accounts are equal, too.

Working with account types

A person using an Administrator account can perform the following functions:

✔ Add or remove other accounts (except your own account), and turn on or turn off "The" Guest account.

✔ Change passwords and require or remove passwords for any account (except Guest).

Say that your PC has two Administrator accounts, called Woody and Justin. Woody can go into Justin's account, change Justin's password, and then log in as Justin and do anything that Justin can do. Woody doesn't need to know Justin's current password to change it. Conversely, Justin can modify Woody's password, log in as Woody, and do anything Woody can do. Even worse, Woody can delete Justin's account and all his data — permanently — even if Justin's account has a password and Woody doesn't know what the password is.

✔ Change Vista read/write/access permissions for any drive, folder, or file.

✔ Create, open, modify, or delete files anywhere on the PC, except in Encrypting File System protected folders.

✔ Change Registry settings for all users.

An administrator can see the contents of any file on the system unless the file's been encrypted by using, say, the Encrypting File System (see http://en.wikipedia.org/wiki/Encrypting_File_System), an application's password-protection mechanism, or Windows' Information Rights Management technology. All three of those file-locking methods operate independently of Vista.

Because Administrator accounts can create files in important places, such as C:\Program Files, and administrators can modify the Registry, you usually need an Administrator account to install a program.

You also usually need an Administrator account to install new hardware.

By contrast, people with Standard accounts can perform the following functions:

✔ Change their own password or require/remove passwords on their own account.

✔ Create, open, modify, or delete files in their own Documents folder.

✔ Create, open, modify, or delete files in the Public folder, provided that the Public folder has been made available (see Technique 41).

 The powers granted to a limited account usually restrict limited user accounts to running programs but not installing them.

The limited account called Guest can do all those limited account things except require a password for the account.

Increasing security with passwords

Many Vista users with stand-alone machines or small (peer-to-peer workgroup) networks think that they can keep other people out of their files by putting a password on their account and then creating new accounts and requiring passwords on those accounts.

As long as you're creating new Administrator accounts, you have no protection.

Here's the fastest, easiest way to keep multiple users on one machine from seeing or clobbering each other's files:

1. **Put a password on your account and** *don't give* **it out.**

   As soon as one person knows your password, he or she can change anything on the computer.

2. **Create a password reset disk (see Technique 55).**

If only one Administrator account exists, you had better have its password backed up ten ways from Tuesday.

3. **Delete any existing Administrator accounts except yours.**

4. **Create new Standard accounts for everyone on your computer.**

5. **Require those accounts to have passwords.**

6. **Resign yourself to the fact that whenever someone wants to install a new program on the computer, you, personally, will have to do it.**

   That's the only way to keep people out of other people's files.

 Of course, you, being the bearer of a password-protected Administrator account, can do anything, including look at any file, anytime (unless the file has been encrypted).

Using simple, common-sense protection

If you need intricate file security — where large numbers of individuals or groups of individuals are allowed access to specific folders — you need more than Vista. You really need a Big Corporate Network, with servers running Active Directory, the horrendously complex network security program.

If your file security needs are relatively modest — say, you want to protect your Documents folder so that only you can see what's inside, and you don't want to allow anyone to delete the files — you can follow the steps in the preceding section and lock down your computer. To get that to work, though, everyone else who uses your PC must have a Standard account. They won't be able to install any programs or new hardware.

 Most individuals, families, and small offices don't need fancy security settings. In most cases, you can keep things simple but secure.

I've boiled down a lot of experience into a handful of recommendations:

✔ Password-protect files that you don't want others to see. Use the password protection available in the application that created the file (such as Word, Outlook, or Excel). Most applications allow you to set a password that's required to open a file and a second password that's necessary to change the file. This doesn't prevent a malicious or misguided person from deleting the file — you always need good backups — but as long as the Recycle Bin isn't emptied frequently, simple password protection works pretty darn well.

✔ If a user can't be trusted to use an antivirus program religiously or has a bad habit of downloading and installing scummy programs from the Internet, give that user a Standard account. If you have more than one such n00b (newbie), make Windows show the Guest account on the Welcome screen (choose Start➪Control Panel and, under User Accounts and Family Safety, click the Add or Remove User Accounts link, click Guest, and then click the Turn On button) and let your neophytes use Guest.

✔ Give everybody else an Administrator account. But be merciless in your insistence that they use antivirus software religiously and that they check out new programs for scum *before* they go on the machine.

✔ Put files in Public folders only if you're willing to see them get deleted.

Creating a New Account

If you have an Administrator account (unless someone has changed it, your account is probably an Administrator account), creating a new account couldn't be simpler. Follow these steps:

1. **Choose Start➪Control Panel. Under the User Accounts and Family icon, click the Add or Remove User Accounts link.**

   You have to click the Continue button in a User Account Control message, and then Vista shows you the Manage Accounts page, as shown in Figure 40-2.

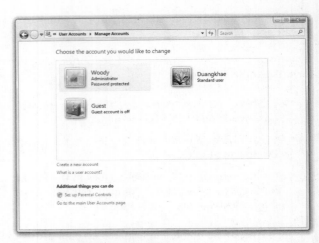

• **Figure 40-2: User Accounts central.**

 Yes, I know. There's a link at the bottom of Figure 40-2 that invites you to go to the main User Accounts page. It's completely bogus. You're already on the main User Accounts page.

2. **Click the Create a New Account link.**

   You see the Create New Account dialog box, as shown in Figure 40-3.

• **Figure 40-3: The name you enter here becomes the name of a folder in the Users folder.**

3. **Type a name, select the type of account you wish to create (see the preceding section), and click the Create Account button.**

To make your life simpler, use a short, simple name, with no spaces or punctuation marks.

The new account becomes available immediately.

Modifying an Account

If you have an Administrator account and you choose Start⇨Control Panel, under the User Accounts and Family icon, click the Add or Remove User Accounts link and then pick an account. You have the following choices (see Figure 40-4):

• **Figure 40-4: Making changes to Duangkhae's account.**

✔ **Change the Account Name:** When you set up the account, the name you choose is permanently, indelibly used as the name of the Users folder for the user. After the account is set up, changing the name changes only what appears on the Welcome screen, at the top of the Start menu, and in this User Accounts dialog box.

 The first time that you enter a user's name — when you set up the new account — choose something short and sweet so that when you go spelunking through the Users folder, you don't have to wade through lots of junk. (You'll probably end up typing the folder name many times, too.) After the account is set up, though, you don't need to be so conservative. Turn the name into John Jacob Jingleheimer Smith, or anything you like.

✔ **Create a Password:** You can force this account to use a password. If you're twiddling with another user's account, setting a password for the user (or changing an existing one) can effectively keep

the user off the machine. And you don't even need to know the user's current password to make the change. Ouch.

✔ **Change the Picture:** Change the picture that appears on the Welcome screen and at the top of the Start menu. If you click this link, Windows responds with the Choose Picture dialog box, as shown in Figure 40-5. Click the picture you want (square pictures work best), click the Change Picture button, and then exit the User Accounts dialog box.

• **Figure 40-5: Pick any picture, and Vista squishes it down to 48 x 48 pixels for you.**

✔ **Set Up Parental Controls:** Aside from a very effective snooper and the ability to set some overly rigid restrictions, there's not much here. See my book *Windows Vista All-in-One Desk Reference For Dummies* (published by Wiley) for details.

✔ **Change the Account Type:** Switch from Computer Administrator to Standard and back again.

✔ **Delete the Account:** Delete another user's account? Yes. That's right. Just like that. You aren't given this option if you're working on your own account. The user who is logged on cannot delete his or her own account.

 When you delete an account, Windows gives you the option of saving some of the files associated with the account (as shown in Figure 40-6). Save the files! After Windows deletes the files, they're gone for good. They're not in the Recycle Bin. They are really gone.

• **Figure 40-6:** Deleting a user removes all of that user's folders. Be careful!

Hobbling the Guest Account

I know, I know. You really want to turn off the Guest account because you know it doesn't have a password and you're worried that some hacker or bad program is going to get into it. Relax.

In the old days, a Guest account on a networked PC served as a convenient way to let people onto a PC or network temporarily. The guest didn't need to know a password to log on, but the guest couldn't perform as many computing functions, either. That's where the term *guest* came from.

In Vista, Windows makes it easy to "turn on" or "turn off" the Guest account. Here's how:

1. **Choose Start⇨Control Panel. Under the User Accounts and Family icon, click the Add or Remove User Accounts link.**

Click the Continue button on a User Account Control message, and Vista shows you the Manage Accounts page, as shown earlier in Figure 40-2.

The Guest account is the last account listed. If Guest appears as one of the accounts on the Windows Welcome screen, you see a Guest / Guest Account Is On icon. If no Guest account is on the Welcome screen (as is the case in Figure 40-2), Windows says Guest / Guest Account Is Off.

Guest gets a bad rap

I'm astounded by how much drivel regarding the Guest account has appeared in print, so let me dispel some false-hoods and misconceptions. If you're feeling nervous about the Guest account, the following points should help calm your fears:

✔ Nobody and nothing can surreptitiously log on to your computer via the Guest account. The Guest account hasn't become a convenient entry point for hackers, as one publication put it. If you decide to put the Guest account on your Welcome screen, it's like any other limited account. If you don't put it on the Welcome screen, nobody can steal it.

✔ Guest is the means by which other users connect to your computer. Say that I have a password-protected Administrator account called Justin on my machine. If someone logs on to my machine from the network with Justin's name and password, that person is not given Administrator account capabilities — even though Justin is an Administrator account. Anyone who logs on from the network is given only the capabilities of the lowly Guest account.

✔ The Guest account is absolutely vital. In addition to providing the means for other people to log on to your computer, Guest operates behind the scenes in Internet Connection Sharing and with File and Printer Sharing. It's okay to hide the account on the Welcome screen, using Vista's settings. But don't follow the advice you occasionally see on the Web to dig deep into Windows and delete the account. You need it.

2. **Click the Guest icon.**

You see the Turn on Guest Account dialog box, as shown in Figure 40-7.

• **Figure 40-7:** Make the Guest account appear on the Windows logon screen.

3. If you want the Guest account to be visible on the Welcome screen, click the Turn On button.

4. Click the red *X* to exit the Manage Accounts dialog box.

   Guest shows up the next time you log off or switch users.

You might assume that this procedure turns the Guest account on or off. It doesn't. Vista is fooling you. In Vista, Guest plays a pivotal role. Among other things, Windows uses Guest to communicate between computers, run print jobs, and perform a plethora of other behind-the-scenes functions. Windows can't let you turn off the Guest account. If you did, all sorts of things would go bump in the night.

You may find detailed instructions on the Web that show you how to really turn off Guest. It's difficult, but it can be done. Resist the temptation. Leave Guest going.

Technique

41

Sharing Drives and Folders

Save Time By

- ✔ Getting your Sharing and Discovery settings right — the first time
- ✔ Letting in the people you want and keeping out the others
- ✔ Assigning access rights to individual drives and folders

You're supposed to share, aren't you? I mean, that's why you bought two computers in the first place. What's the point in having a network if you don't share your drives, data, printers, viruses, and scum-infested smiley icons — the whole nine yards. Sheesh.

Sharing in Vista isn't automatic and it isn't easy. On the other hand, it *is* secure. Kind of like building a giant sports complex and then ringing it with concrete and razor wire and festooning the gates with reinforced titanium locks so that nobody can get in.

 It's time to get out the sledge hammers and pick the locks, sez I.

If you want to live in a locked-out world, where no other computers on your network and no other people on your computer can see your data, it's pretty easy: Tell Vista you have a "Public" network (see Technique 38) and give the other users on your computer Standard accounts (see Technique 40). The razor wire appears like magic.

But if you want to open things up, make your pictures or MP3 music files accessible to everybody, and maybe even share some documents, spreadsheets, or other subversive literature, you have to jump through a couple of additional hoops.

This Technique shows you how.

Sharing the Vista Way

If you're connected to a Big Corporate Network, the Corporate Networkies determine what gets shared, by whom, and when. There's nothing you can do about it. Aside from bribery, which occasionally works.

But if you have one lonely computer, or a small peer-to-peer "workgroup" that you've set up yourself, security lies in your hands — and the hands of anyone who's using an Administrator account (see Technique 40).

Unless you've instituted some truly bizarre security settings, Vista automatically sets up a very limited amount of sharing, as the following list describes:

- ✔ If you use an Administrator account, you can readily open, change, or delete almost any file on the computer. (A few really obscure files are hard to get to.)

- ✔ If you use a Standard account, you can open, change, or delete any file in "your" folders (Documents, Pictures, Music, Desktop, Contacts, Downloads, Links, Favorites, Saved Games, Searches, Videos, and so on). You can also open, change, or delete any file in the computer's Public folders.

- ✔ If you use a Standard account and know an Administrator account's password, you can do anything an administrator can do.

 When you first connect to a network, Vista asks whether it is a *Public* network (like the network in a coffee shop) or a *Private* network (in one dialog box, Private networks are identified as Office or Home — there's no difference between the two). If you specify a Private network, Vista allows other users on the network to "see" your computer, but it still locks down access to your Public folders, other shared folders, and printers.

That's all she wrote. If you want to open up your computer, you have to take the initiative and do it yourself.

In the next section, I show you how to make your computer and its contents accessible to people using other computers on your peer-to-peer "workgroup" network. Among other things, that includes making your Public folders truly public — available to other people on the network.

Then, in the following section, I talk about sharing folders in general — how to allow people using Standard accounts on your computer to look at specific folders, and how to allow people running other computers on the network to get into those folders, too.

 Tackle the sharing problem in this order. It's the fastest way.

Opening Up the Network

If you don't have a network, skip to the next section.

When you attached your computer to the network for the first time, you set its sharing destiny. If you followed along in any of several Techniques in this book, you may have altered the default sharing settings. Now it's time to take control of the way your computer shares. Here's how:

1. **Choose Start, right-click Network, and choose Properties.**

Vista shows you the Network Sharing Center, as shown in Figure 41-1.

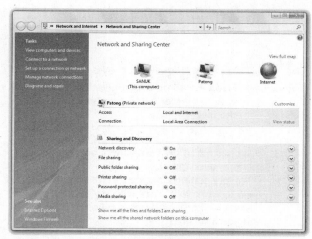

• **Figure 41-1: An almost completely locked-down PC connected to my office network.**

2. **One by one, click the down arrows to the right of Network Discovery, File Sharing (see Figure 41-2), Public Folder Sharing, Printer Sharing, Password Protected Sharing, and Media Sharing.**

If you don't agree with any of the settings that have been made based on Vista's pre-defined settings for your Location Type (Private or Public), change them. Refer to the handy list in Technique 38, Table 38-1.

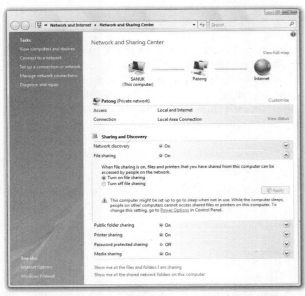

• **Figure 41-2:** Heed the admonition under File Sharing — if your computer falls asleep, you can't get at the files.

 Vista has a horribly convoluted, poorly documented, overlapping set of Sharing and Discovery settings, but hey, that's what we have to work with. Stick with my recommendations for home and home-office networks and you'll be fine.

I leave my home and home-office networks wide open, with all the Sharing and Discovery settings set to On.

 Yes, I know that it doesn't look right to turn Password Protected Sharing off. But if you flip back to Technique 38 and look at Table 38-1, you see that turning this entry off means that you don't require passwords when people using other computers on your network want to get into the files in your Public folder, or

use your shared printer. In most home and home-office settings, that makes sense — you don't want to be in the position of handing out passwords to some members of the family (or the staff) and trusting them to keep the passwords secret from other members of the family (or staff).

3. When you're happy with your settings, click the red *X* to exit the Network and Sharing Center.

You're fully loaded and ready for bear, er, ready to share.

Sharing Folders

Everything you put in a Public folder on your computer is accessible to everyone who uses your computer.

If you set up Public Folder Sharing in the preceding section, everything you put in a Public folder on your computer is accessible to everyone who uses your network. You might require a password (if Password Protected Sharing is set to On) — so anyone who wants to get into your Public folders from another computer has to provide an ID and password that are valid on this computer before they're allowed in.

 Public Folder Sharing has a downside, and you can get burned badly if you ignore it: If someone on another computer deletes a file on your computer, the deleted file does not end up in the Recycle Bin. It's gone. If you have Windows Vista Enterprise or Ultimate, you should be able to get the deleted file back using Restore Previous Versions. But in general, if you don't have a recent backup of the deleted file, you're out of luck.

 So, if you want to share a folder, what's the easiest, fastest, most reliable way to do it? Move the folder to one of the Public folders. Just navigate to the folder you want to share, click it, and drag to move it to the Public folder in the Favorite Links list, as shown in Figure 41-3. Easy. Vista does all the heavy lifting.

• **Figure 41-3: Share the Sandwich Shoppe Signs and Tags folder by moving it to the Public folder.**

Rocket science.

Sometimes you don't want to move a folder to the Public folder. That's okay. As long as you are using an Administrator account, or you have a Standard account and you "own" a folder, you can share the folder — make it available to others on your computer or (if File Sharing is enabled on your computer; see Table 38-1) make it available to others on the network.

Here's how to share a folder quickly:

1. **In Windows Explorer, navigate to the folder you want to share. Click it.**

A Share button appears in the menu at the top.

2. **Click the Share button.**

Vista brings up the File Sharing dialog box, in which you can give permission for others to get into the folder.

3. **Choose the user you want to give permission to get into the folder and click the Add button.**

If you want to allow everyone on your network to get into the folder, choose Everyone. (Note that people using other computers on your

network are controlled by the File Sharing and Password Protected Sharing settings detailed in Table 38-1.)

Vista adds the person (or people) to the allowed list and gives them "Reader" (read-only) permission.

4. **If you want to increase the permission level for a user, click the down arrow to the right of the permission (see Figure 41-4) and select a different level; when you're done, click the Share button.**

A Contributor is allowed to change or delete files; a Co-owner can also set permissions.

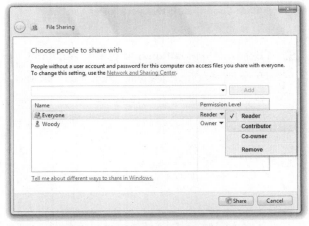

• **Figure 41-4: Give permission beyond read-only in the drop-down box.**

 Don't get too tied up in the details here. Remember that you need to keep these permissions updated — if you don't change them, they stay in effect forever. Even after you forget that you did it.

You have to click the Continue button in response to a User Account Control message, but when Vista is finished, it shows you the dialog box shown in Figure 41-5.

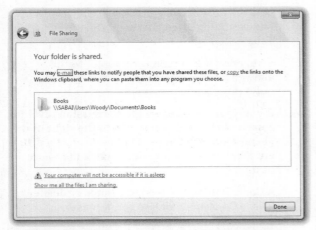

• **Figure 41-5:** Confirmation that your folder has been shared.

5. **Click the Done button and you're, uh, done.**

   The new sharing rules take effect immediately.

If you ever want to see which folders you're sharing, follow these steps:

1. **Choose Start⇨Documents.**

2. **On the left, under Folders, navigate to your Searches folder (see Figure 41-6) and click it.**

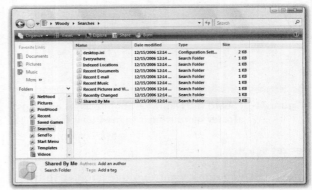

• **Figure 41-6:** Your Shared folders are included in a pre-built saved search.

3. **On the right, double-click the Shared By Me folder.**

   Vista has a pre-built search saved away that lists all your saved folders.

Technique

42

Meeting with Meeting Space

Save Time By

- Knowing when and how to use Meeting Space
- Getting a meeting thrown together quickly
- Using the tools on offer

Ya gotta hand it to the folks at Microsoft who built Meeting Space. They took a Wi-Fi feature that was notorious as a potential security risk — ad hoc networking — built a solid base to it, and produced a system that's genuinely usable. And quite secure.

Meeting Space allows you to set up networks on the fly: If three random people running Vista in an airplane decide that they want to set up a Meeting Space meeting, hey, no problem. The system can work without a hub or a router by skipping among wireless cards. It's smart enough to identify people who ask to be invited to meetings. The person who starts a session can invite others to join. They can look at each other's desktops (similar to Remote Assistance; see Technique 51), work on the same document, give or watch presentations, and pass notes to each other, one on one.

Meeting Space isn't limited to ad hoc networks. You can run it over a traditional peer-to-peer "workgroup" network or even a Big Corporate "domain" Network. That isn't nearly as cool as running ad hoc, but it doesn't bog down as much, either.

 Meeting Space is a typical Microsoft "version 1.0" product. It has a lot of rough edges and plenty of gotchas. It works only for very small groups — connection speed limitations seem to swamp the program as the size of the group grows. But if you're looking for a simple, handy, fast way to hook together a handful of laptops, Meeting Space warrants your consideration.

No, you can't trust it to play Global Thermonuclear War. Meeting Space works only on computers running Vista. You have to use an Administrator account (or have access to an Administrator account's password, which is basically the same thing) to get it going. And so on.

If you have a group of two or more people who are all using Vista on their laptops, Meeting Space is well worth a shot. (Microsoft says it can handle up to ten computers, but that's pushing it.) Give it a try.

After you use it once or twice — there's a learning curve — you may save some time. Mostly, though, you'll have a good feeling for what Meeting Space might be able to do when the next version comes out.

Setting Up Meeting Space

The first time you run Meeting Space, you have to let it pop through your firewall, and you have to set up a Display Name. It's easy. Here's how:

1. **Choose Start⇨All Programs⇨Windows Meeting Space.**

The Meeting Space setup routine presents you with the scary message shown in Figure 42-1.

• **Figure 42-1: Set up Meeting Space by poking through Windows Firewall.**

2. **Even if you don't know a Distributed File System Replication from a Globally Routable IPv6 Address (which you need, too, although the message doesn't warn you), click the Yes, Continue Setting Up Windows Meeting Space icon.**

You have to click the Continue button to get through a User Account Control dialog box.

Vista hems and haws and finally presents you with the Set Up People Near Me dialog box. I bet you never knew that you could set up people near me, but . . . hey, I warned you; this is "version 1.0" techy bafflegab.

Consider. If you go ahead with Meeting Space and click the OK button in the Set Up People Near Me dialog box, any time your computer is alive and you're logged on, Vista can broadcast your display name over the wireless connection.

If that makes you feel a little squeamish, it should. But it's the only way that Meeting Space (or any other application, for that matter) has to identify you, particularly when no network is established. That's why the People Near Me application isn't a default feature in Vista: You have to very deliberately opt in.

3. **Type a Display Name that won't come back to haunt you; then click the OK button.**

Meeting Space appears, as shown in Figure 42-2. Your Display Name is being broadcast. Meeting Space is looking for meetings that you've been invited to. So far, there aren't any.

• **Figure 42-2: Meeting Space is ready.**

Patience, grasshopper.

Holding a Meeting

Want to start a Meeting Space session? I was hoping so.

Here's how to get an ad hoc session going — connecting two computers with wireless cards that are *not* connected to the same network. Nothing to it. Follow these steps:

1. **In the Windows Meeting Space main window (refer to Figure 42-2), click the Start a New Meeting link.**

Meeting Space asks you to give the meeting a name and password (see Figure 42-3).

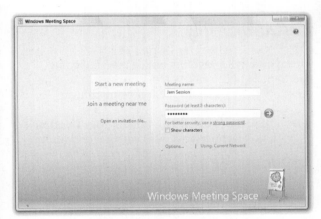

• **Figure 42-3: Pick a name and password.**

2. **Type in a suitable meeting name and password.**

Ho-hum.

In Figure 42-3, note that Meeting Space wants to look for meeting participants over its current network. In this case, as previously noted, I want to set up an ad hoc network. I'm in the office and my laptop is connected to the office network, but I want to force Meeting Space to look at other wireless cards in the vicinity, to set up an ad hoc network. So I click the Options link.

3. **Click the Options link.**

Meeting Space shows you an Options dialog box.

4. **To force Meeting Space to go looking for unattached wireless cards, check the Create a Private Ad Hoc Wireless Network box; then click the OK button.**

You go back to the new meeting dialog box shown in Figure 42-3.

5. **Click the green right arrow to the right of the Password box.**

Meeting Space opens a Meeting window.

A few seconds later, Windows Firewall may tell you, as it did me, that it is blocking Windows Meeting Space, as shown in Figure 42-4.

• **Figure 42-4: You need to unblock the firewall.**

See what I mean about a "version 1.0" product?

6. **In the Windows Security Alert, click the Unblock button.**

You have to click the Continue button through a User Account Control dialog box, and that returns you to the Meeting window.

7. **Back in the Meeting window, click the Invite People link.**

Meeting Space informs you that you can't invite people when you're using an ad hoc network (see Figure 42-5).

• **Figure 42-5:** To invite people by choosing their names or sending them an invitation, you have to use a regular network.

8. **Click the OK, I Guess That's Another Feature Desperately Needed in Version 2 button.**

You go back to the Meeting window described in Step 5.

Other computers running Meeting Space that have working wireless cards see a notification about a new meeting.

9. **Tell all your friends (who are probably huddled over your laptop right now) to click the new meeting notification (in this case, for Jam Session), and give them the password.**

They need the password to join your meeting.

10. **Type the password in the space provided, and click the green right arrow to the right of the Password box.**

Et voilà! Your Meeting Space session has begun (see Figure 42-6).

If you get the feeling that this version of Meeting Space is held together with chewing gum and baling wire (is that what they call "binding"?), well, wait until you see version 3.0. Or 4.0.

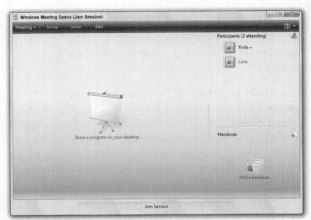

• **Figure 42-6:** The meeting has begun.

Collaborating

After you have a Meeting Space meeting going (perhaps I should say "a Meeting Space meeting meeting"?), you can do the following things:

✔ **Click the Share a Program or Your Desktop link.** Meeting Space asks whether you want other people to see your desktop. When you click the OK button, you're given an opportunity to either share your desktop or to share a file. If you choose to share your desktop, the contents of your desktop appear in the other participants' Meeting Space windows.

✔ **Allow other participants to take control of your desktop.** When you're sharing your desktop, just click the Give Control icon in the upper-right corner of the screen (see Figure 42-7).

• **Figure 42-7:** You can relinquish control, much as you would in Remote Assistance (see Technique 51).

✔ **Connect to a networked projector from Meeting Space.** It takes just a click; it's under the Options icon in the upper-right corner.

✔ **Click the Show Me How My Shared Session Looks on Other Computers link.** It's kind of a hall-of-mirrors effect. You see a window with a window with a window of your desktop (see Figure 42-8).

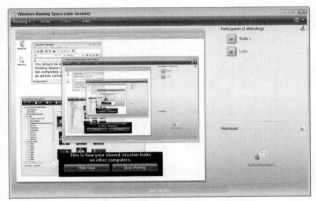

• **Figure 42-8: Hello, hello. Anybody there?**

✔ **Send handouts to all the participants by clicking the Add a Handout link.** Meeting Space makes a copy of the original file and sends the copy to all the participants. They can make changes, which will be reflected in all the other participants' copies — but the original remains untouched.

✔ **Send a note to any single participant.** Right-click the participant's name and choose Send a Note. Compose the note in text or "ink" (see Figure 42-9).

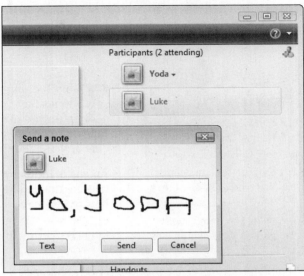

• **Figure 42-9: Ink is an experience for mouse-bound folks.**

 For quick, ad hoc meetings among a small number of participants, Vista's Meeting Space rates as a very cute, possibly useful application. The next version might even be a timesaver.

Technique 43

Controlling Your PC from Afar with LogMeIn

This Technique talks about puppets and puppeteers. How many times have you left on a trip, only to discover about three seconds after the plane takes off that you left an important file behind? How many times have you wished that you could log on to a PC in an Internet café and connect to your PC back at home, or at the office?

An entire industry has grown up to solve that problem. Several industries, actually. They all follow a simple model: You set up your computer before you leave so that it'll act like a puppet. Then you connect to the puppet while you're on the road and pull its strings, watching what happens, just like a puppeteer. Easy concept. Difficult implementation.

Windows Vista ships with a program called Remote Desktop that lets you control one PC from another PC. But . . .

The Remote Desktop "puppeteer" isn't in all versions of Vista; only Vista Business, Enterprise, and Ultimate owners can pull the strings. And it may not work if you have a firewall installed, either on the "puppet" side of the connection or on the "puppeteer." And you may have problems if you try to control a Vista PC from a Windows XP PC. And you may have problems if you try to control a Windows Server 2003 or 2000 Server PC from a Vista PC. And it's slow as a slug over anything but a lightning-fast connection. And . . . well, you get it.

And, oy! The terminology!

Life's too short. Know what I mean?

Yes, some people swear by Microsoft's RDP and RDC and TS and WMI and all that alphabet soup. Network administrators who have some control over firewalls and use Remote Desktop all day, every day get a lot of tools they need — and the power to keep RDP running. Vista's Remote Desktop has some nifty new features (see http://support.microsoft.com/kb/925876) that appeal to people who have to slave over a dozen hot, remote monitors all day. But for most of us, Remote Desktop is too complicated, too error-prone, too slow, and just too much of a time sink. And if you've ever tried to work Remote Desktop through a recalcitrant firewall, you've stared deep into the abyss.

In this Technique, I take you through the steps to get a simple, reliable puppet-puppeteer connection going. Quickly. Free. As long as your puppet computer stays connected to the Internet, you can get to it. Anytime. Anywhere.

Who knows? Maybe on your next trip, you'll "forget" to take your laptop. . . .

Installing LogMeIn

Several excellent free or inexpensive puppet-puppeteer programs are available, the best-known being GoToMyPC (`www.gotomypc.com`), from Citrix Online.

My favorite, though, is LogMeIn, which is free for personal use. Here's how to get it going:

1. **Start on the PC that will serve as a "puppet."**

 Although you can set up a LogMeIn account from any PC, it's faster to work from the PC that will have its strings pulled.

2. **Crank up your favorite Web browser and head to** `www.logmein.com`.

Your browser is immediately redirected to a secure sign-in page like the one shown in Figure 43-1.

3. **Click the Get LogMeIn Free / Click Here button.**

You're transported to a registration page.

4. **Fill in your e-mail address and password (which must be at least six characters long), and take the two-question survey. Uncheck the two Keep Me Informed boxes at the bottom (don't worry, every time you connect as a puppeteer, you get plenty of notification about upgrades). Then click the Go button.**

• **Figure 43-1: LogMeIn — my favorite free remote desktop program.**

5. **In the dialog box that appears, click the Add Computer link to add any computer(s) that you want to act as puppets.**

LogMeIn steps you through the short, simple method for installing the "puppet" software on your computer (see Figure 43-2).

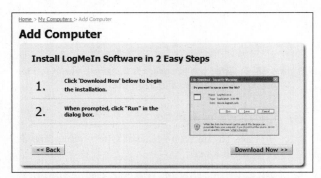

• **Figure 43-2: Follow the instructions to download and install the "puppet" program, called** `LogMeIn.exe`.

6. Click the Download Now button. Depending on which browser you're using, you may have to choose Run, or you may have to click the Save button and then choose to Open (or Run) the downloaded file.

The installer steps you through a very brief wizard that asks for your computer's description.

7. Type in a computer name that you will remember; then finish the wizard.

You need the e-mail address and password that you entered in Step 4.

When the installation is complete, LogMeIn shows you the Setup Completed message shown in Figure 43-3.

• **Figure 43-3:** After the program is installed, you need to run back to the Web site.

8. Click the Finish button.

Go back to the Web browser where you started the installation.

9. Click the Installation Was Successful button.

LogMeIn asks you to log in.

The LogMeIn site sends you a confirmation e-mail. Follow the instructions in that message to confirm your account.

Before you use LogMeIn for the first time, I recommend that you reboot your system. At that point, you're ready to start using LogMeIn.

 You need to install the LogMeIn program only on "puppet" computers. You can play puppeteer — pull the puppet's strings — from any computer with a working Web browser.

Starting, Stopping, and Disabling LogMeIn

After it's installed, the LogMeIn "puppet" program runs every time you start your computer. It appears as an arc-of-dots icon in your system tray, next to the clock.

If you want to turn LogMeIn off, right-click the icon in the system tray and choose Disable LogMeIn. To change your LogMeIn settings, or run through the (comprehensive) Getting Started Guide, right-click the arc-of-dots icon and choose Open LogMeIn.

If you decide that you don't want your computer hooked up to the LogMeIn Web site automatically every time it starts — and I'd hardly blame you for feeling queasy about it — you can simply uninstall it the usual way: Choose Start➪Control Panel and, under the Programs icon, click the Uninstall a Program link.

Using LogMeIn

Playing puppeteer is easy as long as you have LogMeIn installed and running on the "puppet" computer. Here's how:

1. Go to the "puppeteer" computer.

You can use any computer with a working Web browser.

2. Get your favorite browser going, and head to www.logmein.com.

You end up being redirected to a secure login page like the one at the beginning of this Technique (refer to Figure 43-1).

3. **At the top, type your e-mail address and LogMeIn password; then click the LogMeIn button.**

If you haven't yet responded to the account confirmation e-mail message from LogMeIn, the site advises you that you have to confirm.

When all your ducks are lined up — you've verified your account and your puppet computer is running — LogMeIn shows you a My Computers page like the one shown in Figure 43-4.

• **Figure 43-4: LogMeIn shows you a list of all your computers that are logged in to the site.**

4. **Click the name of the computer whose strings you want to yank.**

LogMeIn offers to speed your access by installing a Firefox plug-in (or a similar ActiveX control in Internet Explorer). Although the plug-in (or IE add-on) isn't required for pulling the strings on your puppet computer, it'll make the job go much faster.

5. **As long as you can install the plug-in or control on the PC that you're using (if you're using a PC at an Internet café, that may not be possible), click the Install button.**

Follow the instructions to install the plug-in or add-on.

When Firefox or IE is ready to go, you see a login screen that, as an added security measure, asks you to log in to the puppet computer.

6. **Enter a user name and password *for the puppet computer;* then click the Login button.**

You see the LogMeIn control for the puppet computer, as shown in Figure 43-5.

• **Figure 43-5: Overall controls for the puppet computer.**

7. **Under Remote Control, click the Go button.**

And all of a sudden, you're pulling the puppet's strings, as shown in Figure 43-6. You can do anything that you can do at the puppet computer — check e-mail, search for files, the whole nine yards.

• **Figure 43-6: Whew. There's that picture of Mom I left behind.**

LogMeIn has many tricks up its sleeve. Check the Preferences section in Figure 43-6. The paid version supports direct file sharing, multiple computer access to the same puppet, printing from the puppet computer to a printer on the puppeteer, and much more.

 Unlike some other remote desktop applications, LogMeIn doesn't maintain a connection from the puppet to its Web site to the puppeteer. Instead, after the session is established, all communication goes directly between puppet and puppeteer, over a secure connection. That makes LogMeIn fast — a fact that you'll notice if you have to suffer with a slow Internet connection on either side.

Part VIII

Fast Security Techniques

The 5th Wave   By Rich Tennant

"Well, the first level of Windows Vista security seems good—I can't get the shrink-wrapping off."

Technique 44

Updating Vista Cautiously

Save Time By

- ✔ Dealing with the Security Center's automatic update biases
- ✔ Knowing when to update — and how
- ✔ Protecting yourself against bad updates

Windows Automatic Update is for chumps.

Any large computer program has bugs. Heck, any *small* computer program has bugs. When a program gets as large as Windows — Vista contains 50 to 60 million lines of code, depending on how you count — the bugs start stacking up like planes at O'Hare in a snowstorm.

Microsoft issues hundreds of updates each year. Some of the updates fix bugs that make Windows crash. Many of the updates plug security holes. Most of the updates come in the form of *patches,* which are fixes to an individual Windows program that wasn't working right. Some of the patches are small. Most are big. Many of Microsoft's Security Bulletins, which appear to handle a single bug and its patch, in fact cover many big, frequently unrelated, patches.

You wouldn't need to worry about keeping Vista up-to-date with the latest patches if it weren't for one unavoidable fact: The bad guys are watching. You can bet that some cretin out there, somewhere, will take advantage of one of the patched security holes and come up with a virus or worm that exploits the hole. If you haven't installed the latest patch to plug the hole in Vista, your computer is vulnerable to the cretin's creations.

Microsoft's traditional *Patch Tuesday* — the second Tuesday of every month, which generally sees a host of new patches — now seems to be overshadowed by the next day, *Exploit Wednesday,* where the crackers of the world release malicious programs in two broad categories:

- ✔ **Programs that take advantage of the holes that were patched the preceding day.** By carefully examining the patches that Microsoft releases, sometimes folks in black hats come up with exploits that can clobber computers that haven't yet been patched.

- ✔ **So-called 0day ("zero-day") exploits that take advantage of holes that haven't yet been plugged.** The bad guys like to release their juicy new prey on the day after Patch Tuesday because they know Microsoft is unlikely to fix it until the next Patch Tuesday rolls around.

The only possible way you have to keep up with the latest security patches is Windows Update (or its cousin Microsoft Update, which covers both Windows and Office). I swear by Windows Update, but you have to use it properly.

What happens if something goes wrong and Microsoft's latest update causes yet more problems? It has happened many times before and it will happen again. Historically, by my humble estimate, fully 20 percent of the security patches Microsoft has released in recent history have caused major problems on a significant number of PCs.

 In one of the great acts of computer corporate hubris of all time, on April 24, 2006, Microsoft "pushed" a half-baked update to its Windows Genuine Advantage program onto millions of computers. We Windows consumers only later discovered that the program didn't work right, branding enormous numbers of perfectly legitimate copies of Windows as "not genuine." If you were unlucky enough to have Automatic Updates turned on at the time, you, too, may have had embarrassing warnings pop up on your computer, for no good reason at all. Adding injury to insult, this particularly vile piece of Automatic Update–installed scumware "phoned home" to Microsoft every day, leaving information about Microsoft's customers, their computers, and their software. The ultimate hubris? Microsoft had the temerity to call this Windows Genuine Spyware program a "priority update."

This Technique includes ways to protect yourself against the updates themselves. Caveat updator!

Reining In Windows Update

When you install Vista, or when you first start a new Vista PC, Windows greets you with one of the most biased questions in all of computer-dumb, er, -dom. Windows asks whether you want to "Help protect Windows automatically" with three really bad choices:

✔ **Use Recommended Settings,** which means that you allow Microsoft to turn on Automatic Updates (more about that in this Technique); keep Windows Defender updated automatically; and generally let Microsoft have its way with your computer.

 Those may be Microsoft's recommended settings. They certainly aren't mine.

✔ **Install Updates Only,** which means that you allow Microsoft to turn on Automatic Updates (which isn't a very smart move).

✔ **Ask Me Later,** an option with a big Red *X* — and (you guessed it) my recommendation.

Microsoft wants you to turn on Automatic Updates. Heck, most Windows gurus suggest that you turn on Automatic Updates. One of those gurus says that it's better for Microsoft to automatically install its software on your PC than to leave your system wide open for some malicious kid to install his software on your PC.

He's got a good point.

 Still, I disagree. I believe that Microsoft has proven conclusively that it can't be trusted to produce reliable security fixes. If Microsoft distributes an automatic patch so badly flawed that thousands or tens of thousands of PCs suddenly stop working, the people with those PCs won't have the slightest idea that the culprit was a bad patch from Redmond. In my opinion, savvy Windows users should let the Automatic Update service advise them when new patches are available — but they should wait to apply those patches until some people have had enough real-world experience with the patches to make sure that they solve more problems than they create.

I believe in this issue so strongly that I've devoted a section of my AskWoody.com Web site to tracking Microsoft patches, advising people on whether patches should be applied and how to avoid or work around the problems, even if the solutions involve non-Microsoft products.

It's one of those dammed-if-you-do-dammed-if-you-don't situations that salmon seem to encounter every year (if you'll pardon a fishy metaphor). On the one hand, if you apply Microsoft's patches as soon as they're available, your PC may get all screwed up. On the other hand, if you don't install the patches, some cretin who learned about a security hole when a patch was issued could come along and blast you with a worm. In my experience, at least at this point, if you take some simple precautions (including keeping your antivirus program up-to-date and using Firefox instead of Internet Explorer), your chances of getting clobbered by a bad patch are higher than your chances of getting zapped with a worm. So it makes sense to avoid applying Windows updates until you know that they're solid.

Your first big step in taking control of Windows Update is to turn off Automatic Updates and instead have Windows merely inform you when updates are available. Follow these steps:

1. **Choose Start⇨Control Panel and, under the Security icon, click the Check This Computer's Security Status link.**

You see the Windows Security Center, shown in Figure 44-1.

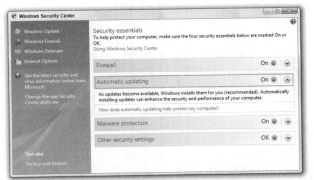

• **Figure 44-1: If Automatic Updating is set to On, you get everything Microsoft pushes down the line.**

2. **If you have Automatic Updating turned on, scold yourself and then click the Windows Update link in the upper-left corner.**

The Windows Update status report appears.

3. **Click the second link on the left, the one that says Change Settings.**

You finally see the dialog box in which Vista lets you turn off Automatic Updates (see Figure 44-2).

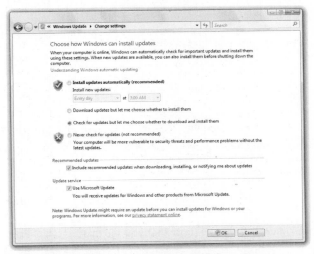

• **Figure 44-2: Turn off Automatic Updates and turn on automatic notification here.**

4. **Consider the ramifications of each of the settings, as I explain in Table 44-1. Choose the updating entry that works best for you; then check the appropriate boxes and click OK.**

You have to click Continue through a User Account Control dialog box to return to the Windows Update status report from the preceding Step 2.

5. **Click X to exit the Windows Update status screen.**

Your changes take effect immediately.

TABLE 44-1: AUTOMATIC UPDATE SETTINGS

Setting	Timesaving Recommendation
Install Updates Automatically (Recommended)	Use this setting only if you trust Microsoft, in spite of its track record, to deliver patches that won't clobber your system. This is a good choice if you're setting up a PC for someone who doesn't have the time, savvy, or inclination to stay on top of the latest updates — because never patching is the worst choice of all.
Download Updates, but Let Me Choose Whether to Install Them	A reasonable choice if you have a slow Internet connection or you don't want to tie it up with downloads while you're working. The only downside comes when Microsoft re-issues a patch, effectively creating a "version 2.0" patch or a patch of a patch. In that case, you have an extra, useless file hanging around.
Check for Updates but Let Me Choose Whether to Download and Install Them	Your best choice if you have a reasonably fast Internet connection. Wait until the patch seems to be working (watch AskWoody.com or your favorite patch watching site) and when the coast is clear, go for it. This choice has the added benefit of allowing you two chances to change your mind and hold off on patching.
Never Check for Updates	The worst of all possible worlds. Avoid it.
Include Recommended Updates When Downloading, Installing or Notifying Me About Updates	I generally avoid recommended updates like the plague — the old "ain't broke, don't fix" theory. Video driver updates, in particular, have caused lost hours and days at the worst possible moment. However, it's good to know when a new driver is available, in the unlikely event that a piece of hardware has been acting flakey. So I like to be notified, but will take extreme caution before installing.
Use Microsoft Update (note that you see this option only if you have an additional Microsoft product, such as Office, installed)	Primarily adds Microsoft Office to the list, although occasionally updates to other Microsoft products occur. For years, Microsoft Update had all sorts of problems, most of which have been ironed out finally. I say go ahead and use it.

Microsoft updates Windows Update so often that you need a scorecard to keep the versions straight. This bit is a brain-twister, but if you don't turn on Automatic Updating, Windows can't update Windows Update itself until you specifically give your permission.

Making the logic even more convoluted, Microsoft in the past has insisted on calling its Windows Genuine Spyware, er, Nagware, uh, Advantage software updates an update to Windows Update. (Say that ten times real fast.)

 To avoid an endless loop of chickens and eggs, you might want to log on to the Windows Update Web site, windowsupdate.microsoft.com, from time to time and allow Windows Update to install patches to itself.

 Microsoft officially releases new security patches on the second Tuesday of every month. (Except when, uh, it doesn't.) If you hear of a security patch coming out on any date other than the second Tuesday of the month, chances are good that Microsoft has heard about somebody attempting to take advantage of the security hole.

Downloading the Big Updates

From time to time, Microsoft releases a big Windows update. It may be called a Service Pack or an Update Rollup or a Version Change or The Greatest Thing Since Sliced Bread. It all depends on what ears the marketeers are wearing at the moment.

There was a giant download for Windows XP Service Pack 1, another one for Windows Media Player 9, another for Windows Movie Maker 2, and then Service Pack 2, and then Windows Media Player 10, and then Internet Explorer 7. . . well, you get the idea. You find out about the big updates from the press, or from the Windows Update pop-up in your notification area (next to the clock on the taskbar) that says updates are available.

If you have just one PC that needs updating, you can simply click the notification bubble and follow the instructions to apply the download to the PC that needs it.

 If you have more than one PC, downloading the same update file repeatedly is a huge, time-consuming chore. For those of you who have unlimited broadband access and enjoy lightning-fast 100MB downloads, I applaud your resourcefulness. Literally. For the rest of us, the idea of downloading a 270MB file four times for four different machines is a bit daunting, to say the least. (Windows XP Service Pack 2 weighed in at 270MB; Service Pack 1, by contrast, ran a sprightly 138MB. On a 56K dial-up modem, downloading one of the big service packs would take about a year, if you lasted that long.)

Fortunately, you can download the big updates as a single file and save them on your PC, so you can use the saved file multiple times. It isn't worth the effort to find and download small updates — ones that can be downloaded in a few minutes. The way to save a whole bunch of Internet time is to look for updates that take 30 minutes or more to download.

To see whether a particular update is available for download in its own file, follow these steps:

1. **Choose Start➪Control Panel and, under the Security icon, click the Check for Updates link.**

   If you have Automatic Updates set to the Check for Updates but Let Me Choose Whether to Download and Install Them option, you should see a summary of available updates, as in Figure 44-3.

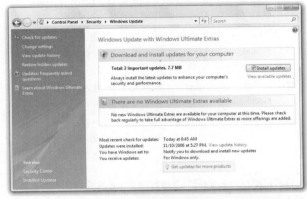

• **Figure 44-3: Search for big, downloadable updates here.**

2. **Click the View Available Updates link.**

   Vista shows you a detailed list of the updates that are available, as in Figure 44-4.

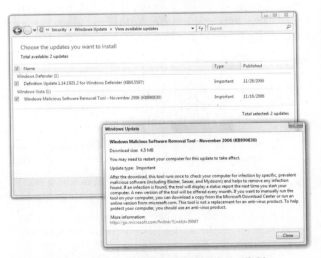

• **Figure 44-4: Look at the details for each available update.**

3. **One by one, right-click each update and choose View Details.**

Vista shows you a Windows Update summary of the patch in a window like the one in the lower-right corner of Figure 44-4. Each summary includes the download size for the patch.

4. **If you might be interested in downloading a patch just once, click the More Information link inside the detailed window.**

Vista starts Internet Explorer and goes to the Knowledge Base article associated with the patch.

5. **Follow the instructions inside the Knowledge Base article to download and install the patch.**

Generally, manual download instructions point to a page at the Microsoft Download Center.

Checking for Small Updates

Although there are powerful reasons for manually downloading just one copy of the big updates, the small ones are far too numerous for most carbon-based life forms to keep track of. As long as you don't mind running Microsoft's Windows Update sniffer program, you can easily deal with those little updates by letting Windows Automatic Update take care of them.

Follow these steps to do a mini update:

1. **If you see a bubble in the notification area, down near the clock, that says updates are available, click the bubble.**

Vista brings up the available updates list, shown earlier in Figure 44-4.

2. **Check the boxes next to the updates you want to install.**

It's a good idea to check an unbiased source to make sure the update won't create more problems than it fixes. My Microsoft Patch Reliability Ratings page should help:

www.AskWoody.com/viewpatch.php

3. **Click the Install button.**

You may need to accept a User License agreement.

You have to click Continue to get through a User Account Control message.

Vista keeps you posted on the progress of the downloads and updates. When Vista finishes, it notifies you of its success (see Figure 44-5).

• **Figure 44-5: The download and install progress report.**

4. **Click X to exit the update scorecard.**

You may need to reboot your PC.

Retrieving and Installing a Declined Update

What if you turn down an Automatic Update and later wonder whether maybe you should've accepted?

No problem. Just follow these steps to get that update:

1. **Choose Start⇨Control Panel and, under the Security icon, click the Check for Updates link.**

Vista brings up the update history, as shown earlier in Figure 44-3.

2. **On the left, click the Restore Hidden Updates link.**

Vista presents you with a list of any updates you may have declined in the past.

3. **Click the update you want to bring back and then click the Restore button.**

Vista puts the update back on the update history and returns you to the window showing available updates (refer to Figure 44-3).

The next time Windows Update scans for updates, it treats the ones you have restored in this way as new and offers them to you again.

Protecting Your PC from Viruses

Y ou can lose a lot of time — not to mention a lot of sleep — over viruses. Some of the worries are justified. Many are not. I've been working with viruses and antivirus software manufacturers since the first Word macro virus infected most of the computers on Microsoft's campus in August 1995. I was the first person to find a Word 97 macro virus, which was posted on Microsoft's Web site, by a Microsoft employee, and was attached to a marketing document. And I've been intimately involved in fighting viruses, Trojans, worms, and other nasties up to and including the current "cyberterrorism" phase. Don't tell anybody, but I've even helped Microsoft at times.

You know what I've discovered?

Viruses aren't anywhere near as bad as most people think. Of course, you need to protect yourself by running a good antivirus program (I show you how to get a good free one in this Technique), setting up a firewall (you already have a decent, but not great, firewall in Vista), and following a few simple rules (which I list in this Technique).

Network administrators need to stay on their toes to block fast-spreading Internet worms. Everybody needs to patch Vista when the time is right (see Technique 44). But for the most part, in spite of what you've read in the papers, well-meaning people trying to fight viruses have done more harm than the viruses themselves have ever caused.

I don't mean to say that you should avoid antivirus software. Jim Allchin, the head honcho for Windows Vista, has been quoted as saying that Vista's "lockdown features are so capable and thorough that he was comfortable with his own seven-year-old son using Vista without antivirus software installed." Jim and I disagree about a lot of things. This is one of the biggies.

If you want to save time, set up an antivirus program following the rules I give in this Technique, get Windows Firewall cranked up (Technique 46), and then get on with your life.

Understanding Viruses — and Hoaxes

So much bad information about viruses is floating around the Internet that it's a wonder anybody gets any work done. Before I look at what a virus is, I offer a look at what a virus isn't. Have you ever received an e-mail message that looks like this?

E-mails with pictures of Osama Bin-Laden hanged are being sent and the moment that you open these e-mails your computer will crash and you will not be able to fix it!!!

This e-mail is being distributed through countries around the globe, but mainly in the U.S. and Israel.

Don't be inconsiderate; send this warning to whomever you know.

Alarming, isn't it, that a picture of bin Laden can crash your computer? I mean, with the Department of Homeland Security issuing a warning that U.S. stock market and banking sites could be attacked by Al Qaeda, and all those jihadists running around with computers in their tents and electric generators strapped to their camels and . . .

Relax. The message is a hoax, passed on by (usually) well-intentioned people who simply haven't got a clue. It takes a sick mind to dream up a hoax like that. But it takes only a gullible clicking finger to pass it on to a hundred people.

My inbox overfloweth with poorly written hoaxes such as these:

- ✔ "Warning READ AS SOON AS POSSIBLE Get this sent around to your contacts ASAP...we don't need this spreading around..... Do not open any message with an attached filed called "Invitation" regardless of who sent it, It is a virus that opens an Olympic Torch which "burns" the whole hard

disc C of your computer . . ." On and on it goes, finally ending with "SEND THIS E-MAIL TO EVERYONE YOU KNOW."

- ✔ ""With this program, THE WORST THING THAT CAN HAPPEN IS YOU LOSE $5 Here are the simple steps....   Firstly, you need a Paypal account - go to www.paypal.com. . . . . . Through Paypal, pay $5 to the email address listed on top of the list below. Delete the first email address listed, move the next 4 up in position and then place your own email address in position 5. Don't be tempted to put your email address in top position, this will lead to a possible short term return and ZERO long term benefits . . ."

It continues to amaze me how many people forward messages like these. But every day, hundreds of millions of copies of hoax virus warnings and chain letters clog the Internet. Between the hoaxes and the phishing messages (that is, messages that try to get you to divulge sensitive information, usually through a tricky e-mail message), it's hard to figure out what's real and what isn't.

No, Bill Gates can't keep track of whom you send e-mail to — and he certainly won't give you $10 each time you click the Forward button. No, the postal service isn't about to impose a fee for using e-mail. No, you won't have your hard drive erased if you view a message entitled WTC Survivor.

Here's how to spot a hoax:

- ✔ Unless the message is an official release from a recognized source — say, a Microsoft Security Bulletin, a Symantec Virus Alert, a CERT Advisory, or a news story from AP or Reuters — there's at least a 90 percent chance that you are looking at a hoax.

- ✔ If one single exclamation point is in the entire message, or more than one word is in ALL CAPS, or the message has more than one or two misspellings, or it warns in breathless terms about all the data on your disk being destroyed, it's a hoax. Bet on it.

✔ If the message refers to a legitimate source — say, the Bugtraq news list or Microsoft or Norton — but doesn't quote directly from the source, it's either a hoax or so hopelessly garbled that you don't stand a chance of understanding the real problem.

✔ Microsoft doesn't distribute files by e-mail. If you get a file attached to a message that purports to be from Microsoft, it isn't. Chances are good that you have a hoax message, with a real virus attached.

✔ If it's too good to be true . . . well, you know the rest of the saying.

Do yourself a favor. If you get junk like this, don't forward it. Forwarding hoaxes does not endear you to most folks. Forwarded hoaxes are indistinguishable from spam. Spam's bad enough without turning it into a cottage industry.

Also, check out a site such as CIAC's Hoaxbusters (hoaxbusters.ciac.org) or Symantec's hoax list (www.symantec.com/avcenter/hoax.html) or Snopes (www.snopes.com) and see whether you're looking at a known hoax. If you are, write to the person who sent the hoax to you and tell him or her about it.

Even if you get a real message warning about a real virus, don't forward it. You only add to the damage caused by the virus — and the information you send may be out of date. The best way to handle a real warning about a real virus is to find a reliable Web site that's reporting on the infection. Then pick up the phone, call your friends, and tell them about the site. That way, you don't add to the volume of e-mail that the virus generates, and you make sure that your friends get the latest, best information from an authoritative source.

That saves your time. It saves your friends' time. And you don't contribute to the volume of e-mail. Spend a few minutes now learning the telltale signs of a virus and you can laugh at messages like the Osama picture hoax.

Dissecting a Virus

A computer *virus* is a program that replicates. That's all. Viruses generally replicate by attaching themselves to files — programs, documents, spreadsheets — or replacing "genuine" operating system files with bogus ones. They usually make copies of themselves whenever they're run. Even relatively benign viruses can sap your time by bloating your files and making your computer do strange things. Most embarrassingly, viruses can take up enormous amounts of time if you send an infected file to someone else and have to warn the person (or, worse, the organization) after the fact.

You probably think that viruses delete files or make programs go belly-up or wreak havoc in other nefarious ways. Some of them do. Many of them don't. Viruses sound scary, but many really aren't. Most viruses have such ridiculous bugs in them that they don't get very far "in the wild."

Trojans (occasionally called Trojan horses) may or may not be able to reproduce, but they always require that the user do something to get them started. The most common Trojans these days appear as e-mail attachments: You double-click an attachment, expecting to open a picture or a document, and you get bitten when some program comes in and clobbers your computer, frequently sending out a gazillion messages, all with infected attachments, without your knowledge or consent.

Worms move from one computer to another over a network. The worst ones replicate very quickly by shooting copies of themselves over the Internet, taking advantage of holes in the operating systems (all too frequently Windows).

Collectively, viruses, Trojans, and worms are known as *malware*. Although some malware can carry bad payloads — programs that wreak destruction on your system — many of the worst offenders cause the most harm by clogging networks (nearly bringing down the Internet itself, at times) and by turning

PCs into *zombies*, frequently called *bots*, which can be operated by remote control.

 If your PC is turned into a zombie, the cretin who infected you may be able to retrieve data from (or destroy data on) your computer. Surprisingly, though, most zombie puppet-masters aren't interested in personal data. Some of them make money by mining e-mail addresses from subverted machines, selling the addresses to spammers. Many of them, though, wait until they can get a bunch of subverted machines to work in unison, bombarding a Web site with so many "hits" that the site shuts down. That's the genesis of the so-called Distributed Denial of Service attack, a technique that has brought down more than a few controversial sites. Most recently, zombies have been used to send out tons of spam, with the spammers lining the pockets of the puppet-masters. 'Tis a brave new world, eh?

The most successful pieces of malware these days run as *rootkits*, programs that evade detection by stealthily hooking into Windows in tricky ways. Some nominally respectable companies (notably Sony, which got socked for its intransigence) have employed rootkit technology to hide programs for their own profit. Rootkits are very difficult to detect and even harder to clean.

All these definitions are becoming more academic and less relevant as the trend shifts to blended-threat malware. Blended threats incorporate elements of all three traditional kinds of malware — and more. Most of the most successful "viruses" you read about in the press these days are, in fact, blended-threat malware. They've come a long way from old-fashioned viruses.

The first really big virus

The world changed when John McAfee appeared on the "Today Show" in March 1992 and told Bryant Gumbel that the Michelangelo virus infected more than a million PCs. One week later, the PC world was supposed to end. All the major wire services ran alarming predictions — millions of dollars were forecast to be lost in the wake of the largest computer virus of all time.

The Big Day arrived and . . . nothing. A few thousand systems got clobbered here and there, but Michelangelo turned into a dud of astonishing proportions. McAfee made millions. The wire services fell silent. We all got huckstered. Does history repeat itself in Internet time?

McAfee was demoted to Chief Technology Officer, then forced out of McAfee Associates — after receiving a rumored $50 million severance package. His antics helped start an entire cadre of antivirus antihucksters. See www.kumite.com/myths/opinion/pamkane.htm.

By and large, malware works in rather predictable ways:

- **By infecting legitimate program files or key discs:** These old-fashioned methods of replicating have all but disappeared because people rarely pass around program files or USB key discs.

 If you find a "lost" key disc, be extremely cautious if you decide to plug it into your computer. At the very least, hold down the Shift key as you plug it in so that you don't automatically run any programs before you can inspect the contents of the drive.

- **By infecting documents:** This type of transmittal works when a user opens an infected document. Other documents on the user's PC become infected. When the user sends copies of those documents to others, the recipients' machines can become infected, too. It's a slow and haphazard approach that's on the wane because antivirus programs have improved enormously and because Microsoft has built antivirus hooks into the Office programs. Whenever you open a file in a recent version of Office, your antivirus program scans the file before the program (Word, Excel, whatever) even touches it.

 A small resurgence in infected Word documents, Excel spreadsheets, and PowerPoint presentations has occurred because of newly discovered "0day" exploits in Word, Excel, and PowerPoint. (A so-called *0day attack* uses a previously unknown, unreported security hole to wreak its havoc.) The 0day targets to date have been very focused — most likely industrial espionage efforts undertaken by sophisticated (and well-paid) crackers.

✔ **By automatically sending copies of infected documents to others:** That's how Melissa (1999) works. If you open a Melissa-infected document in Word, Melissa automatically sends infected documents attached to e-mail messages destined to the first 50 people in your address book. Melissa was so successful that network administrators at hundreds of large installations — including Microsoft and Intel — pulled their networks offline (in some cases for days). Melissa doesn't have a destructive payload, but it completely brought down e-mail communication in many companies.

More recently, many rootkits work this way, shoveling out phishing messages and other types of spam under the control of sophisticated (and well-paid) botmasters. Do you see a pattern here?

✔ **By sending copies of itself attached to e-mail messages:** The ILOVEYOU (2000) worm arrives attached to an innocuous-looking message that says, "Kindly check the attached LOVELETTER coming from me." Anyone using Outlook or Outlook Express who double-clicks the attached file, LOVE-LETTER-FOR-YOU.TXT.vbs, unleashes the worm, which immediately sends copies of itself to everyone in the infected user's address book. It also overwrites files. Ford, the Jet Propulsion Lab, the Space Center in Houston, and even the British Parliament were knocked out by ILOVEYOU. Bill Gates once joked that he received infected messages from people who should know better.

The Anna Kournikova worm (early 2001) works much the same as ILOVEYOU. It arrives as an e-mail attachment called AnnaKournikova. jpg.vbs. If you double-click the attachment, copies of the worm are sent to everyone in your address book. One big difference with Anna: It was written with a virus construction kit, readily available on the Web.

More recently, the people who create such infectious messages have become more brazen and much more sophisticated. One particularly successful category of malware

arrives in a message that claims to contain a virus patch — from Microsoft, no less. Rest assured that any program you receive attached to an e-mail message that seems to come from Microsoft, uh, doesn't.

✔ **By sending copies of itself via e-mail and directly infecting other computers on the local network:** Klez (Spring 2002) is a multi-attack opportunist of this ilk. It sends copies of itself attached to e-mail messages addressed to everyone in your address book. For good measure, sometimes Klez retrieves a legitimate file from the infected computer and sends it along with the program itself. (Highly embarrassing!) Klez also spoofs the From: address (puts a completely bogus return address on the message) by scanning the address book and sticking randomly selected e-mail addresses in the From: line. At the same time, Klez infects other PCs on the local network by dropping copies of itself in network-accessible folders. The copies have random names, so people using other computers on the network might run Klez accidentally, thinking that they're running some different program. MyDoom (2004) also spreads as an e-mail attachment. Variants of both are popular today.

 Your best defense is to install a good antivirus package. Downloading one from the Web takes less than 30 minutes. Setting it up takes another 30 minutes, tops. See the last section in this Technique for quick instructions on installing AVG Free, a very good antivirus program that's absolutely free for personal use. For an hour's investment, you can save days and days of cleanup.

✔ **By attacking computers connected directly to the Internet:** The brave new world of attacks involves worms, such as Code Red (Summer 2001) and Slammer (early 2003), that aggressively look for vulnerable PCs that are directly connected to the Internet. Humans are no longer part of the infecting vector; these worms are completely self-propelled, scanning randomly generated IP addresses. (Code Red 2 goes one step further by focusing most of its attacks on nearby networks, presumably inside a corporate firewall.) Microsoft's own Hotmail servers were brought down by Code Red, which exploited a known, fixed problem with Microsoft's Internet Information Server. (Yes, Microsoft forgot to patch its Hotmail servers.) Slammer took out SQL Server installations. Many PC users have a SQL Server on their machines, disguised as a product called MSDE. Sobig, Blaster, and Sasser (2003–2004) also ran across wide swathes of unpatched Windows systems.

Code Red took about 12 hours to infect most of its intended victims. During the first minute of its existence, Slammer doubled the number of infected systems every 8.5 seconds. Slammer took about 10 minutes from the moment it was unleashed to infect most of its victims. In fact, the single greatest barrier to Slammer's propagation was the Internet's near meltdown due to Slammer's fast propagation.

Fast-propagating worms on the Internet are nothing new. The Computer Emergency Response Team (CERT) was initially formed largely in response to Robert Morris's worm, which essentially brought down the Internet in late 1988.

 I think it's pretty obvious that the future of viruses, worms, and Trojans lies in rootkits, spewing spamming and phishing messages. A lot of money is to be made in these activities. We can certainly expect technological advances in infection methods. But the big push now, it seems, lies in good social engineering — creating a compelling story that will convince you to do something stupid even though you know that you shouldn't.

Discerning Whether Your PC Is Infected

So how do you know whether you're infected?

The short answer is this: Many times, you don't. If you think that your PC is infected, chances are very good that it isn't. Why? Because malware these days doesn't usually cause the kinds of problems people normally associate with infections.

That said, here are a few telltale signs that might mean that your PC is infected:

✔ Someone tells you that you sent him an e-mail message with an attachment — and you didn't send it. In fact, most e-mail malware these days is smart enough to spoof the From: address, so any infected message that appears to come from you probably didn't. Still, some dumb old viruses that aren't capable of hiding your e-mail address are still around. And if you get an infected attachment from a friend, chances are good that both your e-mail address and his e-mail address are on an infected computer somewhere. Six degrees of separation and all that . . .

If you receive an infected message, look at the header to see whether you can tell where it came from. In Outlook 2003 and earlier, open the message and then choose View➪Options. In Outlook 2007, you have to open the message and then click the tiny square with a downward-facing arrow in the lower-right corner of the Options group. A box at the bottom may (or may not!) tell you who really sent the message (as shown in Figure 45-1).

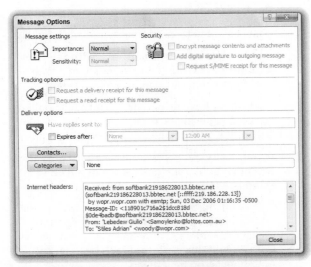

• **Figure 45-1: The box at the bottom contains the e-mail header, which may give you a clue as to its origin.**

✔ If you suddenly see files with two filename extensions scattered around on your computer, beware. Filenames such as `kournikova.jpg.vbs` (a VBScript file masquerading as a JPG image file) or `somedoc.txt.exe` (a Windows program that wants to appear to be a text file) should send you running for your antivirus software.

Always, always, always have Windows show you filename extensions. See Technique 15.

✔ Your antivirus software suddenly stops working. If the icon for your antivirus product disappears from the notification area (near the clock), something killed it — and chances are very good that the culprit was a virus.

✔ Your Internet connection slows to a crawl. Even worse than usual.

Dealing with Your Infected PC

If you think that your PC is infected, follow these steps in order:

1. **Don't panic.**

Chances are very good that you're not infected.

2. **Update your antivirus software with the latest signature file from the manufacturer's Web site; then run a full scan of your system.**

If you don't have an antivirus package installed, run — don't walk — to the final section of this Technique, and download and install AVG Free.

3. **If your antivirus software doesn't identify the problem, hold your nose and run a free Windows Live OneCare safety scan.**

I'm *not* talking about paying for Windows Live OneCare, which I consider to be a protection racket (see sidebar) only half a step removed from early-1900s gangster Frank Nitti, one of Al Capone's top henchmen.

 The free Windows Live OneCare safety scan is a service from Microsoft that frequently catches new malware before any of the commercial products — including Microsoft's own Live OneCare — can detect or fix a problem. I firmly believe that Microsoft offers the free safety scan strictly to keep itself out of court (see the article "MS Live OneCare Halts Flow of Antivirus Info" in *Windows Secrets* newsletter, `windowssecrets.com/comp/061012`). It's slow. It's clunky. It offers no options. But when a new 0day exploit hits the stands, the free safety scan gets its scanner updated first.

To run a free safety scan, make sure you have an hour or two to spare; then follow these steps:

a. *Start Internet Explorer (the safety scanner doesn't work with Firefox) and go to* `safety.live.com` *(see Figure 45-2).*

b. *Click the Protection icon (you don't need or want a "Full Service" scan).*

Windows Live OneCare takes you to the Protection Center, as shown in Figure 45-3.

• **Figure 45-2:** The poorly constructed Windows Live OneCare safety scanner site gets new virus definitions first.

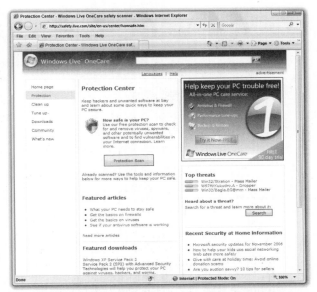

• **Figure 45-3: A free Protection Scan can take a long time, but it's the most up-to-date scan anywhere.**

c. *Click the Protection Scan button.*

You may be required to install software from Microsoft that hooks into the free scanner. To do so, you may need to manually install an ActiveX control and manually enable pop-ups. Follow the instructions to install that software and run a scan.

4. **If you still haven't nailed it, check your antivirus software manufacturer's "alert" page and see whether it notes any known pieces of malware that aren't yet identified.**

Table 45-1 gives the Web addresses for the major antivirus software manufacturers. Note that some sites may have news posted hours before other sites — but it's impossible to tell in advance which will get the story first.

5. **Check one of the following sites to see whether you're the victim of a hoax:**

```
securityresponse.symantec.com/
    avcenter/hoax.html
us.mcafee.com/virusInfo/default.asp
    ?id=hoaxes
hoaxbusters.ciac.org
```

Many of the hoaxes floating around these days sound mighty convincing. Save yourself a lot of embarrassment by ensuring that you're not being pulled by the leg.

6. **If you still can't find the source of the problem, follow the instructions on your antivirus software manufacturer's home page to submit a new virus.**

If you're the first to report a new virus, you're *so* cutting edge.

7. **Do not — repeat, do not — send messages to all your friends advising them of the new virus.**

Messages about a new virus can outnumber infected messages generated by the virus itself — in some cases causing more havoc than the virus itself. Try not to become part of the problem. Besides, you may be wrong.

In recent years, I've come to view the mainstream press accounts of virus and malware outbreaks with increasing, uh, skepticism. The antivirus companies are usually slower to post news than the mainstream press, but the information they post tends to be much more reliable. Not infallible, mind you, but better. We also cover security problems at AskWoody.com.

The Windows Live OneCare Racket

The free Windows Live OneCare safety scan that I discuss in this Technique rates as a slow, bloated, poorly documented and nearly unknown service acting primarily as an advertising come-on to get people to sign up for the $50-per-year Windows Live OneCare.

"Help get confidence and peace of mind with round-the-clock protection and maintenance—virus scanning, firewalls, tune ups, file backups, the whole nine yards." That's what Live OneCare's marketeers say. Vista has a firewall, and entire industries support firewalls, virus scanning, tune-ups, and backups with packages that range from utterly free to very expensive. Not sure where you can buy a whole nine yards, or even half of one, but I'll leave that to the philosophers.

(continued)

TABLE 45-1: MAJOR ANTIVIRUS SOFTWARE VENDORS

Product	Company	Breaking News Web Site
AVG Anti-Virus	GRISOFT	www.grisoft.com
F-Secure Antivirus	F-Secure	www.f-secure.com/virus-info
Kaspersky Antivirus	Kaspersky Lab	www.kaspersky.com
McAfee VirusScan	Network Associates	us.mcafee.com/virusInfo/default.asp
Norton AntiVirus	Symantec	securityresponse.symantec.com
Panda Antivirus	Panda	www.pandasecurity.com
Trend PC-cillin	Trend Micro	www.antivirus.com/vinfo

It burns me up that Microsoft has the temerity to charge for something that should be free, should be unnecessary, and should be part of the deal when we plunk our dollars down for an exorbitantly priced product such as Vista. How many billions of dollars do these guys need to make before they fix what they broke?

The irascible John Dvorak nailed it in *PC Magazine:* "Does Microsoft think it is going to get away with charging real money for any sort of add-on, service, or new product that protects clients against flaws in its own operating system? Does the existence of this not constitute an incredible conflict of interest? Why improve the base code when you can sell 'protection'? Is Frank Nitti the new CEO?"

This much I know for sure: If you're paying Microsoft to protect your computer, you're part of the problem, not part of the solution.

Protecting Yourself — Quickly

Every Vista user needs to follow five simple rules to guard against viruses, worms, Trojans, and the like:

✔ **Install, update, and religiously use one of the major antivirus packages.**

You can use any of the packages listed in Table 45-1; they all work just fine. You can also install AVG Free, the free antivirus package that I use. Follow the instructions in the next section.

If you already own an antivirus package and you're tired of its incessant demands for more money — or if you got snoockered into buying Microsoft's Live OneCare — uninstall the thing (choose Start➪Control Panel and, under the Programs icon, choose Uninstall a Program) and pick something less intrusive.

✔ **Force Windows to show you filename extensions.**

Microsoft's decision to have Windows hide filename extensions — the letters at the end of a filename, such as .doc or .vbs — reeks of trying to put the toothpaste back in the tube. It's a dangerous design mistake that you can fix by following the steps in Technique 15.

The important letters in a filename's extension are the ones following the last period. For example, abc.gif.bat is a batch file that runs if you double-click it. Similarly, def.doc.vbs is a VBScript program — not a Word document — that also runs immediately.

✔ **After you can see filename extensions, watch out for the ones in Table 45-2.**

If you double-click a file with one of those extensions, it runs immediately, with potentially disastrous results.

Yes, it's true: JPEG files (that is, files with the filename extension .JPG) can include potentially harmful programs. How can picture files turn into malicious programs? Because Microsoft screwed up. Dozens of Microsoft programs mishandle JPG files, and the result can be devastating. You need to patch them all. See `www.microsoft.com/security/bulletins/200409_jpeg.mspx` for details.

✔ **Never open or run a file attached to an e-mail message until you (a) contact the person who sent you the message and verify that he or she specifically sent you the file and (b) save the file on your hard drive, update your antivirus software's signature file, and run your antivirus software on the file.**

Infected e-mail attachments are the single most common source of preventable infection at the moment.

✔ **If you get an e-mail message warning you about a virus, don't forward it.**

You're only contributing to the problem even if the warning is valid (and it rarely is; see the first section in this Technique). If the problem sounds dire, find a reference on one of the sites mentioned in Table 45-1 (earlier in this chapter) and then call your friends and tell them to look at the site. That way, they not only get the real story (plus or minus an editorial quirk or three), they also stay informed about new tools to solve the problem.

Follow those five rules and you help not only yourself but also all your co-workers, friends, and colleagues.

TABLE 45-2: FILENAME EXTENSIONS FOR POTENTIALLY UNSAFE PROGRAM FILES

.ade	.adp	.app	.asp	.asx	.bas
.bat	.cer	.chm	.cmd	.com	.cpl
.crt	.csh	.exe	.fxp	.hlp	.hta
.inf	.ins	.isp	.its	.jpg	.js
.jse	.ksh	.lnk	.mad	.maf	.mag
.mam	.maq	.mar	.mas	.mat	.mau
.mav	.maw	.mda	.mdb	.mde	.mdt
.mdw	.mdz	.msc	.msi	.msp	.mst
.net	.ops	.pcd	.pif	.prf	.prg
.pst	.reg	.scf	.scr	.sct	.shb
.shs	.tmp	.url	.vb	.vbe	.vbs
.vsmacros	.vss	.vst	.vsw	.ws	.wsc
.wsf	.wsh				

Installing AVG Anti-Virus Free

 I use an antivirus program called AVG Free. It's free for personal use and it works just great — no nagging about expired licenses, no hassles, no sweat.

Yes, faster products are available. Yes, AVG updates its signature files for its commercial product before it updates AVG Free. But AVG Free installs easily, runs without a hitch, and doesn't cost a cent for personal use. Here's how to get it:

1. **Start your favorite Web browser and go to `free.grisoft.com`.**

The site should look like Figure 45-4.

• **Figure 45-4: The GRISOFT Web site for its AVG Free product.**

2. **Click the link for AVG Anti-Virus Free.**

You end up on a page devoted to AVG Anti-Virus Free (see Figure 45-5).

 It's important that you run an update from the First Run Wizard so that AVG knows how to automatically update in the future. The other steps are optional.

• **Figure 45-5: The link to download AVG Free.**

 AVG has many products. You're looking for the free version (not the trial version) of AVG Anti-Virus.

3. **Click the Download Free Version link and then click the link to the latest version of AVG Free, which is called `avg75free_430a848.exe` or something similar.**

The installation file is more than 15MB, so it can take a while to download.

4. **Run the setup file called `avg75free_430a848.exe` (or something similar) and take all the defaults. The installer brings up the First Run Wizard.**

AVG Free's First Run installation wizard (see Figure 45-6) has you download the latest virus signature file, create an emergency boot disk, then run a full scan.

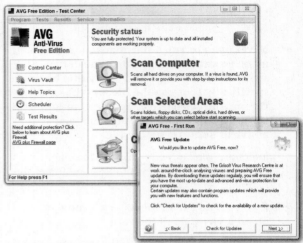

• **Figure 45-6: Follow the First Run Wizard to get AVG Free going quickly.**

5. **When the wizard's done, click Finish. You're one step away from protecting yourself.**

6. **Reboot your computer.**

AVG Free kicks in, and you can say goodbye to those incessant requests for more money.

If you like AVG Free, tell your friends! GRISOFT makes most of its money by selling the regular version of AVG, which includes many more features and a less-congested signature-file download site.

Technique 46

Plugging and Unplugging Windows Firewall

Save Time By

✔ Setting up Windows Firewall for your particular needs

✔ Understanding the outbound Firewall's limitations

✔ Poking holes in the Firewall

So you have Vista, and you know that there's both an inbound and outbound firewall, and you can't figure out how to get the outbound firewall to work.

I know the feeling well.

The reason? Microsoft forgot to build an interface for the outbound firewall.

 And there's a reason that Microsoft forgot to build that interface. Getting an outbound firewall to work reasonably well is an enormously hairy problem. I bet that Microsoft's projected support costs for a "consumer" outbound firewall started to look like the national debt of some small countries.

To make an outbound firewall useful, you have to preload it with a bunch of exceptions for common programs. Then you have to step each customer through a double-edged learning process — a process in which the firewall learns which programs are allowed to send data out and the customer learns to identify suspicious-looking outbound activity.

Vista's outbound firewall doesn't have any of those capabilities. It's as though Microsoft just stopped about halfway along the path toward building a decent firewall. I guess it ran out of money.

I guess you've probably figured out by now that Vista's Windows Firewall isn't a particularly good firewall. If you want a good one, look at ZoneAlarm (www.zonealarm.com).

On the other hand, if you can live with decent protection against the devils outside — and don't mind ignoring the devils within — Vista's Windows Firewall covers the important bases.

This Technique explains key firewalling techniques and then shows you how to poke and prod Windows Firewall. At the end of the Technique, I introduce you to the (so-called) interface that drives the outbound firewall. *"Pleased to meet you. Hope you guess my name."*

Understanding Firewalls

The term *firewall* evokes an image of an impregnable barrier between your computer and the Internet. Alas, in reality, life isn't so simple. A computer firewall is more like a harried cop at a busy intersection than a solid wall.

Although keeping the bad guys out is much more important — that's the function of an *inbound firewall* — after they've jumped over the fence and infected your machine, you have to keep them from spreading their offal through your network (if you have one) and all across the Internet — that's the job of an *outbound firewall*.

If you were infected by a cunning poseur (I won't mention Sony's rootkit by name), or while you had a momentary lapse in Windows Firewall's protection for whatever reason, your PC may have been turned into a *zombie* — also known as a *bot* — so that it operates under the silent control of someone else. Millions, perhaps tens of millions, of PCs have been so subverted. If your firewall doesn't warn you about bad outgoing traffic, you have no way of telling when your PC starts spewing millions of spam messages, or launches a Denial of Service attack on a Web page.

That's why an outbound firewall is important. If you're concerned about not letting the bad stuff out, you need something better than Vista's not even half-hearted attempt at monitoring outbound traffic.

For the home and small office user, firewalls fall into two broad categories:

- ✔ **Hardware firewalls** are built into a box that connects directly to the Internet. Nowadays, all DSL and cable routers, wireless routers, and boxes that handle Internet addresses (see Technique 38) include their own built-in firewalls.

- ✔ **Software firewalls** run on the computer that's connected to the Internet. If you have Vista, you're running Windows Firewall (unless you've disabled it). Windows Firewall does a good job of

playing traffic cop with incoming data. But unless you've changed something, it doesn't even try to catch bad data that's headed out.

Each type of firewall has its pros and cons, as you can see in Table 46-1.

 Blocking bad outbound data isn't merely an exercise in good Internet citizenship. It also adds an extra layer of protection for your own home or office network. A firewall that catches malicious outbound packets tells you whether your PC has been turned into a zombie and is spewing spam or phishing messages or your personal information. It also tells you whether one PC on your network is trying to infect other PCs, retrieve data from them surreptitiously, or use uninfected PCs to break out to the Internet. Attacks are getting more sophisticated every day. If a piece of malware gets in to a specific PC, you should be very concerned about it getting out.

 Every PC should be running a software firewall. In addition, unless you're on the road, you should run a hardware firewall, simply because it adds an independent layer of protection.

A software firewall examines traffic as it leaves your network and goes to the Internet; it also examines traffic from the Internet that's being directed to your network. A good firewall can do the following:

- ✔ **Allow only data into your network that has been requested by someone on your network.** If you ask for a Web page, it appears. But if somebody tries to send something that you didn't request, the unsolicited data gets trashed. The same thing happens on a stand-alone computer: You get only data that you request from the Internet.

- ✔ **Ask you whether it's okay for a specific program to send out data.** That gives you a chance to clear programs such as Firefox (or Internet Explorer) and Trillian (or Windows Live Messenger) that have to send data, but take a look at other programs that may not be so benign.

TABLE 46-1: PROS AND CONS OF HARDWARE AND SOFTWARE FIREWALLS

Type of Firewall	Pros	Cons
Hardware firewalls	Excellent for keeping intruders from getting into your PC or your local network.	Generally don't do much to monitor outgoing traffic (such as data being transmitted by a Trojan that resides, unbeknownst to you, on your system).
	Easy to use.	Hard to set up.
	Run fast.	
Software firewalls	Don't weigh anything — a definite plus if you want a firewall for your portable computer when you're on the road.	Outbound firewalls are more difficult to train because they monitor outgoing traffic; you have to tell the firewall which Internet traffic originating on your machine or network is legitimate so that the firewall can block the rest.
	Easier to customize.	Because software firewalls run on your PC, they slow down your PC whenever you're online.
	After they're trained, they're also easy to use.	

✔ **Block attempts to get at blacklisted Web sites from your network.** If you want to keep everyone on your network from getting at www.IHateBigCompanies.com, you can tell the firewall not to allow any information going out that's bound to that site. It can block other types of outbound traffic as well.

✔ **Make your network (or your computer) invisible to the Internet.** Even if somebody knows your IP address, any attempt to get information from that address is met with silence.

Vista's Windows Firewall scores high on the first point and reasonably well on the last point, but it makes working on the two in the middle excruciatingly difficult. That's why, for all intents and purposes, Windows Firewall rates as a decent inbound firewall but a lost-in-space outbound firewall.

 When you tell Vista that you're connected to a Private network (see Technique 38), Vista applies a set of default firewall settings to the

Windows Firewall. If you switch to a Public network (say, you take your laptop out of your office and connect to the network in an airport, and you tell Vista's wireless connection routine that you're hooking up to a Public network), Vista applies a different set of default firewall settings. That's why your firewall settings may change without your knowledge. Vista protects you — and confounds you at the same time.

Coping with Windows Firewall

The inbound Windows Firewall is relatively easy to modify.

To control outbound firewall activity, you have to dig deep and work through a very difficult interface. See the section "Getting at the Outbound Firewall," later in this Technique, for details.

Checking out the inbound firewall

If you've never looked at Windows Firewall, taking a few minutes right now to look at the high points is worthwhile. Follow these steps:

1. **Choose Start⇨Control Panel and click the Security option on the left.**

The Security window, shown in Figure 46-1, appears.

• **Figure 46-1: The Control Panel Security window.**

2. **Under the Windows Firewall icon, click the Turn Windows Firewall On or Off link.**

Click Continue to go through yet another User Account Control dialog box, and the Windows Firewall Settings dialog box appears.

To understand the precise meaning of each of the three choices on the main firewall dialog box, see Table 46-2.

3. **Click the Exceptions tab (see Figure 46-2).**

 Note that Windows Firewall tells you what kind of network you're attached to — a Private or Public network. Settings on this tab change if you switch from Private to Public or vice versa.

• **Figure 46-2: Programs that are allowed to accept incoming data.**

Windows Firewall allows data packets into your machine only if they were sent in response to a specific request originating on your machine (that's the *stateful* firewall). Exceptions to that rule — either programs, or designated ports (addresses) — are spelled out on this tab, and you can control which exceptions get enforced by checking or unchecking boxes on this tab. I talk about both kinds of exceptions later in this Technique.

4. **Click the Advanced tab.**

Make sure that all the boxes in the Network Connection Settings section at the top are checked. If you uncheck a box, Windows Firewall stops monitoring that connection unless you check the Block All Incoming Connections box on the General tab.

5. **Click OK to get out of Windows Firewall.**

Your changes take effect immediately.

TABLE 46-2: WINDOWS FIREWALL SETTINGS ON THE GENERAL TAB

Setting	What It Means
On (recommended)	Windows Firewall keeps track of requests for information headed out of the computer (for example, requests to retrieve a Web page or download a file) and allows traffic back in only if it can be matched to a specific earlier request. That's called *stateful* monitoring. Windows Firewall allows any exceptions detailed on the Exceptions tab (see the next section). It also monitors all the networking connections that are checked at the top of the Advanced tab.
Block All Incoming Connections	Same as On, but all the entries on the Exceptions tab are ignored and every connection gets monitored, regardless of whether or not it's checked on the Advanced tab.
Off (not recommended)	Turns off Windows Firewall. Anything and everything can come and go.

 If any of the options in Windows Firewall are grayed out, you aren't permitted to change the settings. Usually that happens when you're connected to a Big Corporate Network and somebody has decided that you can't be trusted to control your own computer.

Getting through Windows Firewall

A firewall is a gatekeeper, protecting your computer from other computers that can reach it. Although most people realize that a firewall protects their computer from the big, nasty, wide-open abyss commonly known as the Internet, many people don't realize that a firewall has to protect their computer from other computers on the local network, too.

Windows Firewall is a so-called *stateful* firewall. To a first approximation, that means that Windows Firewall keeps track of what goes out of your computer and allows stuff back in only if it's in response to something that you sent out.

In general, as long as Windows Firewall is working, your computer responds to only three kinds of packets being sent to it, as follows:

- Packets that are in response to something you sent out

- Packets that are sent to a specific program that you put on Windows Firewall's Exceptions list

- Packets sent to specific addresses — called *ports* — that you tell Windows Firewall to ignore

In addition, you can restrict Windows Firewall to allow only packets coming from other computers on your local network — as is the case, for example, with Windows File and Printer Sharing.

Watching a program poke through the firewall

Windows Firewall's job is to keep other computers' stuff from getting into your computer. Unfortunately, in many cases, programs inside your computer need to interact with outside computers to do their job. Windows Live Messenger (which I discuss in Technique 21) is a good example. When one of your contacts logs on to Windows Live Messenger (or the newer Yahoo Messenger, or the Trillian MSN Messenger service), the network sends you a notice that the contact is online. That way, Windows Live Messenger can pop up a little box that says "BillG has just signed in." That notice from the Windows Live Messenger network has to break through the Windows Firewall so that the Messenger can pop up its box.

 Windows Firewall is smart enough to intercept many programs as they first attempt to reach the outside world, and smart enough to ask you whether you are willing to let the program communicate freely with other programs, both on your local network (if you have one) and on the Internet.

If you've never installed Windows Live Messenger, you can watch how the Windows Live Messenger installer pokes a hole through Windows Firewall. Here's how:

1. **Choose Start⇨Control Panel. Under the Security icon, click the Allow a Program Through Windows Firewall link.**

You have to click Continue through a User Account Control message. Then Vista shows you the current Firewall exception settings — a list of all the programs and ports that are allowed to accept data coming into your computer from the Internet.

2. **Scroll down to the bottom of the list so that you can see the entries shown in Figure 46-3.**

 In spite of the wording of the Control Panel link, you aren't actually allowing a program to poke through Windows Firewall. You're just taking a shortcut to the Exceptions tab of the Windows Firewall application. See "Checking out the inbound firewall" earlier in this Technique for an orientation.

3. **Click OK to exit Windows Firewall.**

4. **Go through the steps in Technique 21 to install Windows Live Messenger.**

The first time you attempt to log on, you see the "Windows Firewall has blocked some features of this program" Security Alert.

 Note in particular that the Security Alert dialog box says that you can unblock Windows Live Messenger on Private networks.

5. **Click the Unblock button to poke a hole through Windows Firewall's Private networks settings.**

You need to click Continue through yet another User Account Control message.

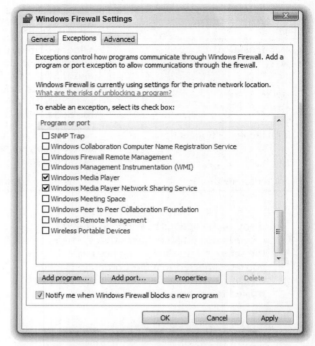

• **Figure 46-3: Firewall Exceptions prior to installing Windows Live Messenger.**

6. **Once again, choose Start⇨Control Panel and, under the Security icon, click the Allow a Program Through Windows Firewall link.**

Once again, you need to click Continue through yet another User Account Control message. Is there an echo in here?

As you can see by comparing Figure 46-4 with Figure 46-3, Vista has poked two new holes through the Windows Firewall, one called Windows Live Messenger, the other called Windows Live Messenger 8.1 (Phone).

The Windows Live Messenger installer is very cavalier about the naming of its Firewall holes, er, exceptions. If you install a version other than 8.1, you may or may not see these two exceptions. You may see more than two. And they may have slightly different names. For example, Windows Live Messenger 8.0 called its Firewall exceptions, simply, "Messenger."

• **Figure 46-4:** Two Firewall exceptions for Windows Live Messenger.

• **Figure 46-5:** Manually poke holes in Windows Firewall here.

7. **Click OK.**

Messenger should be able to accept notices coming in from the Internet.

Making your own firewall exceptions

Here's how to manually modify Windows Firewall to allow a program to receive data sent to it over the Internet, using FileMaker Pro as an example:

1. **Choose Start⇨Control Panel. Under the Security icon, click the Allow a Program Through Windows Firewall link.**

You have to click Continue through yet another User Account Control message, and then the Windows Firewall Settings Exceptions tab appears, as in Figure 46-5.

2. **To put a program like FileMaker Pro on the Windows Firewall Exception list, click the Add Program button.**

Windows Firewall scans a list of installed programs on your computer and comes up with a list of possible programs.

3. **Select the program you want to poke through the firewall. Click Browse to find the program if you don't see it listed. When you're done, click OK.**

Windows Firewall adds the program to its Exceptions list. The program is allowed to accept incoming data from the Internet.

4. **Click OK to get out of Windows Firewall.**

The program can start receiving data immediately.

You can also manually add a port to the Exceptions list, but be extremely cautious when doing so. When you open a port to the Internet, any creepy-crawly piece of garbage trawling the Net may be able to get into your computer. Only open ports when you absolutely have to, and don't leave them open any longer than necessary.

Only add a port to the Exceptions list if a software manufacturer insists — and if you understand the ramifications. Here's how:

1. **Choose Start➪Control Panel. Under the Security icon, click the Allow a Program Through Windows Firewall link.**

You have to click Continue through yet another User Account Control message, and then the Windows Firewall Settings Exceptions tab appears (refer to Figure 46-5).

2. **To put a port on the Windows Firewall Exception list, click the Add Port button.**

Windows Firewall shows you the Add a Port dialog box (see Figure 46-6).

• **Figure 46-6:** Opening a port is risky business.

3. Give the exception a name — preferably a name that reminds you which port you opened — and then type the number of the

port that you need opened. Choose TCP or UDP to conform to the manufacturer's instructions.

TCP and UDP are two different ways of talking across a port. See my *Windows Vista All-in-One Desk Reference For Dummies* for details.

4. **Click OK.**

The port is opened immediately. Don't forget to shut it (uncheck the box next to the exception name) as soon as you can.

I talk about Windows Firewall settings extensively in *Windows Vista All-in-One Desk Reference For Dummies* (Wiley Publishing).

Closing the Inbound Firewall Fast

Every Windows user should be able to lock down the inbound Windows Firewall in a New Yawk minute. If you're using Windows Live Messenger and you think you clicked a dicey link, or if your disk suddenly starts whirring like a tornado's twisting in the box, you're well advised to lock down first, and ask questions later.

Here's the fastest official way I know to tell Windows Firewall to block all incoming traffic:

1. **Choose Start➪Control Panel. Click the Security icon.**

2. **Under the Security icon, click the Check Firewall Status link.**

You have to click Continue to get through a User Account Control dialog box, then you see the main Windows Firewall Settings dialog box.

3. **Check the Block All Incoming Connections box.**

That's Windows Firewall's "lockdown" setting.

4. **Click OK to get out of Windows Firewall.**

Windows Firewall locks down. Finally.

That's a whole lotta clickin', especially if you're feeling a bit panicked.

 Maybe Microsoft will figure out how to make a Fast Firewall Lockdown button for the next version of Windows. Whaddya think? Naw . . .

Getting at the Outbound Firewall

In theory, getting into the outbound side of the Windows Firewall isn't all that difficult.

But in practice, well, the devil's in the details.

Here's how to get into the *sanctum sanctorum:*

1. **Click Start, immediately type firew, and press Enter.**

Vista makes you click Continue through a User Account Control dialog box and then shows you the Microsoft Management Console, with Windows Firewall with Advanced Security (WFwAS) loaded, as shown in Figure 46-7.

• **Figure 46-7: Control the outbound Windows Firewall here.**

Note how WFwAS maintains three separate profiles, one called Domain (to be used when you're attached to a Big Corporate Network), one for Private (associated with the Private network connection type, which incorporates both Home and Office choices), and one for Public (associated with the Public network connection type).

 Also note that, for all three profiles, Outbound Connections that do not match a rule are allowed. In other words, the outbound firewall in Vista is turned off by default.

2. **On the left, double-click the entry marked Outbound Rules.**

Vista shows you an enormous array of outbound rules like the one in Figure 46-8 — none of which matter as long as the outbound firewall is turned off.

• **Figure 46-8: Vista's original crop of outbound firewall rules.**

3. **If you want to create a rule that prevents a specific program from sending data out of your PC, on the right, under Actions, click New Rule.**

Vista's New Outbound Rule Wizard (see Figure 46-9) takes you through the steps to create a rule that blocks a specific program or port.

4. **Unless you're willing to risk completely trashing your computer's ability to communicate, that's as far as you should go. Cancel out of the wizard and choose File➪Exit to exit the WFwAS main dialog box.**

You can find detailed instructions for using this wizard to block Internet Explorer in my *Windows Vista All-In-One Desk Reference For Dummies*.

• **Figure 46-9:** This wizard helps you block specific programs or ports.

I hope that incursion into the outbound firewall convinces you that trying to use Vista's Windows Firewall to monitor outbound traffic amounts to a time sink of the first degree. If you're concerned about controlling outbound communication on your computer, use ZoneAlarm. The predefined outbound rules for common programs, easy identification of outbound traffic, and simple process for creating outbound rules puts ZoneAlarm head and shoulders (and knees and toes) above Vista.

Technique 47

Zapping Scumware

Save Time By

✔ Recognizing scumware — spyware, adware, hijackers, and other lowlifes

✔ Why you can't trust Windows Defender

✔ Getting the scum out

✔ Installing Webroot Spy Sweeper

Scumware's everywhere. Talk about a growth industry.

You have to feel sorry for the folks at Microsoft who deal with the scum. They hit it all the time, both as gatekeepers for scum-attracting services such as Hotmail (which is rapidly morphing into Windows Live Mail) and as regular ol' everyday computer users.

But the 'Softie scum doesn't stop there. In perhaps the worst case of scum-induced time wasting in modern history, the programmers who wrote the installer for Windows XP Service Pack 2 were livid when they discovered that their final release choked on machines that were running a self-described "permission-based contextual marketing network" called T.V. Media (www.totalvelocity.com).

Most people who were running this, uh, contextual marketing network had no idea that the program was installed — and they blamed Microsoft when the Service Pack 2 installer croaked.

Microsoft spent hundreds of millions of dollars on SP2, and this piece of, uh, contextual marketing network software brought the installer to its knees.

And you think you have scumware problems.

 Microsoft has come a long way since that fateful run-in with T.V. Media, most notably creating a scum-busting program called Windows Defender and baking it into Vista. But there are problems with Windows Defender — both by omission and by commission, as I'm fond of saying — and you should not rely on it as your sole defense against scum.

This Technique gives you a quick introduction to scum (as if you couldn't smell it already), steps you through Windows Defender, and then shows you a much better alternative, Webroot Spy Sweeper. Spy Sweeper is one of the few programs I recommend in this book that isn't free.

Unfortunately, unless Microsoft changes its lack-adaisical ways, you need a second scum catcher that tries harder than the free Windows Defender. The $30 for Spy Sweeper is money well spent. You can give it a try and see for yourself.

What Is Scum?

As far as I'm concerned, scumware is in the eyes of the beholder.

To be a leetle bit more specific, *scumware* is a generic term for software that slithers into your system, usually as part of a program that you download and install, but occasionally in the guise of an e-mail attachment. Scumware does annoying things — hijacks your Web browser's home page, keeps track of the things you type or the pages you visit, or pops up ads while you're trying to work. Some types of scumware even download their own updates automatically, without your permission, or "phone home" and deposit information about you on the scumauthor's computers.

Scumware companies frequently call their products "adware," but that's gilding a jet-black lily. It's true that scumware asks before it installs itself on your computer, but frequently the details are buried in hundreds of lines of dense pseudo-legal mumbo-jumbo.

The most successful company in this business, by far, was an outfit that used to be called Gator, which changed its name to Claria. Gator also goes by the acrimonious acronym GAIN — for Gator Advertising Information Network. Remember those names. In my book, they're scumware, and if you're ever given an opportunity to download and install a program that's signed by Claria, uh, Gator, er, GAIN, to coin a phrase, just say No.

In June 2006, Claria claimed to be shutting down the GAIN network (www.claria.com/gainexit) and claimed that it wouldn't collect more data after September 30, 2006. But in the same announcement Claria states, "If you used a GAIN-Supported software

program before October 1, 2006, we may continue to use this previously collected anonymous information in the aggregate." Once scum, always scum.

Microsoft has a detailed discussion of its approach to tackling spyware starting at www.microsoft.com/athome/security/spyware/software/msft/default.mspx.

Knowing When You've Been Slimed

It's pretty hard to define the term *scum* and, as you might imagine, it's even harder to define the term *scumware*. But you can bet that you're looking up the scummy side of the cash cow when

- ✔ Your browser goes bananas. Your home page gets hijacked; IE starts showing you "search" pages that specialize in, uh, barnyard animals with unusual talents, or it suddenly sports a new toolbar, or you get redirected to pages that don't match anything you ever typed.

- ✔ You start getting pop-up ads on your desktop and you aren't even using a Web browser, or you get pop-ups that have nothing to do with the site you're visiting. Yes, they often reference barnyard animals with unusual talents.

- ✔ You have a firewall that monitors outbound traffic (such as ZoneAlarm; see Technique 46) and it keeps warning you that some program you've never heard of is trying to send data out to the Internet. Moo.

If you think you've stepped in it big time, quickly skip to the sidebar, "Using Webroot Spy Sweeper," later in this Technique, to download and run Spy Sweeper.

Using Windows Defender

Microsoft's Windows Defender comes built into Vista. You get it whether you want it or not.

Understanding the problems with Defender

Technically, Windows Defender does a good job of protecting against scumware. Because it's built into the operating system, it has the inside track.

The problems with Windows Defender aren't technical. They're organizational.

Microsoft has an intricate method for determining how scummy a program might be. You can see the details at

```
www.microsoft.com/athome/security/spy
ware/software/msft/analysis.mspx
```

 Problems arise, though, when the results of a Windows Defender scan don't match industry observers' expectations. The, uh, cognitive dissonance came to a head in mid-2005 when researchers discovered that an earlier version of Windows Defender (then known as Windows AntiSpyware) told users to "ignore" detected Claria/Gator/GAIN scum. About the same time, rumors circulated that Microsoft was looking to buy Claria (www.betanews.com/article/MS_Claria_Buyout_Talk_Sparks_Concern/1120148264).

This much I know for sure:

✔ Microsoft has, in the past, made highly controversial recommendations about programs that many experts consider to be scum, including programs from Claria/Gator/GAIN, WhenU, eZula, TopText, and New.net.

✔ The scummy companies change so often that you need a scorecard of scorecards to keep track. For example, on June 7, 2006, Hotbar and 180solutions — two companies that figure prominently on many scum lists — merged to form Zango.

✔ It's horrendously difficult to determine, on any given day, which products Defender blocks. For example, in Figure 47-1, Defender correctly warns against installing the notorious Smiley Guys Screensaver from Zango, a week after the U.S. Federal Trade Commission announced a proposed $3 million settlement against Zango.

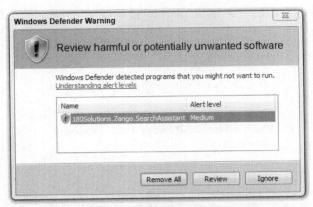

• **Figure 47-1: Windows Defender warns against installing Zango's Smiley Guys Screensaver.**

Unfortunately, Windows Defender places the Smiley Guys Screensaver Alert Level at Medium — quite an understatement for a program that actively spies on what you're doing, hijacks your home page, phones home with Web surfing details, "periodically upgrades automatically," sticks an advertising-laden toolbar on your browser, and displays "several ads per day based upon keywords from your Internet browsing."

✔ Microsoft doesn't publish a list of which products, and which companies, trigger Windows Defender's ire. Good reasons exist for not divulging the precise "bad" list. But given Microsoft's track record, the lack of a definitive list makes it all the more difficult to judge whether Windows Defender does what the scumbusters figure it should.

 Of course, you should use Windows Defender — it's free, it's there, and it does a good job on the products that it catches. But unless you trust Microsoft to keep your best interests at heart, Windows Defender should count as only part of your scum-slaying arsenal.

Removing scum with Defender

Windows Defender runs all the time, scanning for scummy infestations. If you allow scummy programs into your computer, though — for example, by taking the "Medium" alert level in Figure 47-1 at face value and allowing Smiley Guys Screensaver to install itself — Defender may not be able to protect you from yourself.

Here's how to run a Windows Defender scan manually:

1. Choose Start⇨All Programs⇨Windows Defender.

The Windows Defender home screen appears, as shown in Figure 47-2.

• **Figure 47-2: Windows Defender's status report is based on last night's scan.**

 Defender runs only once a day. If you install scummy software and then bring up Defender, it shows the results of only the last scan. It's entirely possible that you could have scummy software on your computer, even if Defender says No Unwanted or Harmful Software Detected.

2. For a quick scan, click the Scan icon.

If you want a thorough scan, click the down-arrow to the right of the Scan icon and choose Full Scan.

Defender comes back with a scan report.

3. If anything untoward appears, click the Review Items Detected by Scanning link.

In this case (see Figure 47-3), Defender reports that 180Solutions.Zango.Sear... has added numerous files plus 41 registry keys, including an

entry in the Windows RUN key, so it runs automatically each time Windows starts.

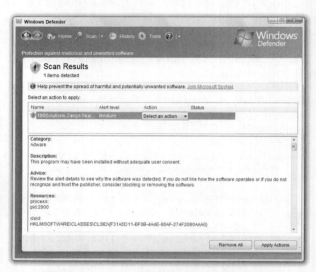

• **Figure 47-3: The report on Smiley Guys Screensaver.**

4. Scroll to the bottom of the Category list and click the View More Information About this Item Online link.

Internet Explorer coughs on the Zango scum. You have to click the Allow button if you want to see Microsoft's More Information page. When IE finally gets through, you see the Malicious Software Encyclopedia entry from 180Solutions.Zango.SearchAssistant (see Figure 47-4). Note how the Threat Overview states that the scum is not circulating, even though it had been downloaded minutes earlier from the Zango Web site.

5. Click X to exit Internet Explorer.

You return to the Windows Defender report (refer to Figure 47-3).

6. Under Action, click the down-arrow next to Remove and choose Quarantine.

It's always safer to quarantine, just in case removing the piece of scum causes other programs to crash.

• **Figure 47-4: This scum watches words on Web pages that you open so that it can deliver targeted advertising.**

7. **Click the Apply Actions button.**

Defender goes out to lunch for a while. When it comes back, Defender reports that it succeeded in quarantining 180Solutions.Zango.SearchAssistant, as shown in Figure 47-5.

8. **Click X to exit Windows Defender.**

 You might want to reboot your computer to make sure all the bad stuff got zapped.

A post-mortem note: After going through all of the preceding steps to quarantine 180Solutions.Zango. SearchAssistant and then rebooting, the first time I started Internet Explorer I was treated to the Zango toolbar, and IE wouldn't start until I finally clicked Allow in response to the message in Figure 47-6.

 I finally got rid of the scum by choosing Start➪Control Panel and, under the Programs icon, clicking Add or Remove Programs. I clicked Zango, answered the uninstaller's

questions, rebooted the computer, and now 180solutions.Zango.SearchAssistant appears to be gone. I think. Windows Defender didn't get rid of it. But the manufacturer's uninstaller did.

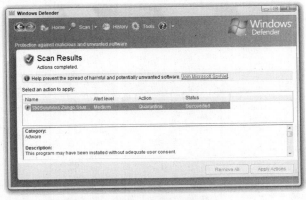

• **Figure 47-5: Successfully quarantined.**

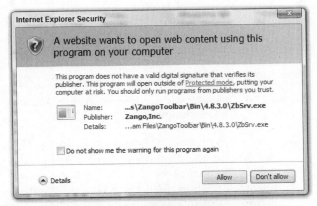

• **Figure 47-6: Even after quarantining with Windows Defender, Internet Explorer still won't start until I click Allow.**

Kinda makes you feel all warm and fuzzy inside, doesn't it?

Running the other parts of Defender

You might find it instructive to poke around Defender a bit. After you start it (choose Start➪All Programs➪ Windows Defender), you can do the following:

✔ Click the History icon to bring up a list of all the Defender actions that were taken by you, or automatically on your behalf.

Don't get too upset by the log. As shown in Figure 47-7, for example, Defender records the fact that it allowed the driver for my USB wireless modem to run.

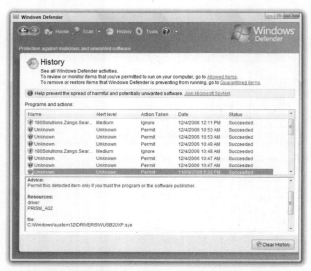

• **Figure 47-7: Defender was watching when I installed my USB wireless modem.**

✔ Click the Tools icon and then the Microsoft SpyNet link. Microsoft wants you to sign up for SpyNet, but you might balk when you learn how much information about you will be collected and sent back to Microsoft's giant database.

Although it may sound exciting (hey, where's my secret decoder ring?), SpyNet is quite intrusive. Although I believe that a case can be made for enabling Internet Explorer's antiphishing tool (which I talk about in Technique 18), the benefits of SpyNet aren't nearly as clear cut.

✔ Click the Tools icon and then the Software Explorer link. From that point, you can bring up a list of programs that are automatically run when you start Windows, all the currently running programs, network connected programs, and programs that hook into your

Winsock communication protocol (see Figure 47-8). I talk about controlling the Startup Programs list in Technique 3.

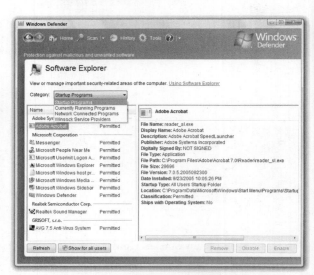

• **Figure 47-8: Windows Defender's startup program blocker catches most programs that start automatically.**

By all means, use Windows Defender. To get a second, independent opinion, see the sidebar.

Using Webroot Spy Sweeper

Spy Sweeper, a product from Webroot Software, Inc., has consistently topped the reviews for its ability to identify and remove all types of scum. The company itself has been in the forefront of antispyware research for many years, with a fearless stand against big scummy companies all over the globe. Spy Sweeper works well with Windows Defender. It offers an excellent second opinion. The only downside? Although you can download a trial version first, the product isn't free. It costs $30 for one year, or $40 for two.

To get your own copy of Spy Sweeper — or try the free version — go to www.webroot.com and follow the links for "Anti-spyware protection."

Technique
48

Checking Your Security Perimeter

Save Time By

✔ Running automated checks to see whether your firewall is working

✔ Finding and plugging holes (before someone else plugs them for you)

✔ Using common sense to increase your network security

✔ Considering BitLocker

A while back I got a call from an old friend who seems to frequently bump into very interesting security problems. My friend was helping a guy set up a home/small office network — and a good one. He spared no expense, and it showed.

That evening, the guy's adolescent daughter was startled to see a message pop up on her PC that was filled with venomous, sexually explicit epithets directed specifically at her. Whoever was responsible for the lessons in vulgar vernacular also transmitted a couple of compromising pictures.

On closer examination, we found that the pictures were fakes and that the attacker was probably known to the family and hiding behind a newly created, virtually untraceable free e-mail account.

In a situation like this, do you need to check your security perimeter? Oh, yes indeed.

 Microsoft's executives love to talk about "trustworthy computing" and how the latest version of Windows can set our minds at ease. Sorry, but I see precisely the opposite: While the technology gets more restrictive with each passing year, the security threats become more pernicious and more time consuming.

You can sit back and hope that your computer won't get clobbered. Far better, in my opinion, is to take a proactive stance and see where your tail is hanging in the wind.

If you don't do it, some cretin is bound to do it for you.

That's what this quick Technique is all about: taking a hard look at your security defenses and figuring out how to protect your system better.

Approaching Your Security Perimeter

If you've followed the steps in Techniques 44 through 47, your computer is all ready for anything the world (or at least the Internet) can throw at it.

Right?

Well, yes and no.

The fact is that you'll never be completely prepared for everything. New threats are surfacing every day. Some of them use old methods that your existing security settings should be able to withstand. Some of them come from out of the blue.

That's why checking your PC and the way that you run your network is important. It's important not because you'll be 100 percent certain that no intruder can ever appear, but because there's a good chance you can do a better job with the tools at hand.

Running Steve Gibson's ShieldsUp!

Steve Gibson's Gibson Research Corp. (www.grc.com) has been protecting PCs since hard drives were powered by little fuzzy chipmunks running in circles. He used to stand next to banks of hard drives and yell, at periodic intervals, "Spin left! Spin right!"

Sorry, Steve. Couldn't resist.

Steve's ShieldsUp! is widely considered to be the granddaddy of all firewall tests. Yes, more probing tests are available. But none of them match the easy-to-use style and no-nonsense explanations of ShieldsUp!.

Besides, it's free.

You should run ShieldsUp! every time you make a major change to your firewall.

To run ShieldsUp!, follow these steps:

1. **Start your favorite Web browser, go to grc.com, and click the ShieldsUp! banner.**

2. **Scroll down the page a bit (Steve always has some interesting projects going) and click the ShieldsUp! link.**

ShieldsUp! checks your IP address to see whether it's listed in a reverse domain name table. As you can see in Figure 48-1, my IP address isn't associated with any particular Web URL.

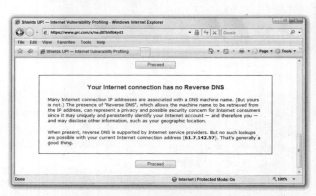

• **Figure 48-1: My IP address flies under the URL radar.**

3. **Click the Proceed button.**

Steve's Port Authority Edition appears.

4. **Click the File Sharing button.**

ShieldsUp! tries to hook up to IIS, an Internet server that should be blocked. It also tries to "ping" port 139, a common trick used by scanners to find computers attached to the Internet. Finally, it tries to wiggle into NetBIOS, an obsolete (and insecure) communication protocol.

Unless you've made security-busting changes to your computer, you should come up with a clean bill of health, as I did in Figure 48-2.

5. **Scroll down the page and click the Common Ports button.**

You get a second report that discusses port blocking. Every one of your tested ports should show "Stealth" status.

6. **If the Common Ports test tells you that an important port is open, you need to reconfigure Vista's Windows Firewall to block it. Check Technique 46 for details.**

You can change Windows Firewall settings, click the Back button in your Web browser, and have ShieldsUp! run the test again.

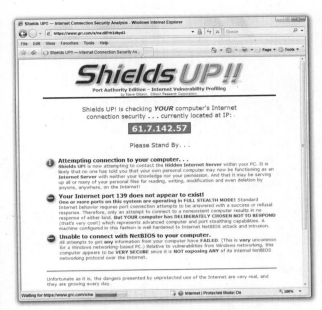

• **Figure 48-2: The major holes are plugged.**

When Vista and Windows Firewall are set up properly, you should get an absolutely clean bill of health.

Just a word or two about ports

At the risk of oversimplifying, a port is a lot like a telephone extension number. If you want to talk to somebody in a big office, you pick up the phone and dial the office's main number. (That's more or less analogous to the computer's IP address; see Technique 38.) After you connect to the switchboard, you need to dial the person's extension. Similarly, after you connect to a computer on the Internet, you have to connect to one of the programs inside the computer.

Each program listens to a specific port or group of ports. So if your PC connects to port 80 on the computer with an IP address of 208.215.179.139, you end up talking to the Web server (which listens to port 80) on `www.dummies.com` (which is at 208.215.179.139). Any rogue cracker on the Internet who tries to get into your machine has to go through a port. The Common Ports test (see Step 5 in the "Running Steve Gibson's ShieldsUp!" section of this Technique) "calls" all 65,535 ports on your PC (or on your router, if you have one) and tells you whether any of them are vulnerable to an outside attack.

Running Microsoft's Baseline Security Analyzer

Microsoft has a tool that examines your system to see whether any important security patches are missing or any obvious security exposures are hanging in the wind. Whereas Steve Gibson's ShieldsUp! probes from the Internet inward (see "Running Steve Gibson's ShieldsUp!," earlier in this Technique), the Microsoft Baseline Security Analyzer looks from the inside out.

The Baseline Security Analyzer goes through your Vista machine and checks most of its major components for missing security patches, gaping security holes, and little nit-picking things that you probably never knew existed (or didn't exist, as the case may be).

To run the Baseline Security Analyzer, follow these steps:

1. **Start your favorite Web browser and go to**

> `www.microsoft.com/technet/security/`
> `tools/mbsahome.mspx`

Make sure that you get the latest version of MBSA (see Figure 48-3). Older "legacy" versions won't work with Vista.

2. **Follow the instructions to download the MBSA program.**

You probably want the English version. The link is at the bottom of the page.

3. **When the download is complete, double-click the icon and follow the wizard to install the program.**

You have to click to get through various security messages. Take all the defaults.

4. **Double-click the icon to start MBSA.**

Again, you get to click through security messages. Ultimately, you see the main screen.

• **Figure 48-3: The MBSA home page.**

5. **Click Scan a Computer and then click Start Scan.**

MBSA produces a very detailed report of potential security exposures (see Figure 48-4).

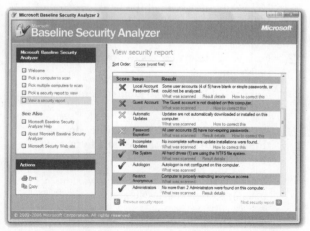

• **Figure 48-4: The MBSA report gives you much insight — but may err on the side of too much security.**

6. **Review the report for real vulnerabilities.**

For example, the report for my production machine identified several vulnerabilities that I don't consider to be problems: Not having passwords on most accounts, for example, doesn't cause me any heartburn. And I don't care to enable automatic updates, thank you very much (see Technique 44). Still, the report is worthwhile, and you should consider any exposures it identifies. If you need tips about the source of the problem or possible solutions, click the How to Correct This link.

 MBSA leaves a lot to be desired because of its infuriatingly convoluted terminology. But it's a powerful self-help utility that every Vista user should stick in his or her bag of tricks.

A bit about BitLocker

If you have Windows Vista Enterprise or Ultimate, you may be interested in using the BitLocker feature, which encrypts an entire drive. That way, even if someone steals your computer (or so the theory goes), the thief won't be able to look at the data on the drive.

BitLocker performs as advertised and does so with a minimum of time-consuming overhead. But it's a pain in the neck to set up — and if you lose the key, heaven help ya.

The trick to setting up BitLocker? You have to form two partitions on the main hard drive, and only one of the two actually gets, uh, BitLocked. The other is a 1.5GB partition that holds key BitLocker files.

If you want to try BitLocker, check out Mark Minasi's description of the commands and incantations necessary to bring it to life at www.minasi.com/newsletters/nws0611.htm.

Part IX

Keeping Your PC Alive

The 5th Wave   By Rich Tennant

"How's the defragmentation coming?"

Running Disk Chores While You Sleep

Save Time By

- ✔ Getting rid of disk dreck
- ✔ Scheduling the cleanup to run automatically
- ✔ Adjusting automatic defrag to run after cleanup

Windows Vista includes a scheduler that runs programs automatically, according to criteria you provide. Want to run the Calculator at 8:00 every Monday morning? Piece o' cake. Want to play "We Will Rock You" every Friday afternoon at 5:00? If you've got the MP3, Vista's got the moxy.

There's a big difference between the Task Scheduler in Vista and the older Windows Scheduler in Windows XP: The one in Vista actually works.

Imagine.

Right out of the box, Vista's Task Scheduler is set up to run a defrag every week at 1:00 on Wednesday morning. It's fast and easy, and you don't have to do a thing.

Vista *doesn't* automatically clean up your hard drive — take out the trash (er, empty the Recycle Bin), delete temporary files, and the like — prior to running a defrag. Why? Because no two people can agree on what should be deleted and what should be left in place. I have no problem if my Internet Explorer cache files go bye-bye on Wednesday mornings, but you may get upset if IE browsing goes slower on Wednesdays. I don't mind getting my Recycle Bin cleaned out every week, but my dad might lose something worthwhile.

This Technique steps you through running a Disk Cleanup and saving your settings. Then I show you how to use Task Scheduler to schedule a cleanup run. Finally, I demonstrate how to adjust the schedule for running a defrag so that you can have the two run back to back.

When you have the procedures in place, you may never have to think about your hard drives again.

Until they start screeching and smoking, anyway.

Fragging Fragmentation

As files on your disk get older, they start falling apart. Something like that.

Fragmentation occurs because Windows divides your hard drive into boxes, called *segments,* that store files. Initially, all the segments on your hard drive get marked as being available for data.

When Windows needs room for a new file, it calculates how many segments are required, figures out which segments are available, divvies up the data into segment-sized pieces, and then writes the segments out to disk.

If Windows needs only part of a segment, it uses the whole segment anyway, and part of the segment "box" is left empty.

When Windows deletes a file or a part of a file, it doesn't actually delete anything. It simply determines which segments are no longer needed and marks those segments as being available for use.

When Windows needs more room for a new file (or an old file that's getting bigger), it calculates how many segments are required, grabs available segments, divvies up the data into segments, and writes the segments out to disk.

Sooner or later, your hard drive starts to look like a checkerboard, with pieces of files scattered all over the place.

Diskeeper, the company that Microsoft turns to when it needs defragmenting help, has an excellent overview of fragmentation and its causes at `www.diskeeper.com/diskeeper/tour.index.html` (see Figure 49-1).

Defragmenting a hard drive involves sifting through all the scattered pieces and reassembling them so that each file (more or less) sits in adjoining segments — with all the boxes stacked next to each other. That arrangement minimizes the amount of time Windows needs to take when it retrieves a file.

It also opens large blocks of free space so that new files are less likely to become fragmented.

Here's the rub: You really should delete files you don't need *before* you run a defrag. That way, the defragmenter can reclaim space for the files you want.

Disk Cleanup and Defrag go together like a horse and carriage. Or dogs and fleas. You get the idea. Read on.

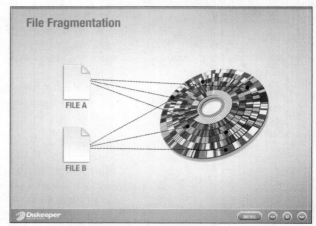

• **Figure 49-1: The Diskeeper multimedia display of a truly fragmented drive.**

Running a Disk Cleanup

If you want to schedule regular automatic runs of Disk Cleanup, getting its settings straight is important.

When you run Disk Cleanup, you tell it what kinds of files you want to clean up — er, delete. If you run Disk Cleanup manually (by choosing Start➪ All Programs➪Accessories➪System Tools➪ Disk Cleanup), the program scans your disk and tells you how much space you can save by deleting specific kinds of files (see Figure 49-2).

If you want to run Disk Cleanup automatically with the Vista Task Scheduler, you need to establish which kinds of files get deleted every time Disk Cleanup runs. In other words, you have to establish the settings for the cleanup run.

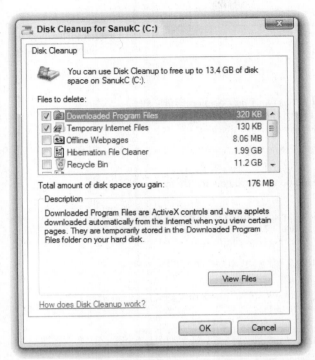

• **Figure 49-2: Disk Cleanup has you specify what kinds of files it should delete.**

There's a very weird method for establishing Disk Cleanup settings. It involves a command line switch — straight from the Days of DOS (trademark pending). If you're into retro, this is just about as retro as Vista gets.

Here's how to save a bunch of Disk Cleanup settings so that they can be reused:

_1._ Choose Start and then immediately type cleanmgr /sageset:3 **and press Enter.**

This action tells Vista to bring up the Disk Cleanup Settings dialog box, which tells you to enter whichever settings you like and then save your settings as set "3." You can use any number you like between 0 and 9. Don'tcha just love the old-style command lines?

It's important that you type a space before the slash in `cleanmgr /sageset:3` but leave no other spaces on the line.

You have to click Continue to get through a User Account Control dialog box. Then Vista brings up the Disk Cleanup Settings dialog box shown in Figure 49-3.

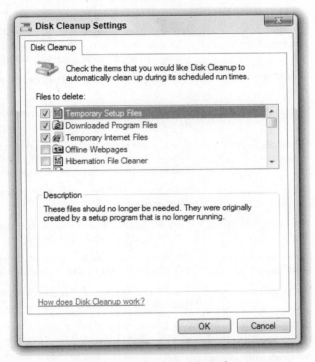

• **Figure 49-3: The Disk Cleanup settings that you want to save.**

_2._ Select the boxes next to the types of files you want to delete.

Use Table 49-1 as a guide. Don't be too surprised if your PC has a list that's slightly different from the one in Table 49-1; the list appears to vary depending on what software is installed.

Keep in mind that if you set Disk Cleanup to run weekly, all of these files will disappear, every week.

_3._ Click OK.

Vista saves your settings as number "3."

TABLE 49-1: CHOOSING WHICH FILES TO CLEAN

Type of File	Contains	Check This Type to Delete These Files?
Temporary Setup Files	Vista and other Microsoft setup files.	✓
Downloaded Program Files	ActiveX controls (used to be called OLE files) and Java applets. Typically these are small programs downloaded from the Internet. They work with "custom" applications: games, Web file viewers, and the like.	✓
Temporary Internet Files	Cached pictures and pages from Internet Explorer (not Firefox).	✓
Offline Web Pages	Pages that are downloaded automatically so that you can see them without being connected to the Internet.	
Hibernation File Cleaner	If you want to reclaim the hibernation file space (which is as big as your system's memory, perhaps 1GB or 2GB), don't check this box. Instead, follow the instructions in the sidebar "Zapping hibernation."	
Debug Dump Files	If Dr. Watson (Microsoft's crash reporting tool) wanted the files, he'd have 'em by now.	✓
Old Chkdsk Files	Lost fragments of files that all the king's horses and all the king's men would never be able to put back together again.	✓
Previous Windows Installations	System files and folders from previous versions of Windows. Chances are good you'll never be able to recover them anyway.	✓
Recycle Bin	I never delete Recycle Bin files automatically. If you're ready to get rid of your old files, delete the files manually by going into the Recycle Bin.	
Setup Log Files	Log files generated when Vista was originally installed.	✓
System Error Memory Dump Files	More Dr. Watson files that you'll never want.	✓
System Error Minidump Files	Ditto.	✓
Temporary Files	Anything in a Temp folder.	✓
Temporary Windows Installation Files	If the Vista installer didn't clean up after itself, these are still sitting on your disk.	✓
Thumbnails	The thumbnail files that sit inside every folder. Save time by keeping them.	
Files Discarded by Windows Upgrade	The Vista installer puts files that it doesn't recognize in a specific location. Unless one of the users on your machine lost files during the upgrade to Vista, you can delete these.	✓
Various Windows Error Reporting Files	More Dr. Watson–style files.	✓

A, uh, Word of warning: Office 2003 sticks hidden installation files in a folder called `\MSOCache` on your hard drive. If you use Disk Cleanup to delete the files, you may trigger very strange error messages. The Office security patch installers should be smart enough to realize that the installation files have been deleted, but on at least two separate occasions, Office 2003 patches have had bugs that stumble on missing installation files. So if you see a line called Office Setup Files in the Disk Cleanup list, don't check the box.

Zapping hibernation

Vista reserves a very large place on your hard drive for a hidden file called `c:\hiberfil.sys`, the Hibernation file. Whenever your system goes into hibernation, a copy of the PC's memory gets written to that file. Thus, `hiberfil.sys` is as big as your system memory. If you have a 2GB machine, that's a sizable chunk.

If you're using a desktop PC that's never allowed to sleep (check the power settings by clicking Start, immediately typing **power**, and pressing Enter) and you want to get back that disk space, you can use Disk Cleanup to turn off hibernation (and thus sleep) mode. To do so, follow the three steps at the beginning of this section to run Disk Cleanup manually, making sure that you check the box marked Hibernation File Cleaner. Checking this box turns off hibernation and deletes `hiberfil.sys` from your hard drive.

If you ever want to reenable hibernation, choose Start⇨All Programs⇨Accessories, right-click Command Prompt, and choose Run as Administrator. Click Continue through the User Account Control warning. Then type **powercfg -h on** and press Enter. Vista doesn't give you any confirmation that the command "took," but your system should have a new, hidden system file called `c:\hiberfil.sys`.

Scheduling Disk Cleanup

So you've run the procedure in the preceding section and you now have a bunch of Disk Cleanup settings called "3."

That isn't quite as exciting as being "Number 6" in the last two episodes of *The Prisoner*, but never mind. . . .

 With the settings called "3" in hand, you're ready to set up Task Scheduler to run Disk Cleanup on a regular basis. Here's how:

1. **Make sure that you're using an Administrator account with a password and that you know your password!**

You may think that you can set up a task without a password, but the task won't run unless you have one!

2. **Choose Start⇨All Programs⇨Accessories⇨System Tools⇨Task Scheduler.**

You have to click Continue through a User Account Control message; then the Microsoft Management Console appears with the Task Scheduler plugged in.

3. **In the Actions pane, click Create Basic Task.**

The Task Scheduler brings up its Create Basic Task Wizard, as shown in Figure 49-4.

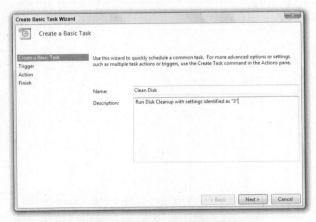

• **Figure 49-4: Create a task to run Disk Cleanup.**

4. Type a name for the task and a description if you like; then click Next.

The wizard asks you how often you want to trigger the task.

5. Assuming that you want to clean your disk weekly, prior to the defrag run, select the Weekly option and click Next.

The wizard asks you to set the time.

6. Choose a time that you feel comfortable with and click Next.

If you set Disk Cleanup to run on, say, Wednesday mornings at 12:30, that gives Cleanup plenty of time to finish before the automatic defrag kicks in at 1:00 a.m.

The Task Wizard asks you to specify which action you want to perform.

7. To run a program, select the Start a Program option and then click Next.

The wizard wants you to pick a program and set its parameters — specify the commands and switches to send the program — as in Figure 49-5.

• **Figure 49-5:** It's important that you type the commands quite precisely.

8. In the Program/Script text box, type cleanmgr and then, in the Add Arguments (Optional) text box, type /sagerun:3 and click Next.

The /sagerun:3 argument tells the cleanmgr program to use the settings established as collection "Number 3." Don't include any spaces. We're talking DOS-style command lines, and they're notoriously unforgiving.

The wizard finishes with a summary of the task that you've constructed.

9. Select the Open the Properties Dialog for this Task When I Click Finish check box and then click Finish.

The wizard shows the properties for this new task, as shown in Figure 49-6.

10. Select the Run Whether User is Logged On or Not option and then click OK.

Task Scheduler asks you to type in a password for this task.

• **Figure 49-6:** The properties for the full task.

11. Type your regular, old, everyday Vista logon password; then click OK.

Task Scheduler appears again, with your new task ready to run.

When the appointed time arrives, Disk Cleanup runs. The cleanup looks like Figure 49-7.

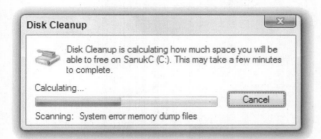

• **Figure 49-7:** An automatically scheduled run of Disk Cleanup in action.

• **Figure 49-8:** The run history for Vista's built-in Defrag task.

Checking Up on Scheduler

At times, you may wonder whether your scheduled tasks ever run. I have gone for months thinking that my scheduled tasks were running fine when, in fact, password problems kept them from running at all.

If you ever want to know the full story about your tasks and what they are (or, more likely, aren't) doing, follow these steps:

1. **Choose Start➪All Programs➪Accessories➪ System Tools➪Task Scheduler.**

You have to click Continue to get through a User Account Control message.

2. **Find the task that you want to check.**

In Figure 49-8, I double-click in the left pane to navigate down to the Microsoft built-in Defrag run, which is in Task Scheduler Library\ Microsoft\Windows\Defrag.

3. **In the lower pane, click the History tab.**

Task Scheduler takes a while to scan all the history logs but eventually produces a list of times that the task was run and how (or if) it was completed.

Adjusting the Timing of Defrags

In general, you can use the Task Scheduler to revise the times any specific tasks run. The preceding section shows you how to get at the task. After you see a task, double-click its name, click the Triggers tab, click Edit, and go from there.

In the specific case of Vista's scheduled weekly defrag runs, though, a much simpler and faster way to alter the schedule is available. You might want to change the schedule so that the defrag runs early Monday morning — or any other time that's best for you.

Here's the fast way to change the scheduled defrag run's schedule:

1. **Choose Start, immediately type** defrag, **and press Enter.**

You have to click Continue through a User Account Control message, but you end up with the Disk Defragmenter on your screen, as shown in Figure 49-9.

2. **Click the Modify Schedule button.**

Vista brings up the Modify Schedule dialog box, as shown in Figure 49-10.

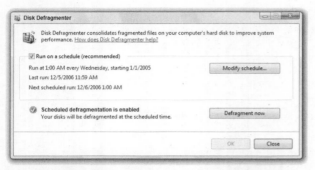

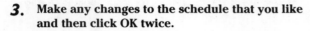

• **Figure 49-9:** The pretty face on the scheduled Defrag run.

3. **Make any changes to the schedule that you like and then click OK twice.**

Your schedule change shows up in Task Scheduler, too.

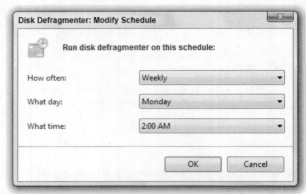

• **Figure 49-10:** Changing the Defrag schedule here is much easier than futzing with Task Scheduler.

Technique 50

Running Periodic Maintenance

Save Time By

- ✔ Buying all the supplies you need in one fell swoop
- ✔ Cleaning on schedule
- ✔ Dealing with spills and stuck CDs
- ✔ Using common tools to get the job done

Ever lost ten minutes looking at a special can of computer monitor cleaner, wondering whether you really need it? Ever open your computer to discover three inches of caked-on gunk clogging the air inlets?

Maintenance is a pain. It takes time, and you know that if you let your teenager (or the housekeeper) try to clean something, it'll take you a half hour to go back and fix it. Still, it has to be done. Otherwise, the inside of your computer will remind you with a bout of spontaneous combustion, and your mouse will start smelling like a dead rodent.

This Technique takes you — quickly! — through the steps necessary to keep your beast alive.

Making Your Maintenance Shopping List

Everything you need to keep your PC in tip-top shape is in this list:

- ✔ Cotton swabs (Q-Tips or something similar)

- ✔ Little balls of cotton

- ✔ Paper towels (good, thick ones — the kind that don't fall apart)

- ✔ Rubbing alcohol (isopropyl alcohol, or isopropanol — they're all the same thing)

- ✔ Glass cleaner

- ✔ If you have a floppy disk drive, you need a disk (just any old floppy disk that's lying around)

- ✔ If you have a disk drive, you also need stamp collectors' 6-inch, round-tip stamp tongs (see the section "Pulling out a stuck disk," later in this Technique) — nope, tweezers and needle-nose pliers don't work as well, unless they're very long and thin

✔ Compressed air

✔ Small pocketknife

✔ A small computer tool kit with screws, screw-drivers, jumpers, and all those little things that seem to get swallowed whenever you open the case

✔ CD lens cleaner (looks like a CD but cleans the CD/DVD lens)

 Make a copy of this list and run through it the next time you go shopping.

Weekly Cleaning

If you're thinking of cleaning each component of your computer, one by one, you're working too hard. Instead, use each cleaning tool once and move from component to component in cleaning phases.

 Set up your computer-cleaning schedule to coincide with your regular house cleaning. That way, you kill two — or five or ten — birds with one stone.

Here's an overview of your weekly cleaning drill:

1. Vacuum.

2. Dust.

3. Clean monitor screens.

4. Ungunk the mouse and its feet.

5. Check the floppy drive if you have one.

I discuss each of these tasks in more detail in the following sections.

Vacuuming strategies

Haul out your vacuum cleaner. (You do that to clean your office anyway, right?) Using the smallest attachment you can find — one of those crevice cleaners works great — vacuum the living daylights out of the following computer components:

✔ **Keyboard:** Unplug the keyboard. Turn it upside down and shake it. Look for loose keys that might be consumed by the vacuum cleaner. If the keys are all hooked on, vacuum every nook and cranny. Turn the keyboard upside down again and repeat once or twice. Finally, shoot compressed air into all the corners and then vacuum again.

✔ **Monitor:** If you have a traditional big monitor, turn it off. Vacuum all those holes in the case to get rid of the dust. Bonus points if you can get at the dust inside. You lose all points, and may go literally down in flames, if anything is obstructing the flow of air into and out of the casing. No, don't open up the casing. Sheesh. You could get electrocuted. Vacuum the base of LCD/flat-panel monitors.

✔ **The computer itself:** Shut down Windows and turn off the power. Then vacuum every single place you can reach. Use your hand to block the largest air intakes so you get maximum suck where you need it most. Push the button to open your CD/DVD drive and vacuum. If you have a disk drive, stick your finger in the drive, push the little flap back or up (depending on the kind of drive), and vacuum like crazy.

✔ **Peripherals:** Turn off your printer, scanner, modem, DSL box, UPS, power distribution bar, network hub, external drives, and everything else, and vacuum, vacuum, vacuum.

 I've tried using many variations on the small vacuum cleaner, but I haven't found anything that works as well as a plain, small, everyday household canister vacuum cleaner with a crevice tool.

Dusting tips

After you vacuum, pull out a cleaning rag and wipe off the plastic case on your computer, the back of the monitor, the printer, the outside of your scanner, the tray on your CD drive that holds the CDs, and any other plastic that's literally sitting around gathering dust. Don't use any cleaners. If some gunk is stuck to a piece of hardware, use a little water and rub gently. If it's still stuck, add a bit of soap and rub gently.

If it's still stuck, get a universal solvent like Goo Gone (www.magicamerican.com/googone.shtml) and go for it. Yeah, I know you aren't supposed to use solvents on plastic cases. But if you're trying to get off tape residue, you don't have much choice. If you use a solvent, make sure you're in a well-ventilated area, and make sure your Aunt Mildred doesn't light up a cigarette while you're in the middle of cleaning.

Cleaning screens

How you clean your screen depends on whether you're using an old-fashioned, full-sized, TV-style monitor or have a flat screen. The working end of a monitor is glass. The panel of an LCD screen is a special kind of plastic. They aren't the same, and they don't clean the same:

Never touch a monitor — a traditional monitor, LCD flat screen, or portable screen — with your finger. Cleaning the smudgy oils in human skin isn't always easy.

✔ To clean a glass screen: Spray or pour a small amount of plain, old, everyday glass cleaner onto a good-quality paper towel.

Don't spray the screen; the cleaner can fall into the electronics. Gently rub down the screen; then rub the glass with a dry piece of paper towel.

I know, I know. You're supposed to use a lint-free cloth to clean a screen. Poppycock. I've been using paper towels for years and I've never seen a scratch yet. In fact, I seem to get the best results with old newspapers. But I don't have the guts to say that in a big book like this. Heh, heh, heh.

✔ To clean a flat-panel screen, including the screen on a laptop: Put a bit of rubbing alcohol (isopropanol) on a ball of cotton. Rub very gently, following quickly with a clean ball of cotton. That's how the manufacturers clean the displays as they leave the assembly line.

I *have* scratched an LCD screen with a paper towel. Use cotton. And don't use a commercial screen wipe unless it specifically says that it works with an LCD. I like to use alcohol preps, which you can buy for a pittance at any medical supply store.

✔ To clean a scanner: Scanner beds are glass, as are monitor screens, and you clean them the same way. But you have to be excruciatingly careful not to let any of the glass cleaner leak over the edges. After the cleaner has dried on the underside of the bed, it takes a screwdriver and a lot of patience to clean things up.

Ungunking the mouse

Nothing drives me nuts faster than a jumping mouse.

Cleaning a mouse involves four steps:

1. **Clean the mouse pad.**

People tend to overlook this vital first step. If your mouse gets dirty, where does the dirt come from? D'oh. Slick, shiny pads are best cleaned with your fingernails. (You can wash them if you must.) Bumpy mouse pads need only a shake. And if you use your desktop for a mousepad — yech. You eat there, don't you?

2. **Clean the gliders.**

The gliders are those little plastic things on the bottom of the mouse that the mouse moves around on. Use your fingernails. If a recessed area is around the gliders, clean the gunk out of there with a toothpick or a knife.

3. **Clean the working part.**

If you have a roller mouse, unplug it first. Flip it over, open the cover, and take out the ball. Wipe off the ball with a paper towel and a little bit of water. Set it aside to dry. Inside the cavity, use a small knife to scrape the big crud off the metal and plastic rollers (many mice have two metal rollers and one plastic roller).

No need to scrape hard, because the rubbing alcohol picks up anything that remains.

Flip the mouse over and pop it against the base of your hand to get the big junk out. Then clean all the rollers with cotton swabs, each dipped in rubbing alcohol. Make sure you rotate the rollers. Blow everything out, reassemble, and you're back in business.

If you have an optical mouse, use rubbing alcohol and a cotton swab or cotton ball to clean the eye. Make sure you don't leave any cotton behind.

4. **If you have a wireless mouse, check the signal.**

Each manufacturer is different, but to check the batteries in a Microsoft mouse, choose Start⇨ Control Panel, click the Hardware and Sound icon, and then click Mouse. If you see a Wireless tab, click it. You see icons for battery status and for signal strength. If the batteries are shot, replace them with cheap NiCads. If the signal strength seems poor, move the base around.

I have a fancy, expensive Microsoft wireless optical mouse, and I used to hate it. Why? At first, it kept clicking those weird side-keys (Microsoft calls them "thumb" keys) for me, even when my fingers were miles away. So when I was working on a Web page and moved my mouse up and to the left, CLICK! The mouse told Internet Explorer that I wanted to go back to the previous Web page. I thought the mouse must have been dirty — even when it was new — so I spent ages trying to clean it. Nope. Ultimately, I disabled the thumb keys using the mouse dialog box, and now I can tolerate the mouse. Barely. I still haven't found a wireless mouse that I really like.

Checking the floppy drive

You can buy a floppy drive cleaning kit if you really want, but few people use floppies frequently enough these days to accumulate much build-up on the recording heads.

Instead, floppies usually die from neglect. Air gets sucked into the PC through the floppy opening, dust builds up, and sooner or later you can't put a disk in or take it out.

That's why I recommend that you simply stick an old disk in the floppy drive every week, make sure you can read it (choose Start⇨Computer⇨3 1/2 Floppy), and then take the disk out.

If your disk gets stuck, see the advice on recalcitrant floppies at the end of this Technique.

Monthly Cleaning

If you keep up with the weekly cleaning, my recommended monthly cleaning comes easy:

1. **Clean the CD/DVD lens.**

You need a special lens cleaner for this, but you can buy one at almost any electronics place and even many grocery stores. It's just a regular CD with a brush (or brushes) attached to the shiny side.

Some manufacturers would have you believe that there's a difference between CD cleaners and DVD cleaners. If there is, I sure can't figure it out. Save yourself some time and money and just get a cheap CD cleaner.

2. **Clean the keys on your keyboard.**

I use my keyboards hard. (Love those old Northgates and Omnikeys.) If you do, too, I suggest you remove the gunk from around the keys once a month. To do so, start with a handful of cotton swabs. Unplug the keyboard (or turn off your laptop, if you're cleaning a laptop). Slowly, carefully, dip a swab in a little bit of rubbing alcohol. Clean around the keys.

Cleaning the keys is tricky (and time-consuming) because you don't want to spill any rubbing alcohol down into the innards of the keyboard.

But keeping the keys clean does prevent big globs of hair and dirt from falling into the keyboard, which makes it well worth the effort.

3. **Clean the inside of your printer.**

Every printer is different. Laser printers usually have a brush stuck on a plastic mount somewhere. Learn how to use it. Check the manufacturer's Web site for details.

Fixing Components As Needed

Here's what you need to know about fixing the other parts of your PC.

Cleaning CDs and DVDs

If a CD or DVD won't work and you have a CD cleaning kit handy, you have it made.

But what if you don't have a cleaning kit handy? Do what I do: Take your CD into the shower with you. Use a little bit of hand soap, lathered in your hands, lightly applied to the shiny side of the CD. When you get out of the shower, use a soft, clean towel and wipe the shiny side from the middle of the CD toward the outside. If you don't have a soft towel, dry your hands and use toilet paper.

Works like a champ — on eyeglasses, too.

Recovering from spilled coffee or soda

Have you ever spilled a latte on your keyboard? Yech. What a mess.

 If you have a run-of-the-mill cheap keyboard, and it stops working after you anoint it, throw it away. Isn't worth the effort.

But if you have a good keyboard — good keyboards are worth their weight in gold — here's how to try to bring it back to life:

1. **Don't panic.**

You can usually bring a good keyboard back — if you're patient.

2. **Disconnect the keyboard.**

3. **Turn the keyboard upside down. Let it sit that way for a few hours.**

4. **Take the screws off the back of the keyboard and pop off as much of the plastic as you can — but leave the keys attached.**

Taking them off is an absolute last resort.

5. **Using a washcloth that's been slightly moistened, clean up as much of the spilled junk as you can.**

You don't want to get more water into the electronics, but most spilled stuff — coffee, soft drinks, fruit juice — responds well to a warm bath.

6. **Pull out a handful of cotton swabs and, using rubbing alcohol, dig into the nooks and crannies.**

That gets out the stuff that's adhered to the grease inside the keyboard before the spill.

7. **Reassemble the keyboard and give it a go.**

Usually that's enough to get it working again.

If you can't get the keyboard to work, you may have to resort to pulling off all the keys. Here's how:

1. **Take a snapshot of the keyboard, or write down the location of all the keys.**

It can save your hide. No kidding.

2. **Take the screws off the back and pull off as much plastic as you can.**

The less plastic, the easier it is to remove keys.

3. **Remove each key cap carefully by pulling it straight up.**

Use extreme caution when taking off the spacebar, the Enter key, and any oversized keys. Frequently, these keys have a spring or a lever that can't be bent.

4. If you can see any electronic contacts, clean them with cotton swabs lightly dipped in rubbing alcohol.

Many keyboards have completely sealed electronics, so trying to clean them is an exercise in futility.

5. Clean the key caps in the kitchen sink and dry them thoroughly.

They're just plastic.

6. Carefully put the key caps back on the way you took them off.

I know. It's much easier said than done.

7. Test the keys before you put the plastic back on.

Almost always, you'll find one that doesn't feel right. Figure out what's wrong with it before the plastic gets wrapped around it.

8. Put the plastic back on and try it out.

Good luck.

The general procedure for a laptop is more drastic — but your chances of bringing a laptop back to life are slim indeed:

1. Turn the laptop off. Remove the battery.

If it's plugged into the wall, unplug it. Electricity is not your friend.

2. Turn it upside down — quickly — and pour off as much of the liquid as you can.

3. If you spilled anything but water into the laptop, take an amount of fresh water equal to the amount you spilled, turn the laptop back upright, and pour the water right on top of the original spill.

You need to rinse off the sugar, coffee, hops . . . whatever.

4. Turn the laptop upside down again and pour off everything.

5. If it's easy to take off the case, do so. If not, don't sweat it.

6. Set the portable upside down on a couple of stacks of books or magazines.

Make sure air can get all around it.

7. If you have air conditioning, turn it on. (AC lowers the humidity in the room.) If you have a fan, aim it toward the laptop. If you have a hair dryer with a "No Heat" setting, blow it into every ventilation slot.

8. Let it dry for at least 24 hours.

Don't put the battery back in or try to start it for at least that long.

9. Reassemble it, turn it on, and pray.

 Remember that coffee can't get into your hard drive, at least not very easily, so even if you lose your portable, you almost certainly haven't lost your data. Unless your portable decided to go for a swim in the pool, of course. That could have a deleterious effect on your hard drive's life expectancy.

Pulling out a stuck disk

As your floppy drive gets older, it starts eating disks. The cause of the problem isn't the drive *per se*. The real problem is the piece of metal on the disk that slides away, revealing the recording surface. If your drive gets a bit dirty, it probably has a hard time putting that slider back in place — and that's why the disk won't come out.

A tool that's absolutely perfect for pulling stuck disks out of sticky drives is a stamp tong. Any kid with a stamp collection can show you one. Philatelists use tongs so that they don't leave dirt and oil from their fingers on their stamps. A good picture of one is at `www.globalstamps.com/tongs.htm`.

When a disk gets stuck, you have to work the stamp tong down into the drive deep enough to release the pressure on the metal slider. Follow these steps:

1. **Shut down Windows and turn off the computer.**

2. **Push open the drive cover with your finger.**

3. **Work the stamp tong back and forth until you feel the disk ease out.**

    You feel a definitive "push" when the slider goes back in place and the disk drive's spring nudges the disk out.

 How to find a stamp tong? Walk into any stamp shop (or most hobby shops) and ask for a round-tip six-inch stamp tong. It should set you back about five bucks. Cheap insurance.

Pulling out a stuck CD

Although getting a disk out of a floppy drive is hard, removing a stuck CD is almost always very easy. Follow these steps:

1. **Shut down Windows and turn off the computer.**

2. **Take a paper clip and unbend it.**

3. **Stick the tip of the paper clip in the little hole at the front of the CD drive. You may have to push just a little bit.**

    No, I'm not talking about the speaker jack. There's a little hole that's just big enough for a paper clip. Look harder.

That's all it takes.

Technique

51

Requesting Remote Assistance

When Remote Assistance works, it's great. Say you're chatting with a friend in Windows Live Messenger and she wants to know how to set up Vista to show filename extensions. (Smart lady.) You can type, type, type, and take her through all the steps. But that's slow and boring. Far better: She clicks Ask for Remote Assistance. You accept. All of a sudden, you're working on her computer while she watches.

And she can terminate the session at any time by pressing the Esc key.

Nothing is faster or better than watching while your problems get solved. If you have a knowledgeable friend who can spare a few minutes — even if your friend lives halfway around the world — and you're both using Vista, you have all you need to solve the problem and find out how the solution works so that you don't need to bug your friend in the future.

 Many people need to use Remote Assistance between Vista and Windows XP machines, but there's a hitch. If the person asking for advice (I call that person the *novice* in this Technique) is running Vista, he or she can get help from anyone running either Vista or Windows XP. But if the "novice" is running Windows XP, the person giving advice (the *guru* in my parlance) has to be running Windows XP. In other words, if you're asking for help, Grasshopper, and you're running Windows XP, the person who gives you help can't be running Vista; your guru has to be using Windows XP.

You'll be pleasantly surprised to know that, with that one exception, few problems occur in going from one version of Windows to the other. The Windows XP version of Remote Assistance supports voice. The Vista version doesn't — you gotta pick up the phone if you really want to talk. Vista lets you pause a session (take a time out with no interaction). Windows XP doesn't.

Remote Assistance running on Windows XP didn't work all the time — it had trouble poking through firewalls and working around various kinds of routers. Vista's Remote Assistance overcomes many (but not all) of those problems.

If you ever wanted to save time, Remote Assistance does it in spades.

Using Remote Assistance Wisely — Quickly

Remote Assistance (RA) rates as one of the best timesaving features of Vista. Rather than dwell on when to use RA (answer: almost anytime you can!), I can tell you that RA doesn't work in these cases:

✔ **If you have a problem that crashes Windows.** As soon as your system crashes, RA goes down with it, and your friend is disconnected. To get RA working again, you have to go through the entire cycle of inviting her to help, accepting the invitation, and so on (see "Requesting Remote Assistance," later in this Technique).

✔ **If you have a problem with a video driver.** Chances are very good that any "artifacts" you see on your screen — weird lines or shading or streaks that appear and disappear mysteriously — won't show up on your helper's screen.

✔ **If you have an intermittent problem.** If you can't reliably replicate your problem, you're only wasting your friend's time. To make matters worse, some problems that occur reliably when RA is not running suddenly clear themselves up when you have an RA connection going. Blame gamma rays and sunspots.

In most other situations, if you can get RA to work, it's a tremendous timesaver.

Coping with Remote Assistance Limitations

Here's what you need to run Remote Assistance:

✔ If the person requesting assistance (the *novice*) is running Vista, the person who gives help (the *guru*) can use Vista or Windows XP. On the other hand, if the novice is running Windows XP, the guru must also be running Windows XP.

✔ If the novice has a dial-up connection, he or she has to stay connected continuously from the time the invitation goes out until the Remote Assistance session ends.

✔ Both of you undoubtedly have a firewall turned on. You should double-check and make sure that Remote Assistance is allowed to poke through the firewall.

In Vista, to make sure your copy of Windows Firewall lets Remote Assistance break through, choose Start➪Control Panel, click the Security icon, and click the Allow a Program Through Windows Firewall link. Make sure the Remote Assistance box is checked (see Figure 51-1).

Just because you open your firewall to allow Remote Assistance connections doesn't necessarily mean that RA can connect. Many variables are involved, and hardware or software firewalls can gum up the connection in many different areas.

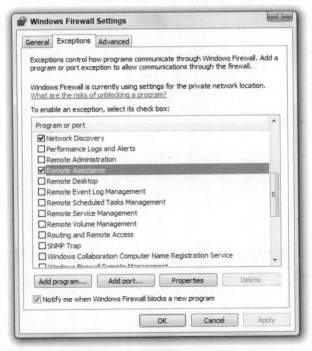

• **Figure 51-1: Windows Firewall must be set to allow Remote Assistance to poke through.**

Don't get your hopes up until you get Remote Assistance to work.

Requesting Remote Assistance

You can ask a friend to help you in one of three ways:

✔ **Windows Live Messenger** (or MSN Messenger or Windows Messenger): This is the easiest option for communicating your need for Remote Assistance. You just start a conversation with your friendly local guru, click a couple of buttons, and Remote Assistance kicks in.

✔ **Send e-mail:** You send an e-mail message. Your friend clicks a link in the e-mail message, and the Remote Assistance session starts. This approach is problematic if you have a dial-up modem or if you're moving around while working with a wireless connection. The invitation that you send to your friend by e-mail is valid only for as long as you remain connected. If you disconnect from the Internet for any reason, or change your connection to a different wireless access point, when you come back on, the invitation won't work.

✔ **Send a file:** This approach is a real pain in the neck but is sometimes the only way that works. You create a file that contains an invitation for Remote Assistance. You then send the file to your friend — perhaps attached to an e-mail message, but you can also send it over a local network or even on a USB key disk. Your friend double-clicks the file, and the Remote Assistance session starts.

Sending a Remote Assistance SOS Using IM

To ask for help via Windows Live Messenger:

1. **Make sure you're using an Administrator account or that you know the ID and password of someone with an Administrator account on your computer.**

   I know it doesn't make sense that you, as a novice, must have an Administrator account in order to let someone help you, but them's the rules.

2. **Log on to Windows Live Messenger.**

   You can also use MSN Messenger or Windows Messenger.

   If you don't have Windows Live Messenger, be sure to follow the timesaving and privacy protecting approach detailed in Technique 21.

3. **Initiate a conversation with your guru — the person who will help you.**

   In Figure 51-2, Duangkhae starts an IM conversation with me and asks me for help. I suggest we use Remote Assistance.

• **Figure 51-2: Start a conversation with your guru.**

4. When you're ready to let your guru see your computer, click the Activities icon (the one that looks like a strip of film with superimposed musical notes); then, in the Share Fun Activities list, choose Request Remote Assistance.

The guru receives an invitation to connect to your computer. The guru clicks the Accept link or presses Alt+C.

You, in turn, receive notification that the guru has accepted (see Figure 51-3) and you are asked to provide a password.

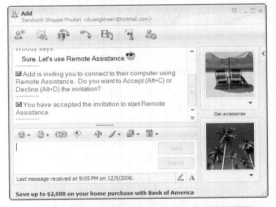

• **Figure 51-3: The novice creates a password.**

5. Enter a password and then enter it again to confirm; click OK.

 At this point, you must communicate the password to the guru. Do NOT send the password via Windows Live Mail. Pick up the phone, for heaven's sake.

The guru receives a prompt to enter the password, as shown in Figure 51-4.

• **Figure 51-4: The guru types in the password.**

6. The guru types in the password and clicks OK.

You receive a confirmation message similar to
```
Would you like to allow askwoody@
hotmail.com to connect to your
computer?
```

7. Click Yes.

Finally, finally! The Remote Assistance session starts.

You (the novice) see the Windows Remote Assistance control window shown in Figure 51-5.

• **Figure 51-5:** The novice continues in full control of the RA session, with a control window.

The guru sees your entire desktop, with his or her screen displaying a set of tools at the top, as shown in Figure 51-6.

• **Figure 51-6:** The guru sees all of the novice's desktop, along with his or her own tools at the top of the window.

In the normal course of events, the guru clicks the Request Control button in the upper-left corner of the Remote Assistance window.

You see a control request similar to `Would you like to allow askwoody@hotmail.com to share control of your desktop?`

8. Unless you're extremely concerned about the guru's abilities (in which case, you should both be asking yourselves why you bother with RA in the first place), select the Allow [your guru] to Respond to User Account Control Prompts box. Then click Yes.

You, the novice — *not* the guru — receive a User Account Control prompt. This is Vista's analog to Alice in the looking glass, but . . .

9. Click Continue when you see the User Account Control prompt.

If the novice simply waits long enough, Vista assumes that the novice *wanted* to click on the Continue button and grants access to the guru.

If you're using a Standard account, you must supply an Administrator's ID and password.

With all the hurdles cleared, your guru can take control of your computer.

Either the novice or the guru can terminate the session by clicking the appropriate icon or pressing the Esc key at any time.

If you want to ask for help by e-mail or by sending a file, look at my *Windows Vista All-in-One Desk Reference For Dummies* book (published by Wiley).

Fine-Tuning Remote Assistance

If you can get it to work, Remote Assistance is one of the best timesaving features in Vista. It does have some limitations, though. A few points worth noting:

✔ Remote Assistance is a one-way street. The guru can see the novice's computer, but the novice has absolutely no way to see the guru's computer. So if you're the guru, you don't need to worry about the novice snooping around your machine.

✔ Remote Assistance exposes everything to the guru. The guru can even make changes to the Registry, which means that you should never invite anyone but a highly trusted friend to help you with Remote Assistance. If you select the Allow . . . to Respond to User Account Control Prompts box (and you should) during a Remote Assistance session, your guru can do anything you can do, short of logging off and logging back on again. If you don't understand what's happening, don't hesitate to press the Esc key.

✔ Both the novice and the guru can control the same mouse pointer and can press keys simultaneously: If the novice and guru both start typing at the same time, the keys they type appear on-screen, interspersed with each other. If both move their mice at the same time, there's no telling where the cursor goes. If one of you doesn't back off, pandemonium results.

 If you can get Remote Assistance to work for you, it's an enormously powerful tool — one of the best reasons to use Vista and/or Windows XP, in my opinion.

Technique

52

Getting Help Fast

Save Time By

- Using Windows Help and Support the smart way

- Creating shortcuts to Help topics — and sending them to friends

- Finding real answers to really vexing questions

Many people get to Vista's Help and Support Center, type a keyword, click a bunch of links, and come away frustrated.

In some cases, that happens because the content in Help and Support Center leaves much to be desired (see the examples in this Technique). In other cases, it happens because you have to know the answer to your question before you can, uh, find an answer to your question.

But in many cases, you probably feel frustrated because the Help and Support Center doesn't work the same as the rest of Windows. Sure, Help and Support has plenty of tools, but they're hard to find and they don't do what you would expect a multi-billion-dollar support system to do. You can't open multiple copies of the Help and Support Center. It has no tabs, no Favorites, no way to keep several topics visible at the same time, and no way to easily navigate from one place to another, except by using the built-in links, which frequently don't go where you want to go. It's slow as molasses, even with a reasonably fast Internet connection.

Besides, when you're sitting in the Help and Support Center, you want help about something that's going wrong — not help about Help, if you know what I mean.

Take a few minutes to figure out how to handle Help, and you can use your newfound knowledge to save yourself loads of time. This Technique shows you how. Quickly.

This Technique also includes previously undocumented information about locating, saving, and navigating to individual Help articles. You have to go to Microsoft's Help Web site, but when you get the hang of it, you can save, bookmark, and send pointers to Help articles in a flash.

The Help and Support Center isn't the only game in town — particularly when you're trying to fix something, and you can't get past the ol' Microsoft Party Line. Fortunately, some non-Microsoft options are worth turning to. In this Technique, I show you some of those, too.

Exploring the Help and Support Center

Think of Vista's Help and Support Center as an ancient version of Internet Explorer, but with all the things that make IE easy to use taken away. That's how I think of it, anyway.

Searching for Help rarely goes as easily as you might think. The other day I wanted to find out how to switch between Vista's two different CD file formats. Windows Media Player wanted to burn my CD in "Mastered" (also known as ISO) format; I wanted to switch to "Live File System" (also known as UDF) format. Microsoft uses the terms "Mastered" and "Live File System" throughout Vista. These sound like good terms to search for, right?

Well, no. You can see the results of my search in the steps that follow. Here's how to search for Help:

1. **Choose Start⇨Help and Support Center.**

The Help and Support Center main window appears, as shown in Figure 52-1. Your main page may look a little different because some hardware manufacturers jimmy the main Help page to add references to their own sites.

2. **Type your search topic in the Search box and press Enter.**

In this example, I typed `live file system` and pressed Enter.

Help searches the massive Help database on the Web and puts together its 30 best results for the query, as shown in Figure 52-2.

3. **Scan the results and click the one that seems to be the best match.**

Looking at the list in Figure 52-2, I see only one entry that seems to have anything to do with the Live File System. It's the sixth entry, entitled `Live File System (definition)`. I click link number six and get the result in Figure 52-3.

• **Figure 52-1: The Help and Support Center main window.**

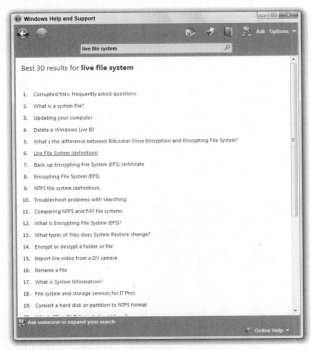

• **Figure 52-2: Help's best matches on** `live file system`.

• **Figure 52-3:** This is the very best help I found on Live File System.

Unfortunately, the definition in Figure 52-3 tells me exactly nothing that I want or need to know, and it gives me no clue where or how to search for the information that I need.

 I should have looked in the index to this book, but nevermind.

4. **If you come up empty, click the Back button in the upper-left corner and try using the Help and Support system's index. Click the Browse Help icon — the one that looks like a blue book, up at the top.**

You can click to drill down into the index. I tried that, as you can see in Figure 52-4, and I'll be hanged if I could find anything about switching from Mastered to Live File System before a burn by going through the index.

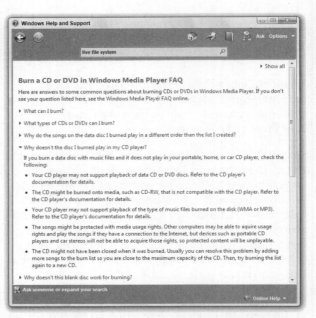

• **Figure 52-4:** Drilling down through the index brings no enlightenment.

5. **If all else fails, click the Home icon to return to the main search window (refer to Figure 52-1).**

6. **Try searching for different terms. Try to avoid the temptation to throw your computer out the window.**

In this case, I remembered that "Live File System" is, in fact, a Microsoft euphemism for UDF format. I finally figured out that by searching for UDF, I could find some information about Mastered and Live File System formats (see Figure 52-5).

 Windows works in strange ways. The Windows Help and Support page you see in Figure 52-5 appeared as a result of searching for UDF — but the term UDF doesn't appear anywhere on the page. Help articles include hidden metadata that help speed searches — but they're inconsistently applied and enormously confusing. I guess some things were never meant to be understood.

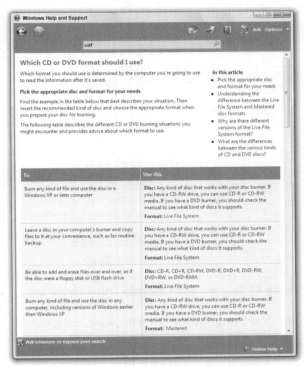

• **Figure 52-5: I didn't get an answer, but at least I got an explanation.**

No, I never found an answer to my question. But by searching for UDF, at least I saw some entries about the topic at hand.

To this day, I don't know how to switch from Mastered (ISO) to Live File System (UDF) format before burning a CD in Windows Media Player. The only work-around I've found involves inserting the CD into the drive and using AutoPlay to select a different format (which messes up Windows Media Player's detection and ultimately ends with WMP telling me that the drive is already in use — long story). That's why you won't find a cool tip in this book about switching CD formats from inside Windows Media Player: If it's possible to switch, Microsoft didn't bother to document it.

Hey, if I get frustrated with this %$#@! Help system, I can only imagine how frustrated you might feel.

Using Help Effectively

Here's what you need to know about Vista's Help and Support Center:

- ✔ **The Search scanner "adapts"** based on what you've searched for in the past. If you type a set of keywords, the 30 best results you get right now will almost certainly be different from the 30 best results you get an hour from now.

- ✔ **Most Help articles are on the Web,** located at windowshelp.microsoft.com. You can get directly at the articles on the Web — and you can use more sophisticated search tools than the ones built into Vista. More about that in the next section.

- ✔ **You can search for terms (by using Find) inside Help articles.** Press Ctrl+F or click the Options button and pick Find (On this Page), and an Internet Explorer Find dialog box appears (see Figure 52-6). It works the same as Internet Explorer Find.

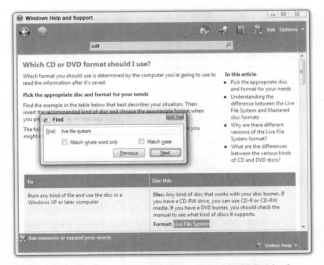

• **Figure 52-6: You can search for text inside individual Help articles.**

The Help and Support Center has no Favorites or bookmarking capability. If you want to bookmark a page, bring up the Help article you want in your Web browser and then use the browser's ability to keep track of your pages.

Saving and Retrieving Help Articles — Quickly

Vista's Help and Support Center ties directly into Microsoft's Windows Help site on the Internet. If you know the trick, you can move directly from a Help article to the same article on the Web. When you're on the Web, you can bookmark the article, save its address (URL), bring up multiple articles at the same time — everything that you can do with Firefox (or Internet Explorer) can be done with Help articles.

E-mailing a Web address is particularly useful because it's very, very hard to tell another Vista user how to get to a specific Help article.

To find a specific Help article on the Web, follow these steps:

1. **Find the Help article that you want to immortalize.**

In this example, I start with the Which CD or DVD Format Should I Use article, shown in Figure 52-5.

2. **Right-click in the body of the article and choose View Source.**

Yes, you need to look in the "source" — the HTML — behind the article. You should see a mass of gobbledygook like that shown in Figure 52-7.

3. **Look for the article's 36-character ID number. It's immediately after text that looks like this: `mshelp://windows/?id=`. Select that text and press Ctrl+C to copy it to the Windows Clipboard.**

In Figure 52-7, I select `2af64e60-60aa-4d79-ab6c-3a5db5806cbe1033` and copy it to the Clipboard.

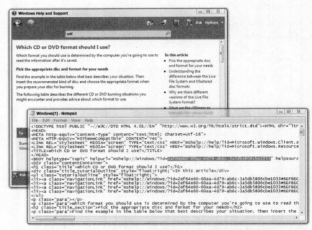

• **Figure 52-7: Underneath the Help article sits the key.**

4. **Start your favorite Web browser and go to the site**

`windowshelp.microsoft.com/Windows/en-US/Help/`

followed by that 36-digit ID number and then `.mspx`.

In Figure 52-8, I use Firefox to go to (hold your breath now) the following:

`windowshelp.microsoft.com/Windows/en-US/Help/2af64e60-60aa-4d79-ab6c-3a5db5806cbe1033.mspx`.

In fact, the page on the Web isn't precisely the same as the Help article — for one thing, Microsoft uses nonstandard formatting on its Web page, so some of the boxes look a little funny in Firefox. There's a navigation bar on the left on the Web site. But the content's identical.

5. **From that point, you can use the Web site any way you would use a "normal" Web site. For example, you can**

▶ Bookmark the site/Help article.

▶ Open a new tab with the site/Help article. (Hint: Ctrl+click to follow a link and put it in a new tab.) You can't do that in Windows Help and Support.

▶ Copy the address and put it in an e-mail message.

▶ Drag a shortcut to the site/Help article onto your desktop.

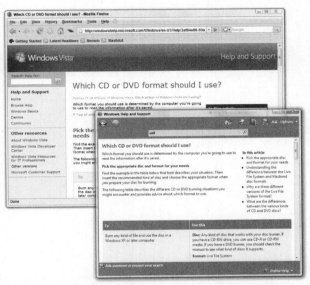

• **Figure 52-8: Sunuvagun. There's the same article, this time on the Web.**

 Someday, Microsoft might make doing simple things with Help easy. Until then, you can take your Help meanderings into your own hands.

Using Other Help Sources

What if the Help and Support Center falls short on help and support?

 Of course, I believe that the first two resources you should turn to for Vista help should be this book and *Windows Vista All-in-One Desk Reference For Dummies* (published by Wiley). But then, I'm a bit biased.

Other sources of accurate, free information:

✔ **Microsoft's Knowledge Base,** `support.microsoft.com`: The ultimate repository of the Microsoft Party Line — but a tremendous source of information, nonetheless.

✔ **AskWoody,** `www.AskWoody.com`, of course: All-volunteer, all the time, with some of the nicest people on the Web. We can't answer every question we get, but we sure do try!

✔ **Brian Livingston's WindowsSecrets Newsletter,** `www.WindowsSecrets.com`: Brian has an uncanny ability to track down some of the most important issues facing Windows consumers and offers many alternatives that most of us overlook. Editor Fred Langa (who's been writing about Windows as long as I have) and, ahem, yours truly, provide useful fodder from time to time.

✔ **Neowin,** `www.neowin.net`: An extraordinarily insightful group of Windows reporters and enthusiasts who have repeatedly changed the course of computing. Frequently the first source of important Windows news.

✔ **Ed Bott's ZDNet blog** (`blogs.zdnet.com/Bott`) and **Mary Jo Foley's All About Microsoft blog,** `blogs.zdnet.com/Microsoft`, carry news, opinions, and rumors about Vista and Microsoft. They, too, have influenced the course of Windows history. Good stuff.

 All these sites do an outstanding job, and they're all free.

Part X

Fast (Nearly Painless) Disaster Recovery

The 5th Wave · By Rich Tennant

"Our automated response policy to a large company-wide data crash is to notify management, back up existing data and sell 90% of my shares in the company."

Making Backups — Fast

Save Time By

- ✔ Choosing the right kind of backup — the first time
- ✔ Knowing a backup's limitations
- ✔ Getting the settings right
- ✔ Using a better backup program

Microsoft's studies reveal that the percentage of Windows users who routinely back up their data runs in the low single digits.

I bet Microsoft would find that the percentage of backup users who recently lost hard drives is in the very high double digits.

Backing up data is like brushing your teeth. If you don't do it, they (your teeth, that is) turn yellow and rot. Or something like that. You have to back up your data. Disks die. It's a cold, hard fact of life.

Vista's backup capabilities run rings around the backup systems in every earlier version of Windows. The Bard would call that "damning with faint praise" because, to a first approximation, the backup programs in earlier versions of Windows didn't work.

Come to think of it, they didn't work to a second approximation, either.

Although Vista's backup works, it suffers from all sorts of incongruous constraints. You can waste all sorts of time trying to figure out how to get Vista to back things up the way you want to back them up — and in the end you'll find that it can't be done, no way, no how.

Vista includes three very different kinds of backups, each of which is completely independent of the other — different programs, different ways of running, different interfaces. Actually, the only thing that all three have in common is the fact that they back up data.

Depending on which version of Vista you use, you may have one kind of backup, or all three.

So what's to like about Vista's backup? Plenty. Whole-drive file backup is drop-dead simple — you can have full backups running in just a few minutes. File backup uses plain, old-fashioned zip files for the backup format, so you can poke around in a backup (using any computer) and unzip the backed up files that you need. In addition, if you have Vista Business, Enterprise, or Ultimate, the Complete PC Backup will create a "ghost" of your entire hard drive, and you don't need to pay for the Norton utilities.

This Technique gives you the quick course.

Using Different Types of Backup

Vista has so many different kinds of backup that it's hard to keep track of them.

Here are the major programs, what they do, and how they do it:

✔ **File Backup.** When most people talk about backing up a computer, they mean backing up their data files. Microsoft's official name for that function is File Backup, although in different places it's also called File and Folder Backup, or the Back Up Files Wizard. Vista's File Backup can run in two different ways:

▶ *Full backups* copy all the selected files. They occur the first time you back up your data; whenever you manually run a backup; and occasionally (according to a formula buried deep inside the program) when Vista figures you need a full backup.

▶ *Incremental backups* copy only changed files. When Vista runs an automatic backup (typically once a week), you usually get an incremental backup.

 Vista uses zip files for File Backup — a commendable decision because your backed-up data can be viewed, sliced, and diced just the same as any other zipped data.

If you have Vista Home Basic, you can perform only manual backups, and you can back up only to "local" drives; if you have a network, with Home Basic, File Backup won't let you put a backup on network drives. With Vista Home Premium, Business, Enterprise, or Ultimate, you can schedule backups, and you can stick the backup in any networked folder accessible to your PC.

✔ **A CompletePC Backup and Restore** image (sometimes called a System Image) is a "ghost" — a bit-by-bit copy — of an entire hard drive. Er, volume. CompletePC Backup is available only in the Business, Enterprise, and Ultimate

versions of Vista — you Home users need not apply. If you burn the image on a DVD or several DVDs, you can boot from the DVD and restore an entire hard drive directly.

CompletePC Backup works completely independently of File Backup.

✔ **Shadow Copies** (also known as Previous Versions) lets you bring back earlier versions of a file that may be deleted or screwed up in some other way. Shadow copies are available only in Vista Business, Enterprise, and Ultimate versions. Shadow copies are stored on the same hard drive as the original, so they won't protect you if your hard drive suddenly does a belly dive.

 To access a shadow copy of a file, navigate to the file, right-click, and choose Restore Previous Versions. If you decide to restore a previous version of a file, make sure that you work with a copy, and don't overwrite the screwed-up version until you're sure that you have salvaged all the data. I talk about shadow copies extensively in *Windows Vista All-In-One Desk Reference For Dummies* (published by Wiley).

✔ **System Restore Points** back up and restore Registry settings, drivers, key system files, and shadow copy files. Restore Points are completely different from File Backups and CompletePC Backups. Every version of Vista creates a System Restore Point every day. You also get automatic Restore Points before most programs and drivers get installed. I talk about System Restore Points in the next Technique.

✔ **Windows Live OneCare Backup** is completely different from any other Vista backup program. In contrast to Vista's File Backup, in which you can take backups and get at the zipped files from any other computer, you must be running Windows Live OneCare on the computer making the backups and on the computer restoring the backups. Also in contrast to Vista's File Backup, Live OneCare Backup allows you to pick which folders will be backed up — a feature that should have been built into Vista itself. I don't recommend that you pay Microsoft for functionality that should be built into Windows, and I explain why in Technique 45.

Understanding Vista File Backup

At least 90 percent of the questions I get about Vista Backup involve the part officially called File Backup, but also called (in various places) File and Folder Backup and the Back Up Files Wizard. Whatever you call it, it's the backup program inside Vista that lets you back up your data files.

Here's what you need to know about File Backup:

- ✔ **You have to use an Administrator account to back up your own files.** You can't even "elevate" by providing an Administrator's ID and password: Vista requires you to physically log on with an Administrator account.

- ✔ **You can't back up individual files or folders or groups of folders.** If you have multiple NTFS drives, you can choose which drives get backed up. But you can't pick specific folders: You get a whole drive or you get nothing. (For the nit-pickers in the audience, if you create multiple partitions, er, volumes on a single drive, you have to choose which volume(s) get backed up.)

- ✔ **You have to back up the drive that contains Windows.** Er, the partition that includes Windows.

- ✔ **You can't back up network drives.** The only drives you can back up are ones attached to your computer.

- ✔ **You can't back up some kinds of files** — for example, you can't back up .exe files.

- ✔ **You can pick broad categories and types of files to back up, but you can't pick and choose the kinds of files you want to back up** — for example, you can back up all your graphics files, but you can't tell Vista to just back up your JPG photographs, or to ignore your BMP clip art files.

- ✔ **You can schedule backups to run in the middle of the night — but you can't tell Vista to "wake up" the machine to run the backups.** (Yes, it's theoretically possible if you dig straight into Task Scheduler. No, I don't recommend that you mess with Mother Nature that intimately.)

 If you're looking for any of those capabilities, don't waste your time with Vista. Flip to the last section in this Technique and get a much more capable backup program, such as ZipBackup.

Running a Quick File Backup

If you're willing to live with Vista File Backup's myriad limitations, running a backup couldn't be simpler, as long as you have an Administrator account. Follow these steps:

1. **Choose Start⇨Control Panel, click the System and Maintenance icon, and click the Back Up Your Computer link.**

Vista shows you the Backup and Restore Center. Depending on the version of Vista that you're running, it may look like Figure 53-1. (Vista Home Basic and Premium users don't have the Complete PC Backup and Restore option. If you've run a file backup before and you don't have Home Basic, you can click the Back Up Files button to find a Change Settings link.)

• **Figure 53-1: A first-time run at the Backup and Restore Center.**

2. **Click the button marked Back Up Files.**

Click Continue on the User Account Control message, and the Back Up Files Wizard asks you where to put the backup. Choose any of your local drives or, if you have a sufficiently savvy version of Vista, a network drive.

3. **Choose where you want your backup and click Next.**

If you specify "shiny media" (geek slang for CD or DVD discs), you need a lot of coasters (school-of-hard-knocks slang for CD or DVD discs) to keep up with the onslaught. After the first backup, though, the demands shouldn't be too great. If you aren't around to put shiny coasters in your DVD drive when Vista starts a scheduled backup, it will wait until you drag your sorry carcass to the computer and insert the appropriate pre-coasterized disc.

If you back up to a drive on your network, Vista prompts you for a computer name, username, and password, as shown in Figure 53-2.

• **Figure 53-2: Enter an Administrator account for the computer that holds the networked drive in this way.**

4. **Type a computer name, username, and password as shown in Figure 53-2. Click OK.**

The account on the computer with the network drive must be an Administrator account, and it must have a password that matches the password you enter *at the time the backup runs*.

If you have more than one drive (more precisely, if you have more than one volume — or partition) on your PC, Vista asks which disks you want to include in the backup, per Figure 53-3.

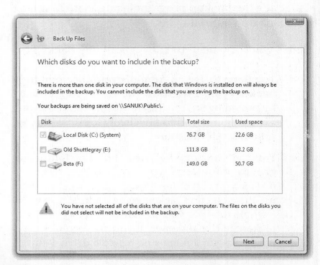

• **Figure 53-3: Choose the drives you want to back up.**

5. **Deselect the boxes next to any drives that you don't want to back up; then click Next.**

Vista forces you to back up the drive (er, volume) that contains Windows.

The wizard asks which types of files you want to back up.

6. **Deselect boxes next to the types of files that you don't want to back up. Click Next.**

 Although Microsoft doesn't appear to document it anywhere, at the very least, a File Backup will back up the specified kinds of files if they sit in the `c:\Program Files` or `c:\Users` folders. All files in the `c:\ProgramData` and `c:\Windows` folders are ignored.

Note that Vista determines a file's "type" by looking at the filename extension. Some types may not be registered properly.

 If you discover that a particular kind of file isn't getting backed up properly, complain to the company that makes the program that handles the file. For example, if you use a non-Microsoft e-mail program, you may need to bug the program's manufacturer to get your e-mail files registered correctly with Vista.

Unless you have Vista Home Basic, the wizard asks how frequently you want to back up your data (per Figure 53-4).

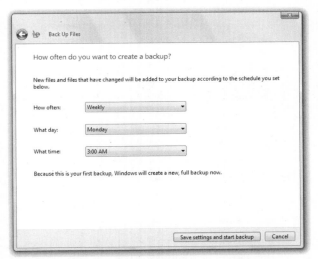

• **Figure 53-4: Pick an automatic backup frequency.**

7. **Pick a frequency and time that you can live with and then click the Save Settings and Start Backup button.**

The backup starts, with a possible long wait to format a DVD or CD. Go have a latte or ten, and avoid the temptation to remove the DVD or disconnect your network, even if very little appears to be happening.

 The files are zipped and then copied to the backup location. They're stored in a folder identified by the name of the originating computer and then the time and date of the backup. For example, backing up files from the computer **SABAI** creates folders `SABAI\Backup Set 2006-12-08 170813\Backup Files 2006-12-08 170813\Backup files 1.zip`, followed by `...\Backup files 2.zip`, and so on (see Figure 53-5).

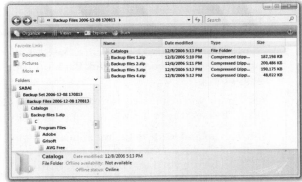

• **Figure 53-5: Your backed up files are in zip files, stored by the original folder name.**

When the backup is finished, a balloon appears in the notification area, next to the system clock.

8. **If you're curious about your backed up files, open the backup folders and browse the zip files.**

The zip files are regular files — you can copy them, open them on a different PC, e-mail them to yourself, extract individual files, or do just about anything with them.

Restoring Backed Up Files and Folders

After you've backed up your PC, resurrecting files and folders couldn't be simpler.

If you have Vista Business, Enterprise, or Ultimate, you should consider using Shadow Copies to retrieve munged files. (*Munged* is another one of those technical terms that can come in handy at dinner parties. "Felix really munged the burgers." Something like that.) In general, you can get at a decent backup faster by working with Shadow Copies. I talk about Shadow Copies extensively in my *Windows Vista All-in-One Desk Reference For Dummies* book (published by Wiley).

Follow these steps:

1. **Choose Start➪Control Panel, click the System and Maintenance icon, and click Back Up Your Computer.**

Yes, I know you want to restore your data, but this is the fast way to get where you want to be.

The Backup and Restore Center appears (see Figure 53-6), but it looks different from the way it looked before you ran a backup (refer to Figure 53-1).

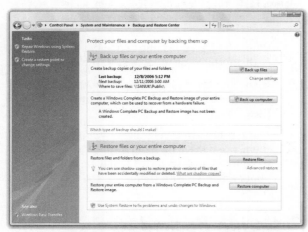

• **Figure 53-6: The Backup and Restore Center as it appears after you've run a backup.**

2. **Click the Restore Files button.**

The wizard asks whether you want to restore files from the latest backup or an older backup.

3. **Unless you've messed up the file badly for an extended period of time, or you're a huge glutton for punishment, choose Files from the Latest Backup and click Next.**

Vista asks which files and folders you want to restore.

4. **Click the Add Files button if you want to restore a file (or files), or the Add Folders button if you want to restore an entire folder (or folders).**

The wizard brings up the Add Files to Restore dialog box (see Figure 53-7), which looks a lot like a regular Windows Explorer dialog box. The only big difference? The files on the right, and the files you can get to from the Favorite Links pane on the left or the Search bar on top, are all backups. Clever.

• **Figure 53-7: It looks like a Windows Explorer window, but you can get only to backed-up files from here.**

5. **Choose files or folders that you want to restore and click Add.**

The wizard keeps a running list of all the files and folders you have chosen, as shown in Figure 53-8.

6. **When you're done choosing files and folders, click Next.**

The wizard asks where you want to save the restored files.

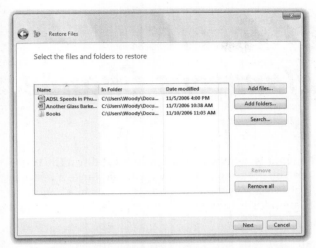

• **Figure 53-8: Choose each file and folder you want to restore.**

7. *Don't* choose In the Original Location. You can clobber good files that way. Instead, click the Browse button and find a new place for the restored files. Then click Start Restore.

My personal predilection is to put the restored files on my desktop, but you may have a better place.

The wizard tells you when it has finished restoring the files.

8. Click Finish and go look at your restored data to make sure you got the files you wanted.

When you're confident that you have the right files and you don't need the old ones, feel free to delete the bad ones and replace them with the restored versions.

Using ZipBackup

Zip Backup from, uh, ZipBackup, Inc. (www. zipbackup.com) was one of the first programs to back up files into the zip format. Doing so makes a whole lot of sense. Also, in contrast to Vista's backup, ZipBackup lets you pick and choose which folders get backed up. It fits right in with Vista's Task Scheduler. It's simple, thorough, and very reliable.

 Vista Backup's artificial restrictions leave me cold. You can't even pick the folders you want to back up, for heaven's sake. There's no way I'll pay Microsoft for Live OneCare. So I have returned to the backup program I've used for many years.

Drop by the ZipBackup site for a free 30-day trial. If you decide to keep it, the package will set you back $29.95. Money well spent, as far as I'm concerned.

Technique 54

Restoring Your System after Calamitous Change

Save Time By

- Making a system restore point before you install something new
- Rolling back immediately with System Restore
- Using the Last Known Good Configuration option in a Windows boot

Ever get the feeling that Windows was about to head down the tubes in a hurry? Before you get to that point, you should make a restore point. That way, after your system has gone to Hades in a handbasket, you can use System Restore to bring it back to its original upright position.

Or something like that.

In spite of what you read in Microsoft's documentation and Help file, System Restore originated with Windows ME, at the turn of the century. System Restore became a key feature in Windows XP, and it has been enhanced (and restore points have grown considerably in size) in Vista.

Finding out how to create system restore points takes only a few minutes. If you create a restore point before you install an unknown piece of software, then even if the installer "forgets" to make its own restore point, you have everything you need to quickly and easily wipe all vestiges of that infernal piece of junk from your system. If you don't make a system restore point, and the naïve (or intentionally obfuscating) installer doesn't work right, oh man, are you in for a wild ride.

Use System Restore right and you can save all sorts of time.

 If you use Vista Business, Enterprise, or Ultimate, you've probably heard that Vista creates and stores shadow copies of data files as part of a system restore point. (I talk about making shadow copies in Technique 53, and in much more detail in *Windows Vista All-In-One Desk Reference For Dummies,* published by Wiley.) What you may not know is that those shadow copies are created only for the main system disk; if you want to save shadow copies of data on other disks, you have to manually go into Vista and make it so. Another one of those things they don't tell you in Vista school, eh?

This Technique shows you how to use System Restore quickly and efficiently — warts and all.

Understanding System Restore's Limitations

Let me just make one thing clear, right off the bat. With one exception, Vista's System Restore is not a backup program. It doesn't back up your spreadsheets, keep track of your e-mail, or create automatic copies of all those Word documents you have lying around.

Rather, System Restore takes snapshots of Vista that include copies of key system files, all the Registry, various settings for each user — basically everything that's necessary to roll back Windows to a previous point in time except for your data. It doesn't back up your programs, either. Just Windows.

The exception? Shadow copies.

 If you use the Vista Business, Enterprise, or Ultimate edition, Vista's system restore points include not only key system files and settings but also backups of the shadow copies of your data files. Vista thinks of shadow copies as system files, as opposed to data files, and in a sense they are. Although System Restore doesn't back up your data, the three jewel-encrusted versions of Vista *do* back up your shadow copies. Confused? Yeah. Me, too.

 The bottom line: No matter which version of Vista you use, you have to make your own file backups, thank you very much. Technique 53 shows you how.

Vista automatically creates snapshots — called restore points — on these occasions:

- ✔ **When you install an application** (if the installer is a recent one and behaves properly by notifying Windows).

- ✔ **When you install a Windows update, patch, or service pack.**

- ✔ **When you run a File Backup**, either manually or via an automated backup (see Technique 53).

- ✔ **When you install an unsigned driver.** An *unsigned driver* is a program that makes hardware work but hasn't been certified by Microsoft's Windows Hardware Quality Labs.

- ✔ **When you manually create a restore point.**

- ✔ **Just before you restore an old restore point** (so that you can, in effect, undo the undo if need be).

- ✔ **Every 24 hours** if you keep your computer on all the time, or when your computer wakes up after sleeping and more than 24 hours have passed since the last restore point. Vista waits until no activity has occurred on the machine for a while before creating a restore point.

When you restore a restore point, only Windows gets restored. (If you're running Vista Business, Enterprise, or Ultimate, shadow copies of your data files get restored, too.) That can lead to some mighty confounding behavior.

 Say you install a program that you think might be unstable. You create a restore point before you install it. The program bombs and takes your system along with it, so you roll back to the restore point. Windows won't know that the program was ever installed — but the program's files are still on your hard drive. If you accidentally try to open one of these files before you have reinstalled the program, there's no telling what might happen.

Turning on System Restore Everywhere

This section applies only to users of Vista Business, Enterprise, or Ultimate editions. If you have any other version of Vista, skip to the next section.

Vista's System Restore program (Microsoft insists on calling it *System Protection*) backs up system files. It doesn't back up data files. Fair enough.

Now things get confusing.

If you use Vista Business, Enterprise, or Ultimate, the term "system files" includes shadow copies of your data files. When you perform a file backup (see Technique 53), before Vista backs up your data files, it creates a restore point — and the restore point contains backups of your shadow copies.

 But if you have more than one drive, the restore point doesn't include backups of *all* your shadow copies.

Vista keeps shadow copies of files on the same drive as the original file. When you run a restore point, Vista normally makes backup copies only of system files on your main hard drive. (For the nit-pickers: If you have multiple partitions on a hard drive, Vista backs up the volume that contains Windows.) So unless you go in and change things, Vista's restore points don't include shadow copies of files on drives (er, volumes) other than your main drive.

Got that?

 If you want system restore points to include shadow copies of data files from drives other than your main drive, you have to go into Vista and turn on System Restore (er, System Protection) for the other drives.

Follow these steps:

1. **Choose Start, right-click Computer, and choose Properties.**

You see the View Basic Information about Your Computer window, shown in Figure 54-1.

2. **In the Tasks pane, click System Protection.**

Vista hits you with another User Account Control message. Click Continue.

You see the System Properties dialog box, which is open to the System Protection tab, as shown in Figure 54-2.

• **Figure 54-1: Get into System Restore through the Basic Information window.**

• **Figure 54-2: To get shadow copy backups on drives other than the system drive, you have to select them here.**

3. Select the boxes next to every drive for which you want to have system restore points generated.

Realize that creating system restore points for additional drives takes more time and space and will therefore slow down installation of new programs and give you halitosis. But it keeps your shadow copies clean.

In Figure 54-2, I checked every drive.

4. Click OK and click X to exit the View Basic Information window.

Vista does not run out and create a new restore point. But the next time a restore point gets generated, it will include shadow copies for all the data files on the newly selected drives.

Creating a Restore Point

Say you have a copy of Uncle Billy Joe Bob's Blaster Beta and you're about to install it. You know that Billy Joe Bob doesn't have a real installer package — one that properly notifies Windows that it's about to install a program and give Windows a chance to create a restore point automatically. It's time for you to ponder your immediate future.

Maybe the Blaster Beta won't do anything bad to your system. Maybe it will. Maybe it has a good installer. Maybe it doesn't.

 When in doubt, run a restore point before you install new software or hardware. It's a quick, easy ounce of prevention.

To manually create a restore point, follow these steps:

1. Choose Start⇨Control Panel, click the System and Maintenance icon, and click the Back Up Your Computer link.

You see the Backup and Restore Center, as shown in Figure 54-3. (See the preceding section for a different way to get to the Restore Point dialog box.)

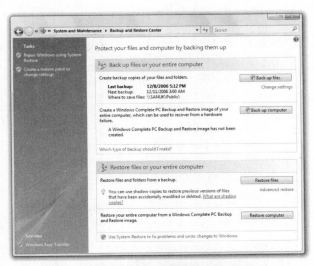

• **Figure 54-3: The Backup and Restore Center.**

2. In the Tasks pane, click the Create a Restore Point or Change Settings link.

Click Continue through a User Account Control warning message, and Vista shows you the computer's System Properties dialog box, which is open to the System Protection tab (shown earlier in this Technique; refer to Figure 54-2).

3. Click the Create button.

Vista asks you to type a description for the restore point (see Figure 54-4).

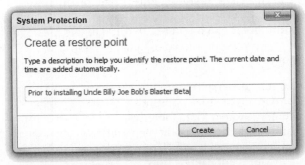

• **Figure 54-4: Give the restore point a name that identifies what you're doing.**

4. **Type a description that you can remember — no need to include the date or time — and click Create.**

The wizard takes a while to gather all the pertinent data, but when it's done, you see a message that says the restore point was created successfully.

5. **Click OK; then click X to exit the System Properties dialog box.**

Vista saves restore points until it runs out of room — which can take a year or two.

See the next section for details on deleting all but the most recent restore point.

Deleting Restore Points

Vista can use up to 12 percent of the total available space (some Microsoft documentation says 15 percent) on your primary hard drive for restore points.

 Think about that for a second. If you have a 200GB C drive, Vista reserves 25GB for restore points. Absolutely incredible, eh? Windows XP included a simple slider that let you adjust the maximum amount of room reserved for restore points. Vista doesn't have the same kind of flexibility.

If you run Vista Business, Enterprise, or Ultimate edition, the volume of data packed away in a single restore point can be quite breathtaking; copies of all the shadow copies can consume an enormous amount of room.

It's unusual — I'm tempted to say "rare" — that you ever use any restore point other than the most recent. Although Vista includes very few tools for dealing with restore point elephantiasis, you can at least tell Vista to delete all the restore points besides the most recent. Here's how:

1. **Choose Start⇨Computer. Right-click your main drive and choose Properties.**

You see the Properties dialog box, probably for your C drive.

2. **Click the Disk Cleanup button.**

Vista asks which files you want to clean up.

3. **Click Files from All Users on this Computer.**

You have to click Continue in the User Account Control dialog box. Disk Cleanup scans your drive and (sooner or later) shows you a list of files available for deleting.

4. **Click the More Options tab.**

Vista shows you a dialog box like the one shown in Figure 54-5.

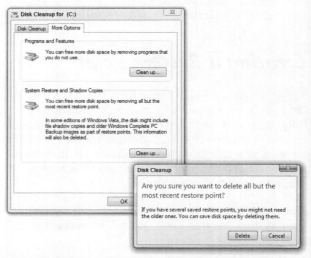

• **Figure 54-5: Delete all but the most recent restore point here.**

5. **At the bottom, under System Restore and Shadow Copies, click the button marked Clean Up.**

Vista asks for confirmation with the Are You Sure You Want to Delete All but the Most Recent Restore Point message.

6. **Click Delete. Then click OK.**

Vista seeks confirmation again — this time with the Are You Sure You Want to Permanently Delete These Files message.

7. **Click Delete Files.**

It takes a minute or two, but all but the most recent restore point get deleted.

Restoring to a Restore Point — *Quickly*

So something has gone terribly wrong with your system, and you want to get Windows back to the way it was a day ago (or, if you installed Uncle Billy Joe Bob's Blaster Beta, maybe just a few seconds ago).

The exact method you use for restoring Windows depends on how bad Windows is hurting.

If Windows isn't running and won't start

If you can't get Windows to start, don't fret. You can restore Windows to the last restore point by following these steps:

1. **Reboot your computer.**

Every PC goes through its self-test a little differently, but typically you see a counter as the PC tests its memory, followed by notices about keyboard and mouse drivers, and finally a notice about your hard drives (assuming that these don't flash by so fast that you see only a blur).

2. **Immediately after you see the message that your hard drive is alive, press F8 and hold it down.**

Vista may show you the Windows Error Recovery screen, as shown in Figure 54-6, or it may show you a similar screen, with more options, called Advanced Boot Options.

3. **Use the down arrow to highlight Last Known Good Configuration (Advanced).**

The Last Known Good Configuration choice simply runs Windows System Restore using the last restore point and then boots normally.

4. **Press Enter.**

```
                         Windows Error Recovery

Windows failed to start. A recent hardware or software change might be the
cause. To fix the problem:

    1. Insert your windows installation disc and restart your computer.
    2. Choose your language settings, and then click "Next."
    3. Click "Repair your computer."

Other options:
If power was interrupted during startup, choose Start Windows Normally.
(Use the arrow keys to highlight your choice.)

      Safe Mode
      Safe Mode with Networking
      Safe Mode with Command Prompt
      Last Known Good Configuration (advanced)
      Start Windows Normally


Description: Start Windows using settings from last successful boot
            attempt.


  ENTER=Choose
```

• **Figure 54-6:** The fast way to restore Windows to the most recent restore point.

Windows automatically makes a restore point when you restore — so if you run through these steps twice in a row (without setting a new restore point), the second time you use Last Known Good Configuration, you get your original (presumably bad!) restore point.

 If you can't get Windows to start, and the Last Known Good Configuration doesn't work — or if you can't even get to the Windows Error Recovery screen — it's time to haul out the big guns. Follow the instructions on the screen shown in Figure 54-6: Grab your Vista installation CD, restart your computer, choose your language, click Next, and then click the Repair Your Computer link. But try using the Last Known Good Configuration first, okay?

If Windows runs

As long as you can coax Windows into running — even if it's in Safe Mode (refer to Figure 54-6, which shows starting in Safe Mode as an option) — you can restore to any restore point that's still available on your computer.

If you're rolling back Windows specifically because of a flaky program, start by uninstalling the program. Follow these steps:

1. **Choose Start⇨Control Panel, click the Programs icon, and click the Uninstall a Program link.**

Vista brings up the Uninstall or Change a Program dialog box.

2. **Select the offending program and click the Uninstall button.**

If the program has a halfway decent uninstaller (not all of them do), this simple step gets rid of most of the program files and other gross pieces of the program. If the uninstaller isn't worth a hill of beans, you may have to run to Google to find an alternate way to get rid of the offensive program.

3. **Choose Start⇨Control Panel, click the System and Maintenance icon, and click the Back Up Your Computer link. Then, on the left, click the Repair Windows Using System Restore link.**

You have to click Continue through yet another User Account Control warning. At that point, one of two things will happen. Either Vista will bring up the System Restore Wizard, which steps you through restoring your system, or Vista will ask whether you want to restore to the most recent restore point (see Figure 54-7).

4. **If you want to look at older restore points, select the Choose a Different Restore Point option and click Next.**

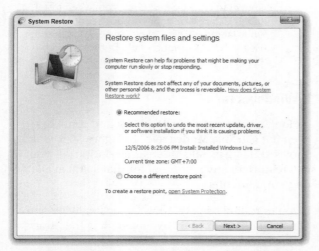

• **Figure 54-7: If you've used the System Restore Wizard before, it offers to restore the most recent restore point.**

The wizard presents you with a list of available restore points, as shown in Figure 54-8.

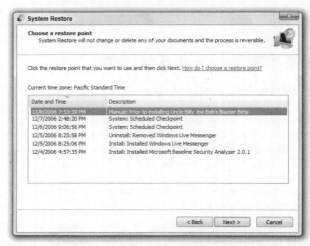

• **Figure 54-8: Choose from among any of the most recent restore points.**

5. **Choose the restore point that will cause the least disruption but still get the job done; then click Next.**

You see the confirmation message shown in Figure 54-9.

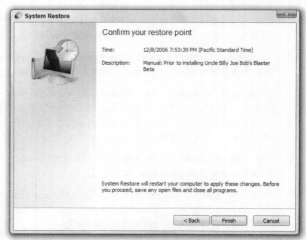

• **Figure 54-9: Make sure you get the right restore point.**

6. **If you're sure you want to restore, click Finish.**

The System Restore Wizard slaps up yet another message reminding you that the system restore can't be interrupted and can't be undone until it's complete, and asks whether you're sure.

7. **Close any open programs and then click Yes.**

In fact, well-behaved programs register themselves with Vista, so they can be restarted when Vista reboots, but it's easier to be safe.

The wizard performs the restore and then immediately shuts down Windows and restarts. When Windows comes back, it tells you that it has been restored.

8. **If you want to undo the restore, choose Start⇨Control Panel, click the System and Maintenance icon, and click the Back Up Your Computer link. Then, on the left, click the Repair Windows Using System Restore link.**

The wizard adds an option to undo, as shown in Figure 54-10.

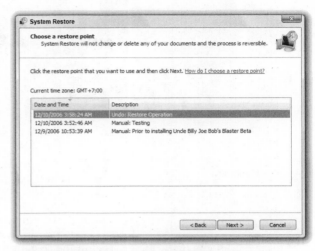

• **Figure 54-10:** Undoing a restore is very easy.

9. **To undo the restore, select Undo: Restore Operation, click Next, and follow the wizard.**

Technique

55

Recovering a Lost Password

Save Time By

✔ Setting up a password reset disk now — before you need it

✔ Using a password reset disk quickly and correctly

✔ Figuring out what to do if you lost your password and don't have a reset disk

Y ou may find out the downside to creating good, strong passwords. What if you forget yours?

If your PC is connected to a Big Corporate Network (BCN; in Microsoft-speak, a *domain*), you can use the password reset disk I discuss in this Technique to get on to your PC — but you can't log on to the network. Should you require files, printers, or anything else on the network, you have to rouse the network administrator and get him or her to change your password. Then you have to log on to the network and change your password once again. It's a pain in the posterior, but there's no alternative. That's how BCNs work.

 If you have a peer-to-peer network (a *workgroup* in Microsoft-speak), or a stand-alone PC, the situation isn't nearly as dire — provided that you're prepared. This Technique's password reset disk can have you going in seconds. A few minutes spent creating a password reset disk can save you hours of hassle and pain.

This Technique shows you how to break your own passwords. Or at least how to set things up ahead of time so that you can break them. It's easy if you know how.

Forget your password? You may be in for some interesting times. At the end of this Technique, I discuss the ramifications.

If you don't have a password on your account, you can pass over this Technique.

Creating a Password Reset Disk

The minute you turn on password protection for an account, you should create a password reset disk for that account. Why? Because any administrator who can get on your PC can switch your password — and you can do nothing about it!

Unless you're using a Big Corporate Network, a password reset disk is a defensive maneuver. It guards you against the slings and arrows of others who use your PC.

Once upon a time, every PC had a floppy drive, and Microsoft assumed that your password reset disk would naturally be a floppy disk. Times change. Nowadays your only real choice is a USB key drive. Or a camera. Yes, a camera — or almost any other kind of drive connected to a USB port, including a SmartCard reader.

Follow these steps to make a password reset disk:

1. **Choose Start➪Control Panel, click the User Accounts and Family Safety icon, and then click the User Accounts icon.**

Sooner or later, you end up at the Make Changes to Your User Account dialog box, shown in Figure 55-1.

• **Figure 55-1: Start the Password Reset Disk Wizard here.**

2. **In the Tasks pane on the left, click the Create a Password Reset Disk link.**

Vista brings up the Forgotten Password Wizard, which steps you through creating a password reset disk. Don't worry. The name's a bit discombobulating. This is the wizard you want to run when you *remember* your password so that you can retrieve all your data if you *forget* your password.

3. **Insert your USB key drive (or other USB-connected drive) or floppy disk — or hook up your camera — *before* you click Next. Then click Next.**

The wizard asks where you want to "create a password key disk" (see Figure 55-2).

• **Figure 55-2: A "password key disk" is a password reset disk.**

This is confusing — to me, anyway. Vista isn't actually creating a password disk but rather putting a small file called `userkey.psw` on the drive.

4. **Choose the drive you want to hold the password reset file and then click Next.**

The wizard asks for the current password, which you must supply to create the disk.

5. **Type the password for the account and then click Next.**

You see a green progress bar that stops at 100 percent complete.

6. **Click Next.**

The wizard warns you that this is the last, best, and only valid password reset disk for this account, as shown in Figure 55-3.

• Figure 55-3: This password reset disk (actually the userkey.psw **file) makes all previous reset disks obsolete.**

7. **Click Finish.**

You can now use your password reset disk. Store the disk — specifically, the file userkey.psw — in a safe place. Anyone who gets the file can log on to your PC without knowing your password.

 Although Microsoft likes to make it sound as though something is magical about the password reset disk, in fact nothing is. The userkey.psw file holds the information that unlocks the account. You can copy userkey.psw onto any disk at all and use it to log in to this particular PC with this particular account. On the other hand, if you use the wizard a second time to create a second password reset disk (in fact, a second userkey.psw), the original password reset disk (userkey.psw) doesn't work anymore.

 No matter how many times you change your password, the last password reset disk (actually, the last version of userkey.psw) created for that account still works. You have no reason to update the disk when you change your password.

Using Your Password Reset Disk

So the sad day has come — you can't remember your password. That's okay. Happens to everybody — except the folks who write their passwords with permanent markers on the front of their screens. But those people have other problems.

You know you've reached that sad state of affairs when the welcome screen greets you with a red *X* and the dour message The user name or password is incorrect.

If you have your password reset disk handy, follow these steps to use it:

1. **On the Vista welcome screen, after you've failed to enter the correct password, click the link that says Reset Password.**

The Password Reset Wizard appears.

2. **Attach any drive containing the latest version of** userkey.psw *before* **you click Next.**

The wizard asks you to choose the "password key disk."

3. **Choose the removable drive that contains** userkey.psw. **Click Next.**

The wizard asks you to provide a new password (see Figure 55-4).

4. **Give the wizard a new password and hint for this account. Click Next.**

The wizard reaches into Vista and changes the password for this particular user. It doesn't matter what the old password was; this new password now takes effect.

• **Figure 55-4: Whenever you use your password recovery "disk," you must provide a new password.**

5. **Click the Finish button and then log on with the new password you specified.**

It's quite remarkable, but the password isn't stored on the password reset disk (nor is it in `userkey.psw`; see Figure 55-5). The password's still on your computer's hard drive, but if you have the password reset disk in your hot little hands, you don't need the password itself to log into Vista — the magical reset disk says "open sesame," and Vista responds, no matter what password may be in force.

• **Figure 55-5: The password isn't stored in** `userkey.psw` **— but** `userkey.psw` **still works, no matter which drive it's on.**

Getting Around Your Own Password

So what do you do if you forget your password, you don't have a network administrator to bail you out, and you didn't create a password reset disk?

In short, you have to go in with a different account and change your password.

 If you forget your password, don't have a password reset disk, and you're using the NTFS file system and its Encrypted File System, don't attempt anything listed here. If you succeed in changing the password, you clobber all those encrypted files. Some companies claim to have software that opens those encrypted files — www.crackpassword.com is among them — but it's far from a sure thing. Spend some time on the Internet and keep trying.

If you're using BitLocker and you forget or lose your key, you're probably beyond help. Google is your friend.

If you are not using the Encrypted File System, try to log on with a different Administrator account, bring up your account, and change your password. This approach really is as simple as it sounds. I describe the process in Technique 40.

 When you change your account's password, you lose any other passwords that Internet Explorer has stored for you, as well as some other stored passwords — so you may have to provide your password again the next time you check out of Amazon.com, for example, and you have to come up with your wireless network password, if you have one. But these inconveniences are usually a small price to pay.

Good luck.

Part XI

The Scary (Or Fun!) Stuff

The 5th Wave   By Rich Tennant

"How do you like that Aero glass interface on Vista? Nice, huh?"

56 Technique

Changing the Registry without Getting Burned

Save Time By

- ✔ Getting in and out of the Registry without breaking anything
- ✔ Knowing when tweaking the Registry is a waste of time (Answer: Usually)
- ✔ Making a few changes . . . just for practice, right?

The Registry is a big, dark, spooky place full of peril and hidden pitfalls. Kind of like, oh, Form 1040. If you aren't very, very careful, you can bring Windows crashing down, and you'll never get it to work again — ever. Click once in the wrong place, and your machine freezes so tight you have to send it back to Boise.

At least, that's what some people think. Personally, I think of the Registry as a big time sink. But scary? Naw.

Sure, you have to be careful, but if you don't go around changing everything in sight, you can dive into the Registry and come back unscathed.

When Vista shipped, several of the screen savers had options that just didn't make it into the final cut — the programmers built the options into the screen saver programs, but they ran out of time when it came to creating a user interface that we could all use. Although Microsoft may have released a PowerToy or Service Pack to hook into those screen saver settings by the time you read this, you may still find it fun and instructive to hack the Registry directly and make the screen savers work a different way.

Severe bragging rights — however fleeting — for Vista cognoscenti await.

This Technique shows you how.

Don't Mess with This?

The Registry is Windows' central repository for all sorts of different settings — the name of your keyboard driver, the size of your desktop, the location of the program that plays MP3 files, and tens of thousands more.

 Nobody understands the Registry. Not completely, anyway. Nobody has ever pulled together a complete description of what all those settings mean. The items are infuriatingly inconsistent, generally entirely undocumented, and stored away in a very nearly random order.

But these items control Windows.

Once upon a time, you had to be able to edit the Registry if you ever hoped to get Windows working efficiently. (Indeed, I would argue, working at all.) Those times have passed. Nowadays, you probably want to go into the Registry for one of three reasons:

- ✔ You read on the Internet that if you change some Registry setting, your copy of Windows works better or faster or both.

- ✔ You have a specific problem that Microsoft says can be fixed only by manually changing a Registry setting. Unfortunately, this type of Registry editing is on the upswing. The MS Knowledge Base is packed with articles that require changes to the Registry.

- ✔ You have a specific problem that Microsoft doesn't talk about, but experts know it can be fixed by changing Registry settings anyway. For example, a lot of Registry tweaks force Windows to bypass (what I believe are) sense-less security restrictions in Outlook.

My favorite quick Vista Registry tweaks, which I detail in this Technique, make the Ribbons and Mystify screen savers look a little different. Nothing earth shattering, but it's a fun way to kick around in the Vista *sanctum sanctorum*.

No matter how much you feel the temptation, it's never a good idea to go into the Registry to "fix" something if you don't know precisely what needs fixing and how. Changing Registry settings willy-nilly to try to fix random prob-lems only lands you in hot water.

Understanding the Registry

The worst part of the Registry isn't the Registry itself — it's the lousy terminology. The Windows Registry has grown up in a hodge-podge way, and terms that (arguably) made some sense back in the days of Windows 3.1 don't mean baloney now. But we're stuck with them.

Historically, Microsoft has put absolutely no emphasis on maintaining consistency inside the Registry. It's kind of like a teenager's closet: You never know what you'll find in there, and any resemblance to organization is entirely coincidental.

The Windows Registry may look like a file or a database, but it's really a conglomeration of many different pieces drawn from several places. You can change some of the entries, but other entries are completely off limits: Your PC generates them inter-nally, and you can't do anything to modify them.

The Registry is organized by *keys,* much as your disk is organized in folders. Just as a folder may have other folders and files inside, Registry keys may have other keys and values inside. Just as Windows Explorer helps you move from a higher-level folder down to a lower-level folder, and down and down before you finally find the file you want, the Registry Editor helps you move from a higher-level key down to a lower-level key, and down and down until you get to the value you seek.

The Registry has five main keys, called *high-level keys.* Confusingly, in different places in Microsoft's documentation (I told you the terminology was bad, eh?), they're also called *root keys* and/or *predefined keys* and/or *hives.* Those five main keys have very long names (see Table 56-1), but the common abbre-viations are HKCR, HKCU, HKLM, HKU, and HKCC. I use those abbreviations in this Technique, rather than the long names, because almost all documenta-tion about the Registry refers to the abbreviations.

Just as you can add or delete folders in Windows Explorer, you can add or delete keys in the Registry Editor. When you delete a folder in Explorer, you delete all the files and folders inside the folder. When you delete a key in the Registry Editor, you delete all the keys and values inside the key.

That's where the similarities end. You can move a folder in Explorer, but you can't move a key in the Registry Editor. And when you delete a key in the Registry Editor, there's no Recycle Bin sitting there helping you recover from your mistakes. After you delete a key, it's gone — for good.

TABLE 56-1: VISTA'S HIGH-LEVEL KEYS

Abbreviation	Means	What It Does	What This Means to You
HKCR	HKEY_CLASSES_ROOT	Associates filename extensions (such as .doc and .exe) with the actions Windows is supposed to take when, for example, you double-click a file. Also associates types of objects (folders, drives) with actions Windows takes when you double-click them.	If you double-click an MP3 file and the wrong program shows up, something is messed up in this Registry key. Don't try to fix the key directly. Use Windows Explorer's File Name Associations dialog box (see Technique 15).
HKCU	HKEY_CURRENT_USER	Controls many settings for the currently logged-on user, from the user's name to his or her desktop background, and tens of thousands of additional Windows entries.	You can make very detailed changes to your Windows desktop by editing entries in this key. Just make sure you know exactly what you're doing before you start tweaking.
HKLM	HKEY_LOCAL_MACHINE	Thousands of settings that apply to all users, no matter who is logged on to the PC at any given moment.	Program settings for all users frequently go in here.
HKU	HKEY_USERS	A collection of all the HKCU entries for everyone who has ever logged on to the PC, in addition to a special entry called .DEFAULT, which is copied when a new user gets added.	This is where you can change desktop settings for all users.
HKCC	HKEY_CURRENT_CONFIG	A tiny key that describes the current hardware configuration and a few basic system settings.	You can change only a few of these settings, primarily the ones associated with basic system functions.

Almost all the changes you make to the Registry involve modifying values: changing, adding, or deleting values (although once in a very blue moon you may need to add a key). Each value in the Registry has a name and data.

For example, in Figure 56-1, the HKCU\Identities key contains seven values. The name of the sixth value is Last Username, and its data is Main Identity.

• **Figure 56-1: Inside the HKCU\Identities key.**

All this would be academic if it weren't for the fact that when you create a new value or change a value, you have to be sure that you use the right data type for the value's data. If the value's data is supposed to be a number, and you type in a bunch of characters, you can mess up everything — even, in very rare cases if you're working with a truly critical key, freeze Windows so tight that you have to reinstall it.

That's why it's very important that you follow instructions for changing the Registry quite precisely.

Table 56-2 shows you the three most common types of value data that you encounter in the Registry. Make sure you stick to the type of data that the value requires.

TABLE 56-2: COMMON REGISTRY DATA TYPES

Type	Description	Use This Info to Save Time
String	Characters — letters, numbers, weird characters.	Anything you can type on the keyboard is fair game. This is the best kind of key because it's hard to mess up!
DWORD	A "double word" 32-bit (4-byte) integer between 0 and 4,294,967,295 in decimal (or hex 00 00 00 00 to FF FF FF FF). When Registry programmers know they're going to need a small integer, they usually use DWORDs because they're easy to work with.	When you type in DWORD data, use only these characters: 0 1 2 3 4 5 6 7 8 9 A B C D E F (or a b c d e f, which are treated the same way). You don't really need to understand that an A is 10 in hexadecimal, but it doesn't hurt. Heh heh heh.
Binary	Similar to DWORD, but binary can be any number of bytes long. Throughout the Registry, many strings are stored as binary data.	In many cases, you have to be very, very careful when you change binary data so that you don't change its length. Follow your instructions precisely and keep track of the binary data's length.

The really confounding fact is that the programmers who set up Registry entries usually don't give a fiddler's fig about data types; programmers frequently put strings in binary values, for example. The problem comes when you want to change a value by hand. When that happens, you need to conform to the way the programmer set up things originally. Otherwise, the program won't understand what you've done — and may start having conniption fits.

In certain rare instances, you have to work with the binary data that sits behind strings. There's rarely any good reason for it. Be very careful when editing the binary numbers behind strings. It's easy to add or lose one number — and throw off the whole string.

Backing Up Data the Registry Way

Before you start spelunking through your Registry, you need to back it up. I recommend that you perform not one but two separate backups:

✔ **Create a system restore point.** That way, if the wheels fall off and you crash Windows utterly and completely, you can restore the Registry to

the point you were at before you started fiddling around (or use the Last Known Good Configuration option on the system boot menu if you can't get Windows to boot). For details about setting a system restore point, see Technique 54.

✔ **Back up the Registry key(s) that you expect to change.** That's what this section is about.

If Windows heads south, you save yourself a lot of time if you have decent backups at hand.

The Registry can store keys and values in many different ways, but you really need to be concerned with only two:

✔ **.reg file:** A text file that contains Registry entries. You can pick a Registry key and have the Registry Editor copy into a text file all the keys and values contained in that particular key. The text file is called a .reg file.

You keep the .reg file as a backup. Restoring from the backup is easy: When you double-click the .reg file, entries in the file overwrite corresponding entries in the Registry. So if you save a .reg file as a backup for a key, mess up something in the key, and then double-click the .reg file, your mistakes get overwritten with the original entries. Very simple.

✔ **Hive:** A bunch of Registry entries stored as a binary file. (Don't be intimidated: A hive is just a bunch of keys under a single key. It's roughly analogous to a folder.) I don't recommend that you use hives because you can't make changes to them by hand, but in some ways, they're better than .reg files. If you're curious about hives, though, a discussion about referencing hives is at www.microsoft.com/resources/documentation/windows/xp/all/proddocs/en-us/regedit_export_hive_file.mspx.

Follow these ultra-simple steps to create a .reg backup file:

1. **Choose Start, type** regedit, **and press Enter.**

   That puts you in Vista's Registry Editor.

2. **On the left, double-click down the tree to navigate to the key you want to save.**

   Typically that's the key you're going to change.

3. **Click once on the key you want to save.**

4. **Choose File⇨Export.**

   The Registry Editor asks for a filename and location.

5. **Give your .reg backup file a name, pick a good location for it (I usually put it on the desktop), and click Save.**

   If something goes haywire, double-click that saved .reg file to go back to your original settings.

I step you through a real-world example, creating a .reg file as a backup for my favorite quick Registry tweaks, in the last section of this Technique.

Making Changes Safely

Here's the general approach to making safe changes in the Registry:

1. **Create a system restore point (see Technique 54).**

2. **Back up the key that you're going to change to a .reg file (see the preceding section).**

3. **Make the changes.**

4. **If necessary, force Windows to recognize those changes.**

   Generally, the most reliable way to do that is to log off and then log back on again.

5. **Test the changes.**

   Depending on the kind of change you made, this step can be quite straightforward or very difficult. For example, testing to see whether a Registry tweak speeds up your Internet connection could be iffy at best. On the other hand, testing to see whether a modified desktop setting (say, a new color for your menus) worked could be as simple as looking at your desktop.

6. **If the change didn't do what you wanted it to do, restore the Registry by double-clicking the .reg file that you saved.**

7. **If something goes very, very wrong, follow the steps in Technique 54 to restore your system to the system restore point.**

Running My Favorite Quick Registry Tweaks

Traditionally, there are very, very few worthwhile Windows Registry tweaks that Microsoft's TweakUI doesn't handle faster, easier, and more reliably. By the time you read this, chances are good that Microsoft will have a Vista-savvy version of TweakUI available. Before you go fiddling with your Registry, use Google to search for *Vista TweakUI* and make Microsoft's product (if it's available) do the heavy lifting.

As we went to press, Vista had a whole bunch of screen saver settings under lock and key — and the only way you could bring them to life was via changes in the Registry. Even if Microsoft has released a PowerToy or extra-cost add-in that brings the screen savers to life, tweaking your Registry to make the screen savers neat (or at least different) counts as a good, safe, fun way to get to know your Registry.

The Ribbons screen saver has two settings that you can change:

- ✔ NumRibbons is the maximum number of ribbons shown on the screen (in hexadecimal).

- ✔ RibbonWidth is the maximum width of the ribbons, expressed in a very weird way. (For the techies in the crowd, it's a floating point representation of an integer value, stored in a DWORD. Weird.)

To see the effect of each of the settings, check out Table 56-3.

TABLE 56-3: RIBBONS SCREEN SAVER SETTINGS

Picture	NumRibbons (DWORD)	RibbonWidth (DWORD)	Looks Like This
	(None)	(None)	The way Ribbons normally looks, before you tweak
	100	3c23d70a	256 thin ribbons
	50	3ded9a8a	128 semi-fat ribbons
	4	3f1ec78a	4 ribbons in need of a diet

Here's how to change your Ribbons screen saver — and learn a bit about the Registry at the same time:

1. **Go through Technique 54 and set a system restore point.**

This is the extra-cautious part. Yes, I'm telling you to put on your training wheels. If you have a system restore point, even if you change every scary setting in the Registry and your whole world comes crashing down, all you have to do is run a System Restore (or boot with the Last Known Good Configuration), and your old Registry returns.

2. **Choose Start, type** `regedit`, **and press Enter.**

The Registry Editor appears.

3. **On the left side, double-click down the tree until you get to HKCU\Software\Microsoft\ Windows\CurrentVersion\Screensavers\ Ribbons.**

Your screen looks like Figure 56-2.

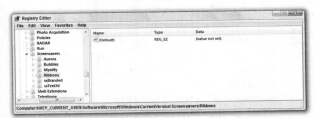

• **Figure 56-2:** Navigate to the settings for the Ribbons screen saver.

4. **Click once on Ribbons, on the left, and then choose File⊃Export. Give your** `.reg` **backup file a name (say,** `Original Ribbons screensaver settings`), **pick a good location for it (I prefer the desktop), and click Save.**

If you don't like this change and want your old Ribbons screen saver back, you can double-click that `.reg` file at any time and return the Registry HKCU\Software\Microsoft\Windows\ CurrentVersion\Screensavers\Ribbon entries to their original states.

5. **On the right, right-click in the big empty area and choose New⊃DWORD (32-bit) Value.**

Regedit creates a new DWORD value and waits for you to type a new name (see Figure 56-3)

• **Figure 56-3:** A new DWORD value ready for a name.

6. **Immediately type** `NumRibbons`.

If you accidentally click somewhere else, click once on New Value #1 and press the F2 key so you can change the name.

7. **Press Enter twice.**

Regedit brings up an Edit DWORD (32-bit) Value dialog box, as shown in Figure 56-4.

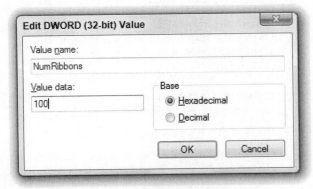

• **Figure 56-4:** Change NumRibbons to 100.

8. **Make sure the Hexadecimal option is selected, and then type 100 in the box marked Value Data. Then click OK.**

That 100 corresponds to the first alternate Ribbons setting shown in Table 56-3.

Regedit shows you the new value's name and data.

9. **Repeat Steps 5 through 8 and create a new DWORD value with the name RibbonWidth and the value 3c23d70a.**

Regedit should look like Figure 56-5.

At this point, you're done with Regedit. Congratulations! Vista's screen saver program doesn't require you to log off and log back on again — much less reboot (which is necessary to get some Registry changes to "take"). So, for the moment, leave Regedit open.

• **Figure 56-5: The new Ribbons screen saver values are in place.**

10. **Take a look at your new Ribbons screen saver — right-click any empty place on the desktop, choose Properties, click the Screen Saver icon, and, in the Screen Saver Settings dialog box, choose the Ribbons screen saver from the drop-down Screen Saver box.**

Bet you're gonna love it. See Figure 56-6.

11. **Before you rest on your rusting laurels, "X" out of the Screen Saver Settings dialog box.**

Don't worry. It's easy to bring it back.

12. **Go back into Regedit. Double-click NumRibbons, change its data per one of the entries in Table 56-3, and then click OK. Then double-click RibbonWidth and change its data.**

13. **Repeat Step 10 and look at your new Ribbons screen saver.**

All together now: ooooooooh! aaaaaaaaaah!

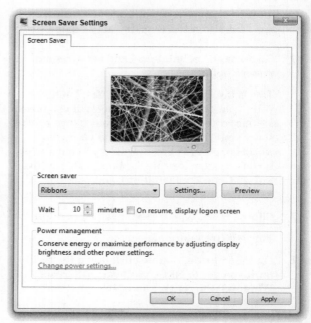

• **Figure 56-6: The Screen Saver Settings dialog box shows a preview of your ribbons.**

14. **Experiment — change the Registry data and see what you can get Ribbons to do. When you're happy with your new screen saver, click OK in the Screen Saver Settings dialog box and "X" out of the Registry Editor.**

All sorts of fun awaits in the Registry — if you're careful.

If you ever change your mind and you want to bring back your old Registry settings, double-click the `Original Ribbons screensaver settings.reg` file, and that Registry key is restored to its old values.

That's the long, boring, safe way to make Registry changes. Once you're familiar with the Editor, you'll probably dispense with running a system restore point, but you should always take a moment to export a `.reg` file before you make any changes.

There's a shorthand for all of the work you just did. If you ever wanted to feel way cool, try the jargon. You can summarize the ten steps as: *Yo, dude. Change HKCU\Software\Microsoft\Windows\CurrentVersion\ Screensavers\Ribbons\NumRibbons to a DWORD 100 hex and \RibbonWidth to DWORD 0x3c23d70a.*

If that isn't enough excitement for you, try making the Mystify screen saver cool by changing HKCU\Software\Microsoft\ Windows\CurrentVersion\Screensavers\ Mystify\NumLines to DWORD hex 15, or maybe DWORD 6. Now that you know the jargon, the steps go quickly, eh?

Technique 57

Making Screen Shots with the Snipping Tool

Save Time By

- ✔ Shooting your screen for fun and profit (no firearm required)
- ✔ Making Vista's built-in Snipping Tool cooperate with Windows Paint
- ✔ Using an industrial-strength screen shooter

"I clicked on my Microsoft and it didn't work."

Wish I had a nickel for every time I've heard that phrase.

I have no doubt that a picture's worth a thousand words. But when it comes to explaining or describing computer stuff, the right picture's worth a million words. Maybe more.

If you're trying to tell someone about an error message you've encountered — or, turning the tables, if you have a friend who's trying to explain some computer hiccup to you — getting a screen shot beats all the arm waving in the world.

Windows has always had a vestigial capability for taking screen shots — press the PrtScr key (on some keyboards, it's called Print Screen), and Windows copies the entire current screen onto the Clipboard; press Alt+PrtScr and the current window gets copied.

Vista brings something new to the party, a lightweight and snappy application called the Snipping Tool that makes taking screen shots a snip . . . er, a snap. (Vista Home Basic users don't get the Snipping Tool, but everybody else can snip along.)

 The Snipping Tool has loads of limitations — for starters, it won't save in TIF or BMP format — but you can work around some of the problems by using Windows Paint. When you combine the best of PrtScr and the Snipping Tool with Paint, you have a fast, free, easy way to take, manipulate, and annotate lots of screen shots.

I take you through both the basics and the advanced course in this short Technique. At the end, I show you how I take screen shots by using a remarkably capable, inexpensive package called SnagIt.

Using Fast Keyboard Shortcuts

How many times have you been typing an e-mail message or working on a document or putting together a presentation and wanted to take the stuff on your screen and stick it in the message, document, presentation, or whatever?

How many times have you encountered a Windows error, a weird thing on the screen, or something so totally incongruous that you just had to save it for posterity?

If you hit something that you want to capture right away, don't bother with the Vista Snipping Tool. Use the built-in Vista keyboard shortcuts, like this:

1. **Set up the screen the way you want to shoot it.**

Try moving the dialog box or window that you want to capture around the screen a bit. You'll see that the colors of the border change. If you have a wallpaper (er, desktop background), it may show through the border — an effect that you may or may not like.

 If you want to shoot against a white background, right-click an empty part of the desktop, choose Personalize, click the link to Desktop Background, and in the Picture Location box, choose Solid Colors. Click the White solid color (it's the second one offered) and click OK. Then "X" out of the Personalize dialog box.

 If you find that desktop icons are getting in the way, right-click an empty part of the desktop, choose View, and uncheck the line that says Show Desktop Icons.

2. **Hold down the Alt key and press PrtScr or Print Screen, whichever appears on your keyboard.**

That copies the currently active window onto the Windows Clipboard.

 If you want to grab the entire screen, don't hold down the Alt key — just press PrtScr.

3. **If you're going to put the screen shot in an e-mail message, a Word document, a presentation, or some other kind of file that can hold pictures, move to the document, click where you want the picture to go, and press Ctrl+V.**

That pastes the contents of the Windows Clipboard — the screen shot — in the document.

4. **If you want to save the screen shot as a picture file, choose Start⇨All Programs⇨Accessories⇨Paint and choose Edit⇨Paste. Then click File⇨Save to save the picture (see Figure 57-1).**

• **Figure 57-1: A screen shot of an Explorer window using Alt+PrtScr and Windows Paint.**

For more tips about using Paint with screen shots, see the section, "Making Paint Behave Itself," later in this Technique.

Interested in the finer points of screen shooting? If you look closely at the screen shot in Figure 57-1, you notice that there are blotches of gray at the corners of the shot; the "glowing red X" in the upper-right corner gets cut off at the top; but the "Close" screen tip appears just fine. If you ever need to make a screen shot that includes Screen Tips, Alt+PrtScr works great.

Cranking Up the Snipping Tool

The Vista Snipping Tool comes into play if you want to take screen shots that extend beyond the narrow boundaries of a selected window — even if you only want to go a little way beyond (see Figure 57-2).

• **Figure 57-2:** The Snipping Tool lets you go beyond the narrow confines of a window.

In fact, the Snipping Tool lets you choose any area on your screen, edit it, and then copy, save, or mail the shot.

 If you're interested in the finer points of screen shooting, take a close look at Figure 57-2. While the Snipping Tool lets you shoot any arbitrary part of the screen, it takes "focus" away from the window that you're shooting. So, as you can see in Figure 57-2, the gray extends all the way around the window, there's no "glowing red X" and no way to capture one, and Screen Tips don't appear at all — they disappear as soon as you start the Snipping Tool.

 The only problem with the Snipping Tool? It's saddled with some really strange default settings, which you can change easily. Here's how to get a good snip:

1. **Choose Start➪All Programs➪Accessories➪ Snipping Tool.**

Vista asks if you want to add the Snipping Tool to your Quick Launch toolbar.

2. **If you want the Snipping Tool on your Quick Launch toolbar (you probably do), click Yes.**

Your screen goes gray (see Figure 57-3) and the Snipping Tool appears.

• **Figure 57-3:** When the Snipping Tool is ready to snip, your screen goes gray.

Straight out of the box, the Snipping Tool puts a garish thick red border around your screen shot.

3. **If you like to put red neon around your shots, don't do anything, but if you have, uh, finer sensibilities, click the Options icon.**

The Snipping Tool Options dialog box appears, as in Figure 57-4.

4. **Refer to Table 57-1 and pick the options you want. Then click OK.**

At the very least, don't let the Snipping Tool save that garish red border.

When you finish setting the options, the Snipping Tool remains open on your desktop, but it's no longer active.

5. **Click the New icon.**

The screen goes gray again, as in Figure 57-3.

6. **Click and drag a box around the section of the screen you want to grab.**

As soon as you release the mouse button, the Snipping Tool's edit dialog box appears, with your screen capture showing and a few basic tools at the top, as in Figure 57-5.

TABLE 57-1: SNIPPING TOOL OPTIONS

What It Says	What It Means	Check This Setting?	Timesaving Tip
Hide Instruction Text	Don't show the two-line instructions at the bottom of the Snipping Tool window.		Show the instructions. The amount of lost space is minuscule.
Always Copy Snips to the Clipboard	As soon as you finish selecting the screen shot area, copy the selected area to the Clipboard.	✓	Saves you an extra click to copy the shot onto the Clipboard.
Include URL Below Snips (HTML Only)	If you take a screen shot while Internet Explorer is running in the active window, and most of the shot includes the IE window, *and* you save the shot as a Microsoft proprietary single-file HTML file (MHT), the Snipping Tool puts the address of the active Web page at the bottom of the shot (see Figure 57-6).	✓	It's a rare combination of events, but if you're working with MHTML files anyway, you probably want the URL.
Prompt to Save Snips before Exiting	If you don't save a shot before leaving the Snipping Tool, it asks if you want to save the file.	✓	You can save yourself time retaking a missed shot.
Display Icon in the Quick Launch Toolbar	Adds a Snipping Tool icon to the Quick Launch toolbar.	✓	Sure. Why not?
Show Screen Overlay When Snipping Tool Is Active	This is the graying-out effect you can see in Figure 57-3.	✓	Having the unselected part of the screen appear in gray helps you quickly select the boundaries of the shot.
Show Selection Ink after Snips Are Captured	The line that you use to select the screen capture area (by default it's red) is saved as part of the picture file.		Yech. Tacky.

• **Figure 57-4:** The way I use the Snipping Tool.

• **Figure 57-5:** The Snipping Tool's edit dialog box.

The Snipping Tool also places a copy of the captured screen on the Windows Clipboard.

7. **Experiment with the Pen and Highlighter tools (click the appropriate icons).**

Note how the Eraser tool erases whatever line or highlight it touches. If you draw a line and decide you don't want it, click the Eraser icon,

and then click anywhere on the line to make the line disappear.

 Edits take place much as you would expect them to, with one exception: Whenever you edit the picture, the Snipping Tool modifies the image on the Windows Clipboard, replacing it with whatever you've added. In other words, the Copy icon is completely superfluous.

8. **When you're done, click the Save icon and save the file.**

You can only save Snipping Tool files as PNGs, GIFs, JPGs, or Single File HTML (MHT).

• **Figure 57-6:** Shoot an IE window and save it in MHT format, and the Snipping Tool puts the URL at the bottom.

Making Paint Behave Itself

Whether you're working with Alt+PrtScr (see the "Using Fast Keyboard Shortcuts" section) or the Snipping Tool to put a screen shot on the Windows Clipboard (see preceding section), Windows Paint may come in handy.

You may want to use Paint to

🗸 Save pictures when using PrtScr or Alt+PrtScr.

🗸 Save pictures in a wider variety of formats when you use the Snipping Tool — Monochrome BMP, 16-color BMP, 256-color BMP, 24-bit BMP, and TIF are all supported in Paint but not supported in the Snipping Tool.

🗸 Make simple edits to screen shots before saving them. Paint's ability to zoom in, select sections of a shot, copy, paste, and propel pasted pieces of pics (say that ten times real fast) around the screen make it a handy, if underpowered, picture editing tool.

 Paint has one bad habit, though, that makes it ornery when dealing with pasted screen shots. When you start Paint, it assumes that you want to create a picture that's 640 pixels wide by 512 pixels high. I don't know why Microsoft chose those dimensions, but they stink. Why? If you have a screen capture smaller than 640 x 512 pixels, and you paste it into Paint, you get a big white margin filling the picture out to 640 x 512. Blech.

Fortunately, there's a workaround, which doesn't appear to be documented anywhere but here:

1. **Choose Start⊃All Programs⊃Accessories⊃ Paint.**

Windows Paint appears on the screen.

2. **Choose Image⊃Attributes.**

You see the Attributes dialog box, shown in Figure 57-7.

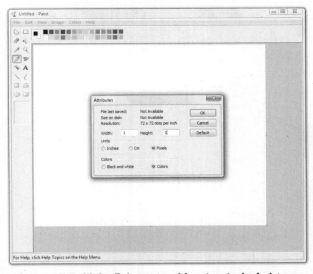

• **Figure 57-7:** Make Paint start with a 1-x-1-pixel picture.

3. **Type 1 in both the Width and Height boxes and click OK.**

Paint shows you a 1-x-1-pixel image.

4. **"X" out of Paint. When Paint asks if you want to save changes to Untitled, click Don't Save.**

The next time you start Paint, it appears with a 1-x-1-pixel image.

Having an initial 1-pixel "picture" makes it slam-dunk easy to use Paint to save screen shots. The general approach goes like this:

1. **Use PrtScr or Alt+PrtScr or the Snipping Tool to create a screen shot and put it on the Windows Clipboard.**

The preceding sections show you how.

2. **Choose Start⊃All Programs⊃Accessories⊃ Paint.**

Paint appears with a 1-pixel picture.

3. **Press Ctrl+V or choose Edit⊃Paste to paste the picture into Paint.**

Paint handles the screen shot just like any other picture coming in from the Clipboard. When you start with a 1-pixel picture, Paint automatically resizes the picture dimensions to exactly match the size of the screen shot.

From that point, you can use Paint to flip, rotate, skew, copy, paste, fill, erase, draw lines, type text . . . the whole nine yards.

 Using Paint's a snap after you get it to avoid sticking in those big white margins.

Going Beyond the Basics

People often ask me how I get screen shots into my books. Hey, with 1,400 pages of Windows Vista books under my belt, I'm picky.

I use a product called SnagIt from a company called TechSmith, and I've been using it for many years. If you take a look at the shot in Figure 57-8, I think you'll see why.

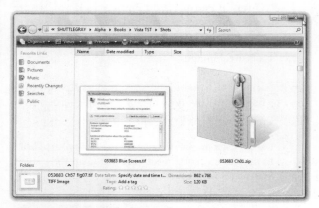

• **Figure 57-8:** A really great screen shot.

SnagIt not only shows the gray border all around the window, but also, when I shoot the window, it stays "active" — so the "glowing red X" appears in all its fiery glory. SnagIt includes options to either shoot the mouse pointer or ignore it, and Screen Tips almost always come through. Compare the shot in Figure 57-8 with the ones in Figures 57-1 (using PrtScrn and Paint) and 57-2 (using the Snipping Tool), and I think you can see immediately how SnagIt's quality runs rings around the others — even in black and white.

 SnagIt has all sorts of additional tools, from automatic sequence numbering to countdown timers to extensive editing tools, and much more. You can get a free 30-day trial at www.techsmith.com, and if you decide to buy it, an individual copy is just $39.95. If you're serious about shooting screens, SnagIt is worth the expense.

Fast, Easy, and Safe Online Shopping

Technique 58

Save Time By

✔ Finding what you want — fast

✔ Ordering with full confidence

✔ Using eBay the right way

One hundred thirty billion bucks. That's about how much consumers in the United States spend while using the Internet in a year. It's a staggering number — but barring some extraordinary calamity, it's going to keep on growing.

You already know why people shop online — it's fast, it's easy, and you don't need to find a parking spot. If you look in the right places, comparing prices can take just a click or two. Although you rarely find the absolute lowest price for most consumer products online, particularly after you pay for shipping, you come pretty darn close.

And you won't waste an hour driving to the mall and back.

Sure, online shopping has its problems. You can't feel the fabric. You can't try on the pants to see if they bag in the butt. You can't hand your kids a five dollar bill and tell 'em to buy the biggest ice cream cone they've ever seen.

But when it comes to saving time, online shopping can't be beat.

Searching for Reliable E-Tailers

Whether you want a genuine first-edition signed Hemingway or an almost-certainly-fake signed *Lincoln in Dalivision,* you find much of what you want — and much more of what you don't want — on the Web.

If you've been on the Web for any time at all, no doubt you've book-marked dozens of places that deserve your hard-earned dollars or euros or yen or shekels or baht.

In this section, I offer you three lists of sites that I think every online shopper should check at least once. This isn't a scientific list or a paid advertisement (which is more than can be said for advertising on some search engines). It's a quick rundown of good places to shop if you're in the mood to save some time.

TABLE 58-1: MY ALL-TIME FAVORITE SHOPPING SITES

Address	Company	Description
www.craigslist.com	Craigslist	Classified ads for the world in every imaginable category, plus community bulletin boards, discussion forums, and jobs.
www.amazon.com	Amazon	The original online bookstore with food, toys, clothes, electronics, and software.
www.bn.com	Barnes & Noble	Giving Amazon a run for the money and staying focused on books.
www.cooking.com	Cooking.com	Absolutely everything a cook could ever want. Shipping is available only to the United States, territories, APO addresses, and Canada, undoubtedly because people who live outside North America don't like to eat.
www.landsend.com	Lands' End	One of the first, and still one of the best. Clothes, shoes, luggage, and more.
www.llbean.com	L.L. Bean	Great clothes, legendary shoes, outdoor gear, and still the best return policy on the planet.
www.oldnavy.com	Old Navy	You call 'em generic; I call 'em cool. Cheap, too.
www.rei.com	REI	Long-time favorite with innovative outdoor products. Includes a tab for REI-Outlet.com.

Table 58-1 lists the e-tailers that I have used for years. They're reliable, the sites are put together so that you can get in and out quickly, and they don't sock you with hidden charges or time-wasting games.

When I want to look for bargains, I go to these three sites:

- ✔ **Overstock.com** (www.overstock.com): Discounted name-brand products in more than a hundred categories — electronics, home, clothes, jewelry, and sports.

- ✔ **Costco.com** (www.costco.com): The big discounter, in cyberspace. Frequently carries items online that you can't find in your local store.

- ✔ **Eddie Bauer Outlet** (www.eddiebaueroutlet.com): An online version of its outlet stores.

The sites are a bit harder to negotiate than the ones in Table 58-1, but that's at least partially attributable to the fact that the merchandise changes constantly.

Here are the sites I use when I know what I want and I'm looking for the best price:

- ✔ **mySimon** (www.mysimon.com): Compare prices from dozens of online retailers. Strong on electronics, computer parts, books, office supplies, clothes, and the like, but not as thorough as it once was.

- ✔ **PriceGrabber** (www.pricegrabber.com): Fast comparisons on cameras, computer products, video games, and DVDs.

- ✔ **BizRate** (www.bizrate.com): Compares prices for computer equipment, cameras, clothes, travel, office supplies, toys, and much more.

- ✔ **Froogle** (froogle.google.com): The new kid on the chopping, er, shopping block lists just about everything, but I found that other sites linked to places with slightly lower prices.

If you aren't sure where to look for a product, you should try:

- **The Google shotgun approach:** Type a description of the product into the Google Search box and press Enter.

- **The Yahoo! indexed approach:** Go to `http://shopping.yahoo.com` and drill down to the product you want.

Paying It Safe

Every major retail site nowadays has adopted the shopping-cart approach. Most online retailers enable you to store information on their Web sites — credit card number, shipping address, and the like — to make it easier for you to make repeated purchases.

 If you want to save something in your shopping cart, you almost always have to enable cookies on your computer. That's how the retailer's computer keeps track of who you are and what you're buying. For more about cookies, see Technique 18.

Choosing a payment method

When you shop online, you're generally offered a number of ways to pay:

- **Credit card:** By far the most flexible and safest option for you (also one of the most problematic sources of income for the retailer).

- **Debit card:** If you have an ATM card or check card in which the full amount of a purchase is deducted from your bank account as soon as you buy something, it's a debit card. In the United States, a debit card purchase is not protected nearly as well as a credit card purchase. Outside the U.S., laws and/or card company policies vary.

- **PayPal or similar third-party payment system:** A very efficient means of paying, with an established conflict resolution method (if you have a PayPal account, see item 15 of the User Agreement at `www.paypal.com/row/cgi-bin/webscr?cmd=p/gen/ua/ua`), but you don't have anything close to the kind of protection given to credit card charges.

- **E-money or micropayments:** Although the first wave of companies died in the dot-com bust, there has been a tiny resurgence of interest. These accounts and/or cards generally reflect some sort of prepaid, stored value. You pay with e-money, and the amount is debited from your card or account.

Getting what you pay for

You should treat a business transaction on the Internet the same way you would treat any other business transaction — only more so.

Before you order a product or service, follow these steps:

1. **Retrieve and save precise details about the product.**

   At the very least, you need a model number and a description of the product. Surf to the page that describes what you're ordering; then print or save the page. To save the page, choose File⇨Save, and in the Save As Type drop-down list, choose Web Page, Complete (or Web Archive, Single File (*.mht) in Internet Explorer) (see Figure 58-1). That saves the page and all the pictures on it in a single file.

• **Figure 58-1:** Save an entire page, including all its pictures, by using the Web Page, Complete option.

2. **Find the company's refund and return policies and save them.**

Again, print or save the appropriate page as Web Page, Complete or Web Archive, Single File (*.mht).

3. **Get the e-mail address or phone number of the customer service people.**

Print it or save it. You know the drill.

4. **Get something in writing about the expected delivery date.**

There should be an explicit statement about delivery somewhere during the checkout process. Make sure that you save (or print) the page with that information.

5. **Make sure that you know how much you will be charged.**

If the final on-screen bill doesn't include shipping and handling, you only have yourself to blame if your product arrives in the back of a Rolls, hand-delivered by a big football star — and you're billed for the privilege.

6. **Print or save the order page.**

Every legitimate retail site e-mails you a receipt. But even under the best of circumstances, sometimes things go awry.

 Most of the time, a specific transaction number is associated with the order. Make sure you have a record of it. Also, many sites send separate e-mail confirmations when the order is placed and when it's shipped. Keep those, too. And if you receive a tracking number for UPS, FedEx, or some other carrier (Amazon, among many others, includes a tracking number in the shipment notification), take a moment and visit the Web site to ensure the package is headed in the right direction. Several times, I've had packages bound for Thailand end up in Taiwan, or ones addressed to Australia go to Austria.

When everything arrives as expected, and your credit card (or debit card, PayPal account, e-account, or whatever) is charged correctly, you can breathe a

sigh of relief. In fact, in my experience, the vast majority of online purchases work just as well as their meatspace analogs. But whether you're clicking online or standing at a checkout counter, it's a whole lot easier to prepare for any eventuality *before* a disaster strikes.

Using reputable Web sites

So how do you know if a specific Web site is on the up-and-up? The short answer: You never really know for sure. Here are a few pointers:

✔ If the Web site has the same name as a store chain you know and trust, you should expect that the policies and services online will be at least as good as what you would receive in person in the store.

✔ If you have any doubt at all about a Web site's credibility, check the Better Business Bureau's online site, www.bbbonline.com. The Better Business Bureau isn't infallible, it covers only the United States and the European Union, and it doesn't have entries for every Web shop, but the 32,000-or-so businesses listed in its directory have gone to extraordinary lengths to ensure that their customers are treated fairly.

✔ If you aren't dealing with a big-name chain, and the Web site isn't on the BBB's list, you have to rely on your own devices. You might be able to find out how long the company has been in business. You can scan the Google newsgroups (groups.google.com) for the company's name. You can look at the site and see if it's well designed: A poorly designed site is a dead tip-off for a company that doesn't care. You can track down a customer service number and call and ask about the company's return policy, product warranties, shipping costs, and so on. More than anything, though, if you start to get second thoughts about dealing with a specific Web site, insist on using a credit card.

 Spend the time up front to save time down the line. When you're sure of a business's reliability, you can shop without fear and save time. Remember that the first rule of buying online is *caveat emptor* — buyer beware — and that a fool and his money soon go separate ways.

On the technical side, you should send out your credit card or other personal information only if the Web site requesting it uses something called the Secured Sockets Layer. You don't need to remember that arcane name, but you should remember to look for the locked (padlock) symbol to the right of a secure page's Web address, either in Firefox or in IE 7 (see Figure 58-2).

• **Figure 58-2: Look for the padlock to the right of the Web page address in Firefox (above) or Internet Explorer (below).**

The locked symbol signifies that it's very, very, very difficult for someone to eavesdrop on your conversation with the Web site. Yes, holes have been discovered in SSL. No, nobody has lost any money because of them.

Handling credit card fraud

If someone steals your credit card and the card was issued in the United States, the Fair Credit Billing Act and the Electronic Fund Transfer Act basically protect you from any charges in excess of $50.

If someone steals your credit card number, as opposed to the card itself, and the card was issued in the United States, your liability for unauthorized charges is zero.

You should call your bank immediately if you find that your card has been stolen, of course.

The situation with U.S.-issued debit cards is different. If your debit card is lost or stolen, you're liable for up to $50 if you report the card stolen to the bank within 48 hours. If you wait longer, you could be on the hook for more, and if you don't report a lost card within 60 days of receiving a statement with a bogus charge on it, you may be held liable for the entire amount in your account.

There don't appear to be any laws about stolen debit card numbers. Call your bank and find out your liability if your debit card number (and not the card itself) is stolen.

I, personally, had a debit card number stolen, and the thief ran up a series of charges at tony boutiques in London. (Pardon the Briticism.) Since I hadn't been in London for more than a decade, my bank went to bat for me, had me fill out the proper forms, and assured that my account was credited for the pilfered amount. It was a hassle — I had to get the card cancelled and re-issued, and my attempts to work with the ripped-off companies fell on surprisingly deaf ears — but in the end, I didn't lose a penny. If it happens to you, I hope your bank is as good as mine.

Laws and credit card company procedures vary in different countries, but many places have laws that are even tougher than those in the United States, and many U.S.-based credit card companies try to match the parent companies' policies overseas.

If you pay for something online with a U.S.-issued debit card or credit card, and if any of these things happen

- You don't receive the goods or service
- You receive something that differs from what was promised
- You were billed for an amount that isn't right

you must immediately contact the credit or debit card company.

It pays to follow through on online fraud — even if you only lose five or ten dollars. Some of the most successful online con men (and women) bilk thousands of customers out of small amounts of money. When you make the effort to correct even small problems, you save time for everyone.

Here's what you need to do:

1. **Make a reasonable effort to resolve the problem with the vendor.**

Conduct all conversations in writing — e-mail or snail mail — and keep copies of everything. Don't let the negotiating go on for more than a couple of weeks.

 When I was ripped off, the vendors in London treated me with indifference, didn't respond, and generally acted like they couldn't be bothered.

2. **If the vendor won't make good on the product or service, write to the credit or debit card company or your bank.**

Theoretically, you're supposed to wait for the bill to come through; but in the case of a debit card, in particular, handling the problem immediately is best — don't wait for your statement. In any case, make sure that your letter arrives at the credit or debit card company within 60 days of when the contested bill was sent to you.

3. **Send the letter certified mail, return receipt requested, or via a bank's secure online message system. Use the address on your credit or debit card statement for billing inquiries or billing disputes.**

If you write to the payment address, you'll never hear a thing.

If you send the notice by mail, keep the return receipt when it comes back. If you send it via a secure messaging system, log on to the site daily and check for a response.

4. **In the letter, include your name, address, telephone number, account number, brief (and I do mean brief) description of the dispute, the amount that's in question, your e-mail address, and copies of everything you can find.**

Make your first shot across the bow overwhelming — not by whining on, page after page, but by presenting the facts clearly and succinctly and supporting what you say with incontrovertible documentation. Ask that the credit card or debit card company contact you by e-mail.

5. **Make copies of everything.**

Keep the whole package stapled together so you can refer to it later.

If you do all those things, the law is on your side.

 There are no laws, at this point, protecting stored-value e-money or micropayment accounts.

If someone takes your money and disappears without supplying the goods you purchased, you have two chances of seeing that money again: slim and none. But if you're smart enough to use a credit card, the credit card company gets the short end of the stick.

 It tickles me when people say they're concerned that someone will steal their credit card number when they order something over the Internet. The fact is that you're far more likely to have your number stolen by a clerk in a store or someone rummaging through a trash can. The largest (known) heist of credit card numbers to date came from a computer hacker who broke into the computers at a credit card processing company. The incident had absolutely nothing to do with online shopping.

For folks in the United States, the Federal Trade Commission has set up a site that helps people handle ID theft and fraud:

    http://www.ftc.gov/bcp/edu/microsites/
    idtheft

Keeping private information private

Many a failing dot-com in the past ten years has discovered that its most valuable asset is its mailing list. As the bubble burst, strapped companies scrambled for negotiable assets. Many "private" mailing lists ended up on the list of assets, right next to manicured office parks and used office chairs.

Never give out any personal information to anyone unless it's absolutely necessary. That's good advice both on and off the computer. Yes, you have to give out your e-mail address if you order online, and you may have to divulge your telephone number. But the site selling you a printer doesn't need to know your job title or annual income — much less your level of education.

Complaining Effectively

Got a beef? Did somebody rip you off online? The Federal Trade Commission wants to hear about it. Really.

Go to `https://rn.ftc.gov/pls/dod/widtpubl$.startup?Z_ORG_CODE=PU03` and fill out the form.

You'll hear back, I bet.

Mastering eBay

So many people use eBay these days that it's worthwhile understanding some of the more arcane bits and pieces of the eBay way.

When you look at an item for sale, a large amount of information about the seller is encoded in some cute icons and staccato notices (see Figure 58-3).

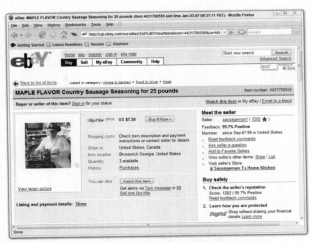

• **Figure 58-3: An eBay Buy It Now listing for maple sausage seasoning.**

Look for these entries:

✔ **The number after the seller's name:** The number (in Figure 58-3, it's 1202) indicates the seller's feedback rating. Feedback is the lifeblood of eBay, and it's what keeps the venue making money while other online retailers and auction venues go belly up. The feedback rating tells you the net number of positive comments that have been submitted about a particular seller. A high number is a good sign, particularly when you realize that the seller gets 1 point for a positive review, 0 points for a so-so review, and –1 for a negative review. (The star icon following the number is a color-coded repeat of the number.)

Don't just go by the feedback rating shown by the seller's name; it only reflects the net positive rating (that is, the total number of positives, minus any negative feedback). Click the number to find out the total number of feedback submissions (see Figure 58-4). For example, it's possible for someone to have a feedback rating of 500, which ain't a shabby feedback rating. But if you click the number, you may find that the seller has received several neutral comments (which don't have any effect on the total rating), or negative feedback comments (which decrease the total shown by the seller's name).

If you're interested in getting a quick look at how to use eBay to shop for bargains, check out *eBay Bargain Shopping For Dummies* by Marsha Collier (Wiley).

• **Figure 58-4:** Sausageman1's feedback is overwhelmingly positive.

✔ A **Power Seller icon:** eBay recognizes its best sellers — ones who sell a lot, remain committed to the eBay rules, and get excellent feedback — with the Power Seller icon.

✔ A **Changed User ID icon:** The icon looks like a pair of bubble boys with an arrow from one to the other. It means that the person hasn't been using eBay long enough to have established a reputation through feedback. Maybe they're new. If an eBay seller changes his or her ID, the new ID gets a Changed User ID icon for the next 30 days. Although the Changed User ID icon doesn't mean anything shady is going on, there's usually a good reason why a member would change his or her ID — and frequently it's because of sketchy feedback.

eBay has a large staff that keeps track of problems and works to resolve the inevitable conflicts that go along with running the world's largest auction house. Before you bid, you should take a look at pages.ebay.com/help/confidence/programs-investigations.html and make sure that you feel comfortable with the safety net that eBay has in place.

Don't let my cautions here turn you off. eBay rates as a tremendous resource. I use it all the time. You have to watch out for the details — inflated shipping and "handling" charges, for example, can turn a bargain into a clunker — but if you follow the nostrums in this Technique, chances are good that eBay will win you over.

Although eBay may or may not be responsible for various aspects of its offerings, keep the following points in mind:

✔ **eBay is not responsible for the item itself.** If you buy a used washing machine and it falls apart the day you install it, eBay is not at fault.

✔ **Every bid is a legal and binding contract between you and the seller.** If you have any questions about the item on offer, you should e-mail the seller and ask. Don't place a bid until you are absolutely sure about every detail of the product, its quality, shipping, insurance, and so on. If you don't ask questions before you place your bid, and you get something that matches the description but it wasn't what you were expecting, that isn't fraud — it's lack of due diligence on your part.

✔ **Beware of anything that's too good to be true.**

✔ **Con men (and women) work eBay, too.** If someone takes your money and runs, you have very little recourse unless you used a credit card. By the time you get to the point where you're asking eBay to investigate, you might as well kiss your money goodbye. A lot of the nefarious schemes that come out of eBay also qualify as Mail Fraud — and the US Postal Service can get involved. See www.usps.com/postal inspectors/fraud/welcome.htm for details.

✔ **eBay says it has enough people on staff to police all their auctions.** If you were in eBay's shoes, what would you say?

Caveat biddor.

Technique 59

Create Your Own Desktop Theme

Ready to have a little fun?

Good. Let's try something different.

You probably know that you can download zillions of themes from the Internet. You probably also know that a very large percentage of all the free themes on the Internet come bundled with spyware, adware, badware, and scumware.

You might not know that it's easy to make your own theme — wallpaper (er, desktop background), colors, icons, screen saver, mouse pointers, even your own custom sounds.

That's pretty cool, especially if you have a good reason to create a theme — like, oh, a new addition to the family.

In this very short Technique, I take you through the steps to make your own theme, save it, and distribute it.

Piece o' cake. And you have a chance to look inside a real, working Registry in the process.

What's in a Theme?

Microsoft created the concept of a Windows desktop "theme" so it could make more money. That probably doesn't surprise you. Starting in the times of Windows 98, Windows Plus! Packs (you may recognize them from the Da Vinci, Nature, or Space themes) made a few coppers for the coffers. Fortunately, you can subvert Microsoft's method for your own porpoises. And dolphins.

A Vista theme includes the following elements:

✔ **A .theme file:** Yep, a file with a filename extension of .theme. Microsoft doesn't talk about it much, but a theme file (see Figure 59-1) contains Registry entries. Fortunately, you don't need to change the Registry entries, but you do have to look inside the .theme file to get it to work. I show you how in the "Distributing Your Theme" section, later in this Technique.

• **Figure 59-1: A .theme file.**

✔ **Big pictures:** A Windows desktop background. A screen saver.

✔ **Little stuff:** Custom advanced desktop settings (such as colors or fonts for all windows), different pictures for the system icons (such as the Recycle Bin), new mouse cursors, and modified colors for buttons.

✔ **Weird stuff:** System sounds. A skin for Windows Media Player. "Visualizations" for the Media Player.

You can try to make your own icons and mouse cursors from scratch, but that's a lot of work. If you want to take the plunge, look at IconCool Editor ($29.95 shareware from Newera Software, www.iconcool.com) for both icons and animated mouse cursors.

It may be better (and it's certainly faster) to download and use free or royalty-free icon and mouse cursor collections, or you can download a theme that

someone else has put together and (providing there are no copyright restrictions) use the icons and cursors from the theme. Tucows has a large selection that's constantly changing. Start at www.tucows.com/Windows/DesktopEnhancements.

A few really scummy companies have taken themes that individuals posted on the Internet and repackaged them, wrapping them with scumware installers. Watch out.

Creating a Theme

Making your own theme couldn't be simpler:

1. **For safety's sake, save your current theme settings, just in case you ever want to use them again. Right-click any empty part of the desktop and choose Personalize.**

   You see the Personalization dialog box, which looks like Figure 59-2.

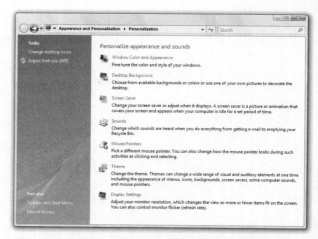

• **Figure 59-2: You can change almost anything from this dialog box and have it apply to your new theme.**

2. **In the Personalization dialog box, click the Theme icon.**

   You see the Theme Settings dialog box, which probably looks like Figure 59-3.

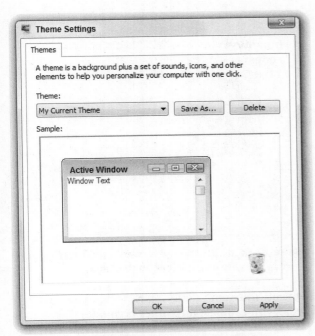

• **Figure 59-3: A typical Theme Settings dialog box.**

If you haven't made any changes at all to your desktop, the Theme drop-down box may say Windows Vista or Satisfied OEM Customer, or it may have some other setting that your computer manufacturer established.

3. **Click the Save As button.**

You see a garden-variety Vista Save As dialog box.

4. **Type a name for your current theme and click Save.**

Consider giving it a name with the current date, or something else that's distinctive, in case you completely mess up your new theme and want to go back.

5. **Click OK to get out of the Theme Settings dialog box.**

6. **If you want to use your own picture for the theme's wallpaper (er, desktop background), take a moment and make sure that the picture is in your Pictures folder.**

 Although Step 6 isn't absolutely necessary, it will save you a bunch of time if you ever want to move your theme to a different computer.

7. **Back in the Personalization dialog box (refer to Figure 59-2), click the Desktop Background link.**

You see the Choose a Desktop Background dialog box, shown in Figure 59-4.

• **Figure 59-4: Look for the wallpaper, er, desktop background that you want to include in your theme.**

8. **Pick the wallpaper that you want to use for your theme, choose how you want it positioned, and change the background color by clicking the link, if you like. When you're done, click OK.**

You can choose any of the standard Vista-supplied pictures, but (as noted in Step 6) if you pick your own picture, make sure it's in your Pictures folder before you choose it.

9. **Back in the Personalization dialog box, click the links to change your Screen Saver, Sounds, or Mouse Pointers. You can also click the tasks on the left to Change Desktop Icons (which is to say, the appearance of standard desktop icons like the Recycle Bin) or Adjust Font Size.**

Although you can click the links to change the Window Color and Appearance or the Display Settings, most of the changes you make in those categories aren't reflected in the theme. Don't ask me why. You really don't want to know.

Well, okay, you dug it out of me. The settings that are reflected in the theme are settings that have been around a long time — at least since the time of Windows XP, and in many cases all the way back to Windows 98. Microsoft didn't change themes in Vista very much, so they didn't bother to include new things like the Aero settings in Vista's themes. At least, as far as I can tell, the Aero settings don't get reliably set in the theme. I guess Microsoft ran out of money. Whaddya think?

10. **When you're happy with all the changes you've made — your new baby as the wallpaper, a complementary background color, swirly icons, those little farting noises when you click the wrong button (that's called a Default Beep) — go back to the Personalization dialog box.**

11. **Click the Theme icon.**

You see the Theme Settings box, and the Theme drop-down list says Modified Theme.

12. **Click the Save As button.**

Vista shows you the Save As dialog box, like the one in Figure 59-5.

13. **Type a name for your current theme and click Save.**

In Figure 59-5, I call my new theme Rubye.Theme.

14. **Click OK to get out of the Theme Settings dialog box, and then "X" out of the Personalization dialog box.**

Anytime you want to bring back this theme, just go the Personalization dialog box, click the Theme icon, and choose Rubye in the Theme drop-down list.

• **Figure 59-5:** My new theme is ready, with a wallpaper of the new addition to the family.

But wait! You aren't done yet! Now that you have a theme, you can take it to other computers!

Distributing Your Theme

If you recall, at the beginning of this Technique, I mention that every theme has a .theme file. In the last step of the preceding section, you created a .theme file, and Vista put it in your Documents folder, of all places.

If you want to move your theme to another computer, you have to gather up all the pieces and move them, along with the .theme file, to the new computer.

How do you know where to find the pieces? You look in the .theme file:

1. **Choose Start⇨All Programs⇨Accessories⇨Notepad.**

Poor, humble (and eminently useful!) Notepad appears on your screen.

2. **Choose File⇨Open.**

You get a run-of-the-mill Open dialog box.

3. In the drop-down box to the right of the File Name box, choose All Files. Navigate to your Documents folder and click the .theme file you created in the preceding section. (See Figure 59-6.) Click Open.

• **Figure 59-6:** Open your .theme file with Notepad.

You see a whole bunch of Registry-style garbage.

4. Look for filenames and locations. Print the .theme file if need be. Then "X" out to close it.

In particular, the Wallpaper entry (see Figure 59-7) points to your %USERPROFILE%\Pictures folder. (I bet you could guess that's your Pictures folder.) If you changed any cursors, the location of the cursor files is in the section marked [Control Panel\Cursors]. If you changed any sounds, the location of the sound files appears toward the end of the .theme file in entries marked [AppEvents\Schemes\Apps\ .Default\.Default\.Current].

5. Copy the .theme file from your Documents folder to the Documents folder on the new

computer. If you chose your own picture as the theme's wallpaper, copy the wallpaper picture from the Pictures folder on the old computer to the Pictures folder on the new computer.

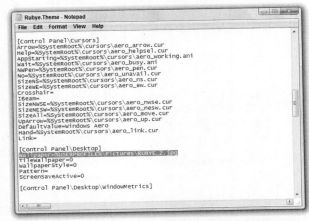

• **Figure 59-7:** Scan the .theme file to see what files you need to move to the second PC and where you need to put them.

6. If you have any custom cursors or icons listed in the .theme file, copy them to the same location on the new computer.

7. On the new computer, right-click any empty part of the desktop and choose Personalize. In the Personalization dialog box, click the Theme icon.

You see the Theme Settings dialog box, looking much like Figure 59-3.

8. From the drop-down Theme box, choose the theme you just moved. Click OK.

Lo and behold, your theme has made the leap.

Technique 60

Saving Time (And Your Eyes) On-Screen

Save Time By

✔ Making characters on your screen easier to see

✔ Choosing the best combination of screen resolution and zoom factor

✔ Adjusting ClearType the right way — the first time

If you're like me, you may have wondered just how much time you have lost because you can't see what's on your %$#@! screen. Even in the best of circumstances, carelessly clicking in the wrong place, deleting the wrong lines, or entering data in the wrong cells is much easier to do than any of us would like to admit.

If your eyes ain't what they used to be, this Technique can save you a great deal of time, money, and (literally!) headaches. I talk about a few commonsense timesavers, changing screen resolution, and zooming in and out to change the appearance of content on-screen.

This Technique also covers ClearType, Microsoft's long-maligned text tweaking technology that's finally come of age. ClearType aims to make text on the screen easier on your eyes. If you used ClearType in earlier versions of Windows, you're in for a treat — for the first time ever, I've become a ClearType fan. Although ClearType originated as a response to the jaggies on LCD monitors (flat screens, laptops, and the like), it has been refined so it does a credible job on traditional CRT (TV-style) monitors.

Applying Basic, Vision-Saving Tactics

All the whiz-bang technology in the world won't save you time unless you set up and use your monitor properly:

✔ **Keep the monitor clean.** On a flat-panel screen, use isopropanol (rubbing alcohol); on a CRT, use any high-quality glass cleaner, but be sure to spray your paper towel (or old newspaper) — don't spray the screen directly. See Technique 50 for more cleaning tips.

✔ **Watch out for glare.** If you can't move your monitor out of direct, bright light, get a glare filter. Yes, fluorescent lights can cause a lot of glare, and some people are very susceptible to fluorescent flicker, particularly when it's reflected on-screen.

✔ **Line up the monitor so that you're face to face** (or face to monitor, as it were). Opinions vary, but if your monitor sits right in front of you, the top of the monitor should be a few inches above your eyes, with the face of the monitor parallel to your face.

✔ **Adjust the darn thing.** Spend a bit of time going through this Technique and apply the options that you're most comfortable using. Whether you're unaware of all the settings or have just been putting off changing them, the most basic adjustments can save you considerable muss and fuss in the long run. Even those "Auto adjusting" LCDs need tweaking.

✔ **Get a bigger/better monitor. Heck, get two.** Although you can't really quantify the amount of time you save by being able to see two documents (or spreadsheets or Web pages) at the same time, there's no question that a larger, better-quality screen can improve your efficiency, and two monitors just double the fun.

 Once upon a time, rotating flat-panel monitors were all the rage — use them normally (in "landscape") for most of your computer activities, but swivel them 90 degrees (to "portrait") when you need to work on documents or narrow spreadsheets. That's changing. ClearType doesn't work right when you rotate the screen. ClearType is designed to look great when a flat-panel screen sits in landscape, but it can't make the flip to portrait. A better solution: If your video card can handle it, buy a second monitor.

Understanding How Characters Appear On-Screen

You and I can whip out a Montblanc and draw swirls and curlicues to our heart's content, but computers have to work with dots. The number of dots, or *pixels* (the word means picture elements), on a screen limits Windows' ability to display characters legibly.

When Windows wants to draw a V on the screen, for example, it looks like Figure 60-1.

• **Figure 60-1: The letter V in 14-point Garamond font on an 1280 x 1024 screen.**

 Jaggies are the stair-step patterns you see when Windows has to draw a line by filling in the dots on-screen.

That's the best Windows can do as long as it can only turn single dots on or off — it must make each pixel either white or black.

Life isn't so simple, nor so black and white. In fact, each pixel on a color monitor actually consists of three subpixels, one each in red, green, and blue — in that order, from left to right. Your brain blurs the subpixels together to make one dot appear for every group of three subpixels.

Judicious manipulation of the red, green, and blue stripes can significantly decrease the jaggies, as shown in Figure 60-2 — the same Garamond "V" but this time with Vista's ClearType enabled.

Many attempts have been made, over the years, to use those three subpixel stripes to improve the legibility of text on a screen. Microsoft calls its approach ClearType.

ClearType is built into Vista, and (unless you've turned it off) it's working right now. I talk about ClearType later in this Technique.

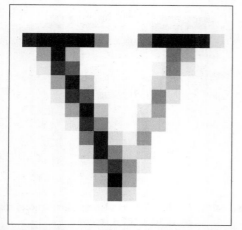

• **Figure 60-2:** Manipulating each subpixel individually greatly increases the clarity of a character.

Flat-panel screens and LCD (liquid crystal display) monitors use three-colored stripes, whereas traditional monitors use subpixels that look more like dots. That difference is the primary reason that ClearType makes text look better on flat-panel displays than it does on traditional monitors. ClearType has been tweaked to produce decent results on traditional monitors, but you won't see the full effect on anything but a flat panel.

 For a detailed description of subpixel character rendering on color screens, take a look at Steve Gibson's excellent explanation at grc.com/cleartype.htm.

Adjusting Resolution Settings

Screen resolution refers to the number of pixels Windows places on a screen. For example, 1024 x 768 resolution has 1024 pixels across the screen and 768 from top to bottom.

LCD displays are generally intended to work optimally for a specific screen resolution (usually 1024 x 768 for 15-inch monitors and 1280 x 1024 for 17-inch, with larger and widescreen displays all over the place). Stick to the intended resolution if you have an LCD monitor. The hardware's designed to work best that way.

If you're shopping for a monitor and wondering if you really need to splurge on a bigger screen, a quick comparison might help. The more pixels you can fit on-screen, the more information you can see at one time. Because of all its boxes, Excel is a good application to illustrate this point:

- ✔ At 1024 x 768 (see Figure 60-3), the resolution of a typical 15-inch display, Excel 2007 shows you about 405 cells.

- ✔ At 1280 x 1024 (see Figure 60-4), typical for a 17-inch display, Excel shows about 760 cells. You get 90 percent more working area by going up a couple of inches and a hundred bucks. That's a pretty darn good improvement for a small amount of money.

- ✔ At 1600 x 1200, a bone-stock Excel screen shows about 1,128 cells, or 50 percent more than 1280 x 1024. Unless you work with giant spreadsheets, you're reaching a point of diminishing returns.

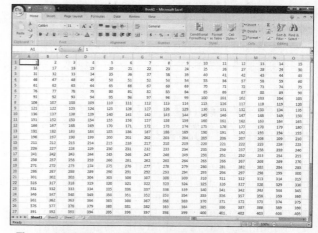

• **Figure 60-3:** A standard Excel 2007 spreadsheet at 1024 x 768 resolution.

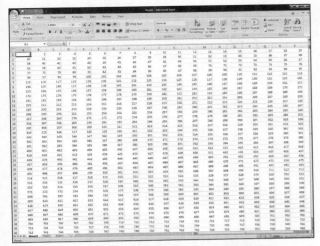

• **Figure 60-4:** The same Excel 2007 spreadsheet at 1280 x 1024.

While you're thinking about changing your screen resolution, you must also take into account the zoom factor. Most major applications these days (including all the Microsoft Office applications) allow you to magnify content within the document, effectively applying a zoom effect to the working part of the application. So you can start at a higher resolution to get more usable area, but then zoom in when you want to see bigger type.

Ready to get confused? Good.

If you're using a flat-panel display, the screen resolution is pretty much a given. You can change it, but the screen never looks as good as it does when it's running at "native" resolution. That part's easy.

Within individual applications, you can almost always change the zoom factor. That's easy, too.

You may not realize it, but you can adjust something very similar to a zoom factor *in Vista itself*. This adjustment works independently of the screen resolution, and it works independently of the zoom factor inside individual applications. It's . . . confusing. At least until you see it work.

Here's how to adjust Vista's DPI (dots per inch) scaling:

1. **Bring up a couple of applications that you use every day and open some real work. Take a screen shot (see Technique 57) and print it if you don't have your normal working programs' appearances seared into your little gray cells.**

In Figure 60-5, I bring up a Word document and an Excel spreadsheet.

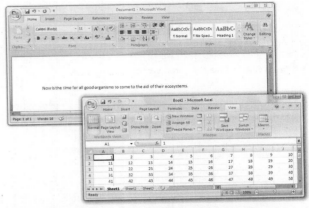

• **Figure 60-5:** Before the change in Vista's DPI scaling.

2. **Right-click any blank part of the desktop and choose Personalize.**

The Vista Personalization dialog box appears, as in Figure 60-6.

3. **On the left, click the link that says Adjust Font Size (DPI).**

You have to click Continue through yet another User Account Control message. Vista shows you the DPI Scaling dialog box, shown in Figure 60-7.

4. **Choose the option that says Larger Scale (120 DPI). Then click OK.**

You can click the button marked Custom DPI if you want to, but I assure you, the ensuing Custom DPI Setting adjustments will drive you crazy. Windows has had something like this since version 3.1, and I doubt that there are more than two people inside Microsoft who understand how it all really hangs together.

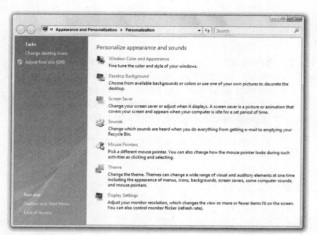

• **Figure 60-6:** The Personalization dialog box.

• **Figure 60-7:** Adjust Vista's zoom here.

5. **Vista tells you it has to restart. Click OK.**

6. **When Vista comes back up, open the same programs that you opened in Step 1 and take a look (see Figure 60-8).**

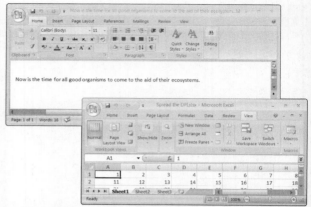

• **Figure 60-8:** After the change to 120 DPI scaling.

Play with your applications a bit. See how the changed DPI scaling affects the text in the titles, as well as the zooming inside the application itself. Take a close look at the text, both inside the application and out on your desktop.

7. **If you don't like the larger fonts — the "zoomed" Vista visual elements — repeat Steps 2 through 5, but in Step 4, go back to 96 DPI scaling.**

You have to restart again, but the effects go away.

High-Resolution Tricks

The higher your screen resolution, the more likely you bump into limitations that Windows' designers used to make Windows work better on tiny screens. If you have a very high-resolution monitor, you might want to change a few settings to accommodate your screen's largesse. Specifically:

✔ **Make the cursor thicker in Vista and some applications.** Right-click any empty spot on the desktop and choose Personalize. In the Personalization dialog box (see Figure 60-6), on the lower left, click the link that says Ease of Access. Click the link that says Make the Computer Easier to See. In the Make the

Computer Easier to See dialog box (see Figure 60-9), increase the value in the Set the Thickness of the Blinking Cursor drop-down box to 2 or 3. Click Save, and then "X" out of the Ease of Access center.

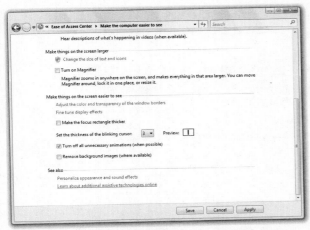

• **Figure 60-9: On a high-resolution display, make the cursor thicker.**

✔ **Adjust the mouse pointer speed.** Mouse travel at higher resolutions may seem sluggish at best. To speed up the mouse, choose Start⇨Control Panel, and under the Hardware and Sound icon, click the Mouse link. In the Mouse Properties dialog box (see Figure 60-10), click the Pointer Options tab. Pull the Select a Pointer Speed slider to the right. While you're there, try unchecking the Enhance Pointer Precision box and see whether your ability to click icons and buttons improves. Click OK and "X" out of the Control Panel.

✔ **Make desktop and Windows Explorer icons bigger (or smaller).** It's easy to adjust the size of icons on the desktop: Hold down the Ctrl key and roll the roller on your mouse. The size of the text underneath the icons changes in tandem. Pick a size that feels right for you — or start out big and, as you get more icons, put 'em on a diet.

✔ **Save your high-resolution settings.** Some day, you may want to retrieve all these settings quickly, so take a moment to give your changes a name. Right-click the desktop, choose

Personalize, and then click the link marked Theme. Click the Save As button. Then give your high-resolution desktop a new name and click OK.

• **Figure 60-10: Speed up the mouse and give yourself more control over precise positioning.**

Fine-Tuning ClearType

Vista ships with a handful of outstanding fonts custom-tuned for ClearType: Cambria, Constantia, Corbel, Candara, Calibri, and Consolas look great with ClearType but, uh, a little gray around the gills on non-ClearType systems.

Vista enables ClearType by default, with a slightly thicker, darker setting than earlier versions of Windows. For almost all the people, almost all the time, it works very well indeed.

As we went to press, Microsoft was putting the finishing touches on the Vista version of its online ClearType adjusting program. The program works (perhaps surprisingly) from the Internet. Chances are good you can find the ClearType Tuner for Vista at `www.microsoft.com/typography/cleartype/tuner/Step1.aspx`.

Keep a few points in mind:

✔ Use Internet Explorer to go to the site and adjust your settings. This is one of the few times that Firefox isn't a good choice.

✔ When you go through the steps to adjust ClearType for your monitor, be sure you press that monitor's "Auto adjust" button before settling on a specific setting. The Auto adjust can make a big difference.

✔ ClearType works best with black text on a white background or white text on a black background. If you use any other color combination, don't be too surprised if the characters look fuzzy. That's just the way subpixel twiddling works.

✔ ClearType works best with small fonts. The effects become much less pronounced at larger point sizes.

✔ If you turn off ClearType in Vista (see next), you also turn it off in Office 2007.

If you ever need to turn ClearType on or off, follow these steps:

1. **Right-click any blank part of the desktop and choose Personalize.**

The Vista Personalization dialog box appears, as shown earlier in Figure 60-6.

2. **Click the link to Window Color and Appearance.**

3. **At the bottom, click the link that says Open Classic Appearance Properties for More Color Options.**

You see the Appearance Settings dialog box, shown in Figure 60-11.

• **Figure 60-11: Turn ClearType on or off here.**

4. **Click the Effects button.**

Vista brings up the Effects dialog box, shown at the bottom of Figure 60-11.

5. **To turn on ClearType, check the box marked Use the Following Method to Smooth Edges of Screen Fonts and select ClearType from the drop-down list. (To turn off ClearType, clear the check mark on the box.)**

6. **Click OK twice and then "X" out of the Window Color and Appearance dialog box.**

You may not notice the effect immediately on your desktop icons, but Vista applications stop using ClearType the next time they're started, and the icon text turns blechy when you reboot.

Top Ten Tiny Timesaving Tweaks

Technique 61

Here's my quick list of the best timesaving tweaks — changes you can make to Vista that will help you get home earlier. All these tweaks are covered elsewhere in this book. I list them here to make it easy and fast for you to refer to them.

Tweak 10: Bring Back Menus

Microsoft decided to hide the menus in Vista's Windows Explorer. I don't know why. I guess they kind of look old and funky, and the general trend tosses out the old stalwarts. Just look at Internet Explorer 7 or Windows Media Player 11, where Microsoft's gone to great lengths to make it very difficult to bring back the old, functional, useful menus. Office 2007 went way off the deep end: The menus are gone, and you can't get them back, no matter how loud you wail.

In Figure 61-1, you see a Windows Explorer window without menus. In Figure 61-2, the old Windows XP–style menus are back.

• **Figure 61-1:** A new, modern, naked Vista Windows Explorer window.

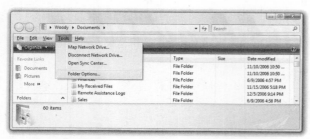

• **Figure 61-2:** The same new, modern Windows Explorer window — but with menus restored to their old Windows XP–era glory.

I say Vista's Windows Explorer should show its menus — you can hunt and peck around for hours looking for functions that sit right there on the menus.

If you want to bring back the menus (hey, you paid for them!), it's easy. To see them immediately, press the Alt key. To bring them back permanently, follow these quick steps:

1. **Bring up Windows Explorer — say, choose Start⟹Documents.**

You see the sorry hairless hound in Figure 61-1.

2. **Press Alt.**

You get your menus back, momentarily, as in Figure 61-2.

3. **Choose Tools⟹Folder Options. Click View.**

You see the View tab, shown in Figure 61-3.

4. **Check the box marked Always Show Menus.**

While you're here, you might also want to check the box marked Display the Full Path in the Title Bar (Classic Folders Only). If you check that box and use Alt+Tab to "cool switch" among running programs, Vista shows you the full path name for any Windows Explorer dialog boxes that are open. No biggie, but kinda cool.

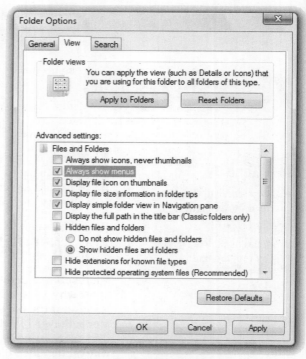

• **Figure 61-3:** Resurrect your menus here.

5. **WAIT! Don't click OK yet. Leave the Folder Options dialog open for the moment, and go on to Tweak 9.**

Tweak 9: Show Filename Extensions/Hidden Files

I rant about this in all my books, including this one. Suffice it to say that Microsoft made a horrible design decision — no, call it a mistake — when they decided that filename extensions were too complicated for the typical Windows user. (Filename extensions are those letters at the end of a filename — like, oh, the `doc` in `BadDecision.doc` or the `vbs` in `ImAVirusAndImGonnaGetYou.txt.vbs`.)

Hogwash. The confusing part comes when you *don't* show filename extensions and all of a sudden you bump into a situation in which you need them.

Here's how to get your filename extensions back — and make Vista show you its hidden files and folders at the same time:

1. **Follow the steps in Tweak 10 to bring up the Folder Options View tab.**

2. **Select the option marked Show Hidden Files and Folders. Uncheck the box marked Hide Extensions for Known File Types. And if you know what you're doing (and won't become suddenly seized with the notion that you should delete system files), uncheck the box marked Hide Protected Operating System Files (Recommended).**

   Vista belly-aches that deleting or editing your system files can make your computer inoperable. Click the button that says, Well, Yes, but Enabling Automatic Updates Can Make My Computer Inoperable, Too, You Stupid Machine. Or something like that.

3. **Click OK.**

   Your system's seat back is now in its normal, upright position.

Tweak 8: Adjust Power Settings

So maybe you like the fact that your desktop PC shuts itself off — er, goes to sleep — after an hour of inactivity, and that you need to log on again after it comes back from the Land of Nod. If that's your feeling, skip on down to the next Tweak.

But if you need to leave your PC on — maybe it's connected to a network printer or drive that you need to use at all hours — or if you habitually leave your screen untouched for 30 minutes at a stretch, try this:

1. **Right-click the desktop and choose Personalize. In the Personalization dialog box, click the Screen Saver link.**

   Vista shows you the Screen Saver Settings dialog box in Figure 61-4.

• **Figure 61-4: Change the automatic "sleep" power settings here, too.**

2. **Choose a Screen Saver if you want one (Photos is pretty cool — check it out). If your PC is in a secure location, make sure the box marked On Resume, Display Logon Screen is unchecked.**

   Some folks need the added security of requiring a logon whenever the computer wakes up. Most people don't.

3. **Click the link marked Change Power Settings.**

   Vista's Power Options dialog box appears, as in Figure 61-5.

4. **If you want to change what Vista does when you push the power button on your PC, click the link marked Choose What the Power Button Does.**

   You can tell Vista to do nothing (in which case, you have to use the Shut Down option on the Start button or yank the power cord out of the wall to turn off your PC), sleep, hibernate, or shut down (which is the default).

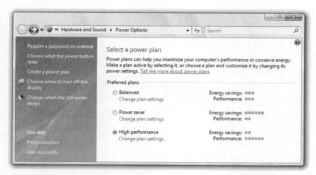

• **Figure 61-5: Power Central.**

5. **Choose the Power Plan you want and then "X" out of the Power Options dialog box.**

You can work through the details if you like, but most people with desktop PCs will want the High Performance setting (20 minutes to turn off the display, and the computer never goes to sleep).

Yes, I know it's weird, but you don't click Apply or OK — just "X" out of the Power Options dialog box.

6. **Back in the Screen Saver Settings dialog box, click OK.**

Your changes take effect immediately.

Tweak 7: Use Trillian

Instant messaging is a polyglot mess with big corporations fighting to lock you in and block others out. Yes, you can use Microsoft's Windows Live Messenger. Yes, you can use the latest version of Yahoo! Messenger. Yes, they'll talk to each other — so if you have a friend with Yahoo! and she upgrades to the latest version of their Messenger, you can actually chat with her using Windows Live Messenger.

But why bother? Why encourage these multi-billion-dollar companies to create and maintain their own little fiefdoms, trading instant messaging users — folks like you and me — like they were baseball cards? Why not help make instant messaging more egalitarian, like, oh, e-mail?

You can do it. With Trillian (free from Cerulean Studios, www.ceruleanstudios.com), you can talk with folks who use Windows Live Messenger, MSN Messenger, Windows Messenger, Yahoo! Messenger, AOL Instant Messenger, Google Talk, and loads of lesser-known programs.

Details in Technique 21.

Tweak 6: Bring on the Eye Candy

Vista packs tons of eye candy, and you should take advantage of the lesser-known pieces. Here are my favorites:

✔ **Network animation.** You can make the network icon down in the notification area (the one that looks like two monitors, next to your clock) blink and sizzle when data's traveling into or out of your computer. Just right-click the icon and choose Turn on Activity Animation.

✔ **Multiple clocks.** Yes, you can put more than one clock gadget on the Vista Sidebar, but did you know that you can also put multiple clocks down in the notification area? They're visible when you hover your mouse over the clock. To add more clocks, right-click the clock that you have now, click Adjust Date/Time, and then choose the Additional Clocks tab. In the Additional Clocks dialog box (see Figure 61-6), check one or both of the Show This Clock boxes, pick a time zone or zones, and type a name for each clock. Click OK.

✔ **Thicken the cursor.** Right-click an empty spot on the desktop and choose Personalize. In the lower left, click the link that says Ease of Access. Click the link that says Make the Computer Easier to See. In the Make the Computer Easier to See dialog box (see Figure 61-7), increase the value in the Set the Thickness of the Blinking Cursor drop-down box to 3. Click Save and then "X" out of the Ease of Access center.

• **Figure 61-6: More clocks for the notification area.**

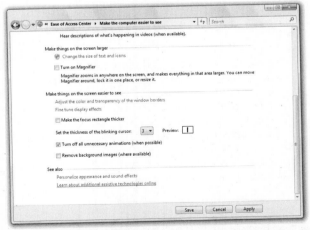

• **Figure 61-7: Make the cursor thicker in many (but not all) applications.**

Tweak 5: Get AI Roboform

If you have more than five online accounts with their own IDs and passwords, you need AI Roboform (www.roboform.com) to keep track of them. Instead of memorizing five (or five hundred) different IDs and passwords, you need to memorize only one, and Roboform takes care of all the details.

I don't know how I ever lived without it. The free version memorizes up to ten IDs and passwords, and it'll run free forever. The unlimited Pro version costs $29.95.

Details in Technique 18.

Tweak 4: Run Webroot Spy Sweeper

Vista's free Windows Defender works well at protecting against scumware, but Microsoft has a spotty track record dealing with big scummy companies — at times you have to wonder if Microsoft has your best interests at heart. (Raise your hand if that surprises you.)

For less than $35 per year, Spy Sweeper (www.webroot.com) keeps you safe and lets you concentrate on more important things. Like, oh, your tan.

Details in Technique 47.

Tweak 3: Dump Your AV Program

Tired of the "free" antivirus program that came with your PC begging for monthly or quarterly infusions of capital?

Dump it.

AVG Free, which is free for personal use (free.grisoft.com), works great, catches the bad stuff, and doesn't give you heartburn. I've used AVG Free for years. Set it and forget it.

Details in Technique 45.

While I'm on the topic, if you're paying Microsoft protection money for Windows Live OneCare, I'm going to take you off my Christmas card list. In my opinion, paying Microsoft to fix problems with its own products is only half a step removed from the old protection rackets.

Tweak 2: Get More Gadgets

Gadgets are great, they save time, and they make Vista a whole lot more fun.

Keep your eyes peeled for good Gadgets. You can look for Microsoft-approved gadgets by clicking the "+" plus sign at the top of the Windows Sidebar. But you'll probably find more interesting ones by occasionally asking Google for enlightenment.

Details in Technique 8.

Tweak 1: Use Firefox

Internet Explorer's okay. Firefox is better.

If you aren't yet using Firefox, all day, every day, run over to www.getfirefox.com and see what you've been missing. Firefox is free. It coexists just fine with Internet Explorer (in fact, it doesn't touch IE in any way). It's fast, it's cool, and it'll definitely add 20 points to your IQ.

Try it and see. Details in Technique 18.

Technique 62

Top Ten Tiny Timesaving Tips

Save Time By

- Keeping Vista at bay
- Looking outside your computer

So you plunked down the cash for Vista, or you bought a new computer with Vista installed. Good for you. *But you aren't done yet.*

Here are my favorite tips for keeping Vista's shiny side up. This list, combined with my Top Ten Tiny Timesaving Tweaks in Technique 61 (say that ten times real fast), should have you up and running right in no time.

Tip 10: Watch Autostarting Programs

It's important that you stay on top of programs that insinuate themselves into your machine. The worst ones figure out ways to hook into Vista and start themselves.

Plenty of good programs figure out how to get themselves running without your assistance (or even your knowledge). But there are plenty of bad apples.

Vista includes a very capable utility for keeping track of autostarting programs, but it's buried deep inside Windows Defender. Here's how to bring it out:

1. **Choose Start⇨All Programs⇨Windows Defender.**

   Defender appears and, no doubt, tells you there's no unwanted software on your computer. Obviously, it's overlooking a few pieces of Vista that you probably don't want, but moving along quickly. . . .

2. **Click the Tools icon. Then click the link to Software Explorer.**

   That's where they hid the list. See Figure 62-1.

3. **Take a hard look at every program on the list. If you see something that doesn't look right, refer to Technique 47 for suggestions.**

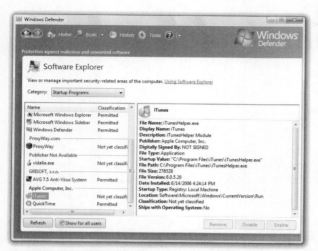

• **Figure 62-1: A detailed list of all the programs that start automatically whenever you log on to Vista.**

Tip 9: Get a USB Drive for Backup

I hate to be the bearer of bad news, but if you don't already own an external USB hard drive — one that sits outside your computer, tethered by a USB cable — you really need one, specifically for backups.

Every hard drive dies sooner or later, and the one(s) inside your computer is no exception. If you have an up-to-date backup on a USB-connected hard drive, restoring your data can take minutes. Okay, okay . . . hours. But at least it won't take years.

I strongly recommend USB-connected hard drives for backup because they're big, cheap, reliable, and mighty easy to transport if worse should come to worst. You don't need a fast one. You need a big one.

 When you have an external hard drive up and running, follow the instructions in Technique 50 to run a full backup onto your USB-connected drive. At the end of the backup routine, Vista asks how frequently it should run backups. They're incremental backups — so you back

up only the data that has been changed since the last backup. Tell Vista to run backups every single night.

You're welcome.

Tip 8: Learn How to Run

Windows XP had a Run command box — click Start➪ Run, type your command, and Windows just ran it. The Run box was very cool for the cognoscenti: You could run the Windows Calculator by typing `calc` or run Word by typing `winword`. Geeky stuff.

In spite of what you think, Vista has a Run command box, too. It's much more flexible than Windows XP's box. But it serves double duty, and you might not have noticed it: Vista's Run command box is labeled Start Search.

 If you feel the hankering to run a command, choose Start (or press the Windows key), type your command, and hit Enter. Yes, the stuff you type goes in the Start Search box. But it works just like the old Windows XP Run command box. Better, in fact, because the Vista version recognizes many more commands than the old Windows XP version.

Tip 7: Change Icon Sizes Quickly

Want to see something startling?

Go out to the Vista desktop, hold down the Ctrl key, and rotate your mouse's wheel. See that? The icons on the desktop — and the text attached to the icons — get bigger and smaller, depending on which way you roll the wheel.

 Now go into Windows Explorer — choose, oh, Start➪Documents. Click once inside the Explorer window. Try the Ctrl+mouse wheel shtick again. You not only cycle through the

Explorer Views — Tiles, Details, List, Small Icons, Medium, Large, and Extra Large Icons — you get several intermediate-size icons that aren't even on the list.

Try the same thing with Windows Photo Gallery (choose Start⇨All Programs⇨Windows Photo Gallery). Click once inside the gallery and then Ctrl+spin.

Cool. And useful.

Tip 6: Use Quick Launch Quickly

No doubt you've used Vista's Quick Launch toolbar — the set of icons to the right of the Start button. I talk about it in Technique 12.

There are two Quick Launch tricks you should check out:

✔ When you find a document that you want to put on the Quick Launch toolbar, hold down the Shift key, right-click the document, and choose Add to Quick Launch. That puts an icon connected directly to the document on the Quick Launch toolbar.

✔ You can use the keyboard to start Quick Launch toolbar items very, very quickly. Hold down the Windows key and press the number corresponding to the item you want to start: `Windows+1` is the same as clicking the first Quick Launch icon, `Windows+2` runs the second, and so on.

Tip 5: Check Your Experience Index

Ready to go out and spend more money on your computer so it'll run Vista mo' betta?

Hold onto your checkbook.

 The Windows Experience Index (see Figure 62-2) *doesn't mean what you think it means.* You have to dig deep to find out how Microsoft measures performance — and the shortcuts they took may surprise you. They may even convince you to spend good money on "upgrades" that don't make Vista faster at all.

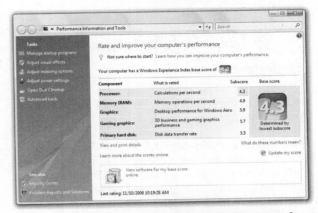

• **Figure 62-2: The Windows Experience Index comes from a hodge-podge of measurements.**

Make sure you read the details in Technique 1 before you part with any cash.

Tip 4: Plug into the Grid

Even if you don't rely on the Internet to deliver your daily news, baseball scores, and steaming lattes, you should still follow what's said online to keep your Vista machine alive and well.

It's easy to keep on top of what's happening in the Vista world if you

✔ Use an RSS reader (like the one available on your Google home page) to scarf up headlines from technology sites. See Technique 19 for details.

✔ Subscribe to — and read — newsletter(s) that specialize in warning you about problems. You can read the Microsoft newsletters if you like, but independent newsletters tend to strike a more balanced view, in my not-so-humble opinion. The number-one online Windows newsletter is Windows Secrets, www.windowssecrets.com.

✔ Watch independent Web sites for the latest news and opinions. My favorites are www.neowin.net, blogs.zdnet.com, and of course my own www.AskWoody.com.

Tip 3: Turn Off Automatic Updates

I've been saying it for years. Windows Automatic Update is for *chumps*.

Microsoft now uses Automatic Update to push insufferable garbage and inadequately tested patches to hundreds of millions of unsuspecting Windows users. The most dire example: Windows Genuine Advantage (which I call "Windows Genuine Spyware") was surreptitiously installed on millions of PCs in the guise of a "priority update." Windows Genuine Advantage started out as a relatively benign program that let Microsoft's customers verify the legitimacy of their copies of Windows: If you wanted one of Microsoft's new Windows add-on goodies, you had to pass muster with WGA before you could install the new add-on. Fair enough. Over time, though, WGA sprouted fangs, with incorrect validations, ugly messages, and the propensity to phone home frequently with details about offending machines. As I describe in Technique 44, the increasingly scummy versions of WGA were pushed onto all Windows PCs with Automatic Update enabled.

Windows Genuine Advantage is baked into Vista: There's nothing you can do about it. But you can keep Microsoft from pushing scummy, unwanted "priority updates" onto your computer without your knowledge or consent.

Microsoft has proven over and over again that it can't be trusted with automatic updating. Set Vista's Automatic Update to notify you when updates are available and ask your permission before installing the updates. See Technique 44 for details.

Tip 2: Don't Buy CRAP Music

Thinking about buying a song from the iTunes Music Store? Really want to hook into Microsoft's Zune music shop? Did you get suckered into, er, did you go out and buy music under Microsoft's Plays For Sure rubric? (You know — the music that doesn't play on iPods or on Zunes, for sure?)

When you buy music online from the big conglomerates, you're helping to ensure that the two big players — Apple and Microsoft — will control our music-listening destiny. Instead of lining the big boys' pockets and helping hurtle us into Big Brother control (and not so coincidentally locking yourself into a music-playing strait jacket), why not get your music the old-fashioned way? Buy a CD and rip it into MP3 files.

It only takes a few minutes, and the MP3 files you rip are yours forever. Unlike songs you buy at the iTunes store, Apple can't suddenly decide that it won't let you copy your MP3 music in a specific way. (Yes, they've done that, retroactively.) Microsoft won't suddenly forget its promise that your music would play for sure. Use MP3s and your music is yours.

David Berlind at ZDNet calls the copy-protected stuff CRAP music (that's Content Restriction, Annulment, and Protection). Right on. Read more about it in Technique 25.

Tip 1: Get a Faster Internet Connection

All the Windows tips and tweaks and tricks in this book, in the other Vista books, on the Internet, in the magazines, and passed along in myriad ways among hundreds of millions of Windows users don't hold a candle to one simple fact:

Windows is becoming less and less relevant.

In the battle between what's "in here" on your PC and what's "out there" in the big wide online world, there's no question where the future lies. There's much more out there. Getting a faster Internet connection helps you find the good stuff out there, and use it in ways that the creators of Vista can hardly imagine. As Windows becomes less relevant, connections take center stage.

The next great strides in computing won't take place on your desktop. They'll pop up on a Web site in Timbuktu. And they'll change your life.

By all means, get to know your PC and the Vista that propels it. But keep your eye "out there." That's where the future's headed.

Index

A

A CompletePC Backup and
Restore, overview, 472
A9 Google Images, search tool, 210
AAC, music format, 269
accelerators, drive, 47–48
Access, application file, 87
ActiveWords, hot keys and, 114
ActiveX control, Internet Explorer
and Firefox, 180
adaptive menu, overview, 67
Add a Contact Wizard, Windows
Live Messenger, 230
Add a Port dialog box, Windows
Firewall, 426
Add Counters dialog box,
Resource Monitor, 25
Add Files to Restore dialog box,
Restoring Backed up Files
and Folders, 476
Add Folder dialog box, Windows
Media Player, 283–284
Add Folder to Gallery dialog box,
Photo Gallery Techniques, 315
Add Search Provider dialog
box, Internet Explorer and
Google, 204
add-in, mlipod, 300
adding
contacts in Windows Live
Messenger, 229–230
directory listings program to
the right-click menu, 172–173
folders in Photo Gallery, 315
locations to the index, 152–154
music to the Media Library,
282–284
Windows components, 132–133

add-on
checking for an, 199
defined, 199
Add-On dialog box, Firefox and
Tor, 262
Add-Ons Disabled dialog box,
Internet Explorer, 37
Add-Ons Installation dialog
box, Anonymous Proxy
Servers, 260
Address Bar
adding to the taskbar, 96
creating shortcuts from the,
197
overview, 95–96
rearranging the, 96
Administrative Tools, Start
Menu, 73
Administrator account, user
account, 376–377
Adobe, indexing and, 151
advanced
search options, 164
searches, 163–165, 206
Advanced Options dialog box,
Building an Index,
151–152, 155
Aero. *See also* Aero Glass; Glass
running, 49–51
switching to another shell
from, 50–52
Vista Basic versus Windows
Standard shell, 50
Aero Glass. *See also* Aero; Glass
overview, 49
Aero shell, features of, 51
Al Roboform
overview, 191–192
timesaving tip, 533
Align to Grid, using, 81
aligning, icons, 80–81

All Programs Submenu
contents of, 67–69
overview, 67
rearranging the, 69–71
AllNetTools, anonymous surfing
and, 257
Amazon, online shopping site, 510
Amplusnet Anonymous Browsing
Toolbar, Internet Explorer,
259
Anonymization.Net Service,
Firefox, 259
Anonymize.net, free anonymizing
site, 258
anonymizing
sites, 258
software, 261–263
anonymous
proxy servers and Firefox,
260–261
surfing overview, 257–258
Anonymouse.org, free anonymizing site, 258
antiphishing
Internet Explorer versus
Firefox, 202
overview, 199
protection and Internet
Explorer, 181
Anti-Phishing Working Group,
Web site for, 255
antivirus, software, 416
AOL Instant Messenger, Trillian
and, 134
AOL Mail, Web-based e-mail services, 238
Appearance Settings dialog box
Aero Glass, 50–51, 54
ClearType, 527–528
Apple iTunes, media player,
272–273

application, shortcuts, 101
archive, Google newsgroups, 207–208
AskWoody, Web site, 467
assembling, files on newsgroups, 215
Attributes dialog box, Windows Paint, 507
AutoComplete, deleting entries, 198–199
AutoComplete Settings dialog box, Internet Explorer, 198
Auto-Hide the Taskbar, taskbar option, 92
automatic backup, Photo Gallery, 319
automatic program startup
    finding and eliminating auto-starting programs, 31–35
    Firefox, 38–39
    Internet Explorer, 36–38
    overview, 30–31
    preventing new auto-starters, 39
Automatic Sync feature, disabling in iPod, 304–306
Automatic Update
    settings, 404
    timesaving tip, 538
    Vista patches and, 133
AutoMovie Generator, Windows Movie Maker, 334
AutoPlay dialog box
    Copying Files to iPods and MP3 Players, 301
    Drive Accelerators, 48
auto-running programs, common, 32
auto-starting programs
    detecting and deleting, 33–35
    main hideouts for, 32–33
    preventing new, 39
    problems with disabling, 35
Autostarting Programs, timesaving tip, 535–536
AV Program, timesaving tip, 533–534

AVG Anti-Virus Free
    installing, 417–418
    software, 416
AVI file, creating an, 337–338

B

Back button, unhijacking the, 196–197
backup
    data through the Registry, 496–497
    timesaving tip, 536
    types of, 472
Barnes & Noble, online shopping site, 510
base score, assembling a, 14
benchmarks
    analyzing performance, 10–11
    benefits of using, 10
Best Quality for Playback on My Computer (Recommended), movie setting, 338
Better Business Bureau, Web site, 512
binaries, defined, 213
Binary, Registry data type, 496
BitLocker, overview, 438
BizRate, online shopping site, 510
BlinkX, Podcasts, 296
blocking, with Windows Firewall, 426–427
book
    conventions used in this, 4
    icons used in this, 4–5
    organization of this, 2–4
Boolean, search capabilities, 160–161
bot, defined, 217, 411, 420
Brian Livingston's WindowsSecrets Newsletter, Web site, 467
Briere, Danny, *Wireless Home Networking For Dummies,* 372
browser
    cache refresh settings, 190
    speeding up your, 186–191
    timesaving shortcuts, 195–196

browsing, tabbed, 94
built-in keyboard shortcuts, using, 98–102
Burn a Disc dialog box, Burning Pictures on a CD, 343
burning
    formats, 290
    a music CD, 291–293
    pictures on a CD, 342–343
    a slide show on a CD, 343–345
business transaction, process of completing a, 511–512

C

C: prompt, opening a, 140
cable
    crossover, 360
    network, 361
cache
    evaluating and resizing in Firefox, 190–191
    overview, 189
    refresh settings, 190
camera
    manufacturer Web sites, 328
    resolution and JPG file sizes, 348
Canon, Web site, 328
Cardinal Rule, of searching, 150
cascading, timesaving tip, 71–75
Casio, Web site, 328
CD
    burning a music, 291–293
    burning pictures on a, 342–343
    burning a slide show on a, 343–345
    cleaning a, 453
    player compatibility, 290
    releasing a stuck, 455
    ripping a, 284–286
CD Audio, music format, 268
CD-R (CD-Recordable), overview, 290
CD-RW (CD-Recordable/Writeable), overview, 290
centered, defined, 341

Change Icon dialog box, hibernating, 56

Choose Details dialog box
Desktop Cleanup Techniques, 78–79
Windows Explorer Techniques, 141

Choose Search Locations dialog box, Saving and Reusing Searches, 166

CIAC Hoaxbuster, Web site, 410

Claria, scumware, 430

cleaning
a CD, 453
files, 41–42
a floppy drive, 452
a mouse, 451–452
screens, 451
up before a reinstall, 131–132
up old icons on the desktop, 78–80
weekly, 450–452

ClearType
overview, 527–528
turning on/off, 528

clips
importing video, 332–334
trimming, 334

Clock, notification area option, 93

Code Red (Summer 2001), malware, 412

codec
defined, 220, 279
MP3, 286
Windows Media Player and, 279–281

coder-decoder. *See* codec

Collier, Marsha, *eBay Bargain Shopping For Dummies,* 516

command line switches
defined, 126
locations for, 128

components
adding Windows, 132–133
of the Start Menu, 64

compression, file, 214

compressor-decompressor. *See* codec

computer
cleaning, 450
Start Menu, 72

Connect To, Start Menu, 73

contact information
author, 4–5
publisher, 5

Contact Wizard, Trillian, 235

contacts, defined, 229

Content Restriction, Annulment, and Protection (CRAP)
music timesaving tip, 538
online music and, 268

Control Panel, Start Menu, 73

controlling, Windows Media Player from the keyboard, 279

Controlling the Assault of Non-Solicited Pornography And Marketing (CAN-SPAM) Act of 2003, 249

Conversation dialog box, Windows Live Messenger, 231

cookie crumb navigation bar
indexing and, 158
Windows Explorer, 139

Cooking.com, online shopping site, 510

copying
files to an MP3 player, 301–303
files quickly in Windows Explorer, 145–146
iPod music to your PC, 306–307

Costo.com, online shopping site, 510

CPU
history graph view, 20
Meter Gadget, 21
monitor, 22–23
Resource Monitor, 23–24

Craigslist, online shopping site, 510

CRAP (Content Restriction, Annulment, and Protection)
Music timesaving tip, 538
online music and, 268

Create New Account dialog box, Creating a New User Account, 380

Create Shortcut dialog box, Bringing Back Word's Last Document, 127

Create Shortcut Wizard
Bringing Back Word's Last Document, 126–127
Hibernating, 55–56
Sending E-mail with a Hot Key, 109
Setting up One-Click E-mail, 82–83
Task Manager Techniques, 22

Create Task dialog box, Scheduling a Nightly Reboot, 58

creating
AVI/WMV files, 337–338
custom reports, 25–26
desktop themes, 518–520
folders for hot key shortcuts, 105
keyboard shortcuts, 103–114
new user accounts, 380–381
password reset disks, 487–488
Podcasts, 297–298
.reg files, 497
Restore Points, 481–482
shortcuts from the Address bar, 197

credit card fraud, handling, 513–515

credits, adding to movies, 336–337

cropping, pictures, 320

crossover cable, using in a network, 360

Customize Start Menu dialog box
Customizing the Start Menu, 74
Search Techniques, 157

customizing
the Details view in Windows Explorer, 141–143
the Start Search bar, 157
the taskbar, 90–95
Windows Explorer for speed, 138–140

D

data types, Registry, 496
Debug Dump Files, Disk Cleanup and, 444
default
    programs, 73
    programs selection, 134–135
    search engine changes, 203–204
defrag. *See also* defragment; partial defrag
    adjusting a scheduled, 447–448
    commands, 44
    help and Diskeeper, 45
defragment. *See also* defrag
    overview, 41
    defined, 442
deleting
    AutoComplete entries, 198–199
    Downloaded Program Files, 42
    files, 41–42
    Restore Points, 482–483
desktop. *See also* desktop theme
    adding icons to the, 77
    aligning icons on the, 80–81
    arranging multiple windows on the, 88
    background picture, 340–341
    cleaning up icons on the, 78–80
    hiding icons on the, 77
    hiding the Recycle Bin on the, 77
    improving one-click e-mail on the, 83–85
    moving icons on the, 81–82
    opening multiple documents at once from the, 85–87
    overview, 76
    resizing icons on the, 77
    screen savers, 82
    setting up one-click e-mail on the, 82–83
    shooting a picture of your, 88–89
    Sidebar, 82
Desktop Background dialog box, Adding Pictures to the Desktop, 340

Desktop Cleanup Wizard, Windows XP, 78
Desktop folder. *See* desktop
desktop theme. *See also* desktop
    creating a, 518–520
    distributing a, 520–521
    overview, 517–518
Destination Folder Access Denied dialog box, Directory Listings, 171
Details view, customizing in Windows Explorer, 141–143
detection, virus, 413–414
dialog box (Aero Glass)
    Appearance Settings, 50–51, 54
    Personalize Appearance and Sounds, 50–51, 52–54
    Save As, 53
    Theme Settings, 53
    Visual Effects, 53–54
    Window Color and Appearance, 50, 52, 54
dialog box (Anonymous Surfing)
    Add-On, 262
    Add-Ons Installation, 260
    Proxy Info, 260–261
    Software Installation, 262
dialog box (Auto-Starting Programs)
    Manage Add-Ons, 37
    WEI, 27–28
dialog box (Backups), Add Files to Restore, 476
dialog box (Desktop Techniques)
    Appearance Settings, 77
    Choose Details, 78–79
    Name the Shortcut, 83
    Properties, 86
dialog box (Desktop Theme Techniques)
    Open, 520–521
    Personalization, 518–520
    Theme Settings, 518–519
    Vista Save As, 519–520
dialog box (Digital Camera Pictures)
    Import Options, 327
    Import Settings, 326

dialog box (Digital Pictures and Movies)
    Burn a Disc, 343
    Desktop Background, 340
    Photos Screen Saver Settings, 342
    Resize/Resample Image, 349–350
dialog box (Disk Techniques)
    Disk Cleanup Settings, 443
    Modify Schedule, 447–448
    Open the Properties, 446
    User Account Control, 443
dialog box (Drives)
    AutoPlay, 48
    Disk Cleanup, 41
    Performance Options, 46
    Properties, 41–42, 48
    System Properties, 46
    User Account Control, 43–44, 46
    View Basic Information about Your Computer, 46
dialog box (Google)
    Add Search Provider, 204
    Manage Search Engine List, 209–210
dialog box (Instant Messaging)
    General Options, 224
    Identities & Connections, 234
    Options, 224
dialog box (Internet Explorer and Firefox)
    Add-Ons Disabled, 37
    AutoComplete Settings, 198
    Internet Options, 182–183, 188, 198
    Microsoft Phishing Filter, 200
    Security Settings - Internet Zone, 182
    Set Home Page, 187
dialog box (iPod), iTunes Preferences, 308
dialog box (Keyboard Shortcuts)
    Name the Shortcut, 109–110
    Properties, 105–106, 110, 111–112, 113

dialog box (Listing Files), 172–173, 175
Destination Folder Access Denied, 171
dialog box (Media Library)
Add Folder, 283–284
Options, 286
Properties, 287
dialog box (Meeting Space)
Set Up People Near Me, 390
User Account Control, 390–391
dialog box (MP3 Player), AutoPlay, 301
dialog box (Network Techniques)
Local Area Connection Properties, 368
Local Area Connection Status, 368
Set Network Location, 363
User Account Control Security, 364
dialog box (Newsgroups), Server Setup, 217
dialog box (Passwords), Make Changes to Your User Account, 487
dialog box (Performance and Reliability Techniques), Add Counters, 25
dialog box (Photo Gallery)
Add Folder to Gallery, 315
Import Pictures and Videos, 317
New Scan, 317
Windows Photo Gallery Options, 315
dialog box (Power Settings)
Power Options, 531–532
Screen Saver Settings, 531
dialog box (Quick Launch Toolbar), Properties, 120
dialog box (Registry), Screen Saver Settings, 500
dialog box (Removing and Reinstalling Programs)
Export Registry File, 131–132
Set Program Access and Computer Defaults, 135
Uninstall or Change a Program, 130, 133

dialog box (Scheduling a Nightly Reboot)
Change Icon, 56
Create Task, 58
New Action, 59
New Trigger, 58
Properties, 56
dialog box (Screen Resolution)
Appearance Settings, 528
DPI Scaling, 525
Effects, 528
Vista Personalization, 525, 528
dialog box (Screen Shots)
Attributes, 507
Snipping Tools Edit, 504–506
dialog box (Search Techniques)
Advanced Options, 151–152, 155
Choose Search Locations, 166
Customize Start Menu, 157
Indexing Options, 151–152, 153–155
Properties, 161
Taskbar and Start Menu Properties, 157
User Account Control, 154
dialog box (Sharing Drives and Folders), File Sharing, 387
dialog box (Shortcuts), Create Shortcut, 127
dialog box (Start Menu), Customize Start Menu, 74
dialog box (System Restore)
Properties, 482
Uninstall or Change a Program, 484
dialog box (Taskbar Techniques)
New Toolbar, 97
Taskbar and Start Menu Properties, 91–92, 94
dialog box (Updating Vista), User Account Control, 403
dialog box (User Accounts)
Create New Account, 380
Turn on Guest Account, 382–383

dialog box (Windows Experience Index)
More Details about My Computer, 16–17
Performance Information and Tools, 11, 12, 14, 16–18
View Basic Information about Your Computer, 14, 16
dialog box (Windows Explorer)
Choose Details, 141
Folder Options, 137–138, 138–139, 142–143
Open, 147
Properties, 144–145
dialog box (Windows Firewall)
Add a Port, 426
User Account Control, 426, 427
User Account Control Security, 422
Windows Firewall Settings, 422
dialog box (Windows Live Mail Desktop)
Options, 243, 245
Window Layout Properties, 242
dialog box (Windows Media Player)
DVD (or CD) Properties, 277
Options, 276
Privacy Options, 273
dialog box (Windows Movie Maker)
Display Properties, 341–342
Import Media Items, 332–333
digital camera pictures
automatically transferring pictures, 325–329
memory card as storage device, 329–330
overview, 324
digital picture, file sizes, 347–348
Digital Rights Management (DRM), online music and, 268
directory listings, showing, 170–173
disabling
Automatic Sync feature in iPod, 304–306
defined, 34

disabling *(continued)*
  Glass, 52
  Microsoft Office speech
    recognition, 35
disk
  releasing a stuck, 454–455
  Resource Monitor, 24
Disk Cache Device, cache utiliza-
  tion report, 190
Disk Cleanup
  Hibernation File Cleaner and,
    444
  Old Chkdsk Files and, 444
  running, 442–445
  scheduling, 445–447
  types of files to clean, 444
Disk Cleanup dialog box, Cleaning
  and Defragmenting
  Techniques, 41
Disk Cleanup Settings dialog box,
  Running Disk Cleanup, 443
Diskeeper, defrag help and, 45
display, speeding up the, 53–54
Display Properties dialog box,
  Screen Saver Slide Show,
  341–342
document
  opening quickly, 121
  opening Word with the last
    opened, 126–128
  Start Menu, 72
Dogpile, search engine, 210
Domkus, Drew, *Podcasting For
  Dummies,* 297
dots per inch (DPI) scaling,
  adjusting, 525–526
Downloaded Program Files
  deleting, 42
  Disk Cleanup and, 444
downloading
  files with NewsLeecher,
    217–220
  Jap Anon (Java Anonymous
    Proxy project), 263
  large updates, 405–406
  the latest versions of Microsoft
    applications, 134
  time, 347–350

DPI (dots per inch) scaling,
  adjusting, 525–526
DPI Scaling dialog box, Adjusting
  Resolution Settings, 525
drive
  accelerators, 47–48
  cleaning a, 41–42
  fragmentation overview, 40–41
  indexing a, 154
  paging a, 45–46
  partitions, 46–47
  running a manual defrag, 43–45
  sharing, 384–385, 386–388
  sharing overview, 384–385
drivers, defined, 30
DRM (Digital Rights
  Management), online music
  and, 268
DSL Reports, Web site, 18, 186–187
dusting, tips, 450–451
DV-AVI (NTSC), movie setting, 338
DVD
  cleaning a, 453
  player compatibility, 290
  slide show, 344–345
DVD and HD versions, movie setting, 338
DVD (or CD) Properties dialog
  box, Windows Media Player,
  277
DVD-R (DVD-Recordable),
  overview, 290
DVD-RW (DVD-
  Recordable/Writeable),
  overview, 290
DWORD, Registry data type, 496
Dynamic, local IP addresses, 367

E

eBay, overview, 515–516
*eBay Bargain Shopping For
  Dummies* (Collier), 516
Ed Bott's ZDNet blog, Web site,
  467
Eddie Bauer Outlet, online shopping site, 510

editing, home movies, 331–338
EFF (Electronic Frontier
  Foundation), The Onion Ring,
  262
effects, applying, 335–336
Effects dialog box, ClearType, 528
`ehTray.exe`, auto-running program, 32
Electronic Frontier Foundation
  (EFF), The Onion Ring, 262
e-mail
  adding a blank message to the
    Quick Launch Toolbar,
    121–122
  attachments security in
    Windows Mail, 245–246
  indexing, 153
  sending with a hot key,
    108–111
  shortcut separators, 85
e-mail programs
  choosing, 238–239
  types of Microsoft, 237–238
  unpinning from the Start
    Menu, 64–65
eMusic, MP3 collection, 288
Ethernet, network, 360
ethics, ripping, 284–285
evaluating, and resizing your
  cache in Firefox, 190–191
Event Log, using the, 28–29
Excel, application file, 87
Excel command line switches,
  Web site for, 128
`Explorer.exe`, auto-running
  program, 32
Export Registry File dialog box,
  Removing and Reinstalling
  Programs Techniques,
  131–132
Extend Volume Wizard,
  Partitions, 47
Extensible Application Markup
  Language (XAML), Internet
  Explorer and Firefox, 181
eye candy, timesaving tip,
  532–533

F

Fastmail, e-mail program, 238
Favorites, Start Menu, 72
Federal Trade Commission, Web
    site, 514, 515
Ferris, Edward, *Wireless Home
    Networking For Dummies,* 372
file format
    choosing when ripping CDs,
        285
    sampling rate and, 286
file listing
    embellishing the, 173–176
    overview, 169–170
    printing a, 175–176
    showing directory listings,
        170–173
file search
    adding locations to the index,
        152–154
    advanced searches, 163–165
    building an index, 150–155
    Cardinal Rule, 150
    changing simple search param-
        eters, 161–162
    finding lost files, 166–168
    modifying a simple search,
        159–160
    overview, 149–150
    rebuilding/moving the index,
        154–155
    saving and reusing searches,
        165–166
    search wildcards, 159
    searching with OR and AND,
        160–161
    setting index file type options,
        151–152
    simple searches, 158–162
    Start button, 156–158
    tips, 156
File Sharing, network, 364
File Sharing dialog box, Sharing
    Folders, 387
file sizes
    digital picture, 347–348
    resolution and JPG, 348

filename associations, changing
    in Windows Explorer, 146–147
filename extensions
    defined, 137
    listing files by, 173–175
    overview, 137
    for potentially unsafe program
        files, 417
    removing from the indexing
        list, 152
    showing, 136–138, 530–531
    .theme, 518
    timesaving tip, 530–531
    worms and, 137
File-Rescue Plus, using, 345–347
files
    adding/extracting from digital
        camera, 330
    assembling on newsgroups, 215
    backup, 473–475
    backup overview, 472–473
    breaking up and posting on
        newsgroups, 214–215
    cleaning, 41–42
    compression for newsgroups,
        214
    copying to an MP3 player,
        301–303
    copying quickly in Windows
        Explorer, 145–146
    creating AVI/WMV, 337–338
    deleting, 41–42
    finding lost, 166–168
    listing, 173–176
    listing by filename extension,
        173–175
    listing quickly, 169–176
    NZB, 214
    opening with a hot key, 111–112
    PAR2, 214
    renaming multiple in Windows
        Explorer, 147–148
    restoring backed up, 475–477
    restoring from iPod to PC,
        307–309
    showing all, 138–139
    sorting by group in Windows
        Explorer, 143

    types to delete, 42
    XML, 17
Files Discarded by Windows
    Upgrade, Disk Cleanup and,
    444
Firefox
    ActiveX control, 180
    adjusting the refresh rate in,
        190–191
    Anonymization.Net Service,
        259
    antiphishing in, 201–202
    checking for add-ons and para-
        sites in, 199
    clearing passowrds out of, 198
    evaluating, and resizing your
        cache in, 190–191
    hiding pictures in, 189
    installing, 184
    Internet Explorer versus, 134
    Live Bookmarks and RSS feeds,
        195
    opening with a blank page, 187
    rearranging close buttons on
        tabs, 185–186
    removing toolbars in, 38–39
    search engines for, 209–210
    setting wallpaper from, 341
    squeezing more tabs in, 186
    subscribing to RSS in, 192–193
    tabbed browsing in, 94
    tabs overview, 184–185
    The Onion Ring and, 262–263
    timesaving tip, 534
    using, 134
    using Internet Explorer and,
        179–180
    X close button preferences,
        186
firewall
    advantages of a good, 420–421
    defined, 420
    exceptions, 425–426
    overview, 420–421
First Run Wizard, AVG Anti-Virus
    Free, 418
Fix Red Eye, in Photo Gallery, 321

Flickr
overview, 352
using, 352–355
Web site for, 208, 351
Flip 3D, using, 51
floppy drive, cleaning, 452
folder
adding in Photo Gallery, 315
applying templates to a, 144
creating for hot key shortcuts, 105
opening with a hot key, 106–107
restoring a backed up, 475–477
setting the behavior of a, 143–145
sharing, 386–388
sharing overview, 384–385
showing all, 138–139
Folder Options dialog box
Filename Extensions, 137–138
Search Techniques, 161
Windows Explorer, 138–139, 142–143
formats, for burning, 290
fragmentation, overview, 40
Froogle, online shopping site, 510
F-Secure Antivirus, software, 416
Fuji, Web site, 328
full backups, overview, 472

G

Gadgets, timesaving tip, 534
GAIN (Gator Advertising Information Network), scumware, 430
Games, Start Menu, 72
Gaming Graphics, Component, 13
Gator, scumware, 430
General Options dialog box, Windows Live Messenger, 224
Gibson, Steve, ShieldsUp!, 436–437
Giganews
news server, 216
newsgroups and, 213
setting up newsgroup access through, 216
special offer from, 220

Glass. *See also* Aero; Aero Glass
defined, 52
overview, 52
Gmail, Web-based e-mail services, 238
Google
Advanced Search page Web site, 206
built-in units converter, 205
Groups search results, 207
Groups search tool, 210
home page overview, 204
home page and RSS feeds, 194–195
online shopping with, 511
PageRank and, 204
patch problems and, 133
search engines, 208
using effectively, 203–206
using to update Sidebar Gadgets, 82
Google Gmail, Windows mail versus, 134
Google Images, Windows Live Search versus, 208
Google News by Date, search tool, 210
Google newsgroups
archive, 207–208
online shopping and, 512
Google Talk, overview, 222
GoToMyPC, Website for, 395
Graphics, Component, 13
Group Policy scripts, auto-starting programs and, 33
Group Similar, taskbar option, 93
grouping, windows, 93–95
Guardster.com, free anonymizing site, 258
Guest account
turning on/off the, 382–383
user account, 377

H

hard drives
defragmenting, 442
running Disk Cleanup, 442–445

Scheduler, 447
scheduling defragmentation, 447–448
scheduling Disk Cleanup, 445–447
hard page fault, defined, 24, 45
hardening
Internet Explorer, 180–183
reason for, 181
hardware
firewall advantages/disadvantages, 421
locating for a network, 361–362
network, 360–361
help. *See also* Help and Support Center
articles on the internet, 466–467
searching for, 463–465
sources, 467
Help and Support Center. *See also* help
Start Menu, 73
using, 463–466
hibernate
icon testing, 56
setting up a shortcut to, 55–56
shortcut linking with a hot key, 56–57
sleep mode versus, 56
turning off, 445
using a Hot Key to, 55–57
Hibernation File Cleaner
deleting, 42
Disk Cleanup and, 444
hidden files, showing, 530–531
Hide Inactive Icons, notification area option, 93
high-level keys, Registry, 495
highest active time percentage, defined, 24
Hive file, Registry, 497
HKCC, high-level key, 495
HKCR, high-level key, 495
HKCU, high-level key, 495
HKLM, high-level key, 495
HKU, high-level key, 495
hoaxes, overview, 409–410
home movies, editing, 331–338

home page
  choosing a fast, 187–188
  defined, 187
hot keys
  ActiveWords and, 114
  creating and organizing,
    104–114
  launching PowerPoint presen-
    tations with, 112–113
  limitations of, 104
  linking the Hibernate shortcut
    with, 56–57
  opening a file with, 111–112
  opening a folder with, 106–107
  opening a Web site with,
    107–108
  overview, 103–104
  Quick Launch Toolbar and, 117
  recommended, 106
  running presentations with,
    112–113
  sending e-mail with, 108–111
  shortcuts, 105
  starting a program with,
    105–106
  unassigning, 113–114
  using for hibernating, 55–57
Hotmail. *See also* Windows Live
    Mail
  Web-based e-mail services, 238
hubs, network, 361
Hupfer, Ryan, *MySpace For
    Dummies,* 356
Hurley, Pat, *Wireless Home
    Networking For Dummies,* 372

I

icon sizes, timesaving tip, 536–537
icon views, Photo Gallery versus,
    140
IconCool Editor, software, 518
icons
  adding to the desktop, 77
  aligning on the desktop, 80–81
  cleaning up old, 78–80
  hiding on the desktop, 77
  lassoing, 81
  moving, 81–82

resizing on the desktop, 77
restoring, 80
used in this book, 4–5
Identities & Connections dialog
    box, Trillian, 234
IE. *See* Internet Explorer
ILOVEYOU (2000), malware, 412
IM, using to request Remote
    Assistance (RA), 458–460
Image Resizer PowerToy, release
    of, 339
images, Google search engine for,
    208
import, settings, 328–329
Import Media Items dialog box,
    Importing and Combining
    Movie Clips, 332–333
Import Options dialog box,
    Transferring Pictures to PC
    Automatically, 327
Import Pictures and Videos dialog
    box, Photo Gallery
    Techniques, 317
Import Settings dialog box,
    Transferring Pictures to PC
    Automatically, 326
importing, video clips, 332–334
inbound firewall
  defined, 420
  overview, 422–423
incremental backups, overview,
    472
index
  adding locations to the,
    152–154
  building an, 150–155
  inside the, 151
  rebuilding/moving the, 154–155
  setting file type options,
    151–152
index building
  adding locations, 152–154
  rebuilding/moving, 154–155
  setting file type options,
    151–152
indexing
  Microsoft Office 2007 and,
    152–153
  offline files, 153

Outlook files, 153
Rich text Format (RTF) files, 151
Indexing Options dialog box,
    Building an Index, 151–152,
    153–155
InfoPath, application file, 87
installing
  AVG Anti-Virus Free, 417–418
  Firefox, 184
  the latest versions of Microsoft
    applications, 134
  Trillian, 233
instant messaging
  choosing a messenger, 222
  pros and cons of, 221–222
  Trillian, 232–236
  Windows Live Messenger,
    223–232
Internet
  Help articles, 466–467
  IP addresses, 366–367
  timesaving tip, 537–538
Internet connection, timesaving
    tip, 538–539
Internet Explorer
  ActiveX control, 180
  adjusting cache settings in, 191
  Amplusnet Anonymous
    Browsing Toolbar, 259
  antiphishing in, 200–201
  antiphishing protection
    and, 181
  breaking the add-on cycle,
    36–37
  checking for add-ons and para-
    sites in, 199
  clearing passwords out of,
    198–199
  Firefox versus, 134
  hardening, 180–183
  indexing Favorites/History
    Folders, 151
  removing toolbars in, 38
  search engines for, 210
  setting a home page in, 188
  setting wallpaper from, 341
  subscribing to RSS in, 193–194
  tabbed browsing in, 94
  using Firefox and, 179–180

Internet Options dialog box
Controlling your Browser, 198
Hardening Internet Explorer, 182–183
Speeding up your Browser, 188
Internet zone, lockdown settings, 183
IP addresses
assigning local, 367–369
Internet, 366–367
IPv6, 369
local network, 367
seeing, 257
switching between static and dynamic, 368–369
iPod
copying music to your PC, 306–307
disabling Automatic Sync feature, 304–306
problems, 300
IPv6, IP addresses, 369
IrfanView
photo software, 321
resizing with, 349–350
ISO, burn format, 290
iTunes
media player, 272–273
using, 134
iTunes Preferences dialog box, Getting Music Off Your iPod, 308

J

Jaggies, defined, 523
JAP Anon (Java Anonymous Proxy project), downloading, 263
JPG file sizes, resolution and, 348
Junk Mail
handling phishers, 254–255
phishing, 250–251
spam, 247–250
spam action, 254
spammeisters/phishers, 251
unsubscribing to, 253

Web Beacons, 251–253
Web crawlers, 253

K

Kaspersky Antivirus, software, 416
KB number, of a patch, 133
Keep the Taskbar on Top of Other Windows, taskbar option, 92
key combinations, windows, 100–101
keyboard
cleaning, 450, 453–454
controlling Windows Media Player from the, 279
keyboard shortcuts
common, 99–100
creating, 103–114
overview, 98–99
using built-in, 98–102, 503
Klez (Spring 2002), malware, 412
Knowledge Base number, of a patch, 133
Kodak, Web site, 328
Konfabulator, Web site, 82

L

Lands' End, online shopping site, 510
lassoing, icons, 81
legality, in newsgroups, 213
Leonhard, Woody
Windows Vista All-In-One Desk Reference For Dummies, 210, 242, 294, 297, 300, 301, 373, 381, 426, 427, 460, 476
Windows XP Timesaving Techniques For Dummies, 2
limitations
of Remote Assistance (RA), 457–458
System Restore, 479
Live File System, burn format, 290
Livingston, Brian, WindowsSecrets Newsletter, 467
L.L. Bean, online shopping site, 510

Local Area Connection Properties dialog box, Network Techniques, 368
Local Area Connection Status dialog box, Network Techniques, 368
local network, IP addresses, 367
lock down, a network, 371
Lock the Taskbar, taskbar option, 92
lockdown settings, internet zone, 183
LockerGnome, Podcasts, 295–296
locking, the taskbar, 91
Logitech, Web site, 328
LogMeIn
disabling, 396
installing, 395–396
using, 396–398
lossy, defined, 268

M

/m command, Word command line switch, 127
Mainstream text newsgroups, Google and, 213
Make Changes to Your User Account dialog box, Creating a Password Reset Disk, 487
malware
defined, 410
how it works, 411–413
Manage Add-Ons dialog box, Internet Explorer and Firefox, 37
Manage Search Engine List dialog box, Browser Choices, 209–210
manual defrag, running a, 43–45
Mary Jo Foley's All About Microsoft blog, Web site, 467
Mastered, burn format, 290
Maxson, Mitch, *MySpace For Dummies,* 356
McAfee VirusScan, software, 416
Media Library, adding music to the, 282–284

Media Sharing, network, 365
Meeting Space
    collaborating, 392–393
    overview, 389–390
    setting up, 390
    starting a meeting in, 391–392
Melissa (1999), malware, 412
Memory (RAM), component, 12–13
Memory, Resource Monitor, 24–25
Memory Cache Device, cache utilization report, 190
memory card, using as a storage device on PC, 329–330
menus
    bringing back, 530
    timesaving tip, 529–530
Merletn.org/uk/anonymizer, free anonymizing site, 258
messages, spreading on newsgroups, 212–213
metadata, defined, 151
Miceli, Dawn, *Podcasting For Dummies,* 297
Microsoft, e-mail programs, 237–238
Microsoft - KB, search engine, 210
Microsoft applications, downloading and installing the latest versions of, 134
Microsoft Baseline Security Analyzer, running, 437–438
Microsoft Knowledge Base, Web site, 467
Microsoft Management Console, defrag runs and the, 44–45
Microsoft Office
    program names, 87
    speech recognition, 35
Microsoft Phishing Filter dialog box, Internet Explorer and Firefox, 200
mlipod, add-in, 300
Modify Schedule dialog box, Scheduling Defragmentation, 447–448
modifying, a simple search, 159

monitor
    basics, 522–523
    cleaning, 450
monthly cleaning, 452–453
More Details about My Computer dialog box, Windows Experience Index, 16–17
Morris, Tee, *Podcasting For Dummies,* 297
mouse, cleaning the, 451–452
movie
    saving the, 337–338
    settings, 338
moving
    icons, 81–82
    the index, 154–155
Mozilla, Web site for tweaks to Firefox, 185
MP3
    codec overview, 286
    making an, 269–270
    music format, 269
MP3 player
    choosing an, 299–300
    copying files to an, 301–303
MSASCui.exe, auto-running program, 32
MSN Home, Windows Live Messenger, 225
multiple documents, opening at once, 85–87
music
    adding to the Media Library, 282–284
    copying from iPod to PC, 306–307
    formats compared, 268–269
    online businesses, 267–268
    Start Menu, 72
    stores online, 270–271
My Microsoft Patch Reliability Ratings, Web site for, 406
Mycroft, overview, 210
mySimon, online shopping site, 510
MySpace, overview, 355–356
MySpace For Dummies (Hupfer, Maxson, and Williams), 356

N

Name the Shortcut dialog box
    Desktop Techniques, 83
    Hot Keys Techniques, 109–110
Neowin, Web site, 467
.NET Framework, Internet Explorer and Firefox, 180
network
    cards, 361
    checking the connection, 365–366
    components, 361
    Ethernet, 360
    File Sharing, 364
    hardware for a, 360–361
    hubs, 361
    interface cards, 361
    locating hardware for a, 361–362
    lock down, 371
    notification area option, 93
    opening the, 385–386
    Password Protected Sharing, 365
    Printer Sharing, 364
    private, 385
    propagating changes, 374–375
    Public Folder Sharing, 364
    public/private, 385
    pulling cable for a, 361
    Resource Monitor, 24
    sharing and discovery settings, 364–365
    Start Menu, 73
    ways to assemble a, 360
    wireless, 360
Network Discovery, network, 364
New Action dialog box, Scheduling a Nightly Reboot, 59
New Outbound Rules Wizard, Firewall Techniques, 427–428
New Scan dialog box, Photo Gallery Techniques, 317
New Toolbar dialog box, Taskbar Techniques, 97
New Trigger dialog box, Scheduling a Nightly Reboot, 58

news, Google search engine for, 208
news reader
  considerations when choosing a, 216–217
  defined, 216
  setting up a, 216–220
news server
  connecting to a, 215–216
  defined, 215
  qualities of a good, 216
newsgroups
  assembling files, 215
  breaking up and posting files, 214–215
  choosing a news reader, 216–220
  connecting to a news server, 215–216
  defined, 212
  Google archive, 207–208
  Google search engine for, 208
  legality and, 213
  limitations of, 212
  overview, 211
  posting on, 206–208
  setting up access through Giganews, 216
  spreading, 212–213
  Usenet, 212
  using, 213–220
NewsLeecher
  news reader, 217
  newsgroups and, 213
  setting up to download a file, 217–220
NIC, network, 361
nightly reboot, scheduling a, 55–59
Nikon, Web site, 328
non-Microsoft replacement products, using, 134–135
Norton Antivirus, software, 416
notification area
  opening Task manager from the, 22
  options, 93
  taskbar, 91
Nullsoft Winamp, media player, 273

NumRibbons, Registry, 498
NZB, file, 214

O

Object Linking and Embedding (OLE). *See* ActiveX control
OCR (Optical Character Recognition), scanning and, 316
Office applications, locating the version of, 126–127
Office Picture Manager, application file, 87
offline files, indexing and, 153
Offline Web Pages, Disk Cleanup and, 444
Old Chkdsk Files, Disk Cleanup and, 444
Old Navy, online shopping site, 510
OLE (Object Linking and Embedding). *See* ActiveX control
Olympus, Web site, 328
one-click e-mail
  embellishing the icon for, 84–85
  improving, 83–85
  setting up, 82–83
online
  copyright issues Web site, 213
  music businesses, 268–269
  music stores, 270–271
online shopping
  author's favorite sites, 510
  credit card fraud, 513–515
  eBay, 515–516
  payment methods, 511
  purchasing safety, 511–515
  reputation of retailers, 512–513
Open dialog box
  Desktop Theme Techniques, 520–521
  PowerPoint 2007, 112–113
Open the Properties dialog box, Scheduling Disk Cleanup, 446
Open With dialog box, Windows Explorer, 147

opening
  a C: prompt, 140
  documents quickly, 121
  a file with a hot key, 111–112
  a folder with a hot key, 106–107
  multiple documents at once, 85–87
  Web pages quickly, 121
  Web site with a hot key, 107–108
Optical Character Recognition (OCR), scanning and, 316
optimization, of screen speed, 49–54
options
  advanced search, 164
  choosing on the Start Menu, 73–75
  notification area, 93
  simple search, 162
  taskbar, 92–93
Options dialog box
  Windows Live Messenger, 224
  Windows Mail, 243, 245
  Windows Media Player, 276, 286
outbound firewall
  defined, 420
  getting into the, 427–428
Outlook
  application file, 87
  e-mail program, 237–238
Outlook 2003/2007, Windows mail versus, 134
Outlook command line switches, location of, 128
Outlook Distribution List, creating a shortcut for e-mailing an, 83
Outlook files, indexing and, 153
Overstock.com, online shopping site, 510

P

PageRank, Google and, 204
paging
  defined, 45
  expanding loads, 46

files defined, 45
overview, 45
Pain, using Windows, 506–507
Panasonic, Web site, 328
Panda Antivirus, software, 416
PAR2, files, 214
parasite
    checking for a, 199
    defined, 199
partial defrag. *See also* defrag
    defined, 43
partitions
    defined, 46
    resizing, 46–47
password
    circumventing your own, 489
    managing in Windows Live
        Messenger, 226
    recovering a lost, 486–489
    removing a saved, 197–199
    reset disk creation, 487–488
    user account, 379
Password Protected Sharing, net-
    work, 365
Password Reset Disk
    creating a, 487–488
    using your, 488–489
Password Reset Wizard,
    Recovering a Lost Password
    Technique, 488–489
pathnames, seeing in Windows
    Explorer, 139–140
payment, methods, 511
PC, copying iPod music to your,
    306–307
performance, components, 12–14
performance benchmarks
    analyzing, 10–11
    problems with, 10
Performance Information and
    Tools dialog box, Windows
    Experience Index, 11, 12, 14,
    16–18
Performance Options dialog box,
    Expanding Paging Volumes, 46
performance/reliability tracking
    Event Log, 28–29
    monitoring performance, 25–26
    monitoring resources, 23–25

redliners, 19–23
reliability report, 26–27
System Health Report, 27–28
periodic maintenance
    checklist, 449–450
    fixing components, 453–455
    monthly cleaning, 452–453
    running a, 449–455
    weekly cleaning, 450–452
peripherals, cleaning, 450
Personal Options dialog box,
    Windows Live Messenger, 228
Personalization dialog box,
    Desktop Theme Techniques,
    518–520
Personalize Appearance and
    Sounds dialog box
    Aero Glass, 50–51, 52–54
    Desktop Techniques, 77
    Display Techniques, 53
phishing
    avoiding, 251
    defined, 250
    overview, 250–251
    rules about, 254–255
Photo Gallery
    adding folders in, 315
    automatic backup and Revert
        capability, 319
    changing pictures in the,
        318–321
    correcting problems with,
        314–316
    cropping, 320
    Fix Red Eye, 321
    icon views versus, 140
    limitations of, 313–314
    revert feature, 319, 321–323
    scanning into, 316–317
photos, touching up, 318–323
Photos Screen Saver Settings dia-
    log box, Screen Saver Slide
    Show, 342
pictures
    automatically transferring to
        PC, 325–329
    burning on a CD, 342–343
    changing in Photo Gallery,
        318–321

changing the resolution of,
    348–350
cropping, 320
decreasing download time of,
    347–350
making the desktop back-
    ground, 340–341
recovering deleted from cam-
    era, 345–347
Start Menu, 72
pinning
    defined, 64
    an icon to the Start Menu, 85
    to the Start Menu, 65–67
pixel, defined, 347, 523
placeholder pictures, showing,
    188–189
Podcast Alley, Podcasts, 296
Podcasting For Dummies (Morris,
    Terra, Miceli, and Domkus),
    297
Podcasts
    creating, 297–298
    finding, 295–297
    LockerGnome, 295–296
    overview, 294–295
Podscope, Podcasts, 296
Podzinger, Podcasts, 296
port
    manually adding to a firewall
        exception list, 426
    overview, 437
Power Options dialog box, Adjust
    Power Settings, 531–532
power settings
    adjusting, 531–532
    timesaving tip, 531–532
PowerPoint, application file, 87
PowerPoint command line
    switches, Web site for, 128
PowerPoint presentation, using
    hot keys to launch a, 112–113
presentations, running with a hot
    key, 112–113
previous versions. *See* shadow
    copies
Previous Windows Installations,
    Disk Cleanup and, 444

PriceGrabber, online shopping site, 510
Primary Hard Disk, component, 13–14
Printer Sharing, network, 364
Printers, Start Menu, 73
Privacy dialog box, Windows Live Messenger, 229
privacy options, Windows Media Player, 275
Privacy Options dialog box, Windows Media Player, 273
private network, defined, 385
Processor, component, 12
program names, Microsoft Office, 87
programs
    adding/removing from the Quick Launch Toolbar, 118
    adding to the right-click menu, 172–173
    allowing other users to run your, 125–126
    automatic startup overview, 30–31
    launching most-used, 117–122
    permanently removing, 129–131
    removing and reinstalling, 129–135
    running when Windows starts, 123–125
    selecting default, 134–135
    starting with a hot key, 105–106
project, overview, 334
propagating, network changes, 374–375
Properties dialog box
    Cleaning and Defragmenting the Hard Drive, 41–42
    Desktop Techniques, 86
    Directory Listings, 172–173, 175
    Drive Accelerators, 48
    Hot Keys, 105–106, 110, 111–112, 113
    Quick Launch Screen Tips, 120
    Restore Points, 482
    Scheduling a Nightly Reboot, 56

Windows Explorer, 144–145
Windows Media Player, 287
Proxify.com, free anonymizing site, 258
Proxy Info dialog box, Anonymous Proxy Servers, 260–261
proxy server (anonymizing sites), 258
ProxyWay, proxy server, 260
Public Folder Sharing
    disadvantage of, 386
    network, 364
public network, defined, 385
public proxy server (anonymizing sites), 258
Publisher, application file, 87

Q

Quick Launch Screen Tips, changing, 119–121
Quick Launch Toolbar
    adding a blank e-mail message to the, 121–122
    adding programs to the, 118
    advantage of using the, 117
    making room on the, 118–119
    overview, 65
    removing programs from the, 118
    turning on the, 118
    using the, 117–118

R

RarSlave, newsgroups and, 219
read receipts, Windows Mail, 244
ReadyBoost, drive accelerator, 47–48
ReadyDrive, drive accelerator, 47
Really Simple Syndication (RSS). *See also* RSS feeds
    overview, 192
    subscribing in Firefox, 192–193
    subscribing in Internet Explorer, 193–194

reboot
    importance of after uninstalling, 130
    scheduling a nightly, 55–59
rebuilding, the index, 154–155
Recent Items, Start Menu, 72
Recycle Bin
    deleting, 42
    Disk Cleanup and, 444
    hiding on the desktop, 77
Redliners
    opening the Task Manager, 20–21
    reasons for, 20
refresh rate, adjusting in Firefox, 190–191
refresh settings, browser cache, 190
.reg file
    creating a, 497
    Registry, 496
Registry
    auto-starting programs and the, 32
    backing up data, 496–497
    common data types, 496
    high-level keys, 495
    making changes in the, 497
    overview, 493–496
    tweaks, 497–501
Registry Editor, reinstalling and the, 131
REI, online shopping site, 510
reinstall
    cleaning up before a, 131–132
    programs, 129–135
Reliability Monitor, using the, 26–27
reliability/performance tracking
    Event Log, 28–29
    monitoring performance, 25–26
    monitoring resources, 23–25
    redliners, 19–23
    reliability report, 26–27
    System Health Report, 27–28
reliability report, reading the, 26–27

Remote Assistance (RA)
  fine-tuning, 460–461
  limitations of, 457–458
  requesting, 458
  requesting via IM, 458–460
removing
  a filename extension from the
    indexing list, 152
  programs, 129–135
  programs permanently, 129–131
  saved passwords and user-
    names, 197–199
  Windows patches, 133
renaming multiple files in
  Windows Explorer, 147–148
Repair'n'Extract, newsgroups
  and, 219
reports, creating custom, 25–26
Reset Disk, creating a Password,
  487–488
Resize/Resample Image dialog box,
  Picture Resolution, 349–350
resizing
  and evaluating your cache in
    Firefox, 190–191
  with IrfanView, 349–350
resolution
  changing in pictures, 348–350
  JPG file sizes and, 348
  screen, 524–527
Resource Monitor
  adding a shortcut for the, 25
  CPU, 23–24
  Disk, 24
  Memory, 24–25
  Network, 24
  opening the, 23
restart, scheduling an overnight,
  57–59
Restore Point
  creating a, 481–482
  deleting a, 482–483
  restoring to a, 483–485
restoring
  backed up files and folders,
    475–477
  icons, 80

music files from iPod to PC,
  307–309
to a Restore Point, 483–485
reusing, searches, 165–166
Revert feature, Photo Gallery,
  319, 321–323
Rhapsody Music Service,
  Windows Live Messenger, 225
Ribbons screen saver, changing
  the, 499–501
`RibbonWidth`, Registry, 498
Rich Text Format (RTF) files,
  indexing and, 151
ripping
  CDs, 284–286
  choosing a file format and sam-
    pling rate, 285
  defined, 276
  ethics, 284–285
  process of, 286–287
rootkits, defined, 411
routers, network, 361
RSS feeds. *See also* RSS (Really
  Simple Syndication)
  defined, 192
  indexing and, 151
  ways to view the news, 194–195
RSS (Really Simple Syndication).
  See also RSS feeds
  overview, 192
  subscribing in Firefox, 192–193
  subscribing in Internet
    Explorer, 193–194
Run, Start Menu, 73
Run command, timesaving tip, 536
`Rundll32`, auto-starting programs
  and, 35
running
  Disk Cleanup, 442–445
  manual defrag, 43–45
  Microsoft Baseline Security
    Analyzer, 437–438
  periodic maintenance, 449–455
  quick File Backup, 473–475
  ShieldsUp, 436–437
  Windows Defender scan,
    manually, 432–433
  Windows Media Player,
    273–275, 278–279

S

Sage, add-on, 195
Salami RarSlave, newsgroups
  and, 213
sampling rate
  choosing when ripping CDs,
    285
  file format and, 286
SANS Internet Storm Center,
  patch problems and, 133
Save As dialog box, Display
  Techniques, 53
saving
  the movie, 337–338
  screen shots with Windows
    Paint, 507
  searches, 165–166
scan, Windows Defender, 432–433
scanning, in Photo Gallery,
  316–317
Scheduled Tasks, auto-starting
  programs and, 33
Scheduler, checking, 447
scheduling
  a nightly reboot, 55–59
  an overnight restart, 57–59
screen, characters overview,
  523–524
screen resolution
  adjusting, 524–526
  defined, 524
  high, 526–527
screen saver
  Ribbons settings, 498
  slide show, 341–342
  using, 82
Screen Saver Settings dialog box
  Adjusting Power Settings, 531
  Registry Techniques, 500
screen shots
  Snipping Tool and, 89
  taking, 88–89
  using SnagIt for, 507–508
  using Windows Paint to save,
    507
screen speed, optimization of,
  49–54

screen speed optimization
  Aero Glass, 49–52
  altering the display, 53–54
  reclaiming visual elements, 54
Screen Tips
  changing Quick Launch,
    119–121
  for Microsoft Office applica-
    tions, 119
screens, cleaning, 451
Scripting, Internet Explorer and
  Firefox, 180
scumware, defined, 430
search
  advanced, 206
  for a message in the Google
    newsgroups archive,
    207–208
  options for an advanced, 164
  options for a simple, 162
  Start Menu, 72
  tricks combined, 205
  wildcards, 159
search engine
  changing the default, 203–204
  Firefox and Internet Explorer,
    209–210
search parameters, changing simple, 161–162
Search PowerToy, overview, 160
search terms
  ignored words list, 205
  timesaving tips with, 204–206
searches
  advanced, 163–165
  Boolean search capabilities,
    160–161
  saving/reusing, 165–166
  simple, 158–162
security perimeter
  Microsoft Baseline Security
    Analyzer, 437–438
  running ShieldsUp!, 436–437
security recommendation, user
  account, 379–380
Security Settings - Internet Zone
  dialog box, Internet Explorer
  and Firefox Techniques, 182
segments, defined, 442

Server Setup dialog box,
  Newsgroup Techniques, 217
Set Home Page dialog box,
  Internet Explorer and Firefox
  Techniques, 187
Set Network Location dialog box,
  Network Techniques, 363
Set Program Access and
  Computer Defaults dialog
  box, Removing and
  Reinstalling Programs
  Techniques, 135
Set Up People Near Me dialog
  box, Meeting Space
  Techniques, 390
settings
  automatic update, 404
  changing on the taskbar, 91–93
  import, 328–329
  index file type options, 151–152
  movie, 338
  network sharing and discov-
    ery, 364–365
  Windows Firewall, 423
Setup Log Files, Disk Cleanup
  and, 444
shadow copies
  file cleanup and, 42
  overview, 472
shortcuts
  adding for the resource
    Monitor, 25
  application, 101
  creating from the Address bar,
    197
  creating a folder for hot key,
    105
  field in e-mails, 85
  keys, 99–100
  separators in e-mail, 85
  using built-in keyboard, 503
  using to hibernate, 55–56
  windows, 102
  windows explorer, 102
Show Quick Launch, taskbar
  option, 93
Show Window Previews
  (Thumbnails), taskbar
  option, 93

shutdown command, switches for
  the, 57
ShySurfer.com, free anonymizing
  site, 258
Sidebar Gadget
  Google and, 82
  resizing the, 195
  using, 82
Sidebar.exe, auto-running program, 32
signatures, Windows Mail,
  244–245
simple search, modifying a, 159
Singingfish, Podcasts, 297
Slammer (2003), malware, 412
sleep mode, hibernation
  versus, 56
slide show
  burning on a CD, 343–345
  making a DVD, 344–345
  screen saver, 341–342
SnagIt
  screen shot program, 89
  using for screen shots, 507–508
Snipping Tool
  options, 505
  screen shots and the, 89
  using the, 504–506
Snipping Tools Edit dialog box,
  Screen Shots Techniques,
  504–506
Snopes, Web site, 410
software
  anonymizing, 261–263
  antivirus, 416
  IrfanView, 321
  photo, 321
Software Explorer, using, 33–35
software firewalls,
  advantages/disadvantages,
  421
Software Installation dialog box,
  Anonymous Surfing
  Techniques, 262
Sony, Web site, 328
Sort By, settings, 81
sorting, files by group in
  Windows Explorer, 143

spam
    defined, 248
    overview, 248–250
    rules about, 254
spammeisters, avoiding, 251
speech recognition, disabling
    Microsoft Office, 35
SpyNet, overview, 434
Standard, user account, 377–379
Start button, searching from the,
    156–158
Start Menu
    advantages/disadvantages of
        options on the, 74–75
    All Programs Submenu, 67–71
    Cascading, 71–75
    choosing options on the, 73–75
    components of the, 64
    indexing and, 153
    options, 71–73
    overview, 63–64
    pinning an icon to the, 85
    pinning/unpinning, 64–67
Start Search bar
    changing the behavior of the,
        157
    customizing the, 157
startup, running a program dur-
    ing Windows, 123–125
Startup folders, auto-starting pro-
    grams and, 32
StartupMonitor, using, 39
stateful firewall, defined, 423
Static, local IP addresses, 367
stretched, defined, 341
String, Registry data type, 496
SuperFetch, drive accelerator, 47
surfing
    anonymously, 256–263
    anonymously overview,
        257–258
switches, network, 361
Symantec hoax list, Web site, 410
System Error Memory Dump
    Files, Disk Cleanup and, 444
System Error Minidump Files,
    Disk Cleanup and, 444
System Health Report, generating
    a, 27–28

System Image. *See* A CompletePC
    Backup and Restore
System Properties dialog box
    Expanding Paging Volumes, 46
    System Restore Techniques,
        480–481
System Protection. *See* System
    Restore
System Queued Windows Error
    Reporting Log, deleting, 42
System Restore
    creating a restore point,
        481–482
    deleting restore points, 482–483
    limitations of, 479
    Points overview, 472
    restoring to a restore point
        quickly, 483–485
    turning on, 479–481
System Stability Index, using the,
    26–27

T

tabbed browsing, advantages of,
    94
tabs
    overview in Firefox, 184–185
    rearranging close buttons in
        Firefox, 185–186
    squeezing more on the screen,
        186
    timesavers, 184
Task Manager
    CPU history graph, 20
    icon in the notification area,
        21–22
    increasing the sampling rate of
        the, 20
    opening from the notification
        area, 22
    opening the, 20–21
Taskbar
    adding a new toolbar to the, 97
    Address Bar, 95–96
    changing settings on the, 91–93
    customizing the, 90–95
    extending the, 90–91
    locking/unlocking the, 91

navigating from the, 97
    options, 92–93
Taskbar and Start Menu
    Properties dialog box
        Search Techniques, 157
        Taskbar Techniques, 91–92, 94
templates, applying to folders, 144
Temporary Files
    deleting, 42
    Disk Cleanup and, 444
Temporary Internet Files
    deleting, 42
    Disk Cleanup and, 444
Temporary Setup Files, Disk
    Cleanup and, 444
Temporary Windows Installation
    Files, Disk Cleanup and, 444
Terra, Eva, *Podcasting For
    Dummies,* 297
The-cloak.com/anonymous-
    surfing-home.html, free
    anonymizing site, 258
The Onion Ring
    anonymizing software, 261–263
    Firefox and, 262–263
theme. *See* desktop theme
Theme Settings dialog box
    Desktop Theme Techniques,
        518–519
    Display Techniques, 53
thrashing, defined, 24–25
Thumbnails
    deleting, 42
    Disk Cleanup and, 444
tiling
    defined, 341
    windows, 88
timeline, defined, 334
timesaving tip
    Automatic Updates, 538
    Autostarting Programs, 535–536
    CRAP (Content Restriction,
        Annulment, and Protection)
        Music, 538
    icon sizes, 536–537
    internet, 537–538
    internet connection, 538–539
    Run command, 536
    USB Drive for Backup, 536

titles, adding to movies, 336–337
Toolbar
    adding a blank e-mail message
      to the Quick Launch,
      121–122
    adding programs to the Quick
      Launch, 118
    adding to the taskbar, 97
    making room on the Quick
      Launch, 118–119
    Quick Launch, 117–118
    removing in Firefox, 38–39
    removing in Internet
      Explorer, 38
    removing programs from the
      Quick Launch, 118
    turning on the Quick Launch,
      118
    using an anonymous, 258–259
Tor. *See* The Onion Ring
transitions, applying, 335–336
Trend PC-cillin, software, 416
triggers, ActiveWords and, 114
Trillian
    adding contacts in, 235–236
    Contact Wizard, 235
    installing, 233
    instant messenger program,
      134
    overview, 232, 532
    timesaving tip, 532
    using, 233–236
    Windows Live Messenger ver-
      sus, 233
trip, defined, 334
Trojans, defined, 410
Trusted Sites, default security
    level of, 182–183
Turn on Guest Account dialog
    box, User Account
    Techniques, 382–383

U

UDF, burn format, 290
unassigning, hot keys, 113–114

Uninstall or Change a Program
    dialog box
    Removing and Reinstalling
      Programs Techniques, 130
    System Restore Techniques,
      484
Uninstall an Update dialog box,
    Removing and Reinstalling
    Programs Techniques, 133
Uninstalling, a program, 130–131
unlocking, the taskbar, 91
unpinning, from the Start Menu,
    64–65
unsigned driver, defined, 479
unsubscribe from spam, 253
updates
    downloading large, 405–406
    retrieving declined, 406–407
    settings for automatic, 404
    small, 406
updating, overview, 401–402
URGE, online music store, 270–271
U.S. Federal Trade Commission,
    Web site for, 255
USB Drive, timesaving tip, 536
Usenet
    daily posting statistics, 212
    newsgroup postings overview,
      206–207
    overview, 212
user account
    creating a new, 380–381
    modifying a, 381–382
    passwords, 379
    reasons for adding a, 377
    security recommendations,
      379–380
    types of, 376–380
User Account Control dialog box
    Defragmenting, 43–44
    Disk Cleanup Techniques, 443
    Meeting Space Techniques,
      390–391
    Partitions, 46
    Search Techniques, 154
    Updating Vista Techniques, 403
    Windows Firewall Techniques,
      422, 426, 427

User Account Control Security
    dialog box, Network
    Techniques, 364
user ID, overview, 225–226
`userinit.exe`, auto-running
    program, 32
usernames
    removing saved, 197–199
    Start Menu, 71–72
Users, indexing and, 153

V

vacuuming, tips, 450
Various Windows Error Reporting
    Files, Disk Cleanup and, 444
version, locating on Office appli-
    cations, 126–127
video clips
    importing, 332–334
    trimming, 334
video effect, defined, 335
view, changing in Windows
    Explorer, 140–143
View Basic Information about
    Your Computer dialog box
    Expanding Paging Volumes, 46
    Windows Experience Index,
      14, 16
virtual memory, defined, 45
virus
    dealing with a, 414–416
    defined, 410
    detection, 413–414
    overview, 409–410
    protection, 416–418
    types of, 410–411
virus protection
    overview, 408
    tips for, 416–418
Vista Basic, Aero versus Windows
    Standard shell versus, 50
Vista File Backup, overview, 473
Vista networking
    preparing for, 362
    turning on, 362–365
Vista patches, Automatic Update
    and, 133

Vista Personalization dialog box, Resolution Techniques, 525, 528
Vista Save As dialog box, Desktop Theme Techniques, 519–520
Vista search, overview, 149–150
Vista Sidebar Gadget
  CPU Meter, 21
  resizing the, 195
  RSS feeds and, 195
Visual Effects dialog box, Display Techniques, 53–54
visual elements, reclaiming, 54
Volume, notification area option, 93

W

wallpaper
  making a picture the, 340–341
  setting from Internet Explorer or Firefox, 341
Web Beacons, overview, 251–253
Web browser, unpinning from the Start menu, 64–65
Web Bugs. *See* Web Beacons
Web crawlers, overview, 253
Web pages
  opening quickly, 121
  pinning to the Start Menu, 66–67
Web sites
  opening with a hot key, 107–108
  using anonymous, 258–259
Web surfing, approach to safe and fast, 180
Webroot SpySweeper
  timesaving tip, 533
  using, 434
website, DSLReports test, 18
weekly cleaning
  dusting, 450–451
  floppy drive, 452
  mouse, 451–452
  screens, 451
  vacuuming, 450
WEI (Windows Experience Index)
  analyzing the, 14–16
  calculating the, 11–14

caps for Memory (RAM) Component, 13
  overview, 9
  performance benchmarks, 10–11
  seeing your computer's, 11
WEI (Windows Experience Index) dialog box, 27–28
Wikipedia (3rd Party - Google), search engine, 210
Williams, Ryan, *MySpace For Dummies,* 356
Winamp, media player, 273
Window Color and Appearance dialog box, Aero Glass, 50, 52, 54
Window Layout Properties dialog box, Windows Mail, 242
windows
  grouping, 93–95
  key combinations, 100–101
  patches, 133
  running a program during startup, 123–125
  shortcuts, 102
  tiling, 88
Windows components, adding, 132–133
Windows Defender
  history icon, 434
  problems with, 431
  running a scan with, 431–433
  Software Explorer link, 434
  SpyNet link, 434
  using, 33–35, 433–434
Windows Experience Index (WEI)
  analyzing the, 14–16
  calculating the, 11–14
  caps for Memory (RAM) Component, 13
  dialog box, 27–28
  overview, 9
  performance benchmarks, 10–11
  seeing your computer's, 11
Windows Explorer
  changing filename associations in, 146–147
  changing views in, 140–143

cookie crumb navigation bar, 139
copying files quickly in, 145–146
customizing the Details view in, 141–143
customizing for speed, 138–140
renaming files in, 147–148
seeing pathnames in, 139–140
setting a folder's behavior, 143–145
shortcuts, 102
showing filename extensions, 136–138
sorting files by group in, 143
timesaving techniques, 138
zipping, 146
Windows files, adding/extracting from digital camera, 330
Windows Firewall
  blocking incoming traffic fast, 426–427
  inbound, 422–423
  modifying, 425–426
  outbound, 427–428
  settings, 423
  watching a program get through, 423–425
Windows Firewall Settings dialog box, Windows Firewall, 422
Windows Live Mail
  e-mail program, 238
  starting, 239–242
  Web-based e-mail services, 238
  Windows mail versus, 134
Windows Live Messenger
  adding contacts in, 229–230
  advanced features of, 232
  advantages/disadvantages of, 222
  background of, 223–224
  conversing on, 231–232
  installing, 224–225
  managing your password in, 226
  setting up an account, 226–229
  setup translator, 225
  Setup Wizard for Instant Messaging with Microsoft and Trillian, 224

Windows Live Messenger
  (continued)
  Shortcuts, 225
  Trillian and, 134
  Trillian versus, 233
Windows Live OneCare
  backup overview, 472
  safety scan, 414–416
Windows Live Search, Google
  Images versus, 208
Windows Live Sign-In Assistant,
  Windows Live Messenger, 225
Windows Live Toolbar, Windows
  Live Messenger, 225
Windows Mail
  arranging your desktop,
    242–243
  e-mail attachment security,
    245–246
  e-mail program, 238
  read receipts, 244
  send/receive settings, 243
  signatures, 244–245
Windows Media Player
  controlling from the keyboard,
    279
  iTunes versus, 134
  making improvements to,
    276–278
  Media Library, 282–284
  overview, 272–273
  privacy options, 275
  ripping CDs, 284–287
  running, 278–279
  starting, 273–275
  working with codecs, 279–281
Windows Media Portable Device,
  movie setting, 338
Windows Media VHS Quality,
  movie setting, 338
Windows Movie Maker
  adding titles and credits,
    336–337
  AutoMovie Generator, 334
  importing and combining clips,
    332–334
  limitations of, 331–332
  saving the movie, 337–338

trimming clips, 334
  using transitions and effects,
    334–336
Windows Paint
  using, 506–507
  using to save screen shots, 507
Windows patches, removing, 133
Windows Photo Gallery Options
  dialog box, Photo Gallery
  Techniques, 315
Windows Standard shell, Vista
  Basic versus Aero versus, 50
Windows Update
  using, 402–404
  Web site, 404
*Windows Vista All-In-One Desk
  Reference For Dummies*
  (Leonhard), 210, 242, 294,
    297, 300, 301, 373, 381, 426,
    427, 460, 476
*Windows XP Timesaving
  Techniques For Dummies*
  (Leonhard), 2
WinSAT
  viewing the log, 17–18
  Windows System Assessment
    Tool, 11
Winword.exe, locations for, 128
wireless, network, 360
wireless access point, defined,
  360
wireless base stations/cards, net-
  work, 361
*Wireless Home Networking For
  Dummies* (Briere, Hurley, and
  Ferris), 372
wireless network
  propagating changes, 374–375
  Wireless Router Setup Wizard,
    371–374
Wireless Network Setup Wizard,
  Securing Your Wireless
  Network Technique, 375
Wireless Router Setup Wizard,
  running the, 371–374
Wizard, Create Shortcut, 82–83,
  109, 126–127
WMA, music format, 269
WMPlugins, Web site, 280

WMPNSCFG.exe, auto-running
  program, 32
WMV file, creating a, 337–338
Word
  application file, 87
  opening with the last opened
    document, 126–128
Word 2003, screen tips for, 119
Word 2007, screen tips for, 119
Word command line switch, /m
  command, 127
Word 2000, 2002, and 2003 command line switches, Web site
  for, 128
Word 2007 command line
  switches, Web site for, 128
Worms
  defined, 410
  filename extensions and, 137
WpcUmi.exe, auto-running program, 32
wrapper program, defined, 35

X

XAML (Extensible Application
  Markup Language), Internet
  Explorer and Firefox, 181
XML file, overview, 17

Y

Yahoo!
  Groups, 356
  Mail Web-based e-mail serv-
    ices, 238
  Messenger and Trillian, 134
  online shopping with, 511
  Podcasts, 297

Z

zip files, indexing, 151
ZipBackup, using, 477
zipping, overview, 146
zombies, defined, 411, 420
ZoneAlarm, overview, 428

USINESS, CAREERS & PERSONAL FINANCE

0-7645-9847-3

0-7645-2431-3

Also available:
- Business Plans Kit For Dummies
  0-7645-9794-9
- Economics For Dummies
  0-7645-5726-2
- Grant Writing For Dummies
  0-7645-8416-2
- Home Buying For Dummies
  0-7645-5331-3
- Managing For Dummies
  0-7645-1771-6
- Marketing For Dummies
  0-7645-5600-2
- Personal Finance For Dummies
  0-7645-2590-5*
- Resumes For Dummies
  0-7645-5471-9
- Selling For Dummies
  0-7645-5363-1
- Six Sigma For Dummies
  0-7645-6798-5
- Small Business Kit For Dummies
  0-7645-5984-2
- Starting an eBay Business For Dummies
  0-7645-6924-4
- Your Dream Career For Dummies
  0-7645-9795-7

HOME & BUSINESS COMPUTER BASICS

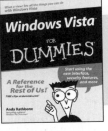

0-470-05432-8

0-471-75421-8

Also available:
- Cleaning Windows Vista For Dummies
  0-471-78293-9
- Excel 2007 For Dummies
  0-470-03737-7
- Mac OS X Tiger For Dummies
  0-7645-7675-5
- MacBook For Dummies
  0-470-04859-X
- Macs For Dummies
  0-470-04849-2
- Office 2007 For Dummies
  0-470-00923-3
- Outlook 2007 For Dummies
  0-470-03830-6
- PCs For Dummies
  0-7645-8958-X
- Salesforce.com For Dummies
  0-470-04893-X
- Upgrading & Fixing Laptops For Dummies
  0-7645-8959-8
- Word 2007 For Dummies
  0-470-03658-3
- Quicken 2007 For Dummies
  0-470-04600-7

FOOD, HOME, GARDEN, HOBBIES, MUSIC & PETS

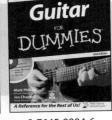

0-7645-8404-9

0-7645-9904-6

Also available:
- Candy Making For Dummies
  0-7645-9734-5
- Card Games For Dummies
  0-7645-9910-0
- Crocheting For Dummies
  0-7645-4151-X
- Dog Training For Dummies
  0-7645-8418-9
- Healthy Carb Cookbook For Dummies
  0-7645-8476-6
- Home Maintenance For Dummies
  0-7645-5215-5
- Horses For Dummies
  0-7645-9797-3
- Jewelry Making & Beading For Dummies
  0-7645-2571-9
- Orchids For Dummies
  0-7645-6759-4
- Puppies For Dummies
  0-7645-5255-4
- Rock Guitar For Dummies
  0-7645-5356-9
- Sewing For Dummies
  0-7645-6847-7
- Singing For Dummies
  0-7645-2475-5

INTERNET & DIGITAL MEDIA

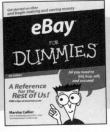

0-470-04529-9

0-470-04894-8

Also available:
- Blogging For Dummies
  0-471-77084-1
- Digital Photography For Dummies
  0-7645-9802-3
- Digital Photography All-in-One Desk Reference For Dummies
  0-470-03743-1
- Digital SLR Cameras and Photography For Dummies
  0-7645-9803-1
- eBay Business All-in-One Desk Reference For Dummies
  0-7645-8438-3
- HDTV For Dummies
  0-470-09673-X
- Home Entertainment PCs For Dummies
  0-470-05523-5
- MySpace For Dummies
  0-470-09529-6
- Search Engine Optimization For Dummies
  0-471-97998-8
- Skype For Dummies
  0-470-04891-3
- The Internet For Dummies
  0-7645-8996-2
- Wiring Your Digital Home For Dummies
  0-471-91830-X

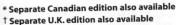

Available wherever books are sold. For more information or to order direct: U.S. customers visit www.dummies.com or call 1-877-762-2974.
U.K. customers visit www.wileyeurope.com or call 0800 243407. Canadian customers visit www.wiley.ca or call 1-800-567-4797.

SPORTS, FITNESS, PARENTING, RELIGION & SPIRITUALITY

0-471-76871-5

0-7645-7841-3

Also available:
- Catholicism For Dummies
  0-7645-5391-7
- Exercise Balls For Dummies
  0-7645-5623-1
- Fitness For Dummies
  0-7645-7851-0
- Football For Dummies
  0-7645-3936-1
- Judaism For Dummies
  0-7645-5299-6
- Potty Training For Dummies
  0-7645-5417-4
- Buddhism For Dummies
  0-7645-5359-3

- Pregnancy For Dummies
  0-7645-4483-7 †
- Ten Minute Tone-Ups For Dummies
  0-7645-7207-5
- NASCAR For Dummies
  0-7645-7681-X
- Religion For Dummies
  0-7645-5264-3
- Soccer For Dummies
  0-7645-5229-5
- Women in the Bible For Dummies
  0-7645-8475-8

TRAVEL

0-7645-7749-2

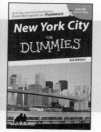

0-7645-6945-7

Also available:
- Alaska For Dummies
  0-7645-7746-8
- Cruise Vacations For Dummies
  0-7645-6941-4
- England For Dummies
  0-7645-4276-1
- Europe For Dummies
  0-7645-7529-5
- Germany For Dummies
  0-7645-7823-5
- Hawaii For Dummies
  0-7645-7402-7

- Italy For Dummies
  0-7645-7386-1
- Las Vegas For Dummies
  0-7645-7382-9
- London For Dummies
  0-7645-4277-X
- Paris For Dummies
  0-7645-7630-5
- RV Vacations For Dummies
  0-7645-4442-X
- Walt Disney World & Orlando
  For Dummies
  0-7645-9660-8

GRAPHICS, DESIGN & WEB DEVELOPMENT

0-7645-8815-X

0-7645-9571-7

Also available:
- 3D Game Animation For Dummies
  0-7645-8789-7
- AutoCAD 2006 For Dummies
  0-7645-8925-3
- Building a Web Site For Dummies
  0-7645-7144-3
- Creating Web Pages For Dummies
  0-470-08030-2
- Creating Web Pages All-in-One Desk
  Reference For Dummies
  0-7645-4345-8
- Dreamweaver 8 For Dummies
  0-7645-9649-7

- InDesign CS2 For Dummies
  0-7645-9572-5
- Macromedia Flash 8 For Dummies
  0-7645-9691-8
- Photoshop CS2 and Digital
  Photography For Dummies
  0-7645-9580-6
- Photoshop Elements 4 For Dummies
  0-471-77483-9
- Syndicating Web Sites with RSS Feeds
  For Dummies
  0-7645-8848-6
- Yahoo! SiteBuilder For Dummies
  0-7645-9800-7

NETWORKING, SECURITY, PROGRAMMING & DATABASES

0-7645-7728-X

0-471-74940-0

Also available:
- Access 2007 For Dummies
  0-470-04612-0
- ASP.NET 2 For Dummies
  0-7645-7907-X
- C# 2005 For Dummies
  0-7645-9704-3
- Hacking For Dummies
  0-470-05235-X
- Hacking Wireless Networks
  For Dummies
  0-7645-9730-2
- Java For Dummies
  0-470-08716-1

- Microsoft SQL Server 2005 For Dummies
  0-7645-7755-7
- Networking All-in-One Desk Reference
  For Dummies
  0-7645-9939-9
- Preventing Identity Theft For Dummies
  0-7645-7336-5
- Telecom For Dummies
  0-471-77085-X
- Visual Studio 2005 All-in-One Desk
  Reference For Dummies
  0-7645-9775-2
- XML For Dummies
  0-7645-8845-1